THE ENCYCLOPEDIA
OF THE
SPANISH-AMERICAN AND
PHILIPPINE-AMERICAN
WARS

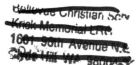

THE ENCYCLOPEDIA OF THE SPANISH-AMERICAN AND PHILIPPINE-AMERICAN WARS

A Political, Social, and Military History

VOLUME II: M–Z

Dr. Spencer C. Tucker
Volume Editor

James Arnold and Roberta Wiener
Editors, Documents Volume

Dr. Paul G. Pierpaoli Jr.
Associate Editor

Dr. Jack McCallum
Dr. Justin D. Murphy
Assistant Editors

A B C ⬩ C L I O

Santa Barbara, California   Denver, Colorado   Oxford, England

Library of Congress Cataloging-in-Publication Data
The encyclopedia of the Spanish-American and Philippine-American wars : a political, social, and military history / Spencer C. Tucker, editor.
     p.   cm.
     Includes bibliographical references and index.
     ISBN 978-1-85109-951-1 (hardcover : alk. paper) — ISBN 978-1-85109-952-8 (e-book)   1. Spanish-American War, 1898—
Encyclopedias.   2. Philippines—History—Philippine American War, 1899-1902—Encyclopedias.   I. Tucker, Spencer, 1937–
     E715.E53 2009
     973.8'903—dc22

                                        2009012422

13 12 11 10 9   1 2 3 4 5

This book is also available on the World Wide Web as an ebook.
Visit abc-clio.com for details.

ABC-CLIO, LLC
130 Cremona Drive, P.O. Box 1911
Santa Barbara, California 93116–1911

This book is printed on acid-free paper ∞
Manufactured in the United States of America

About the Editors

Spencer C. Tucker, PhD, held the John Biggs Chair of Military History at his alma mater, the Virginia Military Institute in Lexington, for 6 years until his retirement from teaching in 2003. Before that, he was professor of history for 30 years at Texas Christian University, Fort Worth. He has also been a Fulbright Scholar and, as a U.S. Army captain, an intelligence analyst in the Pentagon. Currently the senior fellow of military history at ABC-CLIO, he has written or edited 25 books, including the award-winning *Encyclopedia of World War I, Encyclopedia of World War II,* and *Encyclopedia of the Cold War,* all published by ABC-CLIO.

James Arnold is the author of more than 20 military history books and has contributed to numerous others. His published works include *Jeff Davis's Own: Cavalry, Comanches, and the Battle for the Texas Frontier* and *Napoleon Conquers Austria: The 1809 Campaign for Vienna,* which won the International Napoleonic Society's Literary Award in 1995.

Roberta Wiener is managing editor for the John A. Adams Center for Military History and Strategic Analysis at the Virginia Military Institute. She has written *American West: Living the Frontier Dream* and has coauthored numerous history books for the school library market, including *Robert Mugabe's Zimbabwe.*

Contents

List of Entries

List of Maps

General Maps

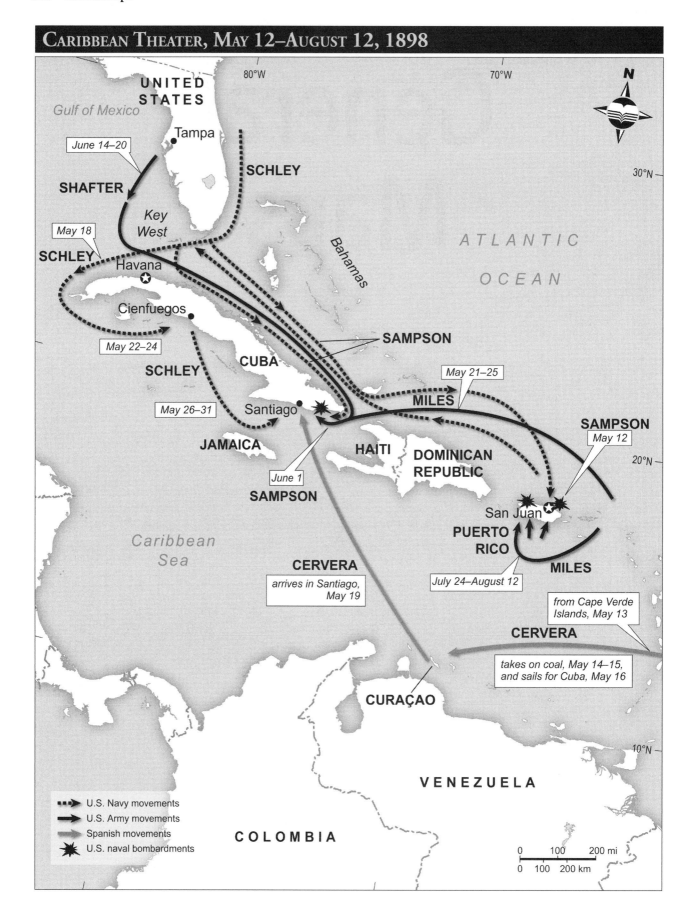

CARIBBEAN THEATER, MAY 12–AUGUST 12, 1898

UNITED STATES

Gulf of Mexico

80°W

70°W

N

30°N

Tampa

June 14–20

SHAFTER

SCHLEY

Key West

May 18

SCHLEY

Havana

ATLANTIC OCEAN

Bahamas

Cienfuegos

May 22–24

SCHLEY

CUBA

SAMPSON

May 21–25

MILES

May 26–31

Santiago

SAMPSON

SAMPSON

May 12

JAMAICA

June 1

HAITI

DOMINICAN REPUBLIC

20°N

SAMPSON

San Juan

PUERTO RICO

MILES

Caribbean Sea

CERVERA

arrives in Santiago, May 19

July 24–August 12

from Cape Verde Islands, May 13

CERVERA

takes on coal, May 14–15, and sails for Cuba, May 16

CURAÇAO

10°N

VENEZUELA

COLOMBIA

0   100   200 mi
0   100   200 km

- ▸▸▸ U.S. Navy movements
- ▸ U.S. Army movements
- ▸ Spanish movements
- ✶ U.S. naval bombardments

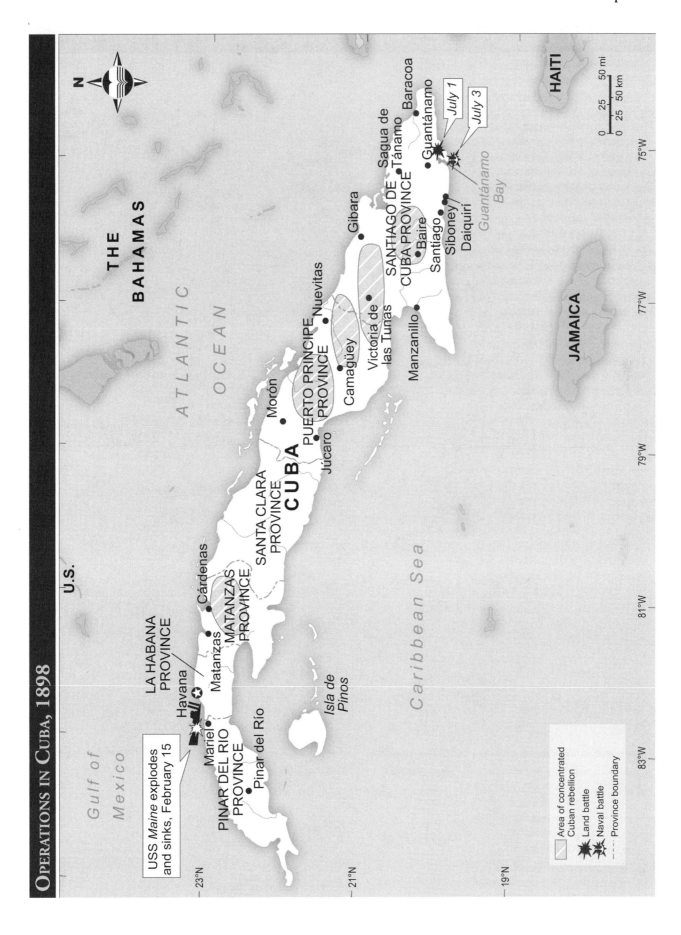

OPERATIONS IN CUBA, 1898

N

U.S.

Gulf of
Mexico

THE
BAHAMAS

ATLANTIC
OCEAN

LA HABANA
PROVINCE

Havana

USS *Maine* explodes
and sinks, February 15

Mariel

PINAR DEL RIO
PROVINCE

Pinar del Río

Matanzas

Cárdenas

MATANZAS
PROVINCE

SANTA CLARA
PROVINCE

CUBA

Isla de
Pinos

Morón

Júcaro

Nuevitas

PUERTO PRINCIPE
PROVINCE

Camagüey

Victoria de
las Tunas

Gibara

Manzanillo

SANTIAGO DE
CUBA PROVINCE

Santiago

Baire

Siboney

Daiquirí

Guantánamo
Bay

Guantánamo

Tánamo

Sagua de

Baracoa

July 1

July 3

Caribbean Sea

JAMAICA

HAITI

23°N

21°N

19°N

83°W   81°W   79°W   77°W   75°W

0   25   50 mi
0   25   50 km

Area of concentrated
Cuban rebellion

Land battle

Naval battle

Province boundary

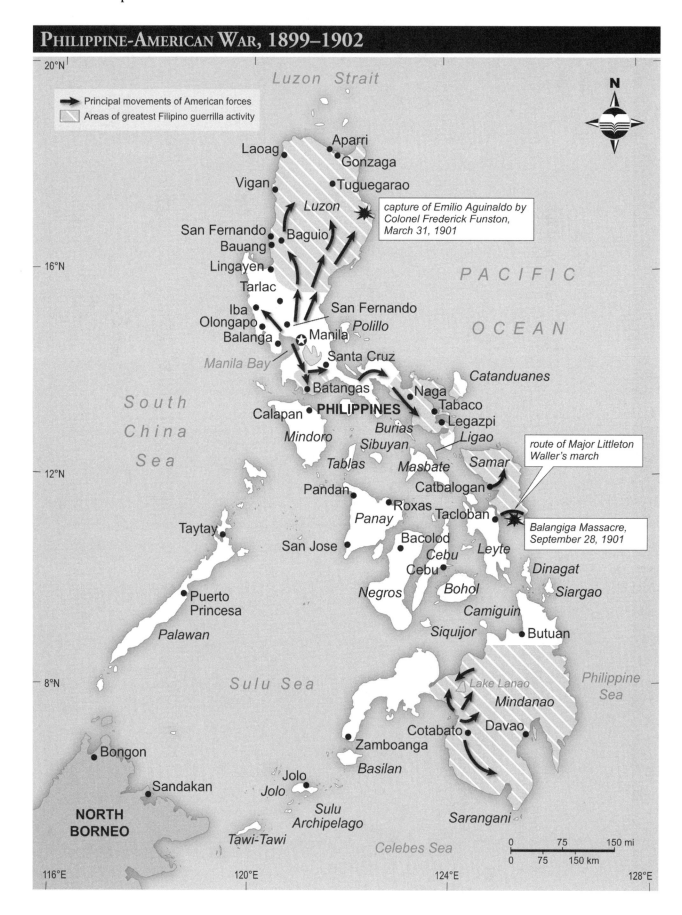

PHILIPPINE-AMERICAN WAR, 1899–1902

Principal movements of American forces
Areas of greatest Filipino guerrilla activity

N

Luzon Strait

20°N

Laoag
Aparri
Gonzaga
Vigan
Tuguegarao
Luzon

capture of Emilio Aguinaldo by
Colonel Frederick Funston,
March 31, 1901

San Fernando
Baguio
Bauang
Lingayen
16°N
Tarlac
Iba
Olongapo
Balanga
San Fernando
Polillo
Manila
Manila Bay
Santa Cruz

PACIFIC

OCEAN

*South
China
Sea*

Batangas
PHILIPPINES
Calapan
Burias
Mindoro
Sibuyan
12°N
Tablas
Pandan
Panay
Roxas
San Jose
Taytay
Bacolod
Cebu
Cebu
Negros
Bohol

Naga
Tabaco
Legazpi
Ligao
Masbate
Samar
Catbalogan
Tacloban

Catanduanes

route of Major Littleton
Waller's march

Balangiga Massacre,
September 28, 1901

Leyte
Dinagat
Siargao
Camiguin
Siquijor   Butuan

Puerto
Princesa
Palawan

Sulu Sea

*Philippine
Sea*

Lake Lanao
Mindanao
8°N
Cotabato   Davao
Bongon
Zamboanga
Sandakan
Basilan
Jolo
Jolo
**NORTH
BORNEO**
*Sulu
Archipelago*
Tawi-Tawi
Sarangani
Celebes Sea

0   75   150 mi
0   75   150 km

116°E   120°E   124°E   128°E

U.S. Acquisitions in the Pacific, 1857–1899

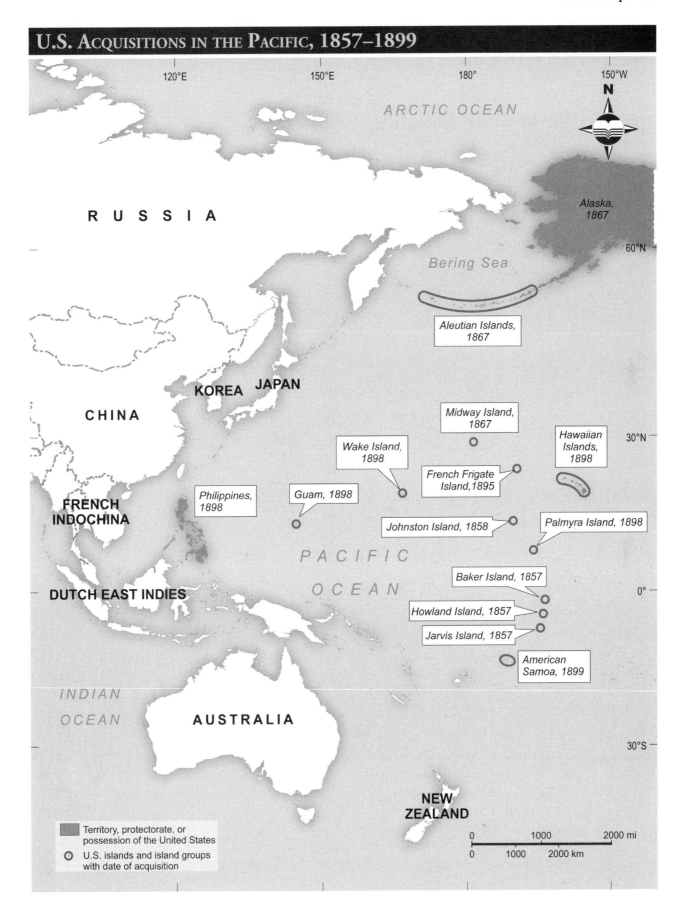

ARCTIC OCEAN

N

RUSSIA

Alaska,
1867

60°N

Bering Sea

Aleutian Islands,
1867

KOREA JAPAN

CHINA

Midway Island,
1867

Hawaiian
Islands,
1898

30°N

Wake Island,
1898

French Frigate
Island, 1895

FRENCH
INDOCHINA

Philippines,
1898

Guam, 1898

Johnston Island, 1858

Palmyra Island, 1898

PACIFIC

DUTCH EAST INDIES

OCEAN

Baker Island, 1857

0°

Howland Island, 1857

Jarvis Island, 1857

American
Samoa, 1899

INDIAN

OCEAN

AUSTRALIA

30°S

NEW
ZEALAND

Territory, protectorate, or
possession of the United States

U.S. islands and island groups
with date of acquisition

0   1000   2000 mi

0   1000   2000 km

M

Maass, Clara Louise
Birth Date: June 28, 1876
Death Date: August 24, 1901

U.S. nurse and medical pioneer. Born in East Orange, New Jersey, on June 28, 1876, Clara Louise Maass was the oldest of 10 children in a devout Lutheran German immigrant family. She helped in an orphanage during her high school years and at age 17 entered the newly established Christina Trefz Training School for Nurses at Newark's German Hospital. She graduated in 1895, and her competence earned her a promotion to head nurse only two years later.

On the outbreak of the Spanish-American War in April 1898, Maass volunteered to serve as a contract nurse for the U.S. Army. From October 1898 to February 1899, she served with VII Corps in Jacksonville, Florida; Savannah, Georgia; and Santiago, Cuba. After her discharge, she joined VIII Corps in the Philippines, which was battling Filipino insurgents in the Philippine-American War (1899–1902). She remained in the Philippines until mid-1900, when she was sent home after having contracted dengue fever, a serious disease of the tropics transmitted by infected mosquitoes.

The wars in which she had served had given Maass considerable expertise in fighting malaria, yellow fever, and other tropical diseases. In October 1900, she returned to the Las Animas Hospital in Havana, Cuba, at the request of Major William Gorgas, chief sanitation officer, and Dr. John Guitares. The U.S. Army's Yellow Fever Board (also known as the Reed Commission), headed by Major Walter Reed, an army physician, had been established in Cuba after the war to find out the means of transmission for this tropical fever and develop effective immunization against it.

In order to determine whether yellow fever was caused by contaminated filth, person-to-person transmission, or the bite of a mosquito, the commission recruited volunteers to test their theories. They were paid $100 for risking their lives, with an offer of an additional $100 if they became ill. In March 1901, experiments revealed that men living in filth without exposure to mosquitoes were not infected with yellow fever. Next, seven volunteers offered themselves to be bitten by infected mosquitoes. One of them was Maass, who contracted a mild case of the fever and recovered quickly; however, two men who volunteered died. Because the other volunteers remained healthy, however, researchers were not sure whether the mosquitoes were truly the carriers of the disease.

On August 14, 1901, Maass volunteered for a second mosquito bite, hoping to prove that her earlier case of yellow fever had immunized her against the disease. This time, however, she became severely ill. She died of yellow fever on August 24, 1901, at the age of 25 and was buried in Colón Cemetery in Havana with full military honors. Her death confirmed the theory of transmission by mosquitoes, but public protest put an end to further experiments on humans. Maass's death also seemed to prove that the body did not produce sufficient antibodies to ward off further infections of yellow fever. In fact, the original illness was almost certainly not yellow fever, and Maass was not immune. Several years later, vaccines would be developed to build the body's defenses against infection.

Maass's body was moved to Fairmont Cemetery in Newark, New Jersey, on February 20, 1902. She has been honored by both Cuba (in 1951) and the United States (in 1976) with a postage stamp, the first nurse to receive such a distinction. In 1952, Newark's German Hospital was renamed Clara Maass Memorial Hospital (now located in Belleville, New Jersey) in her honor, and she was inducted into the American Nursing Association's Nursing Hall of Fame in 1976.

KATJA WUESTENBECKER

U.S. nurse and medical pioneer Clara Maass volunteered for yellow fever studies and subsequently died of the disease. (National Library of Medicine)

See also
Medicine, Military; Reed, Walter; Yellow Fever; Yellow Fever Board

Further Reading
Cunningham, John T. *Clara Maass: A Nurse, a Hospital, a Spirit.* Belleville, NJ: Rae, 1968.
Herrmann, E. K. "Clara Louise Maass: Heroine or Martyr of Public Health?" *Public Health Nursing* 2(1) (1985): 51–57.
Samson, J. "A Nurse Who Gave Her Life So That Others Could Live." *Imprint* 37 (1990): 81–89.
Tengbom, Mildred. *No Greater Love: The Gripping Story of Nurse Clara Maass.* St. Louis, MO: Concordia, 1978.

Mabini, Apolinario
Birth Date: July 22, 1864
Death Date: May 13, 1903

Filipino intellectual, political philosopher, patriot, key adviser to Filipino revolutionary leader Emilio Aguinaldo y Famy, and first prime minister of the First Philippine Republic during 1899. Apolinario Mabini was born on July 22, 1864, in Talaga, Batangas, Philippines, to a poor peasant family. Despite his impoverished upbringing, the bright and precocious Mabini attended the Colegio de San Juan de Latran in the Philippines from which he received an undergraduate degree.

Mabini also worked as a Latin teacher and a clerk for a Philippine court. While doing so, he pursued law studies at the University of Santo Thomas (Philippines) from which he earned a law degree in 1894. An ardent champion of the poor, he dedicated much time to ameliorating the status of impoverished peasants and defending those who could not afford representation.

In 1896, Mabini was struck down by a serious illness, likely polio (infantile paralysis), that paralyzed him from the waist down. From then on he became known as the "sublime paralytic," in part an acknowledgment of his keen intellect. As the unrest in the Philippines intensified, Spanish authorities arrested the still desperately ill Mabini in late 1896 for inciting turmoil. When he proved that he was unable to move his lower limbs and thus unable to participate in the uprisings, he was released and sent to a hospital, where he was able to convalesce.

A member of the Liga Filipina, a reformist group headed by José Rizal, Mabini was initially against the use of violence to effect social change in the Philippines. By 1897, however, he had become convinced that radical change was needed to throw off the shackles of Spanish rule and began to support the concept of armed rebellion. Accordingly, he wrote a number of manifestos urging all Filipinos to unite in the fight against the Spanish.

In May 1898, while he was on holiday in Los Banos, Laguna, Philippines, Mabini was summoned by Aguinaldo to help him establish a government in anticipation of the end to Spanish colonial rule. It required dozens of men to physically carry Mabini's cot to the meeting with Aguinaldo in Kawit. Mabini quickly became one of Aguinaldo's most trusted advisers and certainly his most cerebral. Mabini penned the June 18, 1898, decree that organized local governments under Filipino control. He was also instrumental in establishing an independent judicial system, supervising elections for the revolutionary congress, and crafting the framework of the soon-to-be new government.

When the revolutionary congress first convened in Malolos on September 15, 1898, Mabini immediately found himself at odds with the Filipino elites, who called for the prompt invocation of a constitution. Mabini believed that the role of the congress should be to advise the leaders and to facilitate the pursuit of the revolution. When he was overruled, he wrote his own draft of a constitution, which was rejected by the majority.

After the Malolos Constitution, which represented a compromise document, was adopted and the First Philippine Republic officially organized, Mabini was appointed both prime minister and foreign minister when the government came into force on January 23, 1899. Mabini was immediately confronted with a panoply of problems, not the least of which was negotiating an end to the hostilities between Filipino revolutionaries and U.S. forces. Having failed on several occasions to secure a cease-fire or armistice with the Americans, Mabini cut off negotiations and instead backed the growing guerrilla insurgency. On May 7, 1899, he resigned his posts with the fledgling republic. By then, he had alienated many of the elites in the government and had fallen out of favor with Aguinaldo. Mabini's departure was a significant loss, for no other person within the revolutionary movement had understood the stakes of the struggle as well as he did.

Mabini went into hiding to escape capture but was apprehended by American forces on December 10, 1899. When asked to take an oath of allegiance to the U.S. government, he pointedly refused. He also refused to end his support for the Filipino insurgency. After Mabini spent more than a year in detention, American authorities deported him to Guam. In February 1903, he returned to the Philippines, where he died in Manila on May 13, 1903, only weeks after having sworn allegiance to the U.S. government. During Mabini's imprisonment, he wrote *La Revolución Filipina* (The Philippine Revolution), which was published posthumously in 1907 and remains today one of the most insightful analyses of the Filipino struggle during the 1890s.

PAUL G. PIERPAOLI JR.

See also

Aguinaldo y Famy, Emilio; Liga Filipina; Malolos Constitution; Philippine Republic, First; Rizal, José

Further Reading

Hartendorp, A. V. H., ed. *Mabini: The Sources of His Political Thought.* Manila: Alberto S. Florentino, 1965.

Latorre, Stephen. *Apolinario Mabini.* Manila: Tahana Books, 1992.

Majul, Cesar Adib. *Mabini and the Philippine Revolution.* Quezon City: University of the Philippines, 1960.

Macabebe Scouts

Filipinos from the town of Macabebe in Pampanga Province on the island of Luzon who served with the U.S. military during the Philippine-American War (1899–1902). The residents of Macabebe were longtime foes of the Tagalogs and had a history of providing military service to Spain. As loyal Spanish mercenaries and fierce warriors, the Macabebes had manned outposts, engaged in foreign campaigns, and suppressed domestic disorder. For example, when Francisco Maniago rebelled in Pampanga in 1660, the Macabebes helped quell the uprising. They likewise assisted Spanish authorities in putting down the revolutions of 1896 and 1898, actually compelling a Spanish pledge to remove them to the safety of the Caroline Islands if the revolt prevailed. Once Spain ceded the Philippine Islands to the United States, the Macabebes were essentially abandoned and sought to protect themselves from Tagalog reprisal. Consequently, they tendered their services to the U.S. military upon the beginning of the Philippine-American War in February 1899.

With War Department approval and upon the order of Major General Henry W. Lawton, Lieutenant Matthew A. Batson recruited the first company of Macabebes in the spring of 1899. He proposed to employ the unit in the Rio Grande region, a strategy that Lawton endorsed. By September 10, the 1st Company, Macabebe Scouts, had been established. After training, the unit was armed with Krag

As many as 5,000 Filipino Macabebe Scouts served with U.S. forces during the Philippine-American War. One of their detachments helped capture insurgent leader Emilio Aguinaldo. (Library of Congress)

carbines, and traveling in bancas (outrigger canoes), they at once demonstrated their effectiveness by curtailing raids on military communications.

Major General Elwell S. Otis decreed the creation of a second Macabebe troop on September 21 and a third one on October 6, 1899. In short order, the U.S. Army VIII Corps could rely on the services of a battalion of five companies designated Batson's Macabebe Scouts. It is estimated that as many as 5,000 Macabebe Scouts served with U.S. forces.

Fiercely loyal to the United States, the Macabebes quickly won the trust and admiration of American officers. They were of great assistance in recognizing insurgents posing as friendly natives in crowds. However, the Macabebes were often cruel and inhumane toward their adversaries, and a number of atrocities were attributed to them.

Batson and his colleagues stood by the Macabebes, claiming that the accusations of cruelties were simply insurgent propaganda. Yet the Macabebes did use torture to obtain intelligence, and by 1900 both American troops and their mercenaries turned to, among other excesses, the water cure (force-feeding a suspect with water).

In early October 1899, two companies of Batson's Macabebe Scouts were in the vanguard of Brigadier General Samuel B. M. Young's drive to San Isidro in Nueva Ecija Province, and in March 1900 Colonel Frederick Funston led a combined troop of Macabebes and Americans against an enemy base at Fort Rizal in southern Nueva Ecija. To the southwest, Brigadier General Frederick D. Grant employed Lieutenant Colonel William E. Wilder's Macabebes to sweep southward through the Rio Grande delta to Manila Bay in Bulacan Province. Bancas carried Macabebes into swamps, and there they roused guerrillas who fled to villages, where they were identified and captured. Rifles were seized, but the Macabebes committed atrocities. On March 30, 130 natives were murdered, and there were allegations of rape and arson. Yet American officers on the scene continued to defend the Macabebes. On March 23, 1901, Macabebe Scouts were part of a detail led by Funston (now a brigadier general) that captured Filipino leader Emilio Aguinaldo y Famy at Palanan, Isabela Province, in northern Luzon. Following the Philippine-American War, the Macabebes were folded into the Philippine Constabulary.

RODNEY J. ROSS

See also

Aguinaldo y Famy, Emilio; Atrocities; Funston, Frederick; Grant, Frederick Dent; Lawton, Henry Ware; Luzon Campaigns; Otis, Elwell Stephen; Philippine-American War; Philippine Constabulary; Tagalogs; Wheaton, Lloyd; Young, Samuel Baldwin Marks

Further Reading

Gates, John M. *Schoolbooks and Krags: The United States Army in the Philippines, 1898–1902.* Westport, CT: Greenwood, 1973.

Linn, Brian McAllister. *The Philippine War, 1899–1902.* Lawrence: University Press of Kansas, 2000.

Miller, Stuart Creighton. *"Benevolent Assimilation": The American Conquest of the Philippines, 1899–1903.* New Haven, CT: Yale University Press, 1982.

MacArthur, Arthur
Birth Date: June 2, 1845
Death Date: September 5, 1912

U.S. Army general. Arthur MacArthur was born in Chicopee Falls, Massachusetts, on June 2, 1845. At an early age he moved with his family to Milwaukee, Wisconsin, and was educated in the local schools. With the start of the American Civil War, he secured a commission as first lieutenant with the 24th Wisconsin Regiment of Volunteers and soon distinguished himself in fighting. He was breveted captain following his performance in the Battle of Perryville (October 8, 1862). He also fought effectively at Stone's River (December 31–January 2, 1863), Chickamauga (September 18–20, 1863), and Kennesaw Mountain (June 17, 1864). He was severely wounded at the Battle of Franklin, Tennessee (November 30, 1984). He received brevet promotions for gallantry and was advanced to major (January 1864), lieutenant colonel (March 1865), and colonel (May 1865). By the end of the war, MacArthur, not yet 20 years old, was commanding the 24th Wisconsin. In 1890, he was belatedly awarded the Medal of Honor for his actions in the Union assault on Missionary Ridge.

With the end of the Civil War, MacArthur joined the regular army as a second lieutenant in the 17th Infantry Regiment in February 1866 and was immediately promoted to first lieutenant. He made captain that July. Over the next 20 years, he served in various posts throughout the country. At first posted to Louisiana during Reconstruction, he then commanded a unit that protected the builders of the Union Pacific Railroad in Nebraska and Wyoming. He was also a cavalry recruiting officer in New York and commanded an outpost in the Utah and New Mexico territory. In 1886, Captain MacArthur was posted to the Infantry and Cavalry School at Fort Leavenworth, Kansas. In July 1889, he was promoted to major and assigned to the adjutant general's department. MacArthur won promotion to lieutenant colonel in May 1898.

Shortly after the U.S. declaration of war on Spain, MacArthur was appointed brigadier general of volunteers in May 1898 and assigned to the U.S. expeditionary force sent to the Philippines. He commanded the 1st Brigade of the 2nd Division in Major General Wesley Merritt's VIII Corps. MacArthur led his brigade in the First Battle of Manila (August 13, 1898). Cited for gallantry, he became the provost marshal general and civil governor of Manila.

Promoted to major general of volunteers, MacArthur then commanded the 2nd Division, the chief field force opposing Filipino insurgents led by Emilio Aguinaldo y Famy in the Philippine-American War. MacArthur's forces pacified all of Luzon. Promoted to regular army brigadier general in January 1900, he succeeded Major General Elwell S. Otis as commanding general of the Division of the Philippines and military governor of the Philippine Islands. He was promoted to major general in the regular army that July. After he combined a mixture of vigorous military action and civic action, including advances in education, health care, and legal reform.

Major General Arthur MacArthur distinguished himself in the American Civil War, but he is best remembered for his role in the Philippine-American War, during which he achieved victory through a combination of military force and civic action. (Library of Congress)

Arthur MacArthur's son, Douglas MacArthur, was later chief of staff of the army and rose to the rank of general of the army. Like his father, Douglas MacArthur would have an equally stormy relationship with his superiors.

WESLEY MOODY, PAUL G. PIERPAOLI JR., AND SPENCER C. TUCKER

See also
Aguinaldo y Famy, Emilio; Manila, First Battle of; Manila, Second Battle of; Merritt, Wesley; Taft, William Howard

Further Reading
Linn, Brian McAllister. *The Philippine War, 1899–1902.* Lawrence: University Press of Kansas, 2000.
Young, Kenneth Ray. *The General's General: The Life and Times of Arthur MacArthur.* Boulder, CO: Westview, 1994.

Maceo Grajales, Antonio
Birth Date: June 14, 1848
Death Date: December 7, 1896

Cuban revolutionary and second-in-command of the Cuban Revolutionary Army during the Ten Years' War and the Cuban War of Independence and one of Latin America's most ardent and successful guerrilla leaders. Antonio Maceo Grajales, commonly referred to as the "Titan of Bronze" because of his bravery and skin tone, was born on June 14, 1848, in Majaguabo near Santiago de Cuba. His father, Marcos Maceo, a mulatto farmer of French descent who had fought with the loyalists in Venezuela during the Latin American Wars of Independence, fled Venezuela in 1823 after Simón Bolívar's revolutionary forces liberated northern South America. Settling in Santiago de Cuba, Maceo's father married Mariana Grajales, a black widow of Dominican descent who already had four children. Maceo was the first of five children born to Marcos and Mariana.

Within days of Carlos Manuel de Céspedes y del Castillo's Grito de Yara (October 10, 1868), which began the Ten Years' War, Maceo, his father, and three of his brothers joined the revolutionary cause. Because of his valor, Maceo was promoted to lieutenant colonel by the end of 1868. Participating in dozens of battles, he had been promoted to brigadier general by the end of the war. By 1878, most Cuban revolutionary generals believed that it was futile to continue to resist Spanish attempts to restore colonial rule on the island.

Maceo, however, was unwilling to stop fighting until Cuban independence and the abolition of slavery were achieved. On March 15, 1878, he met with Spanish captain-general Arsenio Martínez de Campos to discuss the terms of the Pact of Zanjón (February 8, 1878), which had ended the Ten Years' War. Although most Cuban revolutionary generals, including Máximo Gomez, had already accepted Martínez's plan for increased Cuban autonomy and the eventual abolition of slavery, Maceo insisted that the terms were insufficient. In addition, he was offended that Spanish newspapers reported that his popularity with the dark-skinned revolutionaries

MacArthur was, however, slow to hand over control to the civilian administrators headed by William H. Taft. MacArthur and Taft clashed repeatedly, and before the year was out, President Theodore Roosevelt had replaced MacArthur with a more pliable military governor. MacArthur's disagreements with Taft and Roosevelt ultimately cost MacArthur the position of commanding general of the U.S. Army.

Returning to the United States, MacArthur commanded in turn the Department of Colorado, the Department of the Lakes, and the Department of the East. In 1905, he went to Manchuria as a military observer for the last stage of the Russo-Japanese War (1904–1905) and then for a few months was the U.S. military attaché in Tokyo. He toured Asia during November 1905–August 1906. On his return to the United States, he commanded the Department of the Pacific, was promoted to lieutenant general, and was the senior officer in the army (September 1906). When Taft, then secretary of war and still bearing a grudge against his old nemesis, named a more junior officer as chief of staff, MacArthur returned to Milwaukee to await orders. When none were forthcoming, he retired in July 1909. MacArthur died in Milwaukee on September 5, 1912, while giving a speech during the reunion of the 24th Wisconsin Regiment.

Cuban revolutionary Antonio Maceo Grajales was known for his bravery and great skill as a leader of guerrillas. He was killed in battle with the Spanish in 1896. (Library of Congress)

of Cuba threatened to unleash a race war in Cuba and convert Cuba into a second Haiti. Concerns expressed by Maceo at the meeting with Martínez at Baragua are known as the Protest of Baragua. Unwilling to accept the Pact of Zanjón and unable to muster enough troops to continue the revolutionary struggle, Maceo went into exile.

Contending that Spain had not honored the provisions of the Pact of Zanjón, Maceo and Calixto García y Iñiguez called for the Little War, or Guerra Chiquita (1879–1880), the second Cuban revolutionary attempt at independence during the 19th century. Unable to return to Cuba before the end of the Little War, Maceo spent the next 15 years living in exile, primarily in Panama and Costa Rica.

On March 31, 1895, Maceo, accompanied by his brother José, returned to eastern Cuba to continue the revolutionary struggle. On May 5, 1895, Maceo, Gómez, and José Martí y Pérez met in Bocucy to devise political and military strategy. Although Maceo's forces defeated Martínez's troops at the Battle of Peralejo on July 12,

Martínez was able to escape. As second-in-command of the Cuban revolutionaries, Maceo directed thousands of Cuban revolutionaries, many of whom were black and were only armed with machetes.

Maceo believed that U.S. entry into the conflict was unnecessary. Following Martínez's replacement by General Valeriano Weyler y Nicolau in January 1896, Maceo faced an opponent who pursued him relentlessly. On December 7, 1896, Spanish forces killed Maceo in battle at San Pedro in Havana Province as he attempted to rejoin Gómez's forces. Maceo's death, however, did not discourage the Cuban revolutionaries. On the contrary, it motivated them to fight all the harder.

Michael R. Hall

See also

Céspedes y del Castillo, Carlos Manuel de; Cuba; Cuban Revolutionary Army; García y Iñiguez, Calixto; Gómez y Báez, Máximo; Martí y Pérez, José Julián; Martínez de Campos, Arsenio; Ten Years' War; Weyler y Nicolau, Valeriano; Zanjón, Pact of

Further Reading

Argenter, José Miro. *Cronicas de la Guerra* [Chronicles of the War]. Havana: Editorial Leteras Cubana, 1909.
Foner, Philip S. *Antonio Maceo: The "Bronze Titan" of Cuba's Struggle for Independence.* New York: Monthly Review Press, 1978.
Pando, Magdalen G. *Cuba's Freedom Fighter: Antonio Maceo, 1845–1896.* Gainesville, FL: Felicity, 1980.

Machine Guns

Efficient manually operated rapid-firing small arms were in operation in the 1860s and 1870s. They included the Agar Coffee Mill (ca. 1860) and Gatling gun (1862) of the American Civil War and the 25-barrel *mitrailleuse* (1869) employed by the French in the Franco-Prussian War (1870–1871). But the Maxim gun of 1884, named for American Hiram Maxim, was the first truly automatic machine gun. Development of the metallic cartridge made rapid loading at the breech possible.

Maxim's innovation was to use some of the energy of the firing to operate the weapon. Using the recoil energy, which he called blowback, Maxim designed a fully automatic rifle fed by a revolving magazine. He then applied the same principle to a machine gun (in effect a machine for killing), which fired as long as the trigger was depressed. In the Maxim gun, the firing of the cartridge drove back the bolt, compressing a spring that in turn drove the bolt forward again, bringing a new round into position for firing. The Maxim gun was both self-loading and self-ejecting.

Maxim demonstrated his prototype machine gun in 1884. It weighed just 60 pounds, in contrast to the 2,000-pound *mitrailleuse*. The Maxim gun was belt fed and water cooled. It fired a .45-caliber bullet at a rate of up to 600 rounds per minute and could be operated by a crew of only five men, one to operate the trigger and four to assist in carrying the weapon and its ammunition as well as loading the ammunition belts. Aided by the British firm of Vickers, Maxim had his gun largely perfected before the end of the 1880s.

The Maxim gun, invented by American Hiram Maxim, was the first truly automatic machine gun. (*Photographic History of the Spanish-American War,* 1898)

The British employed the Maxim gun with great success against the Zulus in South Africa and the Dervishes in the Sudan. Rudyard Kipling proclaimed the importance of the new weapon when he wrote, "Whatever else, we have got the Maxim Gun, and they have not." Maxim was later knighted by Queen Victoria for services to humanity in the false assumption that the machine gun would make wars shorter and thus more humane.

The U.S. Army eschewed the Maxim gun and still employed the .45-caliber rotating multibarrel Gatling gun at the time of the Spanish-American War. Under Captain John H. "Gatling Gun" Parker, a Gatling gun unit saw effective service during the Santiago de Cuba Land Campaign and provided important fire support to the attacking infantry in the Battle of San Juan Hill, perhaps the first time that machine guns were used offensively in combat. Parker placed the guns, which were mounted on rolling carriages, on the flanks of the U.S. troops, moving them forward with the troops. Parker was an enthusiastic advocate of the machine gun and later wrote three books on the subject, noting that the Santiago Campaign had established the machine gun as "a weapon to be reckoned with in some form in all future wars." Although the

Gatling gun itself was abandoned by the U.S. military as obsolete in 1911, its rotating barrels design nonetheless had important applications for the modern era.

The Colt Model 1895 automatic machine gun, developed by John Browning, was rejected by the U.S. Army but became the first automatic machine gun acquired by the U.S. military when the navy purchased several hundred examples. Browning had offered the machine gun to Colt in 1890. The gas-operated Model 1895 fired a 6-millimeter (mm) round. The gun alone weighed 40 pounds. A tripod added 28 pounds and a mount 28.5 pounds, while a light landing carriage without ammunition weighed 146 pounds.

The 1st Marine Battalion took at least two Colt Model 1895s to Cuba in 1898 and employed them at Camp McCalla after its landing at Guantánamo on June 10, 1898. Two additional Colts, belonging to the battleship *Texas,* were landed several days later to provide additional firepower. The U.S. Marine Corps employed some of these Colts in the Battle of Cuzco Well on June 14, and apparently they were instrumental in halting the initial Spanish attack. A tripod-mounted Colt was also employed in the later Battle of Guánica in Puerto Rico.

Two privately purchased tripod-mounted Colts in 7-mm caliber were taken by the 1st Volunteer Cavalry Regiment (the Rough Riders) to Cuba, but apparently they proved to be unreliable and difficult to transport. The Colt is reported to have performed well with American troops in China during the Boxer Rebellion. Later versions were chambered for the .30–06 Springfield rifle cartridge. The Colt continued in service with the U.S. Navy and the U.S. Marine Corps up to World War I.

Although machine guns proved their worth in colonial conflicts, the implications of the modern machine gun for fighting in Europe were ignored, even when revealed in the Russo-Japanese War (1904–1905). At 450–600 rounds per minute, one machine gun could equal the fire of 40–80 riflemen. It also had greater range than the rifle, enabling indirect fire in support of an attack. New light machine guns, such as the British Lewis gun, soon appeared and were destined to play an important role in the trench warfare of World War I.

SPENCER C. TUCKER

See also

Cuzco Well, Battle of; Gatling Gun; Guánica, Puerto Rico; Guantánamo, Battle of; Rough Riders; San Juan Heights, Battle of; Santiago de Cuba Land Campaign

Further Reading

Goldsmith, Duff L., and R. Blake Stevens. *The Devil's Paintbrush: Sir Hiram Maxim's Gun.* 2nd ed. Toronto: Collector Grade Publications, 1993.
Willbanks, James H. *Machine Guns: An Illustrated History of Their Impact.* Santa Barbara, CA: ABC-CLIO, 2004.

Macías y Casado, Manuel
Birth Date: 1845
Death Date: 1937

Spanish general and last Spanish colonial governor of Puerto Rico. Manuel Macías y Casado was born in Teruel, Spain, around 1845. He graduated from the Infantry School as a second lieutenant in 1862, was promoted to lieutenant in 1863, and then was sent to Cuba.

From 1863 to 1865, Macías participated in the occupation of the Dominican Republic and while serving there was promoted to captain. After Dominican independence was restored in 1865, he returned to Cuba and remained there until 1875. His proven valor on the battlefield during the Ten Years' War (1868–1878) brought him a promotion to colonel. In 1875, he returned to Spain to defend the Spanish Crown during the Third Carlist War (1872–1876). After the Carlist revolutionaries were quelled in 1876, he returned to Cuba in October 1876 to participate in the final months of the Ten Years' War. His actions on the battlefield resulted in his promotion to brigadier general in July 1878 at age 33.

In May 1879, Macías returned to Spain and then took command of Spanish troops stationed at Melilla on the Rif coast of northwestern Africa. Leaving Melilla in 1886, he subsequently served as military commander in Albacete and Santoña. On June 9, 1891, he was appointed major general and was made governor of Cartagena. He returned to Melilla as governor in 1893 to quell a local revolt. Because of his success, he was advanced to lieutenant general in August 1893, making him the youngest lieutenant general in the Spanish Army. He then served as the governor of the Canary Islands during 1894–1898.

On January 17, 1898, Macías was appointed governor of Puerto Rico, replacing Lieutenant General Andrés González Muñoz, who had died on the day of his inauguration. Macías was governor of Puerto Rico from February 2 to October 16, 1898. One of his major achievements was the implementation on February 9, 1898, of the Autonomous Charter of Puerto Rico, which had been approved by the Spanish Cortes (parliament) on November 25, 1897. The Autonomous Charter gave town councils complete autonomy in local concerns. As a result, the governor had no authority to intervene in civil and political matters unless authorized to do so by the cabinet. On February 10, 1898, Macías convened the first autonomous cabinet of Puerto Rico. In elections for the Cortes on March 27, 1898, Luis Muñoz Rivera's Autonomist Party won a majority of the seats.

Macías believed that war with the United States was inevitable. On April 21, 1898, he declared martial law, suspended civil liberties, and prepared to defend the island against an expected American invasion. He delegated the defense of Puerto Rico to Colonel Juan Camó. Macías's effort to defend Puerto Rico against American invasion failed, however, and fighting ended on August 13, 1898. On October 16, he and most of his troops departed Puerto Rico. As he left, he was honored with U.S. and Puerto Rican gunfire salutes and cheers from the people of San Juan. He left Ricardo de Ortega y Diez with the responsibility of turning over power to U.S. officials on October 18, 1898.

On November 3, 1898, Macías, in addition to being named governor of Burgos, Navarra, and Vascongadas, became commander of VI Corps of the Spanish Army. He died in Madrid in 1937.

MICHAEL R. HALL

See also

Puerto Rico; Rivera, Luis Muñoz; Ten Years' War

Further Reading

Pico, Fernando. *Puerto Rico 1898: The War after the War.* Princeton, NJ: Markus Wiener, 2004.
Trask, David F. *The War with Spain in 1898.* Lincoln: University of Nebraska Press, 1996.
Van Middeldyk, R. A. *The History of Puerto Rico: From the Spanish Discovery to the American Occupation.* New York: BiblioBazaar, 2006.

Mahan, Alfred Thayer
Birth Date: September 27, 1840
Death Date: December 1, 1914

Prominent naval historian, strategist, and staunch proponent of U.S. imperialism. Born on September 27, 1840, at West Point, New York, Alfred Thayer Mahan was the son of West Point professor

Rear Admiral Alfred Thayer Mahan was a staunch champion of sea power and an advocate of U.S. imperial expansion. His many books on the history of sea power were highly influential in the United States and abroad. (Library of Congress)

Mahan argued that the United States needed a strong navy to compete for the world's trade. He claimed that there was no instance of a great commercial power retaining its leadership without a large navy. He also criticized the traditional U.S. strategy of single-ship commerce raiding (*guerre de course*) because it could not win control of the seas. He argued for a seagoing fleet, an overbearing force that could beat down an enemy's battle line. Its strength had to be in battleships operating in squadrons. Mahan believed in the concentration of forces, urging that the fleet be kept in one ocean only. He also called for U.S. naval bases in the Caribbean and in the Pacific. Mahan had his shortcomings: he overlooked new technology, such as the torpedo and the submarine, and he was not concerned about speed in battleships.

Mahan was president of the Naval War College twice (1886–1889 and 1889–1893). He commanded the cruiser *Chicago,* flagship of the European Station (1893–1896), and was publically feted in Europe and recognized with honorary degrees from Oxford University and Cambridge University. An important apostle of the new navalism, he retired from the navy in 1896 to devote himself full-time to writing.

Mahan was called back to active duty with the navy in an advisory role during the 1898 Spanish-American War. He was a delegate to the 1899 Hague Peace Conference, and he was promoted to rear admiral on the retired list in 1906. He wrote a dozen books on naval warfare and more than 50 articles in leading journals, and he was elected president of the American Historical Association in 1902. Mahan died on December 1, 1914, in Washington, D.C.

Spencer C. Tucker

See also

Roosevelt, Theodore; United States Navy

Further Reading

Hughes, Wayne P. *Mahan: Tactics and Principles of Strategy.* Newport, RI: Naval War College, 1990.

Livezey, William E. *Mahan and Sea Power.* Norman: University of Oklahoma Press, 1947.

Puleston, William D. *Mahan: The Life and Work of Captain Alfred Thayer Mahan.* New Haven, CT: Yale University Press, 1939.

Quester, George R. *Mahan and American Naval Thought since 1914.* Newport, RI: Naval War College, 1990.

Reynolds, Clark G. *Famous American Admirals.* New York: Van Nostrand Reinhold, 1978.

Seager, Robert. *Alfred Thayer Mahan: The Man and His Letters.* Annapolis, MD: Naval Institute Press, 1977.

Dennis Hart Mahan, who initiated the study of military theory in the United States and exerted a profound impact on officers in the American Civil War.

The younger Mahan attended Columbia College for two years and then entered the United States Naval Academy, Annapolis, graduating second in his class in 1859. He then was on the *Congress* in the Brazil Squadron. During the Civil War, he served with the South Atlantic Blockading Squadron and was promoted to lieutenant commander (June 1865) and commander (November 1872). In 1883, he published *The Gulf and Inland Waters,* a book treating U.S. Navy operations during the Civil War. This impressed Captain Stephen Luce, who in 1885, as president of the newly established Naval War College, invited Mahan there to lecture on naval tactics and history. He was promoted to captain in September 1885.

In 1890, Mahan published his lectures under the title *The Influence of Sea Power upon History, 1660–1783.* This very important book is a history of British naval development in its most crucial period, a treatise on war at sea, and a ringing defense of a large navy. The book had particular influence in Britain, Germany, and Japan, but Mahan's lectures and magazine articles on current strategic problems also won an ever-widening audience in the United States that included such individuals as Theodore Roosevelt.

Maine, USS

The U.S. Navy warship *Maine* was authorized by Congress on August 3, 1886, as an armored cruiser (heavy cruiser) but was designated by the navy as a second-class battleship. Built at the New York Navy Yard supposedly on the design of the *Riachuelo,* built by Samuda for Brazil, the *Maine* was laid down in October 1888,

The U.S. battleship *Maine*. On February 15, 1898, the ship exploded and sank in Havana Harbor, killing 266 of its crew. Many Americans held Spain responsible, and the battle cry "Remember the *Maine*, to hell with Spain!" swept the nation. (Naval Historical Center)

launched in November 1889, and commissioned on September 17, 1995. The ship was 319 feet in length overall by 57 feet in beam. It displaced 6,682 tons (7,180 fully loaded) and had a speed of 17.5 knots. Its coal capacity largely limited it to a coastal defense role. Typical of such warships at the time, it had a decidedly mixed battery to allow the ship to fight at long, intermediate, and close ranges. It was armed with four 10-inch guns in twin *en echelon* turrets and six 6-inch guns in the superstructure (two forward, two amidships, and two aft). It also carried seven 6-pounders, four 1-pounders, and four Gatling guns and had six 18-inch above-water torpedo tubes. Protection came in the form of a 180-foot-long steel armor belt 3 feet above the waterline and 4 feet below it. The top portion of the belt tapered from 12 inches in thickness to 6 inches at the lower edge. It also had 2-inch deck armor forward and 2–3 inches aft. Barbette and turret armor was 12 and 8 inches, respectively.

The renewal of fighting in Cuba between revolutionaries bent on independence and Spanish troops determined to prevent that created concern for the security of U.S. interests in Cuba and fears that a European power, most probably Germany, might seek to take advantage of the situation. On January 24, 1898, President William McKinley ordered Captain Charles Sigsbee of the *Maine* to steam from Key West, Florida, to Havana supposedly to protect U.S. interests in Cuba but actually to pressure Spain to change its policies there and to enforce the 1823 Monroe Doctrine. This was certainly a provocative act, much resented by Spain, although Madrid had reluctantly agreed to it. The *Maine* arrived in Havana Harbor on January 25.

Although the Spanish authorities in Havana extended full courtesies to the *Maine*'s crew, Sigsbee refused to allow the sailors shore leave in order to avoid a possible incident. At 9:30 p.m. on February 15, the *Maine* sank in Havana Harbor when its forward magazines, containing nearly five tons of powder charges, exploded. The explosion claimed 266 lives. A total of 260 men died immediately or shortly thereafter. Another 6 men died later from their injuries. The casualties represented nearly three-quarters of the ship's crew. Sigsbee and most of the officers survived because their quarters were located aft in the ship. Spanish ships and the civilian steamer *City of Washington* set about rescuing the survivors.

While the circumstances of the ignition of the magazines remained in controversy, the loss of the *Maine* provided a rallying point for Americans who wanted war. The cry "Remember the *Maine*, to hell with Spain!" swept the country, and the day after the board of inquiry's report, President McKinley sent Madrid an ultimatum that on April 11 led to the U.S. declaration of war against Spain. It may be misleading to say that the explosion aboard the *Maine* in and of itself brought about the war declaration, but it is hard not to conclude that the incident gave the United States a perfect pretense for war and was indeed the last in a long series of U.S.-Spanish clashes over Cuba.

SPENCER C. TUCKER

Further Reading
Blow, Michael. *A Ship to Remember: The Maine and the Spanish-American War.* New York: Morrow, 1992.
Friedman, Norman. *U.S. Battleships: An Illustrated Design History.* Annapolis, MD: Naval Institute Press, 1985.
Rickover, Hyman G. *How the Battleship Maine Was Destroyed.* Annapolis, MD: Naval Institute Press, 1995.
Samuels, Peggy, and Harold Samuels. *Remembering the Maine.* Washington, DC: Smithsonian Institution Press, 1995.
Weems, John Edward. *The Fate of the Maine.* New York: Henry Holt, 1985.

Maine, USS, Inquiries into the Loss of

At 9:30 p.m. on February 15, 1898, the U.S. Navy second-class battleship *Maine* sank in Havana Harbor when its forward magazines, filled with nearly five tons of powder charges, exploded. The explosion claimed 266 lives and proved a rallying cry for those in the United States who wanted war with Spain.

Charles Sigsbee, the captain of the *Maine* and one of the survivors of the explosion, urged that there be no rush to judgment, especially as the Spanish extended every possible resource in rescue and recovery efforts after the ship sank. He noted at the end of his official telegraphed report to Washington, "Public opinion should be suspended until further report."

The navy immediately established a board of inquiry to establish the cause of the explosion of the ship's magazines. This went forward in Havana and extended over a four-week period. The condition of the wreck and the lack of technical experts on the board cast doubt on the report's validity. The board issued its findings on March 28, 1898, and held that an external mine was to blame. Although the board did not attempt to determine who had set the device, there was a clear implication of Spanish responsibility. The day after the official report was issued, U.S. president William McKinley sent Madrid an ultimatum that on April 11 led to the president asking Congress for a declaration of war against Spain.

In 1911, Congress voted the requisite funds to remove the wreckage of the *Maine* from Havana Harbor, where it was a navigational hazard, and the Navy Department ordered a second investigation into the ship's destruction. Toward that end, U.S. Army engineers constructed a coffer dam around the ship, and the water was pumped out. The wreck was then studied and photographed before it was repaired to floating state and towed out to sea to be scuttled. The examining board discovered that the bottom hull

The damaged forward section of the U.S. battleship *Maine* following its sinking. In 1911, army engineers built a coffer dam around the wreckage, pumping out the water and allowing the damage to be studied. (Naval Historical Center)

plates in the area of the reserve six-inch magazine were bent inward, which suggested an external explosion. The board then confirmed the earlier finding of an external explosion.

Although the precise cause will probably never be established, in 1976 Admiral Hyman Rickover and his staff published *How the Battleship Maine Was Destroyed,* a study that relied on the previous two reports as well as several experts on explosions and stress studies of metal in underwater explosions and concluded that the damage was inconsistent with an external mine. Rickover suggested that spontaneous combustion of bituminous coal in one of the ship's bunkers had cooked off ammunition in an adjacent magazine. There had been similar examples of spontaneous combustion in coal bunkers aboard other navy ships, most notably on the cruiser *Cincinnati* while at Key West, Florida, in 1896 and on board the armored cruiser *Brooklyn* in May 1898, but they had been discovered in time. Critics of Rickover's conclusion point out that it is unlikely that such a fire could have gone undetected.

It is hard to see what the Spanish might have thought they could gain from planting a mine. Other possibilities are an accidental explosion in the magazine itself, sabotage, or a mine planted either by right-wing Spanish groups who hated the United States or by Cuban rebels anxious to involve the United States in a war with Spain in which they could secure independence for Cuba. Peggy and Harold Samuels claimed in *Remembering the Maine* (1995), the latest study of this event, that the culprit was a mine set by Spanish extremists. The truth is that we will never know for certain who or what caused the explosion that sank the *Maine.*

SPENCER C. TUCKER

See also
Maine, USS; United States Navy; Warships

Further Reading
Blow, Michael. *A Ship to Remember: The Maine and the Spanish-American War.* New York: Morrow, 1992.
Rickover, Hyman G. *How the Battleship Maine Was Destroyed.* Annapolis, MD: Naval Institute Press, 1995.
Samuels, Peggy, and Harold Samuels. *Remembering the Maine.* Washington, DC: Smithsonian Institution Press, 1995.
Weems, John Edward. *The Fate of the Maine.* New York: Henry Holt, 1985.

Malaria

Systemic disease caused by four species of protozoa of the genus *Plasmodium.* The organism is transmitted by the female of one of several species of the *Anopheles* mosquito, which, on biting a human, ingests the gametocyte, one of several stages in the organism's complex developmental cycle. The malarial organism multiplies in the mosquito's abdominal cavity and then migrates to the salivary glands from which it is injected into whomever it bites next. It migrates through the human bloodstream to the liver, where it multiplies before again being released back into the bloodstream. It then enters red blood cells and feeds on hemoglobin. When the

victim is bitten by another mosquito, the malarial protozoa are ingested, and the cycle is repeated. There are four species of *Plasmodium,* of which *falciparum* is the most lethal. The other three (*vivax, ovale,* and *malariae*) seldom cause death but can cause repeated episodes of fever and debilitation.

Malaria (named from the Italian *mal aria,* or bad air) was endemic in Athens at least as early as the fifth century BC, and its prevalence in Rome probably played a role in the empire's decline. It was brought to the Western Hemisphere by the Spanish slave trade and was a factor in the collapse of the Central and South American indigenous peoples.

Malaria was endemic in Cuba, and more than 30,000 Spanish troops died from infectious diseases in 1897 alone, leading Cuban revolutionary General Máximo Gómez y Báez to comment that the three best insurrectionist generals were June, July, and August. Because the disease was often confused with typhoid (or conflated into typho-malarial fever), it is impossible to arrive at a precise estimate of the disease incidence during the Spanish-American War, but cases were almost entirely confined to Cuba, and malaria was essentially unknown in both Puerto Rico and the Philippines.

Diagnosis and record keeping were better after the war. Between 1898 and 1900, more than 1,000 people a year died from the disease in Havana alone. Ronald Ross, the British Indian surgeon who had worked out the malarial life cycle and proven that the mosquito was its vector, had contacted U.S. Army surgeon general George Sternberg in 1898 and suggested that the invading force consider mosquito control and protective netting, but neither measure was adopted until after the war, when Walter Reed and his co-workers demonstrated that the mosquito was also responsible for yellow fever transmission. Brigadier General Leonard Wood ordered his chief surgeon William Gorgas to institute a comprehensive anti-mosquito program, and both yellow fever and malaria were brought under control. The number of malaria cases in Havana dropped to an average of only 44 a year between 1899 and 1902. In all of 1912, there was only 1 malaria fatality in Cuba's capital city.

JACK MCCALLUM

See also
Gorgas, William Crawford; Sternberg, George Miller; Typhoid Fever; Wood, Leonard

Further Reading
Cirillo, Vincent J. *Bullets and Bacilli: The Spanish-American War and Military Medicine.* New Brunswick, NJ: Rutgers University Press, 2004.
McCallum, Jack. *Leonard Wood: Rough Rider, Surgeon, and Architect of American Imperialism.* New York: New York University Press, 2006.

Malolos, Philippines, Capture of
Event Date: March 31, 1899

Capture of the capital of the First Philippine Republic on March 31, 1899, by U.S. forces during the Philippine-American War (1899–1902). On January 21, 1899, rebels proclaimed Malolos, a town lo-

American soldiers ride into the captured Filipino insurgent capital of Malolos in 1899. (Library of Congress)

cated 25 miles north of Manila in Bulacan Province of the island of Luzon, to be the Philippine Republic's capital. Once hostilities began between American forces and the Army of Liberation on February 4, fighting flared along U.S. positions in Manila, and the Filipinos withdrew northward abreast along the Manila-Dagupan railroad toward Malolos.

Major General Elwell S. Otis prepared the U.S. VIII Corps for operations against Malolos hoping that this might end the revolt in one stroke. Reaching the insurgents' capital would be no easy task, for villages, thick vegetation, swamps, and rice paddies as well as streams, ditches, and deltas impeded the approach. Six rivers, some with no bridges, proved a formidable obstacle.

Otis first planned to sever the insurgents' supply line north from Manila. On March 12, 1899, Brigadier General Lloyd Wheaton led a U.S. brigade east and south to Laguna de Bay, cleaning out pockets of resistance and destroying crops that might be a source of supply to the rebels. Wheaton's operations were successful and ended on March 17.

Otis was now ready to begin operations against Malolos. On March 17, he split VIII Corps into a defensive force to defend Manila and an offensive force to operate against the Army of Liberation at Malolos. The campaign began on March 25. Major General Arthur MacArthur's 2nd Division of 9,000 men was reorganized into three brigades under Brigadier Generals Harrison

Otis (1st Brigade), Irving Hale (2nd Brigade), and Robert H. Hall (3rd Brigade). Wheaton's provision brigade, shifted from the 1st Division, was to act in support.

Hall's brigade was to feint a direct attack along the Caloocan-Malolos road. Two brigades would then proceed northward—Otis's brigade on the left and Hale's brigade on the right—to Novaliches and there separate. Hale was to move against San Francisco del Monte and Bagbag, while Otis pushed to the south of Novaliches. The brigades would then pivot to the west, sever the railway below Polo, and move against the Filipino left and check its retreat. Wheaton was then to begin a frontal attack with his provisional brigade, forcing the Army of Liberation toward Hale and Otis. Although the plan appeared sound, the Spanish maps proved largely worthless, and the Americans soon discovered that serious terrain obstacles, not identified on the maps, severely impeded their progress.

On March 25, Hale's brigade, backed by the Utah artillery battery, attacked and penetrated the Filipino defensive positions. Advancing northward, it faced physical obstructions and tenacious resistance. Supported by the battery, the brigade crossed the Tuliahan River and engaged and outflanked insurgent forces. To Hale's left, Otis's brigade confronted difficult terrain and a spirited Filipino defense.

MacArthur now realized that he could not reach the assigned rendezvous point of Polo in time. He then requested and received permission from Otis to discontinue the drive on Polo and turn below its objective. This effectively ended any chance of blocking the Army of Liberation's withdrawal to Malolos.

On March 26, U.S. troops of the 2nd Division advanced to the northwest near Polo, crossed the Mecauayan Bridge, and engaged Army of Liberation troops, killing more than 90 of them. On March 27, they forded the Marilao River, outflanked the insurgents, and cut the latter's defensive line.

On March 25, meanwhile, Wheaton launched his diversionary attack beyond Caloocan and drove to the Tuliahan River. Despite natural obstacles and stout defenders, the brigade's direct assault carried the position. Once across the Tuliahan on March 26, Wheaton's men drove the Filipinos back. Still, the Filipinos fought hard, killing 26 U.S. soldiers and wounding another 150 before withdrawing.

Otis now ordered MacArthur and Wheaton to combine and drive north, hopefully catching the Army of Liberation before it could gain Malolos. On March 26, the Americans took the town of Malinta, and Filipino troops on its outskirts scattered. Shortly thereafter, MacArthur's and Wheaton's men joined forces. The American trap had thus closed, but the Army of Liberation eluded it.

MacArthur's men were now exhausted, and he was obliged to halt and await resupply. The advance resumed on March 29. A stiff fight occurred at the Bocaue River when the insurgents ambushed the 20th Kansas Regiment and inflicted 27 U.S. casualties, but by now the Filipinos were in full retreat, and there was no climactic battle for Malolos. The Americans entered the town, but as they did so it was in flames, torched by the escaping Army of Liberation.

The campaign to take Malolos was a qualified success. The Americans had failed in their effort to crush nationalist resistance in one stroke, and the American forces had sustained nearly 500 casualties during a span of only a few days. Emilio Aguinaldo y Famy and much of the Army of Liberation had escaped to fight again. Nonetheless, the campaign had also cost the insurgents dearly in terms of equipment, especially Mauser rifles and ammunition.

RODNEY J. ROSS AND SPENCER C. TUCKER

See also

Aguinaldo y Famy, Emilio; Luzon Campaigns; MacArthur, Arthur; Otis, Elwell Stephen; Philippine-American War; Philippine Republic, First; Wheaton, Lloyd

Further Reading

Linn, Brian McAllister. *The Philippine War, 1899–1902.* Lawrence: University Press of Kansas, 2000.

Silbey, David J. *A War of Frontier and Empire: The Philippine-American War, 1899–1902.* New York: Hill and Wang, 2006.

Malolos Constitution

Philippine constitution. Drafted by the Malolos Congress and ratified on November 28, 1898, it served as the working blueprint for the First Philippine Republic. Emilio Aguinaldo y Famy, the republic's first president, signed the document into law on December 23, 1898. The Malolos Constitution was actually the fourth and final constitution written by Filipino nationalists between 1896 and 1899. Of these, it was the first to call for a true representative democracy. Shortly after the Spanish-American War began, Aguinaldo proclaimed independence from Spain on June 12, 1898. Later that month, he called upon Filipinos to elect delegates to a unicameral congress that would write a constitution and establish a framework for government. By July 7, 193 delegates had been selected. They came almost exclusively from the educated political and economic elite, and only about 20 percent were actually elected. Because of wartime conditions and travel difficulties, Aguinaldo appointed the rest. Meanwhile, on August 13, 1898, the Spanish surrendered to the Americans at Manila.

In mid-September 1898, Aguinaldo asked delegates to convene just north of Manila. They met in the convent of Barasoain Church at Malolos (Bulacan Province) from September 15, 1898, to January 21, 1899. In the opening session on September 15, Aguinaldo addressed the delegates. Against the advice of Apolinario Mabini, a close adviser to Aguinaldo and the great theoretician of the revolution, Aguinaldo also asked them to form committees to draft a constitution for the First Philippine Republic. On September 29, 1898, with Japanese and American journalists witnessing the proceedings, the delegates ratified Aguinaldo's Declaration of Independence.

From the start, the convention was fundamentally divided. Some delegates opposed a strong chief executive and secretly favored autonomy or political assimilation under U.S. rule. Influenced by Mabini, a minority held that writing a permanent constitution was premature and would only accelerate U.S. military intervention and occupation.

Debated in Tagalog and Spanish, the Constitución Política (Malolos Constitution) was written entirely in Spanish. Competing proposals were hotly debated, and ordinary Malolos townspeople, no longer fearing reprisals from the Spanish colonialists, also excitedly discussed the constitutional issues. The constitution consisted of 14 articles, several transitory provisions, and 1 additional unnumbered article. Among other issues, the constitution provided for separation of church and state (Title III), individual human and political rights (Title IV), separation of governmental powers (Titles V and VII–X), local assemblies (Title XI), and an amendment procedure (Title XIII). To that extent, the document reflected liberal and Enlightenment views embodied in constitutions of the United States, Belgium, France, Guatemala, Costa Rica, and Brazil, among others.

The Malolos Constitution outlined the governance of a parliamentary republic. However, by limiting the chief executive's freedom of action, it threatened to hamper rapid decision making during wartime. Elected by the Asamblea Nacional (National Assembly), a permanent seven-member legislative commission was to supervise the president at all times (Title VI). Although legislative supervision was ostensibly designed to offset dictatorial tendencies, it also handicapped the government as hostilities with the

United States loomed. Under pressure from Mabini, Aguinaldo held out for a few minor amendments.

On November 29, 1898, the Malolos Congress ratified the constitution. On December 10, however, ratification was upstaged by the Treaty of Paris between the United States and Spain. Under Article II of that agreement, the Americans agreed to pay Spain $20 million for the Philippines. Although the U.S. Senate did not ratify the Treaty of Paris until February 6, 1899, it strengthened the hand of President William McKinley in domestic U.S. politics and gave him a pretext for prompt Philippine annexation. Entreaties by Don Felipe Agoncillo and other diplomats sent by Aguinaldo went unanswered both in Washington and Paris, and their energetic high-profile supporters in the Anti-Imperialist League could not stem the tide of public opinion in the United States that supported annexation.

Despite continuing misgivings about its basic structure and amendments, Aguinaldo signed the constitution on December 23, 1898. He refrained from proclaiming it, however, until January 23, 1899, in a public ceremony held in Malolos. Less than a month later, the Philippine-American War broke out, rendering much of the Malolos Constitution next to impossible to execute.

VINCENT KELLY POLLARD

See also

Agoncillo, Felipe; Aguinaldo y Famy, Emilio; Anti-Imperialist League; Mabini, Apolinario; Paris, Treaty of; Philippine-American War; Philippine Islands, U.S. Acquisition of; Philippine Republic, First

Further Reading

Agoncillo, Teodoro A. *Malolos: The Crisis of the Republic*. Quezon City: University of the Philippines Press, 1960.
Austin, Eduardo Diaz Serrano. "Study of the Rise and the Fall of the First Democratic Republic in the Far East: The Philippines, 1898–1899." Unpublished PhD dissertation, Georgetown University, 1957.
Mabini, Apolinario. *Memorias de la Revolución Filipina* [Recollections of the Philippine Revolution]. Manila: Buró de la Imprenta Pública, 1960.

Malvar, Miguel
Birth Date: September 27, 1865
Death Date: October 11, 1911

Key military leader in the 1896–1898 Filipino uprising against Spanish rule and the anti-American insurgency during the Philippine-American War (1899–1902). Miguel Malvar was born on September 27, 1865, in Santo Tomas, Batangas, Philippines. His father, Maximo, was a hardworking and enterprising farmer and businessman who amassed considerable wealth, making his money from the cultivation of sugarcane and rice in the shadow of Mount Maquiling.

Unlike most Filipinos at the time, the younger Malvar had the benefit of education, although studies were clearly not his strong suit. His early schooling came about through private tutorials with a Roman Catholic priest, Father Valerio Malabanan. Malvar then spent an additional three years in school before turning his sights on business and farming. He enjoyed even more success than his father and before long had cobbled together major landholdings in Batangas and was growing oranges, mainly for export.

By the mid-1880s, many Filipinos had begun to chafe under Spanish rule, which was little changed since the 16th century when the Spanish had first laid claim to the archipelago. Discontent with the status quo was strong in Batangas Province, which lay in the southwestern corner of the island of Luzon. In Batangas, anti-Spanish sentiment had a distinct anticlerical element to it, and before long priests and friars in the region had become targets of Filipino animosity. In 1890, Malvar was elected *gobernadorcillo* (local governor) and immediately began to implement a systematic anticleric campaign. This put him on a collision course with the local clergy, and this confrontation soon blossomed into open defiance of Spanish authorities in general.

Sometime in the early to mid-1890s, Malvar joined the secret Katipunan society, which was dedicated to ridding the Philippines of Spanish control. He began assembling a makeshift army on his own initiative, to be known as the Batangas Brigade, and proved to be an able military leader known for his dogged determination even in the face of likely defeat. His forces collaborated closely with other insurgents on Luzon, and he became a close ally of Emilio Aguinaldo y Famy. Although the insurgency against the Spanish grew in size and intensity, Filipino forces were gradually outgunned by the better-armed Spanish. When Aguinaldo and much of the resistance had taken refuge in Biak-na-Bato, Malvar joined other revolutionary leaders there and reluctantly signed the Pact of Biak-na-Bato in December 1897. He had been opposed to any accommodation with the Spanish, but his view was clearly in the minority.

Malvar left for Hong Kong, per the stipulations of the pact, on December 25. His exile was short-lived, however. When the Spanish-American War commenced in April 1898, American officials requested that Aguinaldo and the other revolutionaries return to the Philippines to help in the fight against the Spanish. Malvar returned to the Philippines in early May and immediately mobilized his Batangas Brigade for action.

The war against the Spanish went well for Malvar. By July, Batangas had been cleansed of Spanish control. It was at this time that Malvar began to assemble a larger force, which he envisioned would be akin to a provincial army. He did so when it became clear that the Americans were not going to allow Filipino independence or autonomy. In February 1899, the Philippine-American War commenced, and Malvar was at the forefront of guerrilla activity, this time against U.S. forces. Like Aguinaldo, Malvar understood well the importance of guerrilla warfare against a force with superior firepower. Thus, he sought to prolong the war as long as possible to wear down American morale, which in turn might help the antiexpansionist Democrats win the 1900 elections in the United States.

In May 1899, Malvar planned an attack on American strongholds in southern Luzon. The offensive never took place, however, as U.S. forces decided to concentrate on pacifying the south. In the summer of 1899, Malvar had retreated to Calamba to effect a defensive perimeter around Batangas. Repeated American thrusts into Batangas began to wear away his forces. It was clear that he had spread his men too thinly. Refusing to give way, Malvar and his remaining troops kept up an insurgency campaign that would last into 1902. Nevertheless, as the fighting dragged on and more and more civilian casualties occurred, he began losing support from the province's elites and small middle class.

Aguinaldo was finally captured by U.S. forces in March 1901, which should have put an effective end to the insurgency movement. Malvar, undeterred, chose to fight on in Batangas. He was also now considered the leader of the entire insurgency effort. For a brief time, his offensives exacted a toll on the American military in late 1901 and early 1902. But he could not keep up the momentum or overcome the lopsided U.S. advantage in firepower. At the same time, Brigadier General James Franklin Bell launched a brutal offensive in Batangas to capture Malvar and decapitate his forces, which included a controversial scorched earth policy that brought high casualties. By early 1902, only two guerrilla units in the Philippines remained, that of Malvar's and forces under Vicente Lukban on Samar. As Malvar's forces suffered one defeat after another and as short supplies brought them to near starvation, defections and desertions skyrocketed.

In April 1902, Malvar finally surrendered to U.S. forces. His position had been revealed by former guerrillas who had defected to the American side. Just a few days before, Lukban had also surrendered. By month's end, nearly all of the Batangas guerrillas had given up, and the battle for Batangas was over.

Malvar had the distinction of being the last guerrilla leader to capitulate during the Philippine-American War. The Americans treated Malvar with honor, and he returned to a quiet life of farming on his native land in Batangas. Malvar died on October 11, 1911.

PAUL G. PIERPAOLI JR.

See also

Aguinaldo y Famy, Emilio; Bell, James Franklin; Biak-na-Bato, Pact of; Katipunan; Lukban, Vicente

Further Reading

Agoncillo, Teodoro A. *The Revolt of the Masses: The Story of Bonfacio and the Katipunan.* Quezon City: University of the Philippines, 1956.

May, Glenn Anthony. *Battle for Batangas: A Philippine Province at War.* New Haven, CT: Yale University Press, 1991.

Welch, Richard E., Jr. *Response to Imperialism: The United States and the Philippine-American War, 1899–1902.* Chapel Hill: University of North Carolina Press, 1979.

Mambises

Term used to describe Cuban rebels, beginning with the Ten Years' War (1868–1878). The origin of the term "Mambi" is not known with certainty. Conjecture has it that it is an Afro-Antillean word that was given to rebels on the island of Hispaniola fighting against Spanish rule in the early part of the 19th century. During that in-

Mambi (rebel) soldiers who fought for Cuban independence from Spain, shown here in 1896. (Library of Congress)

surrection, which was led by a former Spanish military officer named Eutimio Mamby (or Mambi), Spanish troops dubbed the rebels "Mambises." In 1868 when Cuban insurrectionists rebelled against the Spanish and resorted to the machete-wielding tactics of the Mambises on Hispaniola, the Spaniards began referring to them as Mambises as well. Before long, the rebels had adopted the name for themselves. By 1870, the Ten Years' War had produced some 12,000 Mambises, who were bent on driving the Spanish out of Cuba. When the Cuban insurrection of 1895 began, the rebels were once again known as the Mambises.

ARTHUR STEINBERG

See also

Cuba; Cuban War of Independence; Ten Years' War

Further Reading

Kelly, James G. *The Mambi Land.* Philadelphia: Lippincott, 1874.
Martí, José. *Selected Readings.* New York: Penguin, 2002.
Scott, Rebecca J. *Slave Emancipation in Cuba: The Transition to Free Labor, 1860–1899.* Princeton, NJ: Princeton University Press, 1985.

Manifest Destiny

An ideological mind-set used to rationalize the westward territorial expansion of the United States to the Pacific Ocean during the 1840s and 1850s. Manifest Destiny expressed the belief that the United States had the God-given right and indeed duty to occupy the remainder of the continent and that such expansion was clearly justified (manifest) and inevitable (destiny). The concept was also used to legitimize the annexation of Oregon, Hawaii, and the Philippines.

The phrase "manifest destiny" was coined in the summer of 1845 by John L. Sullivan, a journalist and editor of the *United States Magazine and Democratic Review.* In an essay supporting the annexation of Texas, he argued for the "fulfillment of our manifest destiny to overspread the continent allotted by Providence for the free development of our yearly multiplying millions." Even though the phrase became one of the most influential slogans ever coined, O'Sullivan certainly did not originate the sentiment behind the slogan. In the first half of the 19th century, the United States witnessed an extraordinary growth in territory and population. The multiplying millions to which O'Sullivan referred included immigrants from Europe, who had crossed the Atlantic in droves hoping for a better life. Many of these newcomers began looking westward for fertile, unoccupied lands. Expansion across the continent was thus seen as a desirable necessity, and O'Sullivan gave the movement its name. However, Manifest Destiny included more than the will for westward expansion. It was also a belief that the United States was exceptional of all the world's nations—the promised land, the new Israel, and God's own country—and that its people had both a divine mission and the altruistic right to spread the virtue of its democratic institutions and liberties to new realms. Indeed, this thinking can be traced back to the 17th century, when in 1630 the Puritan minister John Winthrop referred to the Massachusetts Bay Colony as a "city upon a hill" that would stand as an example for all people.

The theme of American exceptionalism was heightened during the American Revolution, when the colonists fought for the right to implement their own version of freedom and democracy. With independence came the promise of expansion, which included cheap and abundant land and economic opportunities west and south of the 13 original colonies. The Louisiana Purchase of 1803 and the acquisition of Florida from Spain in the 1819 Adams-Onís Treaty more than doubled the size of the United States, creating a new frontier that offered relief for a growing population.

The Monroe Doctrine of 1823 also exemplified the ideas and the mood behind Manifest Destiny. When President James Monroe warned Europe that the Americas were no longer "to be considered as subjects for future colonization by any European powers," he paved the way for increasing U.S. hegemony over its neighbors by establishing his nation as the legitimate protector of the Western Hemisphere. Thus, the concept of Manifest Destiny became even more important during the Oregon Boundary Dispute with Great Britain and in U.S. relations with Mexico. Regarding Oregon, Great Britain and the United States had agreed in the Anglo-American Convention of 1818 to jointly occupy the Oregon Territory. However, in the years following the treaty, thousands of American settlers had migrated to the Northwest, and calls for annexation of the region became very popular in the 1840s. When Great Britain rejected President John Tyler's proposal to divide the area along the 49th parallel, American expansionists responded with demands for a northern border along the 54°40' line (the slogan at the time was "Fifty-Four Forty or Fight"). The question of the annexation of Oregon played an important role in the election of James K. Polk as president in 1844. After the election, however, Polk did not yield to the extremists and settled the boundary dispute with Britain diplomatically with the Buchanan-Pakenham of 1846, which terminated the joint occupation and divided Oregon along the 49th parallel.

At the same time, expansionist sentiments led to war with Mexico in 1846. Ever since Mexico had opened its province of Texas for colonization in 1823, thousands of settlers from the United States had moved south. The movement was so strong that Mexican authorities soon lost control of the province. In 1835–1836, differences between Anglo settlers and the Mexican government led the new settlers to revolt against Mexico and declare Texas independent. They then sought admittance to the United States. The annexation of Texas was highly controversial among U.S. politicians, however, because it would come in as a slave state. Anxious to keep the delicate balance between slave and free states, the United States rebuffed Texas's request to join the Union. The question of what to do with Texas was an issue in the 1844 presidential campaign because Polk promised annexation should he be elected. Although he agreed to settle the boundary dispute over Oregon diplomatically, he refused to compromise with Mexico after Congress approved the annexation of Texas in 1845.

John Gast's 1873 painting *American Progress,* depicting an allegorical female figure of America leading settlers, telegraph lines, and railroads into the untamed West. The concept of Manifest Destiny represented in the painting held that the United States had a moral and divine mandate to colonize the lands west of the Mississippi. (Library of Congress)

Polk's desire to acquire California as well as annex all of Texas led to war with Mexico in May 1846. In supporting war against Mexico, American expansionists for the first time cited racial reasons for expanding American territory. This reasoning, though, was controversial even among expansionists. Its supporters argued that Manifest Destiny would help improve the Mexicans, while its opponents claimed that Mexicans, as non–Anglo-Saxons, were not qualified to become Americans. When the Mexican War ended in February 1848 with the Treaty of Guadalupe Hidalgo, Mexico ceded to the United States present-day Texas with its boundary at the Rio Grande and what would become New Mexico, Arizona, California, and parts of Nevada, Utah, and Colorado. The United States had now accomplished its goal of expanding its territory to the Pacific Ocean. After the war, Polk offered Spain $100 million for Cuba in an attempt to consolidate his territory even further, but Spain declined.

After decades of internal struggle, civil war, and reconstruction, the belief that Manifest Destiny justified the seizing of Native American and Spanish-held lands was revived in the 1890s. The ideology behind the term, however, now contained elements of social Darwinism and social determinism. Expansionists believed that it was the white man's burden to lead inferior races in other parts of the world to better lives. The British author Rudyard Kipling made this viewpoint famous in his 1899 poem "The White Man's Burden," which was subtitled "The United States and the Philippine Islands" and in which he urged the United States to spread civilization to less-developed peoples. This expanded set of beliefs incorporated ideas not only about race and religion but also about culture and economic opportunities. Expansionists assumed that Americans had the divine right to dominate other lands because they belonged to the most advanced race and had the most developed culture, the best economic system, and the necessary military and technical expertise.

This notion of an international Manifest Destiny was at play in the decision of the United States to intervene in the Cuban War of Independence (1895–1897) and to annex Hawaii and the Philippines in 1898. The United States soon extended its interest into Asia and the Far East with its calls for an open door policy, meaning that U.S. policy makers sought equal trade preferences in places such as China.

During the Spanish-American War, several U.S. legislators called for the annexation of all Spanish territories. As a result of the war, the United States took control of the Philippines, Guam, and Puerto Rico and had occupation troops in Cuba for several years. Despite the extremist expansionists' demands, Cuba was not annexed, however. Yet the 1901 Platt Amendment provided for the establishment of a permanent U.S. naval base on the island at Guantánamo and the right to intervene in Cuba militarily to maintain order.

The Spanish-American War and the Philippine-American War marked U.S. entry into world affairs. President Theodore Roosevelt buttressed the Monroe Doctrine with his 1904 corollary to the Monroe Doctrine, which stated that the United States reserved the right to intervene in the affairs of any nation in the hemisphere if its political system or economic policies threatened the United States or other nations in the hemisphere. The belief that it was a mission of the United States to promote and defend democracy throughout the world would remain an influential part of the political culture within the United States during the 20th century and into the 21st century.

KATJA WUESTENBECKER

See also
Expansionism; Imperialism; Social Darwinism; White Man's Burden

Further Reading
Haynes, Sam W., and Christopher Morris, eds. *Manifest Destiny and Empire: American Antebellum Expansion.* The Walter Prescott Webb Memorial Lectures 31. College Station: Texas A&M University Press, 1997.
Heidler, David S., and Jeanne T. Heidler. *Manifest Destiny.* Westport, CT: Greenwood, 2003.
Sampson, Robert D. "The Pacifist-Reform Roots of John L. Sullivan's Manifest Destiny." *Mid-America* 84(1–3) (2002): 129–144.
Stephanson, Anders. *Manifest Destiny: American Expansion and the Empire of Right.* New York: Hill and Wang, 1996.

Manila

Capital city of the Philippines and the primary political and cultural center of the Philippine archipelago. Manila is located along Manila Bay in the southern portion of the Island of Luzon, the largest island in the Philippines, and has a current metropolitan population of more than 10 million people. The word "Manila" is derived from the Tagalog *may nilad,* a reference to an aquatic plant that grew profusely along the margins of Manila Bay. The city of Manila has always maintained a strong seafaring flavor owing to its situation on one of the finest natural bays in the world and arguably the best in East Asia.

Begun along the banks of the Pasig River near its confluence with the bay as a small tribal community, Manila was a lively town ruled by Rajah Sulayman, an Islamic Malaysian with a royal bloodline, prior to the arrival of the Spanish. Only a year after the first Spanish conquistador landed at Manila, the Islamic town had been torched by the Spaniards and the vestiges of Islam destroyed. Recognizing its strategic potential, Spanish colonial authorities soon

American flags adorn buildings along Escalta Street in Manila on July 4, 1899. (Library of Congress)

established Manila as the principal Spanish outpost on the Philippines and made it the seat of Spanish colonial government beginning in the late 16th century.

Over the course of more than three centuries, the Spanish left their mark on the city, including Roman Catholicism. Indeed, the formerly Muslim enclave became a bastion for Catholics, both native and Spanish. The principal ethnic group found in Manila was the Tagalogs; however, there were also significant numbers of Filipinos from other islands (Visayans, Maranoas, Llocanos) and a sizable community of Chinese. While the Spanish population in Manila was never very large, it certainly held sway over the city and its politics because of its wealth and privileged positions in the government. Like most locales in the tropics, Manila's weather is characterized by hot, rainy summers and warm, relatively dry winters. The city is regularly threatened by typhoons during typhoon season.

The Spaniards developed what came to be known as the Intramuros beginning around 1570. The Intramuros, meaning "within the walls," was a fortified city enclosed within high, thick walls and surrounded by a moat. It was here where the Spanish colonial government was headquartered and here where government officials and other Spaniards of note lived. During Spanish rule, the Intramuros was considered Manila proper. Anything that fell outside of the walls was typically not planned by Spanish colonial officials. Usually, laborers and field hands erected makeshift communities adjacent to, but outside of, the walls.

Formally established by a royal Spanish decree in 1573, the Intramuros was designed after a medieval Spanish castle and enclosed city. Today, the Intramuros (also referred to as the Old City) is remarkably well preserved, although much of it was rebuilt after World

War II. The area is the only part of the city that has retained significant Spanish details. Also to be found in the Intramuros was Fort Santiago, a famous Spanish redoubt first constructed in 1571.

On May 1, 1898, U.S. naval forces under Commodore George Dewey decimated the Spanish squadron in Manila Bay in less than six hours. The city was also the scene of the First Battle of Manila on August 13, 1898, and the Second Battle of Manila on February 5, 1899. When the war ended and the United States annexed the Philippines, the Americans assumed the old Spanish offices and buildings and administered the territory from Manila.

Manila suffered considerable damage during World War II, especially in the Battle of Manila during February 3–March 3, 1945. Particularly hard hit was the Old City, which was heavily shelled. At the time, Manila was one of the largest cities of Asia, with a population of some 800,000 people. By the end of the battle, the Intramuros had been nearly obliterated, and other parts of the city lay in ruins. The Battle for Manila cost the Americans 1,010 killed and 5,561 wounded. The Japanese lost perhaps 16,000 men in and around the city. More than 100,000 Filipino civilians were killed, and perhaps 70 percent of the city was destroyed.

PAUL G. PIERPAOLI JR.

See also

Manila, First Battle of; Manila, Second Battle of; Manila Bay, Battle of; Philippine Islands, Spanish Colonial Policies toward

Further Reading

Doeppers, Daniel F. *Manila: Social Change in a Late Colonial Metropolis.* New Haven, CT: Yale University Press, 1984.

Neveau, Roland. *Eternal Manila: Contemporary Portrait of a Timeless City.* Paris: Les éditions d'indochine, 1998.

Zafra, Nicholas. *The Colonization of the Philippines and the Beginnings of the Spanish City of Manila.* Manila: National Historical Commission, 1974.

Manila, Capitulation Agreement

Official agreement in which the Spanish surrendered Manila in the Philippines to the Americans. The agreement came after the First Battle of Manila during the Spanish-American War. The term "capitulation" (*capitulación*) was used in the agreement rather than the more pejorative "surrender" (*rendición*) because the latter would have resulted in courts-martial for Spanish officers upon their return to Spain.

The agreement was concluded two days after hostilities had officially ended under the terms of the August 12 Protocol of Peace, word of which did not arrive in the Philippines until August 16 because cable communications had not yet been restored. The Capitulation of Manila Agreement was based on a document signed the day before by U.S. commander in the Philippines Major General Wesley Merritt and Spanish governor-general of the Philippines Fermín Jáudenes y Alvarez.

The agreement of August 14 provided that Spanish soldiers were prisoners of war and were to surrender their weapons. But until the conclusion of a formal peace treaty ending the war, the soldiers would simply remain in their barracks under their own officers. Although also prisoners of war, Spanish officers were permitted to retain their quarters as well as side arms, horses, and all private property. The United States would take possession of all public property and Spanish funds (which amounted to more than $1 million), and Spanish authorities were to present a full list of all public property within 10 days. Manila would now come under U.S. military control. Spanish military families in the islands desiring to leave would be free to do so when they wished.

When word of the Protocol of Peace was received in the Philippines on August 16, Jáudenes protested certain provisions of the Capitulation of Manila Agreement because the Protocol of Peace had been signed before the First Battle of Manila had actually occurred. Merritt rejected Jáudenes's argument and insisted on full implementation of the Capitulation of Manila Agreement, and the Spaniard complied under protest. Because of the date of the Protocol of Peace, however, the issue of whether the United States had acquired the Philippines under right of conquest came up at the Paris Peace Conference.

SPENCER C. TUCKER

See also

Manila, First Battle of; Merritt, Wesley; Peace, Protocol of

Further Reading

O'Toole, G. J. A. *The Spanish War: An American Epic, 1898.* New York: Norton, 1984.

Trask, David F. *The War with Spain in 1898.* Lincoln: University of Nebraska Press, 1996.

Manila, First Battle of
Event Date: August 13, 1898

Last battle fought during the Spanish-American War on August 13, 1898, in Manila. The engagement, which pitted troops of the U.S. Army VIII Corps against Spanish forces, was waged after the Protocol of Peace of August 12 had been signed in Cuba, which ostensibly ended hostilities. At the time, the cable linking Manila with Hong Kong had been cut, so field commanders in the Philippines were unaware of the truce agreement.

Manila, the capital and most important city of the Philippines, is located on the east side of Manila Bay on the island of Luzon. As the capital, Manila was the center of Spanish power in the archipelago and understandably the focal point of Filipino nationalists' efforts to overthrow Spanish rule. Following his breathtaking defeat of the Spanish naval squadron at Manila Bay on May 1, 1898, Commodore George Dewey realized that Manila could and should be seized; however, he had no available landing force to undertake such a mission and therefore could only remain in place and await the army's arrival.

Members of the U.S. Army Signal Corps using flags to communicate from an artillery position outside the city of Manila. (Library of Congress)

The Philippine Expeditionary Force (VIII Corps) reached the Philippines in three contingents, departing from San Francisco as ship availability permitted. The first contingent of 2,500 men, under Brigadier General Thomas Anderson, arrived at the end of June, followed in mid-July by 3,500 additional men under Brigadier General Francis V. Greene. The final contingent, numbering some 4,800 troops and commanded by Brigadier General Arthur MacArthur, reached the islands at the end of July, as did commander of VIII Corps Major General Wesley Merritt.

At the end of July, the Spanish still controlled Manila and much of its environs. The city proper was split by the Pasig River, south of which stood the old walled city of Fort Santiago. The Spanish defensive line, known as the Zapote Line, was located 1.5 miles to the south from where a large blockhouse, Number 14, on the Pasay Road extended west to a stone structure known as Fort San Antonio de Abad, located near the shore of Manila Bay. A line of entrenchments connected these two strong points.

Opposing the Spanish positions were some 10,000 Filipino nationalist troops under the overall command of General Emilio Aguinaldo y Famy, who had formally proclaimed the Republic of the Philippines on June 12. Through the early summer, the nationalists had managed to isolate Manila from its source of supplies, in effect leaving it a city under siege. In Manila, food was scarce and mainly consisted of a little horseflesh and some water buffalo. At night the nationalists and the Spanish defenders maintained lively fire between the two lines but undertook no serious offensive movements.

During the course of the U.S. buildup, Greene's troops constructed a series of entrenchments and moved into some of the works created by the nationalists, who abandoned these positions only reluctantly when Greene persuaded them to do so. The arrangement was irregular, however. In places the nationalist forces actually occupied trench works in between the Americans and the Spaniards.

During the two weeks preceding the attack on Manila, heavy rains of the monsoon season had drenched the area. The period was also characterized by frequent exchanges of artillery and rifle fire between the Americans and the Spanish, with Greene's units

LAND BATTLE OF MANILA, AUGUST 13, 1898

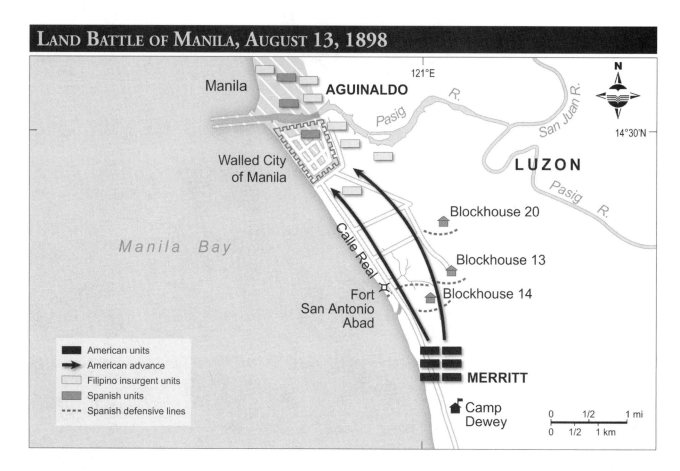

sustaining a number of casualties. In addition, relations between the Americans and Aguinaldo's men, at first cordial, began to deteriorate, as the latter had grown increasingly suspicious of U.S. intentions in the islands.

During the latter part of July, Dewey, now a rear admiral, became convinced that the Spanish would surrender Manila through negotiations. Thus, he met first with Captain-General Basilio Augustín y Dávila and later with his successor, Fermín Jáudenes y Alvarez, to explore possible arrangements. Nevertheless, Greene urged naval gunfire on Spanish positions to relieve the pressure on his command. His troops had dug a line of trenches south of Fort Abad and were taking casualties from Spanish fire every day. General Merritt supported Greene in this request. Dewey, however, was reluctant to open fire from his warships, fearing that doing so would destroy any chance of securing the city by negotiation, an arrangement that he still believed to be entirely possible. Dewey suggested that perhaps the troops could be withdrawn from the trenches until a general attack became necessary. The admiral, however, did agree to support Greene should this prove absolutely necessary. In that eventuality, Greene was to burn a blue light on the beach, and the ships would open fire. Dewey hoped that it would not be necessary.

Merritt had arrived in the Philippines under orders from President William McKinley not to involve the nationalists in taking Manila because to do so would mean including them as partners in future treaty negotiations with Spain. Fermín Jáudenes y Alvarez, who had recently replaced Basilio Augustín as Spanish commander

in Manila, had taken over with orders to hold the city. Inasmuch as peace negotiations were about to get under way, Spain's bargaining position would be weakened by a surrender of the city.

On August 9, 1898, Merritt and Dewey sent an ultimatum to Jáudenes demanding that he surrender Manila. They warned that if he did not, U.S. forces would attack. Jáudenes responded by convening a meeting of his subordinate commanders, putting the issue to a vote. Seven voted in favor of immediate negotiations for a surrender, while seven were opposed. Jáudenes broke the tie, with a decision to continue the present delaying tactics. He informed the Americans that he had no authority to surrender and asked to be able to communicate with Madrid through Hong Kong. On August 10, Dewey and Merritt rejected the suggestion.

In the meantime, Dewey pursued separate negotiations with Jáudenes, working through Belgian consul in Manila Edouard André. Jáudenes then agreed to consider surrendering Manila to U.S. forces but insisted that it would have to appear that a genuine effort had been made to defend the city in order to salvage Spanish honor. Perhaps most important, the Filipino nationalists could not be allowed to enter the city, as Jáudenes feared that they would show no mercy to the Spanish defenders. He also did not want to make it appear as if Spain were surrendering to the Filipinos. Thus, Spain and the United States each had its reasons for wanting to keep Aguinaldo's men from entering Manila.

Finally, the two sides agreed that the Spanish would offer a token defense of their outer works but not of the walled city itself.

However, neither of the U.S. commanders who were to lead the attack, Generals Greene and MacArthur, had been made aware of the pact because General Merritt feared that if they had known of the arrangements, their respective attacks would have lacked authenticity.

Following expiration of the 48-hour truce, Merritt's forces prepared to move. The axis of their attack would be south to north in two essentially parallel columns. Greene's brigade would advance along the northern flank nearest Manila Bay, while MacArthur's brigade was to move along the southern flank. By prearrangement, Dewey's flagship, the *Olympia,* would fire a few token rounds at the heavy stone walls of Fort San Antonio de Abad before raising the international signal flag calling for Spain's surrender.

On the morning of August 13 amid a heavy rain, reveille was sounded. Following the naval bombardment, directed against Fort San Antonio de Abad as agreed, the American artillery opened fire, and the assault moved forward, with the troops advancing under what had turned into a drenching deluge. The Spanish resistance turned out to be heavier than Merritt had expected although not sufficient to thwart the advance. The Spanish defenders gradually fell back, and Greene moved into the city unopposed to accept the Spanish surrender.

On the right flank MacArthur found the going much tougher, exacerbated by Filipino nationalists determined to be involved in the capture of the city. As MacArthur's troops moved north along the Singalong Road, Spanish infantry positioned in a blockhouse inflicted numerous casualties on a regiment of Minnesotans. MacArthur's biggest challenge, however, was in keeping the nationalists from entering the city. As his troops moved closer to Manila, their ranks became increasingly intermingled with those of the Filipinos, and MacArthur was compelled to have his commanders hold the nationalists back from the city.

By the end of the day, U.S. troops had occupied all of Manila proper, but outside the city, Aguinaldo's troops, angry at being denied entrance, were in an ugly mood. Fortunately for the Americans, the heavy tropical storm served to help defuse the hostile mob. On August 14, a joint group of American and Spanish officers agreed to a formal capitulation agreement supplementing a preliminary agreement signed by Merritt and Jáudenes the day before.

The U.S. capture of Manila yielded some 13,000 Spanish prisoners. In addition, the United States garnered 22,000 stands of small arms, 10 million rounds of ammunition, and 70 pieces of artillery. Because Manila had been seized after the Protocol of Peace had been signed, Spanish negotiators in Paris during the autumn of 1898 argued that the U.S. capture of Manila was not valid, a point that the U.S. peace commissioners countered successfully.

JERRY KEENAN

See also
Aguinaldo y Famy, Emilio; Augustín y Dávila, Basilio; Dewey, George; VIII Corps; Greene, Francis Vinton; MacArthur, Arthur; Manila; Manila Bay, Battle of; Merritt, Wesley

Further Reading
Cosmas, Graham A. *An Army for Empire: The United States Army in the Spanish-American War.* College Station: Texas A&M University Press, 1994.
Linn, Brian McAllister. *The Philippine War, 1899–1902.* Lawrence: University Press of Kansas, 2000.
Musicant, Ivan. *Empire by Default: The Spanish-American War and the Dawn of the American Century.* New York: Henry Holt, 1998.
Wolff, Leon. *Little Brown Brother: America's Forgotten Bid for Empire Which Cost 250,000 Lives.* New York: Kraus Reprint, 1970.

Manila, Second Battle of
Event Date: February 4, 1899

The U.S. Army capture of the city of Manila in the Philippines. Relations between the United States and Emilio Aguinaldo y Famy's Philippine Revolutionary Army were strained almost from the arrival of the first elements of VIII Corps in the Philippines in late June 1898. In large part, the friction resulted from the lack of a clear policy on the part of President William McKinley, who was undecided as to exactly what the U.S. role in the Philippines ought to be once Spain was defeated. Interwoven into this political tapestry was a racial bias on the part of U.S. troops against the Filipino people, whom many soldiers regarded as inferior. In addition to vague political directives, there was an attitudinal problem that did not bode well for future relations.

For his part, Aguinaldo sought U.S. recognition of the Philippine Republic and a full partnership in defeating Spain. The McKinley administration, however, was unwilling to recognize any republican government. Indeed, General Wesley Merritt, commanding the Philippine Expeditionary Force, was specifically directed not to enter into any political arrangements with Aguinaldo. Although Merritt's instructions were otherwise ambiguous, McKinley was clear on that point.

During the summer of 1898, however, both sides were largely occupied with the task of defeating Spanish forces around Manila. During the First Battle of Manila (August 13, 1898), the relationship between the forces of Aguinaldo and Merritt deteriorated further when the Americans denied the Filipino revolutionary forces access to the old walled city of Manila; their aim was to shut out Aguinaldo's Army of Liberation from any role in determining the ultimate disposition of the Philippines during later treaty negotiations. Nonetheless, in the nearly five months following the Spanish surrender of Manila in August and the signing of the Treaty of Paris in December 1898, U.S. occupation troops and the Philippine Army of Liberation managed to more or less coexist, although the situation remained volatile.

In the aftermath of Manila's surrender, the United States insisted that the Army of Liberation retract its lines from in front of the capital city as a preventive measure in order to avoid possible exchanges with U.S. troops. Aguinaldo grudgingly acceded to the

U.S. demands, but there were frequent verbal exchanges between Americans and Filipinos, suggesting that a full-scale eruption perhaps was not far off.

That eruption occurred on the night of February 4, 1899. Exactly who fired the first shot remains a matter of dispute. The evidence suggests that the fighting was simply the result of an explosive situation awaiting only the spark needed to ignite a war that was inevitable. At any rate, in the Santa Mesa District northeast of Manila, a patrol of U.S. troops fired on some Filipino troops, supposedly as retaliation against the latter's incursion into what had been agreed to as a neutral zone. The exchange set off what would prove to be a three-year war between the United States and Aguinaldo's republican forces.

The U.S. response to the fighting was swift. On Sunday, February 5, 1899, Brigadier General Arthur MacArthur attacked along his 2nd Division front. Supported by artillery and naval gunfire, some elements of the division advanced through rice paddies, encountering minimal opposition and seizing nationalist positions. Other units had to contend with more difficult terrain and heavy Filipino fire. By the end of the second day of fighting on February 6, MacArthur's troops had driven the nationalists back and secured the high ground north of Manila.

Meanwhile, also on February 6, Brigadier General Thomas Anderson's division attacked Army of Liberation positions south of Manila. Anderson's troops—composed largely of volunteers from the U.S. western states—were also supported by artillery as they steadily advanced. At an old Spanish position on the Pasig River, strong Filipino fire stalled Anderson's advance until supporting cross fire from a California regiment got things moving again. Then, in short order, Army of Liberation forces were in full retreat.

As the Filipinos fled, the U.S. attack lost its cohesiveness in the melee of the pursuit. Units became mixed, and organizational control was temporarily lost. General Anderson had intended to trap the Filipino forces between his two brigades, but the strategy fell apart when the attack splintered. Contributing to the confusion was a breakdown in communications all the way down the chain of command.

The fighting of February 5–6 was heavy, and by the end of the second day, the U.S. forces, and Anderson's in particular, were widely dispersed. Although the area over which much of the action of February 6–7 had taken place was largely secured, pockets of resistance remained, with considerable fighting. On February 16, for example, the Filipinos attacked one of Anderson's brigades in grand style—with trim ranks, bugles blaring, and flags flying—only to be devastated by the Americans' disciplined defensive firepower. On February 19, California and Washington troops, supported by fire from the gunboat *Laguna de Bay,* devastated Filipino positions south of Manila.

In the wake of the fighting of February 5–6, most of the Army of Liberation had fallen back to Caloocan, a dozen miles north of

Filipino insurgents outside the city of Manila in 1898. (Library of Congress)

Manila. MacArthur's plan to strike Caloocan had to be postponed, however, because of an anticipated uprising in the city of Manila itself. Finally, on February 10, MacArthur's division, supported by the guns of Rear Admiral George Dewey's squadron, attacked the Filipino positions in Caloocan, and by day's end the Americans had secured that important rail center on the line to Malolos, the newly proclaimed capital of the Philippine Republic.

Meanwhile, the uprising in Manila, which the United States had learned about through captured nationalist documents, enabled the provost guard of Major General Elwell S. Otis to arrest known revolutionaries and thus shut down the revolt before it really got started. Although some street fighting ensued, it fell far short of a full-scale revolt. The failure of the revolt to materialize—some said because of poor organization within the Army of Liberation—effectively ended the Second Battle of Manila. The next phase of General Otis's effort to defeat Aguinaldo's Army of Liberation began with a spring campaign against the capital of Malolos.

JERRY KEENAN

See also

Aguinaldo y Famy, Emilio; Anderson, Thomas McArthur; Dewey, George; Filipino Nationalist Army; MacArthur, Arthur; McKinley, William; Merritt, Wesley; Otis, Elwell Stephen

Further Reading

Gates, John M. *Schoolbooks and Krags: The United States Army in the Philippines, 1898–1902.* Westport, CT: Greenwood, 1973.

Linn, Brian McAllister. *The Philippine War, 1899–1902.* Lawrence: University Press of Kansas, 2000.

Wolff, Leon. *Little Brown Brother: America's Forgotten Bid for Empire Which Cost 250,000 Lives.* New York: Kraus Reprint, 1970.

Young, Kenneth Ray. *The General's General: The Life and Times of Arthur MacArthur.* Boulder, CO: Westview, 1994.

Manila Bay, Battle of
Event Date: May 1, 1898

The Battle of Manila Bay was the decisive naval engagement of the Spanish-American War. Commodore George Dewey's U.S. Asiatic Squadron was at Hong Kong when he was informed on April 23 by the British acting governor, Major General Wilsone Black, that war had been declared. Black then issued a proclamation of British neutrality and ordered Dewey's ships to leave Hong Kong's territorial waters by noon the next day.

Dewey repaired to Mirs Bay, an anchorage in Chinese waters, and there received a cablegram from Washington ordering him to the Philippines. It instructed him to "commence operations at once, particularly against the Spanish fleet. You must capture vessels or destroy. Use utmost endeavors."

Dewey's squadron consisted of the protected cruisers *Olympia* (flagship), *Baltimore, Boston,* and *Raleigh;* the gunboats *Concord* and *Petrel;* and the *McCulloch,* a revenue cutter that was pressed into service. Dewey left behind the old paddle wheeler *Monocacy,*

but two colliers also accompanied the squadron. He was concerned about his ammunition supply, for when the squadron departed for the Philippines, the ship magazines were only about 60 percent of capacity. Before sailing, he conferred with the former U.S. consul to the Philippines, Oscar Williams, who had left Manila under threat of his life on April 23. Williams briefed Dewey and his commanders on board the *Olympia* only an hour before their departure on April 27, confirming that the American squadron was superior to that of the Spanish, which would most likely be found in Subic Bay, 30 miles from Manila.

That same afternoon, the Americans ships departed Chinese waters. They made landfall at Cape Bolineau, Luzon, at daybreak on April 30. Dewey detached the *Boston* and *Concord,* later reinforced by the *Baltimore,* to make a quick reconnaissance of Subic Bay. The Americans soon determined that the Spanish squadron was not present. Reportedly, Dewey was pleased at the news and remarked, "Now we have them."

Dewey then ordered his ships to steam to Manila Bay, which the squadron entered on the night of April 30. He chose to ignore the threat of mines and the fortifications guarding the entrance to the bay. He selected Boca Grande channel, and the ships steamed in single file with as few lights as possible. Not until the squadron had passed El Fraile rock did the Spanish discover the American presence. Both sides then exchanged a few shots but without damage. The American ships were now into the bay. Detaching his two supply ships and the *McCulloch,* Dewey proceeded ahead, although he did not intend to engage the Spanish until dawn.

The Spanish had some 40 naval vessels in and around Manila, but most were small gunboats. Spanish rear admiral Patricio Montojo y Pasarón's squadron consisted of six ships: the two large cruisers *Reina Cristina* and *Castilla* (of about 3,000 tons each and the latter of wood) and the five small cruisers *Don Juan de Austria, Don Antonio de Ulloa, Isle de Cuba, Marqués del Duro,* and *Isle de Luzon.* Each of these was a very small cruiser of less than 1,200 tons, and none had more than four 4.7-inch guns in its main battery. Other ships were undergoing repairs. The Spanish warships were greatly inferior in armament to the American squadron, the crews of which were also better trained.

Montojo originally had his ships at Subic Bay during April 26–29, but its promised shore batteries were not yet in place, and the harbor entrance had not been mined. The water there was also 40 feet deep. Pessimistic about his chances and reportedly deciding that if his ships were to be sunk he would prefer it to occur in shallower water, Montojo had returned them to Manila Bay. His captains concurred with the decision.

Estimated Casualties of the Battle of Manila Bay

	Killed in Action	Wounded
Spain	167	214
United States	0	8

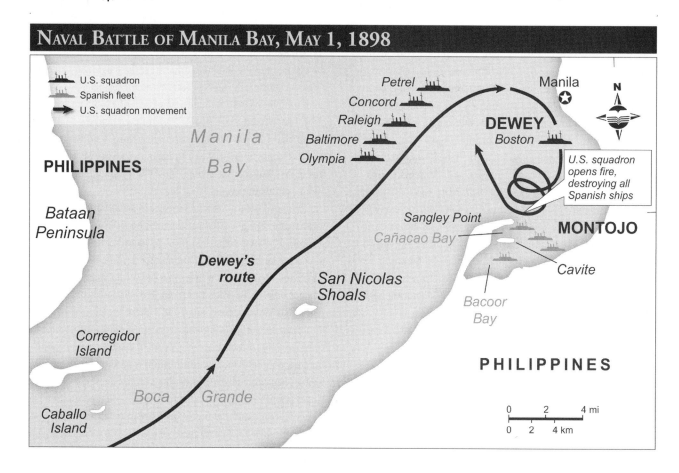

NAVAL BATTLE OF MANILA BAY, MAY 1, 1898

To help offset his weakness in firepower, Montojo anchored his ships in Cañacao Bay just south of Manila off the fortified naval yard of Cavite so that they might be supported by land batteries. There the water was only 25 feet deep, and if the ships were sunk or had to be scuttled, the Spanish crews would stand a better chance of escape. Not believing that there was any immediate threat from the Americans, Montojo went ashore for the night only to be alerted to their presence by the sounds of the exchange of gunfire on Dewey's ships entering the bay.

Early on the morning of May 1, only a week after the declaration of war, Dewey's ships steamed toward Manila, with the *Olympia* leading followed by the *Baltimore, Raleigh, Petral, Concord,* and *Boston*. Off Manila a little after 5:00 a.m., the Spanish shore batteries opened up with wildly inaccurate fire that inflicted no damage. The *Boston* and *Concord* returned fire. Dewey then turned his ships toward the Spanish squadron. As the American ships advanced in single line, two Spanish mines exploded at some distance away from the *Olympia* and without effect. Advancing to about 5,000 yards of the Spanish line, at 5:40 a.m. Dewey turned to his flag captain Charles Gridley of the *Olympia* and said, "You may fire when you are ready, Gridley."

The ships of the American squadron then closed to about 3,000 yards and turned to the west, running parallel back and forth along the Spanish line and pounding it with their guns. The 8-inch guns of the U.S. cruisers, hurling 150-pound shells, exacted the most damage. The Spanish ships and shore batteries responded but failed to inflict significant damage. Dewey then called a halt to assess damage and the status of ammunition stocks, and at the same time he ordered breakfast served to the crews.

At 11:16 a.m., the U.S. ships stood in again to complete their work. Within little more than an hour they had sunk the remaining Spanish vessels firing at them and had secured the surrender of the naval station at Cavite. Dewey then sent a message to the Spanish commander at Manila that if the shore batteries did not cease fire, he would shell and destroy the city. Shortly thereafter, the city's guns fell silent.

In the ships and at Cavite, the Spanish lost 167 dead and 214 wounded, all but 10 aboard the ships. Three of the Spanish ships were later salvaged and pressed into service by the Americans. The Americans had no men killed and only 8 wounded. Rarely was a victory more cheaply obtained.

Dewey then took Cavite and blockaded the city of Manila while awaiting troops to take it. On June 30, Major General Wesley Merritt and 10,000 men arrived. On August 13, the troops, assisted by naval gunfire from Dewey's squadron and Filipino guerrillas under Emilio Aguinaldo y Famy, attacked Manila. After a short nominal defense, the city surrendered. In only 10 weeks' time, the United States had secured an empire from Spain, and it was control of the ocean that had enabled it to do so. The Philippines were secured to provide a bargaining chip to persuade Spain to conclude peace, but in the final peace agreement the United States decided to keep the islands. This led to a war with Filipino nationalists who wanted independence and set up the future confrontation between the United States and Japan.

SPENCER C. TUCKER

See also

Dewey, George; United States Navy

Further Reading

Conroy, Robert. *The Battle of Manila Bay: The Spanish-American War in the Philippines*. New York: Macmillan, 1968.

Dewey, George. *The Autobiography of George Dewey*. 1913; reprint, Annapolis, MD: Naval Institute Press, 1987.

Freidel, Frank. *The Splendid Little War*. Boston: Little, Brown, 1958.

Spector, Ronald. *Admiral of the New Empire: The Life and Career of George Dewey*. Baton Rouge: Louisiana University Press, 1974.

Trask, David F. *The War with Spain in 1898*. Lincoln: University of Nebraska Press, 1996.

Manzanillo, Cuba, Actions at
Start Date: June 30, 1898
End Date: August 12, 1898

Series of U.S.-Spanish clashes at Manzanillo, Cuba, during June 30–July 1, July 18, and August 12, 1898, involving American and Spanish ships. Manzanillo lies approximately 85 miles west of Santiago de Cuba on the Gulf of Guacanayabo. Although surrounded by malarial swamps, during the Spanish-American War it possessed strategic importance because it lay astride an overland supply route to Santiago de Cuba during the U.S. naval blockade of Cuba. U.S. naval squadrons attempted to destroy the Spanish naval forces based at Manzanillo on June 30 and July 1 but were repulsed. A stronger U.S. naval squadron destroyed 10 ships in Manzanillo's harbor on July 18 and bombarded the city on August 12 but ended fire once the armistice had been signed that same day.

Manzanillo also served as a substantial trading port, and as soon as North Atlantic Squadron commander Rear Admiral William T. Sampson obtained shallow-draft naval vessels, he took steps to include Manzanillo in the blockade. On June 30, several small ships—the armed yachts *Hist* and *Hornet* and the armed tug *Wompatuck*—began a reconnaissance of Manzanillo. On their approach, the U.S. squadron encountered and engaged a Spanish armed launch, the *Centinela,* that subsequently sank after being hit by U.S. fire. When the American squadron approached the port of Manzanillo late that afternoon, they were met by the Spanish gunboats *Delgado Perrado, Estrella, Guantánamo,* and *Guardían;* the disabled gunboats *María* and *Cuba Española;* and a shore battery. In the ensuing exchange of fire, the *Hornet* was hit and immobilized, and both the *Wompatuck* and *Hist* were also hit several times. The *Wompatuck* was able to tow the *Hornet* to safety, and the U.S. squadron retired. The U.S. squadron suffered only three injuries (all on board the *Hornet*), while Spanish forces reported two dead and six injured aboard two ships and in Manzanillo itself.

The next day, on July 1, with the Americans believing that they had inflicted much more damage than was the case and that only the Spanish shore battery remained a threat and with the other U.S. ships having gone to Guantánamo to coal, the armed yacht *Scorpion* and the armed tug *Osceola* steamed to Manzanillo to engage the shore battery. Twenty minutes of firing caused no damage to the shore battery, but the *Scorpion* was struck a dozen times by return fire in the 23-minute engagement. Miraculously, it suffered no casualties. The U.S. squadron then withdrew, postponing further attacks until additional ships could be marshaled.

On July 18, 1898, the U.S. gunboats *Wilmington* and *Helena* along with the *Hist, Hornet, Scorpion, Wompatuck,* and *Osceola* steamed into Manzanillo Harbor. Remaining out of range of Spanish shore guns, they proceeded to destroy 10 Spanish ships in the harbor. The Spanish were outgunned and unable to retaliate effectively. Later they transferred remaining naval guns to the shore. U.S. forces suffered no casualties in the engagement, while the Spanish sustained casualties of 3 dead and 14 wounded.

On August 12, 1898, U.S. Navy captain Caspar F. Goodrich called upon the Spanish commander at Manzanillo to surrender. When the latter refused, Goodrich ordered the ships in his squadron— which included the cruiser *Newark;* the auxiliary gunboats *Hist, Osceola,* and *Suwanee;* the transport *Resolute;* and the captured Spanish gunboat *Alvarado*—to shell the port. At the same time, Cuban insurgents attacked by land. The bombardment began in late afternoon and continued intermittently through the night. When Goodrich received word the next morning that the armistice had been signed, he ordered fire ended. This action resulted in no American casualties. Spanish casualties were 6 dead and 31 wounded. Goodrich then sent men ashore to take possession of Manzanillo.

ANDREW BYERS

See also

Cuba, U.S. Naval Blockade of; Goodrich, Caspar Frederick; Sampson, William Thomas

Further Reading

Feuer, A. B. *The Spanish-American War at Sea: Naval Action in the Atlantic*. Westport, CT: Praeger, 1995.

Trask, David F. *The War with Spain in 1898*. Lincoln: University of Nebraska Press, 1996.

Wilson, H. W. *The Downfall of Spain: Naval History of the Spanish-American War*. London: Low, Marston, 1900.

María Cristina, Queen Regent of Spain
Birth Date: July 21, 1858
Death Date: February 6, 1929

Second queen consort of Spanish king Alfonso XII (1879–1885) and queen regent of Spain from 1885 to 1902. María Cristina was born on July 21, 1858, to Archduke Ferdinand of Austria and his wife Archduchess Elisabeth Franziska at Zidlochovice Castle near Brno,

María Cristina, queen regent of Spain during 1885–1902. (James Rankin Young and J. Hampton Moore, *History of Our War with Spain*, 1898)

Moravia (in what is now the eastern part of the Czech Republic). María Cristina was tutored privately and became betrothed to King Alfonso XII, whose first wife had died after less than two years of marriage. The union had produced no heirs.

On November 29, 1879, Alfonso and María Cristina were married in Madrid. Their marriage produced three children (two girls and a boy). The boy was born in May 1886 shortly after his father died and would become Alfonso XIII at the age of 16. Beginning in 1885, María Cristina ruled Spain as queen regent until her son came of age and ascended the throne in 1902.

By most accounts, María Cristina's reign was a smooth one except for some domestic unrest as a result of the Spanish-American War. As a conservative force in Spanish politics, she hoped to maintain what was left of Spain's once grand empire. Complicating her reign were the frequent shifts in Spanish governments, from liberal to conservative and back again. As the situation in Cuba deteriorated during the Cuban War of Independence (1895–1898), the queen made it clear that she not only disapproved of Governor-General Valeriano Weyler y Nicolau's heavy-handed tactics but also believed that he was one of the most pernicious men in the Spanish Empire. Nor did she have much use for the policies of conservative prime minister Antonio Cánovas del Castillo y Vallejo.

As events careened toward war in late 1897 and early 1898, María Cristina tried several times to avert war with the United States by enlisting the help of other European powers. She wrote to Britain's Queen Victoria (the two women were cousins) requesting her assistance in drumming up international support for Spain. Although Victoria would view U.S. motives in the Spanish-American War with suspicion and the war as a potential threat to the British Empire, her views were not shared by Lord Salisbury's cabinet. Consequently, she rebuffed her cousin's plea. María Cristina did not stop there. She also requested aid from both France and tsarist Russia but was again politely rebuffed.

Not willing to give up the last vestiges of the Spanish Empire, María Cristina sullenly agreed to the war with the United States in the vain hope that Spanish troops might prevail. When that did not occur, she quickly approved the Treaty of Paris in March 1899 over the strenuous objections of many of her advisers.

When her son came of age and ascended the throne as Alfonso XIII in 1902, María Cristina largely retired from the public spotlight, although Spaniards continued to respect and honor her for her service to their country. After 1902, she busied herself with family affairs and charitable work. María Cristina died in Madrid on February 6, 1929.

PAUL G. PIERPAOLI JR.

See also

Alfonso XII, King of Spain; Alfonso XIII, King of Spain; Cánovas del Castillo y Vallejo, Antonio; Cuba, Spanish Colonial Policies toward; Cuban War of Independence; France; Gascoyne-Cecil, Robert Arthur Talbot; Great Britain, Policies and Reactions to the Spanish-American War; Spain; Victoria, Queen of the United Kingdom; Weyler y Nicolau, Valeriano

Further Reading

Cancio Y Capote, Rita Maria. *The Function of Maria Christina of Austria's Regency, 1885–1902, in Preserving the Spanish Monarchy.* México City: Ediciones Botas, 1957.

Figueroa y Torres, Alvaro de, Conde de Romanones. *Doña María Cristina de Habsburgo Lorena, la discreta regente de España* [Queen María Cristina of Hapsburg Lorena, the Quiet Regent of Spain]. Madrid: Espasa-Calpe, 1934.

Gould, Lewis L. *The Spanish-American War and President McKinley.* Lawrence: University Press of Kansas, 1982.

Mariana Islands

The northernmost component of Micronesia, the Mariana Islands are an archipelago of 15 islands located in the northwestern Pacific Ocean between the 12th and 21st latitudes. The Mariana Islands encompass just 389 square miles and have a small population. Guam is by far the largest island, covering some 200 square miles. The islands are the southern part of a submerged mountain range that extends over 1,500 miles from Japan to Guam. Geographically, the Mariana Islands can be divided into two categories. The 10 northern islands (Agrihan, Almagan, Anatahan, Asuncion, Farallon de Medinilla, Farallon de Pajaros, Guguan, Maug, Pagan, and Sarigan) are volcanic, while the five southern islands (Aguijan, Guam, Rota, Saipan, and Tinian) are limestone islands surrounded by coral reefs. Because of volcanic activity, the northern islands are virtually uninhabited. Most people, therefore, live on Guam or Saipan. Rising to 2,700 feet, the volcano on Agrihan is the highest point in the Marianas. Except for Farallon de Medinilla and Farallon de Pajaros, the vegetation on the islands is densely tropical and resembles that of the Philippines.

Portuguese explorer Ferdinand Magellan, sailing in the service of Spain, discovered the Mariana Islands on March 6, 1521. He promptly engaged in trade with the local Chamorro people in order to procure fresh supplies. The Chamorro people mistakenly assumed that the Europeans had also traded one of their landing boats, and the confusion resulted in a skirmish with the Spaniards. Three days after arriving, Magellan fled the islands under attack. The European sailors subsequently dubbed the islands the Islas de los Ladrones (Islands of the Thieves). As a result, many sailors simply referred to the islands as the Ladrones. Subsequent navigators and sailors also referred to the islands as the San Lazarus Islands, the Jardines, and the Prazeres.

In 1665, Spanish Jesuit missionary Diego Luis de San Vitores, who had visited the islands in 1662, convinced King Philip IV and Queen Mariana to establish a mission in the archipelago. In 1668, San Vitores named the archipelago Las Marianas in honor of the widow of Spanish king Philip IV. Although the Marianas initially had an indigenous population of more than 50,000 people, they were quickly decimated by diseases brought by the Europeans for which the natives had no immunity. Within 100 years, as a result of disease and miscegenation, less than 2,000 pure Chamorro people remained. During the 19th century, however, the indigenous population, augmented with colonists from the Caroline Islands and the Philippines, increased. The Mariana Islands remained a subsidiary of the Spanish colonial government in the Philippines until the Spanish-American War.

In December 1898, Spain formally ceded Guam to the United States. German protests against U.S. efforts to acquire all of the Mariana Islands with the 1898 Treaty of Paris resulted in Spain's continued political control over the remaining 14 Mariana Islands. On February 12, 1899, Spain sold the remaining islands to Germany for $4 million. The Germans then incorporated the 14 islands and their 2,646 inhabitants into the German Protectorate of New Guinea.

For the Americans, the occupation of Guam was key to their efforts to project power into Asia, protect trade routes, and administer and supply their newfound holdings in the Philippines. Possessing a commodious and accessible harbor, Guam served as a strategic coaling station and became home to a sizable U.S. naval base. Since 1898, Guam has served almost continuously as a key American naval base in the Pacific.

During World War I, Japan invaded the Mariana Islands (except Guam). After the war, the League of Nations gave the Japanese a mandate over the islands. During World War II, Japan occupied Guam for almost three years while the United States sought the islands as a base from which to attack the Japanese mainland. In August 1945, U.S. Boeing B-29 bombers Enola Gay and Bockscar, which dropped the atomic bombs on Hiroshima and Nagasaki, respectively, flew from Tinian Island.

After World War II, the islands were administered by the United States as part of the United Nations Trust Territory of the Pacific Islands. In 1978, the Northern Mariana Islands became a commonwealth associated with the United States. Guam, meanwhile, remains an unincorporated territory of the United States administered by the Department of the Interior's Office of Insular Affairs.

MICHAEL R. HALL

See also

Coaling Stations; Germany; Guam; Japan; Paris, Treaty of; Philippine Islands

Further Reading

De Viana, Augusto V. *In the Far Islands: The Role of Natives from the Philippines in the Conquest, Colonization, and Repopulation of the Mariana Islands 1668–1903.* Manila: University of Santo Tomas, 2004.

Driver, Marjorie, G. *Cross, Sword, and Silver: The Nascent Spanish Colony in the Mariana Islands.* Mangilao, Guam: Micronesian Area Research Center, 1990.

Flood, Bo. *Marianas Island Legends: Myth & Magical.* Honolulu: Bess, 2001.

Mariel, Cuba

Cuban port city situated about 25 miles south-southwest of Havana and the initial U.S. proposed landing and staging site for a ground invasion of Cuba. Mariel lies along the southeast portion of Mariel Bay and is the closest major port to the continental United States. Because of Mariel's proximity to Havana and the United States, U.S. military planners envisioned using the city as a staging area from which American forces would launch an assault against Havana, which was at the heart of the Spanish colonial government. Even before formal hostilities commenced in April 1898, an army-navy advisory board had seen Mariel as key to a ground invasion of Cuba via Havana.

During the second week of May 1898, however, President William McKinley held a series of strategy sessions with his key military advisers. These included Secretary of War Russell A. Alger, commanding general of the army Major General Nelson A. Miles, and Secretary of the Navy John D. Long. The sessions were often contentious mainly because of constant bickering between Long and Alger and interservice rivalry.

The White House, along with the U.S. Navy, advocated a prompt invasion of Cuba, using Mariel as the first landing and staging area. Miles demurred on an immediate invasion, primarily because he knew that the U.S. Army was still ill-prepared for such an expedition. Alger disagreed with Miles and also pushed for an immediate ground assault. The navy, in fact, believed itself prepared for an immediate descent on Cuba, and Long took considerable relish in reminding Miles and Alger of this fact.

Annoyed by Long's posturing, Alger precipitously tasked Miles with preparing for a major ground assault aimed at occupying Havana. Miles was told to prepare for the expedition, which would commence with a landing at Mariel with about 75,000 troops. Miles was frustrated with Alger's impatience but nevertheless began to assemble such a force.

The final plan had U.S. regular forces landing at Mariel, capturing it, and creating a staging area there. That was to be followed by the arrival of reinforcements (largely U.S. volunteer forces) and a joint effort against Havana. On May 10, 1898, V Corps, then still in Florida, was ordered to begin the offensive by landing and taking Mariel. The plan, however, was never implemented.

Several problems led to this plan being shelved. First, the logistics involved in supplying such a large expeditionary force so far from American shores proved daunting. Second, few U.S. Army volunteer units were ready to deploy. Indeed, many of these had been only partly trained, and even more had yet to be properly armed and equipped. Finally, the Spanish decision to deploy its naval forces at Santiago de Cuba meant that those naval assets would have to be defeated or otherwise immobilized before an invasion could take place at Mariel. It was in fact the naval war that decided the U.S. ground strategy in Cuba.

Reducing the Spanish squadron at Santiago de Cuba became a joint army-navy affair, and following the July 3, 1898, U.S. naval victory at Santiago, U.S. invasion forces entered Cuba chiefly through that port, rather than Mariel. Indeed, Havana itself saw almost no action during the brief war, in stark contrast to what might have been the case had the Mariel invasion plan been carried out.

PAUL G. PIERPAOLI JR.

See also

Alger, Russell Alexander; V Corps; Havana, Cuba; Long, John Davis; Miles, Nelson Appleton; Santiago de Cuba, Battle of; Santiago de Cuba Land Campaign

Further Reading

Cosmas, Graham A. *An Army for Empire: The United States Army in the Spanish-American War.* College Station: Texas A&M University Press, 1994.
O'Toole, G. J. A. *The Spanish War: An American Epic, 1898.* New York: Norton, 1984.
Trask, David F. *The War with Spain in 1898.* Lincoln: University of Nebraska Press, 1996.

Marinduque

Philippine island located 11 miles from the coast of Luzon where United States armed forces trained soldiers in pacification tactics and carried out a pacification campaign during the Philippine-American War (1899–1902). Somewhat circular in shape, Marinduque is a small island of 370 square miles in the Sibuyan Sea, south of Luzon's Tayabas Bay in the Philippine archipelago. Despite a rugged topographical interior that inhibits travel, the island is blessed with palm-lined coastlines, green highlands, and dry as well as rainy seasons.

At the start of the insurgency, about 50,000 Filipinos lived on Marinduque. They spoke Tagalog; produced hemp, rice, and coconuts; and raised cattle. The island's landowning and commercial elite exercised political, social, and economic authority and governed from Boac, the provincial capital, through 7 other towns and 96 villages.

The upper classes of Marinduque supported the war of liberation against the Americans. The insurgent leader for the Philippine Republic on Marinduque was Martin Lardizabal, and the insurgent military commander was Lieutenant Colonel Maximo Abad. Abad led the Marinduque Battalion as well as a poorly armed militia. He had at least nominal control of as many as 2,500 part- and full-time guerrilla fighters.

In early 1900, Major General John C. Bates, commander of U.S. forces in southern Luzon, decided to occupy Marinduque to prevent its use as a haven and supply base for Filipino insurgent forces. He also hoped to seize the island's cattle to feed Manila's population. On April 25, 1900, Colonel Edward E. Hardin's battalion of the 29th U.S. Volunteer Infantry Regiment arrived at Marinduque and was later reinforced by Major Charles H. Muir's Company D of the 38th U.S. Volunteer Infantry Regiment. On May 20, Muir defeated Filipino fighters at Santa Cruz and mounted an operation into the interior before being replaced by Captain Devereux Shields's Company F of Hardin's battalion. Filipino harassment and another American campaign into the Santa Cruz area followed, with Shields and 52 soldiers and a hospital corpsman being ambushed in the interior on September 13, 1900, by a force of 250 riflemen and some 2,000 bolomen. After Shields was wounded, the command surrendered.

Santa Cruz then came under insurgent siege, and Bates directed Colonel George S. Anderson to reinforce the garrison. Believing that many of Marinduque's inhabitants supported the guerrillas, Anderson requested additional troops.

In October 1900, Major General Arthur MacArthur ordered two battalions of the 1st U.S. Infantry under Brigadier General Luther R. Hare to Marinduque. MacArthur sent orders to Hare to treat the entire adult male population of the island who were older than 15 years of age as hostile and to arrest as many of them as he could and hold them as hostages until the insurgents surrendered. Hare secured Shields's freedom, arrested all the adult males he could find, and destroyed villages and food stocks. General Bates encouraged Lieutenant Colonel A. W. Corliss, Hare's successor, to continue such aggressive policies. Corliss proceeded to lay waste to much of the island in a series of 30 expeditions during December 1900–January 1901. In the process, Governor Lardizabal was arrested, and many of the elite surrendered. The installation of civil government and Philippine police patrols, including detachments of the Philippine Constabulary, brought some quiet to the island's largest communities.

Major Frederick A. Smith took charge on February 6, 1901, and embraced Corliss's methods with two exceptions. Smith stopped the devastation of livestock and hemp, and he concentrated the population in American-held towns. All civilians were now gathered in six concentration centers to keep them from aiding the guerrillas. Those found to be aiding the insurgency were labeled as enemy combatants and jailed. Reminiscent of the Spanish *reconcentrado* (reconcentration) policy in Cuba, the American tactic did help U.S. officials assert control over the island. Separated from popular support and menaced by repeated U.S. forays into the interior, Abad gave up on April 15, 1901. By early May, Philippine commissioners confirmed the island's pacification and the institution of civilian rule. During the pacification campaign on Marinduque, U.S. forces suffered 27 casualties, apart from the more than 50 men captured. Abad's guerrillas sustained some 100 casualties, while 200 others were taken captive.

RODNEY J. ROSS

See also

Bates, John Coalter; MacArthur, Arthur; Pacification Program, Philippine Islands; Philippine-American War; Philippine Islands

Further Reading

Birtle, Andrew J. "The U.S. Army's Pacification of Marinduque, Philippine Islands, April 1900–April 1901." *Journal of Military History* 61(2) (1997): 255–282.

Linn, Brian McAllister. *The Philippine War, 1899–1902.* Lawrence: University Press of Kansas, 2000.

———. *The U.S. Army and Counterinsurgency in the Philippine War, 1899–1902.* Chapel Hill: University of North Carolina Press, 1989.

Considered by many Cubans to be their national hero, José Martí y Pérez led the fight for independence from Spain. He was killed in battle with Spanish troops in 1895. (Library of Congress)

Martí y Pérez, José Julián

Birth Date: January 28, 1853
Death Date: May 19, 1895

Cuban independence leader, poet, and writer. Considered by many to be the national hero of Cuba, José Julián Martí y Pérez is often called the Apostle of Cuban Independence. Born in Havana, Cuba, on January 28, 1853, he was the son of a professional soldier. Although he was too young to participate in the Ten Years' War (1868–1878), that futile struggle of Cuban nationalists against Spain had an enormous impact on the young Martí, who cultivated and nurtured democratic ideals and the goal of Cuban independence.

A talented painter, Martí enrolled in a professional school in Havana for sculpting and painting. He also began to write inflammatory essays and plays that were critical of Spanish authority and promoted Cuban independence. He published his first political writings in the only edition of the newspaper *El Diablo Cojuelo* in 1869. His well-known sonnet "10 de Octobre" was also written that same year.

In March 1869, the Spanish authorities closed Martí's school and in October arrested him on a charge of treason. Four months later, he was convicted and sentenced, at age 16, to prison for six years. He fell ill and was sent to the Isla de Pinos in lieu of imprisonment. In 1871, he was paroled and sent to Spain, where he studied law and secured a bachelor of arts degree. He also continued to write in support of a free and independent Cuba. He then spent some time in France and also traveled in Latin America.

In 1877, Martí returned illegally to Cuba under an assumed name. In Havana, he continued to agitate for Cuban independence. Arrested and again deported to Spain in 1878, in 1880 he traveled to New York City, where he acted as the joint consul for Argentina, Paraguay, and Uruguay.

Martí traveled the East Coast of the United States, cultivating assistance for the Cuban cause especially from among the Cuban exile community in Florida. In January 1892, he established the Partido Revolucionario Cubano (Cuban Revolutionary Party). He also edited the party's newspaper, *Patria*. His efforts made him the central figure in the Cuban revolutionary movement. While in New York City, he also published his greatest literary works, including his collections of poetry, *Versos Sencillos* and *Versos Libres*.

An idealist and visionary whose life was dedicated to the Cuban cause, Martí firmly believed that Cuba should be built on democratic principles, to apply regardless of an individual's race. He insisted that all citizens should both exercise their political rights and undertake obligations owed to the state. He drew to his ranks other notable Cuban revolutionaries, including Máximo Gómez y Báez and Antonio Maceo Grajales.

The Cuban War of Independence began with the Grito de Baire in February 1895. On March 25, Martí and Gómez issued the "Manifesto of Montescristi" calling for Cubans to take up arms in the fight for independence. Martí arrived in Cuba from Florida with Gómez on April 11 only to be killed in battle with Spanish troops at Dos Ríos on May 19, 1895. His loss was a tremendous blow to the revolutionary cause. However, in no small part due to his unceasing labors on its behalf, the revolution was able to carry on without its most eloquent and determined spokesman. Martí wrote extensively (one edition of his complete work runs 28 volumes). The most popular have been his books for children, of which the best known is *La Edad de Oro* (The Golden Age). José Martí International Airport at Havana and the city of Martí in Cuba are named for him.

JERRY KEENAN AND SPENCER C. TUCKER

See also

Cuban Junta; Cuban Revolutionary Party; Cuban War of Independence; Gómez y Báez, Máximo; Maceo Grajales, Antonio; Ten Years' War

Further Reading

Abel, Christopher, and Nissa Torrents, eds. *Jose Martí, Revolutionary Democrat.* Durham, NC: Duke University Press, 1986.

Foner, Philip S. *The Spanish-Cuban-American War and the Birth of American Imperialism, 1895–1902.* 2 vols. New York: Monthly Review Press, 1972.

Gray, Richard B. *José Martí, Cuban Patriot.* Gainesville: University Press of Florida, 1962.

Kirk, John M. *José Martí: Mentor of the Cuban Nation.* Gainesville: University Press of Florida, 1983.

Ronning, C. Neale. *José Martí and the Emigré Colony in Key West: Leadership and State Formation.* New York: Praeger, 1990.

Thomas, Hugh. *Cuba: The Pursuit of Freedom.* New York: Harper and Row, 1971.

Spanish general Arsenio Martínez de Campos was Spanish captain-general of Cuba during 1895–1896. Believing that a military victory against the Cuban rebels was impossible without inhumane methods, Martínez resigned his position. He was replaced by General Valeriano Weyler. (Library of Congress)

Martínez de Campos, Arsenio
Birth Date: December 14, 1831
Death Date: September 23, 1900

Spanish military officer, politician, and captain-general of Cuba (1876–1879, 1895–1896). Arsenio Martínez de Campos was born in Segovia, Spain, on December 14, 1831. After receiving a military education, he joined the officer corps in 1852 and served in Morocco from 1858 to 1860. He also participated in the 1861 joint British, French, and Spanish seizure of the Veracruz customhouse after Mexican President Benito Juarez declared a moratorium on the payment of his nation's international debt.

In 1868, at the outbreak of the Ten Years' War (1868–1878), Martínez posted to Cuba. He attained the rank of brigadier general in 1869. Believing that the draconian policies orchestrated by Captain-General Blas Villate would be counterproductive to quelling Cuban resistance, Martínez returned to Spain in 1872. He

then fought against the Carlists in the Third Carlist War (1872–1876). In charge of the military garrison in Valencia, he secured several victories against the Carlists in eastern Spain.

On December 29, 1874, Martínez, troubled by the continued inability of the republicans to restore order, announced his support for King Alfonso XII, which led to many other Spanish generals declaring their support for the son of exiled Queen Isabella II. This ultimately resulted in the restoration of the Bourbon monarchy in 1875.

After the defeat of the Carlists in 1876, Alfonso XII sent Martínez to Cuba to end the Ten Years' War. While serving as the captain-general of Cuba from October 1876 to February 1879, Martínez signed the Pact of Zanjón with the Cuban revolutionaries on February 10, 1878. Indicative of his belief that conciliatory gestures would be more successful than force, the Pact of Zanjón granted the Cubans more autonomy and emancipated those slaves who had participated in the revolution. Although the peace treaty failed to attain Cuban independence or the complete end of slavery on the island, it did, albeit temporarily, end hostilities in Cuba. Cuban discontent with the Pact of Zanjón, however, led to the Little War (Guerra Chiquita) from 1879 to 1880, which erupted in August after Martínez had returned to Spain.

Martínez initially supported the Conservative Party led by Antonio Cánovas del Castillo and briefly served as prime minister from March 7 to December 9, 1879, but was forced to leave the Conservative Party after he announced that slavery would be abolished in the Spanish Empire by 1888. Martínez then supported the Liberal Party, led by Práxedes Mateo Sagasta, who made him minister of war in 1881. Martínez founded the Academia Militar General (General Military Academy) in Zaragoza in 1884. He also successfully led Spanish troops in Morocco from September 1893 to January 1894 and negotiated the Treaty of Marrakech, which ended the war with Morocco on January 29, 1894.

Following Cánovas's return to power in March 1895, the Conservative prime minister sent Martínez to Cuba in April 1895 to end the Cuban War of Independence. Unwilling to implement harsh policies, Martínez, who became convinced that a military victory in Cuba was impossible, resigned his post in January 1896 and was replaced by General Valeriano Weyler y Nicolau, who implemented the notorious *reconcentrado* (reconcentration) system. Rather than defeating the Cuban rebels, Weyler's plan led to U.S. intervention in the Cuban War of Independence. Martínez returned to Spain and served as president of the Supreme War and Navy Council until his death in Zarauz, Spain, on September 23, 1900.

MICHAEL R. HALL

See also

Alfonso XII, King of Spain; Cánovas del Castillo y Vallejo, Antonio; Cuba; Cuban War of Independence; *Reconcentrado* System; Sagasta, Práxedes Mateo; Ten Years' War; Weyler y Nicolau, Valeriano; Zanjón, Pact of

Further Reading

O'Toole, G. J. A. *The Spanish War: An American Epic, 1898.* New York: Norton, 1984.
Staten, Clifford L. *The History of Cuba.* London: Palgrave Macmillan, 2005.
Tone, John Lawrence. *War and Genocide in Cuba, 1895–1898.* Chapel Hill: University of North Carolina Press, 2006.

Massiquisie, Battle of
Event Date: September 13, 1900

Battle between U.S. forces and Filipino insurgents during the Philippine-American War of 1899–1902. The engagement took place near the town of Massiquisie on the island of Marinduque on September 13, 1900. Marinduque, an island of about 400 square miles in size, lies just 11 miles off the southern coast of Luzon, southwest of Quezon Province.

Marinduque possesses a rugged, mountainous interior and experiences both rainy (June into October) and dry (November into February) seasons. In 1900, Marinduque, with a population of some 50,000 people, was administered through 5 municipalities, including the capital of Boac, and 96 barrios (towns or villages). Its chief products were hemp and rice. Reportedly, some 250 active guerrilla fighters on the island enjoyed the support of as many as 2,000 part-time insurgents. The principal guerrilla leaders were Martin Lardizabal and Lieutenant Colonel Máximo Abad. In April 1900, Major General John C. Bates, commander of the U.S. military campaign in southern Luzon, deployed a battalion of the 29th U.S. Volunteer Infantry Regiment to Marinduque, and over the next two years the island was occupied by various army units. Although these units conducted patrols in the interior, Abad steadfastly refused to engage in pitched battle with the Americans.

Captain Devereux Shields, commander of Company F of the 29th Volunteer Regiment, was determined to pursue aggressive action. He established a base at Santa Cruz on Marinduque's northeastern corner and carried out 13 operations during July and August. None of these ventured more than 10 miles from Santa Cruz, however. Aided by the local populace and Marinduque's rugged terrain, Abad evaded Shields with little difficulty.

In early September, the presence of the U.S. Navy (ex-Spanish) gunboat *Villalobos* gave Shields the opportunity to deploy his forces to Torrijos, located on Marinduque's southeastern coast. Ordering First Lieutenant M. H. Wilson and 41 soldiers to defend Santa Cruz, Shields and 51 others traveled via the gunboat by water to land on September 11 near Torrijos. There the Americans scattered a group of 20 guerrillas and demolished their compound.

On September 13, Shields and his troops marched into the interior, intending to return to Santa Cruz. Abad then massed virtually his entire insurgent force of some 250 men with rifles and another 2,000 with bolos beside a vertical height overlooking the path. Shields led his detachment right into the trap. Following several hours of fighting, he ordered a withdrawal into a concealed gorge. But this soon became a dash through a rock-strewn stream as he and his men struggled to flee the insurgent flanking columns that were attempting a double envelopment. After withdrawing for more than 3 miles, the harassed Americans took cover in a rice paddy close to the town of Massiquisie; guerrilla rifle fire compelled them to seek shelter behind paddy dikes. Shields was among the wounded.

With no other recourse, Shields surrendered his entire force. Four Americans died in the action, and all others were taken prisoner, 6 of them wounded. The Americans estimated that 30 insurgents had perished in the fight, but this figure was never verified. Following months of stealth, in less than a day of fighting Abad had eliminated a third of the U.S. force on Marinduque.

The Battle of Massiquisie prompted sharp reprisals from the Americans, who reinforced their garrisons on the island and launched a number of stronger punitive raids, which did little to cripple guerrilla activities.

RODNEY J. ROSS

See also

Bates, John Coalter; Marinduque; Pacification Program, Philippine Islands; Philippine-American War

Further Reading

Birtle, Andrew J. "The U.S. Army's Pacification of Marinduque, Philippine Islands, April 1900–April 1901." *Journal of Military History* 61(2) (April 1997): 255–282.

Linn, Brian McAllister. *The Philippine War, 1899–1902*. Lawrence: University Press of Kansas, 2000.

Matanzas, Cuba

City and province located in the northwestern part of Cuba. The city of Matanzas is located approximately 50 miles east of Havana. The Spanish word *matanzas* means "massacre" and is a reference to a massacre of Spanish soldiers as they attempted to cross one of the city's rivers during the early colonial period.

Besides the city of Matanzas, the province's other major cities include Jovellanos, Veradero, and Cárdenas, the latter the site of a brief naval engagement between U.S. and Spanish forces in May 1898. Cuba's second largest province in terms of land mass, Matanzas Province consists of relatively flat terrain. It has a long coastline to the north and south. The northern coast is known for its many small cays (keys, or small islands) and its enormous mangrove swamps. Cárdenas is located on the province's northern coast and sits along Cárdenas Bay (Bahia de Cárdenas), a commodious if shallow body of water. Along the province's southern coast is a huge

marsh, Ciénaga de Zapata, and a peninsula with the same name. Matanzas's southern shoreline also includes the Bay of Pigs (Bahia de Puercos), the site of the failed U.S.-backed Cuban invasion of April 1961.

Matanzas Province served as the center of the sugar and sugar-refining industries. The city of Matanzas, situated along the province's northern shore, has long been noted for its rich Afro-Cuban folklore and is sometimes referred to as the "city of bridges" because of the three rivers that run through it.

Jovellanos, located in the interior section of Matanzas Province, was mainly an industrial area where sugar-processing facilities abounded. Veradero, located on the Hicacos Peninsula, is situated on the eastern end of the peninsula and is renowned for its beautiful beaches. During the 20th century, this seaside resort developed into a major tourist destination and was among the largest resorts in the Caribbean.

Formally established only in 1828, Cárdenas grew quickly owing to the rich surrounding lands and its access to Cárdenas Bay, a wide but shallow body of water that limited access to smaller vessels only. Cárdenas is protected by a large promontory and is strategically positioned between the ocean to the north and hills to the south and southeast. In 1850, the city became momentarily famous when the Venezuelan soldier of fortune Narcisco Lopez launched a filibustering expedition there. After occupying the town for nearly a day, he abandoned it when it had become clear that the locals were not

The armored cruiser *New York* and other U.S. warships shelling the batteries of Matanzas, Cuba, on April 27, 1898. The drawing is by Rufus F. Zogbaum, who was on board the *New York*. (*Harper's Pictorial History of the War with Spain,* 1899)

flocking to his cause. It had been Lopez's intention to free Cuba from Spanish colonial rule.

Although the bay at Cárdenas was too shallow for most naval vessels, including blockade runners, U.S. North Atlantic Squadron commander Rear Admiral William Sampson sought to prevent supplies from reaching the Spanish through Cárdenas or Matanzas. In late April 1898, just days after the declaration of war, a minor naval skirmish took place off the coast of Cárdenas between American and Spanish ships. That same month, U.S. ships blockaded Matanzas, which also came under fire from the battleship *New York,* the protected cruiser *Cincinnati,* and the double-turreted monitor *Puritan.*

The following month, on May 8, 1898, the U.S. torpedo boat *Winslow* entered the bay at Cárdenas and fired on a Spanish gunboat and armed tugs that were present there in an effort to draw them out of the bay where the cruiser *Wilmington* and gunboat *Macias* were lying in wait. This attempt failed, but three days later, on May 11, the *Wilmington, Macias,* and *Winslow* and the revenue cutter *Hudson* returned to Cárdenas. The American ships dueled with the Spanish shore batteries and the gunboats *Alerta* and *Ligera* and the armed tug *Antonio López.* The *Winslow* was seriously damaged in the exchange with a Spanish shore battery and had to be towed out to sea by the *Hudson.* Five crewmen died, and three others were wounded. Among the dead was Ensign Worth Bagley, believed to be the first naval officer killed in the war. On the Spanish side, two ships were damaged, part of Cárdenas was set on fire, and seven people were killed.

PAUL G. PIERPAOLI JR.

See also

Cárdenas, Cuba; Cuba, U.S. Naval Blockade of; Sampson, William Thomas; United States Navy

Further Reading

Gott, Richard. *Cuba: A New History.* New Haven, CT: Yale University Press, 2005.

Nofi, Albert A. *The Spanish-American War: 1898.* Conshohocken, PA: Combined Books, 1996.

Trask, David F. *The War with Spain in 1898.* Lincoln: University of Nebraska Press, 1996.

Mayagüez, Battle of
Event Date: August 11, 1898

Brief skirmish between American and Spanish forces at Mayagüez, Puerto Rico. Mayagüez was located on the west coast of Puerto Rico. At the time the fourth largest city in Puerto Rico with a population of 28,000 people, Mayagüez was unfortified. On August 1, Spanish colonel Julio Soto Villanueva commanded the Mayagüez district with a force of 1,362 men.

Opposing him was a U.S. brigade under Brigadier General Theodore Schwan, assigned to Major General John R. Brooke's I Corps. Schwan's brigade consisted of three battalions of the 11th

U.S. Infantry Regiment, the 1st Kentucky Volunteer Infantry Regiment, Troop A of the 5th U.S. Cavalry Regiment, and two batteries of artillery from the 3rd and 5th Artillery Regiments, in all some 2,900 men.

Schwan's brigade had landed at Ponce, Puerto Rico, on July 31 and then moved westward along the coast to Guánica. The men met only light resistance along the way. Schwan's orders called on him to secure western Puerto Rico. In the process, his men advanced 92 miles in less than nine days, captured nine towns, engaged in two brief battles, and took 192 Spanish prisoners. On August 10, Schwan's brigade took part in the Battle of Silva Heights, the brigade's first real engagement, near Hormigueros, seven miles south of Mayagüez. The Spanish suffered perhaps 50 casualties, while the Americans reported only 17. The Spanish then withdrew, opening the way for the Americans to move into Mayagüez. Colonel Soto Villanueva chose not to fight for the city.

The Americans were well received in Mayagüez. Having secured the city, Schwan's brigade departed the next day and pursued withdrawing Spanish forces toward La Marías, where a skirmish was fought on August 13. Word was then received of the Protocol of Peace of August 12, ending hostilities.

ANDREW BYERS

See also

Brooke, John Rutter; Hormigueros, Battle of; Miles, Nelson Appleton; Peace, Protocol of; Puerto Rico; Puerto Rico Campaign; Schwan, Theodore

Further Reading

Berbusse, Edward J. *The United States in Puerto Rico, 1898–1900.* Chapel Hill: University of North Carolina Press, 1966.

Cosmas, Graham A. *An Army for Empire: The United States Army in the Spanish-American War.* College Station: Texas A&M University Press, 1994.

Trask, David F. *The War with Spain in 1898.* Lincoln: University of Nebraska Press, 1996.

McCalla, Bowman Hendry
Birth Date: June 19, 1844
Death Date: May 6, 1910

U.S. navy officer. Born in Camden, New Jersey, on June 19, 1844, Bowman Hendry McCalla was appointed to the United States Naval Academy, then temporarily located in Newport, Rhode Island, during the American Civil War in November 1861. He graduated fourth in his class in November 1864. His initial service was with the South Atlantic Blockading Squadron.

Following the Civil War, Bowman served successively with the South Pacific Squadron, the Home Squadron, and the European Squadron through 1874. During this period, he experienced rapid promotion, becoming a lieutenant commander by March 1869. He then served as an instructor at the Naval Academy. Following three years as executive officer of the steamer *Powhatan,* he served from

U.S. Navy commander Bowman H. McCalla, who commanded the cruiser *Marblehead* in the blockade of Cuba and whose crewmen cut the cable lines at Cienfuegos. (*Harper's Pictorial History of the War with Spain*, 1899)

1881 to 1887 as the assistant chief of the Bureau of Navigation. He first came to public prominence in April 1885 when he led an expeditionary force of marines and sailors in Panama to protect American interests during an uprising against Colombian control.

From 1888 to 1890, Commander McCalla commanded the steam sloop *Enterprise* in the European Squadron. Known as a strict disciplinarian, he faced a highly publicized court-martial upon his return to the United States for striking an enlisted man and for other discipline-related charges. Convicted on all five counts, he was suspended from duty for three years, losing several places on the navy's seniority list in the process. Upon his restoration to duty in 1893, he served for more than three years as equipment officer at the Mare Island Navy Yard in San Francisco, California. He assumed command of the Montgomery-class cruiser *Marblehead* in 1897.

With the beginning of the Spanish-American War, McCalla commanded U.S. naval forces blockading Havana and Cienfuegos, Cuba, and shelled the port city of Cienfuegos on April 29, 1898. On May 11, members of his ship's crew, along with sailors from the cruiser *Nashville*, cut two of the three telegraph cables located at

Cienfuegos. McCalla later made arrangements with local Cuban insurgents regarding ship-to-shore communications but failed to pass word of the arrangements on to his superiors. This contributed to Commodore Winfield Scott Schley's delay in establishing the blockade of Rear Admiral Pascual Cervera y Topete's squadron at Santiago de Cuba, as Schley erroneously feared that Cervera had taken refuge at Cienfuegos and could not communicate with the insurgents on shore.

The *Marblehead* participated in the blockade before being detached to reconnoiter and seize Guantánamo Bay in southeastern Cuba. McCalla bombarded Spanish positions there on June 7, capturing the outer harbor for use as a supply base for the American blockading squadron. He later supported the landings by the 1st Marine Battalion on June 10. With the *Marblehead*, he remained on station while the marines solidified their positions, taking part in the effective bombardment of a Spanish fort at Cayo del Toro in Guantánamo Bay. In appreciation of his actions, the marines named their encampment Camp McCalla in his honor.

In the dispensation of honors following the war, McCalla was advanced six numbers in grade, restoring him to the seniority he had held before his court-martial. Promoted to captain in April 1899, he commanded the Navy Yard at Norfolk, Virginia, before assuming command of the cruiser *Newark* in September 1899 for service on the Asiatic Station. He then participated in the campaign against Filipino insurgents in the Philippine-American War (1899–1902) and took part in the events of the Boxer Rebellion in China in 1900. He delivered reinforcements to the American legation in Peking in late May 1900 and then led 112 sailors and marines as part of the Seymour Relief Expedition, which unsuccessfully tried to relieve the now-besieged foreign legation in June 1900.

Wounded during the expedition, McCalla received commendations for bravery from Congress, Kaiser Wilhelm II of Germany, and King Edward VII of Great Britain. Following a final tour of sea duty commanding the battleship *Kearsarge* and serving as chief of staff to the commander of the North Atlantic Squadron, McCalla finished his career ashore commanding the Mare Island Navy Yard. Promoted to rear admiral on October 11, 1903, he oversaw the navy's immediate response to the San Francisco earthquake of April 1906, sending ships and men to the aid of the stricken city. He retired in June 1906 and remained in the San Francisco area, where he helped welcome the ships of the Great White Fleet in 1908. McCalla died in Santa Barbara, California, on May 6, 1910.

STEPHEN SVONAVEC

See also

Boxer Rebellion; Cables and Cable-Cutting Operations; Camp McCalla; Cienfuegos, Naval Engagements off; Cuba, U.S. Naval Blockade of; 1st Marine Battalion; Guantánamo, Battle of; Philippine-American War; Santiago de Cuba, Battle of; Schley, Winfield Scott

Further Reading

Blow, Michael. *A Ship to Remember: The Maine and the Spanish-American War*. New York: Morrow, 1992.

Coletta, Paolo. *Bowman Hendry McCalla: A Fighting Sailor*. Washington, DC: University Press of America, 1979.

Feuer, A. B. *The Spanish-American War at Sea: Naval Action in the Atlantic.* Westport, CT: Praeger, 1995.

Trask, David F. *The War with Spain in 1898.* Lincoln: University of Nebraska Press, 1996.

McClernand, Edward John
Birth Date: December 29, 1848
Death Date: February 9, 1926

U.S. Army officer. Edward John McClernand was born in Jacksonville, Illinois, on December 29, 1848. His father was Major General John A. McClernand, who commanded the U.S. Army VIII Corps during the American Civil War. After an education in local schools, the younger McClernand entered the United States Military Academy, West Point, graduating in the class of 1867. He saw much service in the American West during various Indian wars and was attached to the 2nd U.S. Cavalry on June 15, 1870. He soon gained a well-earned reputation as a tenacious fighter and was awarded the Medal of Honor for his gallantry at the Battle of Bear Paw Mountains (September 30–October 5, 1877) in Montana during the Nez Perce War.

When the Spanish-American War began, McClernand was a lieutenant colonel, and on May 9, 1898, he became assistant general adjutant of volunteers. He was subsequently assigned to serve on the staff of Major General William Shafter, commander of V Corps during the Cuba Campaign. As the Santiago de Cuba Land Campaign began in late June 1898, Shafter's considerable weight (300 pounds), an attack of gout, and the tropical heat made it impossible for him to take command in the field. As such, he designated McClernand to act as his liaison with his field commanders.

During the Battle of San Juan Hill (July 1, 1898), McClernand had the unenviable task of transmitting Shafter's orders to the battlefront and reporting back to Shafter on events as they unfolded. At the height of the battle, Brigadier General Jacob Ford Kent criticized McClernand, alleging that he had acted indecisively, but McClernand was not in a position to issue orders; indeed, he was merely acting as a go-between for Shafter.

On July 2, when General Shafter was about to withdraw from the siege of Santiago de Cuba out of fear that his men might fall victim to yellow fever season, it was McClernand who suggested that he immediately demand the city's surrender. Shafter took McClernand's counsel, and the Spanish capitulated on July 17. This move all but ended the war, and Shafter was able to contemplate a withdrawal before tropical disease season set in.

When the fighting was over in the Caribbean, McClernand was assigned to the Philippines, where he was for a time military governor of Cebu Province. He subsequently served in a variety of other army posts and was advanced to brigadier general on August 27, 1912. He retired from active service that December and took up residence in Easton, Pennsylvania, staying active in military matters and writing about his experiences in the Indian Wars and the Spanish-American War. McClernand died on February 9, 1926.

PAUL G. PIERPAOLI JR.

See also
V Corps; Kent, Jacob Ford; San Juan Heights, Battle of; Santiago de Cuba, Capitulation Agreement; Santiago de Cuba Land Campaign; Shafter, William Rufus

Further Reading
Musicant, Ivan. *Empire by Default: The Spanish-American War and the Dawn of the American Century.* New York: Henry Holt, 1998.

Trask, David F. *The War with Spain in 1898.* Lincoln: University of Nebraska Press, 1996.

McCoy, Frank Ross
Birth Date: October 29, 1874
Death Date: June 4, 1954

U.S. Army officer and diplomat. Frank Ross McCoy was born on October 29, 1874, in Lewistown, Pennsylvania. He graduated from the United States Military Academy, West Point, in 1897 and was commissioned a second lieutenant. When the Spanish-American War began in April 1898, he transferred to the 10th Cavalry Regiment (the Buffalo Soldiers), a unit comprised of African American soldiers with white officers. The unit left for Cuba two months later.

During the Santiago de Cuba Land Campaign, McCoy fought at the Battle of Las Guásimas on June 24 and received a leg wound on July 1 at Kettle Hill, part of the Battle of San Juan Hill waged outside Santiago de Cuba. While lying wounded under a tree on the battlefield, he by chance met Colonel Leonard Wood, who came to have a major impact on McCoy's military career. Wood, a physician as well as a field commander, stopped to rebandage McCoy's wound.

After recovering in the United States, McCoy rejoined his unit before it returned to Cuba as part of the occupation force in April 1899. The next year, Wood, who had been appointed military governor of Cuba, requested McCoy as his aide. McCoy reorganized the military government's finances and in June 1901 was promoted to first lieutenant. When the Cuban occupation ended in May 1902, McCoy continued as Wood's aide.

In early 1903, Wood had become the military commander of the Department of Mindanao and governor of Moro Province in the Philippines with McCoy as his aide. In August 1903, McCoy rose to captain. He served at various times as acting secretary and provincial engineer in the Moro legislative council.

As the intelligence officer of the Department of Mindanao, McCoy was often called upon to fight against the Moros. In October 1904, he planned the defeat of the powerful Datu Ali, the last of the hostile Moro chieftains, using American infantry and Philippine Scouts and suffering only one casualty. Both Wood and President Theodore Roosevelt praised McCoy highly for this victory.

On leave in late 1905, McCoy visited Japan and Canton, China, gathering intelligence before returning to Manila in January 1906.

He departed for the United States that June. Later that same year, he served as an aide to the provisional governor of Cuba, William Howard Taft, and his successor before becoming President Theodore Roosevelt's chief military aide in 1907.

McCoy commanded troops along the American-Mexican border during the Mexican Revolution (1915–1916) and became American attaché in Mexico City in 1917. When the United States entered World War I, he transferred to France in the summer of 1917. He fought in several battles and ended the war as a temporary brigadier general. He then served in various diplomatic assignments, including Armenia, Latin America, and Japan. Later he served on the League of Nations Lytton Commission that tried to resolve the Manchurian Crisis.

In 1920, McCoy worked for Wood's unsuccessful campaign for the Republican nomination for president. The following year, McCoy again joined Wood when the latter was appointed governor of the Philippines. McCoy was promoted to brigadier general in 1922 and married Wood's niece Frances Judson in 1924 before returning to the United States in 1925.

McCoy retired from the army as a major general in October 1938. He served as the president of the Foreign Policy Association until 1945. During World War II, he was recalled twice to active duty, and he chaired the Far Eastern Commission in October 1945, overseeing the Allied occupation of Japan and serving in that capacity until November 1949. McCoy died in Washington, D.C., on June 4, 1954.

GREGORY C. FERENCE

See also

African American Soldiers; Las Guásimas, Battle of; Mindanao; Moros; Philippine-American War; Philippine Scouts; Roosevelt, Theodore; San Juan Heights, Battle of; Santiago de Cuba Land Campaign; Taft, William Howard; Wood, Leonard

Further Reading

Bacevich, A. J. *Diplomat in Khaki: Major General Frank Ross McCoy and American Foreign Policy, 1898–1949.* Lawrence: University Press of Kansas, 1989.

Biddle, William S. *Major General Frank Ross McCoy.* Lewistown, PA: Mifflin County Historical Society, 1956.

Linn, Brian McAllister. *The U.S. Army and Counterinsurgency in the Philippine War, 1899–1902.* Chapel Hill: University of North Carolina Press, 1989.

McKinley, William
Birth Date: January 29, 1843
Death Date: September 14, 1901

U.S. politician, congressman, governor of Ohio, and president of the United States (1897–1901). The pivotal figure of the Spanish-American War, William McKinley Jr., was born in Niles, Ohio, on January 29, 1843. In his late teens, he attended Allegheny College, but he did not graduate. As with many others of his generation, his

William McKinley, the pivotal figure of the Spanish-American War, was president of the United States during 1897–1901. (Library of Congress)

American Civil War service as a young Ohio Volunteer officer had a profound impact on his life, and he developed a deep hatred of war. Nevertheless, he performed his duty ably and emerged from the war a brevet major of volunteers.

After the war, McKinley studied law at the Albany Law School in Albany, New York, and was admitted to the Ohio bar in 1867. In 1876, he was elected to the U.S. House of Representatives as a Republican. As chairman of the Committee on Ways and Means, he authored the McKinley Tariff of 1890, which raised tariff rates on many imports, especially sugar, that negatively affected the Cuban economy, already in significant turmoil. That same year, he lost his congressional seat. He went on to serve as governor of Ohio from 1892 to 1896. With the United States mired in the economic depression of 1893–1897, McKinley's longtime mentor, Mark Hanna, worked to secure the Republican presidential nomination for McKinley. In November 1896, McKinley defeated Democratic presidential nominee William Jennings Bryan to become the 25th president of the United States.

Although the campaign of 1896 had focused primarily on monetary policy—McKinley favored the gold standard, while Bryan championed free silver—McKinley's administration would be dominated by foreign policy. When he took the oath of office on

March 4, 1897, the Cuban War of Independence was already two years old and was rapidly becoming a popular issue in the United States. Although the press of the day painted increasingly negative portrayals of Spain's treatment of the Cubans, McKinley nevertheless moved cautiously in forming an official position about Spain. He was not given to falling headlong into a conflict for dubious reasons or because of popular sentiments.

By June 1897, McKinley, who had come to favor Cuban independence, officially demanded of Spain that Cubans be treated in a humane way. In so doing, the president departed from the position of strict neutrality adhered to by his predecessor, Grover Cleveland. As a result of McKinley's prodding, Spain did make an effort to improve relations with the Cubans by offering autonomy and repealing the hated *reconcentrado* (reconcentration) policy. Neither McKinley nor the Cuban revolutionaries, however, were willing to accept anything less than full independence.

During the ensuing months, as tensions with Spain mounted, McKinley ordered the U.S. Navy's Atlantic Squadron to Key West, Florida, as a signal to the Spanish government that the United States regarded the situation as serious business. In addition, he directed the War Department and the Navy Department to prepare war plans.

In February 1898, the infamous Dupuy de Lôme–Canalejas Letter was published. Enrique Dupuy de Lôme, Spanish ambassador to the United States, wrote a dispatch to José Canalejas that was highly critical of McKinley. The communication was intercepted and made available by the Cuban revolutionary junta to the *New York Journal*, which promptly printed it. In his dispatch, Dupuy de Lôme had called McKinley a spineless politician. Amazingly, McKinley himself remained remarkably composed about Dupuy de Lôme's remarks. Publication of the letter was followed by the second and far more provocative event that month, when the U.S. battleship *Maine* blew up in Havana Harbor on the night of February 15. Many Americans blamed the Spanish government for the deed, further inflaming public opinion against Spain.

After the destruction of the *Maine,* McKinley pushed through congressional legislation known as the Fifty Million Dollar Bill, designed to prepare the nation's military services for war. The day after the report of the board of inquiry concerning the loss of the *Maine* concluded that the ship had been sunk by an external mine, McKinley sent to Madrid an ultimatum demanding an immediate armistice, the release of prisoners, and American mediation between Spain and Cuba. Although Spain's formal reply was not satisfactory, the Spanish government did not want war with the United States, and on April 9, Spanish officials in Cuba offered an armistice to the insurgents. The next day, the American minister at Madrid, Stewart L. Woodford, cabled Washington that if nothing was done to humiliate Spain, he could obtain a settlement on the basis of Cuban autonomy or independence or even cession of the island to the United States.

McKinley did not want war, but the Young Republicans in Congress were eager for it, and expansionists saw this as an opportunity to expand American power. McKinley gave in to the view that if he did not give way, the Republican Party would be split. After much prayer and hesitation, he yielded to the interventionists. A year later, the president confessed, "But for the inflamed state of public opinion and the fact that Congress could no longer be held in check, a peaceful solution might have been had."

On April 11, 1898, McKinley requested a declaration of war from Congress, which passed a joint resolution authorizing armed intervention in Cuba on April 19. Three days later, on April 22, the president initiated a naval blockade of Cuba and on April 25 signed the official war declaration against Spain, effective as of April 21.

Overall, McKinley's conduct of the war was efficient, especially in the area of communications. Indeed, he created the nation's first official war room in the White House using the latest technology. President Abraham Lincoln had spent hours in the military telegraph office keeping himself updated on the progress of the American Civil War. McKinley, however, took that concept to the next level. The war room was set up to accommodate 25 telegraph lines and 15 special telephone lines through which he kept close tabs on developments in Cuba. He was in constant and direct contact with his field commanders, usually via telephone.

With the exception of Secretary of War Russell Alger, McKinley's relationship with his cabinet was generally harmonious. Alger, who had performed well enough in a prewar bureaucratic environment, proved to be a poor choice to manage the War Department under the stress of conflict, however. McKinley came to rely on him less and less. The president also came to avoid commanding general of the army Major General Nelson A. Miles, whose frequent squabbling with Alger caused McKinley to turn increasingly to Adjutant General Henry Corbin for military advice. By contrast, McKinley worked well with Secretary of the Navy John D. Long.

Militarily, the war proved to be far less challenging than negotiating the final peace treaty with Spain, and the Philippines turned out to be the sticking point. Had it not been for the U.S. acquisition of the Philippines, McKinley's role in history surely would be much less controversial. At one point early on, he professed to not knowing the exact location of the Philippines, a remark that he perhaps did not intend to be taken literally. He seems to have agonized a great deal as to whether the United States should retain just the port city of Manila, the island of Luzon, or the entire Philippine archipelago.

A strong argument arose against the United States annexing any part of the Philippines because to do so would run counter to U.S. constitutional philosophy. In the end, McKinley reasoned that the islands should not be returned to Spain and that if the United States did not take them, Germany or Japan surely would. Thus, he concluded that the United States should take all of the Philippines, and he instructed his peace commissioners in Paris to stand firm on that point. Because Spain had little bargaining power, it had no choice but to sell the Philippines in exchange for $20 million. In addition to the Philippines, the United States also acquired Puerto Rico and Guam in the Marianas. The terms of the Treaty of Paris further required Spain to evacuate Cuba and called for the United States to oversee that island's preparation for independent government.

If McKinley was not the most controversial occupant of the White House, he was certainly one of the most difficult presidents to know. Pleasant and affable with a wry sense of humor and a fondness for cigars, he somehow appeared more like a country judge than a president of the United States. For all that, however, he was an astute politician who was fully in charge, even if he seemed at times indecisive. His office was open to nearly everyone who wished to see him, and he was the first president to establish a regular format for providing the media with White House news.

In 1900, McKinley ran for reelection, again contesting with Bryan. Enormously popular in the aftermath of the war and having lifted the U.S. out of a serious economic depression, McKinley easily defeated Bryan. McKinley's second term was to last only six months, however, for he was shot on September 6, 1901, while attending the Pan-American Exposition in Buffalo, New York, by anarchist Leon Czolgosz. McKinley was struck by two bullets. One did little harm and was readily removed by doctors. The second, however, had caused extensive damage and would have been exceedingly difficult to extricate. McKinley appeared to be rallying, so doctors decided to leave the second bullet in place rather than risk a serious operation. However, on September 14, 1901, McKinley went into shock and died in Buffalo. This tragic event ruled out the possibility of his further elaborating on some of the controversial issues of his presidency, such as the acquisition of the Philippines. It also resulted in the impetuous vice president, Theodore Roosevelt, becoming president. Many Americans, even Republicans, wondered whether the 42-year-old Roosevelt had the requisite wisdom and foresight to lead the nation at that time.

In the century since the Spanish-American War, historians have debated and sharply differed over McKinley's presidency. In the first two decades following the war, scholars largely supported the McKinley administration for its able prosecution of the war and for the results of the Treaty of Paris, by which the United States acquired its first territorial possessions. Beginning about 1920, however, opinions began to diverge. Some saw McKinley as a reluctant expansionist, but others viewed him as a president who employed clever means to expand U.S. interests, a crafty politician who adroitly managed the acquisition of territorial possessions seemingly without wanting to do so.

The controversy is attributable in large part to the fact that historians have little knowledge of McKinley as a man. He left behind almost nothing in the way of personal correspondence, memos, or a diary through which historians might gain some access to his inner thoughts and feelings. Instead, to evaluate his presidency, scholars have had to rely on the recollections and observations of those with whom he worked closely. As a consequence, he remains something of an enigma, a controversial occupant of the White House during a key transitional period when the United States moved onto the stage of international affairs.

JERRY KEENAN

See also
Alger, Russell Alexander; Bryan, William Jennings; Cuban War of Independence; Dupuy de Lôme-Canalejas Letter; Economic Depression; Hanna, Mark; Long, John Davis; *Maine*, USS; Miles, Nelson Appleton; Paris, Treaty of; *Reconcentrado* System; Roosevelt, Theodore; Spanish-American War, U.S. Public Reaction to; Telephone and Telegraph; Woodford, Stewart Lyndon

Further Reading
Gould, Lewis L. *The Spanish-American War and President McKinley.* Lawrence: University Press of Kansas, 1982.
Morgan, H. Wayne, ed. *Making Peace with Spain: The Diary of Whitelaw Reid, September–December, 1898.* Austin: University of Texas Press, 1965.
Musicant, Ivan. *Empire by Default: The Spanish-American War and the Dawn of the American Century.* New York: Henry Holt, 1998.
Phillips, Kevin M. *William McKinley.* New York: Times Books, 2003.
Smith, Ephraim K. "William McKinley's Enduring Legacy." In *Crucible of Empire: The Spanish-American War and Its Aftermath,* edited by James C. Bradford, 205–250. Annapolis, MD: Naval Institute Press, 1993.

Medicine, Military

The U.S. Army Medical Department was anything but ready for the Spanish-American War. Just four years earlier, Congress had stripped 15 commissioned surgeons and the entire allotment of contract surgeons from a corps that had consistently and justifiably complained that it was incapable of meeting even peacetime requirements.

The Medical Department's organizational structure had not changed since the 1860s. Each regiment had its own surgeons and each division its own hospital. All were under a corps-level chief surgeon. Physicians had an advisory role only over matters directly pertaining to medical care of patients. Hospital administration and evacuation of the wounded were the province of line officers. Even worse, so were camp locations, arrangement, and sanitation.

The department, which still counted 14 veterans of the American Civil War, was led by Surgeon General George Sternberg, an internationally renowned bacteriologist with almost no administrative experience. Besides a severe shortage of physicians, he had no nurses, which left hospital care to a woefully undermanned, untrained, and largely unmotivated collection of stewards assigned to the Hospital Corps. The Medical Department had no transportation resources of its own, being entirely dependent on the Quartermaster Corps. Although war was a near certainty after the February 15 sinking of the U.S. battleship *Maine* at Havana, Sternberg was legally barred from spending any more money to stockpile supplies than had already been budgeted for 1898. He had barely sufficient equipment, hospital supplies, and medicines on hand to take care of the 27,000-man prewar force. The March 9 Fifty Million Dollar Bill intended to fund the war (mostly in the form of coastal defenses) allocated only $20,000 to the Medical Department. Even when purchases were authorized after the declaration of war in April, goods and drugs were almost entirely unavailable on such short notice.

In April 1898, the army numbered 2,143 officers and 26,040 enlisted men. In two calls issued by August, Congress authorized an increase to 2,232 officers and 56,365 enlisted men in the regular army and another 8,785 officers and 207,244 enlisted men in a volunteer army that was to be drawn primarily from the National Guard, supplemented by 3 volunteer cavalry regiments, 1 engineering regiment, and another 10 regiments composed largely of African Americans from the South who were presumed to be immune to yellow fever. On April 22, President William McKinley commissioned 77 surgeons in the Medical Corps and authorized each volunteer regiment to hire 1 surgeon and 2 assistant surgeons. The contract surgeon program was reinstituted, and 700 men eventually served in that capacity, although only 177 of those possessed any military experience. Even at that, the positions proved hard to fill, and the army ultimately closed its medical school and activated the faculty primarily in order to train newly recruited physicians. Operationally, these men fell under the command of Colonel Charles R. Greenleaf to whom they reported for matters pertaining to professional activity, but they remained subordinate to line officers for virtually every other aspect of their day-to-day lives. The contract surgeons, because they had neither rank nor military background, were typically accorded the same level of respect as hired teamsters and packers.

The volunteer regiments were authorized "one acting hospital steward and one private, one hospital and one common tent, one ambulance and necessary animals fully equipped in order to preserve the regimental organization." Their physicians were in no way superior to the contract surgeons. Most had obtained their positions through political influence, and since Abraham Flexner's reform of medical education was still a decade away, their professional training and qualifications were wildly variable and, with distressing frequency, wholly inadequate.

Surgeons were instructed to bring their own instruments, supplies, and medications. What they lacked their regiments lacked as well. To make matters worse, there was no standard pharmacopoeia, and the volunteer surgeons complained incessantly about the lack of their favorite compounded remedies. Of the various state units, none had a complete medical kit, and 16 had no medical supplies at all, a situation they shared with the majority of the regular regiments.

After Congress authorized purchases, supply depots were established at Lytle, Georgia, and at Tampa, Florida. But because of the difficulty in buying what was needed and transporting it, noth-

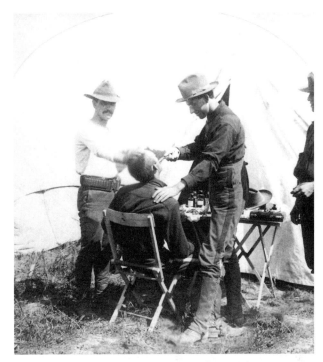

A dentist at work in a U.S. Army camp during the Spanish-American War. (Library of Congress)

ing arrived in either place for more than a month. When the trains finally started coming in, the system was overwhelmed. Cars were backed up all the way from Tampa to Charleston, South Carolina. Freight was seldom labeled, and one complete field hospital was found only after the war had ended. Still, to their great credit, Sternberg and his staff found and distributed 272,000 first-aid packets, 7,500,000 quinine pills, 18,185 cots, 23,950 blankets, and 2,259 litters in 1898.

The flood of regulars and volunteers had to be collected and trained, and to that end, the army established training camps in the southern United States to acclimate the men to a hot, damp climate: Camp Alger in Fairfax County, Virginia; Camp Thomas at the Chickamauga and Chattanooga National Military Park in North Georgia; and Camp Cuba Libre at Jacksonville, Florida. In the first few weeks, disease was not a problem, but no one yet realized that typhoid could be carried by asymptomatic individuals, and the disease tore through camps crowded with men unaccustomed to the necessities of outdoor sanitation. By August, 260 of the 15th Minnesota's 1,323 men were infected. More than 90 percent of the volunteer regiments had typhoid within eight weeks of arriving in camp, and not a single regiment escaped the disease. In the end, far more men died in camp than in battle, and 80 percent of those succumbed to what was likely typhoid, although the disease was often confused with malaria.

The Medical Corps initially planned for 1 percent of the volunteer force to require hospitalization while in camp, but the folly of that estimate was quickly evident, and a network of military hospitals had to be created. General hospitals were built at Key West,

Comparison of Casualties between the U.S. Army and the U.S. Navy during the Spanish-American War

	U.S. Army	U.S. Navy
Killed in action or died of wounds or injuries	345	47
Died of disease	2,565	56
Wounded	1,577	68

Nurses with the U.S. Army VII Corps mobilized in Savannah, Georgia, during the Spanish-American War, 1898. (National Library of Medicine)

Fort McPherson in Atlanta, Fort Monroe in Virginia, at Chickamauga, and in Washington, D.C. In addition, post hospitals in New York City, at the Presidio in San Francisco (later Letterman General Hospital), and at Vancouver Barracks in Washington state were enlarged enough to be essentially general hospitals. Two more hospitals were later opened at Manila and Honolulu (later to become Tripler General Hospital). On July 17, a 300-bed general hospital was opened in the newly captured city of Santiago, Cuba. After July, a number of civilian hospitals—especially in Philadelphia and New York City—were employed, and a number of the sick and injured were simply discharged to seek care at facilities near their homes. Transport within the United States was assisted by a 10-car hospital train operated by the Medical Department.

At the war's outset, Sternberg decided to replace the regimental hospitals with 200-bed division hospitals staffed with 6 officers, 99 enlisted men, and an ambulance company comprising 6 more officers and 114 enlisted men responsible for getting men to dressing stations and then on to rear-area hospitals. The regiments were left with only 1 surgeon, 1 steward, and a Hospital Corps private, the remainder being seconded to the division hospital, a decision that proved efficient but profoundly unpopular both with the physicians and the soldiers.

When the war began, nursing care was provided by the 791 noncommissioned officers and privates of the Hospital Corps since the Medical Corps had no female nurses. It proved much more difficult to get volunteers for the Hospital Corps than for line regiments, a deficit that was often made up by forced transfer of unwilling soldiers. To help alleviate the problem, Congress authorized the hiring of female nurses on contract, and the Daughters of the American Revolution (DAR) was recruited to find and hire those women. The DAR committee led by Anita Newcombe McGee, a physician and vice president of the organization, included the wives of both Sternberg and Secretary of War Russell Alger. In August 1898, the Army Nurse Corps Division of the Surgeon General's Office was formed and placed under Dr. McGee, who was made an acting assistant surgeon. A total of 1,563 women were hired, with a maximum of 1,158 serving at any one time, but since the first American nursing school had only been founded 25 years earlier, the supply of trained nurses was quite limited.

Besides their service in hospitals in the United States, 76 members of the Nurse Corps were sent to Cuba, 9 to Puerto Rico, 30 to the Philippines, 6 to Honolulu, and 8 to the hospital ship *Relief*. Typhoid struck 140 of the nurses, and 12 died from the disease. One nurse, Clara Maass, died of yellow fever acquired as a result of the Reed Commission's experiments. By the end of the war, nurses had largely been accepted as important to patient care in ways other than seeing to adequate diets and clean linen.

Although the Army Dental Corps was not established until 1901, army steward J. W. Horner, who was serving in VII Corps, set up a free tooth extraction clinic for soldiers stationed at Camp Cuba Libre.

When Major General William Shafter's V Corps left Tampa for Cuba, it took with it 79 medical officers and 89 newspaper correspondents. At the time of embarkation, most of the force's drugs were still lost on trains scattered north from Florida. A system dating to Jonathan Letterman's American Civil War plan called for stretcher bearers to carry men to collecting stations two or three miles behind the lines, where they could be dressed and transferred to ambulances that would take them another two or three miles to a base hospital. There was, however, a general shortage of litters, with few regiments having more than two and some having none at all. All but three ambulances were left in Tampa, and those that were taken had been disassembled and were not taken off the transports. The general lack of equipment would turn out to be immaterial to the initial landing at Daiquirí since the harbor was unprotected and the single dock was not even adequate for unloading military animals and equipment. Draft animals were simply shoved overboard with the hope that they would swim ashore. Many were lost. Chief surgeon Lieutenant Colonel Benjamin A. Pope and his division surgeons Majors Marshall W. Wood, Henry S. Kilbourne, and Valery Havard were largely left to their own devices.

By the time of the initial skirmish at Las Guásimas, there was no facility for the 52 wounded ashore, so those needing more than minimal care were transferred to the *Olivette,* a freighter converted to a hospital ship. Later, a field hospital was established at Siboney, and the wounded from San Juan Heights and El Caney were treated there. That facility had an adequate supply of surgical instruments and dressings and was able to keep six operating tables working around the clock. Men in the field had a good supply of first-aid packs and splints, and most of the men—who were transported to Siboney on a short-haul railroad pressed into service for that purpose—were well splinted and well dressed.

A combination of antisepsis, anesthesia, and relatively clean wounds from the high-velocity Spanish Mauser rifles resulted in cleaner injuries and better surgical results than in prior wars. Of the 1,142 men wounded in the Battle of San Juan Hill and the Battle of El Caney, the War Department reported a mortality of less than 1 percent. The Surgeon General's Report for 1898, however, said that 1,457 men were injured by guns that year, with a mortality rate of 6 percent. Regardless, the death rate from gunshot wounds was strikingly less than in prior wars.

Although the number of battle injuries was relatively low and the complications less frequent than in earlier wars, disease was a major problem. By mid-July, V Corps had 1,500 men sick with fever, and 10 percent of those had yellow fever. The death rate from disease peaked at 6.14 per 1,000 in August, with malaria being the most common problem and yellow fever the most feared.

As many as 75 percent of the American forces in Cuba may have ultimately suffered from malaria, with typhoid, dysentery, and other diarrheal diseases also common. In 1898, there were 217,072 cases of disease or injury among the men serving in the U.S. Army. The rate of men reporting for sick call was 2,146 per 1,000 per year. Battle wounds were numerically almost insignificant. In fact, significantly more men were disabled by rupture (the contemporary term for cases of inguinal hernia) than by gunshot wounds. Dis-

ease, however, became such a problem that in late July the city of Siboney was burned to the ground as a sanitary measure.

The land-based facility at Siboney had been largely replaced by three hospital ships, the *Olivette, Relief,* and *Missouri.* The *Olivette* was a former commercial passenger steamer that accompanied V Corps from Tampa and, because it also carried hospital equipment, was quickly converted to a 280-bed floating hospital after its arrival at Cuba. The *Missouri* was a former cattle boat given 10 days to convert to medical use. Its entire below-deck plumbing consisted of a hole in the deck and a funnel that had been used as a shower for the former captain. The *Relief* had been the Long Island passenger steamer *John Englin* before being sent to Cuba.

One immediate effect of the outbreak of disease was the Round-Robin Letter in which Shafter and his general officers demanded the immediate return of the American force to the United States. Because there was a widespread fear that returning soldiers would bring yellow fever with them, the decision had been made to build what was in essence a quarantine facility at Camp Wikoff on eastern Long Island. The Round-Robin Letter led to a hurried transfer of almost all of Shafter's troops to that facility in spite of the fact that transport ships were disastrously underequipped and the camp not nearly finished. The facility was divided into five detention camps for 1,000 men each and one 500-bed general hospital.

The short Puerto Rico Campaign resulted in only 3 enlisted men being killed and 4 officers and 36 enlisted men being wounded. There were no large concentrations of men, and as a result, no serious infectious disease outbreaks.

Although Commodore George Dewey had defeated the Spanish Navy in Manila Harbor on May 1, 1898, he lacked the manpower to occupy the capital. A force of 13,000 regulars and 2,000 volunteers under Major General Wesley Merritt left San Francisco two weeks before Shafter left Tampa. VII Corps was better organized than the Cuban invasion force. Chief surgeon Lieutenant Colonel Henry Lippincott's force (Ashburn called Lippincott "a kindly old man nearing retirement") was well staffed except for stewards and was well supplied. The force arrived on July 25, 1898, and, after a brief and prearranged battle, took the city from the Spanish on August 13. The medical purveyor to the expedition noted that every man was comfortably dressed and in bed by 7:00 p.m. after the engagement. No Americans were killed, and only 50 were wounded.

There were a handful of military medical innovations attributable to the Spanish-American War. Difficulty in identifying dead and seriously wounded men led to the use of metal identification tags subsequently worn by all soldiers. X-rays were used both in hospitals in the United States and on hospital ships to locate metallic foreign bodies and to visualize fractures. But the biggest changes came as a result of the postwar investigation of shortcomings in medical care led by Major General Grenville Dodge. Colonel Jefferson R. Kean called the resultant Dodge Commission Report the Medical Department's charter. The report recommended a sharp increase in the number of commissioned medical officers and the establishment of a volunteer hospital corps and a permanent corps of trained nurses. It also recommended maintenance of a stockpile of medical stores sufficient to supply an army four times as large as that maintained in peacetime and a separate transport service dedicated to medical needs. Virtually all of the commission's recommendations were adopted, and the changes in the Medical Department formed the basis of its preparation for the larger wars to come.

JACK MCCALLUM

See also

Alger, Russell Alexander; Camp Wikoff; Casualties; Daiquirí Beachhead, Cuba; Dewey, George; Dodge Commission; Dysentery; El Caney, Battle of; Fifty Million Dollar Bill; Hospital Corps; Las Guásimas, Battle of; Malaria; Manila, First Battle of; Manila Bay, Battle of; Merritt, Wesley; Round-Robin Letter; San Juan Heights, Battle of; Sternberg, George Miller; Typhoid Fever; Yellow Fever

Further Reading

Ashburn, P. M. *A History of the Medical Department of the United States Army.* Boston: Houghton Mifflin, 1929.

Cirillo, Vincent J. *Bullets and Bacilli: The Spanish-American War and Military Medicine.* New Brunswick, NJ: Rutgers University Press, 2004.

Cosmas, Graham A. *An Army for Empire: The United States Army in the Spanish-American War.* College Station: Texas A&M University Press, 1994.

Gillett, Mary C. *The Army Medical Department, 1865–1917.* Washington, DC: Center of Military History, United States Army, 1995.

Mario García Menocal served in the Cuban revolutionary forces during the Spanish-American War and served as president of Cuba during 1913–1921. (Library of Congress)

Menocal, Mario García
Birth Date: December 17, 1866
Death Date: September 7, 1941

Cuban engineer, soldier, politician, and third president of the Republic of Cuba (1913–1921). Mario García Menocal was born in Hanábana, Matanzas Province, Cuba, on December 17, 1866. His father owned a sugar plantation. When Menocal was only about 2 years old, his father was forced to flee Cuba with his family because of his revolutionary activities. The family went first to the United States and then settled in Mexico. There Menocal's father resumed his livelihood of growing sugarcane at San Juan Bautista, in Tabasco. At age 13, Menocal left Mexico to be educated in the United States, first at the Chappaqua Institute in New York and then at the Maryland College of Agriculture. In 1884, he entered Cornell University, graduating with an engineering degree in 1888.

Menocal spent nearly three years working with his uncle Aniceto Menocal on the commission studying the possible construction of an isthmian canal across Nicaragua. In 1891, the younger Menocal returned to Cuba, a stranger to his native land. For a time he worked as an engineer for a French Company that owned salt works and banana plantations on Cayo Romano Island. Then he worked in railroad construction, doing surveying for a rail line from Camagüey to Santa Cruz del Sur.

Menocal was also soon in the middle of Cuban revolutionary activities. When the Cuban War of Independence began in 1895, Menocal joined forces under General Máximo Gómez y Báez. He continued to serve in the field until the final victory following U.S. intervention as a consequence of the Spanish-American War of 1898. Menocal served under three well-known Cuban generals: Máximo Gómez, Mayía Rodriguez, and Calixto García y Iñiguez. Menocal won recognition in the battles of Yerba de Guinea, La Piedra, and La Aguada and also in the capture of Fort Loma de Hierro, for which he won special distinction and was rewarded with the rank of colonel. For his participation in the siege and capture of Guáimaro in Camagüey, he was advanced to brigadier general in the Cuban revolutionary forces. The Battle of Victoria de las Tunas marked the climax of his military career.

Following the Spanish-American War, Menocal helped organize the Lighthouse Service, a post he held for a short time. He then worked for the Cuban American Sugar Company helping to construct its factory at Chaparra, said to be the largest sugar factory in the world at the time. He also became a leading figure in the Conservative Party. In 1908, he received his party's nomination for the presidency but failed to win the election. In 1912, he again ran for the presidency from the Conservative Party and this time won.

Menocal served as president of Cuba from May 20, 1913, to May 20, 1921. As president, he championed closer ties with the United States, administrative and financial reform, and strict fiscal conservatism. He was criticized in some quarters for his strong support of large corporations and businesses and rampant corruption. He won reelection in 1916, but the race was so close that members of the opposition Liberal Party took to the streets in an armed uprising, which for a time threatened to overturn the government and was put down only with some loss of life and property destruction. Menocal's close relations with the United States may be seen in the fact that Cuba declared war on Germany on April 7, 1917, only a day after the U.S. declaration. Menocal left office in 1921. He ran again for the presidency, without success, in 1924. Attempting a revolution in 1931, on its failure he went into exile in the United States. He returned to Cuba within five years and in 1936 again ran unsuccessfully for president. Menocal died on September 7, 1941.

SPENCER C. TUCKER

See also

Cuban War of Independence; García y Iñiguez, Calixto; Gómez y Báez, Máximo

Further Reading

Bethell, Leslie, ed. *Cuba: A Short History.* New York: Cambridge University Press, 1993.

Staten, Clifford L. *The History of Cuba.* London: Palgrave Macmillan, 2005.

Merriam, Henry Clay
Birth Date: November 13, 1837
Death Date: November 18, 1912

U.S. Army officer and commander of the Department of California during the Spanish-American War. Henry Clay Merriam was born in Houlton, Maine, on November 13, 1837. After attending Colby College, in 1862 during the American Civil War, he enlisted in the army and raised a volunteer company from Houlton. He was then commissioned a captain, in command of Company H, of the 20th Maine Regiment. He saw action in various engagements during the Civil War, including the Battle of Antietam and a daring assault on Fort Blakely on April 9, 1865, during which 600 Confederates were captured. For this action, he was awarded the Medal of Honor.

Following the Civil War, Merriam briefly read for the law but then again cast his fortunes with the military, becoming a major of the 38th Infantry Regiment. He was involved in numerous campaigns against Native Americans and served in a variety of frontier posts. On June 30, 1897, he was promoted to brigadier general.

When the Spanish-American War began in April 1898, Major General Wesley Merritt, VIII Corps commander, employed Merriam and his staff in the Department of California to help muster men into VIII Corps and organize what would become the Philippine Expeditionary Force. San Francisco was Merriam's headquarters, so he and his staff were well placed to assist. Some of

Merriam's tasks included housing, supplying, and training the troops of VIII Corps. In so doing, he worked closely with Merritt's chief deputy, Major General Elwell S. Otis.

On May 7, 1898, Camp Merriam—named as was customary for its commander—was officially established. The camp was located on a series of hills just beyond the Lombard Street entrance to the San Francisco Presidio. Conditions at the camp were deemed satisfactory, and there were ample supplies of fresh water and adequate bathing facilities. However, Camp Merriam was not a large facility in area and soon became overcrowded.

Shortly after Camp Merriam opened, the U.S. Army decided to increase the size of VIII Corps and designated San Francisco to be the staging area for the Philippine Islands Expeditionary Forces. In consequence, toward the end of May, a second camp, located along the northern border of Golden Gate Park, was established and was named for Major General Wesley Merritt. The camp was probably known as Camp Richmond prior to Merritt becoming commander. Toward the end of May, most of the soldiers from Camp Merriam were moved to Camp Merritt as the new recruits began arriving en masse. At that time, Merriam turned command of the camps over to Merritt. Unlike the sometimes chaotic planning for the Caribbean expeditions, planning in San Francisco for the Philippine expedition was both smoothly executed and well organized, thanks in good measure to General Merriam's assistance.

In May 1898, Merriam was promoted to major general of volunteers. In February 1899, he was advanced to major general (regular army), and from 1900 to 1901, he commanded the Department of Colorado. Merriam retired from active service in February 1903 and settled in Portland, Maine, where he died on November 18, 1912.

PAUL G. PIERPAOLI JR.

See also

Camp Merriam and Camp Merritt; Merritt, Wesley; Otis, Elwell Stephen

Further Reading

Cohen, Stan. *Images of the Spanish-American War.* New York: Pictorial Historians Publishing, 1997.

Cosmas, Graham A. *An Army for Empire: The United States Army in the Spanish-American War.* College Station: Texas A&M University Press, 1994.

Merrimac, USS

U.S. Navy collier (a coal-carrying ship designed to resupply other ships) scuttled in an attempt to block the channel to the harbor of Santiago de Cuba in order to bottle up the Spanish squadron there. The mission occurred on June 3, 1898. The *Merrimac* had been the Hogan line *Solvieg* before the U.S. Navy purchased it for $342,000 on April 12, 1898. It was renamed in honor of the U.S. Navy steam frigate secured by the Confederates and turned into the ironclad ram *Virginia.*

In late April 1898, a Spanish squadron commanded by Rear Admiral Pascual Cervera y Topete departed the Cape Verde Islands,

The U.S. Navy collier *Merrimac*, shown here at the Norfolk Navy Yard early in 1898. In a daring operation, the ship was scuttled in an unsuccessful effort to block the channel to Santiago Harbor. (Naval Historical Center)

ultimately anchoring in the harbor of Santiago de Cuba. Once its presence was known to the United States, the far superior North Atlantic Squadron, commanded by Rear Admiral William T. Sampson, established itself off the narrow harbor entrance. In order to thwart an escape attempt at night by Cervera's squadron, the American ships illuminated the harbor channel during hours of darkness with searchlights.

The entrance and much of the harbor were protected naturally by high cliffs. The meandering ship channel varied in width from 350 to 450 feet. Over the years, the Spanish had erected a number of batteries along both sides of the entrance, and they had sowed the channel with electronically detonated mines. These mines and American intelligence estimates of the strength of the Spanish defenses led Sampson to attempt to incapacitate Cervera's squadron by blocking it in the harbor instead of taking it on directly. To accomplish his plan, conceived prior to his leaving Key West, Florida, Sampson selected the collier *Merrimac* to be scuttled at a strategic spot at the channel mouth. The *Merrimac*, which had frequently broken down and had to be towed to Santiago, was on the list of expendable U.S. Navy ships.

Lieutenant Richmond Pearson Hobson of the battleship *New York* commanded the attempt. When a call went out for men to assist Hobson in what many regarded as a suicidal mission, hundreds

volunteered. Six were selected, while a seventh man stowed away in order to participate.

To scuttle the *Merrimac*, 10 electronically detonated mines, each filled with 78 pounds of gunpowder, were lashed to the port side of the ship below its waterline. The plan called for Hobson and his crew to steer the *Merrimac* toward the harbor entrance, pass Morro Castle, then turn to port, drop anchors fore and aft, and detonate the charges. Because the *Merrimac* was 333 feet long, if properly positioned it would completely block the channel for larger ships. Their mission accomplished, the crew were to escape via a lifeboat that was towed astern.

Problems delayed an attempt on the night of June 1–2, and it was then called off. The mission was rescheduled and began at 3:00 a.m. on June 3. It started out well, with the *Merrimac* able to proceed up the channel some distance before it was discovered by a Spanish picket boat. It and Spanish shore batteries then opened fire. The Spanish also exploded a number of their electronically detonated mines, according to Hobson six in the first line and two in the second. Also, one of the Spanish shots disabled the *Merrimac*'s steering. Hobson ordered the sea cocks opened; the mines exploded, but only two went off. Both the bow and stern anchor were dropped, but the stern anchor was shot away, and the bow anchor cable parted under the strain. The strong current straightened out the sinking vessel, which finally went down inside Santiago Harbor but past the entrance. The placement of the ship did not block egress for ships.

In the exchange of fire, the Spanish suffered a number of casualties from cross fire, while the Americans involved received only minor injuries in the operation. Hobson and his crew were picked up by a Spanish steam launch at 6:00 a.m. and taken prisoner. The Spanish praised the men for their brave deed, and that afternoon Captain Joaquín Bustamante y Quevedi came out under a flag of truce to inform Sampson that all the crewmen were safe and prisoners.

The failure of the attempt with the *Merrimac* forced Sampson into a close blockade. A month later, the Spanish squadron sortied only to be destroyed in the Battle of Santiago de Cuba. The crew of the *Merrimac* was released in an exchange of prisoners on July 6. All were subsequently awarded the Medal of Honor.

GREGORY C. FERENCE AND SPENCER C. TUCKER

See also

Cervera y Topete, Pascual; Hobson, Richmond Pearson; Morro Castle; Sampson, William Thomas; Santiago de Cuba, Battle of

Further Reading

Feuer, A. B. *The Spanish-American War at Sea: Naval Action in the Atlantic.* Westport, CT: Praeger, 1995.

Hobson, Richmond Pearson. *The Sinking of the "Merrimac": A Personal Narrative of the Adventure in the Harbor of Santiago de Cuba and of the Subsequent Imprisonment of the Survivors.* New York: Century, 1899.

Pittman, Walter E. *Navalist and Progressive: The Life of Richmond P. Hobson.* Manhattan, KS: MA/AH Publications, 1981.

Merritt, Wesley

Birth Date: June 16, 1836
Death Date: December 10, 1910

U.S. Army officer. Wesley Merritt was born in New York City on June 16, 1836. He attended the United States Military Academy, West Point, graduating in the middle of his class in 1860. Following graduation, he served in Utah with the 2nd Dragoons. The American Civil War brought Lieutenant Merritt's transfer to the East. There he turned out to be a superb cavalry officer. As a captain, he distinguished himself in the Gettysburg Campaign in the Battle of Brandy Station (June 9, 1863), the largest cavalry engagement in the history of North America. Receiving further notice, he was breveted brigadier general of volunteers and commanded the reserve cavalry of the Army of the Potomac.

Assigned temporary command of a division in May 1864, Merritt again fought with distinction in the Battle of Todd's Tavern on May 7, the largest dismounted cavalry engagement of the war. Following further distinguished service, especially the Battle of Yellow Tavern on May 11, he received permanent command of the 1st Cavalry Division of Sheridan's Army of the Shenandoah, leading it in a number of important Union victories. During the Appomattox Campaign of April 1865, Merritt commanded the Cavalry Corps as a brevet major general of Volunteers.

During the Spanish-American War, U.S. Army major general Wesley Merritt (shown here as a brigadier general) commanded VIII Corps, the expeditionary force sent to the Philippines. (Chaiba Media)

Following the Civil War, Merritt remained with the regular army as a lieutenant colonel and commander of the 9th Cavalry Regiment, one of two African American regiments in the army. This began 17 years of service on the frontier and extensive fighting against hostile Native Americans in the West. In 1876, he received promotion to colonel and took command of the 5th Cavalry Regiment, fighting in the Great Sioux War of 1876, the pursuit of the Nez Perce and in the Bannock War (1877–1878), and the Ute War (1879).

In 1882, Merritt became superintendent of West Point, serving in that position until his promotion to brigadier general in 1887. He then assumed command of the Department of the Missouri at Ft. Leavenworth, Kansas. From 1895 to 1897, he commanded the Department of the Missouri, the Department of Dakota, and Department of the East, respectively. In 1893, he wrote a book, *The Armies of Today*. In the book and in articles, he advocated a large and modern regular U.S. Army. He also supported U.S. imperial expansion.

Nearing retirement age at the beginning of the Spanish-American War, Major General Merritt was the second-ranking officer in the army. On the outbreak of war, he asked for command of VIII Corps. Appointed to that position on May 12, he was informed that the corps would be headed to the Philippines. On May 19, he received his instructions to defeat the Spanish, pacify the islands, and hold them for the United States but not to ally his forces with those of Filipino insurgent leader Emilio Aguinaldo y Famy. Although the instructions left vague the future of the islands, Merritt assumed that they would be annexed by the United States.

Merritt did what he could to organize his corps prior to departure, making it a point to secure suitable tropical uniforms and supplies for the soldiers, which may have reduced deaths from heat-related illness and disease. He sailed for the Philippines in the *Newport,* departing San Francisco on June 29 and arriving at Manila in late July.

Styling Aguinaldo a "Chinese half-breed adventurer," Merritt followed his instructions of operating independently of the insurgent forces, which had surrounded Manila. Rear Admiral George Dewey negotiated with the Spanish commander, General Fermín Jáudenes y Alvarez, agreeing to stage a small symbolic battle on August 13 to satisfy Spanish honor while at the same time excluding the Filipino revolutionaries. The occupation of Manila on August 14 proceeded smoothly, and Merritt's troops quickly established order in the city. He issued a proclamation promising support and protection to all those cooperating with the U.S. troops.

On August 30, Merritt transferred command of VIII Corps to Major General Elwell S. Otis and departed the islands for Paris to brief the U.S. peace commissioners meeting with their Spanish counterparts in Paris. There, Merritt told the commissioners that it was his opinion that the United States should annex the Philippines and that the majority of Filipinos would welcome American rule.

In December 1898, Merritt assumed command of the Department of the East. He retired from the army in 1900 and died in Natural Bridge, Virginia, on December 10, 1910.

DAWN OTTEVAERE NICKESON AND SPENCER C. TUCKER

See also
Aguinaldo y Famy, Emilio; VIII Corps; Filipino Revolutionary Movement; Manila, First Battle of; Spain, Army; United States Army

Further Reading
Alberts, Don E. *Brandy Station to Manila Bay: A Biography of General Wesley Merritt.* Austin, TX: Presidial, 1980.
Feuer, A. B. *America at War: The Philippines, 1898–1913.* Westport, CT: Praeger, 2002.
Trask, David F. *The War with Spain in 1898.* Lincoln: University of Nebraska Press, 1996.

"Message to Garcia, A"
Event Date: February 22, 1899

Essay written by American writer and publisher Elbert Hubbard on February 22, 1899, to extol the virtues of self-reliance. First published in the March 1899 issue of *Philistine* magazine, which Hubbard was then editing, "A Message to Garcia" was meant as filler

material and carried no title. Much to Hubbard's surprise, the essay, which praises the initiative taken by an American soldier at the outset of the Spanish-American War, became an instant success. Before long, Hubbard republished it as a stand-alone pamphlet and then in book form.

The essay recounts the actions of Andrew Summers Rowan, a U.S. soldier and 1881 graduate of the United States Military Academy, who was ordered to carry a message to Cuban revolutionary Calixto García y Iñiguez just prior to combat operations in Cuba. García, who had been struggling for Cuban independence since the Ten Years' War (1868–1878), had repeatedly sought American assistance in liberating Cuba from Spanish colonial rule. U.S. military officials hoped to contact García to coordinate the U.S. Army's land invasion of Cuba. In his essay, Hubbard applauds Rowan's dogged dedication to duty and his willingness to accomplish his task without asking questions or raising any objections. Rowan's success in delivering the letter to García made him the prototype of the American can-do mentality. For many years, even after World War II, Hubbard's inspiring story became a popular cultural allusion, showcasing Yankee ingenuity and self-reliance. Leaders in both the military and business frequently used "A Message to Garcia" to motivate their subordinates.

More than 4 million copies of the essay have been published in 37 languages, and it was required reading for all U.S. servicemen during both world wars. The essay was the basis of two motion pictures: a silent film released in 1916 and another one in 1936 that starred Wallace Beery, Barbara Stanwyck, and Alan Hale.

MICHAEL R. HALL

See also
García y Iñiguez, Calixto; Hubbard, Elbert; Journalism; Ten Years' War

Further Reading
Garcia, Gerardo Castellano. *Tierras y Glorias de Oriente* [Lands and Success in the East]. Havana: Editorial Hermes, 1927.
Hubbard, Elbert. *A Message to Garcia.* Mechanicsburg, PA: Executive Books, 2002.
Martin, John H. *Saints, Sinners and Reformers: The Burned-Over District Re-Visited.* Hammondsport, NY: Crooked Lake Review, 2005.

Middletown, Pennsylvania
See Camp Meade

Midway Island

A coral atoll in the North Pacific Ocean annexed by the United States in August 1867 as the Unincorporated Territory of Midway Island and administered by the U.S. Navy. Midway Island is located in the north central Pacific Ocean at 28°12' north latitude and 177°12' west longitude, about one-third of the way between

Honolulu and Tokyo. It is considered a distant part of the Hawaiian Islands chain.

Midway, just 2.4 square miles in area, is almost circular and surrounds a shallow lagoon about 15 miles in circumference. The largest and most important parts of Midway are two islands, Sand and Eastern, that lie on the southern edge of the lagoon. Midway has a subtropical climate that is characterized by warm, dry summers and cool (but not cold), wet winters. Its native flora includes beach morning glory and bunchgrass. The most common animal life consists of seabirds such as the tern and albatross.

U.S. Navy captain N. C. Middlebrooks discovered the uninhabited atoll in July 1859, but the tiny island chain was largely ignored in the ensuing years despite general interest in Pacific islands for their deposits of guano, which was commonly used as fertilizer. In August 1867, the Department of the Navy sent Commander William Reynolds to take possession of Midway Island for use as a coaling station, and the United States annexed Midway later that year. The relatively early acquisition of Midway kept it out of the reach of other seagoing powers such as Great Britain and Germany, which were seeking to acquire coaling stations in the North Pacific. The possession of Midway and America's new land acquisitions resulting from the Spanish-American War helped contain Germany's strategic influence in the Pacific.

After 1903, Midway became a cable station along the Guam-to-Hawaii portion of the first transpacific telegraph cable. In the late 1930s, the island served as a stop on Pan American Airline's civilian air route between San Francisco and Manila. The U.S. Navy began constructing a submarine base and an air station on Midway Island in 1940 as war clouds loomed. As such, it was an important part of the American war effort in the Pacific during World War II. There were two seaplane landing areas carved into the coral of the lagoon's bottom, and although many parts of Welles Harbor on the western side of Sand Island were adequate to accommodate many ships, oceangoing vessels used a man-made channel between the two islands to berth at the larger island. President Franklin D. Roosevelt assigned control of the airspace and ocean surrounding Midway to the navy in 1941. The atoll is perhaps most famous for the Battle of Midway, fought near there during June 4–7, 1942. Midway Island remains a U.S. possession. Since 1996, it has been administered by the Department of the Interior.

MATTHEW J. KROGMAN

See also

Coaling Stations; Hawaiian Islands

Further Reading

Skaggs, Jimmy M. *The Great Guano Rush: Entrepreneurs and American Overseas Expansion*. New York: St. Martin's, 1994.

Trask, David F. *The War with Spain in 1898*. Lincoln: University of Nebraska Press, 1996.

United States Coast Survey: United States, Hawaiian Islands, Midway Islands. Washington, DC: U.S. Department of Commerce, National Oceanic and Atmospheric Administration, National Ocean Service, 2005.

Miles, Evan
Birth Date: 1838
Death Date: 1908

U.S. Army officer. Born in 1838, Evan Miles saw service in the American Civil War and remained in the U.S. Army afterward, assigned to the 21st Infantry Regiment as a captain. Serving in the American West, he took part in the Bannock War in 1878. Rising to the rank of major, during the Spanish-American War he first commanded the 1st Infantry Regiment and then the 2nd Brigade of the 2nd Division in V Corps during the Santiago Campaign. The 2nd Brigade comprised the 1st, 4th, and 25th Infantry Regiments. Initially held in reserve, the brigade saw service at El Caney on July 1, 1898. Advanced to brigadier general of volunteers on October 6, 1898, Miles retired from the army in 1899 and died in 1908.

JAMES R. MCINTYRE AND SPENCER C. TUCKER

See also

El Caney, Battle of; V Corps

Further Reading

Musicant, Ivan. *The Spanish-American War and the Dawn of the American Century*. New York: Henry Holt, 1998.

Trask, David F. *The War with Spain in 1898*. Lincoln: University of Nebraska Press, 1996.

Miles, Nelson Appleton
Birth Date: August 8, 1839
Death Date: May 15, 1925

U.S. Army officer and commanding general of the army during the Spanish-American War. Nelson Appleton Miles was born on a farm near Westminster, Massachusetts, on August 8, 1839. After attending public school, in 1856 he moved to Boston, where he worked as a store clerk. Interested in the military, he received some instruction from a retired French colonel.

At the outbreak of the American Civil War, Miles recruited some 100 men for the Massachusetts Regiment of Volunteers and was commissioned a captain. At first considered too young for battlefield command, he initially served in a staff position during the 1862 Peninsula Campaign. He soon demonstrated a natural capacity for battlefield leadership and began a meteoric advance in rank. After the Battle of Seven Pines (Fair Oaks), he was promoted to lieutenant colonel. He then fought in the Seven Days' Campaign and the Battle of Antietam (Sharpsburg). Promoted to colonel, he was wounded in the Battle of Fredericksburg and again in the Battle of Chancellorsville. For his actions at Chancellorsville, he received the Medal of Honor in 1892. He commanded a brigade of II Corps in the 1864 Overland Campaign and saw combat in the Battle of the Wilderness and the Battle of Spotsylvania Court House, after which he was breveted a brigadier general of volunteers in May 1864. He commanded a division in the Siege of Petersburg and, briefly (at age 26), a corps. He suffered his fourth wound of the war in the Battle of Reams Station.

U.S. Army major general Nelson A. Miles distinguished himself in the American Civil War and in fighting against Native Americans in the West. He was commanding general of the army during the Spanish-American War. (Library of Congress)

Following the war, in October 1865 Miles was advanced to major general of volunteers and assumed command of II Corps. In the reorganization of the army in 1866, he became a colonel and commander of the 40th Infantry Regiment, an African American unit. In 1869, he took command of the 5th Infantry Regiment. He saw extensive service in the American West and became renowned as one of the army's finest commanders in the ensuing Native American wars. He was largely responsible for the quick end of the Red River War of 1874–1875. In 1876 and 1877, he fought in the Sioux Wars and the Nez Perce War, and he personally took the surrenders of Sioux war chief Crazy Horse and Nez Perce chief Joseph.

Miles was promoted to brigadier general in the regular army in December 1880. From 1880 to 1885, he commanded the Department of the Colombia, and from 1885 to 1886, he had charge of the Department of the Missouri. In 1886, he took command of the Department of Arizona, overseeing the final surrender of Geronimo and the Chiricahua Apaches in September 1886. Miles then engaged in a public dispute with Brigadier General George Crook over the subsequent exile of the Apaches, including the loyal scouts, to Florida.

In 1888, Miles took command of the Division of the Pacific. He was promoted to major general in April 1890 and commanded the Department of the Missouri. He had overall charge of the suppres-

sion of the Sioux Ghost Dance Uprising but was angered by the bloodshed at Wounded Knee on December 19, 1890. He wanted to court-martial Colonel John W. Forsyth, in command during that action. Although Miles relieved Forsyth from command, the War Department reinstated him. In 1894, Miles was called upon to employ troops in suppressing the Pullman Strike. He next commanded the Department of the East. On October 5, 1895, he succeeded Lieutenant General John M. Schofield as commanding general of the army.

Miles opposed the Spanish-American War, believing that diplomacy could resolve the differences between Spain and the United States. He also held that fighting the war would be best left to the regular army rather than recruiting a volunteer force. Thus, he thought that the invasion of Cuba should be carried out by regular troops with volunteers replacing the regulars at home, where they would garrison the coast defense works against a possible Spanish attack. Unlike Secretary of War Russell Alger with whom he was continually at odds, Miles recognized the impracticality of expanding the nation's army to several times its prewar strength and expecting to employ it virtually overnight. He opposed an invasion of Cuba during the summer, the tropical disease season, and believed that initially the United States should rely on a naval blockade and support for the Cuban insurgents.

Originally, U.S. strategy focused on Havana, but Miles persuaded President William McKinley that the city was not a good choice because it was the strongest Spanish position on the island. The revised strategy settled on an assault against Santiago de Cuba. Miles urged postponing any invasion until the Spanish squadron there had been destroyed. He seemed to have a realistic understanding of the problems in creating and organizing a large army, and his recommendations regarding it were generally sound.

Miles supported the choice of Major General William R. Shafter to command the Cuban Expeditionary Force of V Corps. In July 1898, Miles, undoubtedly chafing at not having a more active role in the war, visited Shafter in Cuba but, to his credit, did not interfere in operations there even though as commanding general of the army he was Shafter's superior.

Once Santiago was secured, Miles received approval to proceed with his own invasion of Puerto Rico, an assignment he had sought early on. Indeed, he had originally argued for an invasion of Puerto Rico before attempting to seize Cuba. Originally, he had planned to land at Fajardo on the eastern coast but en route changed his mind because of anticipated heavy losses. On July 25, 1898, his troops came ashore at Guánica on the southwestern coast. Miles conducted a highly successful campaign in Puerto Rico but was angered that the armistice of August 12 denied him the capture of San Juan.

In the aftermath of the war, Miles was the central figure in the notorious Embalmed Beef Scandal. He alleged that the Commissary Department had issued spoiled beef to the troops, but others claimed that the meat was safe, just not very palatable. On December 21, 1898, Miles gave sensational testimony before the Dodge Commission, headed by former Civil War general and railroad builder Grenville Dodge, investigating the scandal.

Miles's allegations brought a strong response from Brigadier General Charles P. Eagan, the army's commissary general, who called him a liar in the hearings. Eagan was severely reprimanded for his outburst, but Miles did not escape unscathed. He too was reprimanded by the Dodge Commission for making charges that were proven to be substantially unfounded. Miles's old enemy, Secretary of War Alger, sought to take advantage of the situation by requesting that Miles be relieved of his command, which President McKinley rejected.

In February 1901, Miles was promoted to lieutenant general. President Theodore Roosevelt, who called him a "brave peacock" for his love of excessive uniform display, also crossed swords with Miles, as did Secretary of War Elihu Root, who found Miles in sharp opposition to his plan to create a general staff and do away with the position of commanding general of the army, substituting for it the new position of chief of staff.

While Root was carrying out his reforms, Miles was sent on an inspection tour of the Philippines in 1902 to get him out of Washington. From the Philippines he wrote to condemn the U.S. Army's torture of prisoners in order to extract information from them. Such criticism was not welcome in Washington and was suppressed.

Miles retired from the army on his 64th birthday in 1903. Combative, vain, and ambitious, he was, despite his leadership qualities in battle, a commanding general who displayed little political sense and did not fit in well with the new 20th-century army. In 1917 when the United States entered World War I, he offered his services, but the offer was not accepted. In retirement, he wrote articles and several books, including a two-volume memoir. Miles died in Washington, D.C., on May 15, 1925.

JERRY KEENAN AND SPENCER C. TUCKER

See also

McKinley, William; Roosevelt, Theodore; Root, Elihu; Shafter, William Rufus

Further Reading

Cosmas, Graham A. *An Army for Empire: The United States Army in the Spanish-American War.* College Station: Texas A&M University Press, 1994.

DeMontravel, Peter R. *A Hero to His Fighting Men: Nelson Miles, 1839–1925.* Kent, OH: Kent State University Press, 1998.

Johnson, Virginia. *The Unregimented General: A Biography of Nelson A. Miles.* Boston: Houghton Mifflin, 1962.

Miles, Nelson A. *Personal Recollections and Observations of General Nelson Miles.* 2 vols. Lincoln: University of Nebraska Press, 1992.

Wooster, Robert. *Nelson Miles and the Twilight of the Frontier Army.* Lincoln: University of Nebraska Press, 1993.

Miley, John David

Birth Date: September 1862
Death Date: September 19, 1899

U.S. Army officer. John David Miley was born in Belleville, Illinois, in September 1862. He graduated from the United States Military Academy, West Point, in 1887, ranking 20th in a class of 64, and was commissioned a second lieutenant of artillery. His initial assignments included Fort Adams in Rhode Island; Fort Schuyler in New York; and the Presidio in San Francisco. While stationed at Fort Schuyler, he graduated from Columbia Law School in 1889. In 1894, he was promoted to first lieutenant.

In 1897, Miley became aide-de-camp to Major General William Shafter, who at the beginning of the Spanish-American War in April 1898 took command of V Corps. Shafter then led V Corps with more than 15,000 troops from Tampa, Florida, to Cuba, with the taking of Santiago de Cuba his primary strategic task.

U.S. forces landed at Daiquirí, east of Santiago, during June 22–24, 1898. By July 1, they had advanced to San Juan Heights, which dominated the approaches to Santiago. Since arriving in Cuba, Shafter's size (he weighed 300 pounds), the frenetic activity of the campaign, and the hot climate all combined to cause him serious health problems. He was thus forced to rely extensively on his aides to bring him reports and relay orders. Early on the morning of July 1, as the assault on San Juan Heights was about to begin, General Shafter and Lieutenant Miley visited the troops and surveyed the area. By the time the attack began at approximately 10:00 a.m., however, Shafter had taken ill and was unable to personally direct operations. Miley and Colonel Edward J. McClernand, Shafter's adjutant, set up a forward command post at El Pozo, about four miles east of San Juan Heights, and employed messengers to relay situation reports and orders between Shafter at general headquarters, a mile farther east, and his subordinate commanders.

Miley was positioned with the troops and served as Shafter's forward observer and coordinator for the operation. Miley's most distinct contribution came as American units were forming at the base of the hill complex and taking heavy casualties from Spanish rifle fire from the top of the hills. At that point, assault unit commanders Brigadier Generals Jacob F. Kent, Samuel S. Sumner, and Hamilton S. Hawkins met with Miley. Hawkins reported that his command was taking heavy casualties and was unable to withdraw because of congestion on the trails behind them. Kent considered delaying the assault until the arrival of Brigadier General Henry Ware Lawton's 2nd Division, but Miley concurred with Hawkins that a withdrawal was not practical and that the troops could not continue to maintain their exposed positions indefinitely. The lieutenant then gave the command to the generals, under the authority of General Shafter (but without his input), to initiate the assault that ultimately resulted in Hawkins's brigade securing San Juan Hill and Sumner's cavalry division securing Kettle Hill.

Following the Battle of San Juan Hill, Miley led an expedition to secure the surrender of outlying Spanish garrisons. This assignment was accomplished without further fighting. Later, he was appointed a member of the U.S. commission that negotiated for the Spanish surrender of Santiago de Cuba.

Following the war, Miley wrote a book, *In Cuba with Shafter* (1899). He transferred to the Philippines in 1899, where he was promoted to lieutenant colonel of volunteers and became inspector general for Major General Elwell S. Otis, commander of U.S. forces in the Philippines. Miley died in Manila on September 19, 1899, from complications of typhoid fever, which he had contracted in Cuba soon after the conclusion of the campaign there. In 1900, the military reservation on Point Lobos in San Francisco was renamed Fort Miley in his honor.

LOUIS A. DiMARCO

See also

Hawkins, Hamilton Smith; Kent, Jacob Ford; Lawton, Henry Ware; Mc-Clernand, Edward John; Otis, Elwell Stephen; San Juan Heights, Battle of; Santiago de Cuba, Capitulation Agreement; Santiago de Cuba Land Campaign; Shafter, William Rufus; Sumner, Samuel Storrow; Typhoid Fever

Further Reading

McClure, Nathaniel F., ed. *Class of 1887 United States Military Academy: A Biographical Volume.* Washington, DC: P. S. Bond, 1939.

O'Toole, G. J. A. *The Spanish War: An American Epic, 1898.* New York: Norton, 1984.

Trask, David F. *The War with Spain in 1898.* Lincoln: University of Nebraska Press, 1996.

United States Army Center of Military History. *Correspondence Relating to the War with Spain, Including the Insurrection in the Philippine Islands and the China Relief Expedition, April 15, 1898 to July 30, 1902.* Washington, DC: Center for Military History, 1993.

Military Intelligence

In the period leading up to and during the Spanish-American War, the organized gathering of military intelligence was still in its infancy. The United States had no civilian government agency charged with information gathering. Although the U.S. Army and U.S. Navy had their own intelligence agencies, there was little coordination between them. Organized espionage became a uniformly acceptable method of gaining intelligence only in the period after the American Civil War. To supplement the data from the intelligence agencies, individual military commanders created and utilized their own espionage networks to gain tactical information, often through local insurgents. Counterintelligence did exist and was handled by a civilian agency, the Treasury Department's U.S. Secret Service.

The most successful intelligence agency was the U.S. Navy's Office of Naval Intelligence (ONI), founded in 1882. Prior to the war, the agency confined its activities to the compiling of data on foreign naval capabilities through reports from naval attachés serving with the diplomatic corps in various countries. The attachés provided data on the state of preparedness as well as on strength and movements of naval forces through such sources as open observation and newspaper accounts. Later, as the war appeared inevitable and the clash began, the ONI, headed by Commander Richardson Clover, successfully supplemented the data with information gathered through espionage. The ONI managed to provide fairly accurate data on the condition, location, and order of battle of the Spanish naval forces.

The ONI's most successful espionage effort was that of Lieutenants William Sims and John Colwell in Europe. Although not necessarily working together, the pair created spy networks that were able to gain information from all over Europe and as far away as Egypt. The network's efforts at espionage, disinformation, and direct action became particularly important in dealing with the threat posed by Spanish admiral Manuel de la Cámara's y Libermoore's squadron to the U.S. Asiatic Squadron in the Philippines.

The U.S. Army's intelligence wing was the Military Information Division (MID), which was organized in 1885. Like the ONI, the MID collected reports from military attachés and similar sources. During the Spanish-American War period, the MID, headed by Major Arthur Wagner, was generally successful, with its greatest achievements being in Cuba, where it determined the Spanish order of battle and gained useful information on the island's geography and topography.

To supplement the official data from their respective intelligence agencies, individual commanders created their own espionage systems. Commodore George Dewey supplemented official reports from the Philippines, such as those from U.S. consul Oscar Williams, with data from American businessmen operating in the area and from his own aide, Ensign Frank Upham. Upham, posing as an inquisitive civilian traveler, would meet incoming ships arriving at Hong Kong from the Philippines and question the crews regarding conditions there. The navy also landed in Cuba men such as Lieutenant Victor Blue, who infiltrated the Spanish lines to verify the arrival of Cervera's squadron at Santiago de Cuba. The army used similar methods. Lieutenant Henry Whitney was sent to Puerto Rico under the guise of being a British sailor traveling and gaining important data on climate, topography, harbors, and the attitude of the population. Lieutenant Andrew Rowan aided the army by posing as an English traveler to gain access to Cuba, where he met with the Cuban insurgents, gaining data from them and through direct observation. Rowan's actions became popularized in *A Message to Garcia.*

The greatest coup in military intelligence, however, was not the result of the efforts of either the ONI or the MID. Through an acquaintance of U.S. Navy captain Charles Sigsbee, who commanded the battleship *Maine,* a system was set up to obtain information directly from the palace of the Spanish governor-general in Havana, Cuba. The system, eventually turned over to the U.S. Signal Corps, utilized a Cuban agent, Domingo Villaverde, who was a telegraph operator within the governor-general's palace. Villaverde relayed data obtained from communications of high-level Spanish officials to a contact at a subsidiary of the Western Union Telegraph Company. The data was then forwarded directly to the White House. The existence of this connection was such a closely guarded secret that even U.S. secretary of the navy John D. Long did not know of it.

Although uncoordinated and limited, the intelligence-gathering efforts during the war were generally successful. Failures did occur, however. The most dramatic failure of intelligence was that in-

U.S. Secret Service employees at work, circa 1906. The Secret Service of the Treasury Department carried out counterintelligence operations in the United States during the Spanish-American War. (Library of Congress)

volving the independence movement in the Philippines. The strength of the movement for an independent Philippines was greatly underestimated by the Americans. This lack of understanding led to failed policies toward the movement, which ultimately precipitated the Philippine-American War.

During the Philippine-American War, little centralized military intelligence was initially gained and passed to the field commanders to aid them in pursuing the war. To overcome this lack of information about the Philippine independence movement and its forces, Major General Elwell Otis created the Bureau of Insurgent Records (BIR) to translate and interpret captured documents. The small agency was completely overwhelmed with the amount of data, however, and little useful information was passed back to field commanders. In 1900, Brigadier General Arthur MacArthur reorganized the BIR into the Division of Military Information (DIM), which finally began providing useful data to field commanders. Eventually, a system was created by which field commanders also provided data back to the DIM to allow for more comprehensive understanding of the overall conditions.

Counterintelligence efforts in the United States were directed by the U.S. Treasury Department's Secret Service. The Secret Ser-

vice's most notable success was the destruction of a Spanish spy network being organized in Canada. After departing the United States as war approached, the former naval attaché of the Spanish Washington legation, Lieutenant Ramon Carranza, traveled to Montreal. There he began creating a spy network that included former U.S. Navy cruiser *Brooklyn* crewman George Downing, former artillerist Frank Mellor, and others. The ring was successful in obtaining data on the movement of naval vessels, etc. However, the major informants in the United States were caught and jailed. Carranza was forced to leave Canada but was still transmitting data as late as June 15, 1898.

The Spanish-American War prompted a significant improvement in military intelligence gathering. With the war, the government changed from relying solely on reports available through its diplomatic corps to using organized espionage to gain important information. Improvements were made in espionage methods and practices, although no central agency was charged with coordinating and disseminating military intelligence. The agencies of the U.S. Navy and the U.S. Army were, however, generally successful in gaining useful but limited military intelligence.

PATRICK MCSHERRY

See also

Blue, Victor; Cámara y Libermoore, Manuel de la; Dewey, George; MacArthur, Arthur; "Message to Garcia, A"; Otis, Elwell Stephen; Rowan, Andrew Summers; Sigsbee, Charles Dwight; Sims, William Sowden; Whitney, Henry Howard

Further Reading

Cooper, Diane E. "Diplomat and Naval Intelligence Officer: The Duties of Lt. George L. Dyer, U.S. Naval Attache to Spain." In *Crucible of Empire: The Spanish-American War and Its Aftermath,* edited by James C. Bradford, 1–22. Annapolis, MD: Naval Institute Press, 1993.

Cosmas, Graham A. *An Army for Empire: The United States Army in the Spanish-American War.* College Station: Texas A&M University Press, 1994.

O'Toole, G. J. A. *The Spanish War: An American Epic, 1898.* New York: Norton, 1984.

Trask, David F. "American Intelligence during the Spanish-American War." In *Crucible of Empire: The Spanish-American War and Its Aftermath,* edited by James C. Bradford, 23–46. Annapolis, MD: Naval Institute Press, 1993.

Militia, Naval

Personnel from state naval militias who augmented the U.S. Navy during the Spanish-American War. The modern naval militia system began in 1889 when the Massachusetts and New York legislatures each passed measures establishing state naval militias, the first such organizations since the Revolutionary War. Recognizing the need for a source of trained, experienced seamen for use in wartime, U.S. naval and congressional leaders in the late 1880s attempted to secure funding to organize a federal naval reserve force. Failing in this endeavor, Congress supported the two fledgling state naval militias by instituting what became an annual appropriation for arms and equipment in March 1891.

In 1894, Congress bolstered its support for the naval militia program and authorized the loaning of ships to the then 11 state militias for training purposes. By 1898, 16 states sponsored naval militias with federal assistance, providing a potential source of trained maritime manpower for use by the U.S. Navy.

In January 1898, the U.S. Navy numbered 1,232 officers and had an authorized strength of 11,750 enlisted men. At peak strength in the Spanish-American War, the U.S. Navy numbered 2,088 officers and 24,123 enlisted men, 4,316 of whom came from state naval militias for employment in naval operations and coastal defense. At this time, there was no legal mechanism for mustering these forces into federal service, so state governors allowed state naval militiamen to temporarily resign their state obligations or granted them leave to allow them to serve in the U.S. Navy.

Naval militiamen during the Spanish-American War served either in the Coast Signal Service or the Auxiliary Naval Force (sometimes referred to as the Mosquito Squadron). The Coastal Signal Service, part of the U.S. Coastal Defenses, was manned entirely by state naval militia forces. The service established 36 signal stations along the Atlantic and Gulf coasts cooperating closely with personnel from the Life Saving Service, the Weather Bureau, and lighthouses. These forces kept lookout for the approach of enemy vessels and used various methods of communication including telephone, telegraph, torches, and International Code flags.

Naval militiamen also augmented crews of U.S. naval vessels during the course of the war and provided the entire crew for four naval auxiliary cruisers. The Auxiliary Naval Force was formally established by Congress on May 26, 1898, as a temporary measure to strengthen the naval ship complement for the protection of U.S. cities and ports on the Atlantic, Gulf, and Pacific coasts for the duration of the war. Ten American Civil War–era recommissioned monitors, joined by 31 purchased, chartered, or donated vessels in nine districts along the coasts, patrolled local waters, conducted target practice, protected minefields, and enforced quarantine regulations. Almost entirely manned by naval militiamen, these forces were augmented by a small percentage of merchant mariners.

Naval militiamen entirely manned the four naval auxiliary cruisers *Dixie, Prairie, Yankee,* and *Yosemite.* The personnel came from the state naval militias of Maryland, Massachusetts, New York, and Michigan, respectively. The cruisers served in blockade duty, in engagements, and as transports to and from Cuba, Puerto Rico, and other areas of the Caribbean theater. The naval militia programs of several states continued with federal support until World War I and served as a precursor to today's Naval Reserve Service.

MARK C. MOLLAN

See also

Coastal Defenses, U.S.; Naval Vessels, U.S. Auxiliary; United States Auxiliary Naval Force; United States Navy

Further Reading

Trask, David F. *The War with Spain in 1898.* Lincoln: University of Nebraska Press, 1996.

United States Navy. *Annual Report of the Secretary of the Navy, 1898.* Washington, DC: U.S. Government Printing Office, 1898.

Militia Act of 1903

U.S. congressional legislation passed on January 21, 1903, that marked the beginning of federal funding and recognition of the National Guard, composed of the Reserve Militia and the Organized Militia (National Guard). The Militia Act of 1903 is also known as the Dick Act for its sponsor, Republican senator Charles W. Dick, also a general in the Ohio National Guard. The act offered federal funds to each state to train and equip its own contingent of National Guardsmen. Also under the provisions of the act, the Organized Militia could be deployed upon presidential order for an initial period of nine months. The states, however, operated both reserve and organized militias. The Militia Act was part of Secretary of War Elihu Root's efforts to reorganize, reform, and streamline the American military establishment, a need that had been sorely apparent during the often chaotic and tumultuous mobilization for the Spanish-American War.

Militia units had been part of the American defense system since December 1636, when the General Court of the Massachusetts Bay Colony organized three militia regiments to defend the settlements against the growing threat of Native American attacks. The term "national guard" was first used by Marie Josephe Motier, Marquis de Lafayette, to describe citizen forces mobilized during the French Revolution in the 1790s. The militia was initially patterned after the British militia systems and was later regulated by the Militia Act of 1792. Yet the federal government provided no funding for the militias, and most states allowed their militias to deteriorate, which made them quite ineffective in subsequent wars. By 1903, it was clear that a militia act that was more than 100 years old had to be revised.

In 1902, Dick became president of the National Guard Association. He was determined to elevate the National Guard to the same level as the regular army. However, the final version of the law was a compromise between the association's demands for better funding and training and the government's request to free the militias from complete state control. The 1903 Militia Act consisted of 26 sections, which set forth provisions that had previously applied only to the regular army. Among other things, male citizens between the ages of 18 and 45 were divided into the Organized Militia (National Guard) and the Reserve Militia. Furthermore, Congress mandated that within five years the National Guard's organizational structure, pay scale, equipment, and discipline had to be identical to that of the regular army. Membership in the National Guard units remained voluntary, and state governors retained control over their National Guard regiments' mobilization. To be eligible for federal funds, the states' National Guard units were obliged to undertake 24 drills and 5 days of summer training camps per year, allow for federal inspections, conform to U.S. Army rules, and meet all federal requirements.

Federal funding for the National Guard increased substantially within the next few years. Whereas the militia's budget in 1887 had been a meager $400,000, Congress allocated $53 million to the National Guard between 1903 and 1916. To supervise training, the U.S. War Department created the Division of Militia Affairs. In 1908, the Militia Act was amended to allow guardsmen to serve outside the United States and nullified the nine-month cap for active duty. The June 1916 National Defense Act further expanded the National Guard's role and increased federal regulation of it. This act stipulated that National Guard regiments could be called into federal service, at which point they would be part of the regular army and not the state militia. In addition, the term "National Guard" became mandatory, and the president was given the power to deploy the National Guard in case of war or other national emergency.

KATJA WUESTENBECKER

See also

Roosevelt, Theodore; Root, Elihu

Further Reading

Colby, Elbridge. "Elihu Root and the National Guard." *Military Affairs* 23(1) (Spring 1959): 28–34.

Cooper, Jerry M. *The Rise of the National Guard: The Evolution of the American Militia, 1865–1920.* Lincoln: University of Nebraska Press, 1997.

Cosmas, Graham A. *An Army for Empire: The United States Army in the Spanish-American War.* College Station: Texas A&M University Press, 1994.

Doubler, Michael D. *Civilian in Peace, Soldier in War: The Army National Guard, 1636–2000.* Lawrence, KS: University of Kansas, 2003.

Mindanao

Second largest island in the Philippine archipelago. Geographically, Mindanao is the southernmost Philippine island and encompasses some 36,000 square miles, about the size of the state of Indiana or one-third of all of the landmass of the Philippines. At the time of the Spanish-American War, much of the island was mountainous and heavily forested and was rich in natural resources such as gold, nickel, and copper.

Mindanao has the highest peak in the Philippines, Mount Apo, that soars to 9,692 feet above sea level. The island includes the Sulu Archipelago, which runs to the southwest of the main island. To the north is the Visayas island chain. The island's principal city is Davao in the south. Mindanao is currently home to about 18 million people and is divided into 6 administrative regions and further subdivided into 25 provinces.

Mindanao's social formation has been distinct from the rest of the Philippines because of its unique history. Spanish colonization beginning in 1565 left Mindanao and the smaller islands of Sulu and Tawi-Tawi virtually untouched. At best, they were only weakly integrated to Las Islas Filipinas, the Spanish term for the Philippine Islands. By 1898, about one-third of Mindanao's inhabitants were Muslims, or Moros as the Spanish called them. In the nearly five centuries between Spanish colonization and the Spanish-American War, the Moros waged frequent warfare against their colonial overlords in an attempt to keep themselves separated from the rest of the Filipino population, much of which was Christian by the early 1800s.

Economically, Mindanao was and still is an important region. At the turn of the 20th century, it was a great source of fertile lands officially classified as belonging to the public domain. Most of its land was available for agricultural use except for a few patches occupied by Moros and various tribal groups, whose combined population was only about 380,000 people according to the 1903 census. Thus, the frontier on Mindanao offered a vast potential for agricultural development. American colonial administration initiated steps to open this region by encouraging foreign venture capitalists to invest in the region and invited settlers onto the island to harness its rich, largely untapped resources.

Field artillery on the move at Camp Vicars on the island of Mindanao in the Philippines. (Library of Congress)

While no fighting occurred on Mindanao during the Spanish-American War, the island was the scene of periodic and pitched engagements between rebellious Moros and U.S. Army forces during 1902–1903. The Moros, who steadfastly refused to yield to American governance, continued their long tradition of resisting rule by outside forces. In 1902 and 1903, U.S. forces under Colonel Frank Baldwin and then Captain John J. Pershing conducted a series of punitive raids against entrenched Moro encampments in the Lake Lanao region of the island. Thanks to Pershing's intrepid military skills and sharp diplomatic savvy, the threat posed to U.S. forces by the Moros was sharply diminished after the Lake Lanao Campaigns. Mindanao has remained a hotbed of rebel agitation, however, into the 21st century.

Today, Mindanao is host to various industries engaged in extracting or producing agricultural products (coconuts, pineapples, bananas, sugar, abaca, rubber), deep-sea fishing, mining, and other industrial ventures. The Davao Province was once dominated by Japanese colonists, who pioneered abaca plantations that ushered in the development of this province during the 1930s until the outbreak of World War II.

Following World War II and after the Philippines gained its independence, Mindanao attracted millions of landless settlers from Luzon and the Visayas seeking to acquire and develop its abundant lands. The government passed laws to encourage such mass migration, which contributed largely to the peopling of the southern frontier during the 1950s–1970s. Between 1948 and 1960, for instance, Mindanao's population grew at a rate more than double the national average of 2.9 percent. This pattern of migration eventu-

ally diluted the indigenous culture and overshadowed the native peoples, who became minorities in their own homeland.

Today, Mindanao has become a mainly Christian community except for five predominantly Muslim provinces and a few towns inhabited mostly by tribal communities. Mindanao has become a source of political strain and warfare associated with the secessionist struggle waged by the Moros since the 1970s. Since then, the Philippine government has been engaged in a peace process with the Moro National Liberation Front and lately with the Moro Islamic Liberation Front. The Armed Forces of the Philippines also conducts periodic punitive operations against militant Islamic elements on Mindanao, notably the Abu Sayyaf Group and the Rajah Soliman Movement, which emerged in the 1990s.

FEDERICO MAGDALENA AND PAUL G. PIERPAOLI JR.

See also

Baldwin, Frank Dwight; Bayang, Battle of; Lake Lanao Campaigns; Moros; Pershing, John Joseph; Philippine-American War; Philippine Islands

Further Reading

Bernad, Miguel A. *The Great Island: Studies in the Exploration and Evangelization of Mindanao.* Manila: Ateneo de Manila University Press, 2004.

Canoy, Reuben R. *The History of Mindanao.* Cagayan de Oro, Philippines: International School Publication, 2001.

Tadem, Eduardo C. "The Political Economy of Mindanao: An Overview." In *Mindanao: Land of Unfulfilled Promise,* edited by Mark Turner, R. J. May, and Lulu Respall Turner, 7–30. Quezon City, Philippines: New Day, 1992.

Mines

The 19th century saw development of the modern mine and the automotive torpedo, both of which came to have profound impact on war at sea. The first mines were known as torpedoes, after the electric ray fish that shocks its prey. Modern underwater mine warfare may be said to have originated during the American Revolutionary War when Yale University student David Bushnell released floating kegs of powder in the Delaware River. These contact mines were triggered by a flintlock arrangement inside the keg; the hammer was released by the shock of the mine striking an object. The mines took too long to reach their target, and premature explosion of one of them apparently alerted the British.

During the Napoleonic Wars, the American Robert Fulton tried to interest first the French and then the British in mines of his invention. These were intended to drift down in pairs on their target, be caught by the anchor chains of a target vessel, and then explode by means of a timer on a delay of up to four hours. In October 1804 and again in October 1805, Fulton tried the mines against the French at Boulogne with no apparent effect. In October 1805, he used a mine to blow up the 200-ton captured Danish brig *Dorothea,* the first time in history that such a large vessel had been destroyed by a mine. In another such test in July 1807, he blew up a 200-ton

During the Spanish-American War, U.S. seaports were protected by tethered mines that could be electrically detonated from the shore or that exploded when a ship came into contact with them. (*Photographic History of the Spanish-American War,* 1898)

brig in New York Harbor. During the War of 1812, the Americans made several attempts to destroy British ships with mines, but none were successful.

During the Crimean War of 1853–1856, the Russians used mines to try to prevent Allied access to their coastal forts. In 1839, Tsar Nicholas I appointed Prussian émigré Moritz-Hermann Jacobi as head of a scientific committee to conduct experiments in the development of a galvanic (electronic) mine. As early as 1782, Tiberius Cavallo had demonstrated that gunpowder could be detonated by means of an electric current. Building on the work of Cavallo, Americans Fulton and Samuel Colt and Russian baron Pavel L'vovich Schilling von Cannstadt, Jacobi developed working mines by the time of the Crimean War. The Russians subsequently deployed these mines to help protect access to St. Petersburg. Jacobi's mines consisted of zinc canisters filled with gunpowder and were set off by a detonator, a glass tube filled with acid, that when broken ignited the main charge. During the war, the Russians used chemical, contact, and electrical command-detonated mines in both the Baltic Sea and the Black Sea. Although several of the mines went off against British ships, they were too small to inflict significant damage.

The Confederacy made extensive use of mines during the American Civil War. Influential Confederate Navy officer and scientist Matthew Fontaine Maury was an early proponent of mines and conducted experiments with them. Civil War naval mines and torpedoes were of a variety of types. Either scratch-built or constructed from barrels as casings, they were essentially stationary weapons, a sort of buoy held in place at an appropriate distance from the surface by a cable anchored to the sea bottom by a weight. The Confederates positioned them in rivers or harbors to explode against the hulls of Union warships. The two basic types of detonation were contact and electricity. The first type detonated when horns surrounding the charge were broken; this set off a chemical reaction that ignited the charge. The second was fired by means of electrical

connections from batteries on shore. The first type was more certain to explode but was unable to distinguish its victim and hence was also dangerous to friendly vessels. The second type could only be employed close to shore.

More often than not, such early mines failed to explode as a result of faulty detonating equipment or becoming waterlogged, or they were swept away by the current. Powder charges in Civil War mines ranged from approximately 50 pounds to up to a ton of explosive. In all, 50 ships were sunk or damaged by mines during the war, four-fifths of them Union vessels. Only one Confederate ship, the *Albemarle,* was lost to a Union mine. Most of the Confederate vessels sunk were victims of their own mines.

The Royal Navy in 1870 brought into service a towed mine known as the Harvey torpedo after its inventors, Captain John Harvey and Commander Frederick Harvey, both of the Royal Navy. They merely updated the Fulton concept. The Harvey torpedo made use of the principle that an object towed from the bow of a ship usually diverges from the vessel's course at a 45-degree angle. The towing vessel approached the target vessel at a maximum speed of 10 knots and then veered off to the side while the torpedo swung in a wider arc, struck the target ship, and exploded against it. Various chemical fuses were used to ignite the 33 pounds of gunpowder in the torpedo explosive charge; later this was increased to 66 pounds of wet guncotton. Another version was fired by electricity. However, there were many problems with the Harvey torpedo, including the low approach speed by its delivering vessel and difficulties with the torpedo parting its tow and prematurely exploding.

Despite the proven effectiveness of mines during the Civil War, the U.S. Navy largely ignored their use thereafter. Although the Spanish employed mines during the Spanish-American War in both the Philippines (at Subic Bay and off Manila) and in Cuban waters, these mines were either avoided or failed to explode. Mines produced no casualties during the war. This may have been the result of maintenance problems or incorrect mooring depths or locations. Of course, the perception that a Spanish mine had destroyed the U.S. battleship *Maine* had a great deal to do with bringing on the war in the first place.

Mines really came into their own during the Russo-Japanese War of 1904–1905. During World War I, both sides deployed vast numbers of mines with considerable effect. A total of some 309,800 mines were reportedly laid during the war. Of this number, some 45,000 German mines reportedly claimed more than 1 million tons of Allied shipping sunk.

SPENCER C. TUCKER AND PAUL E. FONTENOY

See also

Maine, USS; Maine, USS, Inquiries into the Loss of; Torpedo Boats; Torpedoes, Automotive

Further Reading

Bradford, R. B. *History of Torpedo Warfare.* Newport, RI: U.S. Torpedo Station, 1882.

Melia, Tamara Moser. *Damn the Torpedoes: A Short History of U.S. Naval Mine Countermeasures, 1777–1991.* Annapolis, MD: Department of the Navy, Naval Historical Center, 1991.

Truver, C. *Weapons That Wait: Mine Warfare in the U.S. Navy.* Annapolis, MD: Naval Institute Press, 1991.

Missionaries

In the immediate aftermath of the Spanish-American War, Protestant missionaries traveled in large numbers to the Philippines and Cuba in an effort to evangelize foreign nationals. As early as the 16th century, shortly after the arrival of Spanish explorers, Catholic missionaries—usually monks or young priests—had spread Christianity in Cuba and throughout the Philippine Islands. With the exception of the people of Mindanao, which retained Islamic influences, the Filipinos converted en masse to the new religion while still keeping their cultural and animist roots. Local and foreign Catholic leaders quickly established powerful positions within communities and local governments.

Missionary efforts had long been part of the Protestant evangelical tradition, which required an individual and enthusiastic conversion in order to receive salvation. Most Protestant missionaries believed that Catholics were not true Christians, so they became targets for missionary evangelism. Additionally, Protestant missionary efforts often targeted nonwhite, or so-called heathen, populations as being less civilized than whites and therefore in greater need of the morality and discipline that religious practice and salvation would provide. The roots for such evangelical missions can be seen in early Protestant efforts to evangelize and civilize frontier Indian populations and immigrants. Thus, these Protestant missionaries fit well within the paradigms of imperialism, expansionism, ethnocentrism, and Progressivism of the late 19th and early 20th centuries. Most missionary efforts to the Philippines and to Cuba began after major fighting had ceased.

In 1899, the American Missionary Society publicly announced praise for Rudyard Kipling's poem "The White Man's Burden," which suggested that white people had a God-given mandate to civilize nonwhite societies as part of God's plan for the world. Soon after the Spanish-American War, President William McKinley, himself a Methodist, addressed the General Mission Committee of the Methodist Episcopal Church and explained his reasoning for annexing the Philippines. In addition to diplomatic and strategic reasons, he suggested that it was the mission of the United States to educate, uplift, civilize, and Christianize Filipino society. His public statement clearly emphasized the extent to which missionary and political objectives converged.

American churches responded to the annexation of the Philippines and continued involvement in Cuba by sending hundreds of missionaries to both countries. In 1899, the Foreign Christian Missionary Society, an organization of the Christian Churches, Churches of Christ, and the Disciples of Christ, sent two couples to Cuba. Sending couples into the mission field was a common practice for many Protestant denominations. In Cuba, Protestant missionaries met with limited success, as most Cubans were deeply instilled with Catholic beliefs and dogma.

In the Philippines, however, missionaries were in a more precarious situation. The Philippine-American War (1899–1902) placed American missionaries in the middle of a contest for control of the Philippines. Most important, American missionaries and their churches in the United States had to respond to Philippine nationalism. They had to balance American fears of Filipino nationalism and self-government with the need to train Filipino nationals as clergy and lay church leaders. Even in the second area, however, white missionaries consistently expressed doubt that Filipino nationals could effectively lead churches. In 1902, Filipino leader Gregorio Aglipay led a schism against the Catholic Church in the Philippines and established the Iglesia Filipina Independiente (Independent Filipino Church). Protestant reactions to the schism were mixed: some supported this nationalist movement against the Catholics, while others viewed the movement and its leader as opportunistic and bound to stir up unrest.

According to some scholars, missionary efforts such as these should also be viewed within a larger context of American cultural imperialism. In their assessment, missionaries to foreign countries preceded the cause of the flag and advanced the creation of new markets and imperialism. For example, Sanford Ballard Dole, the leader of the Americans who overthrew the Hawaiian monarchy in 1893, was the son of Protestant missionaries. In addition to spreading American ideas about religion, democracy, and culture throughout the Philippines and Cuba, missionaries also acted within the United States to create a national consensus about expansionism in general. Others contest the idea that missionaries were directly implicit in the hegemonic and imperialist policies of 19th-century politicians, but they generally recognize that religion constitutes an inseparable part of the larger culture. Therefore, some argue that even if missionaries' efforts were purely theological or religious in nature, their actions cannot be considered apart from the wider imperial context.

JACQUELINE E. WHITT

See also

Churches and the War; Dole, Sanford Ballard; Expansionism; Hawaiian Islands; Imperialism; Kipling, Rudyard; McKinley, William; Progressivism; Social Gospel Movement; White Man's Burden

Further Reading

Clymer, Kenton J. *Protestant Missionaries in the Philippines, 1898–1916: An Inquiry into the American Colonial Mentality.* Champaign: University of Illinois Press, 1986.

———. "Religion and American Imperialism: Methodist Missionaries in the Philippine Islands, 1899–1913." *Pacific Historical Review* 49(1) (February 1980): 29–50.

Kwantes, Anne C. *Presbyterian Missionaries in the Philippines: Conduits of Social Change (1899–1910).* Quezon City, Philippines: New Day, 1989.

Neill, Stephen. *Colonialism and Christian Missions.* New York: McGraw-Hill, 1966.

Varg, Paul A. "Motives in Protestant Missions, 1890–1917." *Church History* (March 1954): 68–92.

Yaremko, Jason M. *U.S. Protestant Missions in Cuba: From Independence to Castro.* Gainesville: University of Florida Press, 2000.

Monroe Doctrine

Seminal principle of U.S. foreign policy enunciated on December 2, 1823, by President James Monroe during his annual message to Congress. Monroe's declaration came just eight years after the end of the Napoleonic Wars, which had resulted in the dissolution of much of the Spanish Empire and the declarations of independence of several Latin American countries between 1810 and 1822. The United States now perceived a threat from France and Spain, together with the Holy Alliance of Russia, Prussia, and Austria, to return colonial rule to many of these new republics. Washington was also concerned over Russia's intentions in northwestern North America. Indeed, Tsar Alexander I had recently declared the waters off Alaska closed to foreign ships.

Concerns in Washington were also shared in London. The British wanted to expand trade with Latin America. In September 1822, British foreign secretary George Canning suggested to the American minister to London, Richard Rush, that Britain and the United States issue a joint declaration designed to prevent European intervention in the New World. Although Secretary of State John Quincy Adams persuaded Monroe to go it alone, Canning later boasted that he had "called the New World into existence to redress the balance of the Old." Any declaration by the Americans would have the support of Brain's Royal Navy, the world's most powerful navy.

Monroe's speech included three primary positions. First, European powers ought not to attempt to establish colonies in the continents of North or South America. Second, European monarchs should not meddle in the internal politics of the Americas, especially to attempt to overthrow republics and replace them with monarchies. Third, the United States would continue to refrain from interfering in the internal politics of any European power. Monroe warned that European interference in the Americas would be viewed by the United States "as dangerous to our peace and security" and "as the manifestation of an unfriendly disposition toward the United States." While not enforced at first, the Monroe Doctrine became a basic tenet of American foreign policy and a justification for American intervention throughout the Western Hemisphere.

Monroe's declaration was a response to these specific threats rather than the formulation of a fundamental doctrine governing American foreign policy. In fact, for two decades the United States did not act decisively to uphold Monroe's principles despite the fact that European powers continued to meddle in the politics of the Americas. Even if U.S. leaders had chosen to enforce Monroe's dictates, however, the nation lacked the military power to do so.

President Monroe's declaration began to be transformed into a doctrine in 1845 when President James K. Polk invoked it during the dispute with Mexico over the boundary of Texas, which the United States had annexed in March 1845. Texas had declared independence from Mexico in 1836, but Mexico had not ratified the treaty imposed on General Antonio López de Santa Anna after the Battle of San Jacinto. Consequently, Mexico recognized neither Texas independence nor its claim of the Rio Grande as the boundary with Mexico when the United States annexed Texas. Concerned over European potential interference in Texas and in Mexico generally (which included the territory of California, where both Britain and France had interests) and similarly concerned over British interests in the Oregon territory, Polk explicitly invoked Monroe's principles and warned European powers not to intervene militarily or interfere politically. Polk also enlarged those principles by prohibiting European powers from acquiring territories in the Americas through peaceful transfers (e.g., of California to Britain) but allowing such territorial transfers to be made to the United States (e.g., Texas). Finally, Polk warned that the United States would vigorously enforce these policies in North America even though the Monroe Doctrine had not been upheld in Central and South America heretofore.

American public support for the Mexican-American War (1846–1848) was bolstered by a belief in Manifest Destiny, the concept that divine providence had destined the United States to span the entire continent, from the Atlantic to the Pacific. The annexation of Texas was seen as partial fulfillment of this destiny. American victory in the war forced Mexico to transfer more than half its territory to the United States, including present-day California, Arizona, and New Mexico and parts of Colorado, Nevada, and Utah. This immense territorial acquisition further strengthened belief in Manifest Destiny, which lent additional support to the Monroe Doctrine. The outcome of the war also effectually defended the principles of the Monroe Doctrine as a preemptive action that kept European powers from establishing colonies in that territory or acquiring it through transfer.

Now established and enlarged, the Monroe Doctrine was directly challenged during the American Civil War (1861–1865) when

This 1896 political cartoon, originally captioned "The old horse was too slow for Uncle Sam," criticizes U.S. foreign policy. To the anger of other countries, Uncle Sam has abandoned the horse, whose saddle says "Monroe Doctrine," in favor of "coasting" on a bicycle with "Eastern Hemisphere" and "Western Hemisphere" for wheels. (Library of Congress)

France invaded Mexico, overthrew the republic, and established a puppet monarchy headed by Austrian prince Ferdinand Maximilian. While at the time the United States was unable to forcibly resist these events, Secretary of State William Seward negotiated with France to withdraw its forces, which led to the overthrow of Maximilian in 1867. Although the Monroe Doctrine was not explicitly invoked during this dispute, Seward's diplomacy was most certainly guided by its principles.

The Monroe Doctrine finally found respect in Europe after a dispute between Great Britain and the United States over the boundary between British Guiana and Venezuela. In 1895, Secretary of State Richard Olney invoked the Monroe Doctrine explicitly in his correspondence with Great Britain demanding that it accept U.S. arbitration over the boundary dispute. While the British initially refused to acknowledge the authority of the Monroe Doctrine in international law, they ultimately submitted to American arbitration, which further vindicated the doctrine.

The Monroe Doctrine was again invoked and further extended by expansionists in favor of the Spanish-American War in 1898. The United States had long been interested in Cuba, where the Cuban War of Independence against Spanish rule commenced in 1895. In 1854, the Americans had attempted to purchase the island from Spain, which declined the offer. The revolution provided an opportunity to help force Spain out of Cuba and perhaps out of the Caribbean entirely, goals that further extended the Monroe Doc-

trine by intervening in the internal politics of a European power already possessing a colony in the Americas.

At the successful conclusion of the Spanish-American War, the United States acquired the Philippines, Guam, and Puerto Rico from Spain. And while the United States did not annex Cuba, the Platt Amendment guaranteed its interests and presence there, which would prove to be considerable until the 1959 Communist Revolution brought Fidel Castro to power. In this case, then, invocation and extension of the Monroe Doctrine contributed to the creation of an overseas empire, or an extraterritorial Manifest Destiny.

From 1823 to 1898, the Monroe Doctrine matured and was transformed into a doctrine justifying intervention by the United States in the Americas to preempt European interference. In December 1904, President Theodore Roosevelt made this transformation even more explicit by seeking to have the United States exercise "an international police power" in the Americas. In 1928, President Calvin Coolidge revoked the Roosevelt Corollary to the Monroe Doctrine, a step that led to President Franklin D. Roosevelt's Good Neighbor Policy of the 1930s. Nevertheless, the transformation of the Monroe Doctrine from being primarily a demand of European nonintervention in the Americas to a justification for intervention by the United States remains a key part of the development of U.S. hegemony in the Western Hemisphere.

S. J. Lange

See also

Manifest Destiny; Monroe Doctrine; Roosevelt, Theodore; Roosevelt Corollary

Further Reading

Dent, David W. *The Legacy of the Monroe Doctrine.* Westport, CT: Greenwood, 1999.

Merk, Frederick. *The Monroe Doctrine and American Expansionism, 1843–1849.* New York, Knopf, 1968.

Nofi, Albert A. *The Spanish-American War: 1898.* Conshohocken, PA: Combined Books, 1996.

Perkins, Dexter. *A History of the Monroe Doctrine.* Boston: Little, Brown, 1963.

Montero Ríos, Eugenio
Birth Date: November 13, 1832
Death Date: May 12, 1914

Spanish politician, jurist, and member of the Spanish delegation that negotiated the Treaty of Paris on December 10, 1898, that officially ended the Spanish-American War. Eugenio Montero Ríos was born on November 13, 1832, in Santiago de Compostela, Spain. After studying canon law at the Universidad de Santiago de Compostela, he subsequently taught that subject at the Universidad de Oviedo (1859), the Universidad de Santiago de Compostela (1860), and the Universidad Central de Madrid (1864).

A member of the Partido Progresista (Progressive Party), Montero was elected a deputy to represent Pontevedra in the aftermath of the Revolution of 1868, which overthrew Queen Isabella II. An ardent supporter of Juan Prim, primary architect of the Revolution of 1868, Montero was appointed minister of justice in 1870. Working to separate church and state, he introduced civil marriage into the Spanish legal system.

Montero supported Prim's efforts to offer the Spanish throne to Prince Leopold von Hohenzollern-Sigmaringen, which sparked the Franco-Prussian War (1870–1871). When the duke of Aosta, son of King Victor Emmanuel II of Piedmont-Sardinia, became king of Spain as Amadeo I in 1871, Montero supported his anticlerical stance and continued to push for legislation to strengthen the separation of church and state, much to the chagrin of many powerful elements of Spanish society. When Amadeo I, regarded as a foreigner by the Spanish people, was unable to win support, he abdicated in February 1873. Montero drafted his letter of abdication and followed the monarch into exile in Lisbon, Portugal.

In late 1873, Montero supported Cristino Martos's creation of the Partido Republicano Democrático (Democratic Republican Party). For the remainder of his life, Montero oscillated between republicanism and liberal monarchism. Unable to establish his own liberal party, in 1884 he joined Práxedes Mateo Sagasta's Partido Liberal (Liberal Party). Montero served as Sagasta's minister of justice in 1892.

In 1898, Montero, then the president of the Spanish Senate, was appointed president of Spain's Peace Commission sent to Paris to negotiate a formal end to the Spanish-American War. Other Spanish members of the commission included Buenaventura de Abarzuza, José Garnica, Wenceslao Ramirez de Villa-Urrutia, and Rafael Cerero. Never a supporter of a Spanish colonial empire, Montero was not opposed to relinquishing Spanish colonial authority of Cuba, Puerto Rico, Guam, or the Philippines. He was willing to give up all of these without indemnity provided that the United States absorbed all their debts. He also sought European arbitration to resolve the impasse. Ordered by his government on November 25 to sign the treaty, he threatened to resign but was persuaded to remain and did sign the treaty.

Following Sagasta's death in 1903, Montero led the radical faction of the Liberals while Segismundo Moret led the conservative faction. Montero was prime minister from June 23 to December 1, 1905. During his brief tenure, the *Cu-Cut!* debacle erupted. In November 1905, Barcelona's small Catalan weekly journal *Cu-Cut!* published a cartoon satirically contrasting the political victory of antimilitarist proseparatist politicians in Barcelona with the Spanish defeat in the Spanish-American War. On November 24, 1905, approximately 200 junior officers attacked the offices of *Cu-Cut!* Military officers demanded a law placing press attacks on the army under military jurisdiction. Montero, however, refused to agree to legislation curtailing freedom of the press. On November 30, 1905, King Alfonso XIII announced his support of the army's demands, prompting Montero's resignation on December 1. The *Cu-Cut!* Affair was a prelude to the end of the civil-military power sharing arrangement implemented by the Bourbon Restoration.

Montero again served as president of the Senate from 1911 to 1913. He died in Madrid on May 12, 1914. Interestingly, in his will, he renounced all royal decorations and honors.

MICHAEL R. HALL

See also

Alfonso XIII, King of Spain; Paris, Treaty of; Sagasta, Práxedes Mateo; Spain

Further Reading

Esdaile, Charles J. *Spain in the Liberal Age: From Constitution to Civil War, 1808–1939*. Oxford: Blackwell, 2000.

Offner, John L. *An Unwanted War: The Diplomacy of the United States and Spain over Cuba, 1895–1898*. Chapel Hill: University of North Carolina Press, 1992.

Pierson, Peter. *The History of Spain*. Westport, CT: Greenwood, 1999.

Montgomery, USS

U.S. protected cruiser. The *Montgomery*, namesake of its class, displaced 2,094 tons, making it one of the smallest ships of its type in the U.S. Navy. The *Montgomery* was launched in December 1891 at Baltimore, Maryland, and was originally armed with nine 5-inch guns, six 6-pounders, two 1-pounders, and three 18-inch torpedo tubes. The ship was commissioned at Norfolk, Virginia, on June 21, 1894, under Commander Charles W. Davis. It joined the North Atlantic Squadron after its shakedown and embarked on routine service in both the Atlantic and Caribbean.

In February 1898, the *Montgomery*, now captained by Commander George A. Converse, visited several Cuban ports, including Santiago de Cuba, in conjunction with the visit to Havana of the U.S. battleship *Maine*. While there, Converse submitted reports to the Navy Department detailing the appalling conditions faced by Cuban civilians. Following the loss of the *Maine* on February 15, 1898, Converse brought the *Montgomery* to Havana on March 9 to assist briefly in the official investigation of the disaster. The *Montgomery* soon left for Key West, Florida, amid fears by Converse and Captain Charles D. Sigsbee of the *Maine* that the cruiser might suffer the same fate as the *Maine*.

Following the declaration of war against Spain in April 1898, the *Montgomery* escorted the transport *Panther*, carrying the 1st Marine Battalion (Provisional) from Hampton Roads, Virginia, to Key West. The *Montgomery* then joined the squadron of Rear Admiral William T. Sampson in the blockade of Havana on May 1 and captured two Spanish sailing ships, the *Lorenzo* and *Frasquito*, on May 5. On May 12, the *Montgomery* participated in the shelling of the Spanish forts guarding the harbor at San Juan, Puerto Rico, where Sampson had gone in search of Rear Admiral Pascual Cervera y Topete's squadron. The ship played a minor role but helped to silence Fort Canuelo during the bombardment.

The *Montgomery* then resumed its station with the blockade of Havana, remaining there when Sampson took most of his squadron to Santiago de Cuba, where Cervera had sought refuge.

The U.S. Navy protected cruiser *Montgomery* participated in the blockade of Cuba during the Spanish-American War. (Naval Historical Center)

In late May, the *Montgomery* served as the flagship of Commodore John Watson, commander of U.S. naval forces along Cuba's northern coast. The ship later participated in the Puerto Rico Campaign, which was still ongoing when hostilities came to an end on August 12, 1898.

In early 1899, the *Montgomery* joined the South Atlantic Squadron and patrolled the South American coast until it was decommissioned in September 1900. Recommissioned in May 1902, it served in the West Indies until decommissioned again in September 1904. The *Montgomery* was recommissioned in January 1908 and served as a torpedo experimental vessel in the Fifth Naval District, having all its armament except its torpedo tubes and four 6-pounder guns removed. From 1914 to 1918, the ship served with the Maryland Naval Militia. Renamed the *Anniston* on March 14, 1918, the ship then served with the American Patrol Detachment along the Atlantic coast and the Caribbean until its final decommissioning on May 16, 1918. The *Anniston* was sold on November 14, 1919.

STEPHEN SVONAVEC

See also

Cervera y Topete, Pascual; Converse, George Albert; Cuba, U.S. Naval Blockade of; *Maine,* USS; Puerto Rico Campaign; Sampson, William Thomas; Santiago de Cuba, Occupation of; Sigsbee, Charles Dwight; Watson, John Crittenden

Further Reading

Blow, Michael. *A Ship to Remember: The Maine and the Spanish-American War.* New York: Morrow, 1992.
Chadwick, French Ensor. *The Relations of the United States and Spain V1: The Spanish-American War.* Reprint ed. Kila, MT: Kessinger, 2007.
Feuer, A. B. *The Spanish-American War at Sea: Naval Action in the Atlantic.* Westport, CT: Praeger, 1995.
Trask, David F. *The War with Spain in 1898.* Lincoln: University of Nebraska Press, 1996.

Montojo y Pasarón, Patricio
Birth Date: September 7, 1839
Death Date: September 30, 1917

Spanish admiral, intellectual, novelist, and essayist who commanded the Spanish squadron in the Philippines during the Spanish-American War. Born in El Ferrol, Corunna Province, Spain, on September 7, 1839, Patricio Montojo y Pasarón studied at the Naval School in Cádiz and joined the Spanish Navy as a midshipman in 1855. Promoted to sublieutenant in 1860, he was assigned that same year to the Philippines, where he fought against the Moros on the island of Mindanao. Returning to Spain in 1864, he served on the frigate *Almansa* and fought in the Battle of Abato and the Battle of El Callao under Admiral Casto Méndez Núñez, commander of the Spanish Pacific Fleet, in the Chincha Islands War (1864–1866) against Peru and Chile. Montojo was then secretary to Admiral Méndez Núñez and served in the Admiralty Secretariat in Madrid.

Promoted to commander in 1873, Montojo then commanded Spanish warships on Havana station and in the River Plate. Advanced to commodore, he again served in the Philippines before returning to Madrid in 1890. Promoted to rear admiral and reassigned to the Philippines, he took command of all Spanish naval forces in the islands, the command he held at the start of the Spanish-American War.

Montojo had few options in prosecuting the Spanish-American War. Although he possessed some 40 ships, most were small gunboats. Only his 6 cruisers were capable of offering any real resistance to U.S. commodore George Dewey's Asiatic Squadron, and even these were not as well armored and were greatly inferior in armament to the ships in the American squadron. Montojo originally had his ships at Subic Bay 60 miles west of Manila, but the water there was 40 feet deep, and its defenses were unready. Reportedly, he decided that if his ships were to be sunk, he would prefer it to occur in shallower water. He then returned them to Manila Bay. To help offset his weakness in firepower, he anchored his ships off the fortified naval yard of Cavite so that they might be supported by land batteries.

Following the virtual destruction of his fleet in the May 1, 1898, Battle of Manila Bay, during which he was wounded in the leg (both his sons also participated in the battle on the Spanish side, and one was also wounded), Montojo withdrew to the city of Manila. There, he continued to exercise his command responsibilities until the surrender of that city on August 13.

A Spanish government decree of September 1898 officially relieved Montojo of his duties. On his return to Spain that November, he was imprisoned and then court-martialed. Absolved by the court of responsibility for the destruction of his squadron, he was nonetheless retired from active duty. One of his chief defenders was Read Admiral Dewey. Montojo later wrote an account of the Battle of Manila Bay. He died in Madrid on September 30, 1917.

SPENCER C. TUCKER

See also
Asiatic Squadron; Dewey, George; Manila Bay, Battle of

Further Reading
Conroy, Robert. *The Battle of Manila Bay: The Spanish-American War in the Philippines*. New York: Macmillan, 1968.
Montojo, Patricio. *El desastre de Cavite, sus causas y sus efectos* [The Causes and Effect of the Disaster at Cavite]. Madrid: La España Moderna, 1909.

Trask, David F. *The War with Spain in 1898*. Lincoln: University of Nebraska Press, 1996.

Moret y Prendergast, Segismundo
Birth Date: June 2, 1833
Death Date: January 28, 1913

Spanish politician and writer. Born in Cádiz, Spain, on June 2, 1833, Segismundo Moret y Prendergast was educated in Britain and at the University of Madrid, where in 1858 he became a professor of political economy while at the same time continuing to study law.

Moret was elected to the Spanish Cortes (parliament) in 1863 and reelected in 1868. He was one of the authors of the Spanish Constitution of 1869 following the Glorious Revolution (1868) in Spain. In 1870, he became colonial minister in the cabinet headed by General Juan Prim and advocated the abolition of slavery and a constitution for Puerto Rico. In 1871, Moret became minister of the treasury and the next year was appointed Spanish ambassador to Great Britain but resigned from that post after some months to become director of a British bank. Following the restoration of King Alfonso XII in 1875, Moret returned to Spain. Reelected to the Cortes in 1879, he rallied to the restored Bourbon monarchy in 1882. The next year, he became minister of the interior, and in 1885, he joined the Liberal Party of Práxedes Mateo Sagasta and under him held a number of cabinet posts, including minister of foreign affairs (1885–1888) and minister for overseas colonies (1897–1898).

Appointed colonial minister in October 1897 in the Sagasta government, Moret was the most outspoken cabinet advocate of a conciliatory policy toward both Cuba and Puerto Rico, and he was the author of the November 1897 autonomy decrees in an effort to avoid secession of the two islands from Spain. He opposed war with the United States as a hopeless venture for Spain and, in consequence, sought mediation by other European governments to end the crisis over Cuba. Moret favored a positive Spanish response to President William McKinley's ultimatum of March 27, 1898, in the belief that this would give the Spanish government more time to resolve the situation short of war.

Because he had opposed war, when it occurred Moret found himself under fire from Spanish nationalists for having proposed concessions beforehand. He was dropped from the cabinet on May 15, 1898, and replaced by Vincente Romero Girón. Consulted by Sagasta regarding the Protocol of Peace in August 1898, Moret approved signing it provided it was limited to Cuba and Puerto Rico.

Following the death of Spanish premier Sagasta in 1903 and a period of political struggle, Moret became the leader of the Liberal Party. He was premier of Spain during 1905–1906 and again during 1909–1910. He was serving as president of the House of Representatives at the time of his death in Madrid on January 28, 1913.

SPENCER C. TUCKER

See also
Cuba; McKinley, William; Peace, Protocol of; Puerto Rico; Sagasta,
    Práxedes Mateo

Further Reading
Carr, Raymond. *Spain, 1808–1975*. New York: Oxford University Press
    USA, 1982.
De Madariaga, Salvador. *Spain: A Modern History*. New York: Praeger,
    1958.

Morgan, John Pierpont, Sr.
Birth Date: April 17, 1837
Death Date: March 31, 1913

American financier and banker and one of the wealthiest and most
influential men in the United States during the Spanish-American
War. John Pierpont Morgan's activities facilitated the Industrial
Revolution, which gave an impetus to overseas economic and territorial expansion at the end of the 19th century. Born in Hartford,
Connecticut, on April 17, 1837, he was the son of Julius Morgan, a
wealthy financier. After attending the University of Göttingen in
Germany, the younger Morgan worked as an accountant for Duncan, Sherman, and Company, a New York City banking firm, from
1857 to 1861. At the outbreak of the American Civil War, he
avoided military service by paying for a substitute soldier to take
his place, a practice that was legal at the time and not unusual for
men in his position. During the war, he first worked for George
Peabody and Company, then moved to Dabney, Morgan, and
Company from 1864 to 1871. He joined the Philadelphia firm of
Drexel, Morgan, and Company as a partner in 1871. After the death
of the firm's founder, Anthony J. Drexel, in 1893, Morgan became
the senior partner of the firm. The firm, which became J. P. Morgan and Company, grew to be one of the most powerful banking
houses in the world.

Morgan bought, consolidated, or restructured many U.S. railroads during the last two decades of the 19th century. By 1900, he
controlled more than 5,000 miles of rail lines. He also implemented
regulations and standards that the federal government was either
unwilling or unable to enact. His vast holdings in the railroad industry included the New York Central, the New Haven and Hartford, the Pennsylvania, the Reading, and the Chesapeake and Ohio
networks. In 1902, he organized the Northern Securities Company
as a trust for his railroad holdings only to have it dissolved two years
later by a landmark antitrust suit. In 1892, he financed the formation of General Electric by merging Edison General Electric and the
Thomson-Houston Electric Company. In 1896, General Electric was
one of the first companies listed on the newly formed Dow Jones
Industrial Average. During the economic depression of 1893–1897,
Morgan supplied the U.S. government with $62 million in gold to
issue government bonds, which restored a surplus in the U.S.
Treasury. This financial coup helped to return the nation to economic prosperity.

American financier and banker John Pierpont Morgan was one of the
richest men in America and a dominant figure in the U.S. economy
during the late 19th and early 20th centuries. (Library of Congress)

In 1901, Morgan financed the creation of the United States Steel
Corporation by purchasing the interests of Andrew Carnegie and
other steel-producing industrialists. At the time of its creation, the
United States Steel Corporation, which became the world's first billion-dollar corporation, was the largest steel producer in the world
and accounted for two-thirds of all U.S. steel production. Federal
antitrust legislation unsuccessfully attempted to break up U.S. Steel
in 1911. Increased steel production greatly facilitated the role of the
United States as a great power during and in the aftermath of the
Spanish-American War.

In 1902, Morgan facilitated the creation of the International
Mercantile Marine Company by financing the purchase of the
Leyland Line and other British steamship companies operating
in the Atlantic Ocean. Among the companies purchased was the
White Star Line, which built and operated the ill-fated ocean liner
Titanic. Indeed, Morgan was to have been a passenger on the
ship's maiden voyage, but business activities in Europe kept him
from departing on the doomed ship in 1912.

Morgan's financial interests exerted a tremendous influence on American foreign policy and domestic politics. Having acquired the assets to the defunct French company that had attempted but failed in its efforts to build a canal in Panama, he used his considerable political influence to ensure that Panama, rather than Nicaragua, would be the preferred American site for a canal. When Colombia balked at the Hay-Herrán Treaty, in part because Colombia was offered only $10 million up front and $250,000 annually for a 100-year lease compared to $40 million for Morgan's Panama Canal Company, the Theodore Roosevelt administration supported a revolution in Panama that resulted in independence from Colombia in 1903. Morgan's manipulation of financial markets was exposed in the Pugo Committee hearings in 1911 and contributed to the creation of the Federal Reserve System in 1913.

Often vilified in the press as a cold-hearted robber baron, Morgan made substantial contributions to charities, churches, hospitals, and schools during his lifetime. He died in Rome, Italy, on March 31, 1913, and his son, J. P. Morgan Jr., inherited his father's financial empire.

MICHAEL R. HALL

See also

Economic Depression; Panama Canal; Railroads

Further Reading

Auchincloss, Louis. *J. P. Morgan: The Financier as Collector.* New York: Harry N. Abrams, 1990.

Chernow, Ron. *The House of Morgan: An American Banking Dynasty and the Rise of Modern Finance.* New York: Grove, 2001.

Morris, Charles R. *The Tycoons: How Andrew Carnegie, John D. Rockefeller, Jay Gould, and J. P. Morgan Invented the American Supereconomy.* New York: Times Books, 2005.

Morgan-Cameron Resolution

Resolution passed by Congress on April 6, 1896, two years before the start of the Spanish-American War that served as an indicator of congressional sentiment regarding Cuba. In the midst of an ongoing debate in the United States over what approach the nation should take regarding the Cuban War of Independence and with strong support from the Cuban exile lobby, in February 1896 expansionist Democratic senator John T. Morgan of Alabama and Republican senator Donald Cameron of Pennsylvania joined to introduce a resolution that recognized Cuban belligerency against Spain and called for Cuban independence. The bill passed the Senate on February 28. The House passed its own version of the resolution on March 2.

Following reconciliation between the two versions, the resolution was passed overwhelmingly on April 6. Although the Morgan-Cameron Resolution was not binding, it did serve notice on President Grover Cleveland and Secretary of State Richard Olney of congressional sentiment in support of the Cuban rebels and against Spain.

KATJA WUESTENBECKER AND SPENCER C. TUCKER

See also

Cleveland, Stephen Grover; Cuba; Cuban Junta; Cuban War of Independence; Olney, Richard; Ten Years' War

Further Reading

Auxier, George W. "The Propaganda Activities of the Cuban Junta in Precipitating the Spanish-American War, 1895–1898." *Hispanic American Historical Review* 19(3) (August 1939): 286–305.

O'Toole, G. J. A. *The Spanish War: An American Epic, 1898.* New York: Norton, 1984.

Moro Campaigns
Start Date: 1902
End Date: 1913

Under the terms of the Treaty of Paris of December 10, 1898, the United States acquired the Philippine archipelago from Spain. Yet the end of the war with Spain was only the beginning of hostilities for American forces in the Philippines. The northern islands had been in revolt against Spanish rule since 1896, and U.S. forces would spend nearly three years (1898–1902) defeating the Filipino independence movement in what was commonly called the Philippine Insurrection and is today known as the Philippine-American War.

The southern islands of Sulu and Mindanao in the Philippines had never been completely conquered by the Spanish despite more than 400 years of sporadic warfare. The U.S. Army would spend 11 more years (1902–1913) fighting on the southern islands against the Moros with only limited success. In the course of these Moro campaigns, some 130 American soldiers died in the fighting, and 16 Medals of Honor were awarded.

The southern portion of the Philippine archipelago was controlled by a people the Spanish called the Moros, meaning "Moors." The Moros were Austronesians who had migrated from Taiwan and had been converted to Islam beginning in the 14th and 15th centuries and enjoyed a fierce reputation as pirates and warriors. The Spanish had established isolated garrisons in small fortresses along the coastline but had never penetrated the thick jungle interior. The Moros had remained neutral throughout the Philippine-American War, for rule by a Christian-dominated Republic of the Philippines was as distasteful to them as rule by the Americans. Indeed, the Moros fought their Christian and pagan neighbors as hard as they had fought the Spanish.

When U.S. Army forces occupied Sulu and Mindanao, they were not content to remain barricaded along the coastline. Instead, they attempted to Americanize the entire island. This meant bringing an end to slavery, blood feuds, and the piracy that had been a way of life for the Moros for centuries. On August 20, 1899, Brigadier General John Bates signed a treaty with the sultan of Sulu ostensibly giving the United States control over the islands, ending slavery and piracy, and guaranteeing the sultan certain rights, including an annual stipend.

U.S. Army brigadier general Samuel Sumner meeting with the sultans of Bayang and Oato at Camp Vicars on Mindanao in 1902. (Library of Congress)

The Bates Treaty had little effect, however, for the sultan had little control over Sulu and Mindanao. Real power lay in the dozens of tribal datus (chiefs), who strongly resisted U.S. control over their territories and carried out isolated attacks against American troops and all other foreigners. Although the Moros were skilled with rifles taken from the Spanish and Americans, their principal weapon was a short sword, known as the kris.

The Moros were masters at guerrilla warfare, attacking at night and ambushing stragglers and small patrols. They used the jungle cover to their advantage and could be within stabbing distance with the kris before their enemies could return fire. The Moros often charged into gunfire, continuing to rush their enemies despite being hit several times. One consequence of the Moro Campaigns was the U.S. Army decision to change its official side arm from the .38 revolver to the semiautomatic .45 because the .38 round did not have the power to stop a charging Moro warrior.

Although isolated attacks occurred against U.S. troops from the beginning of the occupation, they were at first considered the work of solitary bandits. This changed in the spring of 1902 when more than 200 Moros ambushed 18 soldiers patrolling Lake Lanao on Mindanao. In the attack, a soldier of the 15th Cavalry Regiment was killed, and all of the horses were taken.

Colonel Frank Baldwin, who had won the Medal of Honor in both the American Civil War and the Indian Wars, commanded expeditionary troops against the datu of Binadayan. The resulting Battle of Bayang on May 2, 1902, led to 51 Americans killed or wounded of a force of 470 men. Some 300 Moros died, with fewer than 30 escaping. Although the Moros were masters of jungle warfare, when attacked they retired to their cottas, which were small castlelike structures with thick, high walls. Cottas dotted the landscape and were almost impenetrable without artillery. In the Battle of Bayang, U.S. soldiers were forced to scale the walls of the cottas using improvised ladders.

Captain John J. Pershing, the future commander of the American Expeditionary Forces in World War I, was also a veteran of the Moro Campaigns. He led several campaigns in the Lake Lanao area. In April 1903, U.S. forces destroyed the cotta at Bacalod following a three-day siege that killed 120 Moros. In the Battle of Taraca on May 4, 1903, U.S. forces killed another 250 Moros. Only two Americans died in action, although 18 others succumbed to disease. Pershing was involved in both of these operations.

In August 1903, Major General Leonard Wood became the civilian governor of the Moro islands. He immediately launched a campaign into the interior in an attempt to capture Datu Ali, the leader of the resistance on Mindanao. In this operation, Wood employed not only the U.S. Army but also the Philippine Constabulary of native Filipinos. During the ensuing months, more than 130 cottas were destroyed, and hundreds of Moro warriors were slain.

On March 5–7, 1906, the largest battle of the Moro Campaigns occurred on the extinct volcano of Bud Dajo on Jolo Island. One thousand Moro warriors—both men and women—fiercely resisted 800 American soldiers and Filipino Constabulary troops. The

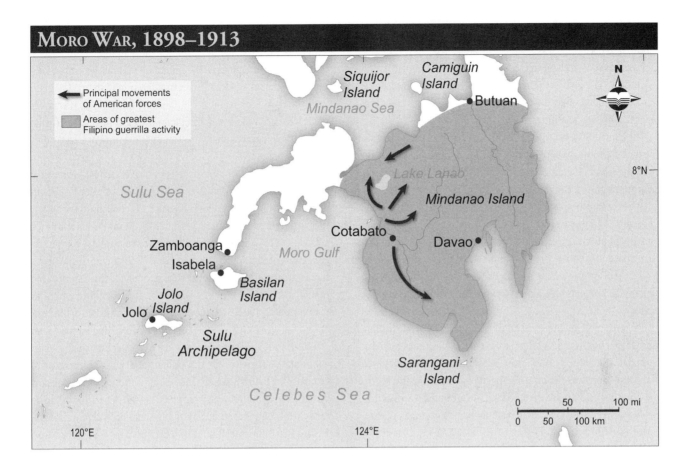

Moro War, 1898–1913

Principal movements of American forces

Areas of greatest Filipino guerrilla activity

Mindanao Sea

Siquijor Island

Camiguin Island

Butuan

N

Sulu Sea

Lake Lanao

Mindanao Island

8°N

Zamboanga

Isabela

Cotabato

Davao

Moro Gulf

Jolo Island

Jolo

Basilan Island

Sulu Archipelago

Sarangani Island

Celebes Sea

0   50   100 mi

0   50   100 km

120°E   124°E

Moros used to great effect the area's natural fortifications and a series of cottas. When the brutal, sometimes hand-to-hand fighting was over, more than 700 Moros lay dead along with 21 Americans and Filipinos.

The next several years were relatively quiet, with only sporadic violence. By now, most Moros had begun to realize that the U.S. government had no intention of trying to convert them from Islam to Christianity as the Spanish had attempted to do. This removed a major incentive for Moro resistance.

The last major engagement of the Moro Campaigns occurred on the island of Jolo during June 11–15, 1913. Recently promoted Brigadier General John Pershing led U.S. Army forces in what came to be known as the Battle of Bud Bagsak. In four days of fierce combat, some 500 Moros were killed along with 15 Americans. The battle broke the last significant resistance to American rule in the southern Philippines.

As with all American actions in the Philippines, there were negative reactions to the Moro Campaigns. This was chiefly because of the high casualties inflicted on the Moros in comparison to the number taken prisoner. On the other hand, there was little U.S. soldiers could do, considering that most Moros chose to fight to the death rather than surrender. During the Moro Campaigns of 1902–1913, some 130 American soldiers died in combat, while more than 500 others died of various diseases.

WESLEY MOODY

See also

Bates, John Coalter; Bayang, Battle of; Bud Bagsak, Battle of; Bud Dajo, Battle of; Cottas; Lake Lanao Campaigns; Mindanao; Moros; Pershing, John Joseph; Philippine Constabulary; Wood, Leonard

Further Reading

Baldwin, Alice Blackwood. *Memoirs of the Late Frank D. Baldwin, Major General, U.S.A.* Edited by W. C. Brown, C. C. Smith, and E. A. Brininstool. Los Angeles, CA: Wetzel, 1929.

Birtle, Andrew J. *U.S. Army Counterinsurgency and Contingency Operations Doctrine, 1860–1941.* Washington, DC: Center of Military History, U.S. Army, 2003.

Hurley, Vic. *Swish of the Kris: The Story of the Moros.* New York: Dutton, 1936.

Lane, Jack C. *Armed Progressive: General Leonard Wood.* San Rafael, CA: Presidio, 1978.

Smith, Gene. *Until the Last Trumpet Sounds: The Life of General of the Armies John J. Pershing.* New York: Wiley, 1999.

Moro Province

Philippine province created on June 1, 1903, by U.S. occupation authorities. Moro Province was inhabited largely by Filipino Muslims, or Moros as they were known by the Spanish. Moro Province included a large part of the island of Mindanao and the Sulu Archipelago, which was traditionally considered part of greater Mindanao. Moro Province covered five districts of Mindanao:

Lanao, Cotabato, Zamboanga, Davao, and Sulu (Tawi-Tawi was part of Sulu because it was ruled by the Sulu sultanate). Each district was administered by an U.S.-appointed governor, also a military officer. The districts were subdivided into tribal wards, with key datus (chiefs) serving as ward chiefs and lesser datus serving as sheriffs, deputies, and judges.

The United States formed Moro Province in an attempt to subdue the hostile Moros and separate non-Muslim Filipinos from the Moro Rebellion. The unique administrative setup was designed to incorporate the Moros' existing political structure in which personal ties with ruling officials were deemed important.

Luzon, the Visayas, and a portion of Mindanao, including their constituent provinces, came to be administered by civilian authorities operating under the Philippine Commission headed by William H. Taft. But a large section of Mindanao, inhabited by intractable and often hostile Moros, was governed directly by the U.S. military.

The area of Mindanao was home to some 278,000 Moros and more than a dozen tribal groups (their numbers were estimated at more than 100,000) in 1903. Most American authorities believed that using force was the only way to subjugate the hostile Moros and other rogue elements on the island. Governing the Moros militarily was deemed necessary so that they could eventually be integrated with Christian Filipinos.

The relationship between Muslim and non-Muslim Filipinos had been characterized by mutual prejudice and animosity to the other, largely as an outcome of Spanish colonization policies and by the fact that the Christianized natives had often been conscripted into military campaigns against the Moros. The Moros posed a formidable problem for the U.S. colonial government, such as during the Spanish regime, because they lived under their own laws (sharia) and traditions (adat) and recognized no power except their own system of government under the sultans and datus. The mission of the military regime was to civilize the Moros and educate them to the ways of modernity. The American civilizing efforts applied both might and persuasion in alternating sequences. Many American soldiers, however, operated under the assumption that "a good Moro is a dead Moro."

Brigadier General Leonard Wood, a veteran American Indian fighter, was appointed the first military governor of Moro Province; his tenure lasted from 1903 to 1906. He was succeeded by two other military governors: Major General Tasker Bliss (1906–1909) and Brigadier General John Pershing (1909–1913). The military governor on Mindanao exercised vast powers and influence, which were likened to those of Roman proconsuls. He was directly responsible to the governor-general of the Philippines and the Philippine Commission, located in Manila. Laws and ordinances applicable to the Moro Province were charged to the Legislative Council, composed of the governor, a secretary, a treasurer, an engineer, a superintendent of public schools, and the provincial attorney, all Americans.

Military rule of the Moro Province spanned only a decade, but its consequences on the social and political structures of the Moros

and tribal communities cannot be overemphasized. Under the American military regime, economic development had begun to flourish, with foreign capital opening up various agricultural and industrial pursuits. Also, Christian migration to the region began with the encouragement of U.S. military authorities. It was Pershing who received the most credit for transforming Moro Province and making it amenable to a system of government based on the Western rule of law.

American officials were usually perceived as just, benevolent, and patriarchal; some were even called "father" by some local datus. However, defiant village chiefs occasionally challenged the authorities with armed resistance, even after the Moro Province was dissolved in 1913, usually over issues related to taxation, compulsory education of children, and mandatory enlistment in the armed forces, among others. Bloody revolts punctuated the history of Moroland, as the Moro Province was also called, ranging from the infamous May 2, 1902, Battle of Bayang to the massacres in the Battle of Bud Dajo (March 5–8, 1906) and the Battle of Bud Bagsak (January 13–15, 1913). There were, of course, smaller but equally violent confrontations between the U.S. military and other disaffected tribal groups. This pattern of resistance would continue on a small scale through the Commonwealth era (1935–1945), when Mindanao became firmly entrenched as part of the emerging Philippine state.

In a sense, the transitional system of military governance broke the backbone of the age-old sultanate (although it did not go away altogether). At the same time, however, the new ways provided avenues for upward mobility for those at the bottom of the social hierarchy. The fruits of these policies became evident when hundreds of low-status Moros eventually rose to prominent positions in government and the civil service sectors as teachers, clerks, and local officials.

Despite all the various difficulties in modernizing and integrating Moro Province, the policy of Filipinization had largely worked. The military governance of Moro Province ended in 1913, at which time the Moro insurgency had been largely neutralized. Civilian administrator Frank Carpenter then replaced Pershing as governor. The province was formally integrated with the three largely Christian provinces of Mindanao (Agusan, Misamis, and Bukidnon) and became a new administrative region known as the Department of Mindanao and Sulu under a civilian governor. This was followed by a series of administrative changes and jurisdictional rearrangements as independence neared during the 1930s and owing to the 1916 Jones Act, which accelerated the Filipinization of the islands. Central to these bureaucratic shifts was the gradual transfer of authority from Americans to the more educated and politically mature Christian Filipinos and educated and articulate Moros.

FEDERICO MAGDALENA AND PAUL G. PIERPAOLI JR.

See also

Bliss, Tasker Howard; Bud Bagsak, Battle of; Bud Dajo, Battle of; Bud Dajo Campaign; Lake Lanao Campaigns; Mindanao; Moro Campaigns; Moros; Pershing, John Joseph; Philippine Commission; Philippine Islands; Taft, William Howard; Wood, Leonard

Further Reading

Abinales, P. N. *Making Mindanao: Cotabato and Davao in the Formation of the Philippine Nation-State.* Quezon City: Ateneo de Manila University, 2000.

Gowing, Peter Gordon. *Mandate in Moroland: The American Government of Muslim Filipinos, 1899–1920.* Quezon City: University of the Philippines Press, 1977.

Magdalena, Federico V. *The Battle of Bayang and Other Essays on Moroland.* Marawi City, Philippines: Mindanao State University, 2002.

Tan, Samuel K. *The Fillipino Muslim Armed Struggle, 1900–1972.* Makati, Philippines: Filipinas Foundation, 1977.

Moros

Native Muslims of the Philippines. The term "Moros" is Spanish for "Moors," referencing the North African Muslims who conquered Spain in 711 CE. Most of the Moros resided in the southern Philippines in an area called Bangsamoro on the island of Mindanao. They also lived in the long archipelago of small islands to the south and west of Mindanao. There were, however, Muslim enclaves and influences as far away as Manila. The Spanish called all Muslims they encountered during the Age of Exploration Moros, but only in the Philippines did the name take hold. The group that became known as the Moros is believed to have come to the Philippines as part of the Great Polynesian Migration in about 100 CE. By the late 15th century, when the Moros had been converted to Islam by merchants from India, they already had a reputation as fierce warriors and pirates.

Islam had arrived in the Philippines only 60 years before the Spanish. The Spanish conquered and Christianized the northern islands, while the southern islands of Mindanao and Sulu became Muslim strongholds. For more than 300 years, the Spanish battled the Moros for complete control of the archipelago. The Moros traditionally allied themselves with Spain's enemies, the British and the Dutch, when the European powers were at war with one another. They also constantly preyed on Spanish merchant ships.

During the Spanish-American War and the Philippine-American War that immediately followed, the Moros remained neutral. Indeed, it was not until the Christian Filipinos had been conquered that the Moros and U.S. Army forces began to clash. A series of bloody confrontations followed between 1902 and 1913 that cost the United States more than 600 men. Finally subdued through a mix of military force and civic action, the Moros came under U.S. civilian administration, as did the entire Philippines.

During World War II, the Moros resisted Japanese occupation, and after Filipino independence in 1946, the Moro Islamic Liberation Front (MILF) began a terrorist campaign to win independence for the southern Muslim-dominated Filipino islands. Today the MILF receives funding from several international terrorist organizations, including Al Qaeda.

WESLEY MOODY

Early 20th-century photograph of Moros near the shores of Lake Lanao on the island of Mindanao in the Philippines. (Hulton-Deutsch Collection/Corbis)

See also
Bud Bagsak, Battle of; Bud Dajo, Battle of; Bud Dajo Campaign; Mindanao; Moro Campaigns

Further Reading
Hurley, Vic. *Swish of the Kris: The Story of the Moros.* New York: Dutton, 1936.
Rabasa A. *Political Islam in Southeast Asia: Moderates, Radicals, and Terrorists.* London: Routledge, 2003.

Morro Castle

A fortification situated at the entrance to the harbor of Santiago de Cuba. Also known as Castillo de San Pedro de la Roca, Castillo del Morro, San Pedro de la Roca Castle, and simply the Morro, the redoubt sits atop a bluff 207 feet high on the eastern headland of the harbor's entrance some six miles south of the city of Santiago itself. The Spanish began construction of the fort in the 16th century as part of a network of batteries at the mouth of the harbor and along the approximately 400-foot-wide channel that leads to it. During the Spanish-American War, Morro Castle was garrisoned by 411 soldiers and served as an observation post, an artillery position, and a prison.

During the war, the castle's handful of antiquated guns rarely fired at U.S. Navy ships, but the presence of the castle and the surrounding batteries was a consideration in the U.S. plans to bottle up Admiral Pascual Cervera y Topete's squadron in the harbor by sinking the collier *Merrimac* in its narrow approach channel. An idea to trick the defenders into thinking it was a Spanish ship was rejected in favor of moving the block ship surreptitiously into position, in part because of the fort's close proximity. During the actual mission on June 3, 1898, the mission commander, Navy lieutenant Richmond Pearson Hobson, decided to forego the gradual approach and order full steam when the castle's profile could be clearly seen in the early dawn and he became convinced that the ship must have been observed from only 2,000 yards away. The expedition ultimately failed, and the ship's skeleton crew, including Hobson, was captured and interred in Morro Castle.

Intelligence from Cuban insurgents, however, revealed the location of the prisoners, so the American ships that bombarded other defenses on June 6 and again on June 16 did not target the castle. It received only incidental damage in the actions. Lookouts on the castle were the first Spaniards to observe the dozens of ships that made up the American invasion fleet, and it was from the fort that Cervera learned of their presence. A sentinel on the castle also reported the departure of Rear Admiral William T. Sampson's flagship, the *New York,* from the blockading squadron outside the harbor's entrance on July 3.

Morro Castle was probably most important as a deterrent. Sampson was unwilling to send his ships through the Spanish defenses along the narrow approach to attack Cervera in his harbor refuge. Although Sampson believed that a determined bombard-

Morro Castle, a 16th-century fortification that sits above the harbor entrance to Santiago de Cuba. (Library of Congress)

ment could have silenced all of the castle's batteries, he was also very concerned about mines in the channel controlled from onshore installations.

Morro Castle still stands today more than 500 years after its construction. In 1997, the United Nations Educational Scientific and Cultural Organization (UNESCO) declared it and its associated works a World Heritage Site as the largest and most complete example of European Renaissance military architecture.

Matthew J. Krogman

See also
Cervera y Topete, Pascual; Hobson, Richmond Pearson; Morro Heights; Sampson, William Thomas; Santiago de Cuba, Battle of

Further Reading
O'Toole, G. J. A. *The Spanish War: An American Epic, 1898.* New York: Norton, 1984.
Trask, David F. *The War with Spain in 1898.* Lincoln: University of Nebraska Press, 1996.

Morro Heights

A high bluff commanding the entrance to the harbor of Santiago de Cuba, situated on Cuba's southeastern coast. The headland lies six miles south of the city on the eastern side of the narrow channel that serves as the only sea approach to the city from the open ocean. The channel is no more than 400 yards wide at its greatest width.

Located on the heights were the Spanish-built Morro Castle, a Renaissance-style fortress first constructed in the 16th century, and nearby Morro Battery on the high ground. These were part of a larger system of fortifications that included the Estrella and Punta Gorda batteries to the north and the Upper and Lower Socapa batteries on the somewhat lower western side of the channel. During the Spanish-American War, the defensive network contained about three dozen large guns of varying caliber and quality. Two 6.3-inch pieces in the upper Socapa battery were the largest in the defenses, but there were only some 100 rounds of ammunition for them. Most of the pieces were antiquated muzzle loaders, and some dated to 1724.

On June 3, 1898, rapid-fire guns and machine guns on the heights fired upon the U.S. collier *Merrimac,* commanded by Richmond Pearson Hobson, as the Americans tried unsuccessfully to block the channel by sinking the ship at its most narrow point. The mission failed, and Hobson and his crew were taken prisoner.

Rear Admiral William T. Sampson's blockading U.S. Navy warships bombarded Morro Heights on June 6, 16, and 21 but largely refrained from shelling the installations directly because accepted doctrine held that battleships should not engage shore batteries. American officials were also concerned about Hobson and his crew, who were being held in Morro Castle. Although the larger Spanish guns lacked the range and accuracy to pose a serious threat to the blockading squadron, Sampson nonetheless worried about mines in the harbor and the channel controlled from the batteries as he considered whether to enter the harbor to attack Rear Admiral Pascual Cervera y Topete's sequestered Spanish squadron and support the U.S. Army in its advance toward Santiago.

Sampson's desire to neutralize the defenses created a significant interservice dispute when he asked the army to capture Morro Heights from the rear so that minesweeping teams could work unimpeded. Having taken an interior route toward Santiago and fearing the digression would result in high casualties, U.S. ground force commander Major General William R. Shafter declined the request and suggested that the navy should challenge the guns and steam into the harbor directly.

Sampson did not follow suit, and the ships held their stations while the army fought toward the city. On July 3, the guns on Morro Heights saw their most sustained action of the campaign as they ineffectually fired on the U.S. blockading ships during the Spanish squadron's egress from the harbor in the prelude to the decisive Battle of Santiago de Cuba later that same day. Morro Heights was again a factor on July 6 when the U.S. Army and the U.S. Navy made plans for a coordinated attack on its defenses so that the navy could clear the mines, enter the harbor, and bombard the city itself. This plan was not carried out, and the ships instead bombarded the city from the sea for two days before a truce went into effect that lasted until the formal surrender on July 17.

MATTHEW J. KROGMAN

See also
Cervera y Topete, Pascual; Hobson, Richmond Pearson; Morro Castle; Sampson, William Thomas; Santiago de Cuba, Battle of; Shafter, William Rufus

Further Reading
O'Toole, G. J. A. *The Spanish War: An American Epic, 1898.* New York: Norton, 1984.
Trask, David F. *The War with Spain in 1898.* Lincoln: University of Nebraska Press, 1996.

Music

The musical scene during the Spanish-American War was particularly interesting, owing much of its variety and popularity to recent inventions such as the gramophone and phonograph, which for the first time allowed Americans to listen to quality music that had been prerecorded. In an age before radio, television, or even movies with sound, listening to music, playing music, and dancing to music were favorite American pastimes. Spectacularly popular song writers and band leaders, such as John Philip Sousa, dubbed the "March King," and new forms of musical expression also lent to the music scene its own unique richness. Patriotic music and songs also played a central role in keeping civilians as well as soldiers enthusiastic about the war effort.

In addition to the gramophone and phonograph, which few people in fact could afford, the majority of Americans in the 1890s listened to music in person in such venues as dance halls, vaudeville and minstrel shows, concert halls, and outdoor band shells.

Many Americans were also introduced to new music and new musical genres by sheet music, which was sold for piano and for parlor singing at home. At the time, pianos were household fixtures in many middle- and upper-class American homes. The companies holding the rights to sheet music would often send musicians on musical tours so that the songs could be performed and sales of sheet music encouraged. These tours were usually performed by young and up-and-coming musicians who would one day become highly popular songwriters, musicians, and singers. Advertisements for sheet music were to be found in both magazines and newspapers. The covers of sheet music were often dramatically and elaborately illustrated to help sales and set a mood for the music.

During the 1890s, a section of New York City known for its high density of musicians, songwriters, and music publishers—dubbed Tin Pan Alley—became a fertile testing ground for new songs and genres of music. Ragtime, considered by many to be the precursor of jazz, had become enormously popular by the late 1890s. Among its most illustrious composers were Scott Joplin and Vess Ossman. A sort of hybridized form of marches with roots also in African American music, ragtime began as up-tempo dance music written usually in 2/4 or 4/4 time that featured highly syncopated melodies. Ragtime would come to feature a wide array of styles during its heyday.

Among the more popular songs during the Spanish-American War were "Hot Time in the Old Town Tonight," a very popular song among U.S. troops who often sang it in camp; "After the Ball"; John Philip Sousa's "El Capitan March," another favorite among soldiers and military bands; "My Wild Irish Rose"; and "Sweet Rosie O'Grady." When the U.S. Asiatic Squadron began its voyage to

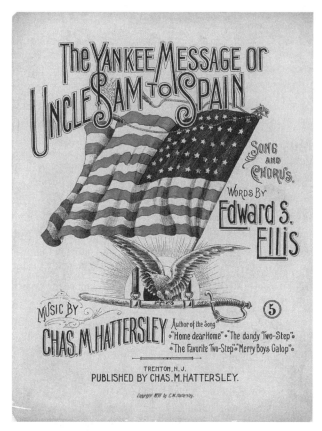

Cover to a piece of patriotic American sheet music titled "The Yankee Message; Uncle Sam to Spain," published in 1898. (Rare Book, Manuscript, and Special Collections Library, Duke University)

Manila Bay in 1898, the band on board the *Olympia,* Commodore George Dewey's flagship, played "El Capitan March."

Songs dealing specifically with the war and military service were very popular among soldiers and were designed to stress esprit de corps and war propaganda all at the same time. "Brave Dewey and His Men" celebrated the American victory at the Battle of Manila Bay, while "The Charge of the Rough Riders" immortalized the service of Theodore Roosevelt and the Rough Riders at San Juan Hill. Songs such as "The Belle of Manila" and "Ma Filipino Babe" spoke of American intervention in the Philippines and the hard-ships it had engendered. The emphasis in many of these songs was undiluted patriotism and sacrifice for a noble cause. Other such songs were blatantly racist and spoke of African Americans' service in the war as well as Filipino insurgents whom U.S. forces began to fight in February 1899.

Undoubtedly the most popular and influential musician of the time was Sousa, who had led the U.S. Marine Band for 12 years before retiring and branching out on his own in 1892. He became an instant sensation, known not only for the plethora of jaunty and memorable marches he wrote but also for his leadership of his own band of handpicked musicians that toured the nation exhaustively throughout the 1890s. Sousa was indeed the forerunner of a present-day rock-and-roll superstar.

Musically speaking, Sousa was the right man for the times. His unflinching patriotism, long affiliation with the U.S. Marine Corps, and rousing marches all fed into the upsurge in American patriotism during the 1890s. His quintessentially American sound also helped the great masses of immigrants become instantly familiar with a key part of American culture. Of course, the timing of the Spanish-American War could not have been better, for Sousa's marches were played nearly ad nauseum in civilian parades, military reviews, and the like. His most famous march, "The Stars and Stripes Forever," composed in 1896, was written less than 18 months before the Spanish-American War began in April 1898. In an age prior to electronic media, with no radio or television, Sousa's music took its place as a musical form of propaganda, stirring American patriotism and showcasing Americans' newfound pride as a nation on the edge of greatness.

PAUL G. PIERPAOLI JR.

See also

Dewey, George; Manila Bay, Battle of; Propaganda; Roosevelt, Theodore; Sousa, John Philip

Further Reading

Agay, Denes. *Best Loved Songs of the American People.* New York: Doubleday, 1975.

Davis, Ronald L. *History of Music in American Life,* Vol. 2, *Gilded Years, 1865–1920.* Malabar, FL: Krieger, 1981.

Zannos, Susan. *The Life and Times of John Philip Sousa.* Hockessin, DE: Mitchell Lane, 2003.

N

National Guard, U.S.

The U.S. National Guard was essentially an organized volunteer militia controlled by the state governors. The federal government could call the National Guard into service only for the constitutional purposes of keeping internal order or repelling foreign invasion. For foreign wars, Washington could ask only that its members volunteer, with the presumption that in a national emergency members of the National Guard would volunteer as whole units and that the U.S. military establishment would thus be dramatically increased in size. In theory, these units would all be well officered, well trained, and effectively equipped. It did not work out that way in practice, however.

In April 1898, the National Guard consisted of 45 independent state militia organizations enrolling a total of 115,627 men (9,376 officers). Most of the guard units were infantry, although there were a few units of cavalry and artillery. Because governors were reluctant to share their authority, there was no overall coordinating National Guard agency. Training was lax, weaponry was obsolescent (the National Guard was still equipped with .45-caliber Springfield rifles utilizing black powder), and most of its units functioned more as social organizations than well-honed military units.

Both the state governors and members of the National Guard fought strongly to preserve the organization, opposing both expansion in the regular army and creation of an army reserve. On the eve of the war with Spain, a compromise was reached with the William McKinley administration in the April 22, 1898, Volunteer Army Bill, which permitted the president to designate general officers and staff officers for divisions as well as commissioned officers for the U.S. Volunteers. The National Guard could be sworn as entire units, retaining their own officers.

McKinley originally planned to call for only 60,000 volunteers, and although his call on April 23 for 125,000 volunteers shocked army planners, the president was determined not to repeat President Abraham Lincoln's mistake at the beginning of the American Civil War in calling up too few men. Besides, the 125,000-man figure, no doubt by design, only slightly exceeded the number of National Guard members and would therefore blunt any possibility of criticism that certain state guard units had been excluded.

Generally, National Guard units arrived at training camps poorly equipped and untrained, and most did not see service. Only 35,000 guardsmen were sent overseas or even assigned to units designated for overseas service by the time the Protocol of Peace was signed on August 12, 1898. A few performed occupation duties in Cuba and Puerto Rico after the war, but most were mustered out of service in the fall after the end of hostilities. However, three-quarters of the men of the Philippine Expeditionary Force (VIII Corps) were volunteers and presumably a large number of them were from the National Guard.

The war revealed weaknesses in the U.S. military system and led to the Militia Act of 1903 (Dick Act) and the National Defense Act of 1916. The Militia Act of 1903 repealed the Militia Act of 1792, ending the universal military obligation for able-bodied adult males. The act recognized the National Guard as the organized militia and first-line military reserve. The act stipulated that the National Guard was to be organized, trained, and equipped identically to the regular army, and the federal government undertook providing its weapons and equipment as well as regular army officers to serve as instructors. The act also provided for the setting of minimum standards of weekly drills and an annual encampment. The 1916 National Defense Act provided for the gradual expansion of the National Guard to 400,000 men.

Spencer C. Tucker

Cavalry Squadron A of the New York National Guard. The squadron served in Puerto Rico during the Spanish-American War. (*Photographic History of the Spanish-American War,* 1898)

See also
Militia Act of 1903

Further Reading

Alger, Russell A. *The Spanish-American War.* New York: Harper Brothers, 1901.
Cooper, Jerry. *The Militia and the National Guard in America since Colonial Times: A Research Guide.* Westport, CT: Greenwood, 1993.
Doubler, Michael D. *Civilian in Peace, Soldier in War: The Army National Guard, 1636–2000.* Lawrence: University Press of Kansas, 2003.
Trask, David F. *The War with Spain in 1898.* Lincoln: University of Nebraska Press, 1996.

Naval Ordnance

Both the United States and Spain entered the Spanish-American War with modern naval ordnance on board many of their warships. Aboard the largest warships, the primary batteries were those guns greater than 6.3-inches (160-millimeter [mm]), with the largest in the war being the U.S. 13-inch. The Spanish 180-mm, 200-mm, and 240-mm and American 8-inch guns were sometimes referred to as intermediate guns. Secondary batteries consisted of 3.4-inch (87-mm) to 6.3-inch (160-mm) guns. The smallest guns, known as the auxiliary batteries, were usually housed in open unarmored positions with a gun shield usually the only protection for its crew.

Heavy guns were built up; that is, they were made of an inner steel tube with an outer jacket. Ordnance is always locked in a race with armor, so one of the period's principal demands was for increased muzzle velocity in order for shells to penetrate enemy armor. This required longer gun lengths and slow-burning propellants that would allow the shell to gain the maximum muzzle velocity.

The United States had begun experimenting with steel shells in 1882. In 1883, the U.S. Navy Gun Foundry Board recommended that the obsolescent naval artillery—largely left over from the American Civil War—be replaced with modern naval ordnance. By 1887, modern naval artillery was being manufactured in the United States, and by 1894, U.S. Navy battleship main battery guns were firing a 13-inch shell weighing 1,100 pounds and capable of penetrating a 17-inch-thick plate of Harvey process nickel steel. The first U.S. manufacturer of modern guns was the Bethlehem Iron Company, which adopted the methods employed by the British Elswick Company. Naval guns were also assembled at the Washington Naval Yard.

The Spanish Hontoria Company was the chief supplier of ordnance to the Spanish Navy. Hontoria was a large state-owned

Upper turret of two 8-inch guns on the battleship *Massachusetts.* (James Rankin Young and J. Hampton Moore, *History of Our War with Spain,* 1898)

foundry at Trubia, outside of Oviedo. The French Schneider-Creusot Company had a contract to assist Hontoria, and the German Krupp firm also had some influence there. Hontoria would purchase several pattern pieces, usually from Creusot, and then modify them for domestic production. As a rule, the Hontoria gun was considered less efficient than models from other manufacturers. Some of the older Spanish warships still carried obsolescent Creusot-designed Model 1875 steel-tube guns with iron hoops. Some older warships even carried British Armstrong muzzle loaders. Hontoria then adopted the French Model 1883, which was designed for black powder and did not lend itself well for later conversion to quick-fire use. The end result was that many of the 5.5 quick-fire guns carried on the Spanish armored cruisers had a very slow rate of fire and, in some cases, were inoperable.

Another dimension of naval ordnance of the period was the adoption of quick-fire guns. The goal here was to be able to produce a rain of shells on an enemy warship, especially on its unarmored sections. This was deemed necessary in thwarting attacks by torpedo boats. American quick-fire guns were the new 4-inch and 5-inch guns carried on the most modern of their warships. The one exception was the protected cruiser *New Orleans,* built by the British and purchased from the Brazilian government. It carried Elswick 6-inch and 4.7-inch quick firers. But the older 6-inch and

smaller guns in the secondary battery were still capable of more rapid fire than guns in the primary battery. Spanish quick firers were limited to the Hontoria converted 5.5-inch and 4.7-inch guns, guns purchased from Krupp, and Italian-made Ansaldo guns.

The quick-fire gun with its brass cartridge had a maximum rate of fire of five rounds per minute for the American 5-inch gun and seven to eight rounds per minute for the 4-inch gun. Rates of fire for the Spanish Hontoria designs were much slower, while Krupp or Elswick guns under ideal conditions had a slightly higher rate of fire than a comparable American gun. That rate, however, was never achieved by the Spaniards in combat.

The auxiliary batteries were made up principally of quick-firing 6-pounders and 1-pounders as well as machine guns. A few 3-pounders were found on the older Spanish warships and their torpedo craft. The Spanish destroyers carried new 12-pounder or 75-mm guns. Spain relied on the extremely reliable American-designed Hotchkiss guns and also had some Nordenfelt guns in service. The United States did adopt some machine guns and related ordnance known as Driggs-Schroeder guns. The Americans also utilized Hotchkiss and Nordenfelt guns.

Representative American and Spanish guns included the largest-size 13-inch Mark I mounted on the Oregon-class battleships, which weighed 60.5 tons and fired an armor-piercing round

Gunners manning 1-pounder guns aloft on the U.S. battleship *Texas*. (*Photographic History of the Spanish-American War,* 1898)

weighing 1,100 pounds at a rate of fire of one round per 3.5 minutes. Spain entered the war with the primary battery being the 280-mm Model 1883 gun. It weighed 32 tons and fired an armor-piercing round weighing 585 pounds or a common shell weighing 693 pounds. The rate of fire was one round every two minutes.

The American intermediate 8-inch, 35-caliber Mark III gun was mounted on both its first-class battleships and armored (heavy, protected) cruisers and weighed 13.1 tons. It fired an armor-piercing round weighing 250 pounds and had a rate of fire of one round per 77 seconds. The Spanish intermediate gun most utilized in the war was the Hontoria 140-mm Model 1883. It weighed 4.1 tons and fired an armor-piercing round weighing 86 pounds or a common shell weighing 75 pounds. It had a rate of fire of four rounds per minute. The American 5-inch rapid-fire gun weighed 3.1 tons and fired a 50-pound shell. Its rate of fire was five rounds per minute. A widespread Spanish secondary gun was the Hontoria 120-mm Model 1883 gun that weighed 2.6 tons. It fired an armor-piercing round weighing 53 pounds or a common shell weighing 47 pounds with a firing rate of about seven rounds per minute.

Complementing these guns were numerous light machine guns. They were primarily Maxim and Nordenfelt machine guns used by both navies; some older American warships carried Gatling guns. In 1896, Spain pressed the 1.45-inch Maxim machine gun into service, while the United States that same year brought the Colt .236-caliber machine gun into service. Machine gun rates of fire were usually 400–500 rounds per minute.

The United States had one unique gun, which was used in bombarding Santiago de Cuba. This was the so-called dynamite gun carried on USS *Vesuvius.* The ship had three fixed at 18 degrees elevation bow-mounted pneumatic tubes used to project the shells. The three shells carried were those of 500, 200, and 50 pounds, respectively. The 500-pound shell had a maximum range of 1,700 yards. The propellant charges were fired by electrical circuit. The guns were not very accurate, but the explosions from their large shells were impressive.

Shells used by both Spain and the United States were of three main types. The armor-piercing shell carried a smaller bursting charge. The common shell with a base fuse had less penetrating power but carried a larger bursting charge. There were other common shells that had the fuse on the cap of the shell. Shrapnel shell was available, but it saw little service. Shrapnel was designed for firing on light torpedo boats and for firing at troops on land. High-explosive shell, introduced by the French in 1888, was not utilized in the conflict by either side.

American gunfire accuracy in the war was poor and only appeared effective when compared to the abysmal Spanish accuracy. In 1897, the U.S. Navy had doubled its gunnery practice time, but this does not seem to have made a major impact. At the May 1, 1898, Battle of Manila Bay, out of 1,257 American 6-inch and 5-inch shells fired, only 28 hit their mark, for an accuracy rate of just 2.2 percent. Of 157 8-inch shells fired from the *Olympia* and *Baltimore,* just 13 hit their target. The 6-pounders fired 2,124 rounds and struck only 31 of the intended targets.

At the July 3, 1898, Battle of Santiago de Cuba, the 47 13-inch shells fired did not score even once, while of 39 12-inch shells fired, only 2 struck their mark. Of the 219 8-inch shells fired, 10 hit, while of the 744 6-inch and 5-inch shells fired, just 17 struck their target. Overall, of 9,400 total rounds fired, there were 122 hits, for a 1.3 percent accuracy rate. Following the war, the U.S. Navy introduced sophisticated range-finding equipment and more regular gunnery practice.

JACK GREENE

See also

Artillery; Dynamite Gun; Gatling Gun; Machine Guns; Manila Bay, Battle of; Santiago de Cuba, Battle of; Spain, Navy; United States Navy

Further Reading

Feuer, A. B. *The Spanish-American War at Sea: Naval Action in the Atlantic.* Westport, CT: Praeger, 1995.
Garbett, H. *Naval Gunnery.* Wakefield, Yorkshire, UK: S. R. Publishers, 1971.
Hovgaard, William. *Modern History of Warships.* Annapolis, MD: Naval Institute Press, 1971.
Laughton, L. G. Carr. *The Naval Pocket-Book.* London: W. Thacker, 1903.
Nofi, Albert A. *The Spanish-American War: 1898.* Conshohocken, PA: Combined Books, 1996.

Naval Strategy, Spanish

When news of the American blockade of Cuba reached Madrid, large numbers of Spaniards clamored to enlist in the navy. Convinced of Spanish naval strength following more than a decade of showy reconstruction and foreign purchases, many Spaniards pressed for its immediate employment. These sentiments were echoed by many politicians in the Cortes (parliament) and throughout the civilian administration.

Pundits and opinion makers expected Rear Admiral Pascual Cervera y Topete to sortie immediately with his squadron from the Cape Verde Islands and challenge the U.S. Navy in the Caribbean. Many Spaniards believed that while the Americans were distracted in the Caribbean, the navy could also easily raid the vulnerable U.S. Atlantic seaboard. General Valeriano Weyler y Nicolau, who had been recalled to Madrid by the queen regent, even glibly proposed that 50,000 Spanish troops be disembarked to wreak havoc along the U.S. eastern shoreline.

Such grandiose schemes, of course, went well beyond the capabilities of the Spanish Navy. Spanish professional naval officers realized that although numerous, few of their warships were capable of campaigning effectively on the high seas against their more powerful American opponents. Set-piece battles against an enemy fleet were not part of the Spanish Navy's mentality or training. Indeed,

the Royal Spanish Navy's defensive strategy had been codified as early as 1886 by naval minister Vice Admiral José María Beránger.

When current minister Rear Admiral Segismundo Bermejo y Merelo, in office scarcely seven months, bowed to political pressure and reluctantly drew up orders for Cervera to steam to the Caribbean, he attempted to deflect the public clamor for his squadron to charge headlong into battle. Indeed, Cervera was to proceed stealthily toward the sanctuary of San Juan de Puerto Rico, avoiding any unfavorable clashes at sea. He was also authorized to proceed on to Cuba, depending upon the situation.

To Cervera, even such modest goals seemed ill-advised. After meeting with his officers, he cabled back a proposal that his warships proceed no farther than the Canary Islands, taking up station there so as to steam to the aid of any threat against Spain itself. In proposing this strategy, he pointed out that U.S. naval forces were "immensely superior in number and class of ships, armor, and gunnery, as well as in state of readiness" to his own problem-plagued command.

Yet such a timid course as Cervera proposed was impossible for political reasons, so Bermejo's initial orders were repeated. At midnight on April 29, 1898, Cervera slipped out of San Vicente in the Cape Verde Islands with his four cruisers, three destroyers, and a hospital ship. While running across the Atlantic, he learned that Rear Admiral Patricio Montojo y Pasarón's squadron had been destroyed in the

The destruction of the Spanish armored cruiser *Vizcaya* during the Battle of Santiago de Cuba, July 3, 1898. (Library of Congress)

Battle of Manila Bay on May 1 and that the shore batteries guarding San Juan, Puerto Rico, had been shelled by Rear Admiral William Sampson's powerful North Atlantic Squadron. Therefore, with considerable skill and good fortune, Cervera was able to coal at Curaçao and steal into Santiago Bay on May 19.

Only the day before, Bermejo had been compelled to resign as minister of the navy amid a great public outcry against the unexpected Spanish defeat at Manila. In order to mitigate the recriminations being hurled against the navy's disappointing performance, the notion of attacking the U.S. eastern seaboard was revived. Although a full-scale invasion was clearly impossible, it was suggested that a pair of transatlantic sorties might be launched. While no significant strategic advantage could realistically be achieved by such a feat, naval professionals at least consoled themselves that the distraction might ease some of the American pressure on blockaded Cuba.

Thus, Captain José Ferrándiz was ordered to prepare to strike out in the direction of the Caribbean with his aged battleship *Pelayo* plus the even older coast guard vessel *Vitoria* and the destroyers *Osado, Audaz,* and *Proserpina.* This sortie was to be merely a feint, though, as all five were to quickly reverse course and return to Spanish waters and assume coastal patrol.

The real thrust was to be made by Admiral Manuel de la Cámara y Libermoore, who under cover of this initial diversion was to slip out for Bermuda with his armored cruiser *Carlos V* accompanied by three fast, lightly armed liners that had been converted into auxiliary cruisers—the 12,000-ton *Patriota*, 11,000-ton *Meteoro*, and 10,500-ton *Patriota*—as well as the dispatch vessel *Giralda.* After coaling at Bermuda, this strike force was to ply the eastern seaboard of the United States as commerce raiders, wreaking as much havoc as possible, while working its way northward into Canadian waters. From Halifax, Admiral Cámara's small force was then to head east into the Atlantic as if returning to Spain before actually veering south to emerge amid the Turks and Caicos islands for more interceptions of American ships.

Finally, anticipating that U.S. naval forces would be obliged to redeploy into the North Atlantic to hunt for this elusive force, a second small squadron of commerce raiders was to steam from Spain under Captain José Barrasa. With his aged cruiser *Alfonso XII* plus the auxiliary cruisers *Antonio López* and *Buenos Aires,* he was to make landfall near Brazil's Cape San Roque, then prey upon the busy American ship lanes rounding South America.

Yet all these offensive notions were scrapped when it was learned that the United States intended to dispatch an expeditionary force to occupy the Philippines. Hoping to beat them to the archipelago, Spanish naval strategy turned around completely. Admiral Cámara was ordered to convoy transports carrying 4,000 troops to the Philippines. This Spanish force was to move through the Suez Canal so as to arrive in Philippine waters prior to the U.S. invasion army and disembark the Spanish troops on the islands of Jolo and Mindanao to spearhead a local resistance.

Cámara's original 13 vessels were to be augmented by the transport *Isla de Panay* as well as the colliers *Colón, Covadonga, San Agustín,* and *San Francisco,* the latter four ships because the only reliable supplies of coal for the Spanish squadron would be found at the neutral Italian ports in Eritrea as well as French ports in Indochina. Accompanied by the dispatch vessel *Joaquín del Piélago,* Cámara's lumbering squadron reached Port Said, Egypt, by June 22, 1898, only to be delayed in gaining access to the Suez Canal.

Meanwhile, political pressure continued to mount in Madrid regarding the navy's lackluster performance, with feelings running especially high against Cervera's lengthy stay inside Santiago Bay. Fearful that the anchored Spanish warships would be forced to surrender without firing a shot once Santiago fell to its American besiegers, yet another new and hard-pressed navy minister, Captain Ramón Auñón y Villalón, ordered Cervera's squadron to sortie. Fully as Cervera had predicted, it was annihilated after exiting the harbor on July 3. This shocking loss collapsed public morale and also led to the recall of Cámara's expedition from the Red Sea. The Philippines had been openly abandoned to U.S. seizure, soon to be followed by Cuba and Puerto Rico, as Spain could only look on helplessly.

If allowed to pursue their prewar strategy, the high command of the Royal Spanish Navy would have preferred to fight a defensive struggle, sortieing occasionally from their fortified harbors with single ships or swift, small squadrons to make a sweep or to relieve a beleaguered outpost. Instead, unrealistic expectations generated by public opinion and pushed by the politicians had resulted in demands for a naval strategy that the professional navy did not want and could not perform.

DAVID F. MARLEY

See also

Asiatic Squadron; Bermejo y Merelo, Segismundo; Cámara y Libermoore, Manuel de la; Cervera y Topete, Pascual; Manila Bay, Battle of; Montojo y Pasarón, Patricio; Naval Strategy, U.S.; North Atlantic Squadron; Santiago de Cuba, Battle of; Spain, Navy; United States Navy

Further Reading

Almunia Fernández, Celso Jesús. "La opinión pública española sobre la pérdida del imperio colonial: De Zanjón al desastre (1878–1898)" [Spanish Public Opinion toward the Loss of the Imperial Colonies: From Zanjon to the Disaster, 1878–1898]. *Imágenes y ensayos del 98* (1998): 205–252.

Calvo Poyato, José. *El Desastre del 98* [The Disaster of 1898]. Barcelona: Plaza & Janés, 1997.

Cervera Pery, José. *La guerra naval del 98: a mal planeamiento, peores consecuencias* [The Naval War of 1898: Poor Planning, Worse Consequences]. Madrid: San Martín, 1998.

Feuer, A. B. *The Spanish-American War at Sea: Naval Action in the Atlantic.* Westport, CT: Praeger, 1995.

Smith, Joseph. *The Spanish-American War: Conflict in the Caribbean and the Pacific, 1895–1902.* New York: Longman, 1994.

Naval Strategy, U.S.

Beginning in the mid-1880s, the U.S. Navy had undergone a dramatic transformation. Although still small by European standards,

The U.S. Navy armored cruiser *New York,* flasghip of Rear Admiral William T. Sampson's North Atlantic Squadron. (*Photographic History of the Spanish-American War,* 1898)

the navy began receiving modern steam-driven steel ships armed with modern breech-loading rifled ordnance. The intellectual underpinnings of U.S. naval strategic thought came principally from the writings of naval historian and strategist Captain Alfred Thayer Mahan. In his landmark work *The Influence of Sea Power upon History, 1660–1783* (1890), he postulated that world power rested on sea power. He eschewed the traditional U.S. Navy strategy of a *guerre de course* (war against commerce) in favor of a battle fleet capable of winning control of the sea. Such a task could only be accomplished by battleships operating in squadrons. To support the projection of naval power, the United States would need overseas bases and coaling stations. Among Mahan's admirers were President William McKinley and Assistant Secretary of the Navy Theodore Roosevelt. They along with others within the administration, many in Congress, industrialists, and leaders from many segments of American society pushed for naval expansion to be concentrated in capital ships. It was this new American navy that made possible the victory over Spain in 1898.

With tensions increasing between the United States and Spain over Cuba, the U.S. Naval War College developed a strategy for fighting a naval war with Spain. This strategic plan was revised annually right up to the beginning of the Spanish-American War. In

addition, the Navy Department also drafted contingency plans for a conflict with Spain. Some contingency plans envisioned a war that would involve fighting the combined navies of Spain and Great Britain. Seizure of Cuba from Spain, however, was at the center of planning in the half decade before the war.

At the beginning of the war, the immediate Spanish threat came in the form of Spanish rear admiral Pascual Cervera y Topete's squadron of two cruisers and four destroyers. The U.S. public grossly exaggerated the squadron's actual power, and there were loud calls from alarmists in East Coast cities for ships to protect them from a Spanish naval blockade or even attack. Such action was utterly beyond Cervera's means. In any case, the manning of coastal forts, armed for the most part with obsolete ordnance, helped to quiet fears, as did a compromise naval strategy.

The Navy Department was determined that the North Atlantic Squadron should be kept together in keeping with Mahanian principles. No matter where Cervera might appear in the Caribbean, the Atlantic Squadron would thus be able to mount a retaliatory strike. To quiet East coast anxieties over Cervera, however, the Navy Department agreed to a compromise arrangement. While the bulk of U.S. naval strength was still concentrated in the North Atlantic Squadron under Rear Admiral William T. Sampson based at Key

West, Florida, for a descent against Cuba, part of Atlantic naval strength was formed into the Flying Squadron, under Commodore Winfield Scott Schley, to serve as a mobile protection force for the vulnerable Atlantic seaboard. In addition, a small Northern Patrol Squadron of obsolete warships was organized to defend the coast from the Delaware Capes northward.

On April 22, 1898, the Navy Department ordered Sampson to establish a naval blockade of Cuba. On April 25, Congress declared that a state of war had existed since April 21. Initially, the U.S. blockade was to extend from Havana around the western tip of Cuba as far as Cienfuegos on the southern coast of the island. It was later extended as more ships became available. The blockade was designed to prevent Spain from supplying or reinforcing its sizable military strength in Cuba while the United States prepared its own invasion forces. In the war at sea, the United States enjoyed a tremendous geographical advantage over Spain. U.S. ships on Cuban station could be easily resupplied from nearby Florida ports, whereas to reach that island the Spanish ships would have to cross the Atlantic Ocean. Meanwhile, on April 29, Admiral Cervera departed Cape Verdes for Puerto Rico and eventually found his way to Santiago de Cuba.

U.S. secretary of the navy John D. Long left naval deployments and planning largely up to Roosevelt, who ordered an aggressive strategy for the Pacific theater of war. Roosevelt cabled Commodore George Dewey, commander of the small U.S. Navy Asiatic Squadron of four cruisers, two gunboats, and a revenue cutter, directing that in the event of hostilities with Cuba, Dewey was to mount offensive action against the Spanish squadron in the Philippine Islands. When war came, Dewey immediately steamed the 600 miles to the Philippines and in the Battle of Manila Bay (May 1, 1898) destroyed the Spanish squadron of Rear Admiral Patricio Montojo y Pasarón. After taking the Spanish naval base at Cavite, Dewey then blockaded Manila to await the arrival of ground troops.

In the Caribbean theater, meanwhile, the U.S. Navy steadily built up its naval strength, assisted by the eventual arrival of the battleship *Oregon* from the Pacific coast. The navy not only maintained a blockade of Cuba but also cut cable communications with Spain and supplied Cuban insurgent forces ashore. Sampson wanted a descent on Havana, believing that the U.S. capture of the Cuban capital city would bring the war to a close. Long disagreed, citing the facts that the army was unready for an amphibious operation, that the Atlantic Squadron was divided between Norfolk and the Caribbean, that Cervera's Spanish squadron was still at large, and that the U.S. warships would be at risk from Havana's shore defenses. The new Naval War Board agreed.

Meanwhile, there was the problem of Cervera. Guessing that the Spanish admiral would head to San Juan, Puerto Rico, to coal, Sampson partially lifted the naval blockade of Cuba on May 3 and made for that island with two battleships, a cruiser, two monitors, and a torpedo boat. Slowed by the monitors, which had to be towed, he did not arrive off Puerto Rico until May 19 and then contented himself with a brief bombardment of the San Juan shore defenses,

inflicting little damage. Mahan, who condemned Sampson's move, had advocated only the dispatch of scout cruisers to provide warning of Cervera's arrival. They could then notify Sampson. Only then, Mahan believed, should Sampson venture forth with his squadron to seek a decisive encounter.

As it turned out, Cervera outguessed Sampson and slipped undetected into Santiago on Cuba's southern coast on May 19. Meanwhile, Schley, sent by Sampson to locate Cervera, wasted valuable time at Cienfuegos in the belief that Cervera might be there. Schley did not arrive at Santiago until May 28, and he was soon joined by Sampson and the remaining ships of the North Atlantic Squadron. Although the U.S. Navy's June 3 attempt to scuttle the monitor *Merrimac* failed to block the narrow channel into Santiago Harbor, Cervera remained quiescent, allowing the U.S. Navy to blockade Santiago.

With Cervera bottled up at Santiago, the U.S. invasion of Cuba could proceed. Still, the U.S. Navy demanded that the army invade at Santiago and do so quickly in order to destroy Cervera's squadron. U.S. strategic thinking now shifted definitively from Havana to Santiago. On June 22, members of the army's V Corps Expeditionary Force under Major General William R. Shafter began coming ashore at the port of Daiquirí, some 16 miles east of Santiago. Although Shafter wanted the navy to shell the forts, steam up the channel, and engage Cervera's ships at Santiago, Sampson held that this was impossible given the Spanish shore batteries and threat of mines in the narrow channel. He wanted Shafter's troops first to attack and reduce the shore batteries at the mouth of the channel. Despite Sampson's belief that there was agreement on that course of action, Shafter moved inland to attack Santiago itself. In any case, following U.S. victories on land on June 1 and the closing of the U.S. ground force on Santiago, on July 3 Cervera finally attempted to escape Santiago de Cuba to sea. The ensuing naval battle at Santiago de Cuba resulted in the utter destruction of his squadron by the far more powerful U.S. blockaders. The other factor in the defeat was the fact that the Spanish ships had to exit the narrow harbor mouth in single file, making them vulnerable to American fire one at a time.

With the Spanish naval threat gone and with Santiago having surrendered, the navy then transported an army expeditionary force to Puerto Rico. Meanwhile, the threat of a Spanish naval squadron under Rear Admiral Manual de la Cámara y Libermoore, consisting of a battleship, three cruisers, and two transports lifting 4,000 troops and dispatched from Spain to the Philippines by way of the Mediterranean and the Suez Canal, evaporated when it was called home from the Red Sea. Dewey maintained a blockade of Manila Bay and, with the arrival of U.S. ground forces, assisted the army in the capture of Manila in August. The war ended on August 12, 1898, with the United States in possession of Cuba, Puerto Rico, and the Philippines. In the subsequent fighting of the Philippine-American War, the navy provided valuable assistance to army operations ashore, including the conduct of amphibious operations.

RICK DYSON AND SPENCER C. TUCKER

See also

Cámara y Libermoore, Manuel de la; Cervera y Topete, Pascual; Coaling Stations; Dewey, George; Long, John Davis; Mahan, Alfred Thayer; Manila Bay, Battle of; McKinley, William; Montojo y Pasarón, Patricio; Naval Strategy, Spanish; Naval War College; Roosevelt, Theodore; Sampson, William Thomas; Santiago de Cuba, Battle of; Schley, Winfield Scott; Shafter, William Rufus; Spain, Navy; United States Navy

Further Reading

LaFeber, Walter. *The New Empire: An Interpretation of American Expansion, 1860–1898.* Ithaca, NY: Cornell University Press, 1963.

Livezey, William E. *Mahan on Sea Power.* Norman: University of Oklahoma Press, 1947.

Schoonover, Thomas. *Uncle Sam's War of 1898 and the Origins of Globalization.* Lexington: University Press of Kentucky, 2003.

Seager, Robert. *Alfred Thayer Mahan: The Man and His Letters.* Annapolis, MD: Naval Institute Press, 1977.

Trask, David F. *The War with Spain in 1898.* Lincoln: University of Nebraska Press, 1996.

Naval Vessels, U.S. Auxiliary

Ships purchased by the U.S. government to augment the nation's naval forces immediately prior to and during the Spanish-American War. At the beginning of the 1880s, the U.S. Navy consisted primarily of a small force of wooden vessels and American Civil War–era ironclads. Congress first appropriated significant funds for a new modern, all-steel navy in 1883, but even 15 years later on the eve of the Spanish-American War, the navy included an inadequate number of modern warships to carry out all the missions expected of the navy in the event of war with Spain.

Accordingly, just three days after Congress passed a $50 million national defense bill on March 9, 1898, the Navy Department appointed a special board to communicate with the owners of suitable privately owned vessels and determine who among these would be interested in selling or leasing their ships to the navy. The department further tasked the board with inspecting the vessels and ascertaining their suitability for auxiliary naval service.

Secretary of the Navy John D. Long placed Assistant Secretary of the Navy Theodore Roosevelt in charge of buying all auxiliary naval vessels. Between March 16 and August 12, 1898, Roosevelt and his successor, Charles H. Allen, expended $21.4 million to purchase 102 vessels. The first and most expensive ships purchased were the *Albany* and *New Orleans,* protected cruisers being built in England for the Brazilian government. The *Albany* did not see service during the war, but the *New Orleans* was commissioned almost immediately

The protected cruiser *New Orleans* arrives at the New York Navy Yard after crossing the Atlantic in April 1898. The United States purchased the ship from Brazil while it was still under construction in England, hence the Brazilian Navy paint scheme and the commissioning pennant flying from the main mast. (Naval Historical Center)

and took part in the blockade of Cuba. Several other combatant ships were acquired from overseas, including the gunboat *Topeka* and torpedo boat *Somers,* but most of the auxiliary ships were American-owned vessels in merchant service.

The Navy Department also chartered four large ships from the American Line shipping company, paying an aggregate $9,000 a day for their use. The American Line vessels and a number of the other merchantmen were armed and employed as auxiliary cruisers. Most saw action in the Caribbean theater. The *Saint Louis* in particular had an interesting war record, successfully cutting Spanish cables near San Juan and Santiago de Cuba and later transporting Spanish rear admiral Pascual Cervera y Topete as a prisoner of war.

In all, 131 auxiliary ships served in the U.S. Navy during the Spanish-American War. In addition to foreign-made combatants and merchant ships, the navy acquired 15 revenue cutters, 4 lighthouse tenders, 2 Fish Commission vessels, and an iceboat. The navy also obtained a number of steam yachts including the *Gloucester* and *Vixen,* both of which participated in the Battle of Santiago de Cuba on July 3, 1898.

In total, the Navy Department spent nearly $5 million preparing its auxiliary vessels for service. Shipyard workers strengthened superstructures, repaired and improved steam machinery, installed gun batteries, and removed flammable materials. Generally, the money was well spent, as auxiliary ships bolstered the North Atlantic Fleet, the Asiatic Squadron, and the Auxiliary Naval Force. In particular, many of these ships effectively supported the Cuban blockade. At war's end, the navy retained some of the auxiliary ships, but the majority were sold, scrapped, or returned to their original owners.

TIMOTHY S. WOLTERS

See also

Allen, Charles Herbert; Asiatic Squadron; Cables and Cable-Cutting Operations; Cuba, U.S. Naval Blockade of; Fifty Million Dollar Bill; Long, John Davis; North Atlantic Squadron; Roosevelt, Theodore; Santiago de Cuba, Battle of; United States Auxiliary Naval Force; United States Revenue Cutter Service; Warships

Further Reading

Bauer, K. Jack, and Stephen S. Roberts. *Register of Ships of the U.S. Navy, 1775–1990: Major Combatants.* Westport, CT: Greenwood, 1991.

Feuer, A. B. *The Spanish-American War at Sea: Naval Action in the Atlantic.* Westport, CT: Praeger, 1995.

Paullin, Charles O. *Paullin's History of Naval Administration, 1775–1911.* Annapolis, MD: Naval Institute Press, 1968.

Silvertone, Paul H. *The New Navy, 1883–1922.* New York: Routledge, 2006.

Trask, David F. *The War with Spain in 1898.* Lincoln: University of Nebraska Press, 1996.

Naval War Board

A committee made up of four U.S. naval officers along with the assistant secretary of the navy created at the behest of Secretary of the Navy John D. Long in March 1898. The purpose of the Naval War Board was to provide the U.S. Navy with planning strategy in the event of war with Spain and to advise the secretary of navy in the conduct of war if such a war came. The board also provided technological expertise when needed and collected military, intelligence, and statistical information.

The Naval War Board's members included Assistant Secretary of the Navy Theodore Roosevelt, Admiral Montgomery Sicard (chairman), Captain Arent S. Crowninshield, Captain Alfred Thayer Mahan, and Captain Albert S. Barker. Commander Richard Clover, head of the Office of Naval Intelligence (ONI), assisted the board in its work by providing current information collected by overseas contacts and operatives and naval attachés as well as information collected by the Naval War College. Roosevelt resigned his position on the Naval War Board on May 9, 1898, to join the Rough Riders. Barker also left in May 1898 to command USS *Newark* for the remainder of the war.

Although the ONI provided the Naval War Board with information prior to the declaration of war against Spain in April 1898, Crowninshield and Sicard were anxious over newspaper and other unconfirmed reports that Spain had already seized the offensive in the Caribbean and was ready to attack U.S. forces deployed in that region. In response to heightened concerns, the board dispatched to Europe two undercover navy ensigns, William H. Buck and Henry Herber Ward, to gather as much information as possible on the Spanish naval force's preparedness and strength and, more importantly, to determine if the Spanish squadron was en route to the Caribbean.

Buck and Ward traveled separately, each in disguise. Buck, who traveled to Europe, was able to report back to Washington via telegraph of the movements of Admiral Manuel de le Cámara y Libermoore's squadron, while Ward's adventure in locating information on the Spanish West Indian Fleet almost cost him his life. Ward traveled to Spain and St. Thomas and eventually ended up in Puerto Rico, where he was arrested by Spanish authorities while in the guise of an English gentleman.

Aside from the adventures of Buck and Ward, the Naval War Board made significant contributions to the U.S. Navy's war plans of 1898. Building on prior war planning done by the Naval War College, the board correctly endorsed and recommended the initial blockade of Cuba prior to the landing of U.S. forces and supported offensive measures by Commodore George Dewey's Asiatic Squadron against the small Spanish squadron under Admiral Patricio Montojo y Pasarón in Philippine waters. In both cases, the Naval War Board's recommendation resulted in successful missions.

The Naval War Board disbanded immediately following the Protocol of Peace signed on August 12, 1898, its mission having been completed to the satisfaction of Long. Strangely, when asked about the workings, findings, and achievements of the Naval War Board after the war, Alfred Thayer Mahan was very critical of the group, favoring a single chief of staff answering directly to the secretary of the navy as opposed to a multiperson board.

RICHARD W. PEUSER

Further Reading

Dowart, Jeffery M. *The Office of Naval Intelligence: The Birth of America's First Intelligence Agency, 1865–1918.* Annapolis, MD: Naval Institute Press, 1979.

Feuer, A. B. *The Spanish-American War at Sea: Naval Action in the Atlantic.* Westport, CT: Praeger, 1995.

Paullin, Charles Oscar. *Paullin's History of Naval Administration, 1775–1911.* Annapolis, MD: Naval Institute Press, 1968.

Trask, David F. *The War with Spain in 1898.* Lincoln: University of Nebraska Press, 1996.

Naval War College

Established in 1884, the Naval War College is the oldest senior-level institution of professional military education in the United States. Commodore Stephen B. Luce, the first president, defined it as "a place of original research on all questions relating to war and to statesmanship connected with war, or the prevention of war."

In 1884, the U.S. Navy was a small, relatively unimportant entity compared with the great navies of Europe. Qualitatively, only the steam frigate *Tennessee,* flagship of the North Atlantic Squadron, could compare with the warships of France and Great Britain. Seemingly at a low point in the existence of the U.S. Navy, events soon heralded the resurgence of the navy and a new definition of its role in national security and world affairs. Establishment of the Naval War College exemplified the new importance assigned to the navy in national security and, in particular, on officer professional education that emphasized strategic thinking, sound decision making, tactical and operational competence, and an understanding of the increasingly vital role of the navy in an industrialized imperial world.

The navy had traditionally been employed in a defensive role, with harbor and coastal defense and protection of maritime trade its primary missions. In the occasional conflict with a European power as in the War of 1812, the navy took on the role of commerce raiding, or *guerre de course* strategy, against Britain. Even during the American Civil War, when the navy grew to be the second largest in the world, its essential roles were enforcing the blockade, conducting riverine operations with the army, and hunting down Confederate commerce raiders on the high seas. There was no doctrine regarding power projection in distant waters or fleet operations.

The Naval War College at Newport, Rhode Island, circa 1900. (Library of Congress)

With the evolution of steam propulsion and steel ships by the 1870s, coinciding with aggressive European imperial expansion, many naval and military affairs commentators argued for the evolution of U.S. strategic naval doctrine. Among these forward-looking thinkers were Luce and Captain Alfred Thayer Mahan. Both officers advocated a more aggressive high seas fleet built around modern, powerful battleships able to concentrate on and defeat the great navies of Europe in decisive battle so as to establish sea control to ensure the security of U.S. coasts and maritime commerce. To prepare American naval officers for this new role, the navy established the Naval War College in 1884.

Officer professional development at the new college was intended not only to emphasize strategy, tactics, logistics, and naval history but also to examine the role, functions, limitations, and broader national security issues inherent in naval and maritime power. Under the umbrella of the term "sea power," coined by Mahan, the college began classes at Coasters Harbor Island (ceded to the federal government by Rhode Island in 1881) on Narragansett Bay just outside of Newport, Rhode Island, in September 1885. The navy converted the three-story former Newport County poorhouse and asylum for the deaf (now the Naval War College Museum) into the first college facility.

Luce, appointed to command the North Atlantic Squadron in 1881, the most prestigious command in the navy at the time, had long been concerned with training, education, naval administration, and organization, which made him not only the natural advocate but also the best choice to head the new institution. Luce believed that with individual reading, research, and contemplation conducted within a collaborative group setting (hence the college's seminar format), an officer could discern the immutable laws that governed individual and state actions. Through this cooperative and contemplative learning process, aided by a study of history, American naval officers would be more capable of sound decision making, critical strategic thinking, and analysis, thus preparing themselves and the navy for the challenges of the evolving modern world. Both comparative and inductive learning techniques through the lens of history, naval art and science, and international politics and law would be part of the new program.

The curriculum's goal was to educate officers who could then take specific events and, through broad analytical thinking, draw broader observations. Thus, the case study and seminar discussion techniques complemented by a series of elective courses on topics germane to international law and relations, history, political science, and technology have been the academic pattern since the Naval War College's founding. Tactical exercises were also to be part of the curriculum. Initially based on the close location of the North Atlantic Squadron, the concept of war gaming, a largely tactical and operational exercise, quickly took root, and war gaming became an inherent part of the student experience.

With this theoretical concept in play, on October 6, 1884, General Order 325 formally established the U.S. Naval War College as an "advanced course of professional study." The first class of four lieutenant commanders and five lieutenants began instruction on September 4, 1885. The following year, two U.S. Marine Corps officers joined the student population of 21 in the enlarged ten-week course, thus quickly establishing the inherently joint nature of the college. The second-year curriculum reflected the concepts laid out originally by Luce, including 16 lectures on naval gunnery, 20 on international law and the relations of nations, and 18 on military and naval tactics, strategic principles, and operational art.

The second paramount faculty addition was the arrival in September 1886 of Mahan as a lecturer in naval strategy and tactics and an advocate of a more powerful and aggressive sea service as an inherent component of an integrated national security strategy. Charged with presenting lectures examining the interrelationship among strategy, tactics, diplomacy, and national power, he evolved his lectures into his seminal book, *The Influence of Seapower upon History, 1660–1783,* published in 1890 and widely responsible for the revolutionary transformation in international naval thought at the beginning of the 20th century.

Over the years, the Naval War College has expanded its offerings and functions, including a distance education program (beginning in 1914 with a correspondence course), seminars at more than 20 sites across the country (Fleet Seminar Program), programs for international officers of allied and friendly nations (Naval Command College and Naval Staff College), the War Gaming Department, the Strategic Studies Group, the Center for Naval Warfare Studies (research), the International Law Department, the Center for Maritime History, and the Warfare Analysis Department. Thus, from the beginning, the curriculum and mission, through many iterations and evolutions, have essentially remained firmly grounded in the original concepts laid out by the first president of the Naval War College.

STANLEY D. M. CARPENTER

See also

Luce, Stephen Bleeker; Mahan, Alfred Thayer; Naval Strategy, U.S.; United States Navy

Further Reading

Hattendorf, John B. *Naval History and Maritime Strategy; Collected Essays.* Malabar, FL: Krieger, 2000.
Hattendorf, John B., et al. *Sailors and Scholars: The Centennial History of the Naval War College.* Newport, RI: Naval War College, 1984.

Newcomb, Frank Hamilton
Birth Date: November 10, 1846
Death Date: February 20, 1934

U.S. Navy seaman during the American Civil War (1861–1865) and officer in the U.S. Revenue Cutter Service (the forerunner of the U.S. Coast Guard) during the Spanish-American War. Frank Hamilton Newcomb was born on November 10, 1846, in Boston, Massachusetts. In 1861, at the age of 15, he enlisted in the Union Navy and served throughout the Civil War as an acting master's mate.

When the war ended, he joined the U.S. Revenue Cutter Service and, at the beginning of the Spanish-American War in April 1898, was a first lieutenant and commander of the revenue cutter *Hudson.* Built essentially as a harbor tugboat, the *Hudson* displaced 128 tons and was 96 feet in length.

In March 1898, a month before hostilities began, Assistant Secretary of the Navy Theodore Roosevelt prevailed upon President William McKinley to dispatch a number of revenue cutters to join naval ships being readied for war. On March 24, 1898, McKinley ordered that 10 revenue cutters be temporarily attached to the U.S. Navy, the first time this had occurred since the Civil War. Newcomb's ship was among them. Reclassified as a U.S. Navy auxiliary vessel, the *Hudson* was hardly a warship in the traditional sense. It mounted two 6-pounders fore and aft and a single 6-millimeter machine gun.

When Secretary of the Navy John Davis Long ordered a blockade of Cuba's northern coast beginning in late April 1898, Newcomb and his crew steamed toward Cárdenas, a port city located on the northern coast of Cuba in Matanzas Province, some 75 miles east of Havana. Although the bay at Cárdenas was too shallow for most naval vessels, including blockade runners, U.S. North Atlantic Squadron commander Rear Admiral William Sampson sought to prevent supplies from reaching the Spanish through the city. In late April 1898, just days after the declaration of war, a minor naval skirmish took place off the coast of Cárdenas between American and Spanish ships.

On May 8, the U.S. torpedo boat *Winslow* entered the bay and fired on a Spanish gunboat and armed tugs in an effort to draw them out of the bay where the cruiser *Wilmington* and gunboat *Macias* were lying in wait. This attempt failed, but three days later, on May 11, the *Wilmington* and the torpedo boat *Macias,* the armed revenue cutter *Winslow,* and the tug *Hudson* returned to Cárdenas. The American ships dueled with the Spanish shore batteries as well as the gunboats *Alerta* and *Ligera* and the armed tug *Antonio López.* The *Winslow* was seriously damaged in the exchange with a Spanish shore battery.

Seeing that the *Winslow*'s steering mechanism had been shot away and that the vessel was in serious distress, Newcomb risked his own ship to tow the stricken *Winslow* to safety and out of the range of Spanish guns. Newcomb and his crew were lauded for this action. On May 3, 1900, a joint session of Congress awarded Newcomb and his crew with the Cárdenas Medal of Honor, a specific award granted only to those involved in the naval battle of Cárdenas. Five crewmen died and three others were wounded aboard the *Winslow.* Among the dead was Ensign Worth Bagley, believed to be the first naval officer killed in the war. Without Newcomb's actions, the death toll would certainly have been significantly higher, and the *Winslow* might have been lost or captured.

Following the Spanish-American War, Newcomb remained with the U.S. Revenue Cutter Service, which in 1915 became the U.S. Coast Guard, and retired as a commodore. He died in Los Angeles, California, on February 20, 1934.

PAUL G. PIERPAOLI JR.

See also

Bagley, Worth; Cárdenas, Cuba; United States Revenue Cutter Service

Further Reading

Nofi, Albert A. *The Spanish-American War: 1898.* Conshohocken, PA: Combined Books, 1996.

Trask, David F. *The War with Spain in 1898.* Lincoln: University of Nebraska Press, 1996.

Newspapers

Daily and weekly newspapers played a major role in American life in the late 19th century by conveying day-to-day information to a mass audience. Indeed, in the absence of electronic or broadcast media, most educated people read several daily and weekly papers. In particular, the latter half of the 1890s was a period a great prosperity for the newspaper industry, as a strong economy spurred the advertising industry to buy large amounts of ad space at high rates. By the end of the decade, advertisements occupied half of the space in most newspapers.

Most dailies also shifted distribution to the afternoon to cater to people leaving work, who bought papers on a daily basis in increasing numbers. Cable, the telephone, and the telegraph allowed people to read about events only a day after they happened. Other developments that contributed to the success of the industry included the expanded use of the typewriter and the telephone and the creation of a process to make newsprint cheaply from wood pulp. Also, the look of papers recently changed when multicolumn headlines became possible, while color printing and the ability to print half-tone photographs developed. Although the technology existed to allow for the electronic transmission of photographs, as a practical matter publishing illustrations still required an artist to draw a sketch or make an engraving. As a result, their renditions of photographs, people, scenes, and maps appeared only in feature stories.

The leading papers of the era were the *New York Herald, New York Journal, New York Sun,* and *New York World,* all of which had their headquarters along Park Row in New York City, making the city the center of the nation's newspaper industry. In the early part of the decade, the *Herald* had the largest circulation, in part because wealthier New Yorkers supported it. At five cents per copy, the paper was relatively expensive. Daily editions ran from 12 to 20 pages and carried more news, illustrations, and advertisements

Prominent New York Newspapers during the Spanish-American War

Newspaper	Owner
New York Herald	James Gordon Bennett Jr.
New York Journal	William Randolph Hearst
New York Sun	Frank Andrew Munsey
New York World	Joseph Pulitzer

Newspaper correspondents aboard a steamer during the Spanish-American War. One of the men shown may be Richard Harding Davis. (Library of Congress)

successfully increased readership by employing the sensationalism that characterized yellow journalism. Large, screaming headlines about scandals and crime grabbed the interest of the masses, and the copy itself was quite evocative. Combined sales of the *World*'s morning and evening editions reached 1 million per day by 1897, and the *Journal*'s Sunday edition reached 600,000 in sales by 1898. Meanwhile, the *Herald*'s James Gordon Bennett Jr. maintained an authoritative, conservative, and even-handed tone for his paper even though his father had pioneered the effort to increase the popular appeal of newspapers during his tenure. Subscribing to a morning daily increased one's status, but many readers supplemented them with more interesting afternoon tabloids.

The growing conflict in Cuba, which began in earnest in 1895, was a common topic for these and other New York papers, including the *Times, Evening Post, Telegram,* and *Tribune*. After Captain-General Valeriano Weyler y Nicolau's appointment as governor-general in Cuba in 1896, Spanish atrocities—real and invented—became a mainstay for the New York press. Horatio Rubens, legal counsel for the Cuban Junta, regularly hosted a group of more than 40 different reporters, informally called the Peanut Club because of the snacks he provided. He also gave the reporters handouts emphasizing Cuban victories and Spanish wickedness that the newsmen accepted at face value and used extensively in their articles.

The papers also spent a great deal of money putting people and other assets in place to cover the more interesting aspects of the growing conflict. The *World, Herald, Sun,* and *Journal* each had between 5 and 20 permanent correspondents in Cuba. Many of them were experienced war reporters such as James Creelman, Edward Marshall, and Murat Halstead. Others, such as Frank Norris, John Fox, and Stephen Bonsal, were primarily authors. Newspapers also retained noted artists, including R. F. Zogbaum, W. A. Rogers, and John T. McCutcheon. Hearst hired a duo made up of celebrity novelist Richard Harding Davis and artist Frederic Remington and sent them to the island. When Remington asked to come home because he believed that there would be no war, Hearst reportedly told him to provide the sketches and he (Hearst) would provide the war. Davis actually got permission to travel in the countryside and visited one of the Spanish fortified trenches, called a trocha, and wrote a moving story called "The Death of Rodriguez" about the execution of a young Cuban farmer by a Spanish firing squad. Davis also wrote a provocative account of how several young Cuban women who supported the insurgency were strip-searched three times before being sent into exile. However, he omitted the fact that the searches had been conducted in private by female authorities. The drawing that accompanied the article featured leering Spanish soldiers conducting the search.

Hearst sent correspondent Karl Decker to rescue Evangelina Cisneros, daughter of famed Cuban revolutionary Salvador Cisneros Betancourt, who was imprisoned for allegedly helping organize an assassination attempt on the military governor of Cuba's Isle of Pines. The rescue, the stuff of a Hollywood movie, was trumpeted with great fanfare in the United States. Acclaimed American

than any of its contemporaries. The first two pages displayed a dense text of death notices and similar announcements surrounded by personal ads and commercial advertisements. News, especially sensational local stories, appeared in the next portion of the paper, which was heavily illustrated. Unsigned editorials usually appeared on page 8. Remaining pages were illustrated and contained shipping notices, sports, interviews, reprints from other papers, political cartoons, society pages, weather, and financial information.

Papers in other cities routinely reprinted articles from the *Herald,* but its position weakened after Joseph Pulitzer took over the rival *World* in 1893. Within two years, the rival paper's Sunday edition was the most popular. Sunday editions were quadruple the size of an average weekday edition and were always more widely read. Morrill Goddard, head of the *World*'s Sunday staff, included several pages of news and editorial but also created large page spreads about sordid topics to attract readers' attention. Regular features related advice for relationships, happenings in high society, and profiles of popular sports topics. Another source of the paper's success was the eight-page comic section that included the famous "Yellow Kid" strip among four colored pages. This helped to coin the term "yellow press."

William Randolph Hearst's acquisition of the *Journal* in 1895 led to a famous circulation war in which both the *World* and the *Journal* novelist Stephen Crane also spent time with the Cuban rebels and reported on their point of view.

Most American reporters stayed in Havana, where they interviewed Weyler or the American consul general, Fitzhugh Lee. Many reporters had low standards for journalistic integrity and cared more about interesting copy than accuracy. For instance, men who never left Havana often submitted alleged eyewitness reports of action in the countryside. Those who ventured forth into rural areas often related the revolutionaries' side of the conflict because the most lurid, and therefore attractive, stories involved the mistreatment of Cubans. Common topics included imprisonment in horrid conditions, brutal executions, and mistreatment in the *reconcentrado* (reconcentration) camps. The Spanish authorities required journalists to submit their dispatches to a military censor, who often drastically revised the copy.

Both the American public and the papers had generally negative attitudes toward Spain that were fed by the yellow press. Hearst disliked the Spanish monarchy and was genuinely sympathetic to the Cubans, and his paper reflected his views. Editorials and political cartoons critical of Spain were actually common in all the leading papers for three years leading up to the Spanish-American War, however. The *Herald*'s choice of news stories promoted war sentiments, but unlike the other three papers with reporters in Cuba, it did not promote war in its editorials because victory was not assured, the U.S. military was not adequately prepared, and the war would increase costs for the government. The *Herald* even urged restraint in the wake of the sinking of the U.S. battleship *Maine* in February 1898.

Although other papers such as the *Evening Post* and the *Tribune* also avoided condemning Spain, the two leading yellow journalism papers seized on the opportunity to exploit the explosion. The *Journal* immediately blamed Spain and repeatedly attacked President William McKinley in editorials and political cartoons for his non-interventionist policy, while the *World* claimed that it had information that Spain had perpetrated the act. Newspapers also readily acted as a venue for the expression of policy makers' opinions. Senator William E. Chandler, Republican from New Hampshire, told a newspaper publisher that the McKinley administration was not "militaristic" enough in its policies toward Spain.

When the war did come in April 1898, reporters had good access to Cuba during hostilities. Eighty-nine correspondents rode aboard various vessels in the invasion fleet that carried troops to Cuba. *Herald* correspondents learned of the conflicting priorities of the U.S. Army and the U.S. Navy regarding how to best put pressure on the defenders of Santiago de Cuba and made the interservice rivalry public. Newspaper tugs accompanied various naval squadrons and made runs back and forth between Cuba and Key West to send cables. Several correspondents were employed by the military to make contact with Cuban insurgents and establish lines of communication. Some reporters even participated in combat. James Creelman of the *Journal* led an attack on a small fort. One group of newsmen followed American soldiers through the surf during an assault near Abolitas Point despite the proximity of the firefight.

The Spanish-American War had a dramatic impact on the newspaper business. The tension in Cuba and the subsequent war provided a steady stream of content for its pages. Readership increased as the crisis deepened. Daily circulation for the *World* surpassed the 1 million mark during the war, and the *Journal* had almost 1.5 million readers at one point, while about a half million read the *Herald*. Pulitzer, who had military experience, backed away from a jingoistic approach during the war and began to advocate for an early end to the hostilities. Even postwar activities stimulated the industry as papers ran exposés decrying various examples of incompetence and inefficiency in the Cuba Campaign and the various camps in the United States.

For their part, newspapers in the Spanish-American War left a legacy all their own. Although less than a third of the papers in New York City were yellow presses at the time, a sensationalist brand of journalism remained for 20 years and persists in some ways today. In their quest to capture the public's attention, they exposed much of the gritty reality of city life and thus created an awareness that laid the foundation for Progressivism, which flourished from 1900 to 1920 or so. They also pioneered investigative journalism techniques that have allowed newspapers to promote democracy by exposing abuses of government power. However, the traditional view that the yellow press played a large role in creating war with Spain has lost much of its popularity because the papers that advocated the most drastic action were not located in New York, and there is little evidence that the yellow press unduly influenced policy makers.

MATTHEW J. KROGMAN

See also

Artists and Illustrators; Bennett, James Gordon, Jr.; Chandler, William Eaton; Cosio y Cisneros, Evangelina; Crane, Stephen; Creelman, James; Cuban Junta; Davis, Richard Harding; Hearst, William Randolph; Jingoism; Journalism; Lee, Fitzhugh; Peanut Club; Progressivism; Propaganda; Pulitzer, Joseph; Remington, Frederic Sackrider; Trocha; Weyler y Nicolau, Valeriano; Yellow Journalism

Further Reading

Bouvier, Virginia M. "Imaging a Nation: U.S. Political Cartoons and the War of 1898." In *Whose America? The War of 1898 and the Battles to Define the Nation,* edited by Virginia M. Bouvier, 91–122. Westport, CT: Praeger, 2001.
Mott, Frank Luther. *American Journalism, A History: 1690–1960.* New York: Macmillan, 1962.
O'Toole, G. J. A. *The Spanish War: An American Epic, 1898.* New York: Norton, 1984.
Procter, Ben. *William Randolph Hearst.* 2 vols. New York: Oxford University Press USA, 1998, 2007.
Stevens, John D. *Sensationalism and the New York Press.* New York: Columbia University Press, 1991.

Nipe Bay

Large bay located on Cuba's northern coast. Nipe Bay is situated in the Holguín Province at the eastern end of the island, about 50 miles to the north of Santiago de Cuba. It is a well-sheltered inlet with a narrows linking it with the open sea. The narrows are approximately 14 miles long and 8 miles wide. A mainly forested mountain range known as the Sierra de Micaro frames part of the area, beyond which lay fertile agricultural lands. In October 1492, Christopher Columbus landed in the area near Nipe Bay.

During preliminary planning for the Spanish-American War, U.S. strategists at the Naval War College at Newport, Rhode Island, drew up a plan in which Nipe Bay was to play a key role. The plan was predicated on the anticipated movement of significant Spanish naval assets to Cuba at the beginning of the war. American warships would then proceed to Nipe Bay, capture and occupy it, and use it as a base from which they would engage Spanish vessels. Naval War College planners also envisioned using the area as a coaling station for U.S. ships, enabling them to engage Spanish ships or launch operations against other parts of Cuba or Puerto Rico. These plans were never implemented.

Nipe Bay was, however, the scene of a brief and relatively inconsequential naval engagement on July 21, 1898. As plans evolved for the Puerto Rico Campaign in the early summer of 1898, U.S. Army commanding general Major General Nelson A. Miles pinpointed Nipe Bay as a logical and natural site for a staging area for the island of Puerto Rico to the east of Cuba. On July 18, four U.S. naval vessels were ordered to Nipe Bay with the task of clearing the harbor mines there and taking control of the inlet. On July 21, the gunboats *Annapolis* and *Topeka* steamed into the narrows leading to Nipe Bay. They were accompanied by the newly commissioned armed steam yacht *Wasp* and the armed steam tug *Leyden.*

After a tense passage during which the four ships navigated by the mined part of the bay, the Americans spotted a Spanish gunboat at anchor. The *Wasp* opened fire first and was soon joined by the other U.S. warships. After a brief exchange of fire, the American vessels easily overwhelmed the antiquated Spanish gunboat *Don Jorge Juan,* which began to take on water. The Spanish crew scuttled the gunboat, which quickly sank. This marked the end of organized Spanish resistance in the area of Nipe Bay, and the Americans quickly went about the task of clearing the minefields there. The following day, July 22, the *Annapolis* steamed out of the bay and made for Puerto Rico, where it supported the U.S. Army's capture of Ponce, Puerto Rico, on July 30. On July 23, the *Wasp* also departed the bay for Puerto Rico, followed by the remaining two ships. In the end, Nipe Bay was never used as a staging area, which was shifted to Guantánamo Bay, located farther to the east.

Paul G. Pierpaoli Jr.

See also

Miles, Nelson Appleton; Naval Strategy, Spanish; Naval Strategy, U.S.; Puerto Rico Campaign

Further Reading

Marolda, Edward J., ed. *Theodore Roosevelt, the U.S. Navy, and the Spanish American War.* New York: Palgrave, 2001.
Trask, David F. *The War with Spain in 1898.* Lincoln: University of Nebraska Press, 1996.

North Atlantic Squadron

U.S. Navy squadron. Redesignated the North Atlantic Fleet in June 1898, the North Atlantic Squadron was one of five operational units of the U.S. Navy. When the Spanish-American War began in April 1898, the squadron was assigned the mission of blockading Cuban and Puerto Rican ports and neutralizing Spanish naval forces in the Caribbean Sea.

In January 1898, the Navy Department ordered the North Atlantic Squadron, commanded by Rear Admiral Montgomery Sicard, to assemble at the navy base at Key West, Florida, for winter maneuvers. The squadron was comprised of the armored cruiser *New York* (flagship); the battleships *Iowa, Indiana, Maine, Massachusetts,* and *Texas;* the cruisers *Detroit* and *Montgomery;* and the torpedo boats *Cushing, Dupont,* and *Ericsson.* The deployment was also designed as a show of force to remind the Spanish government of U.S. naval might.

As tensions mounted between Cuban rebel forces and the Spanish Army in late 1897, U.S. consul general at Havana Fitzhugh Lee requested that the U.S. Navy be ready to deploy a force there to protect American interests should it become necessary. Captain Charles D. Sigsbee of the *Maine* received orders to remain in constant communication with Lee and to steam to Havana if so requested. On January 24, 1898, the *Maine* was indeed ordered to Havana.

With the sinking of the *Maine* at Havana Harbor on February 15, 1898, the North Atlantic Squadron went on heightened alert with the assignment in the event of war with Spain of meeting and defeating any Spanish warships in the Caribbean to allow the safe passage of U.S. ground forces to these islands and of blockading Cuban and Puerto Rican ports to prevent the reinforcement of Spanish ground forces.

In mid-April, newly promoted Rear Admiral William T. Sampson of the squadron flagship *Iowa* replaced the ailing Sicard as squadron commander and immediately commenced preparation for the blockades. The initial cordon would isolate the ports of Cuba and the friendly strongholds along the western half of Cuba's northern coast, including Havana, Matanzas, and Mariel, as well as the southern port of Cienfuegos with a strategic railroad line.

Throughout the war, the Navy Department regularly allocated more ships, allowing Sampson to expand the blockade. Sampson, however, clashed with the army leadership, especially V Corps commander Major General William R. Shafter, in fashioning strategy and providing tactical support while deflecting pressure of Secretary of the Navy John D. Long to expand the blockade with less-than-sufficient means.

On May 10, the squadron included the armored cruiser *New York* (flagship); the battleships *Iowa, Massachusetts,* and *Indiana;* the monitors *Amphitrite, Puritan,* and *Terror;* the cruisers *Cincinnati, Detroit, Marblehead, Montgomery,* and *Vesuvius;* the torpedo boats *Cushing, Dupont, Ericsson, Foote, Porter,* and *Winslow;* the gunboats *Castine, Helena, Machias, Nashville, Newport, Wilmington,* and *Vicksburg;* the dispatch boats *Dolphin* and *Samoset;* the armed tug *Leyden;* and the supply steamer *Fern.*

Return of Rear Admiral William T. Sampson's fleet from Cuba to New York Harbor in August 1898, as seen from the battleship *Oregon*. (Naval Historical Center)

While Sampson strengthened the squadron's blockade of northwestern Cuba and Cienfuegos and continued to add ships, Spanish rear admiral Pascual Cervera y Topete and his naval forces slipped into the port of Santiago de Cuba undetected on May 19. After a series of miscommunications between Sampson and Flying Squadron captain Winfield S. Schley during the subsequent 10 days, Cervera and his squadron were contained in the southern Cuban port until their doomed July 3 sortie.

On June 20, ships of the North Atlantic Squadron escorted General Shafter's V Corps to Cuba's southern coast. From June 22 to June 26, Shafter's forces landed at Daiquirí and Siboney, and the North Atlantic Squadron provided naval artillery cover fire for the successful landings. The squadron also transferred Cuban rebel forces from Aserraderos to Siboney and subsequently brought naval artillery power to bear for the attacks on Santiago de Cuba, which began on July 1. In addition to these duties, Sampson planned and helped execute the sinking of the collier *Merrimac* in the harbor channel at Santiago de Cuba to block Cervera's exit. This mission was unsuccessful.

With Cervera bottled up at Santiago de Cuba, the Navy Department reorganized U.S. naval forces to strengthen Sampson's command. On June 21, the North Atlantic Squadron became the North Atlantic Fleet, which was divided into the First and Second North Atlantic Squadrons, initially commanded by Captains John C. Watson and Winfield S. Schley, respectively, with Sampson leading all operations of the fleet.

In the wake of U.S. military successes in the area and with the absence of Sampson, who was en route from Santiago de Cuba to confer with Shafter, Cervera decided to pick up anchor and sortie his squadron out of the harbor at Santiago de Cuba at 9:35 a.m. on July 3, 1898. Within four hours, the Spanish squadron was destroyed, giving the U.S. Navy uncontested control of the Caribbean.

In addition to its activities in Cuba, the North Atlantic Squadron also conducted operations in Puerto Rico. Searching for Cervera's forces early in the conflict, Sampson briefly bombarded San Juan on May 12. In late July, several warships of Sampson's force escorted and supported Major General Nelson A. Miles's I Corps expedition force to Puerto Rico. Still other ships were being prepared to conduct an attack on the Spanish mainland under the auspices of the Eastern Squadron. The North Atlantic Fleet entered New York City Harbor on August 20, 1898, to a tumultuous reception. The fleet was dissolved in 1906 with the establishment of the U.S. Atlantic Fleet.

MARK MOLLAN AND ARTHUR STEINBERG

See also

Cervera y Topete, Pascual; Cuba, U.S. Naval Blockade of; V Corps; I Corps; Flying Squadron; Lee, Fitzhugh; Long, John Davis; *Maine,* USS; *Merrimac,* USS; Miles, Nelson Appleton; Puerto Rico Campaign; Sampson, William Thomas; Santiago de Cuba, Battle of; Santiago de Cuba Land Campaign; Schley, Winfield Scott; Shafter, William Rufus; Sicard, Montgomery; Sigsbee, Charles Dwight; Watson, John Crittenden

Further Reading

Chadwick, French Ensor. *The Relations of the United States and Spain V1: The Spanish-American War.* Reprint ed. Kila, MT: Kessinger, 2007.

Feuer, A. B. *The Spanish-American War at Sea: Naval Action in the Atlantic.* Westport, CT: Praeger, 1995.

Hendrickson, Kenneth E., Jr. *The Spanish-American War.* Westport, CT: Greenwood, 2003.

Trask, David F. *The War with Spain in 1898.* Lincoln: University of Nebraska Press, 1996.

Northern Patrol Squadron

U.S. Navy squadron formed just prior to the Spanish-American War to patrol the East Coast of the United States from Delaware north to Maine. The Northern Patrol Squadron was created principally to allay public fears of a Spanish naval assault against the northeastern United States. In early 1898, as the threat of war between the United States and Spain increased, the U.S. Navy took steps to concentrate its forces to protect the United States against Spanish attacks while also carrying out offensive operations. This included recalling overseas squadrons and, when the two nations finally declared war on each other in late April, establishing new squadrons in home waters.

With many Americans along the Atlantic coast expressing fears of a potential Spanish naval attack, politicians and other public figures called on the navy to provide protection. Although navy officials considered a Spanish attack on the northeastern United States extremely unlikely, it did authorize the creation of a small squadron to assuage these concerns.

Commodore John A. Howell, commander of the recently recalled European Squadron, now assumed command of the Northern Patrol Squadron. He was charged with patrolling the East Coast

U.S. Navy protected cruiser *San Francisco* patrolled the East Coast of the United States during the Spanish-American War as the flagship of the Northern Patrol Squadron. (*Photographic History of the Spanish-American War,* 1898)

of the United States from the Delaware Capes to Bar Harbor, Maine, and assumed command on April 20, 1898. His squadron included the cruiser *San Francisco* (flagship) and the converted cruisers *Prairie, Dixie, Yankee,* and *Yosemite.* These ships, some of which did not finish their conversions until early May, were primarily manned by members of the Naval Militia, which had been mobilized to augment the regular navy. In May 1898, the navy added the cruiser *Columbia* and the converted cruisers *Badger* and *Southery* to Howell's command. Meanwhile, the *Yankee* was detached on May 29, the *Yosemite* on May 30, and the *Dixie* on June 13, with all three vessels reassigned to duty off the coast of Cuba under the command of Rear Admiral William T. Sampson. The cruiser *Minneapolis* was administratively attached to the Northern Patrol Squadron on June 9 but remained at Newport News, Virginia, to guard battleships under construction.

As expected, the Northern Patrol Squadron did not encounter any Spanish warships during its patrols, and by the end of June the events of the war allowed the navy to discontinue its operations. On June 25, 1898, with the only potential Spanish threat coming from Rear Admiral Pascual Cervera y Topete's squadron blockaded by Sampson at Santiago de Cuba, Howell was ordered to take the remaining ships of the Northern Patrol Squadron to Key West, Florida, for duty in the blockade of Cuba. Upon arriving there on July 1, he was designated the commander of the 1st Squadron of the North Atlantic Fleet, and the Northern Patrol Squadron passed out of existence.

STEPHEN SVONAVEC

See also

Cervera y Topete, Pascual; Cuba, U.S. Naval Blockade of; Howell, John Adams; Militia, Naval; North Atlantic Squadron; Sampson, William Thomas; United States Navy

Further Reading

Blow, Michael. *A Ship to Remember: The Maine and the Spanish-American War.* New York: Morrow, 1992.

Chadwick, French Ensor. *The Relations of the United States and Spain V1: The Spanish-American War.* Reprint ed. Kila, MT: Kessinger, 2007.

Feuer, A. B. *The Spanish-American War at Sea: Naval Action in the Atlantic.* Westport, CT: Praeger, 1995.

Trask, David F. *The War with Spain in 1898.* Lincoln: University of Nebraska Press, 1996.

Nuevitas, Cuba

Port city located along Cuba's northern coast in the Camagüey Province. Nuevitas is situated south-southeast of Havana and almost due north of Santiago de Cuba. The city was founded in 1775 but was relocated to its current locale in 1828. On his first trip to the New World in 1492, Christopher Columbus wrote about the area around present-day Nuevitas. By the end of the 19th century, Nuevitas had become the location of light industry and, because of its ample port facilities, served as an embarkation point for Cuban

agricultural products. Camagüey Province, Cuba's largest province, was home to rich agricultural interests, including sugarcane and sugar by-products.

Nuevitas is situated on the Guincho Peninsula and is protected by a large harbor that is capable of accommodating large ocean-going vessels. The city's industrial base grew in the 20th century, as did its ports. By the 1920s, in fact, it boasted a main port and two ancillary ones. It was well served by railroads and highways as well. Located not far from Nuevitas is La Playa Santa Lucia (Saint Lucia Beach), a famous seaside playground among Cubans for several generations.

Nuevitas was perhaps most famous for a failed filibustering expedition launched by Irish-born John "Dynamite Johnny" O'Brien, a renowned adventurer, soldier of fortune, sometime pirate, and sea captain. He earned his name after he had transported dynamite in the hold of his ship to Panamanian rebels in 1888. Never one to turn down an adventure much less publicity, he sailed for Cuba in the autumn of 1896 with supplies for the Cuban rebels. He also had aboard ship Ralph Paine, a newspaper reporter dispatched by publishing magnate William Randolph Hearst. Paine had been given the assignment of delivering a jeweled saber to Cuban rebel leader and military commanding general Máximo Gómez, a personal gift from Hearst. Hearst believed that reports from a filibustering excursion would make good copy and sell more newspapers. He also hoped to play up the Cuban struggle against Spanish colonial rule during the Cuban War of Independence (1895–1898).

O'Brien's party arrived in the *Three Friends* off the coast of Nuevitas on December 19, 1896. As the party made preparations to go ashore, it was spotted by a Spanish gunboat. Without hesitation, O'Brien put a Hotchkiss gun to work and kept the gunboat at bay. O'Brien's ship managed to escape, but the expedition was canceled. Gómez did not receive his saber until after the Spanish-American War, but the affair was vintage O'Brien and also vintage yellow journalism. Paine was later apprehended and briefly held by U.S. authorities for violating the U.S. neutrality law. As he had done in the past, O'Brien eluded seizure or prosecution.

Before the Spanish-American War began, U.S. Army commanding general Major General Nelson A. Miles planned to use Nuevitas as a staging area for an attack on Havana. When the military focus changed from Havana to Santiago de Cuba, however, that plan changed, and Nuevitas saw no action during the brief conflict.

PAUL G. PIERPAOLI JR.

See also

Filibuster; Gómez y Báez, Máximo; Hearst, William Randolph; Miles, Nelson Appleton; Yellow Journalism

Further Reading

O'Toole, G. J. A. *The Spanish War: An American Epic, 1898.* New York: Norton, 1984.

Trask, David F. *The War with Spain in 1898.* Lincoln: University of Nebraska Press, 1996.

O

O'Brien, John
Birth Date: April 20, 1837
Death Date: June 21, 1917

Leader of filibuster expeditions to Cuba prior to the Spanish-American War. John O'Brien was born in New York City on April 20, 1837. Learning to sail at age 13, he became a cook aboard a fishing boat without his family's knowledge. After being returned to his family, he was given a formal seaman's apprenticeship at the city's Thom School. Much of his life—especially his early years—is surrounded by some degree of mystery. He claimed to have served during the American Civil War as an officer on the *Illinois,* a vessel chartered by the U.S. Navy for the purpose of ramming the Confederate ironclad *Virginia,* although no attempt was ever made.

O'Brien's first filibuster expedition occurred during the Civil War when he commanded the schooner *Deer* on an expedition to Matamoros, Mexico, hauling arms bound for the Confederacy. He replaced the expedition's commander and carried out the mission, being well paid for his work. After the war, O'Brien became licensed as a river pilot in New York, guiding ships through the East River's dangerous Hell's Gate section.

In the mid-1880s, O'Brien commanded a number of filibuster expeditions, including several in support of Marco Aurelio Soto, former president of Honduras. However, it was during an 1888 filibuster mission that he gained his "Dynamite Johnny" nickname by transporting 50 tons of the explosives—bound for Cuban expatriate revolutionaries—from New York to Colon, Panama.

In 1896, O'Brien was contacted by supporters of the year-old Cuban War of Independence. His initial Cuban filibuster cargo included thousands of rifles, carbines, and pistols; a field gun; and 1,000 pounds of dynamite. However, the most important cargo was a passenger, Cuban rebel General Calixto García y Iñiguez, who was returning to the island after exile in Spain. Avoiding nearby Spanish warships, O'Brien landed the supplies and the general safely in Cuba. On his return to the United States, O'Brien was indicted as a filibuster and arms smuggler, but no formal action was taken against him.

These expeditions were the first of many carried out by O'Brien to supply the Cuban rebellion. Using a number of vessels such as the *Three Friends* and *Dauntless,* he routinely eluded U.S. Revenue Cutters, naval vessels, and Secret Service agents in the United States as well as Spanish naval and land forces in Cuba. Between 1895 and 1898, he made as many as 40 landings in Cuba. One of the best documented occurred in 1896. Among those accompanying O'Brien was reporter Ralph Paine. Paine described O'Brien's crew using a field gun it was transporting against a pursuing Spanish gunboat. A chance shot to the Spanish ship's pilot house put it out of action. O'Brien also transported to Cuba mercenary Frederick Funston, who later gained fame in the Philippines. Once, after having been publicly threatened by Cuban governor-general Valeriano Weyler y Nicolau, O'Brien claimed to have landed a shipment of supplies just a mile and a half from Havana's Morro Castle.

On February 15, 1898, the night that the U.S. battleship *Maine* was sunk in Havana Harbor, O'Brien was landing supplies between Matanzas and Neuvitas. Following the war, he became a harbor pilot in Havana. On February 13, 1912, the aft portion of the *Maine* was refloated and ceremoniously sunk in deep water. O'Brien was its pilot and sole passenger on the voyage, while the hulk was towed by four tugs. When a boarding party began scuttling the ship, O'Brien was the last man to depart.

Eventually, O'Brien returned to New York City for medical treatment. On his 80th birthday, he was honored with a reception by the

Dynamite Johnny O'Brien (indicated by the arrow) led filibuster expeditions to Cuba between 1895 and 1898 to support the revolutionaries there prior to the Spanish-American War. (Ralph D. Paine, *Roads of Adventure*, 1922)

Cuban government. O'Brien died shortly afterward on June 21, 1917, in New York City, revered as a hero by the Cuban people.

PATRICK MCSHERRY

See also

Cuban War of Independence; Filibuster; Funston, Frederick; García y Iñiguez, Calixto; *Maine*, USS; Nuevitas, Cuba; Weyler y Nicolau, Valeriano

Further Reading

Blow, Michael. *A Ship to Remember: The Maine and the Spanish-American War.* New York: Morrow, 1992.

Garcia, José Antonio Quintana. "John Dynamite–The Adventures of a Filibuster." *Irish Migration Studies in Latin America* 5 (March 2007): 31–34.

O'Toole, G. J. A. *The Spanish War: An American Epic, 1898.* New York: Norton, 1984.

Paine, Ralph D. *Roads of Adventure.* New York: Houghton Mifflin, 1922.

Smith, Horace. *A Captain Unafraid: The Strange Adventures of Dynamite Johnny O'Brien.* New York: Harper and Brothers, 1912.

O'Donnell y Abréu, Carlos Manuel

Birth Date: July 1, 1834
Death Date: February 9, 1903

Spanish politician and foreign minister prior to the Spanish-American War who sought to convince other European nations that U.S. intervention in the Cuban War of Independence (1895–1898) would threaten the national interests of all European nations. Descended from a noble Irish family that had lived for generations in Spain, Carlos Manuel O'Donnell y Abréu was born in Murcia, Spain, on July 1, 1834. He inherited his aristocratic title, Second Duke of Tetuán, from his uncle Leopoldo O'Donnell y Jorris, who had been awarded his title by Queen Isabella II of Spain after he successfully led the Spanish invasion of Morocco at the Battle of Tetuán in 1860. After joining the military, the younger O'Donnell served in the Philippines in 1854 and Italy in 1859. He accompanied his uncle on the Morocco Campaign and took part in the Battle of Tetuán, where he was wounded. Because of his valor in that battle, Queen Isabella II awarded him the Cruz de San Fernando (Cross of Saint Ferdinand).

O'Donnell began his political career in 1863 when he was elected to the Spanish Cortes (parliament) as a deputy in October 1863. A member of the Union Liberal, a political party formed by his uncle to cross the traditional Progressista, Moderado, and Carlist factions, O'Donnell represented Valladolid for three years. While in parliament, he advocated laissez-faire politics and governmental policies. He also supported the September Revolution of 1868 that sent Queen Isabella II into exile. He was subsequently reelected in 1869 and 1872 to represent Valladolid. He supported the restoration of the Bourbon monarchy in 1875, which greatly enhanced his political career. He then served in the Spanish Senate, representing the province of Castellón de la Plana, and held ambassadorial posts in Lisbon, Vienna, and Brussels. He served as the Spanish foreign minister on four occasions: May 16, 1879, to December 7, 1879; June 5, 1890, to December 11, 1892; March 23, 1895, to January 19, 1896; and March 5, 1896, to October 4, 1897.

During his third and fourth tenures as foreign minister, O'Donnell was preoccupied with the revolutionary movement in Cuba. He was convinced that the failure of Spain to either crush the Cuban revolutionary movement or grant significant autonomy to the Cuban revolutionaries would lead to the intervention of the United States in the conflict. In early 1896, Prime Minister Antonio Cánovas del Castillo instructed O'Donnell to solicit European support against the eventuality of U.S. intervention in Cuba. Thus, in the summer of 1896, O'Donnell drafted a memorandum calling for joint European action against possible American intervention in the Cuban crisis.

In the memorandum, O'Donnell argued that U.S. intervention in Cuba might well result in the loss of Cuba and the overthrow of the Spanish monarchy, which could set off a chain reaction that could destabilize or overthrow other European monarchies. In addition, he argued that American attempts to enforce the 1823 Monroe Doctrine in the Caribbean would threaten other European colonies in the Caribbean. He also wanted the U.S. government to promise to restrict the activities of Cuban revolutionaries in the United States. Although all of the major European ambassadors in Madrid initially viewed the secret memorandum favorably, in August 1896 British ambassador to Spain Henry Drummond Wolff informed U.S. ambassador to Spain Hannis Taylor of the memorandum and its contents. Taylor then told O'Donnell that once he leaked the Spanish plot to the press, the Grover Cleveland administration would consider the document a hostile act. O'Donnell thus jettisoned his plan.

Following the return to power of Prime Minister Práxedes Mateo Sagasta in 1897, O'Donnell left government service. He died on Madrid on February 9, 1903.

Michael R. Hall

See also

Cánovas del Castillo y Vallejo, Antonio; Cleveland, Stephen Grover; Cuban War of Independence; Sagasta, Práxedes Mateo; Spain

Further Reading

Bleiberg, Germán, et al. *Diccionario de Historia de España* [Dictionary of Spanish History]. Madrid: Alianza Editorial, 1979.

O'Toole, G. J. A. *The Spanish War: An American Epic, 1898*. New York: Norton, 1984.

Wolff, Henry Drummond. *Rambling Recollections*. London: MacMillan, 1908.

Olney, Richard
Birth Date: September 15, 1835
Death Date: April 8, 1917

Lawyer, politician, attorney general of the United States (1893–1895), and U.S. secretary of state (1895–1897). Born into a promi-

Richard Olney was attorney general of the United States during 1893–1895 and secretary of state during 1895–1897, in which position he proved to be an effective and aggressive spokesperson for U.S. interests. (Library of Congress)

nent, wealthy family in Oxford, Massachusetts, on September 15, 1835, Richard Olney enrolled at Brown University in Providence, Rhode Island, graduating with an undergraduate degree in 1856. Two years later, he earned a law degree from Harvard University. In 1859, he was admitted to the bar and began the practice of law in Boston. Owing to his impeccable credentials and keen legal mind, he soon became a sought-after attorney.

A nominal Democrat, Olney tried his hand at politics briefly when he served in the Massachusetts House of Representatives from 1873 to 1874. Realizing that elective office was not to his liking and that he could make far more money as a full-time attorney, he returned to the practice of law in Boston when his term of office expired.

In early 1893, President-elect Grover Cleveland tapped Olney to be his attorney general. The appointment came as a surprise, particularly to Democratic Party stalwarts, because Olney had never been in the national public arena. Cleveland, however, selected Olney chiefly because of his impressive legal career rather than on political criteria alone. Olney was sworn into office in March 1893. Cleveland had no sooner taken office when a Wall Street panic and deep economic depression set in, the worst to that point in the nation's history. The resultant economic uncertainty precipitated considerable labor unrest and agitation as laborers lost their jobs or saw their wages cut as prices increased.

Olney soon found himself in the middle of one of the country's biggest management-labor showdowns when some 4,000 workers of the Pullman Palace Car Company, a manufacturer of passenger railway cars, staged a strike in Chicago in May 1894. Before long, the strikers had blocked all rail traffic west of Chicago. The strike grew when the American Railway Union, led by Eugene V. Debs, refused to work on trains carrying Pullman cars. The strike continued into June and brought the U.S. economy—already struggling amid a depression—to a virtual halt. Because Chicago was the nation's largest rail hub, the strike meant that few goods were getting through and that passenger traffic was virtually gridlocked. As the strike endured, property damage also increased (mainly to the railroads), as did sporadic violence.

Believing that the strike was placing the nation in peril by impeding commerce and the delivery of mail, Olney counseled the president to undertake stern measures. Olney ordered U.S. district attorneys in Chicago to obtain from federal courts writs of injunction that forbade the strikers from engaging in violence or destruction of property. This was the first time the federal government intervened in a strike using injunctions, which would come to be used by the government many times in the future. When the strikers refused to go back to work or unblock rail lines, Olney insisted that Cleveland authorize the use of troops to break the strike by force. After a fire on July 5 that was blamed on strikers, Olney received authorization to send in federal troops. U.S. marshals and 2,000 army troops under commanding general Major General Nelson A. Miles finally broke up the protests, the first time that federal troops had been employed to stop a labor strike.

When Secretary of State Walter Q. Gresham died in office, Cleveland named Olney to replace him, and he took the oath of office on June 10, 1895. As secretary of state, Olney, who had no experience in diplomatic affairs, turned out to be an effective and aggressive spokesman for U.S. interests. Indeed, he played a key role in the First Venezuela Crisis (1895–1897), an impasse between the British government and that of Venezuela over the border between Venezuela and British Guiana. When the British refused to accept American arbitration of the dispute, Olney engaged British prime minister and foreign secretary Lord Salisbury in a lengthy letter exchange in which Olney expanded the scope of the 1823 Monroe Doctrine. In his strongest corollary, he asserted bluntly that the United States "is practically sovereign on this continent, and its fiat is law upon the subjects to which it confines its interposition." The crisis was eventually resolved despite rumors of war with Great Britain over the controversy. Olney's muscular stance with the British helped set the stage for the Roosevelt Corollary to the Monroe Doctrine enunciated by President Theodore Roosevelt in 1904.

Another of Olney's bold moves during his brief tenure at the State Department was to make all U.S. foreign diplomatic posts embassies. Until this time, American diplomatic posts abroad were only legations, which did not carry the same clout at embassies. This, he hoped, would elevate America's stature in the international arena. He also advocated a peaceful end to the fighting in Cuba between revolutionaries and Spanish regulars. He did not support an independent Cuba, but he did offer to mediate the dispute, an offer accepted by neither side.

Olney left office in 1897 at the end of Cleveland's term in office and returned to his law practice. Olney died in Boston, Massachusetts, on April 8, 1917.

PAUL G. PIERPAOLI JR.

See also

Cleveland, Stephen Grover; Economic Depression; Monroe Doctrine; Pullman Strike; Roosevelt, Theodore; Roosevelt Corollary; Venezuela Crisis, First

Further Reading

Eggert, Gerald G. *Richard Olney: Evolution of a Statesman.* University Park: Pennsylvania State University Press, 1974.
Graff, Henry F. *Grover Cleveland.* New York: Time Books, 2002.

O'Neill, William Owen
Birth Date: February 2, 1860
Death Date: July 1, 1898

U.S. lawyer, sheriff, politician, journalist, and organizer of Troop A of the 1st U.S. Volunteer Cavalry, the Arizona unit of the Rough Riders. William Owen O'Neill was born on February 2, 1860. His birthplace is disputed, although it is believed that it was either St. Louis or Washington, D.C. He was reared in Washington, D.C., and earned a law degree from the National Law School. Unwilling to lead the staid and sedentary life of a big-city attorney, in 1879 he left the capital city for a new life in the Arizona Territory. The following year, he decided to settle in Tombstone, a small mining town in southern Arizona renowned for its colorful characters and lawless atmosphere.

Once in Tombstone, O'Neill took a position as a reporter for the *Tombstone Epitaph.* At the time, a virtual war was being waged in the small town involving rival gangs and the local sheriff. On October 26, 1881, the infamous gunfight at the OK Corral occurred, a muchvaunted event about which O'Neill reported on firsthand. He had also been a friend of Wyatt and Morgan Earp, who had been involved in the gunfight.

In early 1882, O'Neill relocated to Prescott, Arizona, where he continued his career in journalism and founded his own newspaper, the *Hoof and Horn,* a trade paper for ranchers. Later, he joined the Arizona Grays, Prescott's local militia unit. O'Neill ultimately held the rank of captain in the outfit. It was in Prescott where he earned the nickname "Buckey" for his penchant of gambling big— and losing big—sometimes known as "bucking the tiger."

In 1887, O'Neill began serving as a judge for Yavapai County in central Arizona. The next year, he ran for the post of county sheriff and won. He reveled in his role of a western sheriff and by all accounts was a fair and effective enforcer of the law. Reportedly the

William Owen O'Neill, organizer of the Arizona unit of the 1st U.S. Volunteer Cavalry Regiment, known as the Rough Riders. (Library of Congress)

best shot in the entire county with his revolver, he formed a posse in 1889 that captured four armed robbers who had held up an Atlantic and Pacific Railroad train in Yavapai County.

Throughout his many careers, O'Neill had also taken a keen interest in the mining business. As an enterprising and fairly shrewd businessmen, he made a tidy sum in investments in copper and onyx mining. By the mid-1890s, he was serving as the mayor of Prescott, a post to which he had been unanimously elected. He also tried three times to win election as Arizona's territorial delegate to the U.S. House of Representatives, each time losing by a razor-thin margin.

In 1898, as tensions between Spain and the United States steadily increased, O'Neill, along with Alexander Brodie and James McClintock, began to assemble a cavalry unit that the men hoped would be comprised solely of Arizona cowboys and lawmen. Although the outfit had a hard time filling its ranks with cowboys alone, when the Spanish-American War broke out in April 1898, Theodore Roosevelt and others, having heard of O'Neill's efforts, decided to incorporate the Arizona contingent into their own cavalry unit. The result was the 1st United States Volunteer Cavalry Regiment, more commonly known as the Rough Riders. After it was mobilized at San Antonio, Texas, O'Neill was commissioned a captain in Troop A and became fast friends with Roosevelt, who saw in O'Neill the embodiment of the courageous and multitalented western frontiersman.

During the Rough Riders' landing at Daiquirí, Cuba, on June 22, 1898, two African American soldiers of the 10th Cavalry Regiment (Buffalo Soldiers) fell from the loading dock and were dragged down by their packs. Witnessing the accident and without a pause, O'Neill leapt into the water, with his uniform on and his officer's saber still attached to his belt, to save the two men. Although he was ultimately unsuccessful in his effort, the event astounded his men. Two days later, O'Neill led his men ably at the Battle of Las Guásimas, helping to capture a contingent of Spanish soldiers there.

On July 1, 1898, during the Battle of San Juan Hill, the Rough Riders had been stationed at the base of Kettle Hill, a somewhat smaller hill than San Juan Hill and located immediately adjacent to it. Before the unit could charge the hill, it came under intense fire from Spanish soldiers who were still positioned at the top of Kettle Hill. At approximately 10:00 a.m., after joking with a subordinate that the Spanish could make no bullet capable of killing him, O'Neill was shot through the mouth; the bullet exited the back of his head, killing him instantly. O'Neill was celebrated as one of the great American heroes of the Spanish-American War.

PAUL G. PIERPAOLI

See also

Las Guásimas, Battle of; Roosevelt, Theodore; Rough Riders; San Juan Heights, Battle of

Further Reading

Samuels, Peggy, and Harold Samuels. *Teddy Roosevelt at San Juan: The Making of a President.* College Station: Texas A&M University Press, 1997.

Walker, Dale L. *The Boys of '98: Theodore Roosevelt and the Rough Riders.* New York: Forge, 1999.

———. *Death Was the Black Horse: The Story of Rough Rider Buckey O'Neill.* Austin, TX: Madrona, 1975.

Open Door Policy

A foreign policy framework based largely on commerce and trade that stipulates that all nations should have equal trade and commercial opportunities in a given area. Although the genesis of the Open Door Policy can be traced back to the mid-19th century, it gained renewed interest at the turn of the 20th century and is most associated with U.S. secretary of state John Hay vis-á-vis the great-power rivalry in China.

The British first conceptualized and enunciated an open door policy in the aftermath of the First Opium War (1839–1843), a conflict fought largely over issues of trading rights. In a series of treaties negotiated between the British government and Chinese officials, both sides agreed—in principle at least—that China should be open to trade and that the Chinese government should not promulgate policies antithetical to that goal. This era was the commencement of Western imperial interests in China, and Great Britain was determined to keep the fabled China Market open to Western interests. During the 1885 Berlin Conference, European leaders tacitly recognized the principle of the open door when they concluded that no African colonial power should erect trade barriers in the Congo. In retrospect, the conference did little to suppress the mad dash for African colonies, but it did institute measures to prevent great-power economic rivalry in the region.

The American enunciation of the Open Door Policy came chiefly as a result of the Spanish-American War and the U.S. annexation of the Philippines and Guam, which for the first time made the United States an East Asian colonial power. Several factors compelled the William McKinley administration to embrace the Open Door Policy. First, as imperial competition and economic rivalry in China heated up, American policy makers feared that a China divided into competing spheres of influence would be disastrous for U.S. territorial and colonial interests in the Far East. Second, many U.S. policy makers viewed the opening of markets in China as key to American economic prosperity, although the power of the China Market in this era was greatly exaggerated. Third, even though the United States had a credible naval deterrent in the Western Hemisphere, it did not have the ability to effectively project its military power in Asia at the turn of the century. Thus, the Open Door Policy was seen as a substitute for U.S. military hegemony in China.

Beginning in September 1899, Secretary of State Hay sent a series of diplomatic dispatches (subsequently called the Open Door Notes) to the major colonial powers: Great Britain, France, Germany, Russia, Italy, and Japan. The thrust of his dispatches was a plea that all nations have equal access to trade and commerce in China. The British, who had already applied the Open Door Policy in their own affairs, affirmed their commitment to the policy in China. The five other nations, however, were studiously noncommittal to the proposal. In November 1899, the Boxer Rebellion began in China as Chinese nationalists sought to rid the country of foreigners and foreign influences. The unrest alarmed nations that had significant interests in China, especially since the moribund Qing dynasty was all but powerless to stop the rebellion. The unrest seemed poised to spur even more imperial rivalry in China as the Japanese and European nations threatened to tighten their grip on the country. All of this prompted Hay to send another letter to the six nations in July 1900. In it he implored all nations involved to respect China's territorial integrity and to keep trade there open and unfettered. This time, the United States received generally supportive—although still vague—replies to Hay's initiative. Be that as it may, the McKinley administration seized on this apparent success and declared that all of the involved powers had agreed—in principle—to maintaining an open door in China. As it turned out, this was mere rhetorical window dressing, because most of the major imperial powers continued to erect miniature empires in China. For the United States, at least, the Open Door Policy guided U.S. policy toward China for nearly 50 years, until the communists led by Mao Zedong took power there in the autumn of 1949. Interestingly enough, the idea of an American commitment to a free and open China for many years fed the perception that the Americans had a special relationship with the Chinese.

Although the Open Door Policy was something of an illusion, McKinley's successor, Theodore Roosevelt, invoked it in 1902 upon Russian usurpations in Manchuria. After the 1904–1905 Russo-Japanese War, American and Japanese officials promised mutual cooperation in Manchuria. Again invoking the Open Door Policy in 1909, the United States sponsored a multinational financing consortium through which all loans to Chinese railroads would be processed. By 1917, however, U.S.-Japanese policies such as the 1917 Lansing-Ishii Agreement, in which the United States recognized Japanese spheres of influence in China, had called into question America's commitment to the principle of free trade in China. By the mid-1920s, the concept of an open door in China was mere fantasy, and by 1931, it was a dead issue when Japan seized Manchuria and annexed it.

In the aftermath of World War II, the principles of the Open Door Policy gained new life on a global scale as Western democracies championed free trade. Believing that economic autarky and spheres of influence had helped ignite World War II, Western policy makers engaged in a number of institutional mechanisms to foster free and unfettered trade. These included the General Agreements on Tariffs and Trade (GATT), the World Trade Organization (WTO), and the European Economic Community (EEC). The idea was to prevent economic rivalry from driving a wedge between nations, which would thereby lessen the likelihood of war. Policy makers also recognized that major trading partners were much less likely to go to war with a nation with which they enjoyed significant trade. Finally, most believed that free trade would help generate general prosperity among all nations and would serve to stabilize national economies in times of economic uncertainty.

PAUL G. PIERPAOLI JR.

See also
Boxer Rebellion; China; China Market; Hay, John Milton; McKinley, William; Roosevelt, Theodore

Further Reading
Bucknall, Kevin B. *China and the Open Door Policy.* Sydney: Allen and Unwin, 1989.
Hunt, Michael H. *The Making of a Special Relationship: The United States and China to 1914.* New York: Columbia University Press, 1983.
Young, Marilyn. *The Rhetoric of Empire: American China Policy, 1895–1901.* Cambridge: Harvard University Press, 1968.

Oregon, USS

Third member of the Indiana class, which were the first truly modern battleships of the new U.S. Navy. On June 3, 1890, Congress authorized construction of the Indiana class as seagoing coastline battleships. They were more limited in size and range than the navy had hoped yet represented the first concrete embodiment of the plans of Secretary of the Navy Benjamin F. Tracy to construct a powerful American fleet on both the Atlantic and Pacific coasts.

The Indiana-class ships were quite powerful. Their main armament consisted of four 13-inch rifled guns in two twin turrets, one

The U.S. Navy battleship *Oregon* made an epic 66-day voyage of more than 14,000 miles from the West Coast of the United States around Cape Horn to join the fleet off Cuba. The voyage emphasized the need for completion of an Isthmian canal. (Naval Historical Center)

forward and one aft. Four wing turrets, one on each corner of the superstructure, mounted a pair of 8-inch guns apiece, and two 6-inch broadside guns were fitted between each pair of wing turrets. Twenty light 6-pounder guns and several smaller weapons provided close-range defense against torpedo craft. These battleships also mounted six above-water 18-inch torpedo tubes. When commissioned, they were the most powerfully armed battleships in the world.

This class of battleships was also very well protected. The main armor belt was 7 feet deep and tapered from 18 to 8 inches in thickness. Seventeen-inch armor barbettes protected the magazines, the main turrets carried 15-inch armor, and the wing turrets, upper hull, and broadside battery were protected by 5–6 inches of nickel steel, most of it of the superior Harveyized material in the *Indiana* and *Oregon*.

Triple expansion machinery generating almost 10,000 horsepower propelled the Indiana-class ships at a top speed of 15–16 knots. Normal coal supply was 400 tons, sufficient to steam about 3,000 miles, but space was available for up to 1,800 tons of fuel. The principal disadvantages of the design were its low freeboard of only 12 feet, blast interference between the guns, cramped accommodations, and relatively slow speed.

The *Oregon* was laid down at Union Iron Works in San Francisco on November 19, 1891; launched on October 26, 1893; and commissioned into the Pacific Station on July 15, 1896. Shortly after the *Maine* exploded in Havana Harbor on February 15, 1898, the *Oregon* was ordered to the Atlantic. The battleship departed San Francisco on March 19, 1898, and steamed around Cape Horn through very severe weather to arrive at Jupiter Inlet, Florida, on May 24 after an epic 66-day voyage of 14,500 miles, during which the *Oregon* had made five stops for coal. The *Oregon* joined Admiral William T. Sampson's fleet and participated in the destruction of the Spanish fleet at Santiago, Cuba, on July 3.

The *Oregon* served on the Asiatic station from 1899 to 1906, but it missed service during the Boxer Rebellion (1899–1901) after striking an uncharted rock while in transit. The battleship then spent the remainder of its operational career on the U.S. West Coast largely in reserve except during World War I. Under the terms of the Washington Naval Treaty of 1922, the *Oregon* was demilitarized in 1924 and became a museum ship at Portland, Oregon. During World War II, the ship became a storage hulk. It broke loose from its moorings at its final station of Guam in 1948. Recovered, it was sold for scrap in 1956.

PAUL E. FONTENOY

See also

Maine, USS; *Oregon*, USS, Voyage of; Sampson, William Thomas; Santiago de Cuba, Battle of; United States Navy

Further Reading

Alden, John D. *The American Steel Navy*. Annapolis, MD: Naval Institute Press, 1972.

Friedman, Norman. *U.S. Battleships: An Illustrate Design History*. Annapolis, MD: Naval Institute Press, 1985.

Sternlicht, Sanford. *McKinley's Bulldog: The Battleship Oregon*. Chicago: Nelson-Hall, 1977.

Webber, Bert. *Battleship Oregon: Bulldog of the Navy*. Medford, OR: Webb Research Group, 1994.

Oregon, USS, Voyage of

Start Date: March 19, 1898
End Date: May 24, 1898

A record-breaking 1898 voyage that began in San Francisco and ended in Jupiter Inlet, Florida, during which the U.S. Navy battleship *Oregon* steamed some 14,500 nautical miles in 66 days.

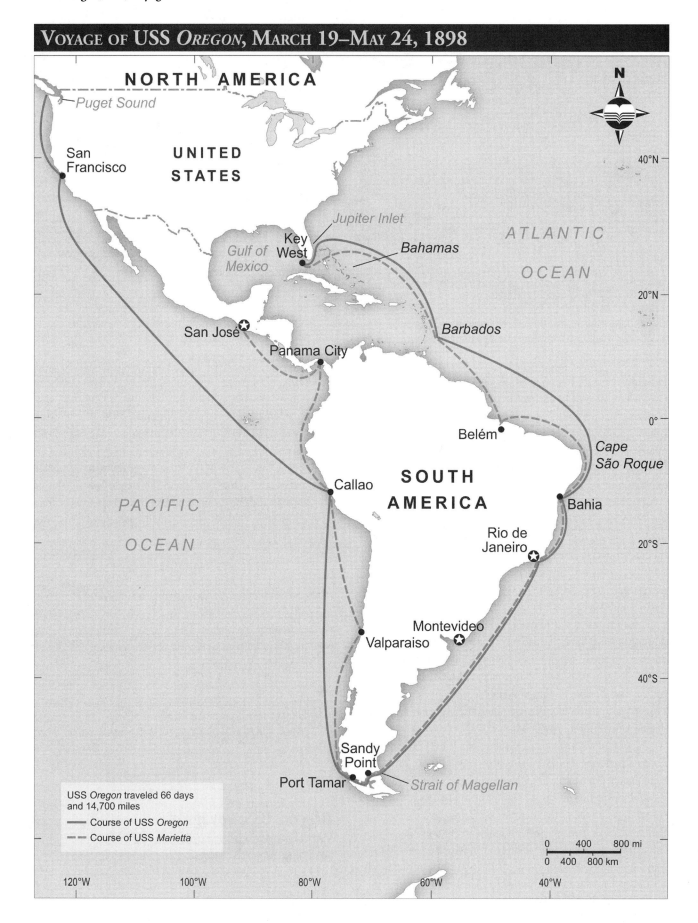

VOYAGE OF USS *OREGON*, MARCH 19–MAY 24, 1898

Lithograph depicting the U.S. battleship *Oregon* transiting the Strait of Magellan in April 1898 en route to join the fleet off Cuba during the Spanish-American War. (Naval Historical Center)

Commissioned in 1896, this Indiana-class battleship was, at the time of the Spanish-American War, one of the newest and most powerful warships in the U.S. Navy.

When the U.S. battleship *Maine* was destroyed in Havana Harbor on February 15, the *Oregon* was at the new navy yard at Bremerton, Washington, where it has been ordered for repair work. As per regulations, all ammunition had been unloaded at Mare Island before the ship had proceeded to Bremerton. With war with Spain looming, U.S. Navy planners, notably Assistant Secretary of the Navy Theodore Roosevelt, began to consider the optimal U.S. fleet disposition. Because Cuba was much nearer to Spain and because Spain's naval presence in the Philippines was known to be limited, the threat from Spain was judged to be greater in the Atlantic. Accordingly, Roosevelt ordered the *Oregon* to provision and steam to Callao, Peru, for final orders.

With all the coal at the yard having been used to supply ships headed for Alaska because of the Klondike Gold Rush, Captain Alexander H. McCormick, commander of the *Oregon,* was unable to get his ship to sea until more coal reached Bremerton on March 6. On March 9, the *Oregon* arrived at San Francisco and immediately began an around-the-clock resupply of ammunition, stores, and coal. In two days, the ship took on 1,600 tons of coal, 500 tons of ammunition, and sufficient stores for six months. McCormick withheld details of the ship's destination for security reasons, although crew speculation centered on the Philippines or Cuba.

The *Oregon* departed San Francisco on March 19, 1898. Two days before sailing, Captain McCormick became seriously ill and had to be relieved of command. Captain Charles Edward Clark replaced him. As the *Oregon* was transiting to Peru, the Navy Department took the final decision to send the battleship to Cuba. While at sea, however, the ship would be out of direct communication with the department. Throughout the long voyage, Clark put the crew through regular drill and gunnery practice to prepare for possible battle with the Spanish.

While Spanish ships were in the Pacific, the chief challenges to the battleship's transit proved to be the elements and geography. The ship's ventilation system also proved a major problem. In the fire rooms and engineering spaces, temperatures could be between 110 and 150 degrees. With the ship's boilers always at full steam, fresh water was also in extremely short supply and had to be sharply curtailed for the crew. Two other problems occurred in the need for the crew to shift coal in order to burn hard bituminous coal that would produce greater speed and then necessitate extinguishing a coal fire in one of the ship's bunkers. Despite these travails, the ship never slackened speed.

The *Oregon* arrived at Callao, Peru, its first coaling stop and 4,100 miles from San Francisco, on April 4. While taking on board 1,100 tons of coal at Callao, Clark received word from the Navy Department that the Spanish torpedo boat *Temerario* had departed Montevideo, Uruguay, and might be searching for the *Oregon*. He also took special security precautions while the battleship was in port. Although the Peruvians appeared to favor the United States in the approaching war with Spain, he ordered the guards doubled and a steam launch constantly patrolling around the ship. He also learned from the Navy Department before departure from Callao that the board of inquiry looking into the sinking of the *Maine* had established the cause of the initial explosion as an external mine.

The *Oregon* departed Callao on April 7. Steaming south, the ship encountered steadily worsening weather. On April 16, the battleship entered the Strait of Magellan for the passage around Cape Horn. There it encountered a great storm, which obscured the shore and placed the ship and its crew in considerable danger. Clark ran for the anchorage at Tamar Island while there was some light and was able to anchor there for the night. Before dawn, the weather moderated sufficiently for the ship to complete the passage.

On April 18, the *Oregon,* having transited the most dangerous part of the Strait of Magellan, again took on coal, which was taken from a hulk in lifting buckets, at Punta Aernas. At Punta Aernas, the battleship was joined by the U.S. Navy gunboat *Marietta.* On April 21, both ships were again under way, entering the Atlantic and bound for Rio de Janeiro. Expecting to encounter the Spanish torpedo boat *Temerario,* both warships steamed with guns loaded and manned.

Delayed by headwinds and rough seas, the two warships did not reach Rio until April 30. There Clark was notified of the U.S. declaration of war on Spain on April 25. A third U.S. ship, the recently purchased dynamite cruiser *Nictheroy,* was in the harbor. The dynamite guns were never installed, and the ship, which mounted traditional armament, became the cruiser *Buffalo.*

Again the *Oregon* and *Marietta* took on coal, this time from barges in the harbor. The Brazilian government placed armed guards on the barges and stationed a cruiser at the harbor entrance. On May 2, the American crews learned of and were jubilant over Commodore George Dewey's spectacular victory in the Battle of Manila Bay (May 1, 1898). The Navy Department also informed Clark that Spanish rear admiral Pascual Cervera y Topete's squadron of four cruisers and three torpedo boat destroyers had left the Cape Verde Islands, its destination unknown. To provide Clark with maximum security against a possible Spanish attack, the Navy Department allowed the captain to plan his own itinerary without first clearing it with Washington.

On May 4, the U.S. ships again sailed, this time for Bahia, Brazil. The Brazilian government delayed the sailing of the *Nictheroy* for nearly a day before permitting it to join the two waiting American warships. The *Oregon* steamed into Bahia on May 8. Word was put out that it would remain there for several days, but it departed again the next day. It then steamed to Bridgetown, Barbados, to coal on May 18. However, neutrality laws there were strictly enforced, and the battleship was allowed to remain in port only 24 hours and was able to take only sufficient coal to reach a U.S. port. The *Oregon* began coaling immediately and departed at 9:00 p.m. with lights lit, then turned off its lights and steamed in another direction,

around Barbados, before making for Key West. On May 24, 1898, the *Oregon* steamed into Jupiter Inlet, Florida. It anchored at Key West, Florida, on May 26. The 14,500-mile voyage had taken 66 days, and the battleship was completely ready for battle. The ship became known as "McKinley's Bulldog."

The American public had closely followed the progress of the *Oregon* in the newspapers, and the voyage inspired popular songs, including "The Race of the *Oregon*" by John James Meehan:

> Lights out! And a prow turned toward the South,
> And a canvas hiding each cannon's mouth
> And a ship like a silent ghost released
> Is seeking her sister ships in the East.
> When your boys shall ask what the guns are for,
> Then tell them the tale of the Spanish war,
> And the breathless millions that looked upon
> The matchless race of the *Oregon.*

Coaled and supplied and having taken on 60 additional crewmen, the *Oregon* sailed again at 1:04 a.m. on May 29 and arrived off Havana that same morning. On June 1, the battleship joined other units of Rear Admiral William T. Sampson's North Atlantic Squadron in blockading Cervera's Spanish squadron at Santiago de Cuba. On July 3, 1898, the *Oregon* was one of eight U.S. warships on blockade duty off Santiago when Cervera sortied with his ships and attempted to escape. In the ensuing engagement, the *Oregon* and the other American ships completely destroyed the Spanish squadron.

In the wake of its triumph in the Spanish-American War, the United States was thrust into the role of global power, with widely dispersed interests around the world. Defending these interests would require a large and highly mobile navy capable of fighting in both the Atlantic and Pacific. Roosevelt, who became president in 1901, vigorously embraced this challenge. Encouraged by navalists such as Rear Admiral Alfred Thayer Mahan, Roosevelt set the United States on an ambitious naval construction program and committed the country to building the Panama Canal. The epic voyage of the *Oregon,* which would have required just 21 days had a canal existed versus the actual 66 days it took, served as a powerful argument for the project in Panama.

Robert M. Brown and Spencer C. Tucker

See also

Cervera y Topete, Pascual; Clark, Charles Edgar; Mahan, Alfred Thayer; *Maine,* USS; *Oregon,* USS; Panama Canal; Roosevelt, Theodore; Sampson, William Thomas; Santiago de Cuba, Battle of; United States Navy

Further Reading

Feuer, A. B. *The Spanish-American War at Sea: Naval Action in the Atlantic.* Westport, CT: Praeger, 1995.

McCullough, David. *Mornings on Horseback.* New York: Simon and Schuster, 1981.

Musicant, Ivan. *Empire by Default: The Spanish-American War and the Dawn of the American Century.* New York: Henry Holt, 1998.

Sternlicht, Sanford. *McKinley's Bulldog: The Battleship Oregon.* Chicago: Nelson-Hall, 1977.

Zimmerman, Warren. *First Great Triumph: How Five Americans Made Their Country a World Power.* New York: Farrar, Straus and Giroux, 2002.

Origins of the War

The American declaration of war on Spain in 1898 is often regarded as marking the beginning of the American Century, an era of de facto U.S. imperialism. At that time, the country attained great-power status in international affairs, becoming the world's unrivaled superpower by the mid-20th century. It is thus quite impossible to understand the rise of American power in the international arena without first understanding how and why the United States went to war in 1898.

On April 20, 1898, Republican president William McKinley signed congressional resolutions declaring war on Spain over that country's treatment of the Caribbean island of Cuba, a Spanish-held colony since 1492, where a native rebellion seeking independence from Spain had been in progress since 1895. Cuba was less than 100 miles from the coast of the United States, and throughout the 19th century, American leaders had shown decided interest in acquiring the island. Ever since the proclamation of the Monroe Doctrine in 1823, the United States had asserted special rights in the Western Hemisphere, demanding that no European imperial nation acquire further possessions in the area or use force to regain colonies that had already won independence. From that time onward, many prominent Americans, including former president Thomas Jefferson, President James Buchanan, and Secretaries of State John Quincy Adams, Daniel Webster, and William H. Seward expressed the hope that in due course Cuba would be annexed into the United States.

Such expectations were in line with the popular belief that it would ultimately be the Manifest Destiny of the United States to expand its borders to encompass all the territory of the North American continent and its contiguous islands. Presidents James Polk, Franklin Pierce, and Ulysses S. Grant all sought unsuccessfully to purchase Cuba from Spain on much the same lines as Seward had acquired Alaska from Russia in 1867. On several occasions in the 19th century, American presidents and secretaries of state also warned Spain that they would not tolerate a Spanish transfer of sovereignty over Cuba to any power other than the United States.

American suggestions that the United States annex Cuba reflected the fact that in the late 19th century, the U.S. government and general public were increasingly assertive internationally, fueled by a nationalistic sense that their country, already one of the world's largest states and strongest industrial economies, had the potential to be a great power whose influence would rank with that of such leading European imperial nations as Great Britain, Germany, France, and Russia. From the 1880s onward, a determined group of American internationalists, including Republican senator Henry Cabot Lodge of Massachusetts, naval officer and strategist Alfred Thayer Mahan, and rising young Republican politician and author Theodore Roosevelt, pushed aggressively for the expansion and modernization of the U.S. Navy.

By the late 1890s, the United States possessed an oceangoing fleet of steel ships that, although still small next to those of most European powers, was quite capable of defending the Western Hemisphere against potential attacks and engaging the more antiquated Spanish Navy. This group of naval expansionists also supported the construction of a canal across the Isthmus of Panama, the narrow bridge of land in Central America connecting North America to South America. Such a waterway would facilitate U.S. commerce, allowing merchant shipping to travel between the East Coast and the West Coast of the United States without needing to circumnavigate South America. The major reason they favored building such a canal, however, was strategic, as it would permit U.S. naval forces to move swiftly from the Pacific to the Atlantic in response to any threat. These internationalists generally adhered to popular social Darwinist views of racial competition and hierarchy, believing that Anglo-Saxons were inherently superior to other races in culture and political and social institutions and were therefore obligated to rule over those races and peoples they considered inferior. They especially admired British imperialism and felt a particular sense of kinship with the British, regarding them as fellow Anglo-Saxons. Although they fundamentally believed their own country to be an improvement even on Britain, they traced American political institutions back to shared British roots and a common heritage.

Watching other late 19th-century great powers compete for colonies around the world, these expansionist-minded internationalists believed that the United States might do well to join in and acquire an empire of its own. Such possessions would, they believed, prove commercially and strategically beneficial to the United States, while the indigenous inhabitants would benefit from benign American tutelage, which would eventually lead them to self-government along American lines.

By the mid-1890s, Americans of both political parties were making expansive statements claiming that the United States enjoyed a special position in the Western Hemisphere. In 1895, during a boundary dispute between Venezuela and the neighboring British colony of Guiana, Democratic president Grover Cleveland and Richard Olney, his secretary of state, convinced Britain to accept arbitration. The Cleveland administration also authorized major increases in naval budgets that substantially expanded the existing U.S. fleet. This decision meant that the United States had the modern ships required to respond with military force when relations with Spain reached a crisis point over Cuba in early 1898.

By the 1890s, Spain's hold on Cuba, one of the sparse remnants of what had once been a massive colonial empire, had become increasingly shaky. About 70 percent of Cuba's population of 1.6 million people were of Spanish descent, either peninsulares (immigrants who had come to Cuba directly from Spain) or the 950,000 descendants of such settlers, known as criollos. The remaining Cubans were either

The U.S. battleship *Maine* entering Havana Harbor, January 25, 1898. (Naval Historical Center)

blacks, whose ancestors had come from Africa, or mulattos. Slavery had not been abolished in Cuba until 1886. The 150,000 peninsulares enjoyed special political and economic privileges and held the great majority of seats in the governing Cortes (parliament), with only 6 out of 430 seats reserved for Cubans. Even these were elected by a very limited franchise, only about 53,000 voters in all, mostly peninsulares. During the Ten Years' War (1868–1878), blacks, mulattos, and some creoles demanded independence from Spain and ravaged Cuba's eastern region. The rebellion was contained and eventually ended by the Pact of Zanjón in 1878, an agreement negotiated by adept Spanish political and military leaders.

By the early 1890s, the Liberal Party, which demanded autonomy for the island, was gaining strength in Spain as well as Cuba itself. The influence of Cuban supporters of Cuba Libre (Free Cuba), who sought complete independence and refused to accept the 1878 agreement, was likewise expanding. Many such dissidents went into exile in the United States, Europe, and Latin America, where they continued to work against the Spanish rule of Cuba.

In February 1895, a second major insurrection against Spanish colonial rule broke out once more in Cuba, led by the Cuban revolutionary José Martí y Pérez and two leaders of the Ten Years' War, Generals Máximo Gómez y Báez and Antonio Maceo Grajales. Martí, who sought to end not just Spanish rule but also economic oppression and racial discrimination in Cuba, was killed while fighting in May 1895, becoming a posthumous inspiration and hero to other rebels, who proclaimed a provisional Cuban government late that summer. Fighting spread throughout Cuba into the wealthy western provinces. Governor-General Valeriano Weyler y Nicolau brutally suppressed Cuban rebels, pursuing scorched earth tactics and forcibly relocating 500,000 villagers, most in the eastern provinces, into concentration camps, or *reconcentrados,* causing more than 100,000 noncombatant deaths and reducing many

others to destitution. Despite this, the Spanish found themselves unable to prevail against guerrilla rebels who avoided pitched battles and melted into the civilian population.

By the end of 1895, the Spanish army in Cuba was 120,000-men strong, and the island was under virtual military occupation. That number rose to more than 200,000 troops by late 1897—representing more than half the regular Spanish Army—facing between 20,000 and 40,000 insurgents. Despite some successes, especially in the western provinces, and the death in battle of Maceo, Spanish forces never succeeded in regaining full control of Cuba. Economically, the insurgency disrupted trade between Spain and Cuba, as rebels raided lucrative sugar and tobacco plantations, destroying the crops. Financing the conflict proved prohibitively expensive for the Spanish government, doubling Spain's national debt, while the sufferings of those confined to the *reconcentrados* provoked international condemnation.

The Cleveland administration at first attempted to mediate in the Cuban conflict, hoping to persuade the Spanish to moderate their repressive methods and grant Cuba independence or at least autonomy, efforts that both Spanish and insurgent forces regarded with considerable distrust. In June 1895, Cleveland and Olney made an official declaration of U.S. neutrality toward both sides in the conflict, and between then and late 1897, U.S. naval forces intercepted 33 insurgent filibustering expeditions bound for Cuba.

President William McKinley, who took office in March 1897, initially continued his predecessor's approach, but within and beyond his administration, other voices demanded a more proactive American stance. Inside the administration, an aggressive internationalist faction led by Assistant Secretary of the Navy Theodore Roosevelt romanticized war and sought to wield the new American steel fleet to win Cuban independence, an event that it believed would enhance American prestige and also facilitate the con-

Cartoon showing a sleeping woman, "Columbia," with Baron Steuben and the Marquis de Lafayette behind her. She is holding a document describing Cuba's repression by Spain. To the left is a man, "Spain," beating a prone woman, "Cuba," who holds a banner "Liberty or death." Cartoon by Victor Gillam appearing in *Judge,* October 19, 1895. (Library of Congress)

struction of a transisthmian canal. The hardships and maltreatment of ordinary Cubans appalled many on the left wing of the Democratic Party, including the agrarian populist William Jennings Bryan, leader of the free silver forces and Democratic presidential candidate in 1896. Bryan and other pro-Cuban Democrats in Congress urged that their country should intervene to assist the Cubans in their quest for independence and assailed the McKinley administration for doing too little to help them. American public opinion, always pro-Cuban, increasingly favored war with Spain. Businessmen and other American residents in Cuba who desired the restoration of peace and stability and restitution for their wartime property and other losses came to believe that only American intervention would guarantee this. With a midterm election approaching, leading Republicans, fearing Democratic gains in Congress, pressured McKinley to take decisive action before voters went to the polls.

Meanwhile, Spain began shifting away from its repressive policies after the August 1897 assassination of Conservative prime minister Antonio Cánovas del Castillo by an Italian anarchist. The controversial Weyler was recalled in October, and in November the new Liberal prime minister, Práxedes Mateo Sagasta, offered Cuba limited autonomy, though not independence; instituted cosmetic political reforms; released various political prisoners; and relaxed

the harsh *reconcentrado* policy. In response, army officers in Cuba rioted in protest, attacking property, including some American-owned businesses. In January 1898, McKinley dispatched the battleship *Maine* to Havana Harbor as a precautionary measure to protect American interests. On February 15, the ship sank, the victim of a mysterious explosion that killed 266 of its crew, now thought to have been caused by spontaneous combustion in a coal bunker but then ascribed to Spanish sabotage.

Further mediation attempts by McKinley, aimed at persuading Spain and the rebels to declare an armistice, proved unavailing. Public opinion, continuously inflamed by the fiercely prointerventionist yellow journalism newspapers of William Randolph Hearst and Joseph Pulitzer, swung toward intervention, as did sentiments in Congress. Historians, including Richard Hofstadter, have suggested that in the late 1890s, Americans—undergoing the disruptive stresses of major industrialization and urbanization and the effort to assimilate a massive wave of immigrants and recovering from a lengthy economic depression—turned to exciting and unifying international adventure in a state of something approximating psychological crisis.

On April 11, 1898, McKinley asked Congress to declare war against Spain, the first occasion on which the United States embarked on hostilities beyond the American continental landmass.

Traditional historiography suggests that he was reluctant to embark on war and was motivated primarily by domestic political pressures and concerns. Revisionist Cuban historians have since suggested that McKinley, alarmed by the prospect of an outright insurrectionist victory, sought to prevent the rebels from winning control of the country and to ensure that any government that took power would be under American tutelage. Democrats in Congress insisted that the resolution declaring war also include an amendment authored by Senator Henry M. Teller whereby the United States renounced all intention of permanent occupation or annexation of Cuba and committed itself to leaving the island once its territory had been pacified. On April 19, both houses of Congress passed a joint resolution recognizing Cuba's independence, although not the provisional government (Cuban Revolutionary Government), and demanding that Spain withdraw immediately from Cuba. The president was also empowered to use the American armed forces for this purpose.

The president signed the resolution the following day, while Spain broke off diplomatic relations and proclaimed its intention to defy the United States. On April 25, a further congressional resolution retrospectively declared that since April 21, a state of war had existed between the United States and Spain. A wave of enthusiasm for the war swept the United States. U.S. naval and land forces immediately embarked on hostilities not just against Cuba but also against all other Spanish colonial territories within reach of the American fleet, including the Caribbean island of Puerto Rico as well as the Philippine Islands and Guam in the Pacific.

PRISCILLA ROBERTS

See also

Cuba Libre; Cuban War of Independence; Democratic Party; Economic Depression; Expansionism; Filibuster; Immigration; Imperialism; Lodge, Henry Cabot; Mahan, Alfred Thayer; Manifest Destiny; McKinley, William; Monroe Doctrine; Panama Canal; *Reconcentrado* System; Republican Party; Roosevelt, Theodore; Social Darwinism; Steel; Ten Years' War; United States Navy; Venezuela Crisis, First; Yellow Journalism; Weyler y Nicolau, Valeriano

Further Reading

Healy, David. *Drive to Hegemony: The United States in the Caribbean, 1898–1917.* Madison: University of Wisconsin Press, 1988.
Musicant, Ivan. *Empire by Default: The Spanish-American War and the Dawn of the American Century.* New York: Henry Holt, 1998.
Offner, John L. *An Unwanted War: The Diplomacy of the United States and Spain over Cuba, 1895–1898.* Chapel Hill: University of North Carolina Press, 1992.
Pérez, Louis A., Jr. *The War of 1898: The United States & Cuba in History & Historiography.* Chapel Hill: University of North Carolina Press, 1998.
Smith, Angel, and Emma Davila-Cox, eds. *The Crisis of 1898: Colonial Redistribution and Nationalist Mobilization.* New York: St. Martin's, 1999.
Smith, Joseph. *The Spanish-American War: Conflict in the Caribbean and the Pacific, 1895–1902.* New York: Longman, 1994.
Trask, David F. *The War with Spain in 1898.* Lincoln: University of Nebraska Press, 1996.
Traxel, David. *1898: The Birth of the American Century.* New York: Knopf, 1998.
Zimmerman, Warren. *First Great Triumph: How Five Americans Made Their Country a Great Power.* New York: Farrar, Straus and Giroux, 2002.

Ostend Manifesto

A secret document advocating the U.S. purchase of Cuba from Spain, written in Ostend, Belgium, in 1854 by U.S. diplomats James Buchanan, U.S. minister to Great Britain; John M. Mason, U.S. minister to France; and Pierre Soulé, U.S. minister to Spain. Cuba, often referred to as the Pearl of the Antilles, with its lucrative sugarcane production, balmy climate, and proximity to the United States, had drawn the attention of leaders in the early republic, including Thomas Jefferson and John Quincy Adams. In 1848, President James K. Polk, whose policies of Manifest Destiny wrested Texas, California, and much of what would become New Mexico, Arizona, Colorado, Utah, and Nevada from Mexico, instructed the American minister to Spain, Romulus M. Saunders, to sound out Spain about selling Cuba to the United States. The Spanish government asserted that under no circumstances would they relinquish control over Cuba.

When these diplomatic overtures were thwarted, some Southerners, who perceived Cuba as a highly desirable slave territory, engaged in filibustering expeditions to seize the island by force. Two such expeditions in the early 1850s were repulsed by Spanish authorities, and the leaders of these invasions were executed, outraging many Southerners.

Relations between the United States and Spain became further strained in March 1854 when Spanish authorities in Cuba seized the American steamer *Black Warrior.* President Franklin Pierce, who supported the expansion of slave territory into Latin America, was prepared to respond forcefully to the Spanish provocation. Thus, he directed Secretary of Sate William Marcy, an expansionist who favored annexation of Cuba, to explore whether Spain could be persuaded to sell Cuba without interference from the English and French. To implement this policy, Buchanan, Mason, and Soulé, gathered in Ostend in the summer of 1854 to strategize. Soulé was an exiled Frenchman who had settled in Louisiana and advocated that the United States acquire Cuba by military action if necessary. His appointment and undiplomatic actions, such as allegedly leading an anti-Spanish riot in New Orleans, exacerbated the deteriorating relations between Spain and the United States.

The three ministers issued their report to Marcy on October 18, 1854. The Ostend Manifesto offered $120 million for the purchase of Cuba but then concluded that if Spain was unwilling to enter negotiations for its sale, the United States would be justified in employing military action to seize the island by force. The bellicose nature of the document was attributed mainly to the influence of Soulé.

Before the Pierce administration could act on the recommendations made at Ostend, word of the Ostend Manifesto was leaked to the American and European press. Reaction in England and France was opposed to the manifesto, while there was a veritable uproar among newspapers in the U.S. North. Passage of the Fugitive Slave Law (1850) as part of the Compromise of 1850 along with introduction of the Kansas-Nebraska Bill in Congress (passed in 1854) convinced many Northerners that Southern slave interests were intent upon expanding slavery and disrupting the sectional balance of power. Because of the political upheaval in the North and opposition from abroad, the Pierce administration disavowed the Ostend Manifesto. Nevertheless, it encouraged sectional divisions and contributed to the rise of the Republican Party.

See also
Cuba; Filibuster; Manifest Destiny

Further Reading

Ettinger, Amos Aschbach. *The Mission to Spain of Pierre Soule, 1853–1855: A Study in the Cuban Diplomacy of the United States.* New Haven, CT: Yale University Press, 1932.
Gara, Larry. *The Presidency of Franklin Pierce.* Lawrence: University Press of Kansas, 1991.
Potter, David M. *The Impending Crisis, 1848–1861.* New York: Harper and Row, 1967.

Otis, Elwell Stephen
Birth Date: March 25, 1838
Death Date: October 21, 1909

U.S. Army general. Born in Frederick City, Maryland, on March 25, 1838, Elwell Stephen Otis graduated from the University of Rochester in 1858 and from Harvard Law School in 1861. During the American Civil War, he was commissioned a captain of volunteers in the 140th New York Infantry Regiment on September 13, 1862. He was advanced to lieutenant colonel in December 1863 and later to colonel. Seriously wounded at Petersburg, he was mustered out of the army on January 14, 1865. In recognition of his distinguished wartime service, he received a brevet promotion to brigadier general of volunteers on March 13, 1865.

As with many other volunteer soldiers, Otis found military life to his liking and secured a regular army commission upon his recovery after the war. In March 1869, he was appointed a lieutenant colonel and assigned to the 22nd Infantry Regiment. Promoted to colonel and assigned to the 20th Infantry Regiment in February 1880, he saw considerable service in the American West during the Indian Wars. He was advanced to brigadier general in November 1893.

With the outbreak of war with Spain in 1898, Otis was appointed major general of volunteers on May 4, 1898, and was sent to the Philippines as second-in-command to Major General Wesley Merritt. On August 30, 1898, Otis succeeded Merritt as commander of VIII Corps and military governor of the Philippines when Merritt was relieved of the command at his own request.

U.S. Army major general Elwell Stephen Otis commanded VIII Corps and was military governor of the Philippines during the Philippine-American War. (*Photographic History of the Spanish-American War,* 1898)

A 36-year army veteran when he arrived in the Philippines, Otis had the misfortune to direct affairs in the Philippines during the initial stages of U.S. involvement in the archipelago. In this capacity, he had to make critical decisions when there were no clear guidelines as to U.S. policy except for President William McKinley's desire to see the Philippines pacified in a kind and compassionate manner. Benevolent assimilation, as it came to be known, was not, however, an easy policy to implement. Furthermore, Otis generally disliked Filipinos. He considered Emilio Aguinaldo y Famy's insurgents "a band of looters" and promptly ordered them from Manila. Otis also issued the proclamation of January 4, 1899, in his capacity as military governor of the Philippines that proclaimed U.S. sovereignty over the islands.

Otis rarely left his office and constantly sent off overly optimistic reports that led the McKinley administration to underestimate the troop strength required to win the war. Otis's refusal to acknowledge the limitations of his military resources, particularly the troop strength necessary to respond effectively to the movements of the Filipino Nationalist Army, exacerbated a difficult situation. Otis's field commanders had to execute his directives while being compromised by the logistic problems of campaigning in extremely difficult conditions against an elusive foe and without sufficient manpower.

Otis also had to deal with the problem posed by volunteer troops who wanted to go home once the war with Spain had ended. These men had volunteered to fight the Spanish, not the Filipinos. Otis had difficulty dealing with the volunteers despite the fact that he had once been a volunteer soldier himself and had led volunteer troops with distinction during the American Civil War. The state volunteer units were eventually sent home, but until replacements arrived, Otis had to make do with the regular army units that were available.

Perhaps the most controversial of all Philippine commanders, Otis was sharply criticized by some of his senior subordinates. Rear Admiral George Dewey, his naval counterpart, thought him "a pincushion of an old woman." Otis's strict censorship of news stories did not endear him to the press either, and reporters often painted him in a critical light. Indeed, the alleged feud between Otis and Brigadier General Henry Lawton, his most outspoken critic, may have been largely a press creation.

Otis was succeeded as military governor of the Philippines in May 1900 by Brigadier General Arthur MacArthur. On Otis's return to the United States in October 1900, he took command of the Department of the Lakes, headquartered in Chicago. He reached mandatory retirement age on March 25, 1902. He was promoted to regular army major general on the retired list on June 16, 1906. Otis retired to Rochester, New York, and died there on October 21, 1909.

JERRY KENNAN AND SPENCER C. TUCKER

See also

Aguinaldo y Famy, Emilio; Benevolent Assimilation; Lawton, Henry Ware; MacArthur, Arthur; McKinley, William; Merritt, Wesley

Further Reading

Gates, John M. *Schoolbooks and Krags: The United States Army in the Philippines, 1898–1902.* Westport, CT: Greenwood, 1973.

Linn, Brian McAllister. *The Philippine War, 1899–1902.* Lawrence: University Press of Kansas, 2000.

Wolff, Leon. *Little Brown Brother: America's Forgotten Bid for Empire Which Cost 250,000 Lives.* New York: Kraus Reprint, 1970.

P

Pacification Program, Philippine Islands

Filipino nationalists fought U.S. forces in a war for independence from the United States during February 1899–July 1902. This conflict, known as the Philippine-American War, occurred after U.S. military forces had defeated Spanish forces in the Philippines and occupied Manila. The war began with an incident at the San Juan Bridge in Manila on February 4, 1899, and ended when the major Filipino operating forces were defeated or had surrendered by April 1902. The U.S. Army declared the insurrection to be over on July 4, 1902, although various bandits and other independent belligerents continued hostilities on a minor scale until 1913.

The Philippine insurrection came as something of a surprise to the United States. Americans hoped that over time, the independence movement would falter and that Philippine insurgent forces would disband. Initially, the Filipino nationalists fought the U.S. Army conventionally. This operational approach failed miserably, as by February 1900 the U.S. Army had won several important victories that destroyed most of the Filipino conventional military capability. The insurrectional leadership, principally General Emilio Aguinaldo y Famy, then changed strategy. The new strategy emphasized guerrilla tactics meant to strike swiftly and avoid decisive combat with large American forces. The goal of the strategy was twofold. First, the insurgents sought to keep the cause of Philippine independence alive and viable. Second, Aguinaldo was determined to influence the American presidential election of 1900 by causing as many casualties as possible to U.S. forces. He hoped that domestic American disagreement on Philippine policy would result in the election of anti-imperialist and antiwar candidate Democrat William Jennings Bryan.

The American response to the guerrilla strategy was slow to evolve but ultimately became a sophisticated pacification program informed by experience in the American Civil War and fighting against the American Indians in the West. One of the guiding policies for the pacification program was General Order 100, which specifically gave field commanders guidance on authorized actions against guerrillas, civilians supporting guerrillas, and the civil population at large. The order was actually a reissue of the same order that had been issued in 1863 and used to define the army's legally permissible actions during the American Civil War.

A total of 26 of the 30 American generals who served in the Philippines were veterans of the various Indian campaigns, as were numerous junior officers. The American pacification effort was a two-pronged program, which at its peak involved some 69,000 troops. Security was the focus of one aspect of the strategy. Called the chastisement component, it was designed to destroy the insurgency by force. The other major approach of the strategy was the policy of attraction. It was designed to win the support of the Filipino people to the American cause by demonstrating the material benefits of American control.

The chastisement policy was brutal but effective. U.S. commanding general and military governor in the Philippines Major General Arthur MacArthur unleashed the policy after the 1900 American elections. The policy spawned a variety of tactics, techniques, and procedures that systematically diminished the military capabilities of the insurgents. These techniques included offensive operations against the insurgents, separating the insurgents from their support base, and direct attacks on the insurgent leadership.

Most offensive operations against the insurgents took the form of highly decentralized local efforts conducted on a relatively small scale. These patrols, called hikes by the American troops, were largely ineffective in locating and destroying insurgent bands. Although not showing significant results in combat, they gave the

Americans the initiative in the war and forced the insurgents to concentrate on evasion and survival rather than on offensive operations. Other operations were large-scale offensive affairs designed to pursue and kill or capture major insurgent groups and their supporters. Such operations included the destruction of crops and means of sustenance to deny these to the insurgents. Such operations, like the smaller scale hikes, kept the insurgents on the run.

The Philippine archipelago numbers more than 7,000 islands, making pacification a very difficult affair. An important technique that greatly aided the pacification of the islands was the use of maritime assets to control travel, trade, and information passing between the islands. Although the U.S. Navy had the primary mission for interdicting unauthorized maritime traffic, the U.S. Army assisted these efforts with a small gunboat contingent. The navy operated a fleet of more than 25 seagoing gunboats to interdict traffic between the islands, while the army maintained 12 shallow-draft river steamers to support shore operations. U.S. control of waterborne travel in the islands helped fragment and isolate the insurgency.

American commanders quickly recognized that an element of insurgent strength was the support of the local civilian population. The insurgents gained support through genuine appeals to nationalism, taxation through a shadow government, and coercion. The U.S. Army broke down this relationship through a variety of techniques. One was centrally locating the population. The army sought to concentrate the rural population in towns and villages, where small army detachments could monitor them closely. The army was largely successful in avoiding forcible relocations. The reconcentration was accomplished through various incentives, including the building of town markets, as well as requiring all food distribution in the towns. These techniques, combined with destroying food and residences outside of the towns, had the effect of forcing the population to concentrate without orders to that effect. Once the population was concentrated, restrictions on travel and curfews kept it controlled. The concentration of the population resulted in large numbers of civilian deaths, however. At least 11,000 perished in the concentration areas from disease, malnutrition, poor sanitation, and other health problems.

Another more direct means of separating the population from the insurgency was through retribution actions launched against the population. The army sought to make the population more fearful of the army than of the insurgents. In their least extreme forms, such actions included burning homes in the areas where telegraph wires had been cut, burning homes and crops in an area where ambushes occurred, widespread arrests of suspected insurgents and their family members, deportations, and fines. In the most extreme cases, army commands executed individuals in response to the murder of Americans or friendly Filipinos. Although not officially condoned, individual soldiers and units also employed torture to extract information from captured or detained individuals who were suspected of being or supporting insurgents.

During the war, American operations became increasingly effective because of improved intelligence. American officers real-

Three Filipinos enter American lines in 1899 during the Philippine-American War. U.S. forces sought to concentrate the Filipino population by ensuring that food was only distributed in towns. (Library of Congress)

ized very early in the campaign that effective intelligence was absolutely essential to target insurgents and their camps effectively. Toward this end, the army developed a multilayered intelligence capability that included paid informants, spies, translators, and native scouts and guides. As part of the intelligence effort, the Americans, recognizing the central importance of the civilian population, systematically documented noncombatants. They organized a national census and issued identity cards. The intelligence system operated at the local, regional, and national levels. Officers who specialized in intelligence operations and who had success, including Lieutenant William T. Johnson and Major Edwin F. Glenn, traveled throughout the area of operations assisting other commands in organizing and coordinating their efforts. Increased effectiveness of intelligence allowed commanders to effectively employ their superior combat power.

Another technique that proved very effective in the pacification effort was the use of indigenous Filipino forces. Soon after arriving, the Americans began organizing Filipino forces to support the counterinsurgency. These forces took the form of the Philippine military units (Philippine Scouts and Macabebe Scouts) and police units (Philippine Constabulary).

American officers trained and led both these units. The Americans screened members of the indigenous forces carefully to ensure their loyalty. This vetting process dramatically slowed the pace of recruiting and training. Indigenous forces had the advantage of knowing the terrain, culture, and language and of being acclimatized to the tropical conditions. They also undermined the morale of the insurgents and their supporters because they served as a visible sign that parts of the population were supporting American goals. By 1902, the Philippine Scout forces numbered more than 50 companies, and the Philippine Constabulary numbered 5,000 men.

Effective intelligence and indigenous forces greatly increased the U.S. Army's counterinsurgency capability. This increased capability allowed the army to focus resources on neutralizing the individual leaders of the insurgency. The most famous and successful example of the success of these efforts was the capture in March 1901 of Aguinaldo, the leader of the insurgency from its inception until his capture. The Americans were able to locate Aguinaldo when they captured a courier who had a letter from him requesting more troops. The courier provided Aguinaldo's location. With this information, Brigadier General Frederick Funston led a contingent of Philippine Scouts disguised as insurgents into the insurgent camp. There they captured Aguinaldo and then escaped to a waiting navy ship. Subsequently, Aguinaldo agreed to support the American effort and was influential in inducing a great many insurgents, including senior leaders, to surrender.

While the bulk of the army was involved in the operations designed to destroy insurgents and provide security, the army also waged a very effective attraction campaign. This campaign was designed to win Filipino loyalty by demonstrating the benefits of American rule. This was a multifaceted program designed to implement President McKinley's stated goal of benevolent U.S. administration. At its foundation was the concept of public education. The army built thousands of schools and detailed soldiers to function as teachers when required. As American civil administration became operational, thousands of civilian American teachers were brought to the Philippines to run the schools and train Filipino teachers. A vigorous economic infrastructure program that built roads and bridges and installed telegraph lines backed the education program. Americans also sought to improve the overall health and welfare of the population through inoculation programs, instruction in proper sanitary practices, and the enforcement of hygiene regulations. Finally, the army assisted in the development of a civil administration, based on a democratic model, that provided for a civilian judiciary, election of local officials, and the transition of Philippine policy and administration from the authority of the army's commanding general to a civilian U.S. governor.

For the first 18 months of the war, the attraction aspects of policy were the main focus. Commanders and the American civil leadership alike understood that the long-term relationship between the Philippines and the United States could not be fundamentally based on coercion. However, commanders also realized that an attraction policy by itself could not be successful as long as an intelligent and ruthless enemy remained free to intimidate and propagandize the population. Thus, for the last 18 months of the war the policy of chastisement had priority. In reality, the two aspects of the pacification program reinforced each other. Without the other, each individual component of the pacification program, the attraction policy and the chastisement policy, were doomed to failure. However, the combination of the two policies proved very effective in inhibiting the operations of the insurgents and ultimately achieving unchallenged control of the islands.

Louis A. DiMarco

See also

Aguinaldo y Famy, Emilio; Atrocities; Benevolent Assimilation; Bryan, William Jennings; Funston, Frederick; Gunboat Operations, Philippine Islands; Macabebe Scouts; MacArthur, Arthur; McKinley, William; Military Intelligence; Philippine-American War; Philippine Constabulary; Philippine Scouts

Further Reading

Birtle, Andrew J. *U.S. Army Counterinsurgency and Contingency Operations Doctrine, 1860–1941.* Washington, DC: Center of Military History, U.S. Army, 2003.
Boot, Max. *The Savage Wars of Peace: Small Wars and the Rise of American Power.* New York: Basic Books, 2002.
Karnow, Stanley. *In Our Image: America's Empire in the Philippines.* New York: Random House, 1989.
Linn, Brian McAllister. *The Philippine War, 1899–1902.* Lawrence: University Press of Kansas, 2000.
Miller, Stuart Creighton. *"Benevolent Assimilation": The American Conquest of the Philippines, 1899–1903.* New Haven, CT: Yale University Press, 1982.

Panama Canal

Isthmian canal linking the Pacific and Atlantic that traverses the Central-American nation of Panama. The canal was built by the United States between 1904 and 1913. The Panama Canal is roughly 41 miles in length. Still in use today, the canal is capable of handling ships ranging in size from small yachts to large container vessels and most, but not all, modern naval ships. It takes an average of nine hours for a ship to navigate through the Panama Canal's system of channels, locks, and lakes. In 2005, an average of 40 ships traversed the canal daily. The Panama Canal, still considered one of the greatest engineering marvels of modern times, not only greatly facilitated commercial shipping but also was a boon to the U.S. Navy, which could use the canal to dispatch ships to either the Atlantic or Pacific with much greater speed. Indeed, the construction of the canal was entirely in keeping with naval strategist Alfred Thayer Mahan's ideas about the importance of a powerful and modern navy, which would require coaling station and bases located around the globe. President Theodore Roosevelt, a former assistant secretary of the navy and a staunch adherent of Mahan's worldview, was highly influential in the construction of the Panama Canal, which began under his watch.

Prior to the construction of the Panama Canal, which opened to maritime traffic in 1914, a ship moving at a good clip had to travel about 14,000 miles to make the journey from San Francisco to New York City. The long voyage required ships to pass through the Drake Passage and around Cape Horn, where the waters are often treacherous. After 1914, the very same journey would require a ship to cover only some 6,000 miles using the Panama Canal. The amount

Under the direction of Lieutenant Colonel George Goethals, the U.S. Army Corps of Engineers played a major role in the construction of the Panama Canal. The canal was completed in 1913. (U.S. Army Corps of Engineers)

of time traveled, fuel used, and manpower required for such long voyages was reduced markedly. This was not, of course, lost on naval and war planners, who saw in the canal a far easier and faster way to shift naval assets from one ocean to another. Also, it would substantially reduce the need for a large navy to cover both coasts and hemispheres. An isthmian canal also gave the United States better and far faster access to Central and South America in case of war and significantly bolstered America's command of the Caribbean Sea and the Gulf of Mexico.

If nothing else, the lack of an isthmian canal during the Spanish-American War and the Philippine-American War prompted war planners and naval experts to push for the construction of one in all due haste. Forced to transit South America, the U.S. battleship *Oregon* spent 66 days steaming from San Francisco to Key West, Florida, during the war. Fighting a simultaneous war in the Pacific and the Atlantic placed great stress on the U.S. Navy, as it did on commercial shipping, and the navy struggled to keep the supply lines running smoothly over thousands of miles. At war's end, President William McKinley and Congress agreed that the time had come to construct a canal. McKinley's successor, Theodore Roosevelt, threw his considerable weight behind the Herculean project.

The concept of an isthmian canal was far from new in 1904, when construction began. Indeed, the first reference to a canal was mentioned as early as the mid-1500s, when Holy Roman emperor Charles V suggested that an isthmian canal would greatly ease shipping between Central and South America. Several attempts were made to forge such a canal in the 17th and 18th centuries, but they all ended quickly. In 1855, the first railroad linking the two coasts of Panama (then part of Colombia) was completed, and it was then that the idea of building a canal was once again seriously considered. Several plans to dig a canal across the Nicaraguan isthmus were considered, but the Panamanian isthmus finally won out.

Buoyed by the unabashed success of the Suez Canal, which opened in 1869, the promoter behind that venture, Frenchman Ferdinand de Lesseps, formed a new company to construct a sea-level canal through Panama. Many Frenchmen invested all their savings in the venture. Construction began in January 1880. The Panama Canal Company might have succeeded had de Lesseps followed the advice of eminent French engineer Adolphe de Lepiney and sought to construct a lock canal rather than one at sea level. But de Lesseps refused despite mounting evidence that a sea-level canal was impractical. The Americans almost made the same mistake a quarter of a century later.

De Lesseps's decision substantially added to the canal's cost and difficulty. The excavation of the canal was daunting enough, but the climate and diseases of the region (mainly yellow fever and malaria) proved too much for the French effort. Thirteen years and millions of francs later, de Lesseps and his company went bankrupt. A staggering 22,000 workers had lost their lives working on the canal. Most were felled by disease.

Too often, the French effort in Panama is considered one of corruption and mismanagement alone. This was not the case. The vast bulk of the money raised was indeed spent on the project, and the Americans would later be the beneficiaries of magnificent French hospitals, considerable equipment, large machine shops, and the excavation of 30 million cubic yards of earth.

When Theodore Roosevelt ascended to the presidency in 1901, one of his first goals was to pursue the construction of a canal across the Panamanian isthmus, which would be constructed and controlled by the United States. Before this could be done, however, the equipment that had been left behind from the French had to be purchased, and the isthmus itself had to be secured. Secretary of State John Hay immediately began the process of negotiating with the British, with whom the United States had earlier promised in the Clayton-Bulwey Treaty to cooperate in any canal project. The result was the Hay-Pauncefote Treaty, signed on November 18, 1901, that superseded the earlier agreement and essentially gave the United States carte blanche to do what it wished in terms of an isthmian canal.

Meanwhile, Colombia had been offered $10 million to cede to the United States a narrow strip of land in the Panama Province, where the canal would be built. In 1902, when the United States was scheduled to purchase the French equipment and old excavations for $40 million from a consortium headed by American financier John Pierpont Morgan, the Colombian Senate balked at the Hay-Herrán Treaty, which offered just $10 million up front and $250,000 annually for a 100-year lease of the 10-mile-wide canal zone. Instead, Colombia demanded an additional $10 million and refused to turn over any equipment or land to the Americans. The Roosevelt administration, outraged at this slight, arranged for the province to declare its independence from Colombia, thereby allowing the United States free rein in the area. Working closely with Panamanian businessmen, headed by Philippe Bunau-Varilla, who were eager to cooperate with Washington, a brief and largely phony revolution was staged in Colombia with the help of the U.S. government and U.S. naval forces off the coast of Panama.

On November 3, 1903, the Republic of Panama was officially proclaimed, the constitution for which had already been drafted by Americans in Washington. Almost immediately thereafter, the United States signed the Hay–Bunau-Varilla Treaty that promised Panama $10 million and annual payments of $250,000 in compensation for the establishment of the Panama Canal Zone, to be controlled and operated solely by the United States. The treaty also provided for the purchase of French equipment and their excavations. The United States would exercise sole control over the Panama Canal for 100 years. A subsequent treaty negotiated by the Jimmy Carter administration in 1978 provided for a transition to total Panamanian control, which was completed in December 1999.

On May 4, 1904, American construction on the Panama Canal began under the direction of Lieutenant Colonel George Washington Goethals, who as chief engineer and chairman of the Isthmian Canal Commission oversaw a plethora of U.S.-owned engineering and construction companies. To avoid the problems that plagued the earlier French efforts, the Roosevelt administration commenced a vigorous program under future surgeon general Dr. William C. Gorgas to eradicate yellow fever and malaria from the area. Under the watchful supervision of the U.S. Army, sanitation and quarantine facilities as well as hospitals were established to contain and eliminate the spread of infectious diseases. Commissions were also formed to carefully monitor laborers' health. A large part of the disease-eradication effort was the systematic elimination of mosquitoes, which carried the diseases. This included the eradication of stagnant water and the draining and filling of swamps and wetlands, where mosquitoes thrived. Insecticides were also widely used, and thin films of oil were often spread over ponds and lakes to discourage mosquito activity.

The army's aggressive and innovative approach to mosquito and disease control was highly successful. By 1906, yellow fever was virtually eliminated in the Canal Zone, and other diseases such as malaria had been curbed significantly. Finally, the hospitals in the Canal Zone were among the best in the world, meaning that the construction of the Panama Canal was a crowning achievement both for engineering and public health.

The Panama Canal was opened officially on August 15, 1914, when the cargo ship *Ancon* made the first commercial voyage through the canal. This was almost 12 months ahead of schedule. In all, some 5,600 laborers died while working on the canal between 1904 and 1914. Many were killed in accidents rather than by disease.

Following negotiations between the United States and Panama, the canal reverted to Panamanian control in December 1999. Panama recently embarked on a major project to widen and improve the canal. Officials estimated that when completed, it would expand traffic through the canal by 20 percent.

PAUL G. PIERPAOLI JR.

See also
Clayton-Bulwer Treaty; Goethals, George Washington; Gorgas, William Crawford; Hay, John Milton; Hay–Bunau-Varilla Treaty; Hay-Herrán Treaty; Hay-Pauncefote Treaty; Mahan, Alfred Thayer; Malaria;

Medicine, Military; Morgan, John Pierpont, Sr.; Naval Strategy, U.S.; *Oregon,* USS, Voyage of; Roosevelt, Theodore; United States Navy; Yellow Fever

Further Reading

Friar, William. *Portrait of the Panama Canal: From Construction to the Twenty-First Century.* Portland, OR: Graphic Arts Center, 2003.

McCullogh, David. *The Path between the Seas: The Creation of the Panama Canal, 1870–1914.* New York: Simon and Schuster, 1977.

Morris, Edmund. *Theodore Rex.* New York: Random House, 2001.

Parker, Nancy Winslow. *Locks, Crocs and Skeeters: The Story of the Panama Canal.* Greenwillow, NY: Greenwillow Books, 1996.

Panic of 1893

See Economic Depression

Paris, Treaty of

Treaty signed in Paris on December 10, 1898, that formally ended the Spanish-American War. The war itself lasted less than three months and resulted in a complete victory for the United States. Following Spanish land and naval defeats in Cuba, a naval defeat in the Philippines, and a U.S. expeditionary force registering significant progress in Puerto Rico, an armistice was arranged to take effect on August 12, 1898.

President William McKinley had wanted the negotiations to take place in Washington, D.C., but on the suggestion of French ambassador to the United States Jules-Martin Cambon, McKinley agreed on Paris. On the formal invitation of the French government, envoys from both the United States and Spain met in Paris on October 1, 1898. The American peace commission, chosen carefully by McKinley, included U.S. senators, prominent Republicans, and expansionists and consisted of William R. Day, Cushman K. Davis, William P. Frye, George Gray, and Whitelaw Reid. The Spanish side was represented by Eugenio Montero Ríos, Buenaventura de Abarzuza, José de Garnica, Wenceslao Ramirez de Villa Urrutia, and Rafael Cerero. Cambon, who had been acting as the official liaison between Madrid and Washington, was also present.

The United States had won an overwhelming military victory in the war, and the only question concerned the extent of concessions to be made by Spain. Territorial discussions included the future of Cuba, Puerto Rico, and Guam; the rights of Spanish citizens living on these islands; the exchange of prisoners; and debt questions. Debate over Cuba lasted nearly a month. The Spanish wanted the United States to annex the island, which would have meant absorbing a $400 million debt. The American commissioner steadfastly refused. The major issue in dispute was the future of the Philippine Islands. The Americans were themselves somewhat in disagreement over the islands, and the Spanish commissioners took the position that because Manila had surrendered after conclusion of the armistice, the Philippines

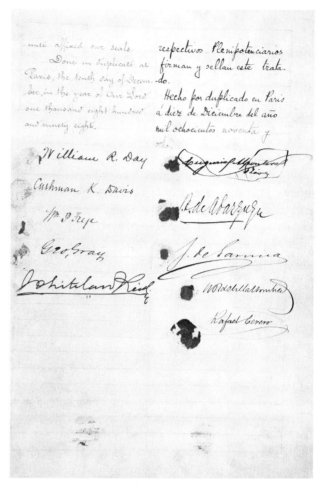

Signatures on the Treaty of Paris of December 10, 1898, which formally ended the Spanish-American War. (Bettmann/Corbis)

could not be considered as an American conquest in the war. In the end, with McKinley having decided firmly in favor of annexation, the Spanish side was forced to yield, with the United States agreeing to pay compensation.

The treaty comprised 17 articles. In Articles 1 and 2, Spain renounced all rights to Cuba and ceded Puerto Rico and other islands in the West Indies and the island of Guam to the United States. In Article 3, the United States agreed to pay Spain $20 million for the Philippine Islands. In Article 4, Spain was granted free access to its ships and goods to these islands for another 10 years. Articles 5 and 6 settled the question of the prisoners of war, who were to be returned to their home countries immediately, and also set timetables for the Spanish evacuation of the islands ceded to the United States. In Article 7, both countries mutually relinquished all claims for indemnity, while Article 8 settled property questions. Articles 9, 10, 11, and 13 dealt with the rights of Spanish citizens and other inhabitants in the islands. Article 12 set up specific rules relating to judicial proceedings in the territories pending at the time of the treaty. In Article 14, Spain was allowed to establish consular offices in its former colonies. Article 15 specified that both countries were to extend to the other's merchant ships the same port charges and duties as for its own vessels. Article 16 granted Cuba independence after a period of U.S. occupancy of unspecified length, the United States having pledged previously in the April 19, 1898, Teller Amendment not to annex the island. Finally, Article 17 called for the treaty to be ratified within six months of its signing.

The treaty was controversial in the United States, and ratification was not a foregone conclusion. The principal issue of friction was the U.S. acquisition of the Philippines. A great public and congressional debate occurred during the ensuing months that pitted imperialists against anti-imperialists. Proponents of U.S. expansion, including Senators Henry Cabot Lodge and Knute Nelson, argued that the United States had a duty to export its "superior" democratic institutions and a mission to further the spread of Christianity (never mind the fact that the Philippines were already overwhelmingly Roman Catholic). Besides, the expansionists argued, if the United States did not move into the Philippines, other powers, most probably Germany, would. Anti-imperialists, such as Senators George Frisbie Hoar and George Graham Vest, maintained that expansionism would turn the United States into another colonial power, suppressing people fighting for their independence, and that it meant violating American values and the constitution because these people would not be represented in Congress. Former president Grover Cleveland and industrialist Andrew Carnegie also petitioned the Senate to reject the treaty. The Senate rejected the Bacon Amendment, which rejected permanent U.S. sovereignty over the Philippines, with Vice President Garret August Hobart casting the tie-breaking vote. On February 6, 1899, the treaty received the necessary two-thirds ratification approval by a vote of 57 to 27. In Spain, there was also considerable opposition to the treaty. Indeed, it required the signature of Queen Regent María Cristina to end a deadlock in the Spanish legislature and permit ratification on March 19, 1899. The Treaty of Paris marked both the end of the Spanish Empire and the emergence of the United States as a world power.

KATJA WUESTENBECKER

See also

Anti-Imperialist League; Bacon Amendment; Carnegie, Andrew; Cleveland, Stephen Grover; Cuba; Day, William Rufus; Dewey, George; Frye, William Pierce; Gray, George; Guam; Hoar, George Frisbie; Hobart, Garret Augustus; Lodge, Henry Cabot; Manila Bay, Battle of; María Cristina, Queen Regent of Spain; McKinley, William; Montero Ríos, Eugenio; Philippine Islands, U.S. Acquisition of; Puerto Rico Campaign; Reid, Whitelaw; Teller Amendment

Further Reading

Benton, Elbert J. International Law and Diplomacy of the Spanish-American War. 1908; reprint, Clark, NJ: Lawbook Exchange, 2005.
Johnston, William. History up to Date: A Concise Account of the War of 1898 between the United States and Spain, Its Causes and the Treaty of Paris. New York: A. S. Barnes, 1899.
McCartney, Paul T. Power and Progress: American National Identity, the War of 1898, and the Rise of American Imperialism. Baton Rouge: Louisiana State University Press, 2006.
A Treaty of Paris between the United States and Spain, Signed at the City of Paris, on December 10, 1898. U.S. Congress, 55th Congress, 3rd Session, Senate Doc. No. 62. Washington, DC: U.S. Government Printing Office, 1899.

Paterno y Debera Ignacio, Pedro Alejandro
Birth Date: February 17, 1857
Death Date: April 26, 1911

Filipino revolutionary, writer, and politician who served as the second prime minister of the First Philippine Republic (1899). Pedro Alejandro Paterno y Debera Ignacio was born into an elite mestizo merchant family in Manila on February 17, 1857. His home was a frequent venue for gatherings of literary artists. As such, it was one of the first attempts to present works by Filipinos to project a national identity. Paterno departed for Spain in 1871 and, after studying at the University of Salamanca, earned a law degree at the University of Madrid in 1880. While studying in Spain, he became acquainted with Fernando Primo de Rivera y Sobremonte, who would twice become governor-general of the Philippines.

In 1880, Paterno published Sampaguitas y Otras Poesias Varias, which became the first book of poetry published by a Filipino in Europe. Sampaguita is the Tagalog term for Jasminum sambac, a species of jasmine native to southern Asia. His detractors at the time called Paterno the sampaguitero. In addition to poetry, Paterno wrote on historical subjects, ethnography, law, politics, and drama. He wrote the first Filipino novel, Ninay, that was published in Madrid in 1885. The novel is an exaltation of the pre-Hispanic traces of civilization in the Philippines. Although not valuable for its literary qualities, the novel did set the stage for subsequent novels that would highlight Filipino identity traits. As with many ilustrados (Filipino intellectuals educated in Europe), Paterno wrote about the downside of European colonization. In 1887, he published his first of many volumes on Filipino history. In La Antigua Civilización Tagala (Ancient Tagalog Civilization), he glorified the pre-Spanish Tagalog culture. Unfortunately, his rich imagination produced historical studies that fall into the genre of historical fiction. His most energetic historical effort was his seven-volume Historia de Filipinas published in Manila between 1908 and 1910.

After living in Spain for more than two decades, Paterno returned to the Philippines in 1894 to become the director of the Museo-Biblioteca de Manila. Although suspected of revolutionary tendencies, he was not arrested by Spanish authorities. In 1897, Spanish governor-general Primo de Rivera appointed Paterno sole mediator in discussions of the terms of peace between Filipino revolutionaries and the Spanish colonial government. After five months of negotiations, both sides agreed to the Pact of Biak-na-Bato and signed the agreement on December 14, 1897. The treaty ended the first phase of the Philippine revolution and resulted in the voluntary exile of Emilio Aguinaldo y Famy and other revolutionary leaders to Hong Kong. Paterno went with Aguinaldo.

Following the return of Aguinaldo and other Filipino revolutionary leaders to the Philippines in May 1898, they renewed their struggle against Spanish colonial authorities. Paterno served as president of the Assembly of Representatives from September 15, 1898, to May 7, 1899. Aguinaldo then appointed Paterno as the prime minister of the First Philippine Republic on May 7, 1899, succeeding Apolinario Mabini. On June 2, 1899, Paterno issued a declaration of war against the United States. Captured by American forces in Benguet in November 1899, he was granted amnesty after the Philippine-American War.

In 1910, Paterno published his recollections of the peace treaty between Spain and the Filipino revolutionaries in *El Pacto de Biak-na-bato* (The Pact of Biak-na-Bato). Of all of Paterno's historical works, *El Pacto de Biak-na-bato* is the most credible and important. Paterno's study serves as a valuable counterpoint to the versions of the negotiations recorded by Governor-General Primo de Rivera and Aguinaldo. Paterno died of cholera in Manila on April 26, 1911.

MICHAEL R. HALL

See also
Aguinaldo y Famy, Emilio; Biak-na-Bato, Pact of; Mabini, Apolinario; Philippine-American War; Primo de Rivera y Sobremonte, Fernando

Further Reading
Balfour, Sebastian. *The End of the Spanish Empire, 1898–1923.* New York: Oxford University Press USA, 1997.
Devins, John Bancroft. *An Observer in the Philippines.* Ithaca, NY: Cornell University Press, 2007.
Paterno, Pedro Alejandro. *Ninay: Costumbres Filipinas.* Madrid: Imprenta de Fortanet, 1885.

Pauncefote, Julian
Birth Date: September 13, 1828
Death Date: May 24, 1902

British diplomat and ambassador to the United States (1893–1902). Born in Munich, Germany, on September 13, 1828, Julian Pauncefote was educated in Paris and Geneva and at Marlborough College in Wiltshire. He was called to the law in 1852. Three years later, he became private secretary to British secretary of state for the colonies Sir William Molesworth.

In 1862, Pauncefote decided to practice law in Hong Kong and became that colony's attorney general in 1865 and then chief justice. In 1873, he was appointed chief justice of the Leeward Islands and was knighted. In 1876, he became assistant undersecretary of state for the colonies and later in the year assumed the same post at the Foreign Office. In 1882, Pauncefote was named permanent undersecretary of the Foreign Office.

In 1889, Prime Minister Robert Gascoyne-Cecil, Lord Salisbury, appointed Pauncefote to be British minister to the United States. In this post, Pauncefote worked to create friendly relations with the

Sir Julian Pauncefote was British ambassador to the United States during 1893–1902. (Library of Congress)

United States, successfully negotiating the Bering Sea fishery dispute of 1890–1892. In April 1893 when the position of minister to the United States was raised to ambassador, Pauncefote became the first British ambassador to the United States. He played a key role in defusing the First Venezuela Crisis (1895–1897), eventually accepting American arbitration of the boundary dispute between British Guiana and Venezuela.

During the events that preceded the Spanish-American War, Pauncefote assisted U.S. secretary of state William R. Day in drafting the Great Powers Note of April 6, 1898, which he then signed for Britain. Upset with President William McKinley's war message to Congress of April 11, 1898, Pauncefote sought to organize a meeting of representatives of the great powers in order to avoid hostilities, but acting British foreign secretary Arthur J. Balfour, who was eager to win the support of the United States and not undercut President William McKinley, rejected this suggestion.

Pauncefote participated in the Peace Conference at The Hague in 1899 and was a member of the Court of Arbitration created by it. Recognized for his services in that regard, he was made Baron Pauncefote of Preston in 1899. Still serving as ambassador to the United States, Pauncefote died in Washington, D.C., on May 24, 1902.

SPENCER C. TUCKER

See also

Balfour, Arthur James; Day, William Rufus; Gascoyne-Cecil, Robert Arthur Talbot; Great Britain, Policies and Reactions to the Spanish-American War; McKinley, William; Venezuela Crisis, First

Further Reading

MacKay, Ruddock F. *Balfour: Intellectual Statesman.* New York: Oxford University Press USA, 1985.

Perkins, Bradford. *The Great Rapprochement: England and the United States, 1895–1914.* New York: Atheneum, 1968.

Peace, Protocol of

Preliminary peace proposal signed between Spain and the United States that formally ended hostilities and served as a basis for the subsequent Treaty of Paris. On July 26, 1898, French ambassador to the United States Jules-Martin Cambon contacted the U.S. government on behalf of the Spanish government. The Spanish requested an immediate cease-fire and negotiations for peace. President William McKinley replied to the offer on July 30 via Cambon, who

had represented Spanish interests during the war. Cambon had also expended effort prior to the beginning of hostilities in an attempt to head off war.

On August 2, 1898, Spain tentatively accepted the U.S. proposals of July 30 but with certain reservations concerning the cession of the Philippines. Before agreeing to a cease-fire, McKinley insisted that a preliminary peace protocol be brokered with the Spanish. Thus, on August 11, U.S. secretary of state William Rufus Day and Ambassador Cambon hammered out a preliminary peace proposal known as the Protocol of Peace. This protocol, signed on August 12, 1898, officially ended hostilities between Spain and the United States and was to serve as the basis for more formal negotiations for a lasting peace agreement. That pact, known as the Treaty of Paris, was signed on December 10, 1898. It was Cambon who suggested Paris as the site of the treaty talks, which McKinley readily accepted.

The Protocol of Peace was quite brief and consisted of only six articles. The first article called for Spain to relinquish all control of Cuba. The second article stipulated that Spain was to cede Puerto Rico and other islands in the West Indies to the United States and also called for the cession of Guam to the United States. The third

President William McKinley (standing right, next to table) and members of the government watch as French ambassador Jules-Martin Cambon signs the Protocol of Peace, a document preceding the formal peace negotiations ending the Spanish-American War. (Library of Congress)

article held that the United States would control Manila and its bay until a formal peace agreement was signed, at which time the final disposition of the Philippines would be determined. The fourth article stipulated that Spain immediately evacuate Cuba, Puerto Rico, "and other islands now under Spanish sovereignty in the West Indies." The fifth article called for both nations to appoint up to five commissioners who would meet in Paris no later than October 1 with the goal of producing a peace treaty. The last article formalized the cessation of hostilities as of August 12, 1898.

Although Cambon had worked to limit the amount of Spanish territory ceded to the Americans, he realized that he had an uphill fight. Once the talk of a cease-fire had begun in July, it became more apparent that the United States would exact steep territorial concessions from the Spanish. At first hopeful that he could get the Americans to limit their sovereignty in the Philippines to the city of Manila, Cambon soon realized that U.S. acquisition of the entire Philippine archipelago was practically a foregone conclusion. Indeed, when the hostilities ended, McKinley was more disposed to taking all of the islands, and Congress had already made its preference known on the issue.

PAUL G. PIERPAOLI JR.

See also

Cambon, Jules-Martin; Day, William Rufus; Guam; McKinley, William; Paris, Treaty of; Philippine Islands, U.S. Acquisition of; Puerto Rico

Further Reading

Cambon, Jules. *The Foreign Policy of the Powers.* Reprint ed. Freeport, NY: Books for Libraries Press, 1970.

Leech, Margaret. *In the Days of McKinley.* New York: Harper and Brothers, 1959.

Musicant, Ivan. *Empire by Default: The Spanish-American War and the Dawn of the American Century.* New York: Henry Holt, 1998.

Tabouis, Geneviève R. *The Life of Jules Cambon.* Translated by C. F. Atkinson. London: Cape, 1938.

Peace Commission

A 10-man commission composed of 5 Americans and 5 Spaniards that met in Paris, France, to negotiate the peace treaty—the Treaty of Paris—ending the Spanish-American War. The commission included politicians, judges, and military leaders and convened from October 1 to December 10, 1898, the day the treaty was signed.

Realizing that defeat was inevitable, the Spanish government in Madrid sent a message to President William McKinley on July 18, 1898, to request a cessation of hostilities and talks that would lead to a permanent peace agreement. The message was relayed to the U.S. government by Jules-Martin Cambon, French minister to the United States. Meanwhile, Spanish Minister of State Juan Manuel Sánchez y Gutiérrez de Castro, Duque de Almodóvar del Río, sent a telegram to the Spanish ambassador in Paris directing him to en-

In this political cartoon by Charles Lewis Bartholomew, Uncle Sam points a miniature battleship at a terrified Spain after winning most of the chips in a "Peace Commission Game." (Library of Congress)

gage the services of the French government to help negotiate a cease-fire. This would serve as a preliminary step to final peace negotiations.

On August 2, Spain accepted the U.S. proposals for peace but with some reservations regarding the disposition of the Philippine Islands because McKinley was not entirely sure what to do with the archipelago. Prior to meeting in Paris, the formal Protocol of Peace was signed in Washington, D.C., on August 12, 1898. It officially ended hostilities between Spain and the United States in Cuba, Puerto Rico, and the Philippines.

By September 16, American and Spanish commissioners for the peace talks had been officially appointed. On the American side, McKinley selected his five-man delegation with care. Three prominent members of the Senate were chosen in an obvious effort to win support for the pact in advance. The U.S. commissioners were William R. Day, U.S. secretary of state who resigned his post (and was succeeded by John Hay) in order to head the peace delegation; William P. Frye, Republican senator from Maine and president pro tempore of the Senate; Whitelaw Reid, Ohio journalist, owner of the *New York Tribune,* minister to France, Republican vice presidential candidate on the 1892 ticket, and a mild imperialist; Democratic senator from Delaware George Gray, a respected jurist; and Minnesota Republican senator Cushman K. Davis, chairman of the Senate Foreign Relations Committee.

The Spanish commissioners included Eugenio Montero Rios, president of the Spanish Senate; Buenaventura Abarzuza, a senator and associate justice of the Supreme Court; José de Garnica y Diaz; Wenceslao Ramirez de Villa Urrutia, envoy extraordinary; and General of the Army Rafael Cerero y Saenz.

Prior to the commencement of negotiations in Paris on October 1, the American commissioners were divided over the issue of Philippine annexation. Day, representing the anti-imperialists and former president Grover Cleveland's "little America," opposed the acquisition of the islands. Senator Frye, an advocate of Hawaii annexation, along with Reid and Davis meanwhile urged the retention of all the islands. It would be these three who would ultimately carry out the president's wishes in this matter.

Before addressing the Philippines, however, a protracted controversy over Cuba took nearly a month once negotiations started. American commissioners insisted on independence for Cuba in keeping with the spirit of the Teller Amendment that denied any intention on the part of the United States to annex the island. The Spanish delegation, however, led by Rios and Urrutia, insisted on handing Cuba over to the United States. The real stumbling block was that annexation would have involved the United States absorbing nearly $400 million in debt incurred by Spanish authorities in their attempts to crush the rebellion. The American commissioners flatly rejected such a course.

The question of what to do with the Philippines occupied even more time. McKinley had instructed his delegation to focus on the commercial advantages of the islands and to insist that the United States could not accept anything less than Luzon, the largest island and home to the principal city of Manila and its valuable harbor. The reality was that McKinley had already decided on an expansionist course and believed that popular opinion would eventually catch up with him. In early November, the Spanish commissioners warned that the demand for all of the Philippines, added to the insistence that Spain assume full responsibility for the Cuban debt, could end the negotiations. Reid, Frye, and Day then suggested that Spain be allowed to retain the southern islands of Mindanao and Sulu. But the new secretary of state, John Hay, then cabled the commissioners that the president would accept nothing less than all of the Philippines. On November 28, the Spanish commissioners reluctantly accepted the American proposal of a $20 million payment for all the islands.

Reid and the other expansionist members of the American commission also entertained the question of the annexation of the Caroline Islands during the course of negotiations. American capitalists were considering prospects for a cable between Hawaii and Manila, making the Carolines an attractive acquisition. But the German government quickly preempted such a U.S. acquisition. In fact, a secret accord was struck in which Spain agreed to sell to Germany the islands of Kusaie, Ponape, and Yap in the Carolines. The Spanish commissioners informed their American counterparts that the Caroline archipelago was beyond the scope of the proposed treaty. The American commissioners acquiesced on the point, paving the way for a final settlement.

On December 10, 1898, the peace commissioners on both sides signed the Treaty of Paris formally ending the Spanish-American War. The treaty dictated that Spain renounce all rights to Cuba and agree to an independent Cuba, cede Puerto Rico and Guam to the United States, and give up possessions in the West Indies. The treaty also stipulated that Spain sell the Philippines to the United States for $20 million. On December 21, McKinley issued his so-called Benevolent Assimilation Proclamation, formally ceding the Philippines to the United States and ordering American troops there to impose American sovereignty over the islands, which was to occur before the U.S. Senate ratified the Treaty of Paris. Although the war with Spain was officially over, the conflict in the Philippines lasted almost three more years.

CHARLES F. HOWLETT

See also
Cambon, Jules-Martin; Caroline Islands; Davis, Cushman Kellogg; Day, William Rufus; Frye, William Pierce; Gray, George; Guam; Hay, John Milton; McKinley, William; Paris, Treaty of; Peace, Protocol of; Philippine Islands, U.S. Acquisition of; Puerto Rico; Reid, Whitelaw

Further Reading
Coy, Richard. "Cushman K. Davis and American Foreign Policy, 1887–1900." PhD dissertation, University of Minnesota, 1965.
Croslin, Michael. "The Diplomacy of George Gray." PhD dissertation, Oklahoma State University, 1980.
Dulles, Foster Rhea. *America's Rise to World Power, 1898–1954.* New York: Harper and Row, 1955.
Duncan, Bingham. *Whitelaw Reid: Journalist, Politician, Diplomat.* Athens: University of Georgia Press, 1975.
Gould, Lewis L. *The Spanish-American War and President McKinley.* Lawrence: University Press of Kansas, 1982.
LaFeber, Walter. *The New Empire: An Interpretation of American Expansion, 1860–1898.* Ithaca, NY: Cornell University Press, 1963.

Peanut Club

Nickname given to daily press conferences held at the Cuban Junta's headquarters in New York City. Sponsored by the Cuban Junta, press conferences were typically held at 4:00 p.m., Monday through Friday, beginning with the Cuban War of Independence (1895–1898). Reporters attending the press conferences dubbed them the Peanut Club because Cuban Junta officials always had copious amounts of peanuts for reporters to eat. Horatio Rubens, a New York City attorney and chief legal counsel to the group, presided over most of the press conferences.

The Cuban Junta was formed in September 1895 shortly after the beginning of the Cuban War of Independence. Its principal purpose was to seek U.S. support for the Cuban cause and to lobby politicians and others in positions of power to champion their effort and pressure the Spanish to abandon Cuba. The Cuban Junta worked closely with the yellow journalists of the day and became a favorite cause of newspaper publishers such as Joseph Pulitzer and William Randolph Hearst. It is believed that the Cuban Junta had two of its agents working directly for two influential American newspapers, the *New Orleans Times-Picayune* and the District of Columbia *Washington Star.*

Perhaps the most visible function of the Cuban Junta was to conduct a far-flung public relations effort designed to sway public opinion to the Cuban cause. While some of the accounts of Cuban troubles were clearly accurate, many were not. Some incidents and reports were purposely exaggerated, while others were fabricated altogether. These stories and reports coming from the Cuban Junta invariably portrayed the Spanish as barbaric aggressors with no moral compass. The Cubans, on the other hand, were portrayed as heroic liberators insistent on the establishment of a pure and independent Cuban democracy.

PAUL G. PIERPAOLI JR.

See also
Cuban Junta; Cuban War of Independence; Hearst, William Randolph; Journalism; Newspapers; Pulitzer, Joseph; Yellow Journalism

Further Reading
Auxier, George W. "The Propaganda Activities of the Cuban Junta in Precipitating the Spanish-American War, 1895–1898." *Hispanic American Historical Review* 19(3) (August 1939): 286–305.

Campbell, W. Joseph. *Yellow Journalism: Puncturing the Myths, Defining the Legacies.* Westport, CT: Praeger, 2003.

Milton, Joyce. *The Yellow Kids: Foreign Correspondents in the Heyday of Yellow Journalism.* New York: Harper and Row, 1989.

Pearl of the Antilles

A commonly used nickname for the island of Cuba. The Antilles are the chain of islands, including Cuba, that form the majority of the West Indies, located in the Caribbean Sea between North and South America. The Antilles are divided between the Greater Antilles and the Lesser Antilles. Included among the Greater Antilles are Hispaniola (present-day Dominican Republic and Haiti), Cuba, Jamaica, and Puerto Rico. The Lesser Antilles lie to the southeast and include the many smaller islands of the Leeward and Windward Islands. The origin of "antilles," a French word, is somewhat obscure, but a variant of it appeared on European maps dating to the late medieval period. During the early period of European exploration in the area, the Caribbean Sea was often referred to as the Sea of the Antilles.

Cuba, the largest island in all of the Antilles, came to be known as the Pearl of the Antilles because it was coveted by all of the major colonial powers beginning in the 16th century. Indeed, Spain, France, and Britain all cast their lot to control the island of Cuba, but in the end Spain maintained control of Cuba practically uninterrupted for nearly 400 years. Christopher Columbus, the first European to visit Cuba, which occurred in October 1492, declared it to be "the most beautiful land human eyes have ever beheld." His arrival was made all the more moving by the warm reception he received from the Siboney Indians who inhabited the island. From that point on, Europeans and especially the Spanish saw in Cuba an infinite land of precious resources and prosperity. Less than a generation later, however, the Spaniards' quest for gold and other sources of wealth in Cuba had seriously undermined the native social fabric of the island. European diseases wiped out native populations, and the Spanish imported African slaves for labor. Besides its rich natural resources, Cuba offered a generally salubrious climate that lent itself well to the cultivation of crops such as sugarcane and cotton, which only increased the island's allure from the European perspective.

By the late 16th century, a prosperous slave-based Cuban economy, much of which was based upon the cultivation of sugar, had turned cities such as Havana into elegant microcosms of European society. Controlling the island of Cuba gave Spain de facto control over much of the Caribbean and the Gulf of Mexico, which was particularly important in defending its interests in Mexico as well as in Central and South America. It also allowed the Spanish to control the strategic Florida Strait and its interests in Florida and along the Gulf Coast. Indeed, long after the once-mighty Spanish Empire began to crumble in the New World, Cuba remained Spain's most stable and prosperous colony. Not until the 1860s would a concentrated rebellion against Spanish rule take root on the island, more than 50 years after revolts had caused Spain to lose many of its other American colonies.

Europeans were not the only people to cast covetous eyes upon the Pearl of the Antilles. Over the years, many Americans—including leading politicians—had shown interest in controlling the island. Thomas Jefferson himself stated bluntly that "we must have Cuba" nearly a century before the Spanish-American War began. Southern planters in the United States also greedily eyed the sugar plantations in Cuba, hoping to one day enjoy a controlling interest in sugar production and trade. They also saw in Cuba an additional slave state for the union.

Cuba's natural beauty and bountiful resources, strategic location in the Caribbean, and proximity to the Americas without a doubt earned it the sobriquet Pearl of the Antilles. Even after the Spanish-American War ended, the United States exercised virtual control over the island until Fidel Castro's 1959 communist-inspired revolution cast away nearly every vestige of American hegemony there. And still, more than 100 years after the war and almost 50 years after Castro's revolution, the United States still maintains a naval base in Cuba at Guantánamo Bay, a powerful sign that Cuba remains the Pearl of the Antilles to the present day.

PAUL G. PIERPAOLI JR.

See also
Cuba; Cuban Sugar; Ostend Manifesto

Further Reading
Musicant, Ivan. *Empire by Default: The Spanish-American War and the Dawn of the American Century.* New York: Henry Holt, 1998.

Staten, Clifford L. *The History of Cuba.* London: Palgrave Macmillan, 2005.

Penny Press

Inexpensive, sensationalistic newspapers that began circulating in the 1830s and were the precursors to the yellow journalism of the

Newsboy selling papers on a street corner in 1896. (Library of Congress)

1880s and 1890s. Unlike the partisan newspapers of the pre–American Civil War period, the penny press papers (that is, newspapers that sold for a penny), such as Edward Bennett's *New York Herald,* emphasized sensationalistic crime stories that appealed to a large working-class reading audience. During the Civil War, the *New York Herald* and other similar newspapers sent reporters directly into the field. Because of the demands of the reading public about facts in the war and the world economy that had been imposed by the telegraph, the penny press changed journalism from partisan publications to fact-based reporting. Indeed, the penny press was the prototype of modern journalism.

Prior to the 1830s, newspapers were often called broadsides and were not cheap to produce. Improvements in printing technology, especially the steam-powered cylinder press (rotary press), led to great reductions in the cost of producing newspapers so that they could be sold for a penny, as opposed to the papers produced by the flat plate process that commonly sold for six cents a copy. Two of the leaders in the penny press, Benjamin Day's *New York Sun* and Edward Bennett's *New York Herald,* were aggressively hawked on the streets by paid salesmen. This led to a remarkable rise in their circulations, which allowed the penny press to rely on higher advertising rates to increase profits. The *Herald* reached a circulation of more than 75,000 before the Civil War even though the price had increased to two cents a copy. These tabloid-style papers also differed from the Jacksonian-era partisan papers, which had as their sole goal the election of candidates from specific parties and which

often were founded and operated by party operatives. The Jacksonian-era presses also benefited greatly from the franking privilege in Congress whereby elected officials could send for free any mail to constituents, bombarding voters with a legislator's most recent speeches or commentary.

Bennett and Day, however, emphasized stories that would appeal to buyers, especially crime and particularly the more sensationalistic and lurid stories that could be found. Relying heavily on police reports, the *Herald* and *Sun* were really the forerunners of today's *National Enquirer,* and while penny presses failed at higher rates, before long every city had one. For example, Philadelphia had the *Daily Transcript,* and Boston had the *Daily Ledger.* These papers appealed to immigrants, and the motto of the *Sun* ("It Shines for All") reflected the alleged democratic effects that they had on mass publishing. Certainly, the penny press made publishers such as Bennett quite wealthy.

The penny press changed reporting, which, after all, had merely meant repeating verbatim politicians' speeches in many of the Jacksonian-era papers. Bennett's reporters fought a number of legal battles to report directly from courtrooms without being held in contempt, and Bennett personally investigated the murder of a young prostitute in 1836. The *Herald* sent a reporter to cover the Mexican-American War and had more than 60 reporters covering the American Civil War. By that time, a revolution in journalism had taken place partly due to the telegraph, which placed a premium on word economy. Flowery and verbose stories were replaced by tightly written fact-based reporting that got to the point quickly.

Some journalism historians argue that the inverted pyramid appeared at this time in which the most important facts were presented first, then facts of lesser importance, and so on. The demand for facts during the American Civil War combined with the appearance of professional publishing managers killed the old partisan papers. Already, the partisan press had been unable to pay for itself. Collections on circulations were always behind, and without subsidies from political parties, the partisan press would have collapsed much sooner. The benefits provided by the franking privilege also aided these newspapers. According to one student of the postal system, shipping a newspaper was about eight times cheaper than shipping a book. This, in turn, drove publishers away from book publishing and into newspaper publishing.

In the years leading up to the Spanish-American War, even the mainstream press had begun to borrow reporting and publishing techniques from the penny press. Indeed, publishing magnates such as Joseph Pulitzer and William Randolph Hearst began publishing sensationalistic and lurid accounts of Spanish atrocities in Cuba, which fed the public's hunger for such reporting and fanned the flames of interventionism. After the United States declared war on Spain in April 1898, the so-called yellow press, a linear descendant of the penny press, dispatched scores of reporters, along with photographers, to the front lines to report to the American public on the war effort. By the turn of the 20th century, journalism in the

United States had become thoroughly modernized, not to mention remarkably lucrative.

LARRY SCHWEIKART

See also

Hearst, William Randolph; Journalism; Pulitzer, Joseph; Telephone and Telegraph; Yellow Journalism

Further Reading

Campbell, W. Joseph. *Yellow Journalism: Puncturing the Myths, Defining the Legacies.* Westport, CT: Praeger, 2003.

Nord, David Paul. *Communities of Journalism: A History of American Newspapers and Their Readers.* Champaign: University of Illinois Press, 2006.

Spencer, David R. *The Yellow Journalism: The Press and America's Emergence as a World Power.* Evanston, IL: Northwestern University Press, 2007.

Whitelaw, Nancy. *William Randolph Hearst and the American Century.* Greensboro, NC: Morgan Reynolds, 2004.

Pershing, John Joseph
Birth Date: September 13, 1860
Death Date: July 15, 1948

General of the Armies of the United States and commander of U.S. forces in France in World War I. Born in Laclede, Missouri, on September 13, 1860, John "Black Jack" Pershing worked odd jobs and taught school to support his family until receiving an appointment to the United States Military Academy, West Point, in 1882. Commissioned a second lieutenant upon graduation in 1886, he joined the 6th Cavalry Regiment in New Mexico and saw limited action in the final subjugation of the Apache Indians. He also participated in the campaign to quiet the Sioux in 1891 following the tragic confrontation at Wounded Knee.

In 1891, Pershing became professor of military science at the University of Nebraska, where he also studied law. He completed a law degree in 1893 and, frustrated by the lack of military advancement, flirted with the idea of a legal career. In 1895, however, he returned to the field with the 10th Cavalry, an African American unit. He joined the staff of commanding general Nelson A. Miles in Washington in 1896 and then was an instructor of tactics at West Point in 1897. Here, cadets unhappy with Pershing's dark demeanor and rigid style labeled him "Black Jack," a derogatory reference to his 10th Cavalry posting.

With the start of the Spanish-American War in 1898, Pershing left his teaching assignment to rejoin the 10th Cavalry for the Cuba Campaign, arriving at Tampa, Florida, just in time to board the regiment's transport for Cuba. His men performed well during the Santiago Campaign, and Pershing distinguished himself in the Battle of Las Guásimas on June 24. In the fight for San Juan Heights on July 1, he drew praise for his own coolness and bravery under fire and was later awarded the Silver Star for this action. Contracting malaria, he returned to the United States to recover. There he was

General of the Armies of the United States John J. Pershing, who commanded U.S. forces in France during World War I, first distinguished himself in Cuba during the Spanish-American War and in Moro Province during the Philippine-American War. (Library of Congress)

promoted to major of U.S. Volunteers in August and was assigned to the office of the assistant secretary of war, where he was given oversight of the War Department's new Bureau of Insular Affairs, charged with administering the Philippines and Puerto Rico. Pershing believed that the United States had acted correctly in acquiring the Philippines and firmly believed in a U.S. civilizing mission there.

In September 1899, Pershing was assigned to the Philippines. There he campaigned successfully against the Moros in the Lake Lanao region in central Mindanao in 1901–1902, attracting further recognition for his ability to win their friendship and trust. Commander in the Philippines Brigadier General Adna Chaffee appointed Pershing commander of Camp Vicars on Mindanao in June 1902, and Pershing put into practice his policy of waging the peace, resorting to force with the Moros only as a last recourse. As recognition of the high esteem in which he was held, the Moros gave him the title of datu (chieftain).

Pershing returned to the United States for General Staff service and to attend the Army War College in 1903. As military attaché to Japan during 1905–1906, he became an official observer of the

Russo-Japanese War (1904–1905). Impressed with Pershing, President Theodore Roosevelt nominated him for direct promotion from captain to brigadier general in September 1906, vaulting him ahead of 862 more senior officers. Pershing spent most of the next eight years in the Philippines, where he continued to display effective leadership as military commander of Moro Province and crushed the last major Moro uprising at Bud Bagsak in January 1912. Returning to the United States, he commanded briefly at the Presidio, San Francisco, before moving to Fort Bliss near El Paso, Texas, in 1914 to confront problems associated with the Mexican Revolution. His wife Frances Warren and their three daughters, who remained at the Presidio, died in a house fire there in 1915.

Following the raid by Mexican revolutionary leader Francisco "Pancho" Villa on the small border town of Columbus, New Mexico, on March 9, 1916, Pershing took charge of a Punitive Expedition of 10,000 men into Mexico with orders to capture or kill Villa and his followers while avoiding conflict with Mexico. The expedition lasted 10 months, cut deep into northern Mexico, and threatened all-out war. Although Villa escaped, Pershing tested new technologies, including machine guns, aircraft, motorized transport, and radio.

Following the U.S. declaration of war on Germany on April 6, 1917, President Woodrow Wilson named Pershing, only recently promoted to major general, to command the American Expeditionary Forces (AEF) in France on May 12, 1917. Pershing, promoted to full general in October 1917, stubbornly refused to have his forces broken up in smaller units as fillers for British and French forces. However, during the crisis occasioned by Germany's 1918 Spring (Ludendorff) Offensives, Pershing offered individual U.S. divisions to the Allied command, and the Americans quickly proved their worth.

Pershing directed American forces in the Aisne-Marne Offensive (July 25–August 2, 1918) and the St. Mihiel Salient Offensive (September 12–17). He hoped to follow up this latter victory with a drive on Metz and beyond, but Allied commander General Ferdinand Foch favored a broad-front strategy and refused. Pershing then redirected American efforts into the massive Allied Meuse-Argonne Offensive (September 26–November 11). He opposed the armistice of November 11, 1918, preferring to fight until Germany surrendered, but was overruled.

After overseeing the demobilization of American forces, Pershing returned to the United States a hero in 1919. Congress confirmed his status as a four-star general with the rank title of general of the armies that September. After serving as army chief of staff during 1921–1924, Pershing retired. In 1923, he also became chairman of the American Battle Monuments Commission, the organization responsible for the administration of all American military cemeteries outside the United States. He continued serving in that capacity until 1948.

Active in public life thereafter, Pershing received the Pulitzer Prize for his memoir, *My Experiences in the World War* (1931). He died at Washington, D.C., on July 15, 1948. A stern disciplinarian

with high standards and a superb administrator with an ability to pick able subordinates, Pershing was also a military diplomat of high order and among the most significant leaders in American military history.

DAVID COFFEY

See also
Bud Dajo Campaign; Lake Lanao Campaigns; Las Guásimas, Battle of; Moros; San Juan Heights, Battle of; Santiago de Cuba Land Campaign

Further Reading
Cooke, James J. *Pershing and His Generals: Command and Staff in the AEF.* Westport, CT: Praeger, 1997.
Smith, Gene. *Until the Last Trumpet Sounds: The Life of General of the Armies John J. Pershing.* New York: Wiley, 1999.
Smythe, Donald. *Guerrilla Warrior: The Early Life of John J. Pershing.* New York: Scribner, 1973.
———. *Pershing: General of the Armies.* Bloomington: Indiana University Press, 1986.
Vandiver, Frank E. *Black Jack: The Life and Times of John J. Pershing.* 2 vols. College Station: Texas A&M University Press, 1977.

Philanthropy

In the last third of the 19th century, U.S. industrialists gave away vast sums. If the last decades of the 19th century were known for their unbridled economic expansion and speculation in the United States, so too were they known for the rise of organized philanthropy on a scale never before witnessed. Indeed, the phenomenon of private philanthropy on a massive scale was distinctly American, and in no other industrialized nation—not even in Western Europe—had such a thing ever occurred. Helping to fuel such philanthropic endeavors were modern industrialization and rapid and massive consolidation within industries, which left solitary individuals in control of dizzying sums of money. Also promoting this trend were U.S. government policies that emphasized a laissez-faire economic philosophy that ensured to businesses negligible taxation and practically unfettered access to markets, expansion, consolidation, and profits.

Since the late 1860s, American industrial expansion had brought about the Gilded Age, a term first used by Mark Twain to describe American society in the Victorian era. That same society had helped produce the so-called robber barons, a pejorative term used to describe some of America's most powerful and wealthy industrialists. During the Gilded Age, industrialists such as Cornelius Vanderbilt, Henry Clay Frick, John D. Rockefeller, and Andrew Carnegie amassed personal fortunes; indeed, not even most of the European aristocracy could lay claim to such monetary empires. The American industrialists lived life large, erecting gigantic homes along New York City's Fifth Avenue that were fit for kings. Indeed, for roughly a three-mile stretch, each mansion that went up seemed larger and more ornate than the other. Nowhere in the world was such wealth concentrated in such a small space. These same wealthy men also built grand cottages along the shore, such as at

Adult reading room in the Carnegie Library of Homestead, Munhall, Pennsylvania, circa 1900. (Library of Congress)

Newport, Rhode Island, where the largest of such summer residences, used just a few weeks per year, was constructed in the 1890s by Cornelius Vanderbilt II. This Renaissance Italianate mansion features 70 rooms and a great hall with 45-foot-high ceilings.

Some decried the lavishness of the 1890s industrialists. In his much-celebrated book *The Theory of the Leisure Class* (1899), the Norwegian-born American economist and sociologist Thorstein Veblen coined the phrase "conspicuous consumption," used to describe the apparently unbridled wealth and consumption of the nation's wealthiest people. Viewing the spectacles of immense wealth with chagrin, Veblen argued that the vast consumption patterns of men such as Vanderbilt were driven by a narcissistic desire to impress and awe with little regard as to how they accumulated their fortunes.

Despite such damning criticisms, there was an upside to the accumulation of great wealth, for many industrialists gave away some if not all of their money, giving rise to admirable philanthropic achievements. The trend had begun more modestly in the early 19th century when John Jacob Astor had funded the Astor Library, which became the foundation for the New York Public Library, the second-largest such institution in the nation and the world's biggest privately financed library.

Not until the 1880s and 1890s, however, did philanthropy become big business. The steel magnate Andrew Carnegie, a proponent of the so-called gospel of wealth, once said that to die rich is to die disgraced. Carnegie donated almost his entire fortune to charity (an estimated $350 million, or approximately $4.3 billion in today's dollars), in the process building 5,000 libraries around the nation and many other such public institutions. John D. Rockefeller, the oil baron, gave away $500 million. The world-renowned financier John Pierpont Morgan, who had accumulated the biggest private art collection in the world, gave away all of it. This formed the core of the Metropolitan Museum in New York and the Wadsworth Atheneum in Hartford, Connecticut. Even Henry Clay Frick, perhaps the most controversial of the robber barons, gave away his impressive art collection to New York City, including his home on Fifth Avenue, and bequeathed $15 million to maintain them, a princely sum at the turn of the century.

Besides the obvious public good that came from such endeavors, such grand philanthropy had turned the United States from a veritable cultural desert in 1800 into an impressive intellectual and cultural mecca by 1900. The foresight of the nation's leading industrialists ensured that U.S. economic power was matched by its urbanity and enlightenment. This groundswell of philanthropy helped to fuel Americans' desire to spread their democratic institutions and economic prowess to other parts of the globe. It also seemed to point to the necessity of expanding into new markets to keep the economy expanding. All of these factors helped to push America into war in 1898 and to acquire a significant overseas empire by the end of the century.

PAUL G. PIERPAOLI JR.

See also

Carnegie, Andrew; Frick, Henry Clay; Gilded Age; Morgan, John Pierpont, Sr.; Robber Barons; Rockefeller, John Davison; Twain, Mark

Further Reading

Cashman, Sean Dennis. *America in the Gilded Age: From the Death of Lincoln to the Rise of Theodore Roosevelt.* New York: New York University Press, 1984.

Gordon, John Steele. *An Empire of Wealth: The Epic History of American Economic Power.* New York: Harper Perennial, 2004.

Josephson, Matthew. *The Robber Barons: The Great American Capitalists, 1861–1901.* New York: Harcourt Brace, 1995.

Philip, John Woodward

Birth Date: August 26, 1840
Death Date: June 30, 1900

U.S. Navy officer and commander of the second-class battleship *Texas* during the Battle of Santiago de Cuba on July 3, 1898. Born in Kinderhook, New York, on August 26, 1840, John Woodward Philip was appointed to the United States Naval Academy, Annapolis, in 1856 and graduated in 1861. During the American Civil War (1861–1865), he served in the South Atlantic Blockading Squadron. In July 1863, he was wounded while aboard the screw gunboat *Chippewa* in an action not far from Charleston, South Carolina. Following the war, he saw duty in a variety of overseas postings.

In October 1897, Captain Philip became the commanding officer of the *Texas*. With the beginning of the Spanish-American War in April 1898, his ship began blockade duty off the Cuban coast on May 21, 1898, and subsequently conducted a bombardment of a Spanish fort in Guantánamo Bay. The *Texas* then spent the month of June in blockade duty off the harbor of Santiago de Cuba, where Spanish rear admiral Pascual Cervera y Topete's squadron was anchored. Half of the battleship's crew were kept on full alert each night in readiness should the Spanish attempt a breakout.

On July 3, 1898, the Spanish squadron attempted to escape to sea. As the principal Spanish warships emerged from the harbor, the *Texas* moved toward them and opened fire with its 12-inch guns on the Spanish flagship, the armored cruiser *Infanta Maria Teresa*. Blinded by smoke from its own guns, the *Texas* narrowly missed colliding with the U.S. armored cruiser *Brooklyn*. The *Texas* next

U.S. Navy captain John Woodward Philip commanded the battleship *Texas* during the Battle of Santiago de Cuba on July 3, 1898. (Naval Historical Center)

engaged the Spanish armored cruisers *Vizcaya* and *Almirante Oquendo*. A shell from the *Oquendo* exploded close to the *Texas*'s bridge. As Philip described it, "I remember pitching up in the air, with my coat tails flying behind me, as if I had been thrown by one of [Theodore] Roosevelt's broncos." The *Texas*'s secondary battery later joined other U.S. warships in hammering two Spanish torpedo boat destroyers, the *Furor* and *Pluton,* that were run ashore and destroyed.

An hour after the battle had commenced, the *Texas* passed the burning *Oquendo,* which had run ashore and raised a white flag. Philip ordered his crew to cease firing on the Spanish ship and told his men, "Don't cheer boys—the poor fellows are dying." As the chase continued, the *Vizcaya* was torn apart by shellfire and run ashore. The *Cristóbal Colón,* the final surviving Spanish ship, was closely pursued by the *Texas,* the first-class battleship *Oregon,* and the *Brooklyn* until the *Cristóbal Colón* began to run out of fuel and ran ashore, ending the battle.

From September to December 1898, Philip served as commander of the 2nd Squadron in the North Atlantic Fleet with his flag on the battleship *New York*. On January 19, 1899, he took command of the New York (Brooklyn) Navy Yard and Navy Station and received his final promotion to the rank of rear admiral in March 1899. Philip died on active duty at the New York Navy Yard on June 30, 1900. Two U.S. Navy destroyers were subsequently named for him.

GLENN E. HELM

See also

Cervera y Topete, Pascual; Santiago de Cuba, Battle of

Further Reading

Appendix to the Report of the Chief of the Bureau of Navigation, 1898. Washington, DC: U.S. Government Printing Office, 1898.

Maclay, Edgar Stanton. *Life and Adventures of "Jack" Philip, Rear-Admiral United States Navy.* New York: Baker and Taylor, 1903.

Trask, David F. *The War with Spain in 1898.* Lincoln: University of Nebraska Press, 1996.

Philippine-American War
Start Date: February 4, 1899
End Date: July 4, 1902

A war between U.S. occupation forces in the Philippines and Filipino nationalist insurgents (Filipino Nationalist Army) led by General Emilio Aguinaldo y Famy. The conflict began on February 4, 1899, and military actions ended on April 13, 1902, upon the surrender of the last Filipino general. The war was officially declared over on July 4, 1902. Armed conflict did not come to a complete halt until 1913, however, with Moro (Muslim) and other armed guerrilla groups continuing to wage sporadic resistance against American forces throughout the archipelago. Many of these conflicts occurred independently from one another. Some historians consider these conflicts to be a continuation of the war beyond 1902.

The origins of the Philippine-American War lie in the American victory over Spain in the Spanish-American War of 1898. Under the terms of the Treaty of Paris, signed on December 10, 1898, the United States acquired the Philippine Islands from Spain for $20 million. President William McKinley proclaimed that the United States would now have sovereign rights over the Philippines, couching his expansionist aspirations in the rhetoric of benevolent assimilation.

By this time, Aguinaldo had already declared independence from Spain on June 12, 1898. Not long after, on January 23, 1899,

the First Philippine Republic was officially inaugurated, complete with a new constitution modeled on those of Mexico, Guatemala, Costa Rica, Brazil, Belgium, and France. Malolos was the capital of the new republic, and Aguinaldo was the first president. Initially, the Filipinos had considered the Americans to be allies in their revolutionary war against Spain, but after the American annexation of the Philippines, American intentions became clear. The United States was not about to grant the Filipinos independence. This precipitated a war that would last much longer and cost far more lives than the Spanish-American War. While American forces sought to enforce their acquisition of the Philippines, the Filipinos fought to uphold the First Philippine Republic. In essence, the two sides were fighting for colonization and independence, respectively.

Tensions between American and Filipino forces first began to mount in Manila in August 1898. Filipino revolutionaries had already wrested control of most of the Philippines from the Spanish except for a tiny walled section of Old Manila called the Intramuros. Some 12,000 Filipino soldiers had amassed around the perimeter of the Intramuros and were playing a waiting game, expecting the Spanish to surrender once their food supplies ran out. Meanwhile, the Spanish governor-general, Fermín Jáudenes y Alvarez, held secret discussions with Commodore George Dewey and Major General Wesley Merritt. Through these discussions, an agreement was reached whereby Spanish and American forces would stage a mock battle so that Spain could save face by surrendering to the Americans instead of to the Filipino rebels. After the staged First Battle of Manila, Spain handed over control of the Intramuros to the Americans on August 13, 1898. From there, U.S. forces set about occupying the rest of Manila, excluding Filipino troops beyond the line of demarcation. It was at this point that relations between the Americans and their former Filipino allies deteriorated rapidly.

The actual Philippine-American War commenced on February 4, 1899, and was sparked by an incident on San Juan Bridge in Manila, where American troops were guarding the boundaries of U.S.-occupied Manila. A group of Filipino soldiers strayed close to the line of demarcation and were ordered to halt. When the orders were not heeded, an American army private shot and killed one of the soldiers. This became the very first shot of the war. The Second Battle of Manila (February 4, 1899) that followed resulted in 250 American and 2,000 Filipino casualties. By March 25, American troops had forced the retreat of the Filipino Nationalist Army from Manila. At the opening of the war, the Filipino army was under the overall command of Aguinaldo, while Major General Elwell Otis was the appointed commander of the American forces. The United

Estimated Casualties of the Philippine-American War

	Total Mobilized	Killed in Action or Died of Wounds	Died of Disease	Wounded	Civilian Deaths
Philippines	80,000–100,000	16,000	Unknown	Unknown	250,000–1 million
United States	126,000	1,500	2,825	2,818	N/A

States began the campaign for its acquisition of the Philippine Islands with a U.S. Expeditionary Force of just more than 20,000 soldiers as of January 31, 1899. By April 16, 1902, it had required 126,000 troops to vanquish the Filipino army. With Manila secure, U.S. troops began their thrust into northern Luzon under Major General Arthur MacArthur. Confronting American forces were Filipino insurgents led by General Antonio Luna. MacArthur's first objective was to capture Malolos, the capital of the First Philippine Republic. This was accomplished on March 31, 1899. The Americans continued to win hard-fought victories, in particular at the Battle of Quingua (April 23, 1899) and the Battle of Zapote Bridge (June 13, 1899). The latter was the largest single battle in the Philippine-American War. During the battle, 5,000 Filipino troops squared off against 3,000 American troops. While the Filipinos had the advantage in numbers, the Americans had the advantage of superior firepower, inflicting more than 500 casualties in just a few hours of heavy fighting, as compared to the 75 casualties suffered by the Americans. Major General Henry Ware Lawton, who commanded the U.S. forces at Zapote Bridge, expressed in his dispatches his admiration for the bravery displayed by the Filipinos in battle.

On November 12, 1899, Aguinaldo dissolved the regular army of the First Philippine Republic and reformed it into a series of guerrilla units. Battles such as the one at Zapote Bridge had made the Filipinos aware of the futility of engaging the Americans in large traditional military formations, especially considering their motley and substandard weaponry. The shift to guerrilla tactics would enable the Filipinos to capitalize on their vastly superior knowledge of the landscape and offset their disadvantaged position in the conflict.

The guerrilla war made the American occupation of the Philippines increasingly more difficult over the next few years, with the Filipino army carrying out frequent and deadly raids and surprise ambushes. In the first four months of the guerrilla campaign alone, the Americans suffered almost 500 casualties. The most famous of the Filipinos' guerrilla victories were the Battle of Pulang Lupa (September 13, 1900) and the surprise attack that came to be known as the Balangiga Massacre (September 28, 1901), masterminded by General Vicente Lukban. Both of these guerrilla actions resulted in decisive Filipino victories and heavy American casualties, sending shockwaves through the U.S. high command. At first, there was speculation that the Filipinos might fight American forces into a stalemate and force them to withdraw. However, the guerrilla tactics propelled the Americans to launch a vicious series of reprisal attacks.

In retaliation for the Balangiga Massacre, Brigadier General Jacob Smith issued the infamous order to kill all males aged 10 and up on the island of Samar and burn all the villages until there was nothing left but "a howling wilderness." This campaign was assigned to a marine detachment under the command of Major Littleton Waller. Besides such scorched earth campaigns, American forces also concentrated civilians into so-called protected zones

U.S. forces firing on Filipino insurgents from Block House No. 13, Manila, during the Philippine-American War. (Library of Congress)

that were, for all intents and purposes, concentration camps in which thousands more died. In the United States, there was instant outrage against American tactics in Samar. Congress also held public hearings concerning the atrocities in the Philippines. For his part, General Smith was deemed to have overstepped his prerogatives and was court-martialed and forced to retire from the army.

The American repression severely weakened Filipino resolve. In addition, the insurgents were steadily losing their top generals. General Luna was assassinated by rivals within the Philippine leadership in June 1899, and Brigadier General Gregorio de Pilar was killed in action at the Battle of Tirad Pass on December 2, 1899. This battle was successfully fought as a delaying action by the Filipinos to allow Aguinaldo to escape from the American advance. It was only a matter of time, however, before Aguinaldo was captured. After continually shifting his base of operations for the duration of the war, evading the American pursuit for as long as he could, Aguinaldo was finally apprehended by Colonel Frederick Funston in Palanan, Isabella, on March 23, 1901. Not long afterward, on April 1, 1901, Aguinaldo pledged his allegiance to the United States at the Malacañang Palace in Manila, publicly calling on his followers to lay down their arms and accept American rule.

Aguinaldo's surrender and about-face came as a shock to those still fighting for Philippine independence. General Mariano Trias replaced Aguinaldo at the helm of the Filipino army but surrendered to the Americans soon afterward. The leadership then fell to General Miguel Malvar, who launched an offensive campaign in the Batangas region of southern Luzon against American-held towns. He achieved several small victories but won the ire of Brigadier General J. Franklin Bell, who pursued him relentlessly. Malvar, along with his entire command, finally surrendered on April 13, 1902. He was the last Filipino general to capitulate. By the end of the month, a further 3,000 of Malvar's men surrendered. Northern Luzon, by this point, had already been pacified, and now southern Luzon followed suit.

On July 4, 1902, President Theodore Roosevelt declared the Philippine-American War (or what the Americans called the Philippine Insurrection) over. While this marked the official end of the conflict, some historians consider the war to have continued unofficially until 1913. Indeed, sporadic resistance against American military forces continued throughout the archipelago, spearheaded in different regions by different guerrilla organizations largely fighting independently from one another. General Macario Sakay led one of the strongest groups. He had been a senior member of the Katipunan, a secret mass nationalist organization that had led the Philippine revolution against Spain from 1895 to 1898. Sakay revived the Katipunan for the new war against the United States and even founded a short-lived independent republic—the Katagalugan Tagalog Republic—in the mountains of southern Luzon. This lasted from 1902 to 1907, when Sakay and the Katipunan leadership were captured and executed by American forces.

Mindanao, in the south of the Philippine archipelago, was the last region to be pacified by U.S. occupation forces. There, the Moros resisted until 1913 in what the Americans called the Moro Rebellion. The Moros were never a part of the Filipino Nationalist Army under Aguinaldo but instead fought independently. Nevertheless, many historians consider the Moro Rebellion to have been the second front in the Philippine-American War. When Roosevelt proclaimed the end of the war in 1902, he added that his proclamation did not include Mindanao, where Moro forces were still refusing to submit. The last major engagement between American and Moro forces was the Battle of Bud Bagsak (January 11–15, 1913). As many as 500–1,000 Moros were killed in an American attack led by Brigadier General John J. Pershing. Not long afterward, much of the Moro leadership surrendered, and on March 22, 1915, the sultan of Sulu signed an agreement with the Americans recognizing and accepting U.S. sovereignty.

In the final analysis, it took the Americans more than three years and $600 million to defeat the First Philippine Republic. Estimates of the number of Filipino soldiers who fought from 1898 to 1902 vary between 80,000 and 100,000, with tens of thousands of auxiliaries. While the Filipinos had the advantage of a superior knowledge of the local terrain, climate, and populace, their lack of adequate weapons, ammunition, and training were serious impediments to their campaign. Many of their rifles and cannon had been taken from the Spanish during the revolution of 1896–1898 or from captured or dead U.S. soldiers. The American ground forces were much better equipped, with added assistance from U.S. warships positioned off the coast when needed. In addition, the Americans were issued the most state-of-the-art weaponry of the time, including the Krag-Jørgenson bolt-action rifle and the Colt M1911 handgun. The latter was developed specifically for the war in the Philippines and was designed so that it could kill a charging Filipino soldier with a single shot.

During the first phase of the war, 1899–1902, the Filipino Nationalist Army suffered an estimated 16,000 military deaths. Filipino civilian deaths are estimated to have been between 250,000 and 1 million, taking into account not just those killed directly by the war but also those who died of malnutrition and disease as a result of the conflict. This was out of a total population of 7 million Filipinos at the time of the outbreak of the war. A further 100,000 Filipino civilians perished in the Moro Rebellion. The U.S. military lost 4,325 soldiers during 1898–1902. Up to 1,500 of these were the result of actual combat, while the rest died of disease. A further 2,818 American soldiers were wounded. American forces continued to suffer periodic casualties in the suppression of the Moro Rebellion in the southern Philippines until 1913.

MARCO HEWITT

See also

Aguinaldo y Famy, Emilio; Atrocities; Balangiga Massacre; Bell, James Franklin; Bud Bagsak, Battle of; Funston, Frederick; Lawton, Henry Ware; Lukban, Vicente; Luna de St. Pedro, António Narciso; Luzon Campaigns; MacArthur, Arthur; Malvar, Miguel; Manila, First Battle of; Manila, Second Battle of; Moro Campaigns; Moros; Otis, Elwell Stephen; Pacification Program, Philippine Islands; Pershing, John Joseph; Philippine-American War, U.S. Reaction to; Philippine Islands; Philippine Islands, U.S. Acquisition of; Pilar, Gregorio del; Samar Campaigns; Smith, Jacob Hurd; Tirad Pass, Battle of; Waller, Littleton Tazewell

Further Reading

Agoncillo, Teodoro A., and Milagros C. Guerrero. *History of the Filipino People.* 5th ed. Quezon City, Philippines: R. P. Garcia, 1983.
Bain, David H. *Sitting in Darkness: Americans in the Philippines.* Boston: Houghton Mifflin, 1984.
Linn, Brian McAllister. *The Philippine War, 1899–1902.* Lawrence: University Press of Kansas, 2000.
Miller, Stuart Creighton. *"Benevolent Assimilation": The American Conquest of the Philippines, 1899–1903.* New Haven, CT: Yale University Press, 1982.
Schirmer, Daniel B., and Stephen R. Shalom. *The Philippines Reader: A History of Colonialism, Dictatorship, and Resistance.* Cambridge, MA: South End Press, 1987.
Shaw, Angel Velasco, and Luis H. Francia. *Vestiges of War: The Philippine-American War and the Aftermath of an American Dream, 1899–1999.* New York: New York University Press, 2002.
Tan, Samuel K. *The Filipino-American War, 1899–1913.* Quezon City: University of the Philippines Press, 2002.

Philippine-American War, U.S. Reaction to

The Philippine-American War that commenced on February 4, 1899, provoked various reactions in the United States, from vocal support to fierce protest. The widely popular Spanish-American War had just come to an end, finalized in the Treaty of Paris of December 10, 1898. In this pact, Spain ceded control of Puerto Rico, Guam, and the Philippines to the United States. The treaty was the

Political cartoon titled "School Begins" showing Uncle Sam lecturing four children labeled "Philippines," "Hawaii," "Porto Rico," and "Cuba" in front of children holding books labeled with various U.S. states. In the background is an American Indian holding a book upside down and a Chinese boy at the door. Cartoon from an 1899 issue of *Puck*. (Library of Congress)

source of intense anti-imperialist debates both in and out of Congress. The outbreak of the Philippine-American War compelled rapid approval by the U.S. Senate of the Treaty of Paris on February 6, 1899, ensuring the transition of the United States to imperial power status.

American citizens were almost immediately polarized over the consequences of imperialism and overseas expansion. Issues of race, class, gender, and religion were all employed to support both sides of the imperialist argument and clearly framed reactions to the Philippine-American War. Political parties and organizations, yellow journalism, and U.S. military actions in the Philippines all influenced these issues and attitudes during the three-year-long insurgency.

Politically, the war was seen as pivotal to the interpretation of the U.S. Constitution and American foreign policy. Democrats, largely anti-imperialists, argued that the Constitution did not allow the United States to hold colonies or infringe on the sovereignty of another nation. They opposed the conduct of the U.S. military in the fighting, and some contended that foreign people of color had no place in U.S. government. Republicans, largely expansionists, asserted that benevolent assimilation and the spread of democracy were important ideals and that the war was a necessary duty to uphold American honor in the face of Filipino aggression. Most Filipinos, mirroring their former Spanish overlords, were Roman

Catholic; nevertheless, many Republicans promoted policies of Christianization (even though the vast majority of Filipinos were already Roman Catholics), uplifting and educating the "little brown brothers" overseas. Much of this mind-set had emerged from the ideas of social Darwinism and the so-called white man's burden, made famous by Rudyard Kipling.

A number of religious leaders responded to the antiwar arguments, although this was not with one voice. There was some religious opposition to war in general, primarily among Quakers, who were traditionally pacifists. But the missionary impulse generally also stirred support for the war from among both Protestants and Catholics. Many African Americans, particularly the black press, identified with the Filipinos, who were publicly portrayed as dark-skinned and inherently inferior. Sympathetic African Americans were vocally anti-imperialist, opposing the white domination of the Philippines.

Public discussions about citizenship and suffrage in the Philippines highlighted the limitations of civil rights within the United States. Thus, African Americans and suffragist women used the war to promote their own agendas. However, white suffragist women did not generally identify with the Filipinos and never organized an anti-imperialist platform. Many American women believed in the idea of social uplift, and some supported the war by traveling to the Philippines to serve there as teachers. Others, however, were shocked by the brutality of guerrilla warfare and counterinsurgency.

The U.S. military had waged a conventional war with the Filipino Republican Army throughout much of 1899. In the United States, both the press and the public argued over whether the Filipinos were savage or civilized. Filipino revolutionary Emilio Aguinaldo y Famy's conventional tactics were intended to sway public opinion in his favor and convince the world that the Filipinos were indeed civilized and capable of governing themselves. When American forces won the Second Battle of Manila (February 4–23, 1899), which pitted Filipino insurgents against U.S. troops, the American public generally supported the war effort against the natives despite Aguinaldo's conventional strategy. Drawing on their experience with Native Americans in the West, U.S. citizens could easily conceptualize the indigenous Filipinos as Indians to be conquered, pacified, and ruled. Newspaper reports often reflected this attitude, comparing battles in the Philippines to the Indian Wars and promoting public support. In December 1899, with the war going against him, Aguinaldo shifted strategy, beginning a guerrilla war that would continue for another three years.

Individuals such as Mark Twain and groups such as the Anti-Imperialist League worked hard to oppose the war, but they were generally in the minority. Some anti-imperialists communicated directly with Aguinaldo, offering support and guaranteeing Philippine independence if McKinley lost the presidential election of 1900. Indeed, Filipino guerrillas began a series of offensive actions before the election hoping that an increase in American casualties would sway opinion in the United States against the war. The campaign was unsuccessful. McKinley's reelection demoralized the anti-imperialist faction, but it nevertheless continued its dissent into the new century.

As the Philippine-American War progressed, Americans worried increasingly about the consequences of the foreign expedition. Issues of immigration and long-term military occupation raised concerns about maintaining racial purity in the United States. Many groups, particularly women's organizations, were concerned with the idea of moral decay induced by contact with tropical peoples and venereal diseases carried by returning soldiers. In fact, anti-imperialists utilized the fear of venereal disease to demand the end of the war and the return of U.S. forces. Their demands went unheeded. Despite these worries, support for the war remained generally strong.

The final Philippine campaigns, however, deeply affected American reaction to the war. In October 1901, Brigadier General Jacob Smith began counterinsurgency operations on Samar, instructing his subordinates to make the island "a howling wilderness." In Batangas, Brigadier General James Franklin Bell began a system of concentration centers to isolate civilians from insurgents. Allegations of torture and other brutalities against civilians and prisoners made headlines, shocking the American public. In the U.S. Senate, the Committee on the Philippines (also known as the Lodge Committee for its chairman, Senator Henry Cabot Lodge) would hear

weeks' worth of testimony about military misconduct in the Philippines, and numerous military officers faced courts-martial for their actions.

By the end of the war in April 1902, many Americans had grown disillusioned about the conduct of American forces abroad. Part of this sentiment was certainly due to rising antiforeign, anti-imperialist ideas, but it was also provoked by the vicious and unpredictable nature of guerrilla or insurgency warfare in which the normal rules of military engagement were rendered moot.

Despite pockets of dissent, the Philippine-American War generally had the support of the American public, at least until its closing months. For three years, the U.S. military carried out a progressive program to promote education, improved sanitation, better communication, and other public works. However, the Samar and Batangas campaigns fundamentally changed the U.S. reaction to the conflict. The visibility and negative reaction to these operations shaped perceptions of the Philippine-American War.

DAWN OTTEVAERE NICKESON

See also

African Americans; Aguinaldo y Famy, Emilio; Anti-Imperialist League; Atrocities; Bell, James Franklin; Benevolent Assimilation; Committee on the Philippines; Democratic Party; Imperialism; Kipling, Rudyard; Lodge, Henry Cabot; Manila, Second Battle of; McKinley, William; Missionaries; Pacification Program, Philippine Islands; Paris, Treaty of; Republican Party; Samar Campaigns; Smith, Jacob Hurd; Social Darwinism; Twain, Mark; White Man's Burden; Yellow Journalism

Further Reading
Hoganson, Kristin. "'As Badly Off as the Filipinos': U.S. Women's Suffragists and the Imperial Issue at the Turn of the Century." *Journal of Women's History* 13 (2001): 9–33.
Karnow, Stanley. *In Our Image: America's Empire in the Philippines.* New York: Random House, 1989.
Linn, Brian McAllister. *The Philippine War, 1899–1902.* Lawrence: University Press of Kansas, 2000.
Miller, Stuart Creighton. *"Benevolent Assimilation": The American Conquest of the Philippines, 1899–1903.* New Haven, CT: Yale University Press, 1982.
Welch, Richard E., Jr. *Response to Imperialism: The United States and the Philippine-American War, 1899–1902.* Chapel Hill: University of North Carolina Press, 1979.

Philippine Commission

Commission formed at the behest of President William McKinley in December 1898 to advise him on effective colonial policies for the newly acquired colony of the Philippine Islands. The acquisition of the island archipelago was formalized by the Treaty of Paris, signed on December 10, 1898. There were actually two Philippine Commissions. The first one lasted from 1898 to 1901; the second endured from 1901 to 1903.

The aim of the first Philippine Commission, as envisioned by McKinley, was to help formulate policy and advise him on how to best incorporate the island into the American system, acculturate

Members of the U.S. Philippine Commission meeting with Filipino nationalist representatives, circa 1899. (Library of Congress)

its inhabitants, and govern the colony. The commission was composed of five members: Jacob G. Schurman, president of Cornell University; Dean C. Worcester of the University of Michigan's Zoology Department; Colonel Charles Denby, former U.S. minister to China; Rear Admiral George Dewey, hero of the Battle of Manila Bay; and Major General Elwell Otis, military commander in the Philippines. All five men opposed U.S. annexation of the islands. McKinley chose these men precisely because of their opposition to annexation, believing that their counsel would be less biased.

To assist the U.S. War Department's so-called policy of attraction, the commission had two goals. First, it hoped to attract Filipino elites to the cause of American rule. Second, it sought to "produce an authoritative record of events on the island" that would justify American actions, attract Filipinos to the American way of thinking, and undermine the arguments of those opposed to annexation.

Arriving in the Philippines in January 1899, the members of the commission met daily, seeking ways to diffuse the growing tensions between the United States and the Filipino nationalist movement. Filipino nationalists had been agitating for years for independence from Spain, and a guerrilla war had been under way before the Spanish-American War. At the conclusion of the war, Filipino guerrillas and various Filipino political groups had pressed the United States for independence.

The Philippine Commission frequently sought input from Filipinos on the nature of American rule and trumpeted the large number of natives who appeared before it. However, the majority

of Filipinos who met with the commission were from the middle and upper classes and from the capital city of Manila. Filipinos from the hinterlands and the working and poor classes never ventured before the commission. The commission did, however, enjoy some considerable success in convincing Filipino elites to support American rule and participate in colonial governance.

A key aim of the Philippine Commission was to identify, classify, and develop a policy for dealing with the myriad ethnic and linguistic groups that made up the archipelago's population. As such, Worcester conducted an exhaustive study of the islands' peoples. Included in the commission's first report was a chapter titled "The Native Peoples of the Philippines," written by Worcester. In it he sought to identify the major peoples constituting the Filipino nation. Worcester identified some 84 distinct ethnic groups in the Philippines. This number was used by those in favor of annexation as proof that the islands were so badly divided as to be incapable of self-rule. Worcester argued that such a large number of competing peoples needed direction and that the demands of governing such a disparate population could lead to chaos. The report identified the Tagalogs as the best candidates for training and education to lead a future independent Philippines. The report's findings, however, were disputed by anti-imperialists in the United States and Filipino nationalists on the island.

The commission suffered from frequent internal bickering as tensions between the civilian members and the military members increased. Both Dewey and Otis thought that the commission was a bad idea and was incapable of solving the major problems confronting the occupation authorities. And in the end, the group was unable to head off the Philippine-American War, which began in February 1899. Schurman resigned from the commission in 1901, which hamstrung the group.

McKinley immediately formed a second Philippine Commission in 1901. This time the commission was headed by William Howard Taft. In addition to Taft, the new commission membership included Worcester, Luke E. Wright, Henry Clay Ide, and Bernard Moses. It received broad legislative powers and was to serve as the incubator of American rule in the Philippines. The second commission became the islands' first colonial administration on July 4, 1901, with Taft becoming the first colonial governor of the Philippines. The commission was charged with helping create provincial and municipal governments throughout the archipelago and paving the way for civilian rule. The commission charge included the instructions to respect local customs as much as possible. The second commission went about its work fitfully, with conflict between Taft and Major General Arthur MacArthur, the American military commander, greatly hampering its work.

RICK DYSON

See also

Colonial Policies, U.S.; Dewey, George; MacArthur, Arthur; McKinley, William; Otis, Elwell Stephen; Philippine-American War; Philippine Islands; Philippine Islands, U.S. Acquisition of; Taft, William Howard; Tagalogs

Further Reading

Kramer, Paul A. *The Blood of Government: Race, Empire, the United States and the Philippines.* Chapel Hill: University of North Carolina Press, 2006.

Linn, Brian McAllister. *The Philippine War, 1899–1902.* Lawrence: University Press of Kansas, 2000.

Trask, David F. *The War with Spain in 1898.* Lincoln: University of Nebraska Press, 1996.

Philippine Constabulary

Paramilitary police organization formed by the United States on August 8, 1901, to assist in pacifying the islands. The Philippine Constabulary was part of the civil government and was a distinct entity from the U.S. Army and the Philippine Scouts. With a cadre of American officer personnel, the constabulary recruited and trained local men to gain critical local area knowledge. Recruits were Filipino males ages 18–25 who were in sound health and were conversant in both Spanish and English. Tasked with taking over the security mission from conventional military units, the constabulary garrisoned population centers to protect them from rebel and bandit raids and hunt down the same. The constabulary was also capable of operating as a military unit and occasionally joined U.S. Army and Philippine Scout units in actions to destroy rebel strongholds.

After the successful capture of Filipino insurgent leader General Emilio Aguinaldo y Famy on March 23, 1901, hostilities continued

Members of the Filipino Constabulary at Manila in the Philippines. The 5,000-man constabulary played an important role on the side of the United States in the Philippine-American War. (Library of Congress)

with the surviving guerrilla elements. The government and public opinion had by then grown tired of the level of effort needed to pacify the islands and of stories emerging about army atrocities. William Howard Taft, the new governor of the islands, decided that a strong police force composed of Filipinos would eventually remove the need for U.S. Army involvement in the Philippines. The creation of a constabulary was officially authorized with passage of the second Philippine Commission's Organic Act Number 175 on July 18, 1901.

The Philippine Constabulary was officially born as the Insular Constabulary on August 8, 1901, with the appointment of 70 hand-picked officers to begin recruiting and training. The majority of the constabulary officers were U.S. army volunteers, with two Filipinos commissioned as third lieutenants, which was a revolutionary move at the time. The first chief of the constabulary was Henry T. Allen, a captain in the U.S. regular army but then serving as a lieutenant colonel of a volunteer cavalry battalion. Allen was elevated to brigadier general of volunteers and served until his retirement in 1907.

The Philippine Constabulary adopted the tactics, rank structure, and command style of the U.S. Army. The first group of officers attended an expedited training course to familiarize themselves with police procedures and Filipino society. Upon completion of the training course, teams consisting of one captain and three or four lieutenants were dispatched to areas with civil unrest to recruit local Filipino enlistees to conduct police duties in coordination with army pacification efforts. Each Philippine province was designated a force of 150 constables, although this number was rarely achieved.

There was no standardized method for recruitment and training of Filipino enlistees, especially in provinces far from Manila. Common practice consisted of an officer being issued a supply of guns and uniforms and a cash advance and then assigned to a specific locality. On-the-job training was usually deemed suitable for preparing the new recruits. Often, as the only representative of the government for miles around, a constable would be called to take on additional duties, such as those of health officer, construction supervisor, school principal, and public works manager.

The Philippine Constabulary focused its efforts on three regions: Luzon, the Visayan islands of Leyte and Samar, and the Moro Provinces. The constabulary's first challenge immediately after its creation was the pacification of central Luzon, where many of Aguinaldo's followers still waged a guerrilla war and raided local villages. While raiding provided the rebels with valuable food, weapons, money, and fame that aided in recruiting new rebels, it also proved a source of dissatisfaction among the local population. The constabulary thus developed a strategy of garrisoning villages to protect the population, conducting manhunts, gathering intelligence from disaffected locals, and assaulting neighboring rebel hideouts. Resistance rarely developed above the level of common banditry, however, and the rebels were often indistinguishable from criminal gangs or bandits, known as *ladrones.* It is estimated that in 1901 alone the constabulary captured or killed at least 3,000 bandits.

There were a few Luzon insurgents who were notorious, however. The charismatic Antonio Colache was a Spanish deserter who had formed a network of civilian supporters that allowed him to supply his forces and evade the Philippine Constabulary's manhunts. Unfortunately for Colache, a constabulary raid that failed to capture him resulted in the revelation of the identities of his supporters. His network now compromised, he himself was taken prisoner in May 1902.

Simeon Ola, another insurgent leader, was able to gather a force of several hundred followers, necessitating the formation of a joint 2,000-man force of Philippine Constabulary, Philippine Scouts, and U.S. Army personnel. The presence of so many troops, food control efforts, and the new tactic of concentrating rural farmers into guarded camps denied Ola his support base and led to his surrender on September 23, 1903.

Macario Sakay was perhaps the greatest insurgent threat because of his ability to organize the disparate rebel leaders of central Luzon and the southern Tagalogs under his command. As a result, he was able to organize larger raiding parties that allowed him to attack and defeat Philippine Constabulary and Philippine Scout garrisons, securing rifles and new followers. To combat Sakay, habeas corpus was suspended, and a tougher antibanditry law was passed to compel insurgents to surrender or suffer tougher penalties. Mirroring the campaign against Ola, a force of 785 constables with more than 2,000 army troops and Philippine Scouts was organized to track down Sakay. Constabulary garrisons were

established in every village, linked by telegraph lines. Once again, rural residents were concentrated into controlled camps. Over time, Sakay's followers were gradually captured until he himself finally surrendered in July 1906. Pockets of resistance continued on the island but never proved a threat to the government's administration and had virtually ended by 1914.

Efforts to pacify the Visayan islands of Leyte and Samar were referred to as the Pulajan Campaign, named after the local Muslim group. The resistance there was a combination of political resistance and religious motivations built on a localized form of Islam. The Philippine Constabulary arrived on Leyte in August 1901 to find a relatively calm, stable situation. The majority of the constables moved on to Samar in response to the September 28, 1901, Balangiga Massacre, which presented a more pressing security concern. Rebel leader Jorge Capile took advantage of their departure and organized forces to push back the fledgling Constabulary garrisons. The authorities found it necessary to bring in more than 200 constables under Colonel Wallace Taylor to pursue Capile until his surrender in June 1902.

An even bigger threat appeared in spiritual leader Papa (or Pope) Faustion Ablena, who used his claims of mystical powers to inspire resistance among the Muslim populations of Leyte and Samar. He sold amulets that would supposedly provide immunity from bullets for the true believer. Ablena's raiding of towns for supplies developed the same level of animosity among local populations as on Luzon. However, he consistently evaded capture and always had a willing supply of recruits to replace losses inflicted by the Philippine Constabulary. By July 1904, constabulary units from neighboring islands were moved to Leyte with a U.S. Army and Philippine Scout contingent to capture Ablena.

On Samar, unlike Leyte, there were many spiritual leaders, or papas, but the greatest was Papa Pablo. The level of violence on Samar was so great despite Philippine Constabulary, U.S. Army, U.S. Marine Corps, and Philippine Scout efforts that Colonel Taylor's constables were transferred from Leyte to Samar after they had defeated Capile, despite ongoing operational needs on Leyte. At the height of the violence, rebels were able to wipe out entire patrols and garrisons.

In November 1905, Philippine Constabulary temporary chief Brigadier General Henry Tureman Allen took personal command of the Pulajan Campaign and brought with him 1,800 constables. The resulting pressure and food control policies allowed the constabulary to reduce rebel forces until Papa Pablo was captured in November 1906 and Ablena in June 1907. The Pulajan Campaign was officially ended in 1907, although pockets of resistance continued to spring up until 1917.

The Philippine Constabulary's greatest challenge was on the islands that make up the southern Philippines, known as the Moro Provinces. Ethnically different from the rest of the islands and Muslim by faith, the area had been ruled by the Spanish in name only. Piracy, rebellion, and internal wars were a culturally accepted norm. Real power belonged to a collection of sultans and local tribal datus (chiefs), none of whom was able to achieve the popularity of Aguinaldo or Ablena. The army had been successful in establishing harmonious relations with the larger port cities and installing garrisons there. Extending authority inland had proved much more difficult, however. The constabulary arrived on the island in 1903 and began to recruit from the local populace, a controversial move because of the locals' apparent hatred of foreign control. They proved to be fierce in battle, and many rebel Moro units were simply annihilated, as they refused to retreat.

The Philippine Constabulary developed a divide-and-conquer strategy that pitted rival datus against each other, making itself a necessary intermediary. Datus who resisted built forts, known as cottas, in remote areas. The constabulary and other security forces engaged in innumerable pitched battles in an effort to eliminate these strongholds. In the battles, the defenders often fought to the death.

The Philippine Constabulary's first major battle took place on the island of Sulu. When regional governor Major General Leonard Wood learned of a datu building a major cotta on Mount Bud Dajo, he ordered a combined army-constabulary force to destroy the outpost. The resulting Battle of Bud Dajo of March 5–8, 1906, ended with only 6 of the estimated 800–1,000 Moro fighters surviving.

By 1909, authorities believed that peace had been established in the south, a notion shattered in 1910. A new group of individuals known as Jurametados, who violently opposed the presence of Christians in Moro lands, emerged. The Jurametados believed that the more Christians they killed, the greater the rewards in heaven. Many operated singly outside of the control of any group and engaged in suicidal attacks against U.S. forces. As a result, the regional governor at the time, Brigadier General John Pershing, issued a disarmament order on September 8, 1911, that many Moros resisted. The Philippine Constabulary found itself in a new round of cotta reductions and pitched battles. Despite a campaign of civil improvement and the recruitment of Muslims into the government and security forces, resistance in the Moro areas continued until the handover of rule to the Commonwealth of the Philippines in 1946. Some Moro violence continues to this day.

From the start of the Philippine Constabulary, Filipinos filled out the enlisted ranks. Some rose to junior-level officer ranks based on their accomplishments in battle. With U.S. involvement in World War I, Filipino officers began to assume senior positions, replacing American officers deployed to France in the summer of 1917. That same year, the Insular Constabulary was officially renamed the Philippine Constabulary, and command was turned over to a Filipino, Brigadier General Rafael Crame. The Philippine Constabulary continued to operate until World War II, at which time it was folded into the Philippine Army.

JAMES E. SHIRCLIFFE JR.

See also

Allen, Henry Tureman; Balangiga Massacre; Bud Dajo, Battle of; Bud Dajo Campaign; Cottas; VIII Corps; Ladrone Islands; Luzon Campaigns; Moro Campaigns; Moro Province; Moros; Pacification Program, Philippine Islands; Pershing, John Joseph; Philippine Islands, U.S. Occupation of; Philippine Scouts; Samar Campaigns; Taft, William Howard; Tagalogs; United States Army; Visayan Campaigns; Wood, Leonard

Further Reading

Hurley, Vic. *Jungle Control: The Story of the Philippine Constabulary.* New York: E. P. Hutton, 1938.

Linn, Brian McAllister. *The Philippine War, 1899–1902.* Lawrence: University Press of Kansas, 2000.

San Gabriel, Reynaldo P. *The Constabulary Story.* Quezon City, Philippines: Bustamante, 1978.

Wolff, Leon. *Little Brown Brother: America's Forgotten Bid for Empire Which Cost 250,000 Lives.* New York: Kraus Reprint, 1970.

Philippine Expeditionary Force

As a follow-up to Commodore George Dewey's naval victory over the Spanish squadron in the Philippines in the Battle of Manila Bay on May 1, 1898, President William McKinley directed that an expeditionary force be sent to the islands. On May 3, commanding general of the army Major General Nelson A. Miles initially recommended to Secretary of War Russell A. Alger the dispatch there of a mixed force of regulars and volunteers, composed of some 5,000 infantry, cavalry, and artillery troops.

Major General Wesley Merritt, veteran of the American Civil War and the Indian Wars and the second-ranking general in the army, was appointed to command the expeditionary force, which was designated VIII Corps. Major General Elwell S. Otis, like Merritt another veteran of the Civil War and Indian Wars, was named its second-in-command. Although the War Department subsequently increased the strength of the expeditionary force to 20,000 men, Merritt argued for a stronger representation of regulars in this force than Miles was willing to allot. Furthermore, Merritt believed that his assignment embraced the entire Philippine archipelago, whereas Miles saw only the city of Manila and its port facilities as the objective. The fact that the army's two ranking soldiers differed to such an extent with regard to the expedition's role underscores the ambiguity surrounding the U.S. mission in the Philippines, about which President McKinley had been vague at best. In any event, a mixed force of 5,000 regulars and 15,000 volunteers was earmarked for VIII Corps.

San Francisco was the VIII Corps assembly and embarkation point. The troops were assigned to Camp Merritt, near Golden Gate Park. Because Merritt was busy in Washington, D.C., Otis had charge of preparing the expeditionary corps for departure. As the various regiments arrived there, they were issued weapons and supplies and given training in simulated battle exercises. In contrast to the confusion experienced by V Corps at Tampa, Florida, which was then sent to Cuba, preparations at San Francisco proceeded relatively smoothly.

Troops being sent to the Philippines knew little or nothing about the islands. It took several months for the Office of Military Infor-

Soldiers of the Philippine Expeditionary Force stand behind a cemetery wall waiting for an insurgent attack in 1899 during the Philippine-American War. (Library of Congress)

mation to distribute its sourcebook, *Military Notes on the Philippines.* In the meantime, the War Department provided such information as was available, including at least one encyclopedia article.

Because the U.S. Navy had bought up most of the available shipping and because the Cuban theater of war had priority, there were insufficient numbers of transports available to accommodate Merritt's entire command in one lift, so VIII Corps had to be divided into three contingents. The first, consisting of 115 officers and 2,386 enlisted men under Brigadier General Thomas M. Anderson, sailed on May 25, 1898. After more than a month at sea, they arrived in Manila Bay on June 30. They were immediately put to work un-

loading supplies at Cavite and establishing camps. A second group, consisting of 158 officers and 3,404 enlisted men under Brigadier General Francis V. Greene, departed on June 15 and arrived in the Philippines on July 17. The third and largest contingent, 198 officers and 4,642 enlisted men under Brigadier General Arthur MacArthur and accompanied by Merritt, sailed on June 27 and arrived at its destination on July 25. The total of these three forces was 10,946 officers and men, all members of VIII Corps, arrived in the Philippines before the capture of Manila.

Merritt's first task was to secure Manila. This First Battle of Manila occurred on August 13, although Merritt was unaware that

Spain and the United States had agreed to the Protocol of Peace the previous day. At his own request, Merritt was relieved of command in the autumn of 1898 because of ill health, and command of the Philippine Expeditionary Force devolved to Otis. Initially, Otis was faced with the difficult task of maintaining peace and order among recalcitrant Filipino revolutionaries who resented the U.S. presence in their islands.

When war broke out between the United States and the Filipino Republican Army, headed by Emilio Aguinaldo y Famy, in February 1899, Otis had to deal not only with Aguinaldo but also increasingly disgruntled U.S. volunteers. Once the war with Spain ended, these volunteers, who had been mustered into federal service to fight Spain, saw no reason to remain in the Philippines and fight a war against Filipino insurgents. Eventually, the volunteers were shipped back to the United States and replaced with U.S. volunteer regiments recruited specifically for the Philippine fighting. The Philippine Expeditionary Force that sailed from San Francisco in the early summer of 1898 had undergone an almost complete transformation by early 1900.

JERRY KEENAN

See also

Aguinaldo y Famy, Emilio; Alger, Russell Alexander; Anderson, Thomas McArthur; Camp Merriam and Camp Merritt; Greene, Francis Vinton; MacArthur, Arthur; Manila, First Battle of; Manila Bay, Battle of; McKinley, William; Merritt, Wesley; Miles, Nelson Appleton; Otis, Elwell Stephen; Philippine-American War

Further Reading

Alberts, Don E. *Brandy Station to Manila Bay: A Biography of General Wesley Merritt.* Austin, TX: Presidial, 1980.

Cosmas, Graham A. *An Army for Empire: The United States Army in the Spanish-American War.* College Station: Texas A&M University Press, 1994.

Linn, Brian McAllister. *The Philippine War, 1899–1902.* Lawrence: University Press of Kansas, 2000.

Philippine Islands

Southeast Asian archipelago composed of more than 7,107 islands located in the western Pacific Ocean between the Philippine Sea and the South China Sea. The location of the Philippines along major trade routes has made the island chain strategically and economically important to both Eastern and Western powers for much of its modern history. The islands cover almost 115,831 square miles and are divided into three main groups: Luzon in the north, the Visayas in the middle, and Mindanao in the south. As it is today, Manila was the capital city of the Philippines during the period of Spanish rule from 1565 to 1898.

Filipinos are Austronesian peoples (from Southeast Asia and Oceania). Significant minorities at the time of the Spanish-American War included Spaniards, Chinese, and Arabs. Except for the Moro (Muslim) population in the Philippines, many Filipinos were Roman Catholic, a reflection of Spanish influence. Many Filipino surnames were Spanish, and a good number of Filipinos spoke at least some Spanish. At the time of the Spanish-American War, Tagalog was the other principal spoken language, and variations of it were spoken throughout the archipelago. There are also at least 12 other regional languages spoken in the Philippines.

The climate of the Philippines is tropical, with hot and humid summers and slightly cooler and drier winters. The mitigating factors of this pattern are altered mainly by proximity to the sea and/or elevation. The Philippines have a number of impressive mountain ranges and volcanoes, some of which are still active. Mount Apo, located on Mindanao, is the Philippines' highest peak at 9,692 feet above sea level. As with many areas of the Pacific Rim, the Philippines are subjected to periodic earthquakes and volcanic eruptions.

Chinese, Arabs, and indigenous peoples of the Pacific Rim actively traded with Philippine tribes as early as 900 CE, often establishing permanent or semipermanent settlements. A wave of Malaysian immigration during the 14th and 15th centuries brought Islam to the southern islands of Sulu and Mindanao. This ethnic mixing resulted in a diverse population that speaks more than 100 languages and dialects and practices a wide variety of religions.

In 1521, Portuguese explorer Ferdinand Magellan, sailing for Spain, led the first European expedition to sight the archipelago. Magellan was soon killed by the Visayan chieftain Lapulapu, who became a symbol of Filipino resistance to colonial domination. A later expedition claimed the islands for Spain and named them in honor of Philip, the Spanish prince who became King Philip II. Spain permanently colonized the Philippines in 1565, establishing Manila as the capital, and soon controlled much of the Tagalog-speaking area of Luzon.

At the time of Spanish settlement, family-based villages, known as barangays, were the primary form of government. This independent village structure facilitated European conquest because the barangays were unable to unite against the Spanish. Resistance, although widespread, was usually localized and on a small scale. In the barangays, male datus (chiefs) traditionally constituted the political and military leadership, while powerful female babaylans controlled spiritual, agricultural, and social processes. As spiritual leaders, babaylans were particular targets of Spanish conversion and often led local revolts. Eventually, Spanish friars converted much of the population of the islands, undermining these traditional forms of self-government, and Catholic orders became the focus of political and economic power.

The barangay was adopted into the Spanish government of the Philippines. Filipinos, often datus, acted as heads of the barangays, which came under the jurisdiction of Spanish priests and provincial governors. These officials answered to the governor-general, who was appointed by the king of Spain. Throughout Spanish rule, upper-level political offices were appointed and held exclusively by Spaniards, excluding Filipinos from most positions of significant power.

Rebellion was common during the Spanish colonial period, especially in Muslim areas. Loss of political and cultural freedom, forced labor, religious differences, and the abuses of the encomienda (feudal-like labor) system contributed to ongoing native unrest. However, Spanish military garrisons were often small and understrength, which resulted in the development of special tactics, techniques, and procedures to support the colonial army mission and keep order.

For example, Spain often enlisted and conscripted Filipino soldiers to suppress regional uprisings and to fight small wars of aggression by foreign powers. For Filipinos living under the restrictions of colonial rule, service in the army offered an opportunity for regular pay and higher social status. Filipino soldiers were instructed in European tactics and military practices, a process that accelerated acculturation of the native population.

Military service also helped the colonial government emphasize ethnic differences and prevent nationalist solidarity, as native soldiers from one region were sent to fight revolts in different areas. This tactic emphasized traditional tribal rivalries and regional differences. In particular, Christianized Filipino soldiers were used to suppress ongoing unrest in the southern islands where the Muslim Moros had never been pacified by the Spanish. Filipino soldiers fought not only in native revolts but also in foreign colonial conflicts. Filipinos, for instance, fought for Spain against the Chinese and Dutch and against the British when they occupied Manila during the Seven Years' War (1756–1763). Spain's utilization of native soldiers helped it maintain its hold on the Philippines.

Spain kept the Philippines closed to the West until the 19th century, using Manila as its center of trade between Asia and Mexico. The China Market was important to this galleon trade, as silk and porcelain were exchanged for silver and other Mexican commodities. Mexican independence disrupted this trading arrangement, and Spain opened the Philippines to trade with the West in 1821, when it formally conceded Mexican independence. Soon, Americans, British, Japanese, French, Germans, Dutch, and other nationalities established banks, businesses, and homes in Manila. Not surprisingly, this influx of foreign settlement and economic interests contributed to social and political changes. Also vitally important to Spanish economic control of the islands were vast farms, or plantations, where highly valued cash crops were raised in large quantities and then shipped to Spain and other parts of its empire.

By the 19th century, Spanish colonialism had significantly changed Filipino life. Society was highly stratified by race and class and influenced by European experiences with revolution. Peninsulares, Spaniards born in Spain or of pure Spanish descent, constituted the upper classes, followed by a small middle class of insulares, who were born in the colonies or were mestizos of mixed Spanish descent. Chinese mestizos and native Filipinos, or indios, were on the bottom of the socioeconomic ladder. Some Filipinos belonged to the landed elite, known as ilustrados, and many of these families educated their children in Europe. Using this education, ilustrado reformers began seeking ways to improve the colonial government, while ilustrado revolutionaries sought Philippine independence. Although a sense of nationalism was slowly develop-

ing, the stark social differences and varied goals for Philippine self-government often prevented cohesion among the Filipino people.

The 1872 Cavite Mutiny helped lay the foundation for the Philippine Revolution of 1896. A workers' strike at the naval shipyard in Cavite led to the arrest of three native priests, Mariano Gómez, José Apolonio Gómez, and Jacinto Zamora. Known collectively as the Gomburza, the three priests were executed by Spanish officials. This event deeply influenced nationalist leaders such as José Rizal and helped create a deeper sense of national identity and patriotism among Filipinos. The Propaganda Movement emerged among liberal Filipinos exiled to Europe after the 1872 executions and among Filipino students studying abroad. These reformers hoped to effect changes in Spanish colonial policy and secure representation for the Philippines in the Spanish Cortes (parliament).

Despite the desire for reform rather than independence, propaganda movement leaders were often arrested when they returned to the Philippines. In 1887, Rizal came back to the islands after writing his controversial anticolonial novel *Noli Me Tangere* (Don't Touch Me) but was soon forced to flee to Europe and then Hong Kong. He returned again in 1892 to form the Liga Filipina, a nationalistic civic organization for Filipinos that stressed education as the key mode with which to move Filipinos toward reform and independence. The Spanish government exiled Rizal to Dapitan, effectively undermining the Liga Filipina, but Andrés Bonifacio soon formed the revolutionary Katipunan, a secret society dedicated to the immediate and violent overthrow of Spanish rule.

Dissent among the Katipunan, however, led to its discovery by Spanish authorities, causing Bonifacio to tear up his *cedula* (residence certificate) and initiate the Philippine Revolution on August 23, 1896. This initial declaration of war caused provincial uprisings throughout the Philippines, including Cavite where ilustrado Emilio Aguinaldo y Famy was leading the revolutionary resistance.

Aguinaldo and Bonifacio established rival governments, weakening the revolution. In a compromise election, Aguinaldo was chosen as president of the military junta, provoking Bonifacio to oppose him. Aguinaldo ordered Bonifacio's arrest and had him executed, but Spain utilized the opportunity to move against the revolutionary army. Aguinaldo and his followers surrendered under the December 1897 Pact of Biak-na-Bato and went into brief exile in Hong Kong.

With the outbreak of the Spanish-American War in April 1898, Aguinaldo believed that Philippine independence was fully attainable. Commodore George Dewey soundly defeated the Spanish in Manila Bay on May 1, 1898, and soon established a repair and coaling station for the Asiatic Squadron in the Philippines. The American consul in Hong Kong, Rounseville Wildman, along with U.S. naval attachés, secured Aguinaldo's cooperation against the Spanish, and Aguinaldo and his lieutenants returned to the Philippines.

The United States did not immediately institute a coherent policy toward the Philippines, and both Dewey and U.S. Army commander Major General Wesley Merritt were uncertain about Aguinaldo's position. The Spanish census of 1898 placed the

Filipino population at close to 5.28 million, while Merritt's expeditionary force had only 12,000 regulars and volunteers. The U.S. Army nonetheless kept Aguinaldo out of Manila and excluded him from the conflict by arranging a Spanish surrender in August 1898.

Aguinaldo moved to the town of Malolos north of Manila and initiated a constitutional convention there in September. The Treaty of Paris officially ended the Spanish-American War on December 10, 1898, with Spain ceding the Philippines to the United States for $20 million, but the Malolos Constitution nevertheless established the First Philippine Republic in January 1899 with Aguinaldo as president.

The U.S. Congress and the American people engaged in heated debates about the consequences of imperialism and acquiring the Philippines as a colony. The Treaty of Paris was not ratified until February 6, 1899, after shots had already been exchanged between U.S. soldiers and Filipino insurgents on February 4, 1899, beginning the Philippine-American War. The Second Battle of Manila was fought on February 4, and by August 1899 there were more than 11,000 U.S. soldiers deployed to the Philippines to suppress the insurrection.

The Filipino Nationalist Army, under the leadership of Aguinaldo, initially fought a conventional war against the U.S. Army but lacked the resources to win such a campaign. By November 1899, Aguinaldo had dispersed his army and began fighting a guerrilla war. These tactics led to atrocities on both sides, causing a variety of reactions from the United States and abroad. On March 23, 1901, forces under U.S. Army brigadier general of volunteers Frederick Funston captured Aguinaldo, effectively destroying the First Philippine Republic. Aguinaldo swore allegiance to the United States just days later, but many of his generals refused to capitulate, and the war continued in earnest until July 1902.

Although the Philippine-American War officially ended in 1902, resistance to the American occupation continued for years thereafter, especially in Muslim areas. The Americans suppressed numerous revolts, including the Pulahan Rebellion in Samar from 1904 to 1907 and the various Moro rebellions in Mindanao, which endured until at least 1913. Meanwhile, Filipino political leaders, such as Manuel Quezon, worked for independence until the Tydings-McDuffie Act was approved by the U.S. Congress on March 24, 1934. Also known as the Philippine Independence Act, Tydings-McDuffie established a 10-year transition period to Filipino self-government. The process was interrupted by the Japanese occupation during World War II, but Manuel Roxas became the president of the independent Philippine Republic in July 1946.

DAWN OTTEVAERE NICKESON

See also

Aguinaldo y Famy, Emilio; Biak-na-Bato, Pact of; Bonifacio, Andrés; China Market; Coaling Stations; Colonial Policies, U.S.; Filipino Nationalist Army; Filipino Revolutionary Movement; Hong Kong; Ilustrados; Katipunan; Liga Filipina; Manila, First Battle of; Manila, Second Battle of; Moros; Philippine-American War; Philippine-American War, U.S. Reaction to; Philippine Republic, First; Rizal, José; Spain, Army; Tagalogs; United States Army

Further Reading

Agoncillo, Teodoro A., and Milagros C. Guerrero. *History of the Filipino People*. 5th ed. Quezon City, Philippines: R. P. Garcia, 1983.

Baclagon, Uldarico. *Military History of the Philippines*. Manila: Saint Mary's, 1975.

Karnow, Stanley. *In Our Image: America's Empire in the Philippines*. New York: Random House, 1989.

Linn, Brian McAllister. *The Philippine War, 1899–1902*. Lawrence: University Press of Kansas, 2000.

University of the Philippines Center for Women Studies. *Women's Role in Philippine History: Selected Essays*. 2nd ed. Quezon City: University of the Philippines Press, 1996.

Woods, Damon. *The Philippines: A Global Studies Handbook*. Santa Barbara, CA: ABC-CLIO, 2006.

Philippine Islands, Blockade of

Start Date: 1898
End Date: 1903

Following the defeat of the Spanish Pacific Squadron at the Battle of Manila Bay on May 1, 1898, the U.S. Asiatic Squadron successfully established a blockade of the Philippine Islands with the chief goal of disrupting the First Philippine Republic's interisland communications and finances, thereby hindering insurgent activity. U.S. Navy gunboats successfully severed waterborne traffic, isolated each island's resistance movement, and prevented both the transfer of reinforcements and the creation of safe havens. Also, the Filipino Nationalist Army was severely limited in its ability to equip itself with modern firearms, having to rely mainly on rifles and ammunition taken from the Spanish.

The blockade also contributed greatly to the already-existing food crisis in the Philippines. Roughly a month after the blockade began, widespread rice shortages throughout southeastern Luzon were reported. Indeed, Brigadier General John C. Bates remarked that the blockade had starved out the natives in Zamboanga and allowed a bloodless occupation by the U.S. Army.

In his annual report of 1899, Secretary of the Navy John D. Long stated that the blockade was to be maintained to the extent laid down by the general policy of the War Department. Rear Admiral John C. Watson, who had replaced Admiral George Dewey on June 20, 1899, as commander of the Asiatic Squadron, intended to utilize the blockade to shut off all illicit traffic. Watson viewed such traffic as vessels that flew the Philippine Republic's flag and traded with closed ports. During most of 1899, only three ports were open for trade—Manila, Iloilo City, and Cebu City—with such items as matches, rice, oil, nipa, and fish listed as contraband.

In order to enhance the effectiveness of the blockade, the Asiatic Squadron was restructured in the autumn of 1898. Instead of utilizing the large steel warships that had won the battle against the Spanish Pacific Squadron, the U.S. Navy turned to 25 gunboats, many of which had been captured from the Spanish after the battle. The gunboats ranged in size from 250 to 900 tons, were armed with cannon and machine guns, and were commanded by junior officers, some hardly out of the United States Naval Academy, Annapolis.

Initially, the gunboats were assigned to a larger mother ship, which helped with administration and resupply. Later, however, the navy divided the archipelago into four patrol areas. Each had its own station. These were located at Zamboanga, Cebu, Iloilo, and Vigan, with gunboats assigned to specific stations.

Not everyone believed that the naval blockade was effective. Lieutenant Colonel Thomas R. Hamer, military governor of Cebu, was a strong critic. He saw the blockade as destructive to Cebuano interests. The majority of Cebu's maritime traders owned small vessels that operated along the coast and neighboring islands. Hamer allowed the small vessels to clear Cebu City for all ports except for two that he believed were still under revolutionary control. He also continued to petition Manila to allow exceptions to the blockade but never achieved his goal.

The Asiatic Squadron played a crucial role in the Philippine-American War by shutting down coastal traffic and disrupting the revolutionaries' efforts to raise and transport arms and funds. The squadron also played a critical role in providing U.S. ground forces with an amphibious capability that the insurgents lacked. This proved vital in numerous military operations.

R. RAY ORTENSIE

See also

Asiatic Squadron; Bates, John Coalter; Dewey, George; Filipino Nationalist Army; Gunboat Operations, Philippine Islands; Long, John Davis; Manila Bay, Battle of; Philippine Republic, First; United States Navy; Watson, John Crittenden

Further Reading

Braisted, William R. *The United States Navy in the Pacific, 1897–1906.* Austin: University of Texas Press, 1958.

Brands, H. W. *Bound to Empire: The United States and the Philippines.* New York: Oxford University Press USA, 1992.

Linn, Brian McAllister. *The Philippine War, 1899–1902.* Lawrence: University Press of Kansas, 2000.

Philippine Islands, Spanish Colonial Policies toward

The Philippine Islands were part of Spain's colonial empire for more than 300 years. During the early years of Spanish rule, the islands were subject to the jurisdiction of the viceroy of New Spain. At the end of the 19th century, the Philippine possession was among the last remaining overseas colonies of Spain and the center of one of the first nationalist movements in Asia.

The Spanish first arrived in the Philippines in March 1521 when explorer Ferdinand Magellan came ashore there during the course of his planned circumnavigation of the globe. He claimed the islands for Spain, naming them the Islas de San Lazaro. Magellan es-

Binondo church and convent in Manila in 1899, a remnant of the successful conversion of the vast majority of Filipinos to Christianity by the Spanish. (Library of Congress)

tablished friendly relations with several tribes and converted some of the natives to Christianity but was later killed by local chieftain Lapu Lapu. The Spanish sent out other expeditions to the islands, however, including one in 1543 led by Roy López de Villalobos. He gave the name of Las Islas Felipinas to Samar and Leyte, for Crown Prince Philip, heir to the Spanish throne, who became king as Philip II. This name was later applied to the entire archipelago.

The Spanish did not establish a permanent settlement in the islands and organize them formally as a colony until 1564, when Philip II sent out Miquel López de Legazpi as the first governor-general. He arrived with an expeditionary force of 500 men in five ships and firmly established Spanish control over the Philippines. Following the defeat of the local Muslim ruler Rajah Solayman six years later, López de Legazpi made Manila the administrative center of the islands. He selected it for its location on Manila Bay and the surrounding rich agricultural lands. Although many of the islands had not been under central rule before, the Spanish established their authority at little human cost except for the Muslim areas in the southern islands, where intermittent resistance continued during the period of Spanish rule. Spanish authorities mounted periodic campaigns against the Muslim provinces until the end of Spanish rule.

The Spanish did little to develop the islands economically. Rather, the Philippines served chiefly as an entrepôt to other Asian markets, particularly China. Manila became a vital link in the Spanish galleon trade between Canton, China, and Acapulco, Mexico. The Spanish imported Chinese silk and porcelain in Chinese junks, paying for the goods in Mexican silver. They then reloaded these goods on galleons to be shipped to Mexico. Because the Philippine economy depended heavily on the galleon trade, there was little incentive for internal improvements.

Because church and state were so closely bound together in the Spanish system, Spain's rule in the islands saw vigorous efforts to convert the natives to Christianity. This was accomplished fairly easily except in the areas where Islam had made converts. Although the majority of the indigenous population became Christians, this heightened tensions with the Muslim areas, especially on Mindanao. Christian ritual in the Philippines incorporated native customs and traditions.

Spanish administration in the Philippines was headed by the governor-general. As a province of New Spain, the Philippines fell under the overall jurisdiction of the Spanish viceroy in Mexico. Following Mexican independence in 1821, the islands were governed directly from Madrid. The governor-general was the representative of the Spanish monarch, commander in chief of military forces in the islands, and vice-patron of the Catholic Church. Spanish rule was indirect, with Spanish officials preferring to exercise their authority through local datus (chiefs). The village chiefs were recognized as a noble landowning class with considerable power. This, however, led to considerable tension with the mass of the population of landless tenant peasants. Indeed, this class division has remained a source of economic, social, and political strife to the present. The colonial government was also marked by extensive corruption. Most of the Iberian-born officials in Manila came out to the islands with the sole purpose of seeking a personal fortune, and few had any interest in developing the colony to the benefit of its people.

Spanish authority was wielded through most of the islands by the local datus and the friars of the Catholic Church. Indeed, the friarocracy of Franciscans, Dominicans, and Augustinians exercised considerable power and ultimately held extensive lands throughout the islands. The extensive authority of the friars became one of the chief causes of the Philippine Revolution in 1896.

Spanish rule began to crumble as a consequence of the British capture of Manila in 1762 during the Seven Years' War (1756–1763), an event welcomed by the persecuted Chinese minority in the islands. Although the Treaty of Paris of 1763 restored Spanish rule, much of the China trade had been lost to the British. The Spanish trade monopoly was also broken, for after the war it was far easier for foreign ships and merchants to trade with the Philippines. In addition, Spanish prestige also suffered considerably in the military defeat at the hands of the British, and frequent unrest and revolts occurred thereafter.

Meanwhile, such developments as the opening of the Suez Canal in 1869 dramatically cut travel time to Spain, and an enlightened upper class of Filipinos, known as the ilustrados, were able to study in Europe. Colonial authorities in Manila were deeply suspicious of educated Filipinos, whom they feared were actively plotting revolts. Although there were some far-sighted liberal governors, such as Carlos Maria de la Torre who implemented reforms during 1869–

1871, the vicissitudes of Spanish politics and frequent changes in administrators made such advances short-lived. Spanish reactionary administrators only served to foster Filipino nationalism and hastened the end of Spanish colonial rule over the islands. Revolutionary agitation broke out in 1896.

DINO E. BUENVIAJE AND SPENCER C. TUCKER

See also
Imperialism; Manila; Mindanao; Moros; Philippine Islands; Tagalogs; White Man's Burden

Further Reading
Steinberg, David Joel. *The Philippines: A Singular and a Plural Place.* 3rd ed. Boulder, CO: Westview, 1994.
Zaide, Gregorio F. *Philippine Political and Cultural History.* Manila: Philippine Education, 1957.

Philippine Islands, U.S. Acquisition of
Event Date: December 10, 1898

The cession of the Philippine Islands by Spain to the United States for a one-time indemnity payment of $20 million was effected with the signing of the Treaty of Paris on December 10, 1898. This treaty marked the formal end of the Spanish-American War following the Protocol of Peace, which had been signed on August 12, 1898. Under the terms of the Treaty of Paris, Spain granted independence to Cuba and, along with the Philippines, ceded Guam and Puerto Rico to the United States.

Negotiations surrounding the treaty first commenced in Paris on October 1, 1898. The U.S. Peace Commission was headed by William R. Day, former secretary of state, who was accompanied by Whitelaw Reid (a journalist and ambassador) and Senators Cushman K. Davis, William P. Frye, and George Gray. The Spanish commission was led by Eugenio Montero Ríos, president of the Spanish Cortes (parliament) at the time, and included four other high-ranking Spanish officials. French diplomat to the United States Jules-Martin Cambon also assisted in deliberations on behalf of Spain. With the exception of Britain, much of Europe was sympathetic to the Spanish side. In the end, the Philippine Islands emerged as the main point of contention in the negotiations. No representatives from any of Spain's contested possessions, including the Philippines, were invited to take part in the negotiations regarding the Treaty of Paris. The commissioners failed to give due recognition to the fact that prior to the Spanish-American War, Filipino revolutionary forces had already been engaged in an active revolt against Spain. On June 12, 1898, a full six months prior to the signing of the treaty, Emilio Aguinaldo y Famy, Filipino leader of the anticolonial movement at that time, had already declared the independence of the Philippines and had set about the task of creating a new revolutionary government and constitution. He had also created a commission to lobby for the official recognition of Philippine independence by foreign governments. Toward this end,

Political cartoon titled "Hit him hard!" showing U.S. president William McKinley about to swat "insurgent Aguinaldo," depicted as a mosquito. Other "insurgent" mosquitoes prepare to attack. Cover of *Judge,* 1899. (Library of Congress)

Aguinaldo appointed Don Felipe Agoncillo to be the diplomatic representative to the United States.

In October 1898, Agoncillo attempted to meet with President William McKinley in Washington but was refused access. Agoncillo then shifted his diplomatic operations to Paris, where he attempted to make contact with the American commissioners involved in the treaty negotiations but was again ignored. Filipinos were incensed at the rebuffs, and by this time, Agoncillo was already advising Aguinaldo to prepare for possible war with the United States.

McKinley had already decided that the Philippines should remain a permanent U.S. possession. Although other alternatives to full annexation had been actively considered—including annexation of only Manila, just Luzon, or the whole archipelago except for Mindanao—McKinley and his top aides ultimately dismissed them. Fearing that the annexation of only Manila or even Luzon would make them difficult to defend, the president decided to push for full annexation. Others in McKinley's camp also pointed out that if the United States did not annex all of the Philippines, other nations would, the most likely being Germany or Japan.

Before the Treaty of Paris could take effect, it had to be ratified by the U.S. Senate. Debate on the treaty occurred between late De-

cember 1898 and early 1899. On December 21, 1898, in what became known as the Proclamation of Benevolent Assimilation, McKinley described the American mission in the Philippines as one intended to do good. The annexation would, however, be carried out "with all possible dispatch," clearly a code for the use of force, if necessary, to subdue native opposition.

Senators George Graham Vest and George Frisbie Hoar were among the loudest opponents of the treaty. One of the arguments against the annexation of the Philippines was that it would be unconstitutional for Filipinos to be administered under U.S. law when not represented by lawmakers in Congress. This was part of a larger debate over whether the United States was a democratic republic or an empire. Some feared that annexation would eventually lead to citizenship for Filipinos, whom they believed were inferior peoples not worthy of full citizenship. This point of view was clearly from the social Darwinist perspective. Still others worried that cheap labor from the Philippines would endanger America's domestic labor market.

Among the most enthusiastic proexpansionists in the Senate were Senators Henry Cabot Lodge and Knute Nelson. They argued that the Constitution only applied to U.S. citizens, a view that the Supreme Court upheld in what became known as the Insular Cases, the bulk of which were decided between 1901 and 1905. These cases held that full constitutional rights did not automatically apply in all areas under U.S. control. On the flip side of the social Darwinist argument, those who were social Darwinists but supported annexation opined that the United States had a moral obligation to bring democracy and free-market systems to the Filipinos.

While the Senate debate was taking place, revolutionaries in the Philippines officially inaugurated the First Philippine Republic on January 23, 1899, with Malolos as the new capital and Aguinaldo as president. Meanwhile, Aguinaldo's diplomatic envoy, Agoncillo, returned to Washington to lobby against the ratification of the treaty on behalf of the new republic. This time, he was able to address the U.S. Senate, although his efforts again proved futile. The Senate rejected the Bacon Amendment, which rejected permanent U.S. sovereignty over the Philippines, with Vice President Garret Augustus Hobart casting the tie-breaking vote. On February 6, 1899, the Senate ratified the Treaty of Paris by a vote of 57 to 27, just a single vote more than the required two-thirds majority.

The United States at this time was already occupying Manila. When the Philippine Army, once allied with the Americans, was excluded from Manila by an American-imposed line of demarcation, relations between the two sides began to deteriorate rapidly. On February 4, 1899, just two days prior to the crucial Senate vote to ratify the Treaty of Paris, the Philippine-American War began, sparked by a U.S. soldier opening fire on four Filipino soldiers who had strayed into the U.S.-occupied zone. The outbreak of hostilities, however, was blamed on the Filipinos. Initially, it had seemed as if the Senate might vote against ratification, but once the war broke out, the mood of the Senate turned patriotic and in favor of annexation. With the ratification of the Treaty of Paris,

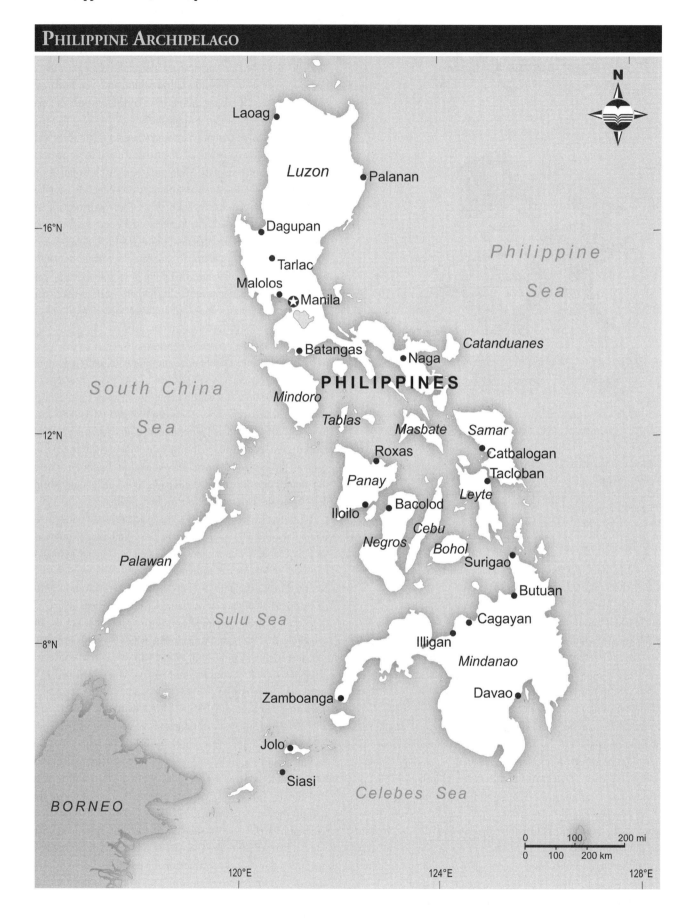

the Philippines came under formal American rule, symbolizing the emergence of the United States as a world power as well as a significant power in Asia.

As popular as annexation may have appeared, it nevertheless met ardent and widespread opposition. In the United States, the Anti-Imperialist League was at the forefront of the campaign against annexation, which it saw as a continuation of the U.S. expansionist agenda in the Pacific beginning with the 1898 acquisition of Hawaii. The league included such notable figures as famed writer Mark Twain, renowned industrialist Andrew Carnegie, former president Grover Cleveland, and 1896 Democratic nominee William Jennings Bryan. The league highlighted the inconsistency of American policy, which, through the Teller Amendment, had ensured that it would not seek to annex Cuba yet still went on to annex the other Spanish colonies of Puerto Rico, Guam, and the Philippines. In the Philippines, resolutions were passed in towns throughout the country decrying American imperialism and expressing allegiance to the First Philippine Republic. There can be little doubt that the annexation of the Philippines helped to inflame passions in the archipelago and played a significant role in the Philippine-American War. Bryan made opposition to imperialism a key platform of his campaign against McKinley in the election of 1900, which Filipinos tried to influence by escalating attacks on the eve of the election.

MARCO HEWITT

See also

Agoncillo, Felipe; Aguinaldo y Famy, Emilio; Anti-Imperialist League; Benevolent Assimilation; Bryan, William Jennings; Carnegie, Andrew; Cleveland, Stephen Grover; Colonial Policies, U.S.; Hawaiian Islands; McKinley, William; Paris, Treaty of; Peace, Protocol of; Peace Commission; Philippine-American War; Philippine Islands; Philippine Republic, First; Social Darwinism; Teller Amendment; Twain, Mark

Further Reading

Agoncillo, Teodoro A., and Milagros C. Guerrero. *History of the Filipino People.* 5th ed. Quezon City, Philippines: R. P. Garcia, 1983.

Pomeroy, William J. *American Neo-Colonialism: Its Emergence in the Philippines and Asia.* New York: International Publishers, 1970.

Schirmer, Daniel B., and Stephen R. Shalom. *The Philippines Reader: A History of Colonialism, Dictatorship, and Resistance.* Cambridge, MA: South End Press, 1987.

Stanley, Peter W. *A Nation in the Making: The Philippines and the United States, 1899–1921.* Cambridge: Harvard University Press, 1974.

Wolff, Leon. *Little Brown Brother: How the United States Purchased and Pacified the Philippine Islands at the Century's Turn.* Garden City, NY: Doubleday, 1961.

Philippine Islands, U.S. Occupation of
Start Date: 1898
End Date: 1901

The U.S. Army occupied the Philippines with the surrender of the Spanish garrison at Manila on August 13, 1898, one day after the Protocol of Peace had been signed. The military occupation lasted almost 23 months under Brigadier Generals Elwell Otis and Arthur MacArthur. The army's occupation formally ended with the appointment of Commissioner William Howard Taft as the first civilian governor of the Philippines and his assumption of executive authority on July 4, 1901. However, even under Taft's and subsequent civilian administrations, subordinate district governors were often army officers operating in districts where insurgent Filipinos were still active.

The U.S. Army occupation of the Philippines was guided by a dual pacification strategy that focused equally on combat operations to eliminate the military power of Filipino nationalist insurgents and on nation-building operations designed to improve the quality of life of Filipinos and win them over to U.S. administration. These two strategies were known as chastisement and attraction, respectively. Military government operations in the Philippines were primarily concerned with components of the strategy of attraction. This program included the promotion of educational opportunities, economic prosperity, Western-style governance, legal reforms, health and sanitation guidelines, and public works.

The U.S. Army placed great emphasis on education as the basis for efficient and effective government of the islands. Toward this end, education was one of the army's top priorities after the conclusion of the conventional phase of the war. In virtually every village and town, army units established schools, and soldiers were detailed to serve as teachers. These early army efforts in education were ad hoc and were largely ineffective in terms of education, however. Nevertheless, they had two very important and lasting legacies. First, they quickly demonstrated to the civilian population that the priorities of the occupying Americans supported the aspirations of the native Filipinos, who placed educational opportunities high on their list of desired reforms. Second, the army established a staff department of education under Captain Alfred Todd that systematically and accurately analyzed the educational needs of the population. Todd's analytical work became the basis for the major educational efforts later undertaken by the civilian administration. By September 1900, the army had in operation more than 1,000 schools that enrolled more than 100,000 students and spent more than $100,000 on school supplies.

The army employed only a few measures in the area of economic reform, although it did recognize the importance of improving the economic conditions to long-term governance of the islands. The army also established the Bureau of Mining and Forestry, which documented resources and sought to preserve them until such time as the government could establish firm procedures for regulating their exploitation and extraction.

The army did not establish a complete or comprehensive system of government in the islands before it was replaced by the civil government. However, it did establish the basic outlines for governance. Otis organized national, provincial, and municipal governments. The national government apparatus was the military

Girls' class at school in Kabayan on the island of Luzon, circa 1900–1923. As a part of the pacification program during and after the Philippine-American War, the U.S. Army built schools in nearly every Filipino town. (Library of Congress)

government headquarters in Manila. Intermediate provincial governments, under a district military governor, were also organized. The district military governor was advised by an elected district council. Finally, local government was organized under the guidance of General Order 43 in 1899 and General Order 40 in 1900. Local municipal government was completely indigenous under the authority of a locally elected mayor supported by an elected municipal council. Guidance for limited suffrage for males over the age of 21 was established by the military and included literacy (in either English, Spanish, or the local language) and property ownership. All local ordinances were determined by the elected officials but subject to approval by the local military commander.

The American military government also took over the Spanish revenue system on the islands. The Americans left most of the Spanish tax system intact. Under U.S. control, the system was simplified and provided greater revenue than it had under the Spanish. This was largely because of the elimination of much of the corruption in the system during Spanish control. The revenue generated was used mainly to support army operations.

The army also took over the Spanish legal system but left it largely intact. The Americans recognized the national supreme court and organized a hierarchy of district courts and local municipal courts. The bulk of Filipino legal officials, judges, and lawyers

remained in their positions. In 1900, army officials overhauled the Spanish criminal code and included many of the characteristics of American law in the new code, including the right to a speedy trial, defense through witnesses, and the rights of bail, retrial, appeal, and habeas corpus. The army also appointed court advisers to ensure that Filipino officials applied the new legal code correctly. During the entire period of military government, military courts operated alongside but independent of the civil courts with overlapping jurisdictions.

A major concern of army officials was health and sanitation. This was both a military operational concern as well as a genuine interest in the quality of life of the general population. The army addressed these issues through strict sanitation guidelines and regulations issued through Manila's Board of Health, which served as the administrator of national health policy for the military government. Army commanders closely supervised the enforcement of sanitation policy at the municipal level. The other aspect of the health and sanitation program was an active national vaccination program, executed through the assigned surgeons of army units garrisoned throughout the country. Occupation authorities supervised the preparation of vaccines within the country, and the army medical service in the Philippines was manned at levels much higher than normally prescribed. The ratio of surgeons to troops

Men in front of a tent with a Filipino woman and a patient sitting on a stretcher, 1st Reserve Hospital, Manila, in 1899. (Library of Congress)

was 1 to every 176 men. Surgeons and their hospital corps assistants provided charity health care to the local population wherever army units were garrisoned. Army health and sanitation efforts had quick and very demonstrative results. Between October 1899 and June 1900, the death rate from disease in Manila was cut in half. Similar results were achieved in most areas of the country by the end of the army occupation.

The Americans also began a significant program of public works as an integral aspect of the occupation. Public works programs were designed to accomplish three goals: assist the operational capability of the army, raise the quality of life of the Filipino population, and employ the local populace for public works projects. The primary focus of public works during the military occupation was road and bridge construction. At the same time, roads and bridges contributed to the military capability of the army and greatly enhanced the local and national economies.

Army occupation policies in the Philippines from 1898 to 1901 were very successful as a comprehensive effort to meet the strategic objectives of the army's mission. At the military campaign level, occupation policies were the heart of the policy of attraction that was a key to the pacification strategy. Occupation policies were also very effective at undermining insurgent propaganda and demonstrating the attractiveness of American administration. At the national strategic level, the army's occupation policies provided a firm basis for the transition of the islands from military to civil government. Ultimately, the occupation policies established by the U.S. Army contributed to building the institutions vital to eventual Philippine independence.

LOUIS A. DIMARCO

See also

MacArthur, Arthur; Otis, Elwell Stephen; Pacification Program, Philippine Islands; Philippine Islands; Philippine Islands, Spanish Colonial Policies toward; Taft, William Howard

Further Reading

Gates, John M. *Schoolbooks and Krags: The United States Army in the Philippines, 1898–1902.* Westport, CT: Greenwood, 1973.

Grunder, Garel A., and William E. Livezey. *The Philippines and the United Sates.* Norman: University of Oklahoma Press, 1951.

Karnow, Stanley. *In Our Image: America's Empire in the Philippines.* New York: Random House, 1989.

Musicant, Ivan. *Empire by Default: The Spanish-American War and the Dawn of the American Century.* New York: Henry Holt, 1998.

Philippine Republic, First
Start Date: 1899
End Date: 1901

Unrecognized independent state established by Filipino leaders at the end of the Philippine insurrection against Spain. Also known as the Malolos Republic, the First Philippine Republic was established by the Malolos Constitution on January 23, 1899. It all but dissolved on April 1, 1901, when president of the Republic, Emilio Aguinaldo y Famy, took an oath of allegiance to the U.S. government after his capture by American forces.

Filipino revolutionaries, led by Aguinaldo, were initially encouraged by the outbreak of the Spanish-American War and considered the United States an ally in their insurgency against Spain. With the United States avowedly fighting Spanish colonialism in Cuba, Aguinaldo declared Philippine independence from Spain on June 12, 1898. U.S. rear admiral George Dewey refused to attend the independence ceremony, not wanting to legitimize a Filipino government as long as the United States was uncertain about the future disposition of the islands. Because U.S. forces then controlled Manila, Aguinaldo established his seat of government in Malolos, Bulacan Province, convening the Malolos Congress to draft a constitution on September 15, 1898. On September 29, 1898, the delegates officially ratified Aguinaldo's Declaration of Independence. Japanese and American journalists witnessed the proceedings.

The Malolos Congress worked throughout the autumn of 1898 to create a republican government in the Philippines. Using European, American, and Latin American models, the delegates outlined the first representative republic in Asia. The constitution created three branches of representative government, delineated the separation of church and state, and recognized the individual rights of citizens. Constitutional committee member Felipe Calderon feared that a strong executive branch would be controlled by Aguinaldo and the armed forces, so he helped frame a dominant legislature to prevent a military oligarchy. In the end, the result was a form of parliamentary republic. The congress ratified the constitution on November 29, 1898, and Aguinaldo signed it on December 23, 1898.

Inauguration ceremony of Emilio Aguinaldo y Famy as president of the First Philippine Republic at Malolos on Luzon, in the Philippine Islands, January 23, 1899. (Library of Congress)

While the congress was still in session, Filipino diplomat Felipe Agoncillo attempted to secure overseas recognition for the fledgling republic. However, the peace commissioners meeting in Paris to negotiate peace between Spain and the United States refused to recognize or include a Filipino representative. In the end, Spain ceded the Philippines to the United States for the sum of $20 million in the Treaty of Paris on December 10, 1898.

Despite lack of support from the international community, the final draft of the Malolos Constitution was accepted by Filipino revolutionary leaders on January 23, 1899. In Malolos that same day, Aguinaldo took the oath of office as the first president of the republic, and Filipino nationalist military forces (later the Army of Liberation) pledged loyalty to the republic. Aguinaldo's first act as president was to pardon Spanish prisoners of war and grant business rights to Europeans and other aliens within the republic. Meanwhile, Agoncillo traveled to the United States to try to prevent ratification of the Treaty of Paris and ensure the sovereignty of the First Philippine Republic, but the outbreak of the Philippine-American War on February 4, 1899, disrupted diplomatic relations. Two days later, the U.S. Senate ratified the treaty. The outbreak of the Philippine-American War and the ratification of the Treaty of Paris made the governance of the republic virtually untenable.

Nevertheless, the republic struggled to survive. It was initially headed by Apolinario Mabini, cabinet president and secretary of

foreign affairs; Teodoro Sandico, interior secretary; Baldomero Aguinaldo, secretary of war; Mariano Trias, finance secretary; Gracio Gonzaga, secretary of welfare; Léon María Guerrero, secretary of agriculture, industry, and commerce; and Máximo Paterno, secretary of public works and communications. Mabini was later succeeded by Pedro Alejandro Paterno y Debera Ignacio as cabinet president and Felipe Buencamino as foreign secretary. Replacing Sandico as interior secretary was Severino De las Alas.

During the Philippine-American War, Aguinaldo's government spearheaded the resistance to American colonial rule. The First Philippine Republic functioned as the unrecognized Philippine government until Aguinaldo's capture by U.S. forces and Macabebe Scouts under the command of Brigadier General Frederick Funston on March 23, 1901, at Palanan, Isabela. Although the Filipino resistance continued, the First Philippine Republic was effectively dissolved by Aguinaldo's oath of allegiance to the U.S. government on April 1, 1901, at the Malacanang Palace in Manila.

DAWN OTTEVAERE NICKESON

See also
Agoncillo, Felipe; Aguinaldo y Famy, Emilio; Funston, Frederick; Mabini, Apolinario; Macabebe Scouts; Malolos, Philippines, Capture of; Malolos Constitution; Paris, Treaty of; Philippine-American War; Philippine Islands, U.S. Acquisition of; Spanish-American War, International Reaction to

Further Reading

Agoncillo, Teodoro A. *Malolos: The Crisis of the Republic.* Quezon City: University of the Philippines Press, 1960.

Agoncillo, Teodoro A., and Milagros C. Guerrero. *History of the Filipino People.* 5th ed. Quezon City, Philippines: R. P. Garcia, 1983.

Arcilla, José S. *An Introduction to Philippine History.* Manila: Ateneo De Manila, 1998.

Austin, Eduardo Diaz Serrano. "Study of the Rise and the Fall of the First Democratic Republic in the Far East: The Philippines, 1898–1899." Unpublished PhD dissertation, Georgetown University, 1957.

Philippine Scouts

A military auxiliary force made up of native Filipinos established to support the U.S. Army during the Philippine-American War (1899–1902). The Philippine Scouts helped American troops navigate the often forbidding terrain of the Philippines and acted as interpreters for a native population that spoke a myriad of dialects.

As a consequence of the Treaty of Paris ending the Spanish-American War, the United States found itself as the colonial ruler of the Philippine Islands, a 7,000-island territory of 10 million people. After a short conventional conflict with American forces that began in February 1899, a Filipino guerrilla army, known as the Army of Liberation and led by Emilio Aguinaldo y Famy, took to the rural areas and began an insurgency aimed at gaining full independence. Among other U.S. military responses to the insurgency was the formation of the Philippine Scouts, a native auxiliary force that would serve alongside U.S. troops in the Philippines for almost 50 years.

The U.S. Army in the Philippines was far from an ideal force to prosecute a conflict that had evolved into a guerrilla war. The approximately 25,000 U.S. troops present in the summer of 1899 were a combination of state volunteer organizations and a growing number of newly recruited regular army personnel. Aside from inexperience, the troops were challenged by the hostile terrain and disease-ridden tropical environment in which they had to operate. The tactical situation dictated that small units, capable of rapid movement and supplied with effective intelligence, would be required to prosecute the counterinsurgency.

In considering this strategy, the U.S. Army could draw upon its experience of the prior 30 years in the struggle against the American Indians of the Great Plains and the Southwest. During that period, the army had routinely employed Indian scouts operating with regular army units with significant success. These scouts brought a unique knowledge of the environment and the enemy and, when coupled with disciplined troop formations, were formidable fighting organizations.

In the Philippines, the mission of the scouts was to conduct reconnaissance in advance of main American units, warn of contact with the insurgents, and fix enemy forces to facilitate their defeat by main forces. At the commencement of hostilities, American soldiers had performed these missions. While they served heroically in an extremely difficult assignment, they were seriously hindered by their ignorance of the terrain, population, and language. In light of this, initiatives were begun to recruit indigenous forces to serve in the scout mission.

In the recruitment of native scouts, historical and tribal considerations loomed large. Much of the support for the insurrection came from the Tagalogs, a tribe dominant in central Luzon. As a result, the vast majority of scouts were recruited from other tribes—the Ilocanos, Visayans, and most notably the Macabebes—a group that had a history of working with the former Spanish colonial government because of their strong hatred for the Tagalogs. This not only motivated them but made them prone to committing atrocities. In the late summer of 1899, Lieutenant M. A. Batson brought the first group of Macabebe volunteers into a U.S. camp. The initial reaction of American military leaders was not enthusiastic. Neither Major General Elwell Stephen Otis, military governor of the Philippines and commander of U.S. forces, nor Brigadier General Arthur MacArthur, commander of the army's 2nd Division on Luzon, believed that they could be trusted enough to be armed.

But the Macabebes, through a series of closely supervised local operations against the guerrillas, gradually gained the confidence of the army and were hired as civilian employees and issued rifles. This first unit of scouts began training in September 1899. A subsequent successful engagement of Philippine guerrillas precipitated the authorization of several more companies, and by the end of 1899, a complete battalion, dubbed Batson's Macabebe Scouts, was in operation.

The first large-scale use of the Philippine Scouts occurred during the Northern Luzon Campaign of October 1899. Aguinaldo's Army of Liberation was still operating in units of significant size in this area, and Otis feared that the rebels would retreat to the mountains and begin a guerrilla war. Accordingly, the Northern Luzon Campaign plan envisioned a quick three-pronged encirclement of Aguinaldo and his fighters. This two-month-long campaign did not achieve its overall strategic purpose, as Aguinaldo escaped and armed resistance continued. Reasons for the failure included extremely wet weather, which hampered mobility and logistics, and questionable tactical decisions on the part of American commanders. The Philippine Scouts, however, acquitted themselves admirably in a series of engagements and grueling marches. Most critically, they earned the trust and respect of all levels of American leadership. The scouts went on to play a significant role in most subsequent military campaigns in the Philippines.

As 1900 began, the Philippine insurrection had assumed the character of a guerrilla war. Aguinaldo had formally declared as much in November 1899, but given his status as a man on the run and the huge geographic area of the country, the insurrection was in reality a large number of localized conflicts. Local American commanders received considerable leeway in the prosecution of a conflict that was both an attempt to win over the people of the Philippines and subdue many diverse groups of guerrillas.

The Macabebe Scouts were some of the first Filipinos to serve alongside U.S. forces during the Philippine-American War. These men fought under U.S. Army lieutenant Matthew Baston. (National Archives)

Throughout 1900, the Philippine Scouts steadily expanded in numbers and came to be a significant factor in achieving the latter goal.

By January 1901, 1,400 Philippine Scouts were in service alongside American troops. Two factors were to more than treble their size within six months. First, American commanders continued to lessen their reflexive distrust of armed native auxiliaries. Second, the looming departure of many U.S. volunteer troops whose tours were up presented U.S. leadership with potential personnel shortages. Accordingly, authority to enlist scouts was delegated to a lower level, and by mid-1901 some 5,500 scouts were serving with the army. Various units of these scouts, usually named after their American commanding officers or tribes from which they were drawn, fought on a number of different islands. Among the most famous were Macabebe, Ilocanos, and Cagayan scouts.

The highly fluid nature of guerrilla warfare, characterized by small units led by junior officers operating far from central authority and often amid the civilian population, unfortunately produced many incidents of atrocities against civilians and abuse of prisoners. Naturally, the Philippine Scouts were implicated in a number of these incidents, most notably on the island of Panay,

where in November 1900 Philippine Scouts were responsible for the burning of some 5,000 houses in the town of Igbaris and the torture of its mayor.

The single most famous feat of arms performed by the Macabebe Scouts was likely their role in the capture of Aguinaldo in March 1901. He had settled in a small town in Isabella Province in Northeast Luzon, where he was effectively protected from army patrols by a network of local agents and observation posts. After intelligence obtained by the U.S. Army from intercepted communications betrayed his position, the district commander, Brigadier General Frederick Funston, designed an elaborate ruse. Aguinaldo's communication had requested reinforcements, so Funston, along with 4 other American officers posing as prisoners, marched into the rebel leader's camp with 80 Macabebe Scouts posing as the reinforcements. Overpowering Aguinaldo's guards, they placed the leader under arrest and returned him to Manila. There, Aguinaldo issued to his guerrillas a proclamation calling for their disarmament.

Thanks to a combination of effective civil affairs efforts aimed at the Filipino people, the destruction of much of the guerrillas' infrastructure by improved American intelligence and tactics (facilitated by the Philippine Scouts), and harsh military retribution on some islands, by mid-1901 many guerrilla leaders had begun to surrender, and the United States declared the Philippine-American War at an end on July 4, 1902.

The record of the Philippine Scouts, while not without its blemishes, was outstanding on the whole. They proved themselves hardy, canny, and extremely dedicated fighters, with a warrior spirit that allowed them to withstand not only savage combat but also the daunting conditions in which they operated. The Philippine Scouts continued to serve with honor throughout the remainder of U.S. rule in the Philippines. After fighting heroically against the Japanese in World War II, the scouts were disbanded in 1950 in the wake of Philippine independence.

ROBERT M. BROWN

See also

Aguinaldo y Famy, Emilio; Atrocities; Funston, Frederick; Luzon; Macabebe Scouts; MacArthur, Arthur; Otis, Elwell Stephen; Philippine Islands; Tagalogs; Visayan Campaigns

Further Reading

Birtle, Andrew J. *U.S. Army Counterinsurgency and Contingency Operations Doctrine, 1860–1941.* Washington, DC: Center of Military History, U.S. Army, 2003.
Gates, John M. *Schoolbooks and Krags: The United States Army in the Philippines, 1898–1902.* Westport, CT: Greenwood, 1973.
Linn, Brian McAllister. *The Philippine War, 1899–1902.* Lawrence: University Press of Kansas, 2000.

Philippines, Committee on the

See Committee on the Philippines

Pilar, Gregorio del
Birth Date: November 14, 1875
Death Date: December 2, 1899

Filipino general during the Spanish-American War and the subsequent Philippine-American War (1899–1902). Gregorio del Pilar was Filipino nationalist Emilio Aguinaldo y Famy's most trusted aide and supporter. Pilar, whose nickname was "Goyong," was born on November 14, 1875, in San José, Bulacan, into an ilustrado (middle-class) family of Filipino nationalists. After completing his bachelor's degree at the Ateneo de Manila in 1896, he joined Andrés Bonifacio's Katipunan, a secret nationalist organization dedicated to ending Spanish colonialism. In August 1896, Pilar returned to Bulacan to fight Spanish troops in his hometown. His success on the battlefield soon caught the attention of Aguinaldo, who by then had become the undisputed leader of the Katipunan following Bonifacio's execution on May 19, 1897.

On December 14, 1897, after suffering numerous military setbacks, Aguinaldo signed the Pact of Biak-na-Bato with Spanish authorities. In return for an indemnity of 400,000 pesos, Aguinaldo and 34 top military leaders, including Pilar, agreed to go into exile in Hong Kong. Aguinaldo, however, who never seriously considered abandoning the nationalist cause, used the money to rearm his revolutionaries with weapons purchased in Hong Kong. After U.S. Navy commodore George Dewey's Asiatic Squadron defeated the Spanish Pacific Squadron in Manila Bay on May 1, 1898, Aguinaldo and his men returned to the Philippines on May 19 to continue their struggle for independence.

Dewey encouraged Aguinaldo and his Filipino revolutionaries to fight the Spanish troops until U.S. ground forces could arrive. On June 1, 1898, Pilar, now a general, landed in Bulacan and without difficulty defeated the Spanish forces occupying that region. After liberating Bulacan, Pilar's troops went on to Manila to continue the struggle for independence.

After the Spanish were finally defeated and the Philippine Constitutional Convention elected Aguinaldo president on January 1, 1899, the U.S. government refused to acknowledge Filipino independence. After the Philippine-American War broke out on February 4, 1899, Aguinaldo and his supporters fled Manila. On April 23, Pilar's forces defeated U.S. troops led by Major James Franklin Bell at Quinqua, Bulacan. The Filipinos, however, were outmanned and outgunned by the U.S. forces. By November 1899, Aguinaldo's forces were in the highlands of Concepcion. On November 22, 1899, Aguinaldo asked Pilar to lead a rear guard of 60 men to defend the Tirad Pass near Concepcion. Pilar's men proceeded to construct a series of stone trenches and barricades to inhibit American advancement up the narrow Tirad Pass. On December 2 during the Battle of Tirad Pass, also known as the Philippine Thermopylae, Pilar's troops held off more than 500 U.S. Marines for five hours, which allowed Aguinaldo and his troops sufficient time to escape capture. Pilar died in the battle on December 2, 1899. After U.S. forces captured Aguinaldo at Palanan, Isabela, on March 23, 1901, Filipino resistance crumbled, leading to the official end of the Philippine-American War in July 1902.

MICHAEL R. HALL

See also

Aguinaldo y Famy, Emilio; Bell, James Franklin; Biak-na-Bato, Pact of; Bonifacio, Andrés; Dewey, George; Katipunan; Pilar, Pio del; Tirad Pass, Battle of

Further Reading

Kalaw, Tedoro M. *An Acceptable Holocaust: Life and Death of a Boy General.* Translated by M. A. Foronda. Manila, Philippines: National Historical Commission, 1974.
Linn, Brian McAllister. *The U.S. Army and Counterinsurgency in the Philippine War, 1899–1902.* Chapel Hill: University of North Carolina Press, 1989.
Miller, Stuart Creighton. *"Benevolent Assimilation": The American Conquest of the Philippines, 1899–1903.* New Haven, CT: Yale University Press, 1982.

Pilar, Pio del

Birth Date: July 11, 1860
Death Date: June 21, 1931

Pio del Pilar was the nom de guerre of Filipino revolutionary and military leader Pio Isidro y Castañeda, who was born on July 11, 1860, in Culi-Culi, Makati, Philippines. His father, Isaac Isidro, a small farmer of Filipino ancestry from Makati, and his mother, a mestizo from the wealthy Castañeda family from Pasay, instilled a revolutionary spirit in their son at an early age. To protect his family from reprisals from Spanish colonial authorities, Pio changed his surname. Historians often incorrectly assert that he was a member of the wealthy del Pilar family from Bulacan. He was not, in fact, related to famed Filipino general Gregorio del Pilar (1875–1899) and his family. Most likely, Pio chose the name to honor Filipino revolutionary Marcelo Hilario del Pilar y Gatmaytan (1850–1896).

Neither Pio del Pilar nor his parents had much formal schooling. In 1867, he was conscripted into the Spanish colonial army, but a family friend, Lorenzo Protacio, intervened on his behalf, and Pilar terminated his military service within four months. While Pilar was still a teenager, his father died, and Pilar had to take control of the family farm. In 1887, while visiting a family friend, he met Filipino revolutionary José Rizal. Although excited by Rizal's Liga Filipina, Pilar did not join the organization. In 1895, Spanish colonial authorities, suspecting Pilar of revolutionary activities, arrested him and subjected him to torture. Ironically, Pilar was not yet a member of any Filipino revolutionary group. After subjecting him to weeks of torture, the colonial authorities released him.

In May 1896, Pilar joined the Katipunan, an ultrasecret Filipino nationalist group. He helped establish the Magtagumpay (triumphant) Chapter of the Katipunan in Culi-Culi, and his cohorts soon began calling him Pang-Una (leader). As with other revolutionary Katipunan cell leaders, Pilar designed a flag for his own chapter that was sewn by his mother. The flag was red with a white triangle. The letter "K" was in each angle of the triangle, which surrounded a rising sun with eight rays. The flag subsequently influenced the current Filipino flag. One of Emilio Aguinaldo y Famy's most trusted generals, Pilar led the eastern flank of Aguinaldo's revolutionaries against the Spanish in the Battle of Binakayan on November 9, 1896. The battle was the first major victory for the Filipino revolutionaries.

On February 16, 1897, Pilar defended the town of Bacoor against a Spanish attack. Following the split between Aguinaldo and Andrés Bonifacio in March 1897, Pilar sided with Aguinaldo. Following the Pact of Biak-na-Bato in December 1897, Pilar remained in the Philippines and received a commission in the Spanish Volunteer Militia. Once Aguinaldo returned to the Philippines from temporary exile in Hong Kong in May 1898, however, Pilar resumed his revolutionary activities until the Spanish surrendered to U.S. authorities.

Unlike Aguinaldo, who initially adopted a conciliatory stance toward the American occupiers of the Philippines at the conclusion of the Spanish-American War, Pilar wanted to continue the nationalist struggle. He had no use for Americans and in fact exhibited a visceral dislike for them. The incident at the San Juan Bridge in Manila on February 4, 1899, that sparked the Philippine-American War involved a member of Pilar's brigade. Following his defeat at the Battle of Zapote Bridge on June 13, 1899, the Filipino insurgency army adopted guerrilla tactics against the Americans.

Pilar was captured by American forces on June 8, 1900, at Guadalupe and was deported to Guam in January 1901. He returned to the Philippines in November 1902 and remained largely out of the public spotlight. Pilar died at Pasay, Philippines, on June 21, 1931.

MICHAEL R. HALL

See also

Aguinaldo y Famy, Emilio; Biak-na-Bato, Pact of; Bonifacio, Andrés; Katipunan; Liga Filipina; Philippine-American War; Pilar, Gregorio del; Rizal, José; Zapote Line

Further Reading

Dery, Luis Camara. *The Army of the First Philippine Republic*. Manila, Philippines: De la Salle University Press, 1995.

Linn, Brian McAllister. *The Philippine War, 1899–1902*. Lawrence: University Press of Kansas, 2000.

Ochosa, Orlino A. *Pio del Pilar & Other Heroes*. Quezon City, Philippines: New Day, 1997.

Zaide, Gregorio F. *History of the Katipunan*. Manila, Philippines: Loyal Press, 1939.

Plant Railroad and Steamship Company

A major transportation and development company that operated a number of southern rail lines, including that serving Tampa, Florida, during the Spanish-American War. The Plant Railroad facilities at Tampa caused much initial confusion and delay in the mobilization of troops and the delivery and unloading of supplies as the U.S. Army prepared for the Cuban expedition in the late spring of 1898. Before and during the war, steamships owned and operated by the Plant Railroad and Steamship Company were used to relay secret dispatches from Cuba to the United States, facilitated by Martin Luther Hellings, a telegrapher for Western Union.

The Plant Railroad and Steamship Company was a large conglomerate founded and operated by Henry Bender Plant, a transportation entrepreneur who had begun his operation during the American Civil War as a parcel delivery company. After the war, he expanded his enterprise by purchasing a series of failing southern railroads, which he bought for next to nothing and then built up. By 1890, he owned 14 thriving railroads and several steamship lines. He had also built a number of high-end resorts and hotels in Florida, all served by his steamships and railways. The Tampa Bay Hotel, finished in 1891, was the most elaborate of these. Indeed,

Rail lines leading to the docks at Port Tampa in 1898 during the Spanish-American War. (*Photographic History of the Spanish-American War,* 1898)

Plant sought to turn the Tampa Bay area into a major commercial, transportation, and resort hub.

By 1898, Plant's dream was nearly realized, as Tampa had become a major seaport and transportation nexus, and his Plant Railroad and Steamship Company had a virtual monopoly over the railways and ports in the city. Goods moving into the area went by rail largely controlled by Plant and were then loaded onto his steamships. His work had helped convince the War Department that Tampa would serve as the major embarkation point for troops and supplies headed to Cuba and later to Puerto Rico.

Most of Plant's railway network ran from Georgia into Florida. Although Plant had modernized and upgraded these rail facilities, they proved to be inadequate to meet the huge demands of the Spanish-American War effort. Two primary factors caused the bottlenecks in Tampa. First, only two railroad companies served the greater Tampa area, and they were bitter rivals. Indeed, Plant did everything in his power to stymie his competitor; this rivalry reached new heights during the war. Second, only a single railroad track—controlled by Plant—served Port Tampa, resulting in gridlock as hundreds of boxcars attempted to navigate the track so that their cargoes might be loaded onto ships.

By mid-May 1898, more than 1,000 full railcars choked the railway yards in Tampa and at Port Tampa. The delays became so bad that boxcars full of uniforms, food, weapons, and ordnance were backed up as far as Columbia, South Carolina, more than 400 miles to the north. The situation was made all the worse because bills of lading had not accompanied the boxcars, and those unloading them had no idea as to their contents.

Although U.S. rail companies performed admirably during the war effort and cooperated quite well with the U.S. government, the situation in and around Tampa did not mirror this. Plant tried to monopolize government contracts, which forced his competitor to follow suit. In the meantime, goods were piling up, and the War Department was having a hard time moving troops into Tampa. In late May 1898, the crisis came to a head when Plant refused to allow any competitor's railcars to traverse his tracks. This would have virtually paralyzed the entire operation in Tampa. Finally, the War Department threatened the Plant Railroad and Steamship Company with a government seizure order, and Plant relented. By mid-June 1898, most of the bottlenecks at Tampa had been resolved.

Paul G. Pierpaoli Jr.

See also
Hellings, Martin Luther; Military Intelligence; Railroads; Tampa, Florida

Further Reading
Cosmas, Graham A. *An Army for Empire: The United States Army in the Spanish-American War.* College Station: Texas A&M University Press, 1994.
Reynolds, Kelly. *Henry Plant: Pioneer Empire Builder.* Cocoa: Florida Historical Society Press, 2003.
Stover, John F. *American Railroads.* 2nd ed. Chicago: University of Chicago Press, 1997.

Platt, Orville Hitchcock
Birth Date: July 19, 1827
Death Date: April 21, 1905

U.S. senator and sponsor of the 1901 Platt Amendment that set the guidelines for U.S.-Cuban relations until 1934. Orville Hitchcock Platt was born on July 19, 1827, in Washington, Connecticut, where he attended local schools before reading for the law in Litchfield, Connecticut. In 1850, he was admitted to the Connecticut State Bar at which time he also moved to Towanda, Pennsylvania. There he began practicing law, but before year's end he moved back to Connecticut and settled in Meriden, where he continued his law practice.

In the mid-1850s, Platt became interested in state politics. Using his legal skills, he secured the post of clerk to the Connecticut Senate, which he held from 1855 to 1856. In 1857, he served as Connecticut's secretary of state. Elected to the Connecticut Senate in 1861, he served in that body until 1862. In 1864 and again in 1869, he served in the Connecticut House of Representatives, acting as its Speaker in 1869.

By now a committed Republican, Platt served as the New Haven County (Connecticut) state attorney from 1877 to 1879. In 1879, the Connecticut legislature elected him to the U.S. Senate, where he would serve until his death in 1905. Not a flashy politician by any means, he nonetheless developed a solid reputation during his many years of Senate service and chaired a number of important committees, including the Committee on Territories and the Committee on Cuban Relations. His work in these areas reflected his interest in the relationship of the United States to its territories, particularly those gained as a consequence of the Spanish-American War.

The Platt Amendment was actually the brainchild of Secretary of War Elihu Root, who in 1901 implored the Senate to pass the legislation and thereby solidify U.S. influence in Cuba. Platt agreed to sponsor the amendment, which was tacked on to the Army Appropriations Act in early 1901. On March 2, 1901, the Senate passed the appropriations bill, including the Platt Amendment. Besides transferring the naval base at Guantánamo Bay to the United States (for which the Americans would pay a token yearly rent), the amendment severely restricted the Cuban government's foreign

Republican senator Orville H. Platt was the sponsor of the 1901 Platt Amendment that outlined the provisions for the withdrawal of U.S. troops from Cuba and defined future Cuban-U.S. relations. (Library of Congress)

policies and its ability to borrow money from overseas. It also granted the United States the right to intervene in Cuban internal affairs if it was deemed necessary.

The Platt Amendment was decried by the Cubans as nothing less than imperialism on the part of the United States designed to keep it in semiservitude to American interests. The Theodore Roosevelt administration insisted that the Cuban government incorporate the Platt Amendment into its own constitution. Although Roosevelt removed the remaining U.S. troops in Cuba in 1902, the United States would intervene in Cuba in 1906, 1909, 1912, and 1917–1923. The Platt Amendment stood until 1934, when President Franklin D. Roosevelt's Good Neighbor Policy abolished it.

Platt died in Mediden, Connecticut, on April 21, 1905.

PAUL G. PIERPAOLI JR.

See also
Cuba; Cuba, U.S. Occupation of; Guantánamo Bay Naval Base; Roosevelt, Theodore; Root, Elihu; Teller Amendment

Further Reading
Coolidge, Louis. *An Old Fashioned Senator: Orville H. Platt.* Port Washington, NY: Kennikat, 1971.

Pérez, Louis A., Jr. *Cuba under the Platt Amendment, 1902–1934.* Pittsburgh: University of Pittsburgh Press, 1986.

Smith, Edwina C. "Conservatism on the Gilded Age: The Senatorial Career of Orville H. Platt." PhD dissertation, University of North Carolina, 1976.

Platt Amendment

U.S. congressional legislation forced upon Cuba that became law in January 1903. The Platt Amendment outlined the provisions for the withdrawal of U.S. troops from Cuba and defined future Cuban-U.S. relations. U.S. troops had been stationed in Cuba since the Spanish-American War began in 1898. Drafted by U.S. secretary of war Elihu Root and presented to the Senate by Connecticut Republican Orville H. Platt, the Platt Amendment was an additional provision attached to the Army Appropriations Act passed by the U.S. Congress on March 2, 1901. The Platt Amendment was a replacement, of sorts, for the 1898 Teller Amendment, which had prohibited American annexation of Cuba.

Following the Spanish-American War and the departure of the Spanish from Cuba in 1898, the United States occupied the island until 1902. During this occupation, the U.S. government organized the Cuban economy and set up educational and health care systems on the island.

The Platt Amendment had several provisions. First, Cuba could never enter into any treaty with a foreign power that would impair its independence. Second, Cuba could not acquire foreign debt beyond its ability to pay from its own revenues. Third, Cuba gave the United States the right to intervene to preserve Cuban independence or to preserve law and order. Fourth, Cuba agreed to cede or lease land to the United States for the purposes of naval or coaling stations (the Guantánamo Bay Naval Base). Fifth, Cuba was required to include the provisions of the Platt Amendment verbatim in the new Cuban Constitution. In effect the Platt Amendment gave the United States a quasi protectorate over Cuba.

Under considerable pressure from the United States, the Cuban Constitutional Convention included the Platt Amendment provisions in its constitution on June 12, 1901. After American troops withdrew from Cuba in May 1902, the United States and Cuba incorporated the Platt Amendment into a formal treaty signed between the two nations on May 22, 1903. As a result of the Platt Amendment, the United States intervened in Cuba in 1906, 1909, 1912, and 1917–1923 to protect American interests. Congress repealed the Platt Amendment in 1934 as part of President Franklin D. Roosevelt's Good Neighbor Policy, which sought to improve relations with Latin American and Caribbean nations. All the provisions of the treaty, except for the U.S. rights to Guantánamo Bay, were nullified. The American presence in Guantánamo Bay continues to this day, and the American lease on the area can be revoked only with the joint consent of both Cuba and the United States.

ANNA RULSKA

See also

Cuba; Guantánamo Bay Naval Base; Platt, Orville Hitchcock; Root, Elihu; Teller Amendment

Further Reading

Benjamin, Jules R. *The United States and Cuba: Hegemony and Dependent Development, 1880–1934.* Pittsburgh: University of Pittsburgh Press, 1977.

Pérez, Louis A., Jr. *Cuba and the United States: Ties of Singular Intimacy.* Athens: University of Georgia Press, 1997.

———. *Cuba under the Platt Amendment, 1902–1934.* Pittsburgh: University of Pittsburgh Press, 1986.

Plüddemann, Max
Birth Date: February 12, 1846
Death Date: January 23, 1910

German admiral who wrote about naval operations in the Caribbean during the Spanish-American War. Max Plüddemann was born in Stettin on February 12, 1846. He entered the Prussian Navy as a cadet aspirant in October 1863 and graduated from the naval academy in 1866 in the same class as future admiral Ernst Otto von Diederichs. Plüddemann was 1 of 6 of a total of 16 midshipmen of that class to make flag rank. He rose steadily in rank and held routine assignments at sea and in the naval administration. In September 1885, as a lieutenant commander and captain of the gunboat *Albatross,* he took possession for Germany of the island of Chuuk in Micronesia. His last post was that of head of the Nautical Department, and he retired from the navy as a rear admiral in June 1897.

Plüddemann was apparently not reactivated when he served as an official observer of U.S. ships of Rear Admiral William T. Sampson's North Atlantic Fleet during the Spanish-American War. Immediately following the war, Plüddemann published an article in the *Marine Rundschau* (Naval Review) with his observations. This article was quickly translated and reprinted that same year by the U.S. Navy as an 18-page booklet.

Among Plüddemann's observations were that the war had brought no major changes in naval warfare; the battleship was still supreme at sea; the U.S. Navy monitors were of little worth; torpedoes were largely ineffective; many Spanish mines were defective and had failed to explode; U.S. Navy ordnance was of high quality, but accuracy of fire was very poor, and claims of damage inflicted were exaggerated; Spanish gunnery was abysmal; the failure of the Spanish to remove combustible materials from their ships had caused the extensive fires on the Spanish ships at the Battle of Santiago de Cuba; and the U.S. Navy repair ship *Vulcan* was a valuable addition to the U.S. fleet.

Plüddemann died in Kleinmachnow near Berlin on January 23, 1910.

SPENCER C. TUCKER

See also

Diederichs, Ernst Otto von; Sampson, William Thomas; Santiago de Cuba, Battle of; United States Navy

Further Reading

Plüddemann, Max. *Comments by Rear Admiral Plüddemann, German Navy (1898) on the Main Features of the War with Spain.* Washington, DC: Washington Printing Office, 1898.

Political Cartoons

Print media and political cartoons strongly influenced public attitudes regarding events leading up to and during the Spanish-American War and also reflected American attitudes toward overseas expansion and the Philippine-American War (1899–1902). This relatively new mode of communication emerged during the American Civil War (1861–1865) and became a major vehicle of political expression in the closing decades of the 19th century. Increasing tensions with Spain prompted a circulation war among major newspapers in the United States, most notably those owned by Joseph Pulitzer and William Randolph Hearst, who were perhaps the greatest paradigms of yellow journalism in the nation. In their newspapers especially, political cartoons played a significant role in defining the stark nature of the conflicts.

The genre of political cartoons greatly appealed to editors who desired graphic representations of Spanish tyranny and oppression. Political cartoons also appealed to readers who preferred a clear pictorial representation of the issues. Many politicians favored the cartoons as a way to garner wide-ranging support from American citizens. As such, the political cartoonists' creativity and political astuteness satisfied these often competing demands.

In the months leading up to the war, political cartoons alerted the American public to the ruthless tyranny of Spanish rule and domination. General Valeriano Weyler y Nicolau, the Spanish commander in Cuba and the architect of the infamous *reconcentrado* (reconcentration) system, was termed "the Butcher" and was vilified by the Hearst papers in a series of cartoons that portrayed mass starvation across generations with great attention paid to the shriveled and emaciated bodies of infants and young children. In contrast, the Spanish were usually portrayed as corpulent beasts. These cartoons helped prompt a strong humanitarian response from most Americans, who were willing to risk war to rescue the allegedly downtrodden Cuban people from the grip of Spanish rule.

On February 15, 1898, the U.S. battleship *Maine* sank in Havana Harbor, and cartoonists quickly produced sketches of heroic acts by the American sailors and pointed to Spanish culpability for the explosion that sank the ship. There was, of course, no hard evidence to indicate Spanish treachery in the affair, but political cartoonists

Cartoon by J. S. Pughe showing Uncle Sam as a large, fat man. Antiexpansionists opposed to the acquisition of overseas territories say, "Here, take a dose of this anti-fat and get thin again!" Uncle Sam replies, "No, Sonny! I never did take any of that stuff, and I'm too old to begin!" William McKinley, as a tailor, is measuring Uncle Sam for clothing. (Library of Congress)

and yellow journalists nevertheless used the incident to further encourage prowar sentiments. In newspapers across the United States, the image of the sinking of the *Maine* competed with mastheads dominated by carefully choreographed American flags bolstered by images of the Founding Fathers.

As in most political cartooning, the visual images from this era relied upon purposeful exaggeration as a means by which to highlight an issue or issues. In one famous cartoon, President William McKinley, drawn in huge proportions and dressed as Uncle Sam bulging out of his too-small clothing, is shown being measured by a tailor for a new suit. On the sleeves are written "Cuba, Puerto Rico, Hawaii, and Philippines," a clear reference to imperialism.

While the Spanish were invariably portrayed as dictatorial tyrants and beasts, Filipinos were often portrayed as diminutive, often feminized characters, particularly during the Philippine-American War. The caricatures were none too subtle: Filipinos were allegedly weak, naive, and childlike, unable to take care of their own affairs. The Americans, who took many forms in these cartoons, invariably played a protective, usually paternalistic, role toward their Filipino "children." Other cartoons were patently racist, likening the Filipino guerrillas to African Americans and referring to them by such incendiary terms as "niggers" and "gugus."

The influence of political cartoonists was significant during the short-lived Spanish-American War and continued to dominate media discourse during the opening years of the 20th century. These artistic expressions reflected competing ideologies, portrayed the hegemony of American expansion, and captured the emotions of many Americans at the turn of the 20th century. While most cartoonists fashioned pictorials to satisfy the inclinations of politically motivated editors and newspaper owners, they nonetheless introduced a potent form of political expression that endures to the present day.

Political cartoons fanned hysteria on the part of many Americans, bolstered ideas of national supremacy, showcased American racism, and helped drum up popular support for a particular point of view. These political cartoons not only provide a chronology of the war but also reflect the attitudes and ideas of the American people toward this global conflict.

JAMES T. CARROLL AND PAUL G. PIERPAOLI JR.

See also

Cuba; Cuba, Spanish Colonial Policies toward; Expansionism; Hearst, William Randolph; Imperialism; Journalism; McKinley, William; Newspapers; Philippine-American War; Philippine Islands; Philippine Islands, Spanish Colonial Policies toward; Pulitzer, Joseph; *Reconcentrado* System; Weyler y Nicolau, Valeriano; Yellow Journalism

Further Reading

Allen, Douglass. *Fredric Remington and the Spanish-American War.* New York: Crown, 1971.

Painter, Nell Irwin. *Standing at Armageddon: The United States, 1877–1919.* New York: Norton, 1987.

Rosenberg, Emily S. *Spreading the American Dream: American Economic and Cultural Expansion, 1890–1945.* New York: Hill and Wang, 1982.

Ponce, Puerto Rico

City in Puerto Rico located about two miles inland from the Caribbean Sea in the central Southern Coastal Plain region of the island, south of Adjuntas, Utuado, and Jayuya. Ponce in 1898 was (and is today) the second largest city of Puerto Rico in terms of population, behind only San Juan. The city is named for Juan Ponce de León y Loayza, grandson of Spanish conquistador Juan Ponce de León. Ponce is often called La Perla del Sur (The Pearl of the South) and La Ciudad Señorial de Puerto Rico (Majestic City of Puerto Rico).

In 1898, Ponce had a population of about 37,500 people and was a center of opposition to Spanish rule. The city had no prepared military defenses. Prior to the U.S. invasion of Puerto Rico on July 25, Spanish colonel Leopoldo San Martín y Gil received orders to defend Ponce with some 500 men: three companies of the Patria Battalion, guerrillas, and volunteers. Many of his men had no weapons, however.

Realizing the importance of Ponce, U.S. expeditionary force commander Major General Nelson A. Miles made plans to take the city. He consigned this to the navy but also ordered Brigadier General George A. Garretson with six companies of the 6th Massachusetts Infantry Regiment and one of the 6th Illinois to move on Ponce by land to Yauco, six miles north of Guánica and on the railroad line and road to Ponce. Yauco was occupied on July 28 following a brief skirmish, allowing troops under Brigadier General Guy V. Henry to march up the highway to Ponce.

At the same time, on July 27, 1899, the U.S. Navy auxiliary cruiser *Dixie,* commanded by Captain Charles H. Davis, arrived at the port of the city, two miles south of Ponce. Several officers came ashore and demanded the surrender of Ponce under threat of naval bombardment. Two other U.S. warships, the gunboat *Annapolis* and armed yacht *Wasp,* then arrived, escorting transports carrying troops under the command of Major General James H. Wilson. Colonel Julison San Martín asked Spanish governor-general Manuel Macías y Casado for instructions, while at the same time foreign consuls and business leaders in Ponce urged Macías to comply with the U.S. demands. Macías agreed, provided that the Spanish garrison was allowed to withdraw unhindered.

An agreement was then reached that called for Ponce to be surrendered, with civilian government there to continue and the Spanish having 48 hours to withdraw their troops. Once the deal was struck, however, Macías repudiated it and removed San Martín, who had already evacuated Ponce, from command and ordered him imprisoned in San Juan. Returned to Spain and court-martialed after the war, San Martín was found innocent by reason of having obeyed a lawful order.

On July 28, the Americans took possession of the port, and the American flag was then raised. Troops under Henry arrived from Guánica, while Wilson's men disembarked from transports at the port and occupied the city proper. In the port of Ponce, the U.S. Navy seized 91 vessels but confiscated only 3 of these as legitimate prizes.

SPENCER C. TUCKER

Street in Ponce, Puerto Rico, in 1898. (Library of Congress)

See also

Garretson, George Armstrong; Guánica, Puerto Rico; Henry, Guy Vernor; Macías y Casado, Manuel; Miles, Nelson Appleton; Puerto Rico Campaign; Wilson, James Harrison; Yauco, Battle of

Further Reading

Cosmas, Graham A. *An Army for Empire: The United States Army in the Spanish-American War.* College Station: Texas A&M University Press, 1994.

Trask, David F. *The War with Spain in 1898.* Lincoln: University of Nebraska Press, 1996.

Populist Party

Significant third party in the United States during the 1890s and the first decade of the 20th century. The Populist Party was formally organized in 1890 by members of the Farmers' Alliance and the Knights of Labor, an omnibus labor organization. The genesis of the Populist Party can be found in the economic cataclysm of 1873, which brought about a deep economic depression and the complete collapse of agricultural prices in the United States. In 1876, this led to the formation of the Greenback Party, which sought to revive American Civil War–era greenbacks, paper money issued by the federal government. More important, the agricultural depression resulted in the formation of the Farmers' Alliance in 1876, formed largely by small independent farmers in Texas who sought cooperative action to ameliorate the agricultural situation in the United States. The alliance grew in size and scope and became strongest in the Great Plains, the South, and the West. It had relatively few adherents in the Midwest or Northeast.

By the end of the 1880s, the Farmers' Alliance had developed a comprehensive agenda for reform designed to help small farmers and rural merchants, many of whom were in debt and barely eking out an existence. The alliance called for heightened regulation of railroads and banks, the abolition of purchasing agents, and the abandonment of the gold standard as a way to counterbalance rising debt and falling prices in the agricultural sector.

Frustrated by its inability to attract serious attention from either the Republican Party or the Democratic Party, especially on the issue of free silver, key members of the Farmers' Alliance decided to form their own political party in 1889. The following year, these same individuals combined forces with the Knights of Labor, and the Populist Party was born.

Although the free coinage of silver—basically an inflationary scheme to help embattled farmers—was the keystone of the new

Political cartoon from the July 11, 1900, issue of *Puck* showing a python with the head of William Jennings Bryan, representing the Populist Party, swallowing the Democratic Party donkey. During the 1896 campaign for U.S. president, the Populists and the Democrats joined together under presidential candidate Bryan in an attempt to wrest control of the White House from the Republican Party. (Library of Congress)

party, there were other components to its platform as well. In 1892, when the Populist Party held its first official national convention in Omaha, Nebraska, it formally put forth its ambitious national agenda. The party platform called for the dissolution of national banks; the direct election of U.S. senators; a graduated income tax; an eight-hour workday for industrial workers; government management of railroads, telegraphs, and telephones; the initiative and referendum; and various civil service and electoral reforms. The 1892 platform clearly demonstrated the Populists' dislike and distrust of large banks and of the East Coast industrial-financial establishment. With former American Civil War brevet brigadier general and 1880 Greenback Party presidential nominee James B. Weaver as its first presidential candidate in the 1892 elections, the Populists garnered just over 1 million votes, not a bad showing for a small upstart political party.

Still, the Populist Party had a long and steep hill to climb if it was to overcome the two main political parties. The party was strongest in the West and the Great Plains and gained some inroads in the South, which was traditionally a Democratic bastion. The western farmers were most insistent on abandoning the gold standard in favor of a free silver or bimetal currency system that would have allowed the government to print greenbacks (dollars) based upon a 16:1 ratio of silver to gold. These individuals believed—rather erroneously—that abandoning the gold standard would

make credit cheaper and more available. In reality, most of the Populist schemes in this regard were little more than inflationary ideas that would not have affected credit as they had hoped. Notably, the Populist Party allowed some women unprecedented access to party decision making, and in the rural South attempts were made to reach out to African Americans, although this effort resulted in little gains for poor blacks.

In 1896, when the rural and Southern Democrats took control of the party from the Bourbon Democrats (most recently led by outgoing president Grover Cleveland), they co-opted most of the Populists' platform after William Jennings Bryan delivered his spellbinding "Cross of Gold" speech at the Democratic Convention in Chicago. In a fateful move, the Populist Party nominated Democrat William Jennings Bryan to be its presidential nominee in the autumn 1896 election. This decision to fuse with the Democratic Party spelled the beginning of the end for the Populists. Bryan lost to William McKinley, and the Populist Party was badly weakened. The party took the biggest hit in the South, which two years later found itself locked in a bitter fight for power with the Democrats. This was a contest that the Populists could not possibly have won.

When Bryan ran for president again in 1900 as the Democratic nominee, a sizable number of Populists supported him, but he again lost to McKinley. The Populists ran candidates in the presidential elections of 1900, 1904, and 1908, but with each passing year their power base continued to shrink. By 1910, the Populist Party existed only on paper and did not participate in national elections thereafter. Be that as it may, the short-lived party left major imprints on the American political scene.

The Democrats ultimately took up many of the Populists' reform agenda, and Populist calls for political reforms became reality during the Progressive era (ca. 1900–1920). In 1913, for example, the 16th Amendment, providing for an income tax, and the 17th Amendment, allowing for the direct election of U.S. senators, were ratified. During World War I, a graduated income tax was instated at the federal level. And the introduction of the initiative, referendum, and recall on the state level were also hallmarks of Populist thinking. In the end, the Populists' decision to fuse with the Democrats in 1896 was a serious tactical error that made their party almost superfluous as an independent political force. Since the early 1980s, several small political groups have taken the name "Populist," but none wielded the influence of the original.

PAUL G. PIERPAOLI JR.

See also

Bryan, William Jennings; Cleveland, Stephen Grover; Democratic Party; McKinley, William; Republican Party; Silver Standard

Further Reading

Brexel, Bernadette. *The Populist Party: A Voice for the Farmers in the Industrialized Society.* New York: Rosen, 2003.
Goodwyn, Lawrence. *The Populist Movement: A Short History of the Agrarian Revolt in America.* New York: Oxford University Press USA, 1978.
Hicks, John D. *The Populist Revolt: A History of the Farmers' Alliance and the People's Party.* Lincoln: University of Nebraska Press, 1961.

Post, Charles Johnson
Birth Date: August 27, 1873
Death Date: September 25, 1956

American illustrator, journalist, and U.S. Army private who served in the Spanish-American War. Charles Johnson Post was born on August 27, 1873, in New York City. Exhibiting a flair for art and writing at a young age, he studied at the Art Student League in New York City under the artistic tutelage of John Twachtman, J. Carroll Beckwith, Harper Pennington, and Kenyon Cox. When the Spanish-American War began in 1898, Post enlisted as a private in the 71st Volunteer Infantry Regiment. Prior to that, he had been an illustrator for the *New York Journal.* Unlike many illustrators, he also wrote commentary that was frequently published. In June 1898, he departed with V Corps for Cuba. Because of his artistic experience and expertise, he was also contracted by the U.S. Army to produce a series of war sketches, many of which would become well known.

After the war, Post enjoyed a storied career as an artist, illustrator, journalist, photographer, and filmmaker. He served as an editorial writer and photographer for the Associated Press and directed the film *The Making of a Sailor* for the U.S. Navy. He was one of the first individuals to successfully demonstrate motion pictures with sound dialogue, and he also invented the process of subtractive color photography. He published numerous books, including *Private Enterprise Did This* and *The Little War of Private Post,* which was published posthumously in 1960. The latter work features an in-depth look at the Spanish-American War through the eyes of Post, serving as a private in the U.S. Army. The book, reprinted in 1999 with an introduction by Graham A. Cosmas and Marylou K. Gjernes, provided vivid commentary and sketches that Post had drawn while on duty. Post died on September 25, 1956.

PAUL G. PIERPAOLI JR.

See also

Artists and Illustrators; Journalism

Further Reading

Post, Charles Johnson. *The Little War of Private Post: The Spanish-American War Seen Up Close.* Lincoln, NE: Bison Books, 1999.
Trask, David F. *The War with Spain in 1898.* Lincoln: University of Nebraska Press, 1996.
Walker, Dale L. *The Boys of '98: Theodore Roosevelt and the Rough Riders.* New York: Forge, 1999.

Powelson, Wilfred Van Nest
Birth Date: September 15, 1872
Death Date: May 20, 1960

U.S. Navy officer who gained temporary fame for his service on the so-called Sampson Board, the navy board of inquiry named after Captain William T. Sampson that first investigated the sinking of the U.S. battleship *Maine.* Born in Middletown, New York, on September 15, 1872, Wilfred Van Nest Powelson was appointed to the United States Naval Academy, Annapolis, in 1889 as a cadet engineer and graduated first in his class in 1893. Intending to join the Corps of Naval Constructors, he was sent to Glasgow, Scotland, for additional education, an honor accorded only top Naval Academy graduates. However, after a year in Scotland, he decided to return to the United States as a line officer.

On his return, Powelson was stationed at the New York Navy Yard, where the *Maine* was being constructed. While waiting for its commissioning, he took the opportunity to examine the new battleship in detail, expecting incorrectly that he would be assigned to it.

Ensign Powelson was ultimately assigned to the dispatch steamer *Fern.* The day after the destruction of the *Maine* on February 15, 1898, the *Fern* steamed into Havana Harbor. Having light duty aboard his own ship, Powelson busied himself by examining the *Maine* wreckage and conversing with the divers exploring it. His background in naval architecture, familiarity with the ship's construction, and conversations with the divers resulted in his transfer to aid in the inquiry by the Sampson Board. He was charged with presenting the divers' findings to the board under oath.

Powelson's most important contribution to the board's conclusion was his observation that the *Maine*'s keel and adjacent steel plates—the structural backbone of the vessel that formed the lowest part of the ship—had been bent upward by nearly 40 feet. The keel itself rested 18 inches below the water's surface, while portions of the adjacent plates actually protruded 4 feet above the surface. This major displacement of the keel was interpreted as evidence suggesting that an underwater mine had caused the ship's sinking. Powelson shared his finding with one of his divers who, in turn, leaked it to the press. This information ultimately encouraged those pushing for war and brought Powelson national recognition. Later studies have suggested that Powelson's findings were either incorrect or could not be substantiated.

With the work of the Sampson Board completed on March 28, 1898, Powelson was assigned to the auxiliary cruiser *St. Paul,* formerly an ocean liner. His transfer was not by chance, for the cruiser was commanded by Captain Charles Sigsbee, former captain of the *Maine,* who had been very impressed by and appreciative of Powelson's testimony indicating that the *Maine* had succumbed to an external mine rather than an internal explosion.

Powelson took part in various actions during the Spanish-American War, most notably on June 22 when the *St. Paul* severely damaged the Spanish torpedo boat *Terror* in an engagement at San Juan, Puerto Rico. The shell that was believed to have put the Spanish ship out of action was from a 5-inch gun under Powelson's command.

The *St. Paul* was decommissioned and returned to civilian service in September 1898. While still aboard the ship as it was awaiting decommissioning, Powelson accidently fell through a hatchway into the hold, breaking his leg and severely injuring his back. On his release from the hospital, he reported to the Navy Bureau of Equipment, to which he had been assigned just prior to the accident.

On March 3, 1899, Powelson was promoted to lieutenant junior grade and then to lieutenant on February 11, 1901. However, he never fully recovered from the injuries from the accident, which forced him out of the navy. On July 3, 1902, he left active service with the rank of lieutenant commander. Upon leaving the navy, he embarked on a successful career as an engineer, at one point serving as a government inspector of General Electric appliances. Powelson died in Fort Lauderdale, Florida, on May 20, 1960.

PATRICK McSHERRY

See also

Maine, USS; *Maine,* USS, Inquiries into the Loss of; "Remember the *Maine*"; Sampson, William Thomas

Further Reading

Blow, Michael. *A Ship to Remember: The Maine and the Spanish-American War.* New York: Morrow, 1992.

Rickover, Hyman G. *How the Battleship Maine Was Destroyed.* Annapolis, MD: Naval Institute Press, 1995.

Samuels, Peggy, and Harold Samuels. *Remembering the Maine.* Washington, DC: Smithsonian Institution Press, 1995.

Weems, John Edward. *The Fate of the Maine.* New York: Henry Holt, 1985.

Pratt, E. Spencer
Birth Date: Unknown
Death Date: Unknown

U.S. diplomat. E. Spencer Pratt was U.S. minister to Persia during 1886–1891 and was serving as U.S. consul to Singapore in 1898. There English adventurer and sometime diplomat Howard Bray introduced Pratt to Filipino insurgent leader Emilio Aguinaldo y Famy. The two men held discussions during April 24–26, 1898. As a result of these talks, Aguinaldo returned to Hong Kong and there was persuaded by American consul Rounseville Wildman to catch passage on an American revenue cutter for the Philippines. During his meetings with Aguinaldo, Pratt is believed to have encouraged the Filipino revolutionary movement in its insurrection against Spanish colonial rule.

Aguinaldo's conversations with both Pratt and Wildman remain controversial, although both men subsequently claimed that they had made no promises to Aguinaldo regarding the future of the Philippines. Aguinaldo subsequently claimed, however, that Pratt had assured him that the United States would recognize the independence of the Philippines under a U.S. protectorate. Bray later confirmed Aguinaldo's claims.

SPENCER C. TUCKER

U.S. diplomat E. Spencer Pratt, believed to have encouraged Filipino nationalists in their efforts to end Spanish rule in the Philippines. (Library of Congress)

See also
Aguinaldo y Famy, Emilio; Dewey, George; Hong Kong; Wildman, Rounsevelle

Further Reading
Leech, Margaret. *In the Days of McKinley.* New York: Harper and Brothers, 1959.
O'Toole, G. J. A. *The Spanish War: An American Epic, 1898.* New York: Norton, 1984.
Trask, David F. *The War with Spain in 1898.* Lincoln: University of Nebraska Press, 1996.

Primo de Rivera y Sobremonte, Fernando

Birth Date: 1831
Death Date: 1921

Spanish Army officer and captain-general and governor-general of the Philippines (1897–1898). Born in Seville, Spain, in 1831, Fernando Primo de Rivera y Sobremonte joined the Spanish Army at a young age. He helped put down the Madrid insurrections of 1848 and 1866. In the Second Carlist War (1846–1849), forces under his command captured Estella, for which he was made Marquess of Estella. He also served briefly as minister of military affairs for King Alfonso XII during 1874–1875. In 1880, Primo de Rivera served as captain-general of Madrid and from 1880–1883 was captain-general of the Philippines. In 1895, he became captain-general of the Spanish Army.

Appointed captain-general and governor-general of the Philippines on March 22, 1897, Primo de Rivera replaced General Camilo García de Polavieja. Primo de Rivera's adjutant was Miguel Primo de Rivera y Orbaneja, his nephew and later dictator of Spain. Believing that he could end the insurrection against Spanish rule by conciliatory measures, Fernando Primo de Rivera issued a number of unconstitutional pardons to the insurgents. When this policy did not have the desired result, he resorted to a harsh policy of military action, especially in Cavite Province near Manila. On May 17, he issued another pardon, which received a better response and led him to consider the possibility of a negotiated settlement with the insurgent leadership. When Pedro Alejandro Paterno y Debera Ignacio offered to serve as a mediator, Primo de Rivera accepted. This decision led to negotiations and, ultimately, the December 1897 Pact of Biak-na-Bato whereby the insurgent leaders received a cash settlement and then went into exile in Hong Kong.

On March 3, 1898, Primo de Rivera cabled Spanish minister of the colonies Segismundo Moret y Pendergast indicating that he had learned from intelligence sources that U.S. Asiatic Squadron commander Commodore George Dewey had orders to attack Manila. Primo de Rivera then worked with Rear Admiral Patricio Montojo y Pasarón to prepare the Philippines, and especially the Manila area, against a U.S. Navy attack. On April 9, however, Primo de Rivera was suddenly replaced on orders from Madrid by Lieutenant General Basilo Augustín y Dávila. Primo de Rivera left the Philippines on April 12, 1898, just days before the U.S. declaration of war.

Primo de Rivera subsequently twice served as minister of war. He died in Madrid in 1921.

SPENCER C. TUCKER AND PAUL G. PIERPAOLI JR.

See also
Aguinaldo y Famy, Emilio; Biak-na-Bato, Pact of; Dewey, George; Hong Kong; Montojo y Pasarón, Patricio; Paterno y Debera Ignacio, Pedro Alejandro

Further Reading
Carr, Raymond. *Spain, 1808–1975.* New York: Oxford University Press USA, 1982.
Ratcliffe, Dillwyn F. *Prelude to Franco: Political Aspects of the Dictatorship of General Miguel Primo de Rivera.* New York: Las Americas, 1957.

Proctor, Redfield

Birth Date: June 1, 1831
Death Date: March 4, 1908

Union Army officer during the American Civil War, well-to-do businessman, and prominent Republican politician. Redfield Proctor was born in Proctorsville, Vermont, on June 1, 1831. His father, Jabez Proctor, was a prosperous farmer, merchant, and a well-respected Whig Party politician. The younger Proctor graduated from Dartmouth College in 1851 and from the Albany (New York) Law School in 1859. Between 1851 and 1857, he was a businessman in Proctorsville, working mainly in the local marble quarry industry. In 1860, he was admitted to the bar and practiced law in Boston until 1861. At the beginning of the American Civil War, Proctor returned to Vermont, where he secured a commission as a major in the 3rd Vermont Volunteer Regiment. He rose to the rank of colonel of volunteers before leaving the army in 1863.

Proctor began practicing law in Rutland, Vermont, in 1863, but he soon became preoccupied with the burgeoning marble industry in the state. By 1869, he had left his law practice and taken up a position as a manager at a local marble quarrying facility. In 1880, two quarries merged to form the Vermont Marble Company, and Proctor served as its first president. He became wealthy as a result of this work.

During the 1860s, Proctor had begun a career in politics. He served in the Vermont House of Representatives from 1867 to 1868 and in the Vermont Senate during 1874–1875. By now a well-known Republican politician, he was elected to serve as Vermont's lieutenant governor (1876–1878) and governor (1878–1880). In 1888, he again served in the state House of Representatives. President Benjamin Harrison named Proctor as secretary of war in 1889, a position he held until 1891 at which time he was appointed to fill a vacancy in the U.S. Senate. He served in the Senate until his death in 1908. By the time he reached the U.S. Senate, he was known as the "Marble King," as the company he now controlled was the largest marble-producing company in the nation.

Proctor enjoyed a stellar reputation in the Senate and was uniformly praised for his hard work, attention to detail, and fair-mindedness. Indeed, he became a frequent adviser to Republican president William McKinley before, during, and after the Spanish-American War. As a member of the Committee on Military Affairs, Proctor supported the appointment of Commodore George Dewey to command the U.S. Asiatic Squadron, which performed brilliantly at the Battle of Manila Bay (May 1, 1898). Proctor had earlier struck up a friendship with Dewey, who considered Proctor something of a mentor.

Before hostilities began between Spain and the United States, Proctor and several of his Senate colleagues went to Cuba to assess the situation there. When Proctor returned, he presented McKinley and his cabinet with a highly persuasive report that called for military intervention in Cuba. Proctor's findings played a significant role in the decision to go to war in April 1898.

Proctor was in many ways a quintessential Republican expansionist. Persuaded by the validity of Alfred Thayer Mahan's writings on naval power and desirous of a wider international role for the United States, Proctor aggressively lobbied for a larger navy and a more activist foreign policy, positions that he took with both the McKinley and Theodore Roosevelt administrations. In other areas Proctor also walked the party line, supporting high tariffs and the gold standard. He died in Proctorsville, Vermont, on March 4, 1908.

PAUL G. PIERPAOLI JR.

See also

Asiatic Squadron; Dewey, George; Mahan, Alfred Thayer; Manila Bay, Battle of; McKinley, William; Roosevelt, Theodore

Further Reading

Bowie, Chester W. "Redfield Proctor: A Biography." PhD dissertation, University of Wisconsin, 1980.

Gould, Lewis L. *The Spanish-American War and President McKinley.* Lawrence: University Press of Kansas, 1982.

Partridge, Frank. "Redfield Proctor." *Vermont Historical Society Proceedings* (1915): 59–123.

Republican senator Redfield Proctor of Vermont, a member of the Committee on Military Affairs and a close adviser to President William McKinley, urged U.S. intervention in Cuba. (Library of Congress)

Progressivism

Far-reaching reform movement in the United States lasting from about 1900 to 1920. Progressivism treated a wide array of issues, including politics, the economy, government, business regulation, organized labor, education, and poverty mitigation. Progressivism was a response to the excesses of the so-called robber barons and the Gilded Age that reigned supreme during the last third of the 19th century. It was also a reaction to the problems caused by frenetic industrialization and massive immigration. Numerous Progressive initiatives had their roots in the Populist movement and Populist Party of the late 19th century. Progressivism was a broad-based bipartisan reform movement that encompassed both Republican and Democratic policy makers.

Presidents Theodore Roosevelt (a Republican) and Woodrow Wilson (a Democrat) considered themselves to be Progressive reformers, although they envisioned somewhat different means to achieve the same ends. Interestingly, American efforts to bring civilization and American values to the Filipinos in the aftermath of the Spanish-American War were infused with Progressive rhetoric and ideology. While Progressives were generally well meaning and earnest about improving American society and government, there was a certain paternalism to their thinking. This reflected the fact that many of them were middle- and upper-class well-educated whites who believed that their status and education made them uniquely qualified to bring about Progressive reforms. The idea of equality in terms of race and ethnicity was not generally part of their mind-set. Nor were many Progressives advocates of gender equality. Indeed, not until 1920 were American women allowed to vote in federal-level elections, and this concession came about largely because of World War I.

Progressivism began largely as a grassroots effort, taking hold first at the local level, then the state level, and finally the federal level. Democratic Party politicians such as William Jennings Bryan and Republican Party politicians such as Robert La Follette lent their substantial political clout to Progressive reform, while Republican presidents Theodore Roosevelt and William Howard Taft and Democratic president Woodrow Wilson added their own momentum to the reform agenda. What made Progressivism in many ways unique among American reform movements was the fact that reformers believed in harnessing the power of the government to bring about change. Both Republicans and Democrats used the government—at all levels—to bring about Progressive reforms. Furthermore, Progressives believed in using newfound social sciences (such as sociology) and statistical analysis to identify problems and then apply solutions to them.

Because Progressivism was such a broad-based reform movement, it borrowed ideas and prescriptions from many different sources. The Populists, for example, had long called for more democratic representation by such mechanisms as the initiative, referendum, and recall. An initiative is a means by which citizens themselves can suggest and even write legislation or laws that can then be considered by deliberative bodies or approved directly by voters. A referendum allows the voters themselves to approve or disapprove laws or legislation passed by lawmakers. The recall empowers citizens to remove elected public officials from office. These measures were adopted by many localities and states during the Progressive era, especially in western states. The Populists also called for the direct election of U.S. senators, which became reality with the 17th Amendment to the Constitution in 1913. Again, the idea was to provide more political power to the people and to make government more accountable to the electorate.

Progressive efforts to mitigate poverty, improve low-income housing, clear slums and ghettoes, and rid city governments of graft and corruption were also holdovers from the late 19th century. The Settlement House Movement popularized by reformers such as Jane Addams provided ample examples of how people's lives in the slums could be transformed with education, adequate housing, and decent medical care. Muckrakers and yellow journalists such as Jacob A. Riis, who made infamous the conditions of U.S. slums in such books as *How the Other Half Lives* (1890) and *Battle with the Slum* (1902), brought the conditions of America's poorest citizens to the fore. In places such as New York City, where the corruption of William Marcy "Boss" Tweed at City Hall had eviscerated the city's treasury, Progressive reformers and politicians found innovative ways to prevent such abuse and make the government accountable for its actions. During the Progressive era, many cities adopted a city-management system whereby the city's day-to-day operations were supervised by a salaried professional who was not a political appointee. Mayors were relegated to more figurehead roles. The commission system, introduced in Galveston, Texas, after the city was devastated by a hurricane in 1900, allowed voters to elect heads of local departments, with the commissioners also serving as a city council.

One of the most notable of Progressive initiatives was the regulation of big business and industry. The government tried to limit the power of certain corporations and industries in order to avoid monopoly and price fixing and worked with labor unions to ensure that their voices were heard but that they did not drown out the in-

Photograph by Jacob Riis of a tenement on Baxter Street in New York City, a neighborhood that Riis covered during his job as a police reporter in the late 1880s. The conditions he witnessed in New York tenements led him to write a photographic exposé, *How the Other Half Lives* (1890). (Library of Congress)

terests of scrupulous businessmen. Numerous states passed laws limiting child labor, establishing maximum work hours, and mandating safer working conditions. As a result, the number of Americans maimed or killed on the job because of unsafe working conditions dramatically diminished. Congress also passed the Meat Inspection Act and the Pure Food and Drug Act in 1906 largely in response to Upton Sinclair's *The Jungle,* which exposed the poor sanitation standards in the meatpacking industry. This was also partly a response to the Embalmed Beef Scandal of the Spanish-American War.

Other Progressive reforms that became law in the first two decades of the 20th century include the Federal Reserve Act of 1913, which provided government supervision of the banking industry; the Clayton Anti-Trust Act of 1914, which strengthened antitrust regulations; and the Federal Trade Commission Act of 1914, which regulated trade practices. More important, the Progressive era resulted in a series of amendments to the U.S. Constitution: the 16th Amendment (1913) established the federal income tax; the 17th Amendment (1913) provided for the direct election of U.S. senators; the 18th Amendment (1919) mandated prohibition of alcohol; and the 19th Amendment (1920) extended the right to vote to women. There were direct links between Progressivism and the

Spanish-American War and Philippine-American War. The U.S. concern with the plight of the Cubans and Filipinos certainly fit into the philosophy of Progressive reform. Indeed, better education and control of communicable diseases such as yellow fever, malaria, and typhoid were high on Americans' agenda in these nations. William Howard Taft, who himself would become a Progressive president from 1909 to 1913 (albeit a conservative one), served as the first civilian governor-general of the Philippines from 1901 to 1903. In this capacity, he used the Philippines as a small-scale laboratory for Progressive reform. He undertook land reform that gave more land to Filipino peasants, built many schools, established medical clinics, and created programs designed to acculturate Filipinos to American society.

Most historians date the end of Progressivism at about 1920. Indeed, World War I and the civil liberty violations it engendered stymied further major reforms. The Russian Revolution and resulting anticommunist Red Scare of 1919–1920 also discouraged new reform legislation. By the early 1920s, Progressives had decided to settle into a conservative cocoon in which they could concentrate on new cultural trends and consumerism. Reflecting this newfound conservatism, the Republican ascendancy of the 1920s was founded upon a small, unobtrusive federal government, hardly the vehicle for advancing reform. Be that as it may, vestiges of Progressivism endured. Indeed, Senator Robert M. La Follette received almost 5 million votes as the Progressive Party candidate in the 1924 presidential election. Subsequent reform movements such as the New Deal of the 1930s and the Great Society of the 1960s traced their ideological heritage to the Progressive movement.

PAUL G. PIERPAOLI JR.

See also

Bryan, William Jennings; Democratic Party; Journalism; Malaria; Populist Party; Republican Party; Robber Barons; Roosevelt, Theodore; Slums; Taft, William Howard; Typhoid Fever; Yellow Fever; Yellow Journalism

Further Reading

Berkowitz, Peter, ed. *Varieties of Progressivism in America.* Palo Alto, CA: Hoover Institution Press, 2004.
Eisenach, Eldon J. *The Lost Promise of Progressivism.* Lawrence: University Press of Kansas, 1994.
Kloppenberg, James T. *Uncertain Victory: Social Democracy and Progressivism in European and American Thought, 1870–1920.* New York: Oxford University Press USA, 1988.
Link, Arthur S., and Richard L. McCormick. *Progressivism.* Wheeling, IL: Harlan Davidson, 1983.

Propaganda

The Spanish-American War was perhaps the first modern conflict in which propaganda employing the modern media of the day (chiefly newspapers and magazines) and enhanced by telegraphs and the newly created telephone played a significant role. There was not, however, a concerted or organized effort on the part of

Stereograph by Keystone View Company in 1899 titled "Cell from which Evangelica Cisneros escaped, Havana, Cuba." Cisneros was a Cuban woman jailed in Havana. William Randolph Hearst secured her alleged rescue. Manipulation of events in Cuba by much of the U.S. press helped to increase public sentiment for war with Spain. (Library of Congress)

the governments involved to engage in propaganda activity. That would not occur until World War I. Rather, propaganda during the Spanish-American War was conducted on a more ad hoc basis, mainly by those in the media. Those involved had varying motives, and not all were tied into the strategic interests of their country. The clearest examples of such propaganda ploys can be seen in the yellow journalism of the day, which publishers William Randolph Hearst and Joseph Pulitzer most closely embodied. Propaganda also made its way into the music of the period by way of patriotic songs and even exhibited itself in a very limited way in the newly emergent medium of film, which was still in its infancy and was limited to short releases with no sound dialogue.

During the 1880s and 1890s, American newspapers engaged in a vicious circulation war, vying for readers' attention and, indirectly, their pocketbooks. In an era in which television and radio were not yet available, newspapers served as the sole source of news and information for a great majority of Americans. This meant that newspaper publishers and journalists played a critical role in the shaping of public opinion. In their quest to best the competition, however, they often played fast and loose with the facts. This was especially the case with Hearst- and Pulitzer-owned publications. Indeed, many

U.S. newspapers began a campaign to discredit and vilify the Spanish while romanticizing the struggle of Cuban rebels after the beginning of the Cuban War of Independence in 1895.

All of the nation's major big-city newspapers either had reporters on-site in Cuba or relied on syndicated reports and columns provided to them by the Hearst and Pulitzer papers in New York City. Thus, there was little in the way of checks and balances to ensure that the reporting was fair and accurate. Through pooled newspaper conglomerates such as the Associated Press, Americans in Boise, Idaho, were able to read the same reports from Cuba or the Philippines as Americans read in Chicago or San Francisco.

As tensions with the Spanish rose, reports from Cuba became more incendiary and more exaggerated. In many cases, reporters submitting stories to their home papers or to the Associated Press were not, in fact, witnesses to the events about which they wrote. Instead, they tended to rely on secondhand accounts or stories written by a single reporter who had claimed to witness an event. Invariably, the Spanish were portrayed as ruthless aggressors bent on subjugating the Cubans with threats and murder. Not surprisingly, the press enjoyed a bonanza when it began reporting on the excesses of the infamous *reconcentrado* (reconcentration) system instituted by Governor-General Valeriano Weyler y Nicolau.

Thanks to advances made in the printing and photography fields, many of these stories were accompanied by emotionally charged illustrations and pictures, which added a new dimension to such over-the-top reporting. The Cubans were almost always portrayed in the best possible light, fighting for the noble cause of freedom against a colonial oppressor. Most of the press thus ignored wrongdoing or atrocities committed by the rebels.

A sure way to stoke the fires of moral indignation at home was to concentrate on the victimization of women in Cuba. This was done routinely and with considerable success. The most brazen example of this was the Evangelina Cosio y Cisneros saga, much of which was staged by William Randolph Hearst. Cisneros's plight became an instant cause célèbre and not only brought Hearst more readers but also further fanned the flames of public resentment toward the Spanish.

When the U.S. battleship *Maine* mysteriously exploded while at anchor in Havana Harbor on February 15, 1898, the yellow press almost immediately concluded that the tragedy had been the result of Spanish treachery. Reporting of this event was based solely on conjecture and was clearly influenced by the strong anti-Spanish sentiment in the United States. The fact that Spain had nothing to gain—and everything to lose—by destroying the battleship did not seem to have a place in reporters' stories on the incident. Nevertheless, the slogan "Remember the *Maine*!" became popularized by those Americans seeking war.

While it is not at all accurate to say that media-inspired propaganda alone pushed the United States to war in April 1898, it did make that decision considerably easier. During the war, the U.S. government exercised some control over the movement of correspondents in the field, but there was no concerted effort to censor

newspaper coverage, just as there was no concerted attempt on the part of the government to create or shape wartime propaganda. In the summer of 1898, a 90-second silent film titled *Tearing down the Spanish Flag* was created at the behest of the War Department. The clip showed the re-creation of a battle scene in which a tattered Spanish flag was hauled down and replaced by a pristine American flag. Few Americans saw the film, however, as commercial film and movie theaters still lay in the future.

During the Philippine-American War (1899–1902), newspapers and magazines again became the main vehicles for propaganda. The U.S. government did not play a large or direct role in the shaping of public opinion, which was left to editors, reporters, and artists. Almost no newspapers openly criticized the U.S. war effort in the Philippines, and Americans were almost always portrayed as paragons of enlightenment and benevolence. On the rare occasions when U.S. atrocities visited upon Filipinos were reported, correspondents were careful to point out that such activities were the products of individual men rather than U.S. policy as a whole.

PAUL G. PIERPAOLI JR.

See also

Artists and Illustrators; Cosio y Cisneros, Evangelina; Cuban War of Independence; Hearst, William Randolph; Journalism; *Maine*, USS; Music; Newspapers; Philippine-American War; Pulitzer, Joseph; "Remember the *Maine*"; Yellow Journalism

Further Reading

O'Toole, G. J. A. *The Spanish War: An American Epic, 1898*. New York: Norton, 1984.

Smythe, Ted Curtis. *The Gilded Age Press, 1865–1900*. Westport, CT: Praeger, 2003.

Stevens, John D. *Sensationalism and the New York Press*. New York: Columbia University Press, 1991.

Trask, David F. *The War with Spain in 1898*. Lincoln: University of Nebraska Press, 1996.

Protocol of Peace

See Peace, Protocol of

Puerto Rico

Caribbean island located between the Caribbean Sea to the south and the Atlantic Ocean to the north, just east of the present-day Dominican Republic. At the start of the Spanish-American War, Puerto Rico was a Spanish colony with a population of approximately 950,000 people. The island was annexed by the United States as a result of the December 1898 Treaty of Paris.

Puerto Rico, part of the Greater Antilles, covers an area of approximately 3,500 square miles. The topography of the island consists of roughly 25 percent level ground, with 40 percent classified as mountainous and 30 percent accented by hills. The climate on the island is comparable to that of its Caribbean neighbors, with the moderate temperatures and plentiful rainfall that characterize the tropics. Major cash crops on the island included coffee, sugarcane, tobacco, and plantains and other tropical fruits. As in Cuba, the Spanish had built a plantation-based economy on Puerto Rico, the mainstay of which was coffee and sugar cultivation. Unlike Cuba, however, the island had little modern infrastructure.

The first European contact with Puerto Rico occurred on November 19, 1493, during Christopher Columbus's second expedition to the region. However, Puerto Rico was not colonized until 1508, when gold was discovered in the northeastern and southwestern portions of the island. Juan Ponce de León led the conquest of Puerto Rico (meaning literally "rich port"), which saw the brutal oppression and enslavement of the Tainos, a native people closely related to the Arawaks. Within a few years' time, the Tainos had been decimated due to disease, harsh working conditions, and Ponce de León's violent quelling of slave rebellions.

Despite the gold deposits found on the island in the 16th century, for much of the colonial period Puerto Rico remained solely a forward military position in the Spanish Empire at the gate to the Caribbean Sea. As a result, the tiny island fortress was repeatedly attacked by other European states. In 1595, for instance, Sir Francis Drake and John Hawkins attempted to take the island for England without success. However, a year later under the Earl of Cumberland, Puerto Rico came into English possession, albeit for a brief 65 days. The island also experienced attacks by other colonial-minded peoples such as the French and the Dutch. The last major attack on Puerto Rico before the American occupation in 1898 occurred in 1797 when yet another British attack was thwarted.

By and large, Spain neglected to develop the island during the colonial period. The limited economy was based on subsistence farming, some cattle ranching, and sporadic smuggling. The chief export was coffee, with sugar a close second. Throughout most of the 19th century, the island lacked major infrastructure needs such as telegraphs, banking institutions, and efficient roadways. Nevertheless, the island experienced periods of relative calm and autonomy. One such case came in 1873 with the abolition of slavery. Yet despite these periods, there were occasional instances of renewed concentration on behalf of the Spanish Crown, as demonstrated in the crushing of the 1868 revolt at Larres.

The island's population remained quite small until the 19th century, when a rapid increase in the number of inhabitants occurred. The population jumped from 163,192 people in 1802 to 953,243 by 1899. Despite this population growth, Puerto Rico retained its rural ways, as only 8.7 percent of the population lived in towns with 8,000 people or more. What is more, by century's end only 32,048 people lived in the capital city of San Juan. This was in stark contrast to the large and bustling capital of Cuba, Havana. The typical dwelling of the Puerto Rican at the time was the *bohio*. It was in essence a cramped windowless cabinlike structure made of wood, hay, dried palm fronds, or a combination of these. These rural dwellings had no running water or other modern conveniences.

It is true that Puerto Rico had once led the Caribbean in illiteracy rates, which stood at more than 83 percent. Indeed, students who wanted to continue their education had to travel to Spain or even in some cases to the United States or France. However, in 1882 Puerto Rico established its first secondary school. Even with the general lack of educational facilities until the close of the 1800s, Puerto Rico produced its own rich culture during this period, which can be seen in the works of both visual and written artists. Moreover, these artists played a key role in the political development of the island, as is seen in the works of poets such as Luis Muñoz Rivera and José de Diego.

The greatest economic growth in Puerto Rico during the 19th century came in agricultural. Similar to Cuba, agricultural development was lacking until the 1800s because of the aforementioned lacked of infrastructure. While coffee was the dominant export until 1899, sugar also held an increasingly critical place in the growing island's economy. The United States was the chief customer of Puerto Rican sugar, importing raw sugar and refining it in stateside mills. There were attempts by Puerto Rican business owners to produce and ultimately sell refined sugar, as was demonstrated in Central San Vicente, but the effort brought little financial success.

As a result of the war with Spain, the United States invaded Puerto Rico on July 25, 1898, staging a landing at Guánica. The United States had been eyeing the island as a place of strategic importance since before the Thomas Jefferson administration. The value of Puerto Rico to the United States can be seen in the commentary of Secretary of State James G. Blaine, who wrote to President Benjamin Harrison on the subject in 1890. Blaine claimed that there were only three locations that were of enough strategic value to be taken with force: Hawaii, Cuba, and Puerto Rico. This idea was undoubtedly reinforced by the notions perpetuated in the 1823 Monroe Doctrine, Manifest Destiny, and the naval theories of Alfred Thayer Mahan. Yet there were economic considerations and opportunities as well. At the beginning of the 20th century, Puerto Rico was the 5th-largest market for U.S. exports in Latin America and 27th in overall global trade. By 1910, those rankings rose to 4th and 11th, respectively.

The conquest of the island by the American forces was proceeding rapidly when it was brought to a close by the Protocol of Peace. Many of the lower-class Puerto Ricans seized upon the U.S. invasion as the opportunity for retribution, and from July 1898 through February 1899, small groups of the impoverished mercilessly attacked Spaniards and those considered members of the upper echelons of society. This activity finally ceased when the military government installed by the United States in October 1898 under the leadership of Major General Guy V. Henry, which was similar to the one established by the United States in Cuba, repressed the rioting. What is more, during the military occupation, there was no major insurrection such as the one in the Philippines.

Article 2 of the Treaty of Paris brought Puerto Rico under the complete control of the United States. The question remained whether the small island should be granted independence, admitted into the Union, or simply left as a colonial possession. The consensus among policy makers in Washington was that Puerto Ricans were incapable of running their own nation, while the question of statehood was complex and hotly debated. Ultimately, Puerto Rico was allowed to exist as a colonial dominion of the United States under the auspices of the 1899 Foraker Amendment. The original proposal called for all Puerto Ricans to be considered citizens of the United States with the extension of rights under the U.S. Constitution. However, the final legislation stipulated neither of these points and gave Puerto Rico only the originally proposed House of Delegates, which served under an American-dominated executive, legislative, and judiciary system. While citizenship was eventually granted to Puerto Ricans under the Jones Act of 1917, the island would not gain commonwealth status and thus the right to draft its own constitution until 1952.

ROB SHAFER

See also

Antilles; Blaine, James Gillespie; Guánica, Puerto Rico; Henry, Guy Vernor; Mahan, Alfred Thayer; Manifest Destiny; Monroe Doctrine; Paris, Treaty of; Puerto Rico Campaign; Rivera, Luis Muñoz

Further Reading

Ayala, César J. *American Sugar Kingdom: The Plantation Economy of the Spanish Caribbean, 1898–1934.* Chapel Hill: University of North Carolina Press, 1999.

Bakewell, Peter. *A History of Latin America.* Malden, MA: Blackwell, 1997.

Martínez-Vergne, Teresita. *Capitalism in Colonial Puerto Rico: Central San Vicente in the Late Nineteenth Century.* Gainesville: University of Florida Press, 1992.

Trias Monge, José. *Puerto Rico: The Trials of the Oldest Colony in the World.* New Haven, CT: Yale University Press, 1997.

Puerto Rico Campaign
Start Date: July 25, 1898
End Date: August 13, 1898

U.S. operations on the island of Puerto Rico that occurred late in the Spanish-American War. Initially, both commanding general of the army Major General Nelson A. Miles and his predecessor, Major

Spanish troops leave Mayagüez, Puerto Rico, to engage the American forces at Hormigueros, August 10, 1898. (Bettmann/Corbis)

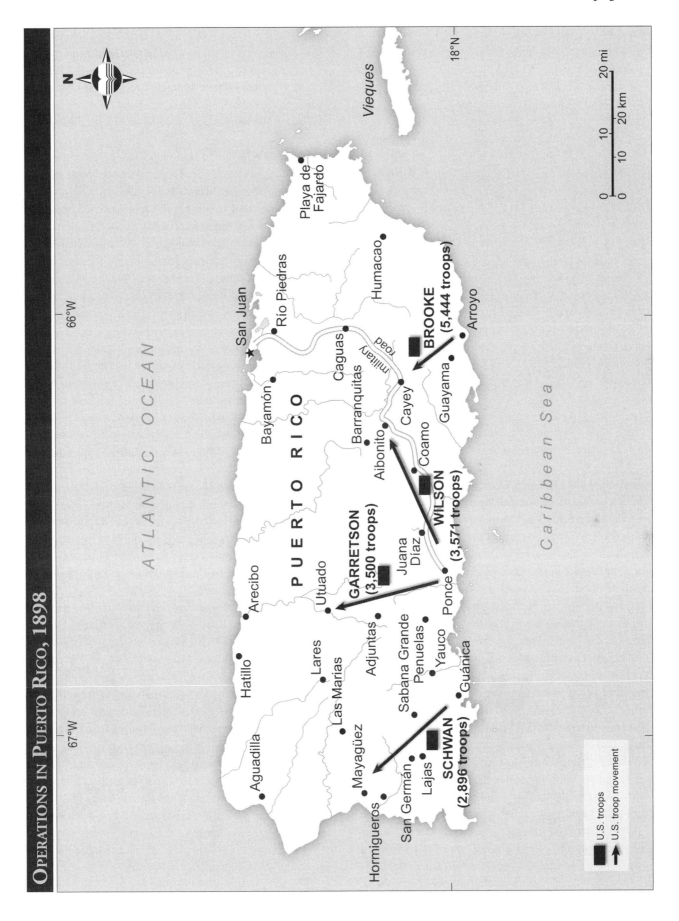

General John Schofield, who acted as a military adviser to President William McKinley during the early weeks of the Spanish-American War, favored a campaign in Puerto Rico over an invasion of Cuba. Miles thought it more strategically sound to strike Puerto Rico first, wait until the yellow fever season in Cuba ended, and then send the navy to defeat the Spanish fleet.

In late May 1898, when Rear Admiral Pascual Cervera y Topete's Spanish fleet sailed into the harbor of Santiago de Cuba, thereby surrendering its strategic initiative, Miles again pressed for a Puerto Rico Campaign, to be followed by an invasion of Cuba. However, McKinley chose to invade Cuba first as a means of supporting the navy in its effort to destroy the Spanish fleet, which remained the primary strategic objective. This move, it was reasoned, would have a more immediate and compelling effect on Spain.

Although the destruction of Cervera's fleet in the Battle of Santiago de Cuba on July 3, 1898, was a stunning victory for the United States, the campaign for Santiago had bogged down, and Miles was directed to proceed to Cuba to support Major General William Shafter's campaign there if needed. Miles sailed from Charleston, South Carolina, on July 8 with a 3,500-man force and steamed to Santiago. But on July 17, Santiago capitulated, and Miles received authorization on the following day to proceed with an invasion of Puerto Rico.

Miles's opposition to a Cuban invasion during the fever season was well founded. By the time Santiago surrendered, a large number of men in Shafter's V Corps had fallen prey to yellow fever and malaria. Miles had originally planned to include a part of V Corps in his Puerto Rico Campaign, but the men were in no shape for more campaigning. Miles had wisely kept his troops with him on ship so as not to expose them to tropical fevers. Now, with authorization finally in hand, he sailed for Puerto Rico with a force of 3,500 men, to be followed by an additional 13,000 men and supporting artillery.

Interservice bickering and rivalry, present throughout the campaign in Cuba, was not absent from the Puerto Rico Campaign. Miles, who never avoided a conflict if he could help it, argued with North Atlantic Fleet commander Rear Admiral William T. Sampson about the size of his naval escort. McKinley, the soul of patience, finally grew tired of the wrangling and directed the navy to provide Miles with whatever ships he needed. But bickering and underhandedness did not end there. In early August, Commander Charles Davis recommended to Sampson that the navy take San Juan alone without the army's participation. Miles learned of the scheme and promptly nipped it in the bud, securing assurance from Washington that the navy would do no more than deliver troops to the island.

Miles departed Guantánamo, Cuba, on July 21 with 3,415 infantry, two companies of engineers, and one signal company, all carried in the transports *Columbia, Macon,* and *Yale.* Captain Francis J. Higginson commanded the naval escort, consisting of the battleship *Massachusetts* (flagship), cruiser *Dixie,* and armed yacht *Gloucester.* Initially, the plan called for Miles to land at Cape Fajardo on the northern coast of Puerto Rico. Once at sea, however, Miles changed the objectives to Ponce and Guánica on the southern coast. From intelligence reports provided to him, he knew that the Spanish were expecting him to land at Fajardo and had prepared accordingly. The city of Ponce, by contrast, was the second largest on the island, only 70 miles from San Juan, and offered a ready source of supplies.

Meanwhile, Manuel Macías y Casado, governor-general of Puerto Rico, was fully aware of the U.S. intent to invade the island even though the point of landing was unknown. Macías's orders were to offer stout resistance, as it was hoped that this would strengthen Spain's bargaining position. As Macías saw it, he had the option of either concentrating most of his military resources around the capital of San Juan or dispersing his forces so as to cover key positions. Although there were other strong points on the island, the bulk of the Spanish defenses were around San Juan.

On July 25, a naval landing party captured Guánica, a small but good deep-water harbor 15 miles west of Ponce, without resistance. On July 27, a detachment from Guánica advanced on Ponce and was joined the following day by some 3,600 troops under the command of Brevet Major General James H. Wilson, whose force had sailed from Charleston on July 20. The combined force compelled the Spanish to surrender the city. On July 26, a column under Brigadier General George Garretson moved on Yauco, a few miles north of Guánica. Following a brief skirmish with Spanish troops, Garretson and his troops captured the town and nearby railroad line. Although the population of Puerto Rico had not risen up against Spanish rule as was the case in Cuba, they did not strongly support the Spanish. Indeed, when in Ponce, Miles proclaimed that the Americans had come as liberators and found that the population responded enthusiastically. Throughout, Miles stressed maneuver to flank and isolate enemy positions rather than direct frontal assaults.

By August 5, additional troops had landed on the island under Major General John R. Brooke and Brigadier General Theodore Schwan with 4,000 and 2,900 men, respectively, so that combined with General Wilson's force, Miles now had some 17,000 troops at his disposal. He estimated Spanish troop strength at more than 8,200 regulars and some 9,100 volunteers. Unlike General Shafter's V Corps, the various elements of Miles's command left the United States fully equipped to conduct the campaign. Miles had 106 mortars, howitzers, and field and siege guns as well as 10 Gatling guns.

Miles learned that the Spanish were organizing their defenses in the low mountainous area separating the northern half of the island from the southern half. A key position in this plan was the strong point at Aibonito, which guarded a gateway through the mountains leading to San Juan, Miles's goal. To attain that objective, he decided to advance with four columns of troops, sweep across the island, and converge on San Juan.

General Schwan was to move from Ponce, northwest along the left flank, to Mayagüez and Arecibo. Garretson's course was due north to Adjuntas and then Arecibo, where he and Schwan would

U.S. volunteer troops from Wisconsin march by the customshouse in Ponce, Puerto Rico, in 1898 during the Spanish-American War. (Library of Congress)

form one column under Brigadier General Guy Henry and move directly on San Juan. Meanwhile, a third column under Wilson was to march northeast from Ponce to Aibonito, the only Spanish strong point on the route to San Juan. Finally, Brooke was directed to march to Cayey, at which point he would be behind the Spanish defenders at Aibonito. It was believed that his presence would compel the defenders to retire, leaving the route from Aibonito open.

Schwan got under way on August 6, aiming to clear western Puerto Rico of any Spanish forces, but he discovered that few troops were there to offer any real resistance. In the course of an eight-day march, Schwan's column captured nine towns and had a sharp fight at Hormigueros, seven miles south of Mayagüez, on August 10, suffering 1 killed and 16 wounded in the process. Brooke commenced his advance, moving west from Arroyo toward Guayama, where he encountered significant resistance and sustained several casualties before finally capturing the position on August 5. On August 9, U.S. forces under Brigadier General Oswald H. Ernst of Wilson's force had a stiff fight at Coamo, some 17 miles east-northeast of Ponce. This hard-fought action ended when the 16th Pennsylvania moved around the Spanish and flanked the defenders out of position before inflicting heavy casualties on them. Some 40 Spanish were killed and wounded, and 170 were captured. American losses were only 6 men wounded. Then on August 12, Wilson's forces had a brief

skirmish at the Asomante Hills near the town of Aibonito on the main road from Ponce to San Juan. The last combat of the Puerto Rico Campaign was another skirmish, at Las Marías, on August 13, a day after the Protocol of Peace had been signed but before word of it had been received. There were no American casualties, but the Spanish suffered 5 killed, 14 wounded, and 56 taken prisoner.

The entire campaign was conducted amid an impending ceasefire. As Wilson was preparing to attack Aibonito after a request for surrender was rejected, Miles received word that the Protocol of Peace had been signed, thereby concluding the campaign on August 13. Brief though it was, the Puerto Rico Campaign moved along smartly, far more so than Shafter's effort in Cuba. There were no tropical diseases to debilitate the troops, and the various columns made surprisingly good time marching over rough terrain. By the time of the armistice, U.S. forces had captured half of the island, fighting six engagements and suffering only 3 dead and 40 wounded. The Spanish sustained at least 10 times that number of casualties.

The Puerto Rico Campaign ensured the U.S. acquisition of Puerto Rico as part of the peace negotiations of 1898 and limited Spanish bargaining power at the conference table. Had the campaign taken longer and proven costlier, it might well have worked to Spain's advantage.

JERRY KEENAN AND SPENCER C. TUCKER

See also

Asomante Hills, Engagement at; Brooke, John Rutter; Cervera y Topete, Pascual; Coamo, Battle of; Guayama, Battle of; Hormigueros, Battle of; Las Marías, Battle of; McKinley, William; Miles, Nelson Appleton; Peace, Protocol of; Sampson, William Thomas; Santiago de Cuba Land Campaign; Schofield, John McAllister; Schwan, Theodore; Wilson, James Harrison; Yauco, Battle of

Further Reading

Cosmas, Graham A. *An Army for Empire: The United States Army in the Spanish-American War.* College Station: Texas A&M University Press, 1994.

Leech, Margaret. *In the Days of McKinley.* New York: Harper and Brothers, 1959.

Trask, David F. *The War with Spain in 1898.* Lincoln: University of Nebraska Press, 1996.

Wilson, James Harrison. *Under the Old Flag: Recollections of Military Operations in the War for the Union, the Spanish War, the Boxer Rebellion, Etc.* 2 vols. New York: D. Appleton, 1912.

Pulitzer, Joseph
Birth Date: April 10, 1847
Death Date: October 29, 1911

Pioneering newspaper reporter, publisher, and sponsor of the Pulitzer Prizes but also associated with the yellow journalism that surrounded the Spanish-American War. Joseph Pulitzer was born in Makó, Hungary, on April 10, 1847, the son of a well-to-do Jewish grain merchant and a devout Roman Catholic German mother. Until the age of 17, Pulitzer was educated by private tutors and at private academies. He then sought to join the military but was rebuffed on at least three attempts because of his poor eyesight and fragile health. While traveling in Germany in late 1864, however, he met a bounty recruiter for the U.S. Army with whom he contracted to enlist as a substitute for an American draftee. Pulitzer sailed for the United States speaking only limited English, although he was fluent in Hungarian, German, and French. He went on to serve for almost a year until the end of the American Civil War in April 1865, assigned to a unit with a number of German-speaking men.

Following the war, Pulitzer worked at a number of odd jobs. Moving to St. Louis, he read voraciously, mastering English and immersing himself in legal studies. In 1868, he took a job as a reporter for a German-language newspaper and quickly distinguished himself. In 1872, he was given controlling interest in the paper, which was teetering on insolvency. From there, the enterprising journalist engaged in a number of risky but very successful business ventures that included the acquisition of other St. Louis–area newspapers. By 1878, he was the owner of the *St. Louis-Dispatch* and had already established a national reputation in journalism and publishing.

It was with his *St. Louis-Dispatch* that Pulitzer, who worked long hours, became known for his gritty mass-appeal journalism and

Joseph Pulitzer was a pioneering newspaper editor and publisher who sponsored the Pulitzer Prizes but was also closely associated with the rise of yellow journalism before the Spanish-American War. (Chaiba Media)

his championing of the average American. Soon, he had pioneered the genre of investigative reporting to uncover government corruption and abuses in private enterprise. In precarious health, in 1883 he and his wife left St. Louis for New York ostensibly for a European vacation. Ever the deal maker, he instead met with New York financier Jay Gould and negotiated the purchase of the *New York World,* a paper that had been on the skids financially. Pulitzer immediately threw himself headlong into his latest acquisition, involving himself in every aspect of the newspaper.

To increase circulation, Pulitzer resorted to sensationalist reporting, the extensive use of illustrations, and staged news events to attract more attention and readers. Indeed, his approach had all the hallmarks of yellow journalism. By the late 1880s, the *New York World* was the nation's most-read newspaper.

By 1890, however, Pulitzer had fallen victim to a vicious circulation war with Charles Anderson Dana, Pulitzer's chief rival in New York and publisher of *The Sun.* Dana had engaged in a despicable personal smear campaign against Pulitzer, whose health was now broken. Nearly blind and suffering from a nervous condition that made him terribly sensitive to any noise beyond a whisper, he spent most of his time in seclusion either aboard his yacht or in his homes in Maine or New York (usually in soundproof rooms). Nevertheless, he kept his hand on the pulse of his newspapers and never entirely relinquished editorial or managerial control.

When William Randolph Hearst bought the *New York Journal,* sparking a circulation war with Pulitzer's *New York World,* Pulitzer upped the ante by engaging in ever more salacious and sensationalistic news stories. Increasingly, the stories focused on events in Cuba. In certain instances, his reporters were encouraged to fabricate stories, which badly hurt Pulitzer's journalistic reputation. Both Hearst's and Pulitzer's papers clamored for war after the February 15, 1898, destruction of the U.S. battleship *Maine* in Havana Harbor. Following the end of the Spanish-American War, Pulitzer turned away from yellow journalism, but unfortunately the damage to his reputation had already been done.

Pulitzer returned to his roots by sponsoring a series of hard-hitting investigative news stories after the turn of the 20th century, although his health prevented him from returning to the newspaper offices he so loved. He died aboard his yacht in Charleston Harbor, South Carolina, on October 29, 1911. Pulitzer had directed in his will that Columbia University should receive a large sum of money from his estate to create a school of journalism. In 1912, the Columbia School of Journalism came into being. It remains one of the most prestigious schools of its kind in the United States. Columbia also created the Pulitzer Prize, which recognizes superlative work in journalism, history, literature, and musical compositions.

PAUL G. PIERPAOLI JR.

See also

Gould, Jay; Hearst, William Randolph; Journalism; *Maine,* USS; Yellow Journalism

Further Reading

Juergens, George. *Joseph Pulitzer and the New York World.* Princeton, NJ: Princeton University Press, 1966.

Noble, Iris. *Joseph Pulitzer: Front Page Pioneer.* New York: Julian Messner, 1967.

Whitelaw, Nancy. *Joseph Pulitzer and the New York World.* Greensboro, NC: Morgan Reynolds, 1999.

Pullman Strike

Start Date: May 11, 1894
End Date: August 2, 1894

Major strike that began with workers at the Pullman Palace Car Company on the outskirts of Chicago and quickly spread to other railway workers. The strike began on May 11, 1894; grew in size and scope into the summer; and finally ended with a defeat for the strikers on August 2, 1894. The Pullman Palace Car Company, which manufactured passenger railway cars and sleeper cars, employed several thousand workers, all of whom were obliged to live in a self-contained town owned and operated by the company. Workers lived in company-provided housing, shopped in company-owned stores, and even worshipped in company-sponsored churches.

As the U.S. economy began to falter in the early 1890s, the Pullman Company began to cut wages to stay profitable. In 1893, the nation was plunged into a serious economic depression that affected all sectors of the economy, and in the late spring of 1894, the company announced across-the-board wage cuts of up to 25 percent. Meanwhile, it stood firm on the rents and prices it charged workers in the company town. This placed an impossible burden on many workers, for they could not afford to pay rent on such reduced wages. And if they sought housing outside the company town, they would be summarily fired. To protest the company's policies, some 4,000 workers staged a wildcat strike beginning on May 11, 1894. When the workers refused to return to work, George Pullman, the owner of the company, ordered a lockout. The affected workers were not only barred from entering the plant but were also barred from their homes in the company town.

Deputies endeavor to operate a train engine during the Pullman Strike of 1894. (Library of Congress)

The workers soon grew desperate and appealed for assistance to the American Railway Union (ARU), then headed by Eugene V. Debs. He pleaded for arbitration on behalf of the strikers but was unsuccessful. On June 26, the ARU announced that none of its members would work on trains that pulled Pullman railcars. Now the strike had mushroomed into a national labor boycott that threatened to severely disrupt the nation's rail service, then the lifeline of the country. Within days, the ARU boycott had brought much of the U.S. rail traffic to a virtual halt. And because Chicago was at the epicenter of the strike and was also the principal rail terminus of the country, practically all rail lines west of Chicago were shut down by the beginning of July.

The paralysis caused by the strike was making a bad economic situation worse and was now threatening to disrupt mail delivery nationwide. President Grover Cleveland finally decided to take action on the counsel of U.S. attorney general Richard Olney, who ordered court injunctions to prevent workers from engaging in sabotage or property damage and to force them back to work. This was the first time in U.S. history that court-ordered injunctions were used against strikers. When the rail workers refused to heed the injunctions and after a July 5 arson fire in Chicago was blamed on the strikers, Cleveland authorized Olney to call in federal troops to crush the strike. This would be the first time the government used federal troops to stop a labor strike. By mid-July, some 2,000 U.S. troops had managed to get most of the trains running again. But Debs was arrested for having violated the earlier court injunctions, and the ARU-inspired strike quickly collapsed when other labor organizations refused to support the strikers. On August 2, 1894, the strike ended after the workers returned to work.

In the end, the Pullman Strike, which saw its share of violence, resulted in 13 strikers killed, 57 others injured, and about $350,000 in property damage. It was a stinging rebuke for organized labor and marked the first significant federal intervention in a labor strike, first through the issuance of court injunctions and then the dispatch of federal troops. Moreover, the uprising was emblematic of the turmoil-ridden 1890s and labor unrest, which had begun two years earlier with the Homestead Steel Strike. On the other hand, the events of 1894 laid bare the paternalistic and unfair treatment of the Pullman workers, called into question the usefulness of company-run towns, and ironically showed the utility and necessity of labor unions in taming the excesses of big business. As the United States mobilized for war in the spring and early summer of 1898, government officials held their breath that no similar rail strikes occurred, which would have been disastrous for the war effort. Thankfully for the United States, none occurred during the Spanish-American War.

PAUL G. PIERPAOLI JR.

See also

Cleveland, Stephen Grover; Debs, Eugene Victor; Homestead Steel Strike; Labor Union Movement; Olney, Richard; Railroads

Further Reading

Adelman, William. *Touring Pullman.* Chicago: Illinois Labor History Society, 1993.

Lindsey, Almont. *The Pullman Strike: The Story of a Unique Experiment and of a Great Labor Upheaval.* Chicago: University of Chicago Press, 1964.

Stein, R. Conrad. *The Pullman Strike and the American Labor Movement in American History.* Berkeley Heights, NJ: Enslow, 2001.

Punta Gorda, Cuba

A peninsula north of the narrow channel connecting the open sea to the harbor at Santiago de Cuba. Punta Gorda lies south of the city of Santiago de Cuba on the island's southeastern coast and in 1898 formed part of the defensive system created by the Spanish to control access to the harbor. At its greatest width, the channel was only about 400 yards.

Punta Gorda was, in fact, only a minor part of the defensive network. The main defenses were located on Morro Heights, a headland six miles south of the city on the eastern side of the narrow channel leading to Santiago Harbor. The Estrella Battery, also located north of the channel, complemented the battery at Punta Gorda. Punta Gorda boasted little in the way of serious armaments, although it did have four breech-loading cannon. The only other guns there were two antiquated howitzers. The Upper Socapa Battery on Morro Heights had the largest Spanish guns: several 6.3-inch pieces.

It was the perceived threat posed by the batteries at Punta Gorda, Estrella, and Morro Heights that had given pause to Rear Admiral William T. Sampson's plans to move with his North Atlantic Fleet against the Spanish squadron, bottled up in the harbor since May 19, 1898. On June 6, 16, and 21, American warships bombarded Morro Heights but to little effect. The defensive positions at Punta Gorda and Estrella would not come under fire until early July. With a tight blockade of Santiago de Cuba now in place, Sampson arrived at Santiago de Cuba on July 1. The American blockade concentrated the principal ships of the North Atlantic Fleet: five battleships (the *Oregon, Indiana, Massachusetts, Iowa,* and *Texas*), two armored cruisers (the *Brooklyn,* Commodore Winfield Scott Schley's flagship, and the *New York,* Sampson's flagship), and a number of smaller cruisers and auxiliaries.

Meanwhile, on June 30, Major General William Shafter, commanding officer of V Corps, had requested that the navy begin bombarding Spanish defensive positions in and around Santiago de Cuba. This was to prepare the area for a full U.S. invasion of the city and, it was hoped, force Rear Admiral Pascual Cervera y Topete to surrender or face U.S. naval assets sitting outside the harbor at Santiago de Cuba. On July 2, Spanish batteries protecting the harbor came under heavy fire from U.S. ships. That same day, the U.S. battleships *Oregon* and *Indiana* concentrated a heavy bombardment on Punta Gorda, which virtually neutralized the Spanish defensive position there. The next day, Cervera's ships steamed out of the harbor at Santiago de Cuba. Badly outgunned

Fortifications at Punta Gorda, Cuba, 1898. Shown here are two 155-millimeter howitzers. (Library of Congress)

and outmaneuvered, Cervera was promptly defeated in a decisive four-hour battle. All six of his ships were either sunk by American fire or scuttled by their Spanish crews. In addition, the Spanish suffered 323 killed and 151 wounded. Another 1,720 became prisoners, including Cervera himself. With the Spanish fleet destroyed and the batteries at Morro Heights, Estrella, and Punta Gorda neutralized, U.S. land forces were able to concentrate on besieging and occupying Santiago de Cuba, which capitulated on July 17, 1898.

PAUL G. PIERPAOLI JR.

See also

Cervera y Topete, Pascual; Morro Castle; Morro Heights; Sampson, William Thomas; Santiago de Cuba, Battle of; Santiago de Cuba Land Campaign; Schley, Winfield Scott; Shafter, William Rufus

Further Reading

Feuer, A. B. *The Spanish-American War at Sea: Naval Action in the Atlantic.* Westport, CT: Praeger, 1995.
O'Toole, G. J. A. *The Spanish War: An American Epic, 1898.* New York: Norton, 1984.
Trask, David F. *The War with Spain in 1898.* Lincoln: University of Nebraska Press, 1996.

Q

Quesada y Aróstegui, Gonzalo de
Birth Date: December 15, 1868
Death Date: January 9, 1915

Cuban author and diplomat instrumental in helping his close friend, Cuban revolutionary José Martí, organize the Cuban independence movement during the 1890s. Gonzalo de Quesada y Aróstegui was born in Havana, Cuba, on December 15, 1868. When he was nine years old, he moved with his family to New York City, joining the growing Cuban exile community in the United States. In 1888, he earned a BS degree from the City College of New York. He officially began his quest for Cuban independence at a commemoration ceremony honoring the Grito de Yara on October 10, 1889, in New York City. During the event, he gave a passionate speech supporting Cuban independence and praising Carlos Manuel de Céspedes and the revolutionaries who had fought in the Ten Years' War (1868–1878). It was also on this occasion that Quesada met Martí. From this point, the two Cuban nationalists formed a lifelong friendship.

Soon thereafter, the Argentine government hired Quesada to be the Argentine consul in Philadelphia. He subsequently earned a law degree from New York University in 1891. That same year, he resigned his diplomatic post to dedicate himself fully to revolutionary activity.

On January 5, 1892, following more than two years of coordination with Cuban nationalists both from inside and outside Cuba, Martí, with Quesada's assistance, officially inaugurated the Cuban Revolutionary Party (Partido Revolucionario Cubano). The party transformed a revolutionary movement into a revolutionary party and paved the way for the Cuban War of Independence, which

began in 1895. From the inception of the party, Quesada served as its secretary. He was also on the board of editors of *Patria*, the official newspaper of the Cuban Revolutionary Party.

Quesada's most important task for the Cuban Revolutionary Party was to lobby on behalf of the Cuban nationalists in Washington, D.C. Although he referred to himself as the chargé d'affaires during his stay on Washington, he did not hold an official diplomatic post. He did, however, cultivate numerous important contacts within the U.S. government. Unlike Martí, Quesada eagerly sought U.S. intervention in Cuba.

When Martí departed for Cuba in 1895, Quesada remained in the United States to continue lobbying for support. In addition to this activity, Quesada was to facilitate the shipment of weapons and supplies needed by the revolutionaries to fight the Spanish colonial authorities. Martí also left Quesada in charge of his personal library, his correspondence, and all documents relating to the formation of the Cuban Revolutionary Party. Quesada ultimately edited and published 35 volumes of Martí's papers. A prolific writer, Quesada also published several books and journal articles about Cuba's struggle for independence.

Following the Spanish-American War and the liberation of Cuba from Spanish rule, Quesada returned to the island and took part in the Cuban Constitutional Convention, which drafted the 1901 Cuban Constitution. Following Cuban independence in 1902, Cuban president Tomás Estrada Palma appointed Quesada ambassador to the United States. On March 2, 1904, Quesada signed the Hay-Quesada Treaty, which was to give Cuba title to the Isle of Pines. It was only after American investigators discovered that the harbors of the Isle of Pines were too shallow for a naval base, however, that the U.S. Congress finally ratified the Hay-Quesada Treaty in 1925. In 1910, Quesada left his post in the United States to serve as Cuban ambassador to Germany. He died in Berlin on January 9, 1915.

MICHAEL R. HALL

See also

Céspedes y del Castillo, Carlos Manuel de; Cuban Revolutionary Party; Cuban War of Independence; Estrada Palma, Tomás; Martí y Pérez, José Julián; Ten Years' War

Further Reading

Quesada, Gonzalo de, and Henry Davenport Northrup. *The War in Cuba: The Great Struggle for Freedom.* Kila, MT: Kessinger, 2004.

Quesada y Miranda, Gonzalo de, ed. *Archivo de Gonzalo de Quesada, Epistolario, II.* Havana: Imprenta El Siglo XX, 1951.

Tebbel, John. *America's Great Patriotic War with Spain: Mixed Motives, Lies, and Racism in Cuba and the Philippines, 1898–1915.* Manchester Center, VT: Marshall Jones, 1996.

Cuban author and diplomat Gonzalo de Quesada helped José Martí organize the Cuban revolutionary movement. (Library of Congress)

R

Racism

Racism against nonwhites profoundly influenced the course of the Spanish-American War and the Philippine-American War. Before these conflicts began in 1898, Spain argued that its colonies in Cuba, Puerto Rico, and the Philippines were incapable of governing themselves. This idea had taken shape by the end of the 19th century as Spain and other Western powers entered an intense phase of nationalistic fervor, colonial competition, militarism, and economic expansion. For Western leaders, establishing colonies was important in terms of measuring a country's status as a world power. But empire-building was also proof positive that Europeans were best able to rule over so-called inferior mixed-race groups. Indeed, xenophobia, scientific racism, and social Darwinism greatly informed these beliefs.

Prior to 1898, race figured prominently in debates within the United States over whether to challenge Spanish power in the Caribbean and the Pacific. Before the American Civil War began in 1861, some political leaders (especially from Southern states) had actively sought annexation of Cuba and Puerto Rico by means of coercion and diplomacy in their quest to expand slavery. Many believed that because slavery had already been established in these areas, the inclusion of these islands as part of an American empire would be a natural fit. However, the efforts to annex Cuba and Puerto Rico were unsuccessful chiefly because of political resistance among Northern politicians.

Following the violent end to slavery in the United States in 1865, new motives emerged to acquire Spain's Caribbean colonies. In 1868, a Cuban independence movement emerged that inspired some Americans to speak openly against Spanish imperialism. Americans' views of the Spanish character were no doubt inspired by the so-called Black Legend, a long-standing representation of Spaniards as backwards, brutal, underhanded, swarthy, and fanatically Catholic. This view extended somewhat to those who lived in Spanish colonies as well. In fact, prominent national newspapers often published visual caricatures of the Spanish colonists as damsels in distress in desperate need of salvation by virile, manly American leaders. These representations are interesting not only for their racist and paternalistic ideas but also for the discourse of gender used in them. Almost unfailingly, American representations of inferior subjugated peoples in the world saw them as female or feminine in nature, with the implication that femininity was inherently weak and was in need of a strong, virile masculinity to protect it.

The destruction of the U.S. battleship *Maine* in Havana Harbor in February 1898 provided the immediate catalyst for the Spanish-American War and also confirmed all of the worst stereotypes about Spaniards. The American press reported widely on the cruelty of Spanish military leaders, particularly that of General Valeriano "the Butcher" Weyler y Nicolau, who conducted a brutal campaign of repression against Cuban civilians. America's quick victory in the conflict only served to validate the idea that the United States should naturally replace Spain as the dominant power in the Caribbean and the Pacific. During the war, American political and military leaders debated whether or not to annex Spain's former colonies outright. They agreed that conditional independence would be granted to Cuba but that the United States would dominate its domestic and foreign affairs. Puerto Rico and the Philippines were annexed outright.

These decisions were based in large measure on the prevailing notion that Cubans, Puerto Ricans, and Filipinos were not adequately prepared to control their own affairs. Accordingly, these newly acquired territories and nations would have to change their societies by encouraging European immigration, building Anglo-Saxon systems of education and law, and establishing close ties with the United States. But American newspapers after 1898 increasingly depicted Cubans as apelike humans incapable of self-rule or democracy.

Indeed, military leaders and administrators in Washington openly questioned whether Cubans, in particular, were prepared to lead their country. This view served to favor prolonging military occupation and discredit emerging Cuban national institutions. In 1899, the passage of the Platt Amendment, which essentially established U.S. dominance over Cuba's foreign policy and the right to intervene in its domestic affairs, exemplified the distrust of the U.S. government toward Cubans. American leaders in Washington also insisted that closely managing elections was the best policy to control popular aspirations. Thus, in 1901, Secretary of War Elihu Root implemented a plan that limited those eligible for suffrage. All voters had to be Cuban males over 20 years of age, literate, own at least $250 in property, or have served in the insurrection military forces. This policy had the practical effect of excluding the vast majority of Cuban men (and all women) from participating in the political process.

Although slavery had been abolished in Cuba in 1888, the vestiges of slavery left sharp racial divisions within Cuban society. A few Cuban leaders, such as José Martí, had promoted racial equality and the idea of Cuba as a racial democracy during the Cuban War of Independence (1895–1898), but this view was not shared by the majority of Cuban elites. After the Spanish-American War, the U.S. occupation government colluded with Cuban elites to deny Afro-Cubans a stake in the political future of their country. In 1899, the U.S. military dissolved the revolutionary army in which Afro-Cubans were overrepresented and denied promotions to Afro-Cubans within the Rural Guard of the new national army. In 1902, the United States also imposed a new immigration law in Cuba that restricted nonwhite immigration in favor of laborers from Northern Europe.

Cuban elites took their cues from American administrators and formed their own parties without black participation. As a result, Afro-Cubans experimented with their own political organizations. The Partido Independiente de Color (Independence Party of Color), created in 1908, advocated equal access to educational institutions, a key component of upward social mobility. However, the new government passed a law prohibiting the existence of political parties based on race. In 1912, Afro-Cubans violently rejected this policy, and a virtual race war began. With U.S. Marines serving as reinforcements, the Cuban government put down the revolt, killing as many as 6,000 Afro-Cubans in the process.

In the Philippines, armed opposition groups, led by Emilio Aguinaldo y Famy, emerged almost as soon as the United States invaded the archipelago. Racism toward Filipinos escalated as the Philippine-American War dragged on into the early 20th century. The U.S. Army conducted intense anti-insurgent operations in the Tagalog Province of southern Luzon, where resistance against occupation was more hostile. In 1901, atrocities against Filipino insurgents and civilians escalated after American troops were massacred at Balangiga on Samar. President Theodore Roosevelt

tacitly approved harsher tactics against the insurgency by promoting commanders, such as Brigadier General Adna Chaffee, who had extensive experience fighting Native Americans in the western United States.

News of specific incidences of atrocities ultimately doomed public support for the Philippine-American War, but the insurgency also died down as a result of Aguinaldo's capture in 1901. Still, racism permeated the ranks of the American forces in the Philippines, with soldiers describing Filipinos as "niggers" and "gooks." At the same time, however, the Philippines became a laboratory for U.S.-style educational, judicial, and bureaucratic institutions.

The Spanish-American War and the Philippine-American War posed a series of dilemmas for African Americans. On the one hand, African Americans did not want to break ranks with President William McKinley and the Republican Party and oppose the wars. In fact, the African American press generally supported the Cuban invasion. African American soldiers also willingly fought in both wars. Indeed, there was a general belief that service in the armed forces would elevate the status of African Americans, but black units were officered almost entirely by whites, and African American soldiers were often subjected to humiliating treatment by white soldiers and officers. Many African Americans joined with antiwar groups, such as the Anti-Imperialist League, because of what they perceived as U.S. imperialism run amok.

JESSE HINGSON

See also

African Americans; Aguinaldo y Famy, Emilio; Anti-Imperialist League; Cuba, Spanish Colonial Policies toward; Imperialism; Martí y Pérez, José Julián; Philippine-American War, U.S. Reaction to; Philippine Islands, Spanish Colonial Policies toward; Root, Elihu; Social Darwinism; Weyler y Nicolau, Valeriano; White Man's Burden; Xenophobia

Further Reading
Cosmas, Graham A. *An Army for Empire: The United States Army in the Spanish-American War.* College Station: Texas A&M University Press, 1994.
Hunt, Michael. *Ideology and U.S. Foreign Policy.* New Haven, CT: Yale University Press, 1987.
Krenn, Michael L. *The Impact of Race on U.S. Foreign Policy.* New York: Garland, 1999.
Love, Eric. *Race over Empire: Racism and U.S. Imperialism, 1865–1900.* Chapel Hill: University of North Carolina Press, 2004.
Smith, Angel, and Emma Davila-Cox, eds. *The Crisis of 1898: Colonial Redistribution and Nationalist Mobilization.* New York: St. Martin's, 1999.
Smith, Joseph. *The Spanish-American War: Conflict in the Caribbean and the Pacific, 1895–1902.* New York: Longman, 1994.
Weston, Rubin Francis. *Racism in U.S. Imperialism: The Influence of Racial Assumptions on American Foreign Policy, 1893–1946.* Columbia: University of South Carolina Press, 1973.

Railroads

At the time of the Spanish-American War, railroads were the very lifeblood of the American economy. Before the advent of aviation,

The 22nd New York Regiment departing Long Island Station for Florida in 1898. (*Photographic History of the Spanish-American War*, 1898)

railroads were the most efficient means of transportation over great land distances. During the war, the railroads also played a vital role in the mobilization for and execution of the war effort. Indeed, because the conflict was the first one waged by the United States on foreign shores, railroads were essential to the war effort and, along with maritime shipping, were the primary mode by which to move massive amounts of matériel and troops over great distances. In general, U.S. railroads did an admirable job of moving men and supplies during the war, and although there were numerous problems early on, it quickly became clear that the vast U.S. network of rail lines, the bountiful supply of locomotives and railcars, and the

efficiency with which they were dispatched were a major advantage to the U.S. war effort.

In the United States, the first commercial railroads made their appearance in the 1820s. These were, however, rudimentary and localized affairs and bore little resemblance to the railroad industry of the 1890s. In 1830, there were just 23 miles of railroad tracks in the entire country. However, as these small local railways proved that trains offered unique advantages in moving goods and people, rail lines were soon built in exponential fashion. In 1840, track mileage in the United States was up to 2,818 miles. In 1850, there were 9,021 miles of track. By 1860, the United States boasted 30,626

Railroads in the United States, 1895–1905

Year	Total Miles of Operating Track	Miles of New Track Built	Number of Operating Railroads	Total Locomotives in Service	Passengers
1895	233,276	1,420	1,104	35,699	507,421,000
1896	239,140	1,692	1,111	35,950	511,773,000
1897	242,013	2,109	1,158	35,986	489,445,000
1898	245,334	3,255	1,192	36,234	501,057,000
1899	250,143	4,569	1,206	36,703	523,177,000
1900	258,784	4,894	1,224	37,663	576,831,000
1901	265,352	5,368	1,213	39,584	607,278,000
1902	274,196	6,025	1,219	41,225	649,879,000
1903	283,822	5,652	1,281	43,871	694,892,000
1904	297,073	3,832	1,314	46,743	715,420,000
1905	306,797	4,388	1,380	48,357	738,835,000

Arrival of the 157th Indiana Volunteer Regiment at Tampa, Florida, 1898. (*Photographic History of the Spanish-American War,* 1898)

miles of rail lines, about 70 percent of which was north of the Mason-Dixon Line and was concentrated most heavily in a belt from Ohio east through Pennsylvania and north to New Jersey, New York, and New England. As the railroads exploded in size and scope, they brought with them new forms of business management and finance that would soon spread to other industries.

It is hard to overemphasize the impact of the railroads on the economy. Over the course of just a few decades, the American economy went from one that was highly localized and fragmented to one that was truly national in both size and scope. Indeed, the nation's rail lines would help catapult the United States into the forefront of world economic power. Railroads greatly increased economic efficiency, allowed for much greater economic output because raw materials and finished products could be brought in and shipped out of factories in quantities unthinkable prior to railways, and could move people in a fast and timely fashion.

The railroad industry itself also spurred industries upon which it relied. These included iron, steel, mining, coal, and glass, among others. The ever-expanding rail industry also required thousands of workers, spread across hundreds of miles, to manage and operate trains, depots, stations, and the like. Railroads even affected the concept of time. Before the railroad companies themselves divided the

nation into four standard time zones in 1883, the United States had been divided by a dizzying array of different time zones. It was not uncommon, in fact, to travel just a few miles and pass through several time zones. The railroads standardized time and in so doing greatly increased efficiency while at the same time reducing shipping problems substantially. By 1890, railroads had also adopted a standard gauge, and this allowed railcars to be transferred from one railway to another without having to transfer the cargo.

On the eve of the Spanish-American War, the United States boasted some 190,000 miles of rail track, more by far than any other nation in the world. The major railroad companies were generally paradigms of efficiency and good management, and the only major concerns were periodic railway strikes, which often threatened the entire national network. Fortunately, no such catastrophic strikes occurred during the war. The only concern faced by war planners was the relative paucity of rail lines in the South, which was to serve as a key mobilization and embarkation region owing to its proximity to Cuba and Puerto Rico. In 1898, Tampa, Florida, for example, was served by just one single-track rail line, which for a time caused monumental problems in moving men and supplies into the area.

Realizing that control over railroads during a modern war might often prove to be the decisive factor in victory or defeat,

American war planners moved quickly to coordinate activities with the various railroad companies. And the railroads were, in general, more than eager to cooperate. They were driven partly by patriotism but also by profits, which they realized in a handsome fashion during the war. In April and May 1898, the War Department contracted with most of the major railway companies to transport certain amounts of men and matériel between predetermined points in the country. Beyond that, the government exercised little control over the railroads, believing that the companies themselves would do the best job of coordinating shipments. Knowing that the war was a potential profit bonanza, rail companies worked closely with quartermasters in depots, stations, camps, and embarkation points. Indeed, many railways constructed additional rail sidings and platforms at such places and many times out of their own pockets.

One infantry regiment needed six trains to transport its soldiers, supplies, and animals. Multiplied over the many regiments that had to be moved, this type of transport added up to staggering numbers of railcars, locomotives, and railway employees. During the Spanish-American War, soldiers were moved in coach cars or sleeping cars, which the War Department insisted upon. This was in stark contrast to soldiers riding in hot, crowded boxcars during the American Civil War. In the South particularly, some railways were short of railcars and locomotives, but the problem never became acute. Occasional problems occurred between soldiers and railway workers in stations and depots concerning the handling of baggage and personal effects, and some cavalrymen groused that their horses were being mistreated. But all in all, such complaints were few and far between.

Leaders of the railroad industry worked closely—and usually in harmony—with quartermasters and war planners. Early on, for example, the unloading of boxcars had been slowed because nobody had labeled the contents therein; this dilemma was solved by railroad employees working closely with the U.S. Army and the War Department, which began to mandate that all boxcars be appropriately identified and labeled. The nation's railroad network worked quite well during the war, and there were few ill effects felt in the civilian economy. From late April to September 1898, the railroads transported some 450,000 men and hundreds of tons of supplies and equipment with no serious mishaps. And they did so at rates well below what they would have charged civilians.

If there was one dark spot in rail efficiency during the war, it undoubtedly occurred in Tampa. Poorly labeled boxcars with no bills of lading meant that railcars piled up in alarming fashion in May 1898. Indeed, by the middle of that month, more than 1,000 boxcars choked the rail yard at Tampa. Because the boxcars were not labeled or were mislabeled, railway workers could only manage to unload two or three per day. To make matters worse, the two railroad companies that operated the line into Tampa worked at cross-purposes in an attempt to garner a monopoly on government contracts. And the company (Plant Railroad and Steamship Company) that actually owned the single-track line to Tampa at first refused to allow railcars from rival firms to use it. The last conundrum was solved when the War Department threatened to seize the line and run it independently.

By June, however, many of the problems with the Tampa rail lines had been solved by the quartermaster general's office in Washington. Indeed, it made sure that cars were labeled properly, that depot managers knew in advance what shipments were due in and when, and that too many cars were not sent in at once. By mid-June, freight cars were being unloaded at the rate of 70 per day, a far cry from the 2 or 3 just a month before. By July 1, the freight pileup in Tampa had been eliminated.

Despite the temporary and relatively minor problems with the railroads during the war, the nation's rail network performed with great efficiency. To be sure, both the war planners in Washington and the railroads learned from their problems and mistakes and made the system even more effective. Less than 20 years later as the United States entered World War I in 1917, America's rail network would once again prove to be a significant part of mobilization and war planning.

PAUL G. PIERPAOLI JR.

See also
Camps, U.S. Army; Plant Railroad and Steamship Company; Steel; Tampa, Florida

Further Reading
Bruchey, Stuart. *The Wealth of the Nation: An Economic History of the United States.* New York: Harper and Row, 1988.
Cosmas, Graham A. *An Army for Empire: The United States Army in the Spanish-American War.* College Station: Texas A&M University Press, 1994.
Gordon, John Steele. *An Empire of Wealth: The Epic History of American Economic Power.* New York: Harper Perennial, 2004.
Martin, Albro. *Railroads Triumphant: The Growth, Rejection and Rebirth of a Vital American Force.* New York: Oxford University Press USA, 1992.
Stover, John F. *American Railroads.* 2nd ed. Chicago: University of Chicago Press, 1997.

Rations

Standardized fixed portions of food issued to soldiers in temporary camps and in the field designed to be carried and eaten easily and to be relatively impervious to rapid spoilage. During the Spanish-American War, rations were handled fairly competently by the Army Subsistence Department, commanded by Brigadier General Charles Patrick Eagan, the army's commissary general. Providing for rations during the war was no easy task. Because this conflict involved U.S. forces on foreign shores and, in the case of the Philippines, thousands of miles from the United States, getting food into the field and storing it properly was an entirely new venture for army planners. Further complicating matters, the hot, tropical climates that prevailed in the Caribbean and the Philippines made the transportation and storage of rations a distinct challenge. While

U.S. Army soldiers organizing rations for distribution, 1898. (*Photographic History of the Spanish-American War,* 1898)

commercial refrigeration was available aboard cargo ships and rail-cars, it was far more scarce and problematic in the field. Finally, American soldiers during the Spanish-American War were issued rations that were remarkably similar to those of the American Civil War, which rendered them rather unsuitable for tropical conditions during the hottest months of the year (June–August).

From a standpoint of quantity, rations for the Spanish-American War were more than adequate. There were, however, distribution bottlenecks in Cuba. Eagan moved quickly to establish a tiered system of rations as the war ramped up. First, he created a supply depot in or near every major camp in the United States where regulars or volunteers went to mobilize or muster in. To ensure timely arrival and reduce possible spoilage, the army utilized supply and purchasing depots in New York City, Baltimore, Chicago, St. Louis, Kansas City, New Orleans, and San Francisco. Food purchased or stored in these cities was distributed to the various camps as well as to the embarkation posts of Tampa and San Francisco. Camps generally received food supplies to meet immediate needs and to maintain a 60-day supply of surplus inventory. The second tier of provisioning occurred in the field and did not operate as smoothly as the first tier.

Interestingly, Eagan's effort to procure rations was so successful that it created an overabundance of food that led to much spoilage. Tampa, for example, received between 6 million and 7 million rations, far more than would have been needed even for a much larger and longer war effort. There was always plenty of food in the mustering-in and mobilization camps, however.

The army did not have the time to adjust rations to the new realities of war in 1898; thus, the basic American Civil War rations were issued with some very minor adjustments. Spanish-American War soldiers received the following daily field ration: 20 ounces of beef (canned for Cuba, fresh for the Philippines and Puerto Rico), 2.5 ounces of sugar, 18 ounces of flour (or bread), vinegar, 10 ounces of potatoes, 64 ounces of salt, .45 ounce of baking soda, .4 ounce of pepper, 2.2 ounces of dried beans, and 1.6 ounces of green coffee. Soap and candles were also part of the daily ration. Rations were often supplemented, based on local availability, with bacon, rice, hominy, and vegetables.

These rations were often unappealing if not unappetizing, and nutritional value was at best questionable. Soldiers in Cuba complained bitterly about the canned beef, which was supposed to be heated before consumption. Lacking time to properly heat the meat, many ate it directly from the can, which sickened a number and led to the Embalmed Beef Scandal after the war ended. Many soldiers also groused about the raw, unground coffee, which necessitated a grinding mechanism that few possessed.

Eagan established Cuba's main food supply depot at Siboney. Those men who served in the Philippines or Puerto Rico were more fortunate in that their rations did not include the dreaded canned beef. Because of the greater distances involved, U.S. transport ships bound for these areas were equipped with large refrigerated lockers that carried fresh meat. Once the initial supplies had been depleted in the Philippines, army commissary officials procured meat, vegetables, and other items chiefly from Australia.

The Army Subsistence Department played no role in the distribution of food below the regimental level, nor was it involved in meal preparation. Approximately every 10 days, regiments would receive a fresh supply of rations. From there, rations were doled out to companies, each of which had an individual or small group of men who were responsible for preparing and serving the meals. At the company level, requisitioning errors, poor food handling, and substandard food preparation became fairly common problems. Meals were prepared for soldiers at the company level only when they were encamped; during expeditions, soldiers were on their own and prepared their own meals from the standard ration. Many times, rations ran low toward the end of the 10-day requisition period. Further adding to the supply problem was the fact that many soldiers discarded their 3-day ration pack to lighten their loads in the stifling heat and humidity.

In spite of the army's best efforts and the general abundance of rations during the war, the amount of food that spoiled in the tropical heat was massive. Spoilage of rations in the field and the consumption of unheated canned beef by soldiers in Cuba led to reports of significant outbreaks of illness, although in some cases it was hard to determine if the illnesses were indeed food-borne. Overall, the mortality rate of soldiers during the war was approximately 14 deaths due to illness for every one death due to combat.

The Embalmed Beef Scandal, which led to the postwar Dodge Commission, was the most serious flap involving food and rations during the Spanish-American War. During his testimony, commanding general of the army Major General Nelson A. Miles set off the controversy when he claimed—with little evidence to support it—that the beef shipped to Cuba had sickened thousands of soldiers. Even worse, he asserted that the Subsistence Department had knowingly purchased substandard meat and had experimented with it by lacing it with chemical preservatives. Although it became clear that Miles's accusations were politically motivated, Eagan lashed out at Miles, which earned him a stern rebuke from the army. The affair embarrassed both Secretary of War Russell A. Alger (who was ultimately forced to resign in July 1899) and President William McKinley. Army rations and procurement procedures were altered in 1901, and the president was given direct authority to change them by executive order.

PAUL G. PIERPAOLI JR.

See also
Alger, Russell Alexander; Eagan, Charles Patrick; Embalmed Beef Scandal; McKinley, William; Miles, Nelson Appleton

Further Reading
Cosmas, Graham A. *An Army for Empire: The United States Army in the Spanish-American War.* College Station: Texas A&M University Press, 1994.
Keuchel, Edward. "Chemicals and Meat: The Embalmed Beef Scandal." *Bulletin of the History of Medicine* 98 (Summer 1974): 65–89.
Roosevelt, Theodore. *The Letters of Theodore Roosevelt.* Edited by Elting E. Morison. 8 vols. Cambridge: Harvard University Press, 1951.
Wooster, Robert. *Nelson A. Miles and the Twilight of the Frontier Army.* Lincoln: University of Nebraska Press, 1993.

Raw Materials

Raw materials are the backbone of a modern economy and are essential to waging war in the industrialized age. Raw materials run the gamut from agricultural commodities such as sugar and hemp to extractive products such as oil, coal, and metals. In the last third of the 19th century, the U.S. economy grew exponentially, fueled largely by massive immigration that provided cheap labor for American factories. Immigration and a swelling population also provided larger domestic markets to which manufacturers could sell their finished goods. As the turn of the 20th century approached, the United States was poised to become the world's largest industrial economy, a feat that it achieved by World War I. As such, the United States also became the world's largest consumer of raw materials. Added to this demand for raw materials was the dizzying expansion of railroads, steamship lines, and naval capacity, all of which consumed massive amounts of coal and lubricating oil.

When the Spanish-American War began in April 1898, U.S. factories were running at near peak capacity. Having weathered the devastating economic depression of 1893–1897, many industries were clearly attempting to make up for lost time. There was thus little reserve capacity in terms of raw material stockpiles. Fortunately, the small scale and short duration of the Spanish-American War meant that there were never any serious shortages of raw materials. Unlike World War I and World War II, the Spanish-American War was not mechanized. There were no airplanes, tanks, or trucks, the construction and operation of which consumed huge amounts of raw materials. The biggest hurdle facing war planners in 1898 was the acquisition of coal to power U.S. naval vessels and trains. These ships transported troops and supplies into and out of the combat zones, while the railroads moved soldiers and supplies to and from embarkation points. The timing of the war, which took place from spring to summer, meant that less coal was being utilized for heating and electricity generation. This ensured that there would be adequate supplies for military operations. Unlike future wars, the federal government did not find it necessary to institute rationing or prioritize industrial production during the Spanish-American War.

A Cuban sugar train. Following the Spanish-American War, Cuba received a tariff reduction on sugar and tobacco exports to the United States. The U.S. consumption of Cuban sugar nearly doubled between 1902 and World War I. (Library of Congress)

Although access to raw materials did not become a military issue during the Spanish-American War, it was nevertheless a key motivating factor in U.S. overseas expansion. Although the United States was one of the best-placed states in the world in terms of stocks of key raw materials, many industrialists and expansionists saw increased access to raw materials and markets for manufactured goods as an absolute must for continued industrial and economic expansion. They realized that the continental United States had a finite supply of raw materials, which necessitated the securing of more materials from abroad. Areas from which raw materials could be extracted would also serve as new markets for finished goods produced in the United States. Given the regularity of economic downturns and uneven growth since the 1870s, U.S. expansionists saw the imperative for opening new markets as key to America's continued economic and industrial ascendancy. Furthermore, the biggest economic competitors of the United States, including Great Britain, Germany, and France, had already assembled extracontinental empires in Asia and Africa. To keep up, American industrialists reasoned, the United States would have to follow suit.

Of course, the American acquisition of the Philippines, Guam, Hawaii, and Puerto Rico meant the acquisition of bases for the projection of naval power in far-flung parts of the world. Prior to the shift to oil-fired ships, the existence of reliable coaling stations was critical to the functioning of navies overseas. Coaling stations would, of course, also serve as forward-based naval stations, which would allow the United States to protect its overseas territories and project power more effectively in the Caribbean and in the Far East.

The United States imposed an economic system on the Philippines (and Cuba) that relied principally on the extraction of raw materials and agricultural products in return for American-made finished products. Although the United States did not exercise de jure control over Cuba after the war, it certainly exercised de facto economic control there. Over the long term, this system was terribly damaging to the economies of these dependent areas. It made them entirely reliant upon the United States and prevented the establishment of native industries, which kept much of the population mired in poverty. This economic system became the focal point for U.S. colonial policies that endured well into the 20th century.

In the Philippines, key raw materials to be found and exploited in 1898 were mainly sugar and sugar-based products, coconut, hemp, and semiprecious metals needed for industrial production. A few years later, rubber would be a key raw material produced by the archipelago. In Cuba, sugar was the number one export to the United States, along with some extractive metals.

PAUL G. PIERPAOLI JR.

See also

Coaling Stations; Colonial Policies, U.S.; Cuba; Expansionism; Imperialism; Philippine Islands

Further Reading

Eckes, Alfred E., Jr. *The United States and the Global Struggle for Minerals.* Austin: University of Texas Press, 1979.

Lipschutz, Ronnie D. *When Nations Clash: Raw Materials, Ideology, and Foreign Policy.* New York: HarperCollins, 1989.

Zeiler, Thomas W., and Alfred E. Eckes Jr. *Globalization and the American Century.* New York: Cambridge University Press, 2003.

Rea, George Bronson
Birth Date: August 28, 1869
Death Date: November 21, 1936

Publicist, lobbyist, journalist, and diplomat. George Bronson Rea was born in Brooklyn, New York, on August 28, 1869. He entered the world of journalism in New York City just as the yellow press was at its most prominent. As a reporter for the *New York Herald,* he began reporting on the Cuban War of Independence beginning in 1895. During 1895–1896, he visited Cuba and, unlike many American reporters of the era, personally traveled into the interior of Cuba with rebel forces and was thus able to provide firsthand reports that other journalists could not. In this regard, he was unique.

In 1897, Rea met with General Máximo Gómez and then accompanied his troops on a number of expeditions. During this time, Rea became disillusioned by what he saw as calculated deception on the part of the Cuban rebels, whom he accused of exaggerating their successes and exaggerating or fabricating alleged Spanish atrocities. He was also put off by their brazen public relations campaign in the United States, which inaccurately portrayed rebel actions. This reporting was quite the opposite of most other journalists, who tended to sympathize with their cause and glorify their exploits.

When Rea returned to New York later in 1897, he was determined to counter the generally very favorable reportage of the rebels in the American press, believing that the American public should be aware of their missteps as well as those of the Spanish. In a book titled *Facts and Fakes about Cuba* (1897), he was highly critical of Gómez and revealed many atrocities committed by the rebels themselves. Rea also excoriated much of the American press for its sensationalist and inaccurate reporting on the Cuban situation. He then turned his attention to developments in the Far East beginning in 1899.

After the war, Rea founded the influential journal *Far Eastern Review* in Manila in 1904. In it he wrote a number of articles dealing with the Far East and U.S. policy there. He served as an adviser to Chinese nationalist leader Sun Yat-sen from 1911 to 1913 and as the head of the Chinese National Railway Corporation from 1913 to 1914. During World War I, Rea served in the U.S. Army and was the assistant military attaché to Madrid from 1917 to 1919. He also served as an adviser to China's delegation to the 1919 Paris Peace Conference. In the late 1920s, Rea lobbied in China on behalf of the U.S. Chamber of Commerce. Most controversially, he served as an adviser to the Japanese-established puppet government in Manchuria (renamed Manchukuo) from 1932 to 1936, writing fa-

vorably of the regime and its actions. Among his many books is the controversial *The Case for Manchukuo* (1935). Rea died in Baltimore, Maryland, on November 21, 1936.

PAUL G. PIERPAOLI JR.

See also

Cuban War of Independence; Gómez y Báez, Máximo; Journalism; Newspapers; Yellow Journalism

Further Reading

Bronson, George Rea. *Facts and Fakes about Cuba.* New York: George Munro's Sons, 1897.

Brown, Charles H. *The Correspondents' War: Journalists in the Spanish-American War.* New York: Scribner, 1967.

Campbell, W. Joseph. *Yellow Journalism: Puncturing the Myths, Defining the Legacies.* Westport, CT: Praeger, 2003.

Reconcentrado System

System instituted by Cuban governor-general Valeriano Weyler y Nicolau in February 1896 whereby 500,000 Cubans were rounded up and placed in *reconcentrado* (reconcentration) centers in an attempt to curtail the Cuban War of Independence (1895–1898).

By 1896, the Cuban insurgents, operating in small guerrilla units, were waging war against the island's sugar industry, crippling the Cuban economy. As the level of violence grew unchecked throughout the island, especially in the west, insurrectionists burned sugarcane fields and mills and destroyed railroads, telegraph lines, and other property. The insurgents hoped to destroy the economy by turning the island into an economic wasteland, thereby forcing the Spanish to concede that it was unprofitable and not worthy of further investment.

To check the spike in violence and put down the rebellion once and for all, the Spanish government inserted more troops into Cuba, but elevated force levels produced limited results. The Spanish attempted to hunt down and confront the insurgents in traditional stand-up battles, but the insurgents failed to cooperate and began conducting irregular warfare. The Spanish Army was unable to adapt to these guerrilla techniques, and conservative Spanish premier Antonio Cánovas del Castillo dispatched Weyler to Cuba in January 1896 to bring an end to the conflict.

Weyler, a professional officer who had risen through the ranks of the Spanish military because of performance rather than politics, worried little about public relations. He had served as an attaché to Washington during the American Civil War and became an advocate of the scorched earth tactics employed by Major General William Tecumseh Sherman. Thus, Weyler set out to break the Cuban independence movement and eliminate popular support for the insurgency through a policy of reconcentration. As devised, the program called for removing civilians from their homes and farms and isolating them in highly fortified towns, thereby breaking the resolve of the detainees as well as the rebels, who relied on the civilians for moral as well as material support.

Distribution of food to *reconcentrados,* rural Cubans relocated in camps. Spanish governor-general Valeriano Weyler hoped to separate the civilian population from the insurgency, but the failure to provide adequate food and medical care to those who were relocated further alienated them from the Spanish government and caused outrage in the United States. (John Clark Ridpath, *Ridpath's History of the World,* 1901)

The reconcentration program had a number of objectives. First, herding the villagers into fortified reconcentration centers would eliminate sources of food and other material support for the insurgents. Second, the program would deprive the insurgents of an efficient intelligence network, which had provided them with valuable information regarding Spanish troop movements. Third, relocating the peasants to the camps would protect them from exposure to insurgent propaganda and seriously impede the insurgents' recruitment efforts. Finally, there was also a psychological component to Weyler's system. The insurgents were likely to have friends or relatives among the *reconcentrados,* so the fear that a relative could be targeted for special abuse by the Spanish might intimidate the insurgents and force them to end the violence.

Upon his arrival in February 1896, Weyler issued the first of a series of reconcentration orders. With these official decrees, some 500,000 people were removed from their homes and farms and herded into four fortified camps. As the villagers abandoned their homes, the Spanish troops swooped in to burn villages, raze crops, and kill livestock to eliminate the rebels' food supply. The economic tactics employed by both the Spanish and the Cubans seriously hurt Cuba's economy, as foreign trade plummeted during the conflict.

In accordance with the program, thousands of *reconcentrados* were held in these fortified areas. Set apart, the camps were in most cases surrounded by a high fence, and housing accommo-dations were extremely limited. More often than not, the detainees were jammed into abandoned warehouses, tents, or dilapidated buildings without the benefit of toilet facilities, running water, or food preparation areas. Food and medicine were in very limited supply. Soon, the detainees were suffering from malnutrition, and the deplorable living conditions became a major cause of communicable disease. Unable to live off the land, some internees resorted to begging or foraging through the garbage. Not surprisingly, discontent among the *reconcentrados* was rampant. Many thousands died in the reconcentration centers, and before long news of the misery had begun to spread abroad, much to the chagrin of Madrid.

Indeed, reports of death and destruction made headlines in American newspapers, evoking sympathy among the American public, which increasingly sided with the insurrectionists. By the summer of 1896, the plight of the Cuban detainees had become the favorite fodder for yellow journalism. The U.S. government protested several times over the human rights abuses in Cuba, but the Madrid government dismissed American pleas and refused to change its policies. In October 1897, a more conciliatory government, headed by Premier Práxedes Mateo Sagasta, recalled Weyler and agreed to terminate the reconcentration system. Nevertheless, the insurgents continued to wage war against their occupiers. In the meantime, the American public provided relief supplies to the *reconcentrados,* while the American press continued to provide lurid accounts of Cuban suffering for popular consumption.

By 1898, many in the U.S. Congress were under intense pressure from their constituents to address the Cubans' suffering. In the early winter of 1898, Republican senator Redfield Proctor went to Cuba to investigate conditions in the camps and to determine if the news accounts were accurate. On March 17, 1898, he arose before the Senate and shared the results of his two-week-long visit. He recounted the dreadful plight of the *reconcentrados,* the devastated Cuban economy, and the Spanish-Cuban conflict in general. He condemned Spanish misrule and contended that the Cubans were capable of self-government. His authoritative voice resonated with conservative business interests and the religious press, galvanizing these groups in a call for intervention on the basis of human rights abuses. Proctor's report on the *reconcentrados,* combined with the explosion of the *Maine* (February 15, 1898), the publication of the Dupuy de Lôme–Canalejas Letter, and other contentious issues, finally pushed the William McKinley administration into war in April 1898.

The reconcentration system was clearly a dismal failure for Madrid. Rather than ending the conflict, the system only widened it. The reconcentration policy made a bad economic situation far worse and engendered the intense disapproval of the international community, especially the United States, which was already biased against Spanish rule in Cuba. In the longer term, the Spanish policy of reconcentration informed the British concentration camps of the South African Boer War and the U.S. Strategic Hamlet program during the Vietnam War.

JEFFERY B. COOK

See also

Cuban War of Independence; Proctor, Redfield; Weyler y Nicolau, Valeriano; Yellow Journalism

Further Reading

Gould, Lewis L. *The Spanish-American War and President McKinley.* Lawrence: University Press of Kansas, 1982.
O'Toole, G. J. A. *The Spanish War: An American Epic, 1898.* New York: Norton, 1984.
Trask, David F. *The War with Spain in 1898.* Lincoln: University of Nebraska Press, 1996.

Red Cross

See American National Red Cross

Reed, Thomas Brackett

Birth Date: October 18, 1839
Death Date: December 7, 1902

Republican politician, U.S. congressman (1877–1899), and Speaker of the House of Representatives (1889–1891, 1895–1899). Born on

Congressman Thomas Brackett Reed was Speaker of the House of Representatives during 1889–1891 and 1895–1899 and an opponent of war with Spain. (Library of Congress)

October 18, 1839, in Portland, Maine, Thomas Brackett Reed attended local public secondary schools and graduated with a BA degree from Bowdoin College in 1860. He read for the law and was admitted to the Maine State Bar in 1865.

Reed began the practice of law in Portland and served in the Maine House of Representatives during 1868–1869. In 1870, he held a seat in the Maine State Senate. He left his seat to become Maine's attorney general from 1870 to 1872. In 1876, he was elected to the U.S. House of Representatives; he would be elected 11 subsequent times.

After enjoying more than a decade of influential service in Congress, Reed decided to pursue the post of Speaker of the House, perhaps the most powerful position in Washington next to the presidency. In 1889, he engaged in a hard-fought battle against U.S. representative William McKinley for the coveted speakership. Reed's chances of victory were given a boost when Theodore Roosevelt, then a young civil service commissioner, threw his support behind Reed. He served as Speaker until 1891 and became a close personal friend and political ally of Roosevelt.

Reed was renowned for his bluntness and biting wit. When asked if he might become a presidential candidate, he retorted, "They could do worse, and probably will." And when a reporter asked if he planned to attend the funeral of a political adversary, he shot back, "No, but I certainly approve of it." Reed moved quickly to consolidate his power as Speaker and headed the Rules Committee himself, virtually guaranteeing that he would control the functions and legislative agenda of the House.

During his second tenure as Speaker, which began in 1895, Reed aggregated unparalleled power and concocted parliamentary rules designed to favor the Republicans and marginalize the Democrats, who were then in the minority. His heavy-handedness became so legendary that he was sometimes called "Czar Reed," while his parliamentary sleights of hand were known as "Reed's Rules." He stymied the Democrats' attempts to by-pass House rules by refusing to answer to a roll call, which often meant that a quorum was not possible. With no quorum, no votes could take place. Instead, Reed began taking a head count at the beginning of a session. If Democrats did not answer a roll call before a vote, he would simply add the names of the absentee legislators to the call, which would result in the necessary quorum. Reed, working closely with Representative Joseph "Uncle Joe" Cannon, who would succeed him as Speaker, managed to revamp and streamline House rules but often to the detriment of the minority.

In 1896, Reed campaigned for the Republican presidential nomination but lost to McKinley. During the 1890s, Reed had an interesting coterie of friends, including expansionists such as Senator Henry Cabot Lodge, John Hay, and Theodore Roosevelt and anti-imperialists such as Mark Twain. Reed was quite influential in the run-up to the Spanish-American War and helped McKinley try to avoid the conflict, which Reed did not support. He remained somewhat on the sidelines during the war and its immediate aftermath because of his position.

Reed stepped down as Speaker and gave up his seat in the House in 1899, returning to the practice of law in New York City. He died of a heart attack on December 7, 1902, in Washington, D.C.

PAUL G. PIERPAOLI JR.

See also

Cannon, Joseph Gurney; Expansionism; Hay, John Milton; Lodge, Henry Cabot; McKinley, William; Roosevelt, Theodore; Twain, Mark

Further Reading

Offenberg, Richard Stanley. "The Political Career of Thomas Brackett Reed." PhD dissertation, New York University, 1963.
Strahan, Randall. "Thomas Brackett Reed and the Rise of Party Government." In *Masters of the House: Congressional Leadership over Two Centuries,* edited by Raymond W. Smock and Susan W. Hammond, 33–62. Boulder, CO: Westview, 1998.

Reed, Walter
Birth Date: September 13, 1851
Death Date: November 23, 1902

U.S. Army doctor who led a team of physicians that proved that yellow fever is transmitted by mosquitoes rather than through direct contact with victims or their personal effects. Walter Reed was born

U.S. Army doctor Walter Reed occupies an honored place in scientific history for his work in ending the scourge of yellow fever. (Library of Congress)

on September 13, 1851, in Belroi, Virginia. His father, a Methodist minister, encouraged him to enroll at the University of Virginia, where he earned an MD degree in 1869. At the time, he was the youngest person to earn such a degree at the university. He earned a second medical degree from Bellevue Hospital Medical College in 1870. On June 26, 1875, he was appointed as an assistant surgeon in the U.S. Army Medical Corps with the rank of first lieutenant. His first assignment was Fort Lowell, Arizona. In 1880, after serving at various posts in the West, he was promoted to captain and transferred to Ft. McHenry, Maryland. During the early 1880s, he attended lectures at Johns Hopkins University in Baltimore. He also studied bacteriology and pathology under the guidance of William Henry Welch, the foremost bacteriologist in the United States. In 1893, after being promoted to major, Reed was appointed professor of bacteriology at the U.S. Army Medical School. He also taught at George Washington University.

Alarmed by the number of U.S. deaths caused by yellow fever during the Spanish-American War, in May 1900 the U.S. Army appointed Reed to head the Yellow Fever Board in Cuba. Reed and his team, which included James Carroll in charge of bacteriology, Jesse Lazear in charge of experimental mosquitoes, and Aristides Agramonte in charge of pathology, arrived in Havana on June 25, 1900. Volunteers were infected with yellow fever, which allowed Reed to prove the hypothesis that mosquitoes caused the disease. He made his conclusions by October of that year. His tests were based on a theory first postulated by Cuban physician Carlos Juan Finlay in 1881 that identified mosquitoes as the carriers of yellow fever. Until Reed had verified Finlay's hypothesis, it had been commonly held that yellow fever was contracted by contact with clothing and bedding soiled by the excrement and body fluids of yellow fever victims. Reed also conducted experiments to determine if survivors were immune to the disease from subsequent mosquito bites. These generated a great deal of controversy when nurse Clara Maass died of yellow fever on August 24, 1901.

As a result of Reed's efforts, Colonel William Crawford Gorgas, the U.S. Army's chief sanitary officer in Cuba, was able to virtually eliminate yellow fever from Cuba by destroying the mosquitoes' breeding grounds. In 1901, Reed returned to Washington, D.C., to resume his duties at the U.S. Army Medical School and George Washington University. Following an appendectomy, he died of peritonitis on November 23, 1902.

Reed's pioneering research stymied the mortality rates caused by yellow fever and facilitated the construction of the Panama Canal from 1904 to 1914. Although there is still no cure for the disease, a vaccine to protect against yellow fever was eventually developed in 1937. Opened in 1909, the Walter Reed General Hospital (Walter Reed Army Medical Center) in Washington, D.C., is named in his honor.

MICHAEL R. HALL

See also

Cuba, U.S. Occupation of; Gorgas, William Crawford; Maass, Clara Louise; Medicine, Military; Yellow Fever

Further Reading

Bean, William. *Walter Reed: A Biography.* Charlottesville: University of Virginia Press, 1982.

Pierce, John R., and James V. Writer. *Yellow Jack: How Yellow Fever Ravaged America and Walter Reed Discovered Its Deadly Secrets.* New York: Wiley, 2005.

Reed Commission

See Yellow Fever Board

Reid, Whitelaw

Birth Date: October 27, 1837
Death Date: December 15, 1912

Businessman, journalist, diplomat, and one of the most influential newspaper publishers of his time. Under Whitelaw Reid's control, the New York *Tribune* grew to have the largest circulation of any newspaper in the United States. Born on October 27, 1837, near

Influential American journalist Whitelaw Reid served as one of the U.S. peace commissioners to negotiate an end to the Spanish-American War and was later U.S. ambassador to Great Britain. (Chaiba Media)

Xenia, Ohio, Reid attended Miami University of Ohio, graduating in 1856 and distinguishing himself especially in foreign languages and writing. While still in school, he had a number of articles published in newspapers as far away as Kansas.

From 1856 to 1858, Reid served as principal of a grade school in South Charleston, Ohio. Finding that work unsatisfactory, he returned to Xenia and purchased *The News,* one of two local newspapers. Politics provided most of the paper's content, and Reid soon became an ardent supporter of the Republican Party. He supported Abraham Lincoln as the best candidate for the party in the 1860 presidential election. At the 1860 Republican National Convention, Reid persuaded the Ohio delegation to rally to Lincoln, although they were already pledged to Salmon P. Chase.

Ill health and a lack of profits forced Reid to sell *The News* and to begin working for the *Cincinnati Gazette.* His skill at covering political events was quickly recognized, and he was soon made city editor. The outbreak of the American Civil War in 1861 provided him with greater opportunities. Traveling with the Union Army as a war correspondent, he quickly proved to be a discriminating observer of military affairs. He criticized the slowness of commanders and the unpreparedness of the soldiers for combat. His journalistic descriptions of the fighting at the Battle of Shiloh (April 6–7, 1862) and the Battle of Gettysburg (July 1–3, 1863) were hailed as masterpieces of comprehensiveness and clarity.

Reid was eventually banned from accompanying the army because of what was regarded as negative reporting. Prevented from taking the field, he was active in Washington, D.C., and became acquainted with Republican leaders. In 1864, he opposed Lincoln's reelection, believing him unequal to the task. Reid's connections secured him positions as librarian of the House of Representatives from 1863 to 1866 and clerk of the Military Committee. He was one of three newspapermen who visited Richmond immediately after its 1865 fall. His descriptions of that event and Lincoln's funeral crowned his wartime reporting.

Immediately after the war, Reid undertook an extended journey through the South with Supreme Court chief justice Chase. Reid returned to the North and to writing, composing the two-volume *Ohio in the War* (1868), which covered both civil and military activities. That work remains valuable today. In the autumn of 1868, he joined the New York *Tribune* and worked as an assistant to Horace Greeley, who became a close friend. Reid was largely responsible for the *Tribune*'s outstanding coverage of the Franco-Prussian War (1870–1871) along with encouraging such writers as Mark Twain and Bret Harte to submit works to the paper.

By 1872, both Reid and Greeley no longer supported President Ulysses S. Grant, and Reid encouraged his boss to run for president on the Liberal Republican ticket. Reid worked to ensure Greeley's nomination and election, but Greeley lost in a landslide. The defeat crushed Greeley, who died soon after the election. In a series of Machiavellian moves, Reid formed an alliance with businessman Jay Gould and obtained control over the *Tribune* from Greeley's heirs. Although Reid never had the flair of Greeley, he expanded the paper's circulation and instituted a number of innovations. He used the linotype machine, which was perfected at the newspaper, to set text, and he initiated the first Sunday edition in 1879. He hired only the best reporters and supported the development of wire services for distant stories. He certainly set the pace and standard of newspaper reporting for the remainder of the century and was the forerunner to publishers such as Joseph Pulitzer and William Randolph Hearst.

Reid publicly declared the *Tribune* to be a Republican paper and refused to support a Democrat for president. He did help elect reformer and Democrat Samuel J. Tilden to the governorship of New York in 1874 but supported Republican Rutherford B. Hayes in 1876 for president. When charges of bribery and fraud were leveled in the disputed election of 1876, Reid published articles declaring that Hayes had won fairly. Reid was delighted when fellow Ohioan James Garfield was elected president in 1880. Garfield relied heavily on Reid's advice regarding political appointments, and his assassination after only a few months in office devastated Reid.

Failing health and other interests led Reid to leave most of the daily operations of the paper in the hands of others. He accepted an appointment as U.S. minister to France from President Benjamin Harrison in 1889 and served until 1892, during which time he helped to negotiate a treaty that improved commercial ties between the two nations. When Harrison ran for reelection in 1892, Vice President Levi P. Morton was passed over. Instead, Reid was selected as a compromise candidate. The campaign was listless, however, and Harrison and Reid went down to defeat.

Reid then returned to his newspaper work. President William McKinley turned down Reid's request that he be appointed minister to Great Britain but did appoint Reid to be one of five peace commissioners to negotiate an end to the Spanish-American War in 1898, which resulted in the Treaty of Paris in December 1898. Following McKinley's 1901 assassination, Reid was finally named minister to Great Britain by President Theodore Roosevelt in 1905. Reid remained in that post until his death in London on December 15, 1912.

TIM J. WATTS

See also
Hearst, William Randolph; Journalism; Paris, Treaty of; Peace Commission; Pulitzer, Joseph; Yellow Journalism

Further Reading
Cortissoz, Royal. *The Life of Whitelaw Reid.* New York: Scribner, 1921.
Duncan, Bingham. *Whitelaw Reid: Journalist, Politician, Diplomat.* Athens: University of Georgia Press, 1975.
Morgan, H. Wayne. *Making Peace with Spain: The Diary of Whitelaw Reid, September–December 1898.* Austin: University of Texas Press, 1965.

"Remember the *Maine*"

A jingoist expression used by American journalists and members of the general public for the pretext for going to war with Spain in April 1898. After a mysterious explosion sank the U.S. second-class battleship *Maine* in Havana Harbor on February 15, 1898, hawkish Americans who were already inclined to go to war with Spain over the situation in Cuba began to use the slogan "Remember the *Maine*, to hell with Spain" as a patriotic rallying cry to increase pressure on President William McKinley to declare war on Spain.

President McKinley had ordered the *Maine* to Cuba to protect American interests and pressure Spanish authorities. The massive explosion that sank the *Maine* resulted in the deaths of 266 sailors. Although the U.S. Naval Court of Inquiry waited until March 28, 1898, to assert that an external mine had caused the explosion, American newspapers, lacking any concrete evidence, immediately reported that the explosion was the result of Spanish treachery.

Joseph Pulitzer's *New York World* and William Randolph Hearst's *New York Journal,* already in fierce competition for readers, exploited the sinking of the *Maine* to boost newspaper sales. The *New York Journal* carried the sensationalistic headline: "The War Ship *Maine* Was Split in Two by an Enemy's Secret Infernal Machine." Below the headline, a drawing of the *Maine* floating in the harbor on top of mines with wires leading to a Spanish fort further enraged American readers. Given its desire to avoid war with the

United States, the Spanish government had no logical reason to sink the *Maine.* Nevertheless, within days of the explosion, Americans across the country, fueled by the persuasiveness of yellow journalism, demanded that McKinley force the Spanish government to relinquish control of Cuba.

The popular phrase, modeled after the equally popular "Remember the Alamo," which had encouraged the people of Texas to support the revolution against Mexico in 1836, served as a powerful catalyst for the Spanish-American War. "Remember the *Maine*" helped shape American public opinion and gave McKinley the support he needed for a declaration of war against Spain in April 1898. Indeed, the rallying cry helped convince many Americans that the war against Spain was a justifiable defense of American national honor.

MICHAEL R. HALL

See also

Artists and Illustrators; Hearst, William Randolph; Journalism; *Maine, USS; Maine, USS*, Inquiries into the Loss of; McKinley, William; Pulitzer, Joseph; Yellow Journalism

Further Reading

Blow, Michael. *A Ship to Remember: The Maine and the Spanish-American War.* New York: Morrow, 1992.
Edgerton, Robert B. *Remember the Maine, to Hell with Spain: America's 1898 Adventure in Imperialism.* Lewiston, NY: Edwin Mellen, 2004.

Remey, George Collier
Birth Date: August 10, 1841
Death Date: February 8, 1928

U.S. naval officer. Born in Burlington, Iowa, on August 10, 1841, George Collier Remey was accepted into the United States Naval Academy, Annapolis, in 1855 and graduated in 1859, the youngest midshipman in his class. Prior to the American Civil War (1861–1865), he served aboard the screw sloop *Hartford,* which saw service in the waters off China and then Japan. During the 1862 Peninsula Campaign, he served in the screw gunboat *Marblehead,* which plied the coastal waters of Virginia. In the spring of 1863, he served as the executive officer of the screw sloop *Canandaigua* and commanded the *Marblehead* during the Union assault on Fort Wagner. On September 7–8, 1863, he participated in the abortive attack on Fort Sumter in Charleston Harbor. Taken prisoner by the Confederates, he was imprisoned in Columbia, South Carolina, for 13 months until he was released during a prisoner exchange. Upon his release, he served as executive officer of the side-wheeler *De Soto,* based at Baltimore, Maryland, until the end of the war in April 1865.

Following the war, Remey served in a variety of assignments, including duty off the coast of Valparaiso, Chile, during the U.S. shelling of that city in 1866 and in the Mediterranean in 1882. Promoted to captain in 1885, he commanded the cruiser *Charleston* in the U.S. Pacific Squadron during 1889–1892. He then commanded

the Portsmouth Navy Yard and, when the Spanish-American War broke out in April 1898, was assigned to command the naval base at Key West, Florida, the U.S. Navy's most important Atlantic base during the war. He was responsible not only for the resupply and repair of naval assets in the blockade of Cuba but also for the convoying of Major General William R. Shafter's V Corps to Cuba. With the end of the war in August 1898, Remey was transferred back to the Portsmouth Navy Yard. He was promoted to rear admiral in November 1898.

In April 1900, Remey took command of the U.S. Asiatic Squadron. He was responsible for providing support for U.S. ground troops fighting the Filipino insurgents during the Philippine-American War (1899–1902). He also played a key role during the Boxer Rebellion (1899–1901), coordinating all U.S. naval operations off the coast of China from his flagship, the cruiser *Brooklyn,* during July–October 1900. Following a tour to Australia, he returned to the United States, where he served for a year as chairman of the Lighthouse Board. He retired from the navy on August 10, 1903, and lived for a time in Newport, Rhode Island, before moving to Washington, D.C. Remey died in Burlington, Iowa, on February 8, 1928.

PAUL G. PIERPAOLI JR.

See also

Boxer Rebellion; V Corps; Key West, Florida; United States Navy

Further Reading

Chadwick, French Ensor. *The Relations of the United States and Spain V1: The Spanish-American War.* Reprint ed. Kila, MT: Kessinger, 2007.
Trask, David F. *The War with Spain in 1898.* Lincoln: University of Nebraska Press, 1996.

Remington, Frederic Sackrider
Birth Date: October 4, 1861
Death Date: December 26, 1909

Painter, illustrator, and sculptor whose images of the Old West shaped American perceptions of the vanishing frontier. Frederic Sackrider Remington was born in Canton, New York, on October 4, 1861. His parents were Seth Pierrepont Remington, a newspaper editor and publisher, and Clara Sackrider. Remington's father served as a lieutenant colonel in the American Civil War for four years, which later influenced his son's art themes of war and conflict on horseback. The younger Remington attended Highland Military Academy in Worcester, Massachusetts, for two years. In 1878, he enrolled at Yale University, studying at the new school of art and architecture. His new passion was football, and he was a starting forward on the varsity team, captained by the founder of American football, Walter Camp. His first published illustration was a cartoon of an injured football player in the *Yale Courant.* Despite his mother's disapproval, he left Yale after only two years when his father died in 1880.

Frederic Remington, a painter, an illustrator, and a sculptor who is best known for his images of the Old West. During the Spanish-American War, Remington was a correspondent and illustrator for the *New York Journal*. (Library of Congress)

Remington worked as a clerk in the office of the governor of New York and other state offices in 1880 but was dissatisfied with the work. In 1881, he was further disappointed when his marriage proposal to Eva Adele Caten was rejected by her father due to Remington's unpromising economic situation. Dejected, Remington decided to experience the American West. His travels to Montana and Wyoming resulted in his first illustration of the frontier, a Wyoming cowboy published by *Harper's Weekly* in February 1882. He returned to the West and bought land in Kansas in 1883 after receiving a modest inheritance from his father the year before. His attempt at sheep farming was not successful, however, and he sold the ranch, returning to friends and family in New York a year later.

Caten's father finally consented to her marriage in 1884, and Remington and his new wife moved to Kansas City, Missouri. He used the remainder of his inheritance to invest in a saloon. The venture was successful, but Remington eventually lost his share due to unscrupulous partners. Eva returned to New York within the year, as Remington could not find steady work. They never had children. He spent the next year traveling through the American Southwest,

working as a cowboy and scout and sketching Native Americans. He returned to New York in 1885, and he and Eva moved to Brooklyn, where Remington began to sell his illustrations of the West to major magazines. His big break came in 1886 when his illustration *The Apache War: Indian Scouts on Geronimo's Trail* became the cover of *Harper's Weekly*.

Remington wanted to develop his talent as an artist and enrolled in classes at the Art Student League, where he worked with watercolors. His exhibition in the National Academy of Design and American Water-Color Society brought him the attention of Theodore Roosevelt, who asked him to illustrate an article he was writing about ranching and hunting in the West. From this initial contact, the two men started a lifelong friendship. Remington spent each summer in the West and in Canada under publisher sponsorship, sketching and photographing scenes for later illustrations as well as collecting Native American and frontier artifacts. In 1888 and 1890, he documented the wars against the Apache and Plains Indians. The demand for magazine illustrations was constant, as new magazine publications had grown from about 700 in 1865 to 3,000 in 1885. Remington published more than 2,700 illustrations in 41 journals. He also illustrated more than 140 books, including Henry Wadsworth Longfellow's *The Song of Hiawatha,* Francis Parkman's *The Oregon Trail,* and Elizabeth B. Custer's *Tenting in the Plains.*

In the late 1880s, Remington began to develop an oil painting career, filling more than 700 canvases with scenes of horses, Indians, and cowboys. He exhibited *A Dash for Timber* at the annual National Academy of Design show. His *Last Lull in the Fight* won a silver medal at the Paris Universal Exposition in 1889. *Harper's Weekly* and William Randolph Hearst's *New York Journal* sent Remington to Cuba to cover the Spanish-American War. His painting *Charge of the Rough Riders at San Juan Hill* helped to foster an image of Roosevelt as soldier hero, which was to become a crucial element in Roosevelt's election as president of the United States.

Remington's first sculpture in 1895 was *The Bronco Buster,* which the Rough Riders later gave to Roosevelt when they returned from Cuba. Remington produced 25 bronze sculptures, all but one emphasizing a western theme.

During his lifetime, Remington was a highly prolific and successful artist. His illustrations have been praised for the authenticity of Native American costumes, soldiers' uniforms, and accurate horse anatomy in all poses. His later paintings were more romantic and captured the disappearing spirit of the Western frontier. Remington said that he knew "the wild riders and the vacant land were about to vanish forever. . . . Without knowing exactly how to do it, I began to record some facts around me and the more I looked the more the panorama unfolded."

Remington was only 48 years old when he died at his home in New Rochelle, New York, on December 26, 1909, due to complications from an appendix surgery.

JOSE VALENTE

See also

Hearst, William Randolph; Yellow Journalism

Further Reading

Nemerov, Alexander. *Frederic Remington and Turn-of-the-Century America.* New Haven, CT: Yale University Press, 1995.

Samuels, Peggy, and Harold Samuels. *Frederic Remington.* Austin: University of Texas Press, 1985.

Republican Party

One of the two predominant U.S. political parties in the United States during the Spanish-American War. Founded in 1854, the Republican Party was a by-product of the building sectionalism over the issue of slavery in the United States. The particular catalyst for the party's creation was the divisive Kansas-Nebraska Act of 1854, which opened the door to slavery in the Kansas and Nebraska territories. Those who founded the Republican Party were adamantly opposed to not only the expansion of slavery into new territories but also any policies that would strengthen the position of slaveholders, whom they feared had too much power. Most Republicans at this point were not true abolitionists; rather, they were against the expansion of slavery beyond where it had already taken root. A good number of adherents to the new party were from the Whig political tradition, and a sizable number of Democrats from the northern states left that party to join the Republicans. There was also an important contingent of Free-Soilers in the party.

Republicans extolled honesty in government and opposed entrenched interests, be they economic, political, or both. They advocated a return to the civic virtue of the founding fathers, which, according to them, was more concerned with the good of the nation than narrow self-interest. Quite progressively minded, the Republican Party advocated better and more accessible higher education, the expansion of the railroads and industry, and a more stable centralized banking system. Unlike the Democrats, Republicans in this era were not against using the power of the government to bring about these changes.

The fateful election of 1860, which led to Abraham Lincoln becoming president, set in motion an era of Republican dominance in the Northeast and Midwest and, of course, sparked the American Civil War. By war's end in 1865, the Republican Party had become known as the party of Lincoln and the party of abolition. Between 1860 and 1890, the Republican Party dominated national politics, especially in the executive branch. In the aftermath of the war, Republicans used their clout to push through myriad congressional acts designed to promote rapid industrialization, create a national banking system, raise taxes via excise and tariff duties, form land grants for colleges and universities, and dole out subsidies to both railroad and agricultural interests in the West. The party also attached itself to protectionism, which meant high tariffs on imported (and especially industrial) goods. Not surprisingly, the Republicans' activist policies resulted in mounting federal budgets.

During Reconstruction (1865–1876), Republicans initially sought to establish a political base in the South among newly freed African American slaves. Toward that end, they pushed through the 14th Amendment, which sought to ensure civil rights to African Americans against state governments, and the 15th Amendment, which guaranteed that the right to vote could not be denied on the basis of race. As southern states were readmitted into the union, however, the Democratic Party regained its dominance in the South and won control of the House of Representatives in the congressional elections of 1874. In the so-called Compromise of 1877, designed to secure the election of Republican candidate Rutherford B. Hayes after the disputed presidential election of 1876, Republicans agreed to withdraw remaining federal troops from the South, effectively ending Reconstruction and abandoning African Americans.

As the American economy grew by leaps and bounds in the 1870s and 1880s, particularly in the Northeast and Midwest, the Republicans' agenda solidified the party's grip on the most populous areas of the nation. By 1890, the Republican Party appealed to big businessmen, small business owners, bankers, midwestern farmers, and the like. It had essentially become the party of business. Also in that decade, the Republicans had become ardent adherents of the gold standard and vehemently opposed the bimetal or free silver schemes of the Democrats and Populists.

Despite the strength of the Republican Party in the decades just prior to the Spanish-American War, Congress remained remarkably and almost evenly split between Democrats and Republicans. During this time, the Democrats benefited from mass immigration, as they tended to appeal to newly arrived immigrants. Indeed, the Democrats shrewdly played off of the Republicans' attraction to business interests by proclaiming that they were for the average worker. The year 1894 was a turning point for the Republicans, as they swept the off-year elections, giving them an impressive mandate in Congress. Economic depression beginning in 1893 further tainted the Democrats, and in 1896 the Republican Party took control of Congress as well as the executive branch with the election of William McKinley. This ushered in an era of remarkable Republican dominance at the national level, which would last practically uninterrupted until 1932.

McKinley was swept into office by promising economic prosperity, industrial growth, protective tariffs, the continuation of the gold standard, and a pluralist agenda that he claimed would benefit all sectors of the American public. He also had a less well-known expansionist agenda that would fully manifest itself in the Spanish-American War. There were, of course, inklings of the Republicans' imperialist proclivities before 1898. In 1894, Democratic president Grover Cleveland had refused to consider the annexation of Hawaii and actually attempted to restore Queen Liliuokalani to the Hawaiian throne. In 1897, however, after McKinley had taken office, he actively pursued the annexation of the islands, which became a reality in 1898.

Generally speaking, the Republican Party supported the annexation of Hawaii, Guam, the Philippines, and Puerto Rico. Republicans saw this as part of a larger plan to make the United States a world power and to expand markets for American-made goods. While there were certainly a fair number of Republican anti-imperialists, the principal roadblock to overseas expansion remained the Democratic Party, which saw expansionism as another way to increase the size and scope of the federal government. The Progressive era (ca. 1900–1920) was often dominated by the progressive agenda of the Republican Party and received its greatest boost under President Theodore Roosevelt, McKinley's successor.

PAUL G. PIERPAOLI JR.

See also

Anti-Imperialist League; Bryan, William Jennings; Cleveland, Stephen Grover; Democratic Party; Economic Depression; Expansionism; Hawaiian Islands; Imperialism; McKinley, William; Populist Party; Roosevelt, Theodore; Silver Standard

Further Reading

Foner, Eric. *Free Soil, Free Labor, Free Men: The Ideology of the Republican Party before the Civil War.* London: Oxford University Press, 1977.

Mayer, George Hillman. *The Republican Party, 1854–1966.* 2nd ed. New York: Oxford University Press USA, 1967.

Sundquist, James. *Dynamics of the Party System: Alignment and Realignment of Political Parties in the United States.* Washington, DC: Brookings Institution, 1973.

Rifles

A shoulder-fired weapon that remains the infantryman's basic weapon for self-defense, position defense, or general security duties. An examination of the prominent rifles used in the Spanish-American War and the Philippine-American War provides an excellent look at one of the most significant periods in military small-arms development: the transition from black powder to smokeless powder cartridges. Smokeless powder, developed in France in 1884, was a technological breakthrough. More powerful than the old coarse black powder, it also left less fouling residue. Smokeless powder had important tactical benefits as well. Black powder emitted thick smoke after each discharge, limiting concealment by marking the shooter's location. At the same time, the smoke served to limit the shooter's vision by obscuring the target. The discharge from smokeless powder, though not completely invisible, allowed riflemen to fire from concealed positions with considerably greater security and accuracy.

In 1898, most of the small arms in the United States' arsenal still used black powder. Although military officials had sought a reliable repeating rifle design since the 1870s, the standard U.S. Army issue weapon until the early 1890s was the single-shot Springfield Trapdoor rifle. The Springfield closely resembled the muzzle-loading rifled muskets of the American Civil War (1861–1865) because they were in fact initially converted from the massive surplus of these weapons left from that conflict. With a portion of the breech of the barrel cut away and with a loading gate (the trapdoor) attached to the weapon, soldiers could load a cartridge quickly and easily rather than ram the powder and a bullet down the muzzle.

With this conversion, the U.S. military successfully turned the outdated muzzle loaders into a faster firing and acceptable weapon. The Springfield was, however, long and heavy. It measured more than 4 feet in length and weighed more than eight pounds. The gun's caliber, or bullet diameter, was reduced from the original .58 (of an inch) to .45. Army officials were happy enough with this design to order newly manufactured trapdoor rifles in the 1870s and 1880s. The last Springfield model, modified in 1889, was praised by many American officers as dependable and accurate.

By the 1890s, however, some military officials warned that the U.S. Army needed an improved standard-issue weapon. In 1892, the army adopted its first smokeless powder rifle, the Krag-Jørgensen (usually known as a Krag). A Danish design, the Krag was a bolt-action weapon that could hold five .30-caliber rounds, which were individually loaded through a gate on the right side of the receiver. The Krag was a few inches shorter than the Springfield but still weighed more than 8 pounds. Shortened versions, known as carbines, were also developed, but these were generally issued to cavalrymen.

Although the Krag was an improvement over most previous American infantry rifles, many officers initially failed to appreciate the new rifle's advantages over the Springfield. Army doctrine emphasized accuracy over individual volume of fire, and some officers continued to believe that single-shot breechloaders did not place soldiers at a disadvantage. In fact, soldiers were initially expected to use the Krag as a single-shot weapon, reloading a cartridge after each shot and keeping the four remaining rounds in reserve. Furthermore, the Springfield fired a larger and heavier bullet, which some argued would be more effective in combat. On the other hand, smokeless cartridges were lighter in weight, meaning that a soldier could carry more Krag cartridges than the heavier and bulkier Springfield rounds.

Despite differing opinions about the weapons, supply issues primarily determined what American soldiers carried into battle. By 1898, the army had only enough Krags for the regular army soldiers but not the thousands of volunteers who enlisted for the conflict. Ammunition problems also plagued the army, and a shortage of smokeless cartridges limited the Krag's use even further. Thus, nearly all volunteer soldiers carried Springfield Trapdoor rifles into combat.

On the other side in the conflict, many Spanish soldiers in Cuba were armed with one of the best military weapons available: the 1893 Spanish Mauser bolt-action rifle. Based on the innovative designs of Germans Peter Paul and Wilhelm Mauser, the Spanish rifle held five 7-millimeter (approximately .28-caliber) smokeless powder cartridges intermittently stacked inside the receiver. The rifle had a smooth, sleek appearance. The length and weight of the Spanish Mauser was comparable to the Krag. A significant difference between the two rifles, though, was the reloading process. Spanish soldiers could load their rifles quickly by pressing five cartridges previously stacked in a thin metal clip down through the open bolt, rather than inserting each round one at a time as with the Krag.

U.S. Army recruits on the rifle range at Camp Townsend, New York, 1898. (*Photographic History of the Spanish-American War*, 1898)

Thus, Spanish soldiers could maintain a higher rate of fire than their American counterparts. American officers and soldiers did not appreciate the value of the clip-loading system until they actually faced persistent fire from Spanish troops in the field.

Spanish forces also fielded a single-shot black powder breechloader, the Remington Rolling Block. To load the rifle, the hammer was placed at half-cock and the breechblock rolled back to allow a cartridge to be placed in the gun. The breech piece was closed, and the rifle was ready to fire. Rolling Block rifles were sturdy and dependable but comparatively slow to load. The rifle was popular with big-game hunters in the American West. The Spanish Army also approved the design and bought, then later manufactured, tens of thousands of the rifles for use in Cuba. As with the Springfield Trapdoor, the Spanish Rolling Block rifle fired a much heavier bullet than the Krag or the Mauser.

Cuban revolutionary soldiers did not have access to standard weapons and had to rely on rifles that could be found, brought in by gun smugglers, or captured from Spanish soldiers. Thus, a variety of military and civilian long arms found their way onto the battlefield, including Spencer lever-action rifles (a successful military firearm dating back to the American Civil War), Springfield Trapdoor rifles, and even shotguns. In the Philippines, nationalist soldiers and Moro fighters also used whatever weapons could be taken or procured.

Combat experience in Cuba and the Philippines proved the effectiveness and necessity of smokeless powder rifles that could operate smoothly and reliably and, perhaps most importantly, reload quickly. As a result of lessons learned in the conflict, the U.S. Army discarded the Springfield and designed a new rifle based on the Mauser—the 1903 Springfield—to replace the Krag. An excellent weapon, the Springfield saw service into World War II.

IAN M. SPURGEON

See also
"Civilize 'em with a Krag"; Machine Guns

Further Reading

Brinkerhoff, Sidney B., and Pierce Chamberlin. "The Army's Search for a Repeating Rifle: 1873–1903." *Military Affairs* 32(1) (Spring 1968): 10–20.

Cosmas, Graham A. *An Army for Empire: The United States Army in the Spanish-American War.* College Station: Texas A&M University Press, 1994.

Markham, George. *Guns of the Wild West: Firearms of the American Frontier, 1849–1917.* London: Arms and Armour, 1993.

Millis, Walter. *Arms and Men: A Study in American Military History.* New York: Putnam, 1956.

Roosevelt, Theodore. *The Rough Riders, an Autobiography.* New York: Library of America, 2004.

Rivera, Luis Muñoz
Birth Date: July 17, 1859
Death Date: November 15, 1916

Puerto Rican politician, journalist, and poet who very briefly headed the Puerto Rican Autonomous Government in 1898 prior to the U.S. invasion in July 1898. Luis Muñoz Rivera was born on July

17, 1859, in Barranquitas, Puerto Rico, to a prominent family. His father had twice been the mayor of Barranquitas, while his grandfather, a captain in the Spanish Army, had been a politician in Puerto Rico. Rivera attended both public and private schools and also worked in his father's commercial ventures. He became interested in politics and sought to ameliorate the plight of Puerto Ricans under Spanish colonial rule. He also exhibited a flare for and keen interest in journalism, believing that he could best advance his agenda by influencing the press. Accordingly, he founded the newspaper *La Democracia* in Ponce in 1890.

In 1887, Rivera helped found the Autonomist Party, which sought political autonomy from the Spanish. He essentially headed the movement. The Autonomist Party under Rivera did not, however, agitate for complete independence; rather, Rivera sought to reach accommodation and accord with Madrid so that the Spanish would reward the island nation by granting it more power over its own affairs. Toward that end, he journeyed to Spain in 1893 to observe the Spanish political system and to learn about its workings. He also managed to meet with key Spanish officials and politicians, which would serve him well in the future. In 1894, he helped draft the Plan de Ponce (Ponce Plan), a blueprint that laid out plans for Puerto Rican political autonomy.

In 1895, Rivera returned to Spain with a group of Puerto Rican politicians to gain Spanish acceptance of the Ponce Plan. Meeting with high-level officials, including prime minister and Liberal politician Práxedes Mateo Sagasta, the Puerto Rican contingent impressed the Madrid government, and two years later, in November 1897, Sagasta authorized the Autonomist Party's charter. Before the year was out, Rivera had been named head and secretary of state of the new autonomous Puerto Rican government. He went on to serve in this capacity until the U.S. invasion of the island in July 1898 during the Spanish-American War.

Disappointed that an American takeover would end political autonomy for Puerto Rico, Rivera went on to champion Puerto Rican rights with the American-imposed government. In 1899, he established *El Territorio,* a newspaper designed to express the concerns of Puerto Rican landowners and farmers who were barred from sending their produce to the United States. Later that same year, he traveled to the United States to lobby Congress for a reciprocal trade arrangement between the United States and Puerto Rico, an effort that was unsuccessful. Determined to continue his fight, he stayed in the United States until 1904. In the meantime, in 1901, he founded in New York City the bilingual newspaper *Puerto Rican Herald,* meant to appeal to the U.S. Puerto Rican community. In its first issue, he excoriated President William McKinley for the passage of the Foraker Amendment, which had created an American-style government in Puerto Rico that allowed for very little local government.

Returning to Puerto Rico in 1905, Rivera went on to found the Unionist Party and in 1906 was elected to the House of Delegates on that party's ticket. In 1910, he became the resident commissioner of Puerto Rico, the chief liaison with the U.S. House of Representa-

tives, a post he held until 1916. He used his position to continue his lobby for Puerto Rican autonomy. His hard work and constant pressure on Washington finally paid off, and in May 1916 the House passed the Jones Act, which extended to Puerto Ricans full U.S. citizenship and authorized the formation of a bicameral Puerto Rican legislature to be elected by universal male suffrage, thereby giving the island nation a significant degree of political autonomy. Unfortunately, Rivera did not live to see the final passage of the bill, which was signed into law by President Woodrow Wilson on March 2, 1917. Rivera died of cancer on November 15, 1916, in Loquillo, Puerto Rico.

In addition to his political and journalistic accomplishments, Rivera also published much poetry, which is held in high esteem even today among Puerto Ricans. In 1891, he published a collection of poems titled *Retamas* (Broom Plants), and in 1902, he published *Tropicales* (Tropicals). His son, Luis Muñoz Marín, also became a well-known Puerto Rican politician and served as the first democratically elected governor of the island territory from 1949 to 1965.

PAUL G. PIERPAOLI JR.

See also
McKinley, William; Ponce, Puerto Rico; Puerto Rico; Sagasta, Práxedes Mateo

Further Reading
Norris, Marianna. *Father and Son for Freedom: The Story of Puerto Rico's Luis Munoz Rivera and Luis Munoz Marín.* New York: Dodd, Mead, 1968.
Reynolds, Mack. *Puerto Rican Patriot: The Life of Luis Munoz Rivera.* London: Crowell-Collier, 1969.

Rizal, José
Birth Date: June 19, 1861
Death Date: December 30, 1896

Filipino nationalist, artist, physician, multilingual writer, and founder of the Liga Filipina (Filipino League). José Rizal (full name José Mercedo y Alonso Realonda Rizal Protacio) was born into a middle-class family on June 19, 1861, in Calamba, Laguna, the Philippines. He received a BA degree from the Ateneo de Manila University in 1877, then studied medicine at the University of Santo Tomas in Manila before leaving for Spain in 1882. He earned his medical degree at the Central University of Madrid two years later, then continued his education in France and Germany, specializing in ophthalmology.

While in Spain, Rizal tried to organize Filipino students to work for reforms back home. In 1887, he published the novel *Noli Me Tangere* (Do Not Touch Me), which criticized Spanish rule in the Philippines and championed Filipino nationalism. The book, which became a classic work, was later banned by the Spanish government. That same year, Rizal returned to the Philippines but was strongly advised by the authorities to leave in 1888.

Writer, physician, and champion of Filipino nationalism José Rizal in 1892 founded La Liga Filipina (Philippine League) to work for peaceful reform in the Philippines. (Library of Congress)

Rizal sailed back to Europe, stopping in Hong Kong, Macau, and Japan before traveling through the United States by train. In Great Britain, he discovered, copied, commented upon, and republished the 17th-century manuscript *Sucesos de las Islas Filipinas* (Events of the Philippine Islands), written by the Spanish colonial administrator Antonio de Morga. This work showed that an advanced civilization had existed in the Philippines well before the Spanish arrival there. Rizal also wrote for *La Solidaridad* (Solidarity), a Barcelona-based periodical championing administrative changes in the Philippines.

In 1891, Rizal published his second novel, *El Filibusterismo* (The Great Pirate), a sequel to *Noli Me Tangere* that again advocated reforms and hinted at a revolution, but not independence, if the Spanish did not grant changes in the Philippines. Later that year he traveled to Hong Kong, where his parents had moved following their exile by the Spanish authorities.

In 1892, Rizal decided to return to the Philippines and founded the Liga Filipina to work for peaceful reforms. He did not advocate violent means to effect change. The Liga Filipina's constitution had two explicit goals. First, it touted an indivisible, strong, and uniform community, which would be essential for national unity, the promotion of a common defense, and the curtailment of internal disorders and injustices. Second, it encouraged educational, agricultural, and commercial pursuits and called for reforms in each.

Despite the less-than-revolutionary agenda of the Liga Filipina, the Spanish colonial government banned it and exiled Rizal to Dapitan on Mindanao. Over the next four years, he helped build there a school, a hospital, and a sanitary water system. He also taught agriculture while continuing to write and draw.

Meanwhile, also in 1892, several cofounding members of the Liga Filipina established the Katipunan, a secret society modeled on the former organization, to work for independence from Spain through armed rebellion. Because Rizal was widely respected, the Katipunan used him as a rallying point and named him honorary president without his knowledge. Nevertheless, he refused to embrace the Katipunan or its ideology. In 1896, members of the Katipunan met with Rizal to discuss his stance on the impending revolution; he warned against it and urged only peaceful means for change.

To distance himself from the Katipunan, Rizal petitioned the government to allow him to serve as a volunteer army surgeon in Cuba, helping victims of yellow fever during the Cuban War of Independence. His request was granted, and he left the Philippines shortly after the rebellion broke out but not before publicly denouncing it.

En route to Cuba, Spanish authorities arrested Rizal on board ship, wrongly linking him to the Filipino revolutionary movement and the Katipunan. He was imprisoned in Barcelona before being transported back to the Philippines to stand trial. He reached Manila on November 3, 1896, and was imprisoned at Fort Santiago. A military tribunal tried him on charges of rebellion, sedition, and conspiracy for organizing illegal societies; found him guilty; and sentenced him to death. On December 30, 1896, he was executed by firing squad in the Luneta in Manila (now Rizal Park). His body was then buried in an unmarked grave. Although he quickly became a martyr and a hero and his death has been designated as a Filipino national holiday, he remains a controversial figure in Filipino history. The hasty Spanish action in executing Rizal only inflamed passions in the Philippines and encouraged the insurrectionists.

GREGORY C. FERENCE

See also
Filipino Revolutionary Movement; Katipunan; Liga Filipina

Further Reading
Abeto, Isidro Escare. *Rizal: The Immortal Filipino (1861–1896)*. Manila: National Book Store, 1984.
Coates, Austin. *Rizal: Philippine Nationalist and Martyr*. Oxford: Oxford University Press, 1968.
Locsin, Teodoro M. *Rizal*. Manila: T. M. Locsin, 1996.
Steinberg, David Joel. *The Philippines: A Singular and a Plural Place*. 3rd ed. Boulder, CO: Westview, 1994.

Robber Barons

A term used to describe industrialists, bankers, and financiers during the last third of the 19th century who often profited by unscrupulous business practices. Men such as John Jacob Astor,

Andrew Carnegie, Jay Gould, Henry Clay Frick, John D. Rockefeller, and Cornelius Vanderbilt were some of the first and most well known of the robber barons. The term "robber baron" is obviously pejorative and tended to be used to describe all wealthy industrialists and financiers whether they engaged in questionable business methods or not. The term itself was borrowed from medieval German history, a time in which lords (or barons) would exact outlandish tolls on ships passing their property along the Rhine River.

Some robber barons engaged in great philanthropic and public works projects after making their fortunes, which tended to soften the public perception of them. Some, of course, simply hoarded their wealth and gave little back to society. Carnegie, for example, believed fervently that it was an absolute responsibility of the wealthy to give back to the society that had enabled them to accumulate great wealth, something that he spelled out in his book *The Gospel of Wealth* (1889). There was a caveat, however, to his thesis, for he believed that those who hold great wealth should direct it to endeavors of their own choosing rather than allowing it to be frittered away on what he believed to be unworthy projects.

In many ways, the robber barons provided the foundation for the industrial powerhouse, which America would become during the Gilded Age. They revolutionized industry by paying attention to details and keeping careful track of where their money went and how it was invested. Utilizing economies of scale, the robber barons revolutionized management techniques and created a small army of professionalized managers who would become the envy of the world. They pioneered vertical integration, allowing firms to control the entire manufacturing process from the extraction of raw materials to sales and distribution. They also did not hesitate to expand their empires through horizontal combination (mergers and buyouts), even if it meant using devious means.

Many, such as Rockefeller and Carnegie, began their rise to fame by arranging special railroad rates in order to move materials more cheaply. Then with cheaper transportation costs in hand, profits rose, and they were able to expand further. When their empires grew large enough, they were able to take over others in their industry. To do this, they would either buy them outright or drive them out of business by lowering the price of their products so that smaller companies could not compete. Carnegie came to control much of the iron industry and Rockefeller much of the oil industry. The term "robber baron" also came to embrace financiers, of course, such as John Pierpont Morgan, who loaned money to industrialists so that they could expand their operations.

American industrial output soared in the last three decades of the 19th century, and in very large measure this was the result of the robber barons. By 1900, the United States had become the world's largest manufacturer of goods and was the largest economy in the world. This was no small feat, for in so doing it had to overtake traditional economic dynamos such as Great Britain and Germany. It also began the rise to economic superpower in the dismal post–American Civil War years, when the nation's economy had been hobbled by four years of terrible war and destruction. The United States was also poised to overtake Great Britain as the world's largest financial center, which was achieved fully by the end of World War I in 1918.

Many Americans at the time hated the robber barons, and history tends not to treat them well. Many of them forced competitors out of business; built huge mansions for themselves in poor company towns; erected extravagant summer cottages in Newport, Rhode Island, and Long Island, New York, that boasted many thousands of square feet; broke labor unions (sometimes by savage means); and were worth hundreds of millions of dollars. But they also helped to stabilize their industries and kept the U.S. economy on a relentlessly upward growth pattern, employing hundreds of thousands of Americans and newly arriving immigrants.

As industrialists were able to sell their products much more cheaply than before, most consumers were happy to pay less thanks to the productive efficiency of the robber barons. In this way, too, they were the driving forces of American industrialization. They also created new types of bonds and securities and steadied the stock market when it was in danger of crashing during economic crises. And many robber barons felt the need to give back to their communities.

There has been disagreement over the years with the term "robber baron," which is not a one-size-fits-all description. Some Americans—even scholars—have chosen to take a different vantage point on the accomplishments of big business during this era. Indeed, some have lionized them as captains of industry and industrial statesmen. These men, some have argued, brought order to the American economy and enabled the United States to become a great world power. Some historians have asserted that the definition of a true robber baron is one who used political clout to build his empire by influence peddling to earn unneeded subsidies from the government, push for protective industrial tariffs, or lobby for legislation that encouraged price fixing and cartelization.

Although Cornelius Vanderbilt gave only $1 million to charitable enterprises during his lifetime, Carnegie gave more than $350 million and Rockefeller more than $500 million. And yet with all that the robber barons gave back, many of their contemporaries found it hard to like them. Some seemed to hate everyone, and Vanderbilt's well-known phrase "The public be damned!" and J. P. Morgan's claim "I owe the public nothing" did not help their reputations. In the end, history often remembers them as men who paid for what legislation they wanted, buying judges when they were opposed, and who fixed prices. Many believed that when the robber barons gave back to their communities, it was based not on their love for the public or generosity but rather on trying to clear their names.

PAUL G. PIERPAOLI JR.

See also

Further Reading
Fulsom, Burton W. *The Myth of the Robber Barons.* Herndon, VA: Young America Foundation, 1993.
Josephson, Matthew. *The Robber Barons: The Great American Capitalists, 1861–1901.* New York: Harcourt Brace, 1995.
Stiles, T. J., and Edward Countryman, eds. *In Their Own Words: Robber Barons and Radicals.* New York: Perigee, 1997.

Rockefeller, John Davison
Birth Date: July 8, 1839
Death Date: May 23, 1937

Leading U.S. industrialist and perhaps the quintessential robber baron. As the moving force behind the Standard Oil Company, John Davison Rockefeller helped create the American petroleum industry and pioneered large-scale systematic philanthropy. Born on July 8, 1839, in Richford, New York, he grew up under the influence of his strict Baptist mother, Eliza Davison Rockefeller, and his shrewd businessman father, William Avery Rockefeller. In 1850, the younger Rockefeller moved with his family to Oswego, New York, and three years later to Cleveland, Ohio. After graduating from Cleveland High School, he had hopes of going to college, but his father insisted that he embark on a career in business, so the serious, reserved young man took courses for three months at a commercial school.

Securing employment as a clerk, Rockefeller joined a commission merchant firm, where he received important training and made contacts with Cleveland businessmen. In 1859, he formed a partnership with Maurice B. Clark, and with $4,000 in capital the two entrepreneurs traded in grain, hay, and meats. During the American Civil War, Clark and Rockefeller made a considerable sum provisioning the Union Army; in fact, the early 1860s brought Rockefeller the capital he needed to expand into other businesses. He did not serve in the war, opting instead to pay $300 to hire a substitute, which the government allowed.

While the war raged, Rockefeller surveyed the developing oil frenzy in northwestern Pennsylvania. The first oil well had been drilled in 1859 in Titusville, Pennsylvania, and new opportunities appeared with the rapid growth of petroleum refining and with the building of a railroad between Cleveland and the oil fields. As the oil arrived in Cleveland, refineries sprang up to process it, and Rockefeller decided that this would be the endeavor to earn him fame and fortune. In 1863, he and several partners constructed the Excelsior Refinery near the Cuyahoga River.

Putting his future prospects in oil, Rockefeller quit the merchant business and in February 1865 bought out all his partners except Samuel Andrews, a move he later referred to as having "determined my career." Before the end of the year, the firm of Rockefeller & Andrews was operating the largest of Cleveland's 30 refineries. Rockefeller then brought his brother, William Rockefeller, into the business and built a second refinery.

Industrialist, robber baron, and philanthropist John Davison Rockefeller was America's richest man and the driving force behind Standard Oil. (Library of Congress)

A postwar drop in the oil market in 1867 wiped out several refineries, but John D. Rockefeller's own remained strong, a credit to his efficiency and commitment. That year, he took in as a partner another talented businessman, Henry Flagler, who entered the partnership with capital, an ability to negotiate lower shipping rates with the railroads, and an austere, puritanical attitude that complemented Rockefeller's own. The firm became known as Rockefeller, Andrews & Flagler. Despite chaotic conditions in an oil industry that was subject to sharp price fluctuations and unrestrained cutthroat competition, Rockefeller and his associates prospered.

To provide a more flexible organization, in 1870 the partners founded the Standard Oil Company of Ohio. Throughout the 1870s, the Standard Oil Company continued to expand. It did so by keeping production costs down, obtaining favorable rates from the railroads in the form of rebates, engaging in occasional price slashing, and buying out competitors (horizontal combination). By the mid-1870s, the company had either absorbed or forced out of business the majority of its rivals. Under Rockefeller's skilled leadership, the company also pioneered in vertical integration within the oil industry, acquiring or building its own pipelines, controlling local distributors, and using its own tank cars. By 1880, Standard Oil had managed to secure a virtual monopoly over oil refining and transportation and had become one of the largest corporations in the United States.

Although Rockefeller's ruthless business practices brought him tremendous wealth, his reputation with the public suffered. With the public resoundingly convinced that everything Rockefeller did was motivated by greed, all of his ventures became tainted by public mistrust. In addition to becoming one of the wealthiest men in America, he entered the export market as well, shipping oil and kerosene to Asia, Africa, and South America. Throughout his career and amid widespread public disapproval, Rockefeller insisted that his drive was to bring order to the chaotic oil industry, known for its boom and bust cycles. He intended to provide the nation with a reliable energy source, and although he made money, accrued power, and crushed competitors, he allegedly saw these as secondary to his greater service.

In 1882, a Rockefeller attorney devised a new organization for the company called a trust, which placed Standard Oil stock and that of its subsidiaries in the hands of nine trustees. Because the trustees rather than the company held the stock, this allowed Standard Oil to circumvent laws that curtailed its right to own property outside Ohio. Within a short time, the term "trust" came to mean any big business combination, a recognition of the drive toward mammoth corporations accelerated by Rockefeller.

Newspapers, politicians, and the public increasingly attacked trusts, especially Standard Oil. Many suspected that Rockefeller and his associates had used illegal tactics and immoral business practices. Although Rockefeller paid fair market value for many companies that he acquired, he drove others into submission through cutthroat attacks, such as selling oil at a loss and then, after the competitor collapsed, driving up prices. He was also directly involved in bribing politicians. One observer commented that Standard Oil had done everything with the Pennsylvania legislature except refine it.

Antitrust legislation by Congress and a decision by the Ohio Supreme Court forced Rockefeller to disband his trust in 1892. He maintained centralized control, however, by simply transferring properties to subsidiary companies in several different states. In 1899, he placed Standard Oil in a New Jersey holding company, with himself as president and Flagler as vice president, in an effort to circumvent the Sherman Anti-Trust Act.

Even as the public criticized and often condemned Rockefeller as a ruthless robber baron, he quietly gave much of his money away to charities and educational institutions, often under the guidance of the Baptist Church. He gave money to Spelman College in Georgia to educate African American women and founded the now-prestigious University of Chicago (ultimately giving it $80 million). He spent a good deal of his time establishing philanthropic institutions, most prominently the Rockefeller Institute for Medical Research, founded in 1901, and the Rockefeller Foundation, chartered in 1913. The latter helped eliminate yellow fever, provided money to hospitals overseas, and extended relief assistance following World War I.

Rockefeller's wealth peaked at about $900 million, an astronomical sum at the turn of the century; indeed, it was almost more than the entire federal budget. His vast fortune qualifies him as the wealthiest man in American history. He ultimately gave away more than $500 million.

Rockefeller had little to do with the corporation by the time Standard Oil endured the widely read attacks from muckraker Ida Tarbell in the *History of the Standard Oil Company* in 1904, and the U.S. Supreme Court ordered the breakup of Standard Oil in 1911 as a company in restraint of trade. Rockefeller died on May 23, 1937. He was an enigmatic business leader who denied a desire for great wealth but obtained it nevertheless, who praised competition but crushed it, and who shunned the public that scorned him but contributed lavishly to help it.

DINO E. BUENVIAJE

See also

Carnegie, Andrew; Railroads; Robber Barons

Further Reading

Chernow, Ron. *Titan: The Life of John D. Rockefeller, Sr.* New York: Random House, 1998.

Fosdick, Raymond B. *The Story of the Rockefeller Foundation.* New York: Harper Brothers, 1952.

Nevins, Allan. *John D. Rockefeller: The Heroic Age of American Industry.* 2 vols. New York: Scribner, 1940.

Segall, Grant. *John D. Rockefeller: Anointed with Oil.* New York: Oxford University Press USA, 2001.

Rodgers, Raymond Perry
Birth Date: December 20, 1849
Death Date: December 25, 1925

U.S. Navy officer. Raymond Perry Rodgers was born on December 20, 1849, in Washington, D.C., and was the son of Rear Admiral Christopher Raymond Perry Rodgers, the brother of Rear Admiral George Rodgers, and the grand-nephew of Commodores Oliver Hazard Perry and Matthew C. Perry. Raymond Rodgers graduated from the United States Naval Academy, Annapolis, in 1868. He held a variety of land- and sea-based posts and was promoted to lieutenant in 1872, lieutenant commander in 1893, and commander in 1899.

Rodgers's expertise came in the area of intelligence, and he was appointed head of the Office of Naval Intelligence (ONI) in April 1885 as chief intelligence officer, a post he held until 1889. He was the second head of the agency, as the ONI had been established only in 1882. Appreciating the significance and importance of his agency, he developed close ties with other branches of the military establishment as well as other government entities, mainly the State Department in its dealings with Panama, Samoa, and Hawaii. His greatest contributions to naval intelligence came in the use of cryptography and technical research and employment of naval attachés to gather useful information. He was especially concerned about European colonial interests in South America within the purview of the 1823 Monroe Doctrine.

The importance of Rodgers's work became apparent when the ONI was transferred from the Bureau of Navigation to the office of the secretary of the navy. Rodgers's tenure also marked a period in which the ONI attracted young and capable talent, people who were eager to learn and make lasting contributions to naval intelligence. As a result of the ONI's contributions, increased demands were made upon it to gather more intelligence.

During the Spanish-American War, Rodgers served as executive officer of the battleship *Iowa* under Captain Robley D. Evans during the blockade of Cuba. As a result of Rodgers's participation in the Battle of Santiago de Cuba on July 3, 1898, during which Admiral Pascual Cervera y Topete's Spanish Squadron was destroyed as it attempted to break the blockade, Rodgers was cited for "imminent and conspicuous conduct" and advanced five number grades in rank.

After the war, Rodgers continued to advance in rank and responsibility. In April 1906, Rodgers, now a captain, was reassigned, again heading the ONI. On July 4, 1908, he was promoted to rear admiral. In May 1909, he left the ONI and retired from the navy shortly thereafter. On November 15, 1909, he was appointed to serve on a board with four other admirals charged with evaluating the expansion of naval yards. Rodgers died on December 25, 1925.

ARTHUR STEINBERG

See also
Cuba, U.S. Naval Blockade of; Evans, Robley Dunglison; Military Intelligence; Santiago de Cuba, Battle of

Further Reading
Angevin, Robert S. "The Rise and Fall of Naval Intelligence 1882–1892." *Journal of Military History* 62(4) (April 1998): 291–312.
Evans, Robley D. *A Sailor's Log: Recollections of Forty Years of Naval Life.* New York: D. Appleton, 1901.
Feuer, A. B. *The Spanish-American War at Sea: Naval Action in the Atlantic.* Westport, CT: Praeger, 1995.

As assistant secretary of the U.S. Navy (1897–1898), Theodore Roosevelt helped prepare the navy for the Spanish-American War but resigned to serve in the 1st U.S. Volunteer Cavalry Regiment (Rough Riders). Roosevelt (shown here as a colonel) won national fame when he led his men on a charge up Kettle Hill in the fighting to secure Santiago de Cuba. This helped catapult him into the presidency (1901–1909). (Library of Congress)

Roosevelt, Theodore
Birth Date: October 27, 1858
Death Date: January 16, 1919

U.S. politician, author, historian, assistant secretary of the U.S. Navy (1897–1898), governor of New York (1899–1901), vice president (1901), and president of the United States (1901–1909). Born on October 27, 1858, in New York City to a prominent and wealthy family, Theodore Roosevelt grew up in a life of privilege, and as a youth he and his family traveled around the world. Although born with poor eyesight, asthma, and nervous digestion, he undertook an exercise regime that transformed him into a physically powerful person. His upbringing in the New York aristocracy taught him a sense of noblesse oblige. Educated by private tutors, he graduated with honors from Harvard University in 1880. He married his first wife, Alice Lee, in 1880 and embarked on a grand tour of Europe.

His wife's death and the death of his mother in 1884, on the same day and in the same house, affected Roosevelt deeply.

Between 1884 and 1886, Roosevelt made a venture in cattle ranching in the Badlands (Dakota Territory), an enterprise he personally supervised. It failed after a disastrous blizzard killed off much of his herd. In 1886, he married Edith Carow, an old acquaintance. He was an especially prolific author who was fascinated with history. Between 1880 and 1900, he wrote many books on history and nature, including the acclaimed *The Naval War of 1812* (1892), the magisterial four-volume frontier history *The Winning of the West* (1889–1896), and *The Strenuous Life* (1900), Roosevelt's vision for leading an active and fulfilling life. As much an intellectual as a politician, he would later become president of the American Historical Association.

Estimated Casualties in the Battles at San Juan Heights (San Juan Hill and Kettle Hill) and El Caney

	Killed in Action	Wounded
Spain	215	376
United States	205	1,177

When Roosevelt was a law student at Harvard, he developed a belief in protecting the common good. He came to determine that he should work for the common good and that politics provided the best means by which to accomplish this. In 1881, he was elected as a Republican to the New York State Assembly. Exposed to the machine politics of the day, he soon developed his commitment to reform. He first gained publicity by attacking New York judge Theodore Westbrook for taking part in an illegal scheme to acquire an elevated train company. Roosevelt was hailed as a breath of fresh air for his candor and willingness to stand up to political machines such as New York City's Tammany Hall.

Roosevelt returned to politics in 1886 after his ranching adventure by running for the office of mayor of New York City but was unsuccessful. Between 1889 and 1895, he served as the civil service commissioner in Washington, D.C., a post that allowed him to pursue his reformist agenda. Indeed, he was allowed to retain the post even after Democrat Grover Cleveland won election in 1892. In 1895, Roosevelt became police commissioner for New York City. In 1896, realizing that he could not defeat Tammany Hall by himself, he tied his hopes to the Republican Party from which he hoped to gain a position after victory in the 1896 elections. Through his connections with Republican senator Henry Cabot Lodge, Roosevelt secured an appointment as assistant secretary of the navy in 1897.

During the 1890s, Roosevelt had been part of an influential circle of people in Washington who believed that the United States should play a larger role in international affairs. He was especially influenced by U.S. naval strategist Alfred Thayer Mahan, who argued that a large navy and adequate coaling stations to provision it were essential for the United States to achieve world power. As assistant secretary of the navy, Roosevelt had a grand vision of the United States, which included the acquisition of Hawaii and islands in the Caribbean, an isthmian canal across Central America, and a large U.S. naval fleet.

The deteriorating situation in Cuba and rising tensions between Spain and America presented a unique opportunity for Roosevelt to apply his world vision. The continuing conflict between Cuban revolutionaries and the Spanish colonial government in Cuba clearly threatened U.S. economic interests on the island. Roosevelt was especially eager to involve the United States in a war against Spain. Indeed, he told President William McKinley that in the event of war, he would immediately resign his post in the Navy Department and enlist in the army. Following the suspicious sinking of the *Maine* in Havana Harbor on February 15, 1898, that claimed 266 American

lives, and even as investigations were under way to determine the cause of the explosion, Roosevelt positioned warships in the Atlantic and the Pacific for action. He ordered Commodore George Dewey, commander of the U.S. Asiatic Squadron, to steam to Hong Kong and be prepared to take action against the Spanish fleet in the Philippines. At this time, Roosevelt had de facto control of the navy, as Secretary John D. Long was not active in its administration.

After the United States declared war on Spain on April 25, 1898, Roosevelt, determined to be a part of the war, promptly resigned his post. He faced skepticism from his friends and colleagues who tried to persuade him that the country required his services as assistant navy secretary more than on the battlefield. Roosevelt was also then 40 years old, not in the best of physical shape, and would be subject to malaria, yellow fever, and typhoid. With the assistance of Colonel Leonard Wood, however, Roosevelt helped recruit the 1st U.S. Volunteer Cavalry Regiment, which came to be known as the Rough Riders, a diverse group of western cowboys, New York policemen, lawyers, and Ivy League college graduates. The Rough Riders were trained in San Antonio before being transferred to Florida in preparation for being sent to Cuba in June 1898, where they would see action by month's end. Initially, Roosevelt held the rank of lieutenant colonel under Wood, but when Wood was advanced to brigadier general of volunteers, Roosevelt replaced him, now with the rank of colonel.

During the Battle of San Juan Hill on July 1, 1898, Roosevelt participated in taking Kettle Hill, a smaller hill adjacent to San Juan Hill. Roosevelt and his men faced Spanish resistance as they ascended the hill, and the torrid heat was affecting the men. Reaching a small trough in the climb, which allowed U.S. troops to regroup, the Rough Riders were now interspersed with men from other units, including U.S. Army regulars. Roosevelt ordered all of the men to charge the hill; many of the regulars refused because they had not received orders from the brigade commanders. Roosevelt simply by-passed them as his regiment pushed on. Near the top, he was forced to dismount. The Rough Riders made it to the top and in so doing became the grist for much propaganda and lore.

Roosevelt gained national prominence during his service with the Rough Riders, particularly at the Battle of Kettle Hill. Frederic Remington painted a famous depiction of this battle, which is erroneously titled *Charge of the Rough Riders at San Juan Hill.* Being a national hero enhanced Roosevelt's political prospects when he returned from Cuba, and he easily won the office of governor of New York in 1898. In that election, he ran again on a Progressive platform against the excesses of big business, particularly the railroads.

In the 1900 election, Roosevelt became the vice presidential candidate of the Republican Party with presidential candidate William McKinley. Party bosses in New York saw this as a way to marginalize Roosevelt politically. The McKinley-Roosevelt ticket won an easy victory. On September 6, 1901, however, McKinley was shot at the Pan-American Exposition in Buffalo, New York, by anarchist Leon Czolgosz and died on September 14. Roosevelt was now president of the United States, the youngest man ever to hold the office.

Secure in his destiny, Roosevelt was not overwhelmed by the presidency, and he went on to transform the image of the presidency. His energy, young family, social prominence, and reputation as a war hero endeared him to the public. His domestic policy was marked by his relentless Progressivism, which aimed at regulating business, breaking up trusts, and giving the American voter a square deal. In 1902, he successfully mediated the disruptive anthracite coal strike. He was also instrumental in the dismemberment of the Northern Securities Company, which John Pierpont Morgan had formed to manage his railroad empire. Roosevelt also conserved 51 million acres of western land as national forests while president. Elected in his own right in 1904 by a landslide, he pushed through a series of landmark progressive reforms: the Hepburn Act (1906) strengthened the powers of the Interstate Commerce Commission to regulate railroad rates, the Meat Inspection Act (1906) regulated the meatpacking industry, and the Pure Food and Drug Act (1906) established the Food and Drug Administration.

As president, Roosevelt applied his own vision for U.S. foreign policy. Victory over Spain announced the arrival of the United States as an international power. Indeed, the United States had acquired Puerto Rico, Guam, and the Philippine Islands. One manifestation of the new, more aggressive U.S. foreign policy, known as the Big Stick, came in 1902 when Roosevelt prevented Germany's encroachment in Venezuela by offering arbitration between both countries over Venezuela's international debts. A similar crisis in the Dominican Republic in 1903 led Roosevelt to announced the 1904 Roosevelt Corollary to the 1823 Monroe Doctrine, which not only stated that the Western Hemisphere was off limits to European exploitation but also asserted that the United States had the right to intervene in the hemisphere when it saw fit to do so.

By far the most controversial event in Roosevelt's Big Stick diplomacy came as a result of his desire to build the Panama Canal. The Spanish-American War had demonstrated the necessity of a canal connecting the Atlantic and the Pacific across Central America. Nicaragua had originally been considered a possible site for construction, but a volcano eruption led to reconsideration of the Panama route. Roosevelt then participated in the intrigues behind the acquisition of the rights to build a canal through Panama. When the Colombian Senate rejected the Hay-Herrán Treaty to purchase land for a canal across the Isthmus of Panama, Roosevelt encouraged a revolt and then prevented the Colombians from suppressing it, allowing the United States to enter into the Hay–Bunau-Varilla Treaty to build the canal with the new country of Panama in 1903.

Roosevelt also fostered a rapprochement with Britain, sought by London because of Germany's decision to build a powerful battle fleet. The resolution of lingering disputes with Britain allowed for full U.S. hegemony in the Western Hemisphere and provided a community of interest that would lead to the United States entering World War I on the side of Britain. In 1905, Roosevelt mediated the end of the Russo-Japanese War (1904–1905), which garnered him the 1905 Nobel Peace Prize. This was followed by his efforts to help mediate the First Moroccan Crisis between France and Germany at the 1906 Algeciras Conference. Before he left the presidency, he sent off the Great White Fleet in 1908 on a cruise around the world as a showcase of U.S. naval power.

Although Roosevelt had easily won a second term in 1904, he had promised not to run for a third term. Before leaving office in 1909, he had groomed William Howard Taft as his successor. Roosevelt hoped that Taft would continue his Progressive legacy. But such was not the case. Taft, who became president in 1909, filled his cabinet with businessmen and establishment scions who had little use for Progressive reforms. Roosevelt broke with Taft and challenged him for the 1912 Republican nomination. When that effort failed, Roosevelt ran as an independent under the Progressive Party (also known as the Bull Moose Party). Roosevelt split the Republican vote, which handed the presidency to Democrat Woodrow Wilson.

Roosevelt continued as a prominent figure in American politics. He also embarked on a series of hunting adventures that earned him much publicity. They included an African safari and an expedition into the Amazon jungle, about which he wrote *Through the Brazilian Wilderness* in 1913. He was openly critical of Wilson's foreign policy, which he claimed was weak, and vociferously worked for U.S. intervention in World War I (1914–1918). In 1918, Roosevelt's son Quentin was killed in action in Europe. Devastated by the loss and hobbled by poor health, Roosevelt died on January 16, 1919, at Oyster Bay, New York.

Dino E. Buenviaje

See also

Imperialism; Kettle Hill, Battle of; Long, John Davis; Mahan, Alfred Thayer; *Maine*, USS; McKinley, William; Remington, Frederic Sackrider; San Juan Heights, Battle of; United States Navy; Wood, Leonard

Further Reading

Brands, H. W. *TR: The Last Romantic.* New York: Basic Books, 1997.
Collin, Richard H. *Theodore Roosevelt, Culture, Diplomacy, and Expansion.* Baton Rouge: Louisiana State University Press, 1985.
Dalton, Kathleen. *Theodore Roosevelt: A Strenuous Life.* New York: Knopf, 2002.
Morris, Edmund. *The Rise of Theodore Roosevelt.* New York: Coward, McCann and Geoghegan, 1979.
———. *Theodore Rex.* New York: Random House, 2001.
Roosevelt, Theodore. *The Letters of Theodore Roosevelt.* Edited by Elting E. Morison. 8 vols. Cambridge: Harvard University Press, 1951.
Samuels, Peggy, and Harold Samuels. *Teddy Roosevelt at San Juan: The Making of a President.* College Station: Texas A&M University Press, 1997.
Tilchin, William. *Theodore Roosevelt and the British Empire: A Study in Presidential Statecraft.* New York: St. Martin's, 1997.

Roosevelt Corollary

Controversial addendum to the Monroe Doctrine by President Theodore Roosevelt in his 1904 address to Congress. Although the

Monroe Doctrine of 1823 had forbade further European colonization in the Western Hemisphere and European interference in the newly independent republics in Latin America, the United States had not been in a position to enforce it at the time. Indeed, the British had called for a joint declaration, but Secretary of State John Quincy Adams had convinced President James Monroe to proceed independently because the United States could count on Great Britain to enforce it. Nevertheless, the United States did invoke the Monroe Doctrine throughout the 19th century, the most notable instance coming after Napoleon III installed Austrian archduke Maximilian in Mexico during the American Civil War. U.S. pressure after the war combined with the need for French troops in Europe prompted Napoleon III to withdraw French forces from Mexico.

As the United States began construction of a modern navy in the 1880s, it gained the means not only to enforce the Monroe Doctrine but also to exert its influence in Latin America. During the 1880s, Secretary of State James G. Blaine pursued a policy of Pan-Americanism that sought to strengthen American economic interests in Latin America and establish the right of the United States to arbitrate international disputes involving Latin American nations. Although Blaine's efforts to secure treaties to this effect were rejected by Latin American countries, who viewed U.S. intentions with suspicion, Venezuela sought U.S. arbitration in 1895 when it became involved in a dispute with Great Britain over its boundary with British Guiana. When the British resisted, Secretary of State Richard B. Olney invoked the Monroe Doctrine, declaring that "Today, the United States is practically sovereign on this continent, and its fiat is law upon the subjects to which it confines its interposition." The British ultimately accepted American arbitration primarily because Britain did not want to risk a conflict with the United States at a time when it faced a potential war with the Boers in South Africa.

With the First Venezuela Crisis (1895–1897) establishing a clear precedent and the United States establishing itself as a world power after the Spanish-American War, the stage was set for the United States to enforce the Monroe Doctrine with or without the request of Latin American nations. When General Cipriano Castro seized power in Venezuela in 1899 and suspended payment of Venezuela's international debts, Germany, Great Britain, and Italy ultimately imposed a pacific blockade of Venezuela. Although the United States did not intervene in the crisis, which was ultimately resolved by the international court at The Hague, the potential for similar crises in the Western Hemisphere prompted Roosevelt to take preemptive action.

In his December 6, 1904, address to Congress, Roosevelt issued his corollary to the Monroe Doctrine, declaring that it "may force the United States, however reluctantly, in flagrant cases of such wrongdoing or impotence, to the exercise of an international police power." When the Dominican Republic faced a default on its debts in 1905, Roosevelt invoked the Roosevelt Corollary, declaring that the United States would not permit a European nation to

forcibly collect debts in the Western Hemisphere and that the United States would assume the responsibility of ensuring that states fulfilled their debt obligations. Roosevelt dispatched troops to Santo Domingo, placed a receiver-general in charge of Dominican revenues, and arranged for 55 percent of receipts to be applied to debts. Within two years, the Dominican Republic's debts had been paid.

Although Roosevelt's intentions were altruistic, the application of the Roosevelt Corollary generated ill will with Latin American nations, especially when combined with the Platt Amendment's authorization of the right of American intervention and the U.S. role in orchestrating a revolution in Panama to secure the Panama Canal Zone. Ironically, President Franklin D. Roosevelt's Good Neighbor Policy marked an abandonment of the Roosevelt Corollary.

JUSTIN D. MURPHY

See also

Blaine, James Gillespie; Hay–Bunau-Varilla Treaty; Hay-Herrán Treaty; Monroe Doctrine; Olney, Richard; Panama Canal; Platt Amendment; Roosevelt Corollary; Venezuela Crisis, First; Venezuela Crisis, Second

Further Reading

Collin, Richard H. *Theodore Roosevelt, Culture, Diplomacy, and Expansion: A New View of American Imperialism.* Baton Rouge: Louisiana State University Press, 1985.
———. *Theodore Roosevelt's Caribbean: The Panama Canal, the Monroe Doctrine, and the Latin American Context.* Baton Rouge: Louisiana State University Press, 1990.
Holmes, James R. *Theodore Roosevelt and World Order: Police Power in International Relations.* Washington, DC: Potomac Books, 2006.
Morris, Edmund. *Theodore Rex.* New York: Random House, 2001.

Root, Elihu
Birth Date: February 15, 1845
Death Date: February 7, 1937

U.S. secretary of war (1899–1904), secretary of state (1905–1909), winner of the Nobel Peace Prize, and U.S. senator (1909–1915). Elihu Root was born in Clinton, New York, on February 15, 1845. After graduating from Hamilton College in Clinton in 1864, he obtained his law degree from New York University Law School in 1867 and became a successful corporate attorney. He became directly involved in politics for the first time when he served as U.S. district attorney for the southern district of New York from 1883 to 1885. In 1894, he managed the state constitutional convention of New York and the following year became that body's president.

When Theodore Roosevelt began his political career by unsuccessfully campaigning for mayor of New York City, Root served as his confidant and adviser. His close relationship to Roosevelt was a major factor in President William McKinley's decision to choose Root as the secretary of war in 1899. At first, Root was reluctant to accept the appointment. He told the emissary of the news, "Thank the President for me, but say that it is quite absurd. I know nothing

Elihu Root was a highly effective secretary of war (1899–1904) who carried out much-needed reforms following the Spanish-American War. He later served as secretary of state (1905–1909) and won the Nobel Peace Prize in 1912. (Library of Congress)

about war." It was not until it was explained to him that it would be his responsibility to establish and direct the governments of the newly acquired colonies of the Philippines and Puerto Rico that Root changed his mind. This was a task for which he believed he was well trained.

Root's immediate problem was to secure adequate manpower for U.S. forces to crush the Filipino insurgency. Although he stressed guarantees of individual liberties in Puerto Rico and the Philippines, he placed the protection of U.S. interests first and accepted responsibility for the army's brutal crushing of the Philippine independence effort.

Root turned out to be one of the most important U.S. secretaries of war. He pushed for a larger U.S. military establishment as necessary to meet the expanded U.S. overseas commitments following the war with Spain and to garrison the new U.S. coast fortifications. He advocated the creation of a staff organization to study military issues and carry out war planning and a similar agency to evaluate weapons and make recommendations regarding them. He wanted a better system of officer promotion and training that would include large bodies of troops. He also saw the need for an extensive reserve system of trained men to augment the regular military es-

tablishment. In addition, he was behind the Platt Amendment, which established a virtual protectorate over Cuba.

In February 1901, Congress fixed the regular army at 30 regiments of infantry, 15 regiments of cavalry, 3 battalions of engineers, and a corps of artillery that included both field batteries and fortress companies. Total manpower would vary between 60,000 and 100,000 men at the discretion of the president. Also in 1901, Root saw his recommendation for creation of the Army War College realized when it was established by executive order.

Roosevelt became president in September 1901 on the death of McKinley. While chiefly interested in the navy, Roosevelt nonetheless supported Root in his reforms. Finally in 1903, after some opposition and compromise, Congress passed bills that established the General Staff and included a compromise with the National Guard (the Militia Act of 1903, also known as the Dick Act).

The new legislation abolished the office of commanding general and replaced it with the position of chief of staff as the highest-ranking army officer and senior military adviser to the president and his secretary of war. He would also have control over the staff bureaus. Previously, the commanding general had been the most senior officer in the army and remained in the office for the rest of his military career. The new chief of staff was appointed for a limited term only. The legislation also did away with permanent appointments to the new General Staff Corps.

The Militia Act of 1903 repealed the Militia Act of 1792. It recognized the wholly volunteer National Guard as the organized militia and the first-line military reserve. The National Guard was to be organized, trained, and equipped as the regular army. Under provisions of the act, the federal government undertook to provide weapons and equipment as well as furnish regular army officers as instructors. The act also imposed minimum standards of drill and an annual encampment.

Root also oversaw the introduction of new weapons, especially the superb Model 1903 .30-caliber Springfield, which was for a generation one of the best rifles in the world. It remained the basic infantry weapon for the army until World War II. The artillery also received new modern field guns to replace the black powder guns on fixed carriages with which it had gone to Cuba.

Root had carried out major reforms in the U.S. military. In 1904, exhausted by his labors, he resigned. But two years later, after the death of John Hay, President Roosevelt appointed Root secretary of state.

As secretary of state from 1905 to 1909, Root worked to improve relations with Latin America and Japan. During a tour of Latin America in 1906, he succeeded in easing tensions that had risen over U.S. actions in Panama. In 1908, he managed to convince Japan to confirm the U.S. Open Door Policy in China with the Root-Takahira Agreement.

In 1909, Root accepted appointment to the U.S. Senate. He had never run for office because he feared the political capital his opponent might make of the fact that Root had been William Marcy Tweed's defense attorney in Tweed's 1873 trial for corruption of urban politics. Tweed, leader of the Tammany Hall political machine, was eventually convicted of establishing political corruption in New York on an unprecedented scale.

The next year, in addition to fulfilling his Senate duties, Root served as chief U.S. consul of the International Court of Justice at The Hague in the North Atlantic fisheries arbitration case. The Permanent Court of Arbitration settled the dispute between the United States and Great Britain over Canadian and U.S. territorial fishing rights in the North Atlantic. In recognition of his work as secretary of state and at The Hague in favor of the use of diplomacy and arbitration to settle international disputes, Root was awarded the 1912 Nobel Peace Prize.

As chairman of the Republican National Convention in 1912, Root ended his long personal friendship with Roosevelt. Root believed himself obligated as a matter of principle to support William Howard Taft's reelection. Roosevelt never fully forgave Root for this.

A strong proponent of the defeat of Germany in World War I, Root was critical of President Woodrow Wilson's policy of neutrality but did not criticize him until after retiring from the Senate in 1915. After the war, Root, with reservations designed to assure critics of American sovereignty, advocated U.S. membership in the League of Nations. In 1920, he helped to create the league's Permanent Court of International Justice. As president of the Carnegie Endowment for International Peace from 1910 to 1925, he worked for the free international exchange of scientific knowledge.

In 1921, Root accepted his last diplomatic appointment. President Warren Harding selected him to be one of the four U.S. delegates to the International Conference on the Limitation of Armaments in Washington, D.C. (commonly known as the Washington Naval Conference). Root died in Clinton, New York, on February 7, 1937.

SPENCER C. TUCKER

See also
Alger, Russell Alexander; McKinley, William; Militia Act of 1903; Platt Amendment; Roosevelt, Theodore

Further Reading
Cosmas, Graham A. *An Army for Empire: The United States Army in the Spanish-American War.* College Station: Texas A&M University Press, 1994.

Jessup, Philip C. *Elihu Root.* 2 vols. New York: Dodd, Mead, 1938.

Leech, Margaret. *In the Days of McKinley.* New York: Harper and Brothers, 1959.

Leopold, Richard W. *Elihu Root and the Conservative Tradition.* Boston: Little, Brown, 1954.

Rough Riders

Popular name for the U.S. 1st Volunteer Cavalry Regiment during the Spanish-American War. The Rough Riders were perhaps the most unusual aggregation of soldiers in the history of the U.S. military. Certainly, it was the most famous and colorful army unit of the Spanish-American War.

As part of the nation's military mobilization for the recently declared war with Spain, a congressional authorization granted President William McKinley the power to enlist special regiments composed of individuals who possessed unique (or at least special) skills. This mandate led to the formation of the 1st U.S. Volunteer Cavalry Regiment, which came to be known as the Rough Riders.

Initially, command of the regiment was offered to Assistant Secretary of the Navy Theodore Roosevelt. He declined, saying that he would agree to serve as second-in-command to his friend Leonard Wood, army doctor and personal physician to McKinley. Wood had distinguished himself in fighting against the Apaches in the American West and had won the Medal of Honor. The gesture by Roosevelt most likely was not made out of modesty but because he recognized that he had no experience in commanding troops and that his own position as well as that of the regiment would be far better served if he accepted the rank of lieutenant colonel and second-in-command.

Once formation of the regiment was announced on April 25, 1898, applications poured in. The press wasted no time focusing on Roosevelt as a story source. Although Wood was the regimental commander and was an officer with considerable experience on the western frontier, he was scarcely mentioned in their reports. But the undue attention accorded Roosevelt seemed not to overly disturb Wood, who left Washington, D.C., for San Antonio, Texas, in early May to prepare for the regiment's training. Roosevelt followed two weeks later.

Recruits from Texas, New Mexico, Arizona, and Indian Territory as well as the East arrived in San Antonio, where the regiment was mustered during May 1–21. The regimental headquarters was the Menger Hotel, the oldest hotel in Texas (and still operating today), which is adjacent to the Alamo. Ultimately, the regiment included 994 enlisted men and 47 officers. More than half of the men came from Texas, New Mexico, and Indian Territory. Ninety were from New York, and almost as many were foreign-born. The regiment included 160 cowboys, young men from the eastern social elite, college students, New York City policemen, Indians and Indian fighters, lawyers, and Texas Rangers, among others.

Accompanying the men were arms, equipment, and horses. The actual training ground for the regiment was at Riverside Park on the San Antonio River, south of the city. The regiment soon developed a reputation both for its dash and lack of discipline. On May 27, the regiment received orders to move to Tampa, Florida, where Major General William R. Shafter's V Corps was assembling for the forthcoming U.S. invasion of Cuba.

The appellation "Rough Riders" was coined early on and was derived from "Roosevelt's Rough Riders." Among names suggested at the time were "Teddy's Terrors," "Teddy's Terriers," and "Teddy's Texas Tarantulas." Insofar as the press was concerned, at least, the unit clearly was Roosevelt's regiment.

Finally, on May 30, 1898, the Rough Riders boarded a train for the journey to Tampa, where they arrived on June 4. The next week was spent preparing for the upcoming Cuba Campaign before or-

Colonel Theodore Roosevelt shown with members of the 1st U.S. Volunteer Cavalry Regiment (Rough Riders) at the summit of San Juan Hill. (Library of Congress)

ders finally came down to board ship. Lack of space on the transport permitted Wood and Roosevelt to take only 8 of their 12 cavalry troops. Moreover, there was no room for the unit's horses except for the personal mounts of the senior officers.

On June 14, 1898, the Rough Riders sailed from Tampa on the *Yucatan.* They disembarked at Daiquirí on June 22. The Rough Riders were assigned to Brigadier General Samuel Young's brigade of Major General Joseph Wheeler's Dismounted Cavalry Division. Consisting of 26 officers and 557 enlisted men, the regiment fought in the Battle of Las Guásimas (June 24, 1898) and sustained casualties of 8 killed and 31 wounded.

When Young fell ill, Colonel Wood replaced him in command of the cavalry brigade, and this led in turn to Roosevelt's appointment to command the Rough Riders. He led the unit during the Battle of San Juan Hill (July 1, 1898) with which the Rough Riders will forever be linked. Contrary to popular belief, the Rough Riders did not actually charge up San Juan Hill but rather charged up nearby Kettle Hill. After securing Kettle Hill, Roosevelt led the regiment across the intervening ground to assist Brigadier General Jacob F. Kent's

infantry in its assault of San Juan Hill, both of which were part of San Juan Heights. In the battle, the unit sustained casualties of 15 killed and 72 wounded.

The Rough Riders departed Santiago, Cuba, on August 8 in the transport *Miami,* landing at Camp Wikoff on Montauk Point at Long Island, New York, on August 14. The remaining Rough Riders who had been left behind in Tampa rejoined the unit at New York, where the unit was disbanded on September 15, 1898, with 1,090 enlisted men and 47 officers. During the war, the Rough Riders had sustained casualties of 26 killed and 104 wounded. Another 20 died from disease, while 12 deserted. The casualty rate of 27 percent for those who saw actual service in Cuba was the highest of any American unit in the war.

JERRY KEENAN AND SPENCER C. TUCKER

See also

Kent, Jacob Ford; Kettle Hill, Battle of; Las Guásimas, Battle of; McKinley, William; Roosevelt, Theodore; San Juan Heights, Battle of; Santiago de Cuba Land Campaign; Wheeler, Joseph; Wood, Leonard; Young, Samuel Baldwin Marks

Further Reading

Cosmas, Graham A. *An Army for Empire: The United States Army in the Spanish-American War.* College Station: Texas A&M University Press, 1994.

Herner, Charles. *The Arizona Rough Riders.* Tucson: University of Arizona Press, 1970.

McCallum, Jack. *Leonard Wood: Rough Rider, Surgeon, Architect of American Imperialism.* New York: New York University Press, 2006.

Samuels, Peggy, and Harold Samuels. *Teddy Roosevelt at San Juan: The Making of a President.* College Station: Texas A&M University Press, 1997.

Walker, Dale L. *The Boys of '98: Theodore Roosevelt and the Rough Riders.* New York: Forge, 1999.

Westermeier, Clifford P. *Who Rush to Glory–The Cowboy Volunteers of 1898: Grisby's Cowboys, Roosevelt's Rough Riders, Torrey's Rocky Mountain Riders.* Caldwell, ID: Caxton Printers, 1958.

Round-Robin Letter
Start Date: July 31, 1898
End Date: August 4, 1898

A controversial sequence of events that transpired between July 31 and August 4, 1898, centered around the fate of the U.S. Army's V Corps, then fighting in Cuba at the height of the malaria and yellow fever season. Immediately following the fall of Santiago de Cuba on July 17, fever cases in V Corps had increased steadily. By July 28, 4,270 men were reported sick, 3,406 of them diagnosed with malaria or yellow fever. As the corps seemingly faced potential annihilation from disease, V Corps commander Major General William R. Shafter convened a special meeting of division and brigade commanders at the Governor's Palace in Santiago. In the ensuing discussions, the assembled officers agreed unanimously that War Department plans to retain V Corps in Cuba until the signing of a peace treaty with Spain would be disastrous for the command, and they recommended immediate evacuation to the United States.

Those present assigned Colonel Theodore Roosevelt, former assistant secretary of the navy and temporary commander of the 2nd Brigade of the Cavalry Division, with conveying this information to the press. He was selected because as a volunteer officer and former high-ranking government official, he was more likely to escape punishment for insubordination than the regular officers present. Initially leaning toward holding a press conference, he was convinced by his friend and commander Brigadier General Leonard Wood to instead compose a letter to Major General Shafter outlining the situation and recommendations.

Simultaneously, Wood dictated an abridged version of Roosevelt's letter for circulation among and signature by all present. In this shorter circular, known as the Round-Robin Letter, Wood and Roosevelt bluntly assessed the situation: "This army must be removed at once, or perish. As the army can be safely moved now, the persons responsible for preventing such a move will be responsible for the unnecessary loss of many thousands of lives."

Both letters were presented to Shafter upon completion. Shafter later refused to acknowledge either of the two letters to Secretary of War Russell A. Alger. Roosevelt reported a different story, however. He asserted that Shafter was aware of the entire process but refused to take any ownership of the letters when presented to him. Instead, he ordered that they be immediately handed off to an Associated Press (AP) reporter present at the meeting.

Regardless of the immediate chain of events, the outcome was soon felt throughout the William McKinley administration. McKinley was outraged by the leak, and Secretary Alger considered a round of courts-martial for all signatories of the letter. The letter itself came at an awkward time, appearing at the start of peace negotiations with Spain. Fears that the Spanish would capitalize on the revelations in the Round-Robin Letter were unrealized, however.

More significant was the public response to the first news that the situation in Cuba was more dire than hitherto reported. A public outcry for the immediate repatriation of V Corps erupted, with many pundits both lionizing Roosevelt for speaking truth to power and condemning Alger for ignoring the plight of American soldiers. Such attacks on Alger were unfounded, however. On July 28, he cabled Shafter of the imminent evacuation of V Corps and its replacement with four regiments of Immunes (troops from southern states who were incorrectly deemed immune to tropical diseases).

That same day, Alger selected eastern Long Island, New York, as the site for a repatriation center and quarantine camp (to be called Camp Wikoff) for V Corps. On August 3, the day before the letter appeared in the press, construction contracts were issued, and the first trainloads of building supplies began to appear at the site. Likewise, a flotilla of hospital ships and hurriedly contracted freighters and steamers were en route for Santiago to begin the evacuation. On August 7, the first units of V Corps began to embark on vessels for the journey north to Long Island.

Yet the damage to Alger's reputation—and the boost to that of Roosevelt—was already done. Dogged by controversy and criticism over the so-called abandonment of V Corps, Alger resigned on September 27, 1899. In his subsequent memoir, he claimed that the Round-Robin Letter had absolutely no effect on the repatriation of V Corps. Alternatively, the Round-Robin Letter did as much for Roosevelt's reputation as his leadership at San Juan Hill. Not only was Roosevelt seen as a bold hero in battle, but he was also portrayed as a strong paternal figure, motivated only by concern for the welfare of the common soldier.

BOB A. WINTERMUTE

See also

Alger, Russell Alexander; Camp Wikoff; V Corps; Malaria; McKinley, William; Medicine, Military; Roosevelt, Theodore; Shafter, William Rufus; Typhoid Fever; Wood, Leonard; Yellow Fever

Further Reading

Gillett, Mary C. *The Army Medical Department, 1865–1917*. Washington, DC: Center of Military History, United States Army, 1995.

Roosevelt, Theodore. *The Rough Riders, an Autobiography.* New York: Library of America, 2004.

Trask, David F. *The War with Spain in 1898*. Lincoln: University of Nebraska Press, 1996.

Rowan, Andrew Summers

Birth Date: April 23, 1857
Death Date: January 10, 1943

U.S. Army officer who enjoyed an entirely undistinguished military career except for a secret mission to Cuba during the Spanish-American War. Born in Gap Mills, Virginia (later West Virginia), on April 23, 1857, Andrew Summers Rowan followed his father, a colonel in the Confederate Army, into the military. Rowan graduated from the United States Military Academy, West Point, in 1881.

Commissioned a second lieutenant of infantry on June 11, 1881, Rowan was assigned to the 15th Infantry Regiment. He held a succession of routine assignments in the American West, serving in frontier posts in Texas, Colorado, and the Dakotas. Pro-

moted to first lieutenant on November 20, 1890, he performed some survey work and also served briefly as military attaché to Chile.

In 1892, Rowan was assigned to the Military Information Division (MID), the forerunner of Army Intelligence. Early in 1898 with war with Spain looming, the head of the MID, Lieutenant Colonel Arthur L. Wagner, dispatched Rowan on a secret mission to Cuba to assess the strengths of Cuban insurgents and Spanish forces on the island. Rowan's knowledge of Spanish, the fact that he had studied the island, and his hobby of mountain climbing all helped earn him the assignment.

Taking a ship to Jamaica, Rowan made contact with Cuban revolutionaries, who arranged for him to enter Cuba secretly by fishing boat on April 24, 1898. Trekking through jungle, he met with General Calixto García y Iñiguez of the Cuban Revolutionary Army. On completion of his 11-day mission, Rowan returned to the United States. For his mission, Rowan, promoted to captain on April 26, was subsequently awarded the Distinguished Service Cross.

Rowan's experience in Cuba was later immortalized in Elbert Hubbard's factually inaccurate account, "A Message to Garcia," published in the March 1899 issue of his monthly magazine, *The Philistine*. The article actually had little to do with Rowan's mission (there was, for example, no message in a "sealed oilskin pouch" from President William McKinley to García) and was largely an

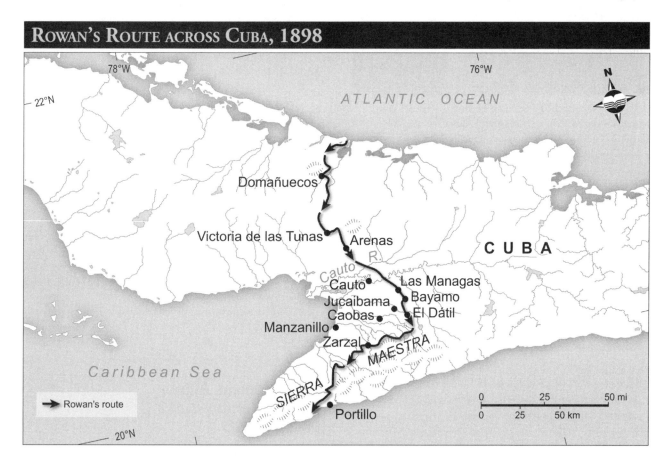

ROWAN'S ROUTE ACROSS CUBA, 1898

Lieutenant (later major) Andrew Summers Rowan served as liaison between the United States and Cuban rebels during the Spanish-American War. His experience was the inspiration for Elbert Hubbard's factually inaccurate tale "A Message to Garcia." (Library of Congress)

unvarnished appeal to workers to obey authority and to place duty above all else. Promoted to lieutenant colonel of volunteers on May 3, 1898, Rowan was mustered out of volunteer service on March 15, 1899. Following the Spanish-American War, he served in the Philippines and spent a year teaching military science in Kansas. Rowan retired from the army as a major in May 1899 and died on January 10, 1943.

SPENCER C. TUCKER

See also

García y Iñiguez, Calixto; "Message to Garcia, A"; Military Intelligence

Further Reading

Goodykoontz, Wells. *Major Andrew Summer Rowan, a West Virginian, the Man Who Carried the Message to Garcia.* Washington, DC: U.S. Government Printing Office, 1926.
Hubbard, Elbert. *A Message to Garcia.* Mechanicsburg, PA: Executive Books, 2002.
Trask, David F. *The War with Spain in 1898.* Lincoln: University of Nebraska Press, 1996.

Rubens, Horatio Seymour
Birth Date: June 6, 1869
Death Date: April 8, 1941

New York City attorney and chief counsel for the Cuban Junta. Born on June 6, 1869, Horatio Seymour Rubens became close friends with José Martí y Pérez, founder of the Cuban Revolutionary Party, and performed free legal work for the organization. Beginning in 1895, Rubens's law office at 66 Broadway in New York City became the headquarters of the so-called Peanut Club, which sponsored press conferences for newspaper reporters, including correspondents from leading New York City newspapers. The conferences, over which Rubens himself usually presided, were so-named because Cuban Junta officials always had copious amounts of peanuts on hand for reporters to eat.

It was Rubens who passed on to the press the notorious private letter critical of President William McKinley written by Spanish minister to the United States Enrique Dupuy de Lôme to Spanish editor and politician José Canalejas. The letter was published in William Randolph Hearst's *New York Journal* on February 9, 1898. In April 1898, learning that the McKinley administration did not intend to recognize the Cuban Republic, Rubens spoke out publicly in strong language, charging that for the United States to invade Cuba without recognition of the insurgent leadership would in effect be a declaration of war against the Cuban revolution. His statement greatly embarrassed the Cuban insurgent leadership.

Following the war, Rubens served as a legal counsel to the U.S. military government in Cuba. In 1932, he published a book, *Liberty: The Story of Cuba.* Rubens died in Garrison, New York, on April 8, 1941.

SPENCER C. TUCKER

See also

Cuban Junta; Cuban Revolutionary Party; Dupuy de Lôme-Canalejas Letter; Hearst, William Randolph; Martí y Pérez, José Julián; McKinley, William; Peanut Club

Further Reading

Auxier, George W. "The Propaganda Activities of the Cuban Junta in Precipitating the Spanish-American War, 1895–1898." *Hispanic American Historical Review* 19(3) (August 1939): 286–305.
Foner, Philip S. *The Spanish-Cuban-American War and the Birth of American Imperialism, 1895–1902.* 2 vols. New York: Monthly Review Press, 1972.
Kirk, John M. *José Martí: Mentor of the Cuban Nation.* Gainesville: University Press of Florida, 1983.
Trask, David F. *The War with Spain in 1898.* Lincoln: University of Nebraska Press, 1996.

Rubín Homent, Antero
Birth Date: February 15, 1851
Death Date: 1923

Spanish general and political leader. Born on February 15, 1851, Antero Rubín Homent followed his father, a career Spanish Army officer, into the military. Rubín joined the army at age 15 in May 1866 and the next year volunteered for service in Cuba. Returning to Spain as a lieutenant, he began his military studies at Vigo and Santiago de Compostella.

In 1869, Captain Rubín returned to Cuba, where he participated in putting down the Cuban insurgency of the Ten Years' War (1868–1878). He also saw service in Spain during the Third Carlist War (1872–1876). Again in Cuba, he was seriously wounded at the outbreak of the Cuban revolt of 1895.

Promoted to brigadier general on February 4, 1898, Rubín took command of the Regimento de María Cristina. During the Spanish-American War, he commanded the 1,500 Spanish troops in the Battle of Las Guásimas on June 24, 1898. He then obeyed orders to withdraw to Santiago in order to avoid being cut off. On July 1, he directed Spanish forces in the Battle of San Juan Hill during which his horse was shot from underneath him.

Rubín emerged from the war with his military reputation intact and was repatriated to Spain in August 1898. Promoted to major general in 1908 and to lieutenant general in 1916, he was appointed captain-general of Galicia in 1917. Rubín retired from the army in 1923 and died that same year.

SPENCER C. TUCKER

See also
Las Guásimas, Battle of; San Juan Heights, Battle of; Santiago de Cuba Land Campaign

Further Reading
Nofi, Albert A. *The Spanish-American War: 1898.* Conshohocken, PA: Combined Books, 1996.
O'Toole, G. J. A. *The Spanish War: An American Epic, 1898.* New York: Norton, 1984.

Rusling, James Fowler
Birth Date: April 14, 1834
Death Date: April 1, 1918

Lawyer, U.S. Army general during the American Civil War, and author. Born in Warren County, New Jersey, on April 14, 1834, James Fowler Rusling graduated from Dickinson College, Carlisle, Pennsylvania, in 1854, and then taught at the Dickinson Williamsport Seminary until 1857. He was admitted to the bar in Pennsylvania that same year and then in 1859 was admitted to the bar in New Jersey, where he set up a private practice in Trenton.

In August 1861 during the Civil War, Rusling was commissioned a first lieutenant of the 5th New Jersey Volunteer Infantry Regiment. That October he was a captain and quartermaster of the 2nd Division of III Corps. Promoted to lieutenant colonel in May 1863, he became quartermaster of III Corps. At the end of the war, he was the inspector of the Quartermaster Department of the army, and in February 1866, he was breveted brigadier general of volunteers.

Rusling left the army and returned to his law practice in September 1867. He wrote several books, among them *The Great West and the Pacific Coast* (1877) and *Men and Things I Saw in Civil War Days* (1899). He was a tax commissioner in New Jersey during 1896 and a trustee of Dickinson College from 1861 to 1883 and again from 1904 until his death.

A devout Methodist who also wrote church hymns, Rusling was a member of the General Conference of the Methodist Episcopal Church. As a member of that church's General Missionary Committee, he was part of a delegation that met with President William McKinley on November 21, 1898. A major issue at the time was the U.S. government's decision to acquire all of the Philippine Islands from Spain. In "Interview with President William McKinley" in the January 22, 1899, issue of *The Christian Advocate,* Rusling published an account of that meeting, reporting the president as having told the group the following:

> The truth is I didn't want the Philippines and when they came to us as a gift from the gods, I did not know what to do about them. . . . I sought counsel from all sides—Democrats as well as Republicans—but got little help. I thought first we should take only Manila; then Luzon; then other islands, perhaps, also. I walked the floor of the White House night after night until midnight; and I am not ashamed to tell you, gentlemen, that I went down on my knees and prayed Almighty God for light and guidance more than one night.
>
> And one night late it came to me this way—I don't know how it was, but it came: (1) that we could not give them back to Spain—that would be cowardly and dishonorable; (2) that we could not turn them over to France or Germany—our commercial rivals in the Orient—that would be bad business and discreditable; (3) that we could not leave them to themselves—they were unfit for self-government—and they would soon have anarchy and misrule over there worse than Spain's was; and (4) that there was nothing left for us to do but to take them all, and to educate the Filipinos and uplift and civilize and Christianize them, and by God's grace do the very best we could by them, as our fellow-men for whom Christ also died. And then I went to bed, and went to sleep and slept soundly.

This account was widely circulated, but there was never any corroboration of it. A further question of the account also arises in that Rusling used much the same language in his 1899 book on the American Civil War in which he describes Lincoln receiving divine inspiration before giving the Gettysburg Address.

Rusling died in Trenton on April 1, 1918.

SPENCER C. TUCKER

See also
McKinley, William; Philippine Islands, U.S. Acquisition of

Further Reading
Bailey, Thomas A. *A Diplomatic History of the American People.* 10th ed. New York: Prentice Hall, 1980.
Pomeroy, William J. *American Neo-Colonialism: Its Emergence in the Philippines and Asia.* New York: International Publishers, 1970.

Wolff, Leon. *Little Brown Brother: How the United States Purchased and Pacified the Philippine Islands at the Century's Turn.* Garden City, NY: Doubleday, 1961.

Russo-Japanese War
Start Date: February 10, 1904
End Date: September 5, 1905

In the 1890s, Russia temporarily set aside its ambitions in the Balkans to seek influence over or outright control of Manchuria and Korea. These would provide warm-water ports to supplement Vladivostok, which was closed by ice part of each year. Control of Manchuria would also allow Russia to establish a more direct rail line to Vladivostok.

Following the 1894–1895 Sino-Japanese War, Russia posed as the defender of Chinese territorial integrity to advance its own position in China, including a lease on the Liaodong (Liaotung) Peninsula, which had been surrendered to Japan in the Treaty of Shimonoseki only to have European powers force Japan to return it to China. The Russians then proceeded to build a naval base at Port Arthur on the Liaodong Peninsula, infuriating the Japanese who became further angered when Russia sent troops into Manchuria during the 1900 Boxer Rebellion and maintained them there afterward.

Tsar Nicholas II and most of his advisers were determined to take Manchuria and even Korea, which the Japanese considered part of their sphere of influence. In 1902, Japan secured an alliance with Great Britain. Directed against Russia, the alliance provided for both powers to maintain a benevolent neutrality in the event of war with another power and, more important, provided for naval cooperation should either face a war with two powers. At the same time, Japan's efforts to secure a compromise agreement with Russia met with delaying tactics from St. Petersburg. Believing correctly that the Russian government was simply stalling, Tokyo then broke off diplomatic relations. Apparently, Nicholas II and most of his advisers wanted war but on Russian terms. They were certain that Japan would never instigate a war. However, the Japanese decided not to wait for Russia's convenience and prepared a preemptive strike against the Russian naval base at Port Arthur to secure control of the seas, an essential precondition for the transportation of troops to Manchuria and Korea.

To the casual observer, the war appeared to be a mismatch. Although Russia was vastly superior in resources and manpower (its army numbered on paper some 4.5 million men), it was seriously handicapped at the outset of the war because it was unable to bring its full strength to bear. The conflict was far distant from the heart of Russia, and troops and supplies had to be shipped 5,500 miles over the single-track Trans-Siberian railway. A gap in the line at Lake Baikal complicated logistical problems.

The Russian Navy was divided into three main squadrons, again widely separated—the Baltic, the Black Sea, and the Pacific—and

Two Russian warships shown here wrecked in the harbor in December 1904 during the Japanese siege of Port Arthur. (Library of Congress)

it was difficult to concentrate them. Russian troops lacked enthusiasm for the war, the purpose of which they either did not understand or did not approve. Indeed, the war never received the wholehearted support of the Russian people. Inefficiency and corruption, which had so often undermined Russian armies in the past, again appeared in this conflict. Finally, it was Russia's misfortune to have a supreme command lacking both initiative and strategic ability.

Japan, on the other hand, had a highly disciplined, efficient, and enthusiastic army and navy. Japan's military was well trained and ably led and was loyally supported by the populace at home. Many of the more powerful ships of the Japanese Navy were new. Furthermore, Japan was in close proximity to the seat of hostilities and, assuming control of the sea, could place its forces in the field with a minimum of difficulty.

On February 6, 1904, Vice Admiral Togo Heihachiro's Combined Fleet departed for Port Arthur. At the same time, Vice Admiral Uryu Sotokichi sailed with a squadron for Korea to ensure the safe landing of transports bearing troops of the army's 12th Division. Two days later, on February 8, Uryu's squadron arrived at Chemulpo (present-day Inchon) and the next day engaged two of three Russian ships there, damaging them. The Russian crews then scuttled all three vessels.

In the Pacific, aside from the warships at Chemulpo, the Russians had at Vladivostok 4 first-class cruisers and 17 torpedo boats. But their most powerful ships—7 battleships and 4 cruisers—were at Port Arthur. Because the Japanese had cut the cable between Port Arthur and Korea early on February 7, the Russians did not know of the Chemulpo attack.

During the night of February 8–9, 1904, Togo launched a surprise torpedo attack against the Russian squadron, then just outside the harbor at Port Arthur. In the attack, two Russian battleships and a cruiser were badly damaged. The next day, Togo brought up his heavy ships to shell the shore batteries, the town, and Russian ships from long range. Although four Russian ships were damaged, most Japanese vessels were also hit, and Togo reluctantly ordered the Combined Fleet to withdraw. There were no pangs of conscience in Tokyo over these surprise attacks, and not until February 10 did Japan formally declare war.

The Japanese were frustrated at their inability to destroy the Russian naval forces at Port Arthur in the initial attack, and they were now obliged to keep up the pressure and adopt attrition tactics. A new Russian commander, Vice Admiral Stepan Ossipovitch Makarov, took command at Port Arthur and initiated a series of sorties to harass the Japanese cruisers while avoiding contact with Togo's battleships. Both sides also laid minefields, but Makarov was killed and his battleship lost when it ran over a known Japanese minefield in April. The Japanese also lost two battleships to mines off Port Arthur. But eventually, Japanese troops cut off Port Arthur from the land side and drove the tsar's forces back to the north.

Following the first Japanese land assault on Port Arthur, Nicholas II ordered Admiral Vilgelm Vitgeft, Makarov's successor, to break free and steam to Vladivostok. Vitgeft was determined to take the whole squadron and on August 10, 1904, sortied with 18 ships. That afternoon, Togo closed on the Russians with 34 ships and 29 torpedo boats. In the Battle of the Yellow Sea, Togo's omnipresent good luck held. Although themselves struck hard, the Japanese ships scored two hits late in the day that killed Vitgeft and put the flagship out of control and the Russian battle line into complete confusion. The Russian squadron then scattered. No Russian ship had been destroyed or taken in the battle, however. Five battleships, 1 cruiser, and 3 destroyers regained in Port Arthur. Most others were interned in Chinese ports and Saigon.

News of the Battle of the Yellow Sea reached Vladivostok on August 11, but not until August 13 did three cruisers under Rear Admiral Nikolai von Essen go to the assistance of the Port Arthur Squadron. On August 14, they ran into Admiral Kammimura Hikonojo's four armored cruisers. In the resulting Battle of Ulsan, the Japanese sank one of the Russian cruisers. The others were able to regain Vladivostok, but Japan now had complete control of the sea.

In the autumn of 1904, Japanese troops under Field Marshal Iwao Oyama defeated the main Russian army under General Alexei Kuropatkin in the August 25–September 3 Battle of Liaoyang and again during October 5–17 at Shao-Ho. On January 2, 1905, Port Arthur surrendered. The remaining ships there had been destroyed the previous month by Japanese siege howitzers. During January 26–27, another land battle occurred at Sandepu (also known as the Battle of Heikoutai), 36 miles southwest of Mukden. Kuropatkin, reinforced with 300,000 men, attacked and came close to defeating

Oyama's 220,000 Japanese. A Russian victory could have changed the entire war, but Kuropatkin failed to press the attack, and the battle ended in stalemate. Then, in the great February 21–March 10, 1906, Battle of Mukden, the Russians lost 100,000 men, while the Japanese lost 70,000.

Following this defeat, Russia's fate appeared to hang on one last-ditch naval effort by the 30 ships of Rear Admiral Zinovi Petrovich Rozhdestvenski's Baltic Fleet, renamed the 2nd Pacific Squadron. It had left its Baltic bases in October 1904 for the Far East. The trip was an incredible odyssey that included the Russians opening fire on the British Hull fishing fleet in the North Sea, fearing that they were Japanese torpedo boats. This Dogger Bank Incident almost brought war with Britain. With little time for training and insufficient gunnery practice, the 2nd Pacific Squadron was destroyed by Togo's well-trained and overhauled Combined Fleet in the May 27–28, 1905, Battle of Tsushima.

In the battle, the Japanese sank, captured, or disabled 8 Russian battleships. Of 12 Russian ships in the battle line, 8 were sunk, including 3 of the new Russian battleships, and the other 4 had been captured. Four cruisers were sunk, and 1 was scuttled; 3 limped into Manila and were interned; and another made it to Vladivostok. Four destroyers were sunk, 1 was captured, and 1 was interned at Shanghai; 2 reached Vladivostok. Three special service ships were sunk, 1 was interned at Shanghai, and 1 escaped to Madagascar.

Togo lost only three torpedo boats. Although other ships suffered damage, all were serviceable. In personnel losses the Russians had 4,830 men killed or drowned and just under 7,000 taken prisoner. Japanese personnel losses were 110 killed and 590 wounded.

In just one day, Russia ceased to be a major Pacific power. Fifty years would pass before it regained status at sea. The battle confirmed Japan as the premier military power of the Far East. It also led the Japanese to believe that wars could be turned on one big battle.

The fighting around Port Arthur and at Tsushima had been decided by main battery guns as well as medium-range quick-firing guns rather than torpedoes, as many navalists had predicted. Ironically, Tsushima was the only major decisive fleet action in the history of the steel battleship. In the future, however, underwater or aerial weapons would come to exercise dominance.

Tsushima led to Russian capitulation on land. Both Kaiser Wilhelm II and U.S. president Theodore Roosevelt had urged peace upon the belligerents. Although Russia, with its vast resources and manpower, might possibly have sent new armies to continue the war, popular discontent and political unrest at home resulted in the Russian Revolution of 1905, alarming the tsar's ministers and making them willing to consider peace proposals. On the other hand, Japan's military efforts had nearly bankrupted the country, so its leaders were also ready to halt military operations.

On Roosevelt's invitation, a peace conference opened in the unlikely venue of Portsmouth, New Hampshire. Sergius Witte, who had opposed the war, ably represented Russia at the conference and succeeded in saving his country from the worst consequences of the defeat. The September 5, 1905, Treaty of Portsmouth transferred Russia's cessions in southern Manchuria to Japan, converting that area into a Japanese sphere of influence. Russia also recognized Japan's preponderant interest in Korea and its right to control and protect the Korean government. In addition, Russia surrendered to Japan the southern half of Sakhalin Island, which Japan had occupied during the war. The treaty, favorable as it was to Japan, was not popular there. Japanese leaders had not obtained the indemnity they wanted, and the Japanese people were unaware of how close the country was to bankruptcy.

The Russo-Japanese War showcased the high stakes involved in great power rivalry in East Asia. The 1890s had witnessed a significant imperial push in the Far East, perhaps best exemplified by the Sino-Japanese War, the Spanish-American War, and the Philippine-American War. Coming on the heels of turn-of-the-century expansionism and the Boxer Rebellion, the Russo-Japanese War capped off a feverish scramble for hegemony in the Far East that was driven by a search for markets as well as by imperial aspirations and military and geostrategic concerns.

Spencer C. Tucker

See also

Boxer Rebellion; Expansionism; Imperialism; Japan; Sino-Japanese War

Further Reading

Busch, Noel F. *The Emperor's Sword*. New York: Funk and Wagnalls, 1969.

Corbett, Julian S. *Maritime Operations in the Russo-Japanese War, 1904–1905*. 2 Vols. Rockville, MD: Sidney Kramer, 1994.

Evans, David C., and Mark R. Peattie. *Kaigun: Strategy, Tactics, and Technology in the Imperial Japanese Navy, 1887–1941*. Annapolis, MD: Naval Institute Press, 1997.

Grove, Eric. *Big Fleet Actions: Tsushima, Jutland, Philippine Sea*. London: Arms and Armour, 1995.

Hough, Richard. *The Fleet That Had to Die*. New York: Viking, 1958.

Warner, Denis, and Peggy Warner. *The Tide at Sunrise: A History of the Russo-Japanese War, 1904–1905*. New York: Charterhouse, 1974.

S

Safford, William Edwin
Birth Date: December 14, 1859
Death Date: January 10, 1926

U.S. Navy officer, botanist, and ethnologist who studied the plants and people of Guam while serving as the U.S. deputy to the naval governor of Guam between 1899 and 1900. A pioneer in the field of ethnobotany (the study of how populations and cultures make use of indigenous plants), William Edwin Safford was born in Chillicothe, Ohio, on December 14, 1859, the son of a judge. While Safford was in primary school, some of his classmates, the children of German immigrants, taught him German. He entered the United States Naval Academy, Annapolis, in 1876 and studied marine biology. Upon graduation in 1880, he was assigned to the side-wheeler frigate *Powhatan.*

From 1883 to 1885, Safford studied botany at Yale University. After completing his studies, he enrolled in graduate courses in marine zoology at Harvard University. He then continued his research in botany and ethnology while serving with the U.S. Navy in the South Pacific. From 1889 to 1891, he was a language instructor at the Naval Academy. Taking a leave of absence from the navy, he served as commissioner to Bolivia and Peru for the Chicago Colombian Exhibition during 1891–1893.

Returning to active duty in 1893, Safford was promoted to lieutenant in March 1897. Following service in the Spanish-American War, in 1899 he was appointed deputy to the U.S. governor of Guam, Richard P. Leary, who delegated most of his responsibilities to Safford. While in Guam, Safford researched the plant life on the small tropical island, especially those plants that had an economic value, and published his findings in the book *The Useful Plants of the Island of Guam* (1905). This work remains the seminal study of plant life on Guam and a pioneering work in the field of ethnobiology and ethnobotany. In addition to studying the plant life of Guam, Safford also studied the island's people. He recorded their history, culture, and folkways and published *The Chamorro Language of the Island of Guam,* a monograph of Chamorro, the native language of the people of Guam, also in 1905. Safford's work remains the most significant study of the Chamorro language.

After Leary's term as governor ended in 1900, Safford left his post in Guam and retired from the navy in 1902. He became a member of the Botanical Society in 1902 and served as president of the association in 1922. He took a post with the U.S. Department of Agriculture as an economic botanist in 1902. While working for the Department of Agriculture, he published *Cactacaea of Northeastern and Central Mexico* (1909), *Edible Plants and Textiles of Ancient America* (1916), *Notes on the Genus Dahlia* (1919), *Natural History of Paradise Key and the Nearby Everglades of Florida* (1919), *Synopsis of the Genus Datura* (1921), *Daturas of the Old World and New* (1922), and *Ant Acacias and Acacia Ants of Mexico* (1923).

While in Washington, D.C., Safford spent much of his time in the National Herbarium. In 1920, he was awarded a doctorate in marine zoology from George Washington University. Although he suffered a debilitating stroke on March 17, 1924, he continued to dictate his research to assistants until his death on January 10, 1926, in Washington, D.C. For his outstanding contributions in the field of botany, the genus of 2 plants, *Saffordia Maxon* (1913) and *Saffordiella Merrill* (1914), were named for him. In addition, 16 species, including *Vicia Saffordii Phil* (1895) and *Dianella Saffordii Fosberg and Sachet* (1987), have been named in his honor.

MICHAEL R. HALL

See also
Guam

Further Reading

Safford, William Edwin. *The Chamorro Language of Guam.* Washington, DC: W. H. Lowdermilk, 1905.

———. *Guam and Its People.* New York: Putnam, 1903.

———. *A Year on the Island of Guam: An Account of the First American Administration.* Washington, DC: H. L. McQueen, 1910.

Schultes, Richard Evans, and Siri V. Von Reis, eds. *Ethnobotany: Evolution of a Discipline.* Portland, OR: Timber Press, 1995.

Sagasta, Práxedes Mateo
Birth Date: July 21, 1825
Death Date: January 5, 1903

Spanish politician and prime minister (1881–1883, 1885–1890, 1892–1895, 1897–1899, 1901–1902). Práxedes Mateo Sagasta was born into a middle-class family in Torrecilla de Cameros, Spain, on July 21, 1825. His parents instilled the values of Spanish liberalism in their son at an early age. In 1842, Sagasta went to Madrid to study engineering and there joined the Progressive Party.

In part because he was a skilled orator, Sagasta quickly rose to prominence in the Progressive Party. In 1854, he was elected to represent Zamora in the Cortes (parliament). Although he lost the election of 1857, he returned to the Cortes in 1858 and served there until 1863. After he left the Cortes, he wrote numerous essays criticizing the increasingly authoritarian Spanish government headed by Queen Isabella II. In 1866, after participating in a failed coup against the government, Sagasta went into exile in France. There he edited a journal and plotted against the Spanish regime.

In 1868, Sagasta returned to Spain to take part in a revolution that overthrew Queen Isabella II. Sagasta conspired with the military, led by General Juan Prim, to overthrow the unpopular regime. Unlike many Liberals, however, Sagasta supported Prim's contention that a constitutional monarchy was the best safeguard to ensure order, stability, and liberalism. Sagasta served in the provisional government that replaced the monarchy, supporting Prim's 1870 search for a European nobleman to assume the throne of Spain. Elected king in November 1870, Amadeus of Savoy arrived in Madrid at the end of December. Prim, however, was shot on December 28 and died two days later.

Sagasta served in Amadeus's ill-fated government until the latter was overthrown in 1873. Amadeus, lacking the support of his strongest backer, Prim, was unable to form a stable government. Amadeus's rule was further weakened by turmoil in Cuba resulting from the Ten Years' War (1868–1878). After Amadeus's abdication, Sagasta served as a cabinet minister in the government of the First Spanish Republic.

The restoration of the Bourbon monarchy in 1875 restored political and economic stability to Spain. Favorably disposed toward the new monarch, King Alfonso XII, Sagasta decided to work within the system to institutionalize liberalism in Spain. In 1880, Sagasta united the Liberals in the Fusionist Liberal Party.

Práxedes Mateo Sagasta was a progressive Spanish politician who found himself in the difficult position of premier of Spain during the Spanish-American War, which he sought to avoid. (Martin Hume, *Modern Spain,* 1899)

For the next two decades, the Liberals and the Conservatives, who were led by Antonio Cánovas del Castillo, alternated in power. In 1885, following the death of Alfonso XII, Cánovas, eager to preserve order and stability, resigned and encouraged the regent, María Cristina, to appoint Sagasta prime minister. It was in 1890 during Sagasta's second term as prime minister that universal male suffrage was reintroduced in Spain. Although universal male suffrage had first been unveiled in the 1812 Cádiz Constitution, the volatile nature of the Napoleonic era and the 1814 restoration of the Bourbon monarchy ended Spain's first experiment with liberalism.

In 1890, Cánovas returned to power. He immediately reversed Sagasta's Liberal economic policies and implemented a protectionist tariff in 1892. This resulted in a serious decline in foreign trade and caused a fiscal crisis that weakened Spain's ability to modernize its navy. A temporary split in the Conservative Party allowed Sagasta to return to office in 1893. Cánovas, however, resumed office in March 1895 immediately after the outbreak of the Cuban War of Independence. Cánovas dispatched General Valeriano Weyler y Nicolau to Cuba to restore order and stability. The American press, however, exaggerated Weyler's draconian *reconcentrado* (reconcentration) policy, which created greater resentment against the Spanish in Cuba and increased tensions with the United States.

Following Cánovas's assassination on August 8, 1897, María Cristina brought in Sagasta as prime minister yet again to bring about a solution to the Cuban war. Sagasta appointed Segismeundo Moret y Prendergast colonial minister and replaced Weyler with the more conciliatory Ramón Blanco y Erenas, who favored a negotiated settlement. Sagasta also curtailed troop shipments to Cuba. In an effort to quell the Cuban War of Independence and diminish the possibility of American intervention, Moret granted local autonomy for the Cubans and on January 1, 1898, extended home rule to Cuba. Most of the revolutionaries, however, rejected this. Moret also attempted to reach some understanding regarding Cuban trade with the United States and to open the island to expanded U.S. imports.

In return for these concessions, Sagasta and Moret expected the United States to clamp down on American assistance to the Cuban revolutionaries and to shut down the Cuba Junta in New York City. Following a series of crises, most notably Spanish ambassador Enrique Dupuy de Lôme's 1898 letter that criticized President William McKinley and the explosion and sinking of the *Maine*, Sagasta found himself in the unenviable position of leading the Spanish government during the Spanish-American War, which erupted in April 1898.

With the war, Sagasta reshuffled his cabinet. He dropped Moret, who favored peace, and brought in a number of talented individuals who, it was hoped, would improve Spain's military performance. Sagasta favored a quick war, no matter the outcome, and approved sending Rear Admiral Pascual Cervera y Topete's Cádiz Squadron from the Cape Verde Islands to the Caribbean in order to assist the Spanish in Cuba and Puerto Rico.

The Treaty of Paris of December 10, 1898, came as a great shock to Sagasta and resulted in the loss of Cuba and Puerto Rico as well as the Philippines and Guam. Most Spaniards blamed him, and shortly after the treaty was signed, he was forced out of office. Sagasta died in Madrid on January 5, 1903.

MICHAEL R. HALL

See also

Alfonso XII, King of Spain; Blanco y Erenas, Ramón; Cervera y Topete, Pascual; Dupuy de Lôme, Enrique; Dupuy de Lôme-Canalejas Letter; *Maine*, USS; María Cristina, Queen Regent of Spain; McKinley, William; Weyler y Nicolau, Valeriano

Further Reading

Garcia, Juan Ramon Milan. *Sagasta: El Arte de Hacer Politica* [Sagasta: The Art of Making Politics]. Madrid: Biblioteca Nueva, 2001.

Ortiz, David. *Paper Liberals: Press and Politics in Restoration Spain.* Westport, CT: Greenwood, 2000.

Ross, Christopher. *Spain, 1812–1996.* London: Hodder Arnold, 2000.

Salisbury, Lord

See Gascoyne-Cecil, Robert Arthur Talbot

Samar Campaigns
Start Date: January 26, 1900
End Date: April 27, 1902

U.S. counterinsurgency and pacification operations lasting from January 26, 1900, to April 27, 1902, during the Philippine-American War. The easternmost and largest of the Visayan group in the central Philippine Islands, Samar is about 5,000 square miles in size and is located across the San Jacinto Straits north of Leyte. Samar proved difficult for U.S. military operations because of its dense jungle interior, lack of roads, and few navigable rivers. These greatly aided Filipino insurgent General Vicente Lukban in carrying out guerrilla warfare against the American forces. In 1900, Samar had a population of some 222,000 people.

There had been little U.S. military activity on Samar early in the war. Rope shortages made the pacification of the island, with its significant hemp production, a priority. On January 26, 1900, U.S. military governor of the Philippines Major General Elwell Otis ordered Brigadier General William Kobbe to employ the 43rd Infantry Regiment and occupy Calbayog and Catbalogan. They forced Lukban to withdraw into the interior. Colonel Arthur Murray and Major Henry Tureman Allen sought to establish civil order on Samar through benevolent assimilation, but Lukban's guerrillas also prevented civilians collaborating with the Americans through the use of intimidation, the burning of towns, and the killing of sympathizers. Allen began offensive operations immediately; however, Major General Arthur MacArthur visited the island in May 1900 and returned the American troops to their defensive garrisons. By July 1900, the first major campaign to secure Samar had failed.

Colonel E. E. Hardin replaced Murray in July 1900 and attempted to interdict trade between Leyte and Samar through naval blockade. By early 1901, however, the small U.S. occupation force on Samar barely held the hemp ports of Calbayog and Catbalogan. This all changed in May 1901 when Leyte was turned over to the Philippine Commission. The pacification of Samar then became a priority, for the rebels across the narrow straits in Samar threatened the pacification of Leyte.

On May 13, 1901, MacArthur transferred Samar back to Brigadier General Robert P. Hughes and ordered him to "clean up" Samar "as soon as possible." A quick inspection trip to Samar convinced Hughes that the situation there was indeed poor, with American troops largely confined to their occupation posts. In June Hughes extended the naval blockade to all the ports of Samar and ordered occupation forces to seize all boats except those used for fishing. Hughes also ordered sweeps of the interior and the destruction of rebel towns and crops. The navy assisted with amphibious operations. These actions deprived the local population of supplies, leading to widespread starvation, but did not break the back of the guerrilla resistance.

Elements of the 9th U.S. Infantry Regiment arrived at Balangiga in the late summer of 1901 at the request of Mayor Pedro Abayan, who had asked for protection from raids against his people. Such raids had in fact virtually ended in the mid-19th century, and Abayan was working for General Lukban.

Captain Thomas W. Connell's Company C of the 9th Regiment occupied Balangiga, and Connell set about trying to clean up the town. Connell instituted local work details that, unknown to him, soon involved some 100 of Lukban's men. To promote a more peaceful atmosphere, Connell also prohibited the carrying of firearms except by sentries. On September 27, the insurrectionists smuggled weapons to the interior in coffins containing the bodies of children who had died in a cholera epidemic, while a number of guerrillas also gained access to Balangga disguised as women carrying the coffins. On the morning of September 28, the rebels struck. They seized an American sentry's weapon and shot him, then rushed the mess hall where most of Connell's men, who were unarmed, were eating breakfast. Some soldiers managed to escape to the arsenal and then by boat to Basey, held by Company G. But 59 of the soldiers, including Connell, were either killed in the attack or died of their wounds on the way to Basey. When an American relief force arrived at Balangiga, it found the town deserted and, after attending to the American dead, burned it to the ground.

The yellow press in the United States immediately compared Balangiga to Custer's Last Stand, and there were immediate demands for revenge. With emotions running high, Major General Adna Chaffee sent 4,000 soldiers to Samar, while Rear Admiral Frederick Rodgers dispatched a marine battalion under Major Littleton W. T. Waller. Chaffee selected Brigadier General Jacob H. Smith to assume command of operations in October 1901. Smith, who was well known for his harsh methods, instructed Waller to take no prisoners, to "kill and burn," and to turn Samar into "a howling wilderness."

Waller soon located Lukban's headquarters in the interior on the Sohotón Cliffs along the Cadacan River. Waller planned a land and amphibious operation. In a sensational success, the marines took the rebel headquarters, killing 30 insurgents with no losses of their own.

Waller then mounted another operation to the interior, planning to cross Samar from east to west. Starting from the army base at Lanang on the eastern coast, he undertook this operation against the advice of the army commander, who could supply only limited rations. The jungle proved virtually impenetrable, and the marines soon ran out of food. The Filipino bearers with the marines claimed not to know what was edible in the jungle and refused to help. Waller then sent half of the force back to Lanang under Captain David D. Porter and pushed on with the remainder. Porter was forced to leave some of his weakened marines behind on the march. An army rescue team subsequently found 9 of them dead, and 1 was never located. Learning that the rest of the bearers had allowed a marine lieutenant to be killed by a bearer, Porter had all 10 of the bearers arrested and sent to Basey.

An ill Waller also made it to Basey, where Lieutenant John H. A. Day had discovered a conspiracy to repeat the Balangiga Mas-

sacre at Basey. Day had the mayor arrested and executed and the local priest imprisoned. Day also secured permission from a delirious Waller to execute all of the bearers arrested earlier, and Waller approved. Day had the 10 men shot in the town square.

On his recovery, Waller reported all of this to Smith, who duly sent it on to Chaffee, who then forwarded the news to the War Department. News of this shocked the American public and empowered American anti-imperialists. Indeed, at the end of January 1902, the U.S. Senate began committee hearings (the Committee on the Philippines, otherwise known as the Lodge Committee) regarding military atrocities in the Philippines.

U.S. forces captured Lukban on February 18, 1902, and continued pressuring the guerrillas, who were by then suffering from starvation and lacked the ability to sustain combat operations. Brigadier General Joseph Grant accepted the guerrillas' surrender on April 27, 1902.

Meanwhile, reaction to U.S. actions on Samar led to Waller's arrest and court-martial. He remained loyal to Smith and did not reveal the latter's orders to him but instead based his actions on American Civil War General Order 100 that authorized actions against guerrillas and civilians who aided them. When Smith testified against Waller, however, and perjured himself by claiming that the latter had acted on his own responsibility, Waller broke his silence and revealed Smith's written orders to him. A parade of witnesses confirmed Waller's testimony. This resulted in Waller's acquittal and Smith's arrest, court-martial, and conviction.

DAWN OTTEVAERE NICKESON AND SPENCER C. TUCKER

See also

Allen, Henry Tureman; Atrocities; Balangiga Massacre; Benevolent Assimilation; Chaffee, Adna Romanza, Sr.; Committee on the Philippines; Lodge, Henry Cabot; Lukban, Vicente; MacArthur, Arthur; Otis, Elwell Stephen; Pacification Program, Philippine Islands; Smith, Jacob Hurd; Waller, Littleton Tazewell; Yellow Journalism

Further Reading

Feuer, A. B. *America at War: The Philippines, 1898–1913.* Westport, CT: Praeger, 2002.
Gates, John M. *Schoolbooks and Krags: The United States Army in the Philippines, 1898–1902.* Westport, CT: Greenwood, 1973.
Linn, Brian McAllister. *The Philippine War, 1899–1902.* Lawrence: University Press of Kansas, 2000.

Samoa

Group of islands located in the Polynesian region of the South Pacific Ocean. Today the islands form the Independent State of Samoa (formerly German Samoa or Western Samoa) and the Territory of American Samoa, which belongs to the United States.

Traders from Germany and Great Britain began arriving in Samoa in the 19th century. They set up plantations and trading houses; exported products such as coconut oil, copra, and cocoa; and used the harbors as coaling stations. In 1878, the United States obtained the strategic harbor of Pago Pago, which led to friction with both Germany and Britain. In 1879, the three Western nations agreed to establish consulates in the capital at Apia to guarantee equal economic opportunities. However, for the next 20 years, the consuls were involved in inner-Samoan conflicts and supplied arms, and in some cases troops, to the warring Samoan parties, further deteriorating the political situation.

When King Malietoa Laupepa ascended the throne in 1881, the German consul felt at a disadvantage, as the new king was purported to be under the influence of the London Missionary Society. The Germans were even more worried when New Zealand demanded stronger British involvement in the region. In 1884, the German consul Oscar Wilhelm Stübel forced Malietoa to sign a Samoan-German contract that favored German interests. When Stübel realized a few months later that this was not sufficient in strengthening his position, he used German troops stationed on the island to invade the royal palace and oust the king. Malietoa's rival Tamasese was then proclaimed as the new ruler. When news of these events reached Europe and Berlin received protests from both Britain and the United States, German chancellor Otto von Bismarck reprimanded Stüber for his unauthorized actions.

The British government, which was then more interested in North Africa, would have favored a solution with Germany over the Samoa question, yet London was forced under pressure from New Zealand to stay involved in the archipelago. Neither of the two countries believed it necessary to include the United States in their negotiations. When Grover Cleveland became president in 1885, however, his administration took a more active role in Pacific affairs. In April 1886, the U.S. consul in Samoa, Benjamim Greenebaum, interfered in Samoan politics. He not only promised to assist King Malietoa but also proclaimed Samoa an American protectorate. U.S. secretary of state Thomas F. Bayard immediately denounced Greenebaum's actions and invited Germany and Great Britain to solve the Samoan conflict at a conference to be held in Washington in June 1887. Both countries agreed to the proposal while at the same time continuing secret negotiations in order to find a compromise of their own. Great Britain assented to recognize German paramount interests in Samoa, hoping that Germany would support its policy in Egypt in return.

Because of these prior Anglo-German agreements, the conference in Washington was doomed to failure before it even began. The United States refused to accept any German control over Samoa and preferred to keep the islands neutral. The conference ended without satisfactory result.

Tensions over Samoa escalated in August 1887 when new German consul in Apia Edward Becker demanded an apology from King Malietoa for insulting the German emperor. When the latter declined, Becker had him taken prisoner and deported him to Kamerun (Cameroon) in Africa. Becker then reinstated King Tamasese and imposed martial law. Soon, German soldiers controlled all the principal buildings. Within a few days, Samoa had become a de facto German possession. The United States demanded an immediate return to the status quo, but Great Britain,

hoping to gain Tonga, protested yet accepted Germany's course of action.

Tensions in the islands increased when followers of Mataafa, another contestant for the throne who was supported by Anglo-American traders, fought Tamasese's troops in the spring of 1888. German soldiers stationed on Samoa were called in to help Tamasese. War between Germany and the United States over Samoa appeared to be a possibility when the German consul declared Samoa to be in a state of war in January 1889 and imposed martial law throughout the archipelago, affecting both British and U.S. nationals.

Public opinion in the United States grew increasingly hostile toward imperial Germany, yet Secretary of State Thomas Bayard insisted on resolving the conflict by diplomacy. President Cleveland, however, ordered U.S. Navy rear admiral Lewis A. Kimberly to Samoa with three ships to protect U.S. interests there. A violent hurricane in Apia Harbor destroyed or damaged a number of German, British, and U.S. warships, effectively ending the possibility of armed conflict.

Bismarck, meanwhile, publicly criticized the German consul's actions and invited Great Britain and the United States to a conference in Berlin. In June 1889, all three countries agreed to solve further Samoan problems mutually by forming a three-power protectorate. The Act of Berlin of that date also restored Malietoa as king. The Samoan monarch was nominally head of the islands yet had virtually no power.

For the next 10 years, Samoan conflicts were kept at bay, while the diplomats of the three countries were involved in trying to find a long-term solution for ruling the archipelago. When Malietoa died in 1898, Germany proposed dividing the islands to prevent further Samoan infighting over the throne. The United States was to receive the island of Tutuila, including Pago Pago; Germany was to keep Upolu and Savaii; and Great Britain was to renounce all rights to Samoa and receive Tonga instead. British prime minister Robert Gascoyne-Cecil, Lord Salisbury, gave in to pressure from Australia and New Zealand and declined the proposal.

In the meantime, the diplomats on Samoa were again taking action into their own hands. When U.S. judge William Lea Chambers, who had been installed as superior judge for Samoa at the conference in Berlin, decided in December 1898 that Malietoa's son, Malietoa Tanu, was to be the next king rather than Mataafa, fighting began again. The Germans backed Mataafa, and the United States and Britain backed Malietoa Tanu. The German diplomats protested Chambers's decision and took command of the courthouse. Chambers ordered British captain Frederick Charles Doveton Sturdee to restore the status quo.

In this crisis, the United States, Great Britain, and Germany all dispatched warships to Samoa with the intention of protecting their interests there. U.S. rear admiral Albert Kautz sent Mataafa an ultimatum to leave Apia. When Mataafa did not respond, Kautz shelled the city, which damaged the German consulate, and ordered all Europeans to leave. Forces from all three countries took part in the Samoan Civil War.

President William McKinley's formal apology for Kautz's actions in March 1899 opened the way for new diplomatic negotiations. Great Britain, facing war in South Africa, was anxious to bring the conflict over Samoa to an end. The Treaty of Berlin of November 1899 abolished the Samoan monarchy and split the archipelago into two parts. The western islands were given to Germany (and became the independent state of Samoa in 1962), while the eastern islands became a U.S. territory. Great Britain gave up its claims in exchange for Tonga, Fiji, and some Melanesian islands.

KATJA WUESTENBECKER

See also
Cleveland, Stephen Grover; Gascoyne-Cecil, Robert Arthur Talbot; McKinley, William

Further Reading
Kennedy, Paul M. "Bismarck's Imperialism: The Case of Samoa, 1880–1890." *Historical Journal* 15 (1972): 261–283.
———. *The Samoan Tangle: A Study in Anglo-German-American Relations, 1878–1900.* New York: Barnes and Noble, 1974.
Masterman, Sylvia. *The Origins of International Rivalry in Samoa, 1845–1884.* London: Allen and Unwin, 1934.

Sampson, William Thomas
Birth Date: February 9, 1840
Death Date: May 6, 1902

U.S. admiral. Born in Palmyra, New York, on February 9, 1840, William Thomas Sampson became an acting midshipman on September 24, 1857, and graduated first in his class from the United States Naval Academy and was promoted to midshipman on June 1, 1861. Sampson began his career as an instructor at the academy. He was promoted to lieutenant on July 16, 1862. Although he saw only limited action during the American Civil War, he nearly lost his life while serving on the monitor *Patapsco* in the South Atlantic Blockading Squadron. On January 15, 1865, the monitor struck a large mine or mines off Charleston, South Carolina, and sank in only about 15 seconds, taking down 62 officers and men. Only 5 officers and 38 men were saved, Sampson among them.

After the Civil War, Sampson served on the steam frigate *Colorado* in the European Squadron and was promoted to lieutenant commander on July 15, 1866. During the three decades between the end of the Civil War and the outbreak of the Spanish-American War, Sampson further enhanced his reputation as an outstanding officer and man of considerable intellect. He was again an instructor at the Naval Academy and served in the Bureau of Navigation and on the screw sloop *Congress*. Promoted to commander on August 9, 1874, he was assigned to the Naval Observatory and then had charge of the Naval Torpedo Station at Newport, Rhode Island. On September 9, 1886, he became superintendent of the Naval Academy. Promoted to captain on April 9, 1889, he fitted out the protected cruiser *San Francisco* at Mare Island Navy Yard and then assumed command of the ship on its commissioning that November.

Rear Admiral William Thomas Sampson commanded the North Atlantic Squadron in the U.S. naval blockade of Cuba and subsequent Battle of Santiago de Cuba during the Spanish-American War. (Library of Congress)

In June 1892, he was assigned as inspector of ordnance at the Washington Navy Yard. He became chief of the Bureau of Ordnance in January 1893.

In June 1897, Sampson assumed command of the new battleship *Iowa*. After the battleship *Maine* blew up in Havana Harbor on February 15, 1898, President William McKinley named Sampson to head the naval board charged with investigating the cause of the disaster. On March 26, 1898, Sampson was advanced to temporary rear admiral and took command of the North Atlantic Squadron, replacing Rear Admiral Montgomery Sicard who had taken ill. Sampson's promotion may have planted the seed of his later troubles with Commodore Winfield Scott Schley, who, along with a number of other officers, was senior to Sampson. Evidence suggests that Sampson was not in the best of health at the time, a fact that he apparently managed to conceal from all but those closest to him. He may have suffered from what we now identify as multiple infarct dementia, caused by a succession of small strokes that can reduce the victim's mental acuity but do not affect the personality. It certainly did not affect his strong leadership of the squadron in the Caribbean theater of war.

On April 29, 1898, a week after the U.S. declaration of war on Spain, Spanish rear admiral Pascual Cervera y Topete, ordered against his recommendations, put to sea with his squadron from the Cape Verde Islands to Cuba. Meanwhile, Sampson had put to sea from Key West for Cuba, his flag on the armored cruiser *New York*. He established a blockade of Havana and the Cuban northern coast and then extended the blockade to the southern coast.

After establishing the blockade, Sampson, with a small task force under his personal command, sailed for San Juan, Puerto Rico, hoping to locate Cervera. Arriving off that port on May 12, Sampson failed to find Cervera and, following a brief bombardment of San Juan's defenses, returned to Key West, where he arrived on May 18 just after Commodore Schley and his Flying Squadron. Schley was then ordered to Santiago but was dilatory in carrying out that order, not establishing a blockade of that port until May 28. Cervera, who had ample opportunity to depart from Santiago, failed to do so, and Sampson arrived on June 1 with his own ships and established a strong presence off Santiago. The blockaders included five battleships, two armored cruisers, and a number of smaller cruisers and auxiliaries. With the Spanish squadron now effectively neutralized, Sampson provided support to the landing of Major General William R. Shafter's U.S. V Corps at Daiquirí and Siboney.

Shafter believed that the navy should enter Santiago Harbor and destroy the Spanish fleet, but Sampson argued that the ground forces should first capture the forts, the guns of which dominated the harbor entrance and posed a serious threat to the navy's ships. Early on the morning of July 3, 1898, Sampson headed east from Santiago in the *New York* (commanded by Captain French Ensor Chadwick) for a conference with Shafter. As luck would have it, Cervera chose that moment to attempt a breakout. In Sampson's absence, Schley had command of the blockading ships and led the attack on the Spanish ships as they emerged from the sanctuary of Santiago Harbor.

Learning of the battle by means of smoke and signal flags, Sampson headed back at flank speed. But the *New York* did not make it back in time to contribute to the near total destruction of the Spanish squadron. Officially, Sampson was credited with the naval victory, which he announced in a cable to Washington as "The fleet under my command offers the nation as a Fourth of July present the whole of Cervera's fleet." It was Schley who received the plaudits in the press, however. Claims and counterclaims over responsibility for the victory led to subsequent controversy and much ill will in the navy.

After the war, Sampson was appointed Cuban commissioner on August 20, 1898, but he assumed command of the Atlantic Fleet that December. In October 1899, he took command of the Boston Navy Yard. All the while, his health had continued to deteriorate, and he retired on February 9, 1902. Sampson died in Washington, D.C., on May 6, 1902.

SPENCER C. TUCKER

See also
Cervera y Topete, Pascual; Daiquirí Beachhead, Cuba; *Maine*, USS, Inquiries into the Loss of; Sampson-Schley Controversy; Santiago de Cuba, Battle of; Schley, Winfield Scott; Shafter, William Rufus; United States Navy

Further Reading
Azoy, A. C. M. *Signal 250! Sea Fight Off Santiago.* New York: David McKay, 1964.
Chadwick, French Ensor. *The Relations of the United States and Spain V1: The Spanish-American War.* Reprint ed. Kila, MT: Kessinger, 2007.
Dawson, Joseph G., III. "William T. Sampson: Progressive Technologist as Naval Commander." In *Admirals of the New Steel Navy: Makers of the American Naval Tradition, 1880–1930,* edited by James C. Bradford, 149–179. Annapolis, MD: Naval Institute Press, 1990.
———. "William T. Sampson and Santiago: Blockade, Victory, and Controversy." In *Crucible of Empire: The Spanish-American War and Its Aftermath,* edited by James C. Bradford, 47–68. Annapolis, MD: Naval Institute Press, 1993.
Trask, David F. "The Battle of Santiago." In *Great American Naval Battles,* edited by Jack Sweetman, 198–218. Annapolis, MD: Naval Institute Press, 1998.

Sampson-Schley Controversy

The Sampson-Schley Controversy grew out of differences of opinion over who should get credit for the July 3, 1898, victory of the American fleet in the Battle of Santiago de Cuba. Acting rear admiral William T. Sampson was in charge of the American naval force blockading the Cuban port of Santiago, but he did not anticipate that Spanish rear admiral Pascual Cervera y Topete's squadron would sortie. Sampson was en route to a conference with V Corps commander Major General William Shafter when the Spanish fleet emerged from the port.

Commodore Winfield Scott Schley was the ranking officer in the blockading squadron in the absence of Sampson and hoisted a signal for all ships to engage the Spanish. But the ships on blockade duty moved to attack the Spanish vessels on their own. At the sound of gunfire, Sampson's ship, the armored cruiser *New York,* turned back to rejoin the fleet but did not arrive until the end of the battle.

Although Sampson claimed credit for the victory in his report to the secretary of the navy, most newspaper reports gave Schley credit for the victory. Alfred T. Mahan argued that victory was due to Sampson's placement of the blockading force and that he deserved the praise.

After the battle, Sampson wrote a confidential report to Secretary of the Navy John D. Long that criticized Schley's actions in the weeks before the battle. When this report became known later, Schley's supporters accused Sampson of duplicity. These supporters grew resentful after both men were promoted to the permanent rank of rear admiral, but Sampson was advanced eight places on the navy list, while Schley was advanced six. Before the war when both were captains, Schley was senior by one. Now, as admirals, Schley was junior by one.

By this time, the Sampson-Schley Controversy was in full bloom, with newspapers, magazines, and individuals in and out of uniform offering their own views. Sampson and Schley did not participate in

Composite image of members of the court of inquiry that convened for three months in 1901 in an effort to settle the dispute between Rear Admiral William T. Sampson and Commodore Winfield Scott Schley over their roles in the Battle of Santiago de Cuba on July 3, 1898. (Naval Historical Center)

the dialogues. In November 1899, Secretary Long issued an order forbidding all officers on active duty to discuss the issue.

The supporters of Sampson eventually forced Schley to ask for a court of inquiry in 1901. The court held that Sampson's conduct was not under review, so only testimony directly concerning Schley was admitted. Schley's lawyer unsuccessfully argued that this was unfair because the actions of both officers were related. Sampson wanted to testify, but his health would not permit it. The court was critical of Schley's conduct prior to June 1, 1898, but said that he was self-possessed and encouraged others during the battle. President of the court Admiral George Dewey issued a separate opinion that dissented from five points at issue prior to the battle. In Dewey's view, Schley was in absolute command and was entitled to the credit for the victory. Many Americans agreed with Dewey. A number of organizations presented gifts of appreciation to Schley.

Sampson, Schley, and Dewey were all dissatisfied for various reasons. Schley appealed to President Theodore Roosevelt for relief from the findings of the court. After studying the record and interviewing the surviving captains in the battle, Roosevelt said that most of the actions that the court censured took place before the battle. He argued that if these actions were censurable, Schley should not have been left in command. Therefore, his shortcomings were in effect condoned by Sampson. As for Santiago, neither Sampson nor Schley exercised command; it was a captain's battle. Roosevelt gave credit to Schley and the captain of his ship for their excellent record in the conflict except for a controversial loop of the ship at the start of the battle. Roosevelt concluded that there was no excuse for keeping this con-

troversy alive. By 1917, the major participants had died, and the matter subsided. But the issues continue to be refought by historians and others almost any time the campaign in Cuba during the Spanish-American War is discussed. The controversy did a great deal of harm to the reputations of Sampson and Schley as well as to other naval officers and administrators.

HAROLD D. LANGLEY

See also

Cervera y Topete, Pascual; Dewey, George; Long, John Davis; Mahan, Alfred Thayer; Roosevelt, Theodore; Sampson, William Thomas; Santiago de Cuba, Battle of; Schley, Winfield Scott; United States Navy

Further Reading

Dawson, Joseph G., III. "William T. Sampson and Santiago: Blockade, Victory, and Controversy." In *Crucible of Empire: The Spanish-American War and Its Aftermath,* edited by James C. Bradford, 47–68. Annapolis, MD: Naval Institute Press, 1993.

Langley, Harold D. "Winfield Scott Schley and Santiago: A New Look at an Old Controversy." In *Crucible of Empire: The Spanish-American War and Its Aftermath,* edited by James C. Bradford, 69–101. Annapolis, MD: Naval Institute Press, 1993.

West, Richard Sedgwick, Jr. *Admirals of American Empire: The Combined Story of George Dewey, Alfred Thayer Mahan, Winfield Scott Schley, and William Thomas Sampson.* Indianapolis: Bobbs-Merrill, 1948.

San Antonio, Texas

See Camp Wood

San Francisco, California

See Camp Merriam and Camp Merritt

San Juan, Puerto Rico, Naval Bombardment of
Event Date: May 12, 1898

Naval bombardment of San Juan, Puerto Rico, by ships of the U.S. North American Squadron on May 12, 1898. Rear Admiral William T. Sampson sailed from Havana, Cuba, to San Juan in search of Rear Admiral Pascual Cervera y Topete's Cádiz Squadron. Sampson's ships arrived off San Juan in the early morning of May 12 and at 5:20 a.m. commenced a bombardment of Spanish military positions ashore. The American ships made three bombardment circuits. The cruiser *Detroit* led, followed by the battleships *Iowa, Indiana,* and *New York;* the double-turreted monitors *Amphitrite* and *Terror;* and the unprotected cruiser *Montgomery.*

The American warships fired a total of 1,360 shells before they broke off the engagement at 7:45 a.m. The Spanish shore batteries fired only 441 shells in reply. Neither side inflicted much damage on the other. American gunnery was abysmal. A majority of the U.S. shells went long, while others fell short. Probably only 20 percent of the shells hit in the general target area, and many of these failed to explode. In the exchange, the U.S. side suffered some minor damage, 1 man killed, and another 7 wounded. Spanish casualties amounted to 13 killed and perhaps 100 wounded, most of these civilians.

The shelling was controversial, for international law clearly required that noncombatants be warned before such an event, but Sampson claimed that his ships were firing not on the city but on its military installations and thus that no prior notification was required. The shelling made little sense, however. Sampson later justified it as a form of naval reconnaissance to ascertain, as he put it, enemy "positions and strength." The shelling did serve to provide the American squadron with a baptism of fire. Secretary of the Navy John D. Long was not impressed and was also upset that Sampson had placed his ships at risk by shelling shore installations before he had concluded the pressing matter of locating and destroying Cervera's squadron.

On May 13, Spanish governor-general of Puerto Rico Manuel Macías y Casado and the island press trumpeted the bombardment as the first Spanish victory of the war, and island merchants distributed food and gifts to the Spanish troops. Sampson, meanwhile, took his squadron to Haiti and then on to Key West, Florida, where he arrived on May 18.

SPENCER C. TUCKER

Lithograph depicting the U.S. Navy bombardment of San Juan, Puerto Rico, on May 12, 1898. (Library of Congress)

See also
Cervera y Topete, Pascual; Long, John Davis; Sampson, William Thomas

Further Reading
Mitchell, Donald W. *History of the Modern American Navy: From 1883 through Pearl Harbor.* New York: Knopf, 1946.
Trask, David F. *The War with Spain in 1898.* Lincoln: University of Nebraska Press, 1996.
West, Richard Sedgwick, Jr. *Admirals of American Empire: The Combined Story of George Dewey, Alfred Thayer Mahan, Winfield Scott Schley, and William Thomas Sampson.* Indianapolis: Bobbs-Merrill, 1948.

San Juan Heights, Battle of
Event Date: July 1, 1898

Key battle that included the Battle of Kettle Hill. The Battle of San Juan Heights took place on San Juan Heights, dominating the eastern approach to Santiago, Cuba, on July 1, 1898.

After defeating the Spanish in the Battle of Las Guásimas on June 24, 1898, the commander of the V Corps expeditionary force, Major General William R. Shafter, devised a strategy for taking Santiago. The strategy involved seizing the high ground east of the city known as San Juan Heights, which included the prominent points of San Juan Hill and Kettle Hill. Shafter's plan called for Brigadier General Jacob Ford Kent's division to attack San Juan Hill while Brigadier General Samuel Sumner's dismounted cavalry assaulted nearby Kettle Hill. It was also expected that Brigadier General Henry Lawton's division would complete its subjugation of El Caney in about two hours, allowing him to participate in the general attack on San Juan Heights. As it turned out, Lawton found himself embroiled in a day-long fight and was unable to add his support to the general attack.

In order to defend Santiago, the Spanish commander, General Arsenio Linares, established a defensive line, the strongest section of which was along San Juan Heights, where some 500 troops, supported by two pieces of artillery, were evenly divided between Kettle Hill and San Juan Hill. The former, some 400 yards northeast of San Juan Hill, was the location of a sugar-refining operation, which included two large iron kettles that gave rise to the hill's name.

Captain George Grimes's light artillery battery of four guns opened up on San Juan Hill from El Pozo at 8:00 a.m. The American fire had little effect, and the Spanish soon managed to locate the guns thanks to telltale clouds of smoke from their black powder charges. Effective Spanish counterbattery fire soon silenced the battery. The order to advance was given at 9:00 a.m., and the three American brigades—the 1st under Brigadier General Hamilton S. Hawkins, the 2nd under Colonel E. P. Pearson, and the 3rd commanded by Colonel Charles A. Wikoff—moved forward. The Spanish artillery had the range, however, thanks to an observation balloon over the Americans that moved forward with the advancing troops. Under heavy Spanish fire, the 71st New York Infantry Regiment of Hawkins's brigade panicked; however, the other units moved into position for the final assault.

All these events delayed the frontal assault across open ground up San Juan Hill, which did not begin until 1:00 p.m. In the lead were the 6th, 16th, and 24th U.S. Infantry Regiments. The men simply charged up the hill without any order. Hawkins's 6th and 16th Brigades moved up the slope through knee-high grass and barbed wire. At first the men made good progress. The Spanish had established their line along the crest of the hill rather than just below at a point where they would have an unobstructed view of the entire slope (the so-called military crest) and thus did not have a good angle from which to fire on the advancing Americans. Some critical support came from Lieutenant John D. Parker's battery of Gatling guns, which raked the Spanish positions for a crucial eight minutes. Also at the same time, Brigadier General Samuel Sumner's dismounted cavalry, including the Rough Riders, had advanced up and secured Kettle Hill. They now provided supporting fire against the Spanish positions on San Juan Hill. When the American troops reached the summit, the Spanish were already in retreat. The Americans on San Juan Hill then dug in and established defensive positions to meet a possible Spanish counterattack, for the new enemy positions were only several hundred yards distant.

In the battle for San Juan Hill, Kent's division lost 89 killed and 489 wounded. Another 35 were killed and 328 wounded on Kettle Hill. Spanish casualties in the entire battles at San Juan Heights and El Caney were fewer: 215 killed, 376 wounded, and 2 taken prisoner.

JERRY KEENAN AND SPENCER C. TUCKER

See also
Black Powder; Kent, Jacob Ford; Kettle Hill, Battle of; Roosevelt, Theodore; Santiago de Cuba Land Campaign

Further Reading
Roosevelt, Theodore. *The Rough Riders, an Autobiography.* New York: Library of America, 2004.
Samuels, Peggy, and Harold Samuels. *Teddy Roosevelt at San Juan: The Making of a President.* College Station: Texas A&M University Press, 1997.
Trask, David F. *The War with Spain in 1898.* Lincoln: University of Nebraska Press, 1996.

Sánchez y Gutiérrez de Castro, Juan Manuel
See Almodóvar del Río, Duque de

Santiago de Cuba, Battle of
Event Date: July 3, 1898

Naval battle off Santiago, Cuba, on July 3, 1898, that led Spain to sue for peace. On April 25, 1898, the United States declared war on Spain. On April 26, Rear Admiral William T. Sampson took command of the U.S. Navy North Atlantic Squadron from Rear Admiral Montgomery Sicard, who had taken ill. Meanwhile, on April 29,

Depiction of the Battle of Santiago de Cuba, July 3, 1898, in which the U.S. North Atlantic Squadron under Rear Admiral William T. Sampson destroyed a Spanish squadron under Rear Admiral Pascual Cervera y Topete. (John Clark Ridpath, *Ridpath's History of the World,* 1901)

Spanish rear admiral Pascual Cervera y Topete's Cádiz Squadron departed the Cape Verde Islands with four cruisers and three torpedo destroyers. Although the Spanish ships were in poor repair and were not well armed, Americans along the coast were terrified of a possible descent by the Spanish squadron. An erroneous sighting of the Spanish ships off New England even led the Navy Department to send two cruisers and other vessels to look for them. Cervera, however, was headed for Cuba.

Sampson first looked for Cervera at Puerto Rico and on May 12 bombarded the shore fortifications at San Juan. But not finding Cervera there, Sampson steamed to Cuba in hopes of intercepting the Spanish ships at sea. Cervera was presumed to be carrying supplies for the Spanish garrison in Cuba. This was not the case, however; indeed, his own ships were themselves desperately short of coal and in acute need of maintenance. Cervera had proceeded via Martinique (where he had left behind one of his destroyers, the *Terror,* which was too unseaworthy to continue) and Curaçao and had put into Santiago de Cuba on May 19. That news was immediately available to the U.S. Navy via an intelligence agent in Havana. Duly informed, Sampson then ordered Commodore Winfield Scott Schley, who had commanded the Flying Squadron formed at Hampton Roads, Virginia, to protect the Atlantic coast from Cervera and had been ordered to Cienfuegos, Cuba, to shift his station to Santi-

ago de Cuba. Schley received these orders on May 23 but for some unknown reason did not take up position off Santiago de Cuba until May 28. Cervera thus had more than a week to leave Santiago de Cuba but in fact had nowhere to go.

Sampson arrived off Santiago de Cuba with his remaining ships on June 1, 1898. The American blockade now concentrated all the principal ships of the North Atlantic Squadron: five battleships (the *Oregon, Indiana, Massachusetts, Iowa,* and *Texas*), two armored cruisers (Schley's flagship the *Brooklyn* and Sampson's flagship the *New York*), and a number of smaller cruisers and auxiliaries. Sampson arranged the ships in a semicircle about four miles from the channel entrance. At night, some of the blockaders closed to two miles and directed their searchlights up the channel in order to detect any Spanish ship movement there.

Sampson took charge of the eastern sector and gave responsibility for the western sector to Schley, his second-in-command. In order to secure a coaling station for his operations, Sampson ordered Commander Bowman H. McCalla and a battalion of marines to seize control of Guantánamo Bay, 40 miles distant. Sampson had managed to conceal from all but a few close associates that he was ill. He was suffering from what was probably multiple infarct dementia. As a consequence, he delegated most of the responsibility to Captain French Ensor Chadwick, captain of the *New York.*

Estimated Casualties of the Battle of Santiago de Cuba

	Killed in Action	Wounded	Captured	Ships Lost
Spain	323	151	1,720	6
United States	1	1	0	0

On the night of June 3, Sampson tried unsuccessfully to block Cervera's ships in the harbor by sinking the collier *Merrimac* at the mouth of the bay. Naval constructor Richmond Pearson Hobson and a crew of seven other volunteers maneuvered the collier through Spanish minefields and the fire of the Spanish shore batteries. The *Merrimac* overshot the mark, however, going down too slowly when only 2 of the 10 demolition charges fired. Hobson and his crew were rescued by the Spanish and promptly imprisoned.

Meanwhile, Major General William R. Shafter's V Corps expeditionary force in Cuba, besieging Santiago de Cuba from the land side after its victories in the battles at El Caney and San Juan Heights on July 1, was in difficulty, its numbers rapidly diminishing from disease. The general wanted Sampson to steam up the channel into Santiago Harbor and engage the Spanish ships, a course of action that the admiral rejected because of the threat of mines. While the Americans were trying to decide how the navy might best assist the army in bringing about a Spanish capitulation, the Spanish solved the problem themselves. On July 1, Cervera's superior, Spanish governor-general in Cuba Ramón Blanco y Erenas, ordered the Spanish admiral to take his squadron to sea. Blanco feared that a failure to attempt to break out would have a disastrous psychological effect on the Spanish war effort. Blanco favored a night sortie, but Cervera vetoed that, certain that his crews would be detected and blinded by the American searchlights. On July 2, Cervera ordered the sorties to take place at 9:00 a.m. on July 3.

That same morning, July 3, Sampson, ordered by President William McKinley to cooperate with Shafter, departed in the *New York* for a meeting with the general at Siboney. This left Schley in the cruiser *Brooklyn* in command. Why Sampson took the flagship for the meeting with Shafter rather than a smaller ship is unknown. At any rate, Sampson remarked to Chadwick that it would be ironic if Cervera chose that time to sortie. That is exactly what happened. Sampson learned by signal that Cervera was departing the harbor and ordered an immediate return, but the *New York* returned too late to take a meaningful role in the action.

Cervera knew that he was badly outgunned. The American blockaders could throw three times the weight of broadside of the Spanish ships, and many of the Spanish batteries were in poor repair. The Spanish ships also were short of reliable ammunition. At 9:00 a.m., smoke from the harbor revealed that the Spanish ships were under way. Cervera's decision to sortie in daylight in fact caught the Americans by surprise. His six ships slowly made their way out of the channel, red and yellow battle streamers at their masts. The ships were the armored cruisers *Maria Teresa* (flagship), *Vizcaya, Cristóbal Colón,* and *Oquendo* and the torpedo boat de-

stroyers *Plutón* and *Furor*. Led by the *Maria Teresa,* the ships exited the harbor one at a time at intervals of about 600 yards and 10 minutes. It took them about an hour to clear the channel.

Cervera hoped to be able to ram the *Brooklyn,* a diversion that might allow his remaining ships to escape. The *Brooklyn* and seven other blockading warships (four battleships, three auxiliaries, and a torpedo boat) quickly converged on the harbor entrance, and the *New York* came up later. Cervera headed the *Maria Teresa* for the *Brooklyn.* The American cruiser was then headed west, and its captain, Francis A. Cook, ordered an immediate turn to the east, a decision with which Schley concurred. This almost led to a collision with the battleship *Texas,* which had to reverse engines. Captain Robley Evans of the *Iowa* hoped to either ram or torpedo the *María Teresa,* but before he could do so, the *Iowa* managed to score hits on the Spanish flagships with shells from the two guns of its forward 12-inch turret.

The Spanish ships were simply overwhelmed by superior U.S. firepower. Engulfed in flames, they tried to make the shore, and the Americans soon turned to rescuing their crews. The last Spanish ship afloat, the cruiser *Cristóbal Colón,* managed to steam some 50 miles along the coast until poor coal enabled the battleship *Oregon* to overhaul it. The captain of the *Cristóbal Colón* then headed his ship to shore and hauled down the flag at 1:15 p.m. Then, in violation of the laws of war, he ordered the sea valves opened and the ship scuttled.

In the four-hour Battle of Santiago de Cuba, the Spanish lost all six ships either sunk or scuttled, and 323 men killed and another 151 wounded. A total of 1,720 were taken prisoner, including Cervera. The U.S. Navy lost only 1 man killed and another injured, both on the *Brooklyn.* As Captain Evans put it, "God and the gunners had had their day." Santiago formally surrendered on July 17.

Later there was a bitter public controversy as Commodore Schley feuded with Sampson over who was responsible for the victory. Schley and his supporters subsequently claimed that Sampson was out of sight when the battle began and that he and not Sampson deserved credit for the victory. Certainly this and the maneuvers of individual ships made no difference in the outcome of the battle, but the controversy damaged the reputations of both men and denied them the satisfaction they deserved for their achievement.

SPENCER C. TUCKER

See also
Blanco y Erenas, Ramón; Cervera y Topete, Pascual; McCalla, Bowman Hendry; *Oregon,* USS; Sampson, William Thomas; Sampson-Schley Controversy; Schley, Winfield Scott; Shafter, William Rufus

Further Reading
Coletta, Paolo E. *Bowman Hendry McCalla: A Fighting Sailor.* Washington, DC: University Press of America, 1979.
———. *French Ensor Chadwick: Scholarly Warrior.* Lanham, MD: University Press of America, 1980.
Muir, Malcolm, Jr. "French Ensor Chadwick: Reformer, Historian, and Outcast." In *Admirals of the New Steel Navy: Makers of the American Naval Tradition, 1880–1930,* edited by James R. Bradford, 97–119. Annapolis, MD: Naval Institute Press, 1990.

Trask, David F. "The Battle of Santiago." In *Great American Naval Battles*, edited by Jack Sweetman, 198–218. Annapolis, MD: Naval Institute Press, 1998.

Santiago de Cuba, Capitulation Agreement

The Spanish capitulation at Santiago de Cuba was negotiated and agreed to by both sides on July 16, 1898, and effectively ended major hostilities between U.S. and Spanish forces in Cuba. The agreement went into effect the next day, July 17. The capitulation set the stage for further negotiations, brokered by the French government and French ambassador to the United States Jules-Martin Cambon. The result of the later negotiations was the August 12, 1898, Protocol of Peace, which set in motion the talks that ended with the Treaty of Paris in December 1898. The capitulation agreement also ended the campaign and siege of Santiago de Cuba, which had begun on June 22 with the landing of V Corps at Daiquirí and Siboney.

Negotiating for the Spanish side was General José Toral y Vázquez, commanding officer of the Spanish garrison at Santiago. Toral had first consulted with General Ramón Blanco y Erenas, the governor-general of Cuba, who had given his approval to the capitulation. When the colonial office in Madrid vacillated on the need for the capitulation agreement, however, Toral took it upon himself to begin talks without the explicit consent of Madrid. As the talks progressed, Toral made it clear that he would be unable to sign an agreement until he received permission from Madrid. The chief negotiators for the United States, Major General Joseph Wheeler and Major General Henry Ware Lawton, refused to allow Toral time to wait for a reply from his home government. They insisted that the capitulation agreement be signed, and they threatened the resumption of hostilities if this was not done in a timely fashion.

Under American pressure, Toral agreed to sign the agreement and let the chips fall where they may. Also signing the agreement for the Spanish were General Federico Escario García, Lieutenant Colonel Ventura Fontán, and Robert Mason, Great Britain's consul in Santiago de Cuba. In addition to Wheeler and Lawton, First Lieutenant John D. Miley also signed the agreement for the Americans. Miley was Major General William Shafter's personal representative.

Throughout the negotiations, it was quite clear that Toral was concerned about maintaining his personal honor and that of his troops. For their part, the Americans were solicitous toward Toral and tried for the most part to allow him to capitulate while keeping intact his honor and that of his men and his country. It was also obvious that Toral was concerned about signing a capitulation agreement without the explicit authorization of Madrid and that he worried about his reception in Spain once the agreement had been concluded. It is worth noting that Toral and Escario insisted on the term "capitulation" rather than the more pejorative term "surrender."

The capitulation agreement stipulated the surrender of not only the garrison at Santiago de Cuba but also the Spanish stronghold at Guantánamo and six other encampments in eastern Cuba as well. The agreement had seven major provisions. First, the agreement was to "absolutely and unequivocally" end hostilities between American and Spanish forces in the vicinity of Santiago de Cuba. Second, the United States was to transport to Spain all Spanish troops in the region as quickly as possible and pay for said transportation. Third, Spanish officers would be allowed to keep their side arms, and all Spanish troops would be allowed to retain their personal property. Fourth, Spanish forces were to remove—or aid

U.S. troops cheering upon news of the Spanish surrender of Santiago de Cuba, July 16, 1898. (Library of Congress)

in the removal of—all explosive mines and other devices in Santiago de Cuba's harbor. Fifth, Spanish commanders were to provide U.S. forces with a complete inventory of weapons and armaments and a full roster of all Spanish troops. Sixth, any Spaniards wishing to remain in Cuba had to surrender their arms and agree not to wage war against Cubans or Americans. Finally, Spanish troops were to march out of Santiago de Cuba with the honors of war, turning in their weapons at a mutually designated location, and await transportation to Spain.

As it turned out, the capitulation agreement of Santiago de Cuba became controversial, not only for Toral and the Spanish but for the Americans as well. Shafter had not included any representatives from the navy in the negotiations, and none had been a signatory to the final agreement. Given the important role of its victory over Spanish naval forces in the Battle of Santiago de Cuba on July 3 and the subsequent actions that aided in the U.S. Army's successful land campaign against Santiago de Cuba, such an oversight did not rest well with the navy. Rear Admiral William T. Sampson learned of the agreement only after he received a copy of it. Understandably perturbed, he insisted that Shafter apologize, which he eventually did. Still, the agreement was yet one more example of the interservice squabbling that became one of the hallmarks of the Spanish-American War.

PAUL G. PIERPAOLI JR.

See also

Blanco y Erenas, Ramón; Cambon, Jules-Martin; Escario García, Federico; V Corps; Lawton, Henry Ware; Miley, John David; Peace, Protocol of; Sampson, William Thomas; Santiago de Cuba, Battle of; Santiago de Cuba, Occupation of; Santiago de Cuba Land Campaign; Shafter, William Rufus; Toral y Vázquez, José; Wheeler, Joseph

Further Reading

Cambon, Jules. *The Foreign Policy of the Powers.* Reprint ed. Freeport, NY: Books for Libraries Press, 1970.

Cosmas, Graham A. *An Army for Empire: The United States Army in the Spanish-American War.* College Station: Texas A&M University Press, 1994.

Musicant, Ivan. *Empire by Default: The Spanish-American War and the Dawn of the American Century.* New York: Henry Holt, 1998.

Santiago de Cuba, Occupation of
Start Date: July 17, 1898
End Date: May 20, 1901

U.S. forces occupied the city of Santiago de Cuba on July 17, 1898, following the Santiago de Cuba Land Campaign that had begun on June 22, the destruction of Rear Admiral Pascual Cervera y Topete's squadron in the Battle of Santiago de Cuba, and a 14-day siege. The city's population of 50,000 came under the control of the U.S. Army's V Corps, commanded by Major General William R. Shafter. Shafter in turn named Brigadier General Leonard Wood as the military governor of Santiago de Cuba on July 20, 1898. Wood had pre-

viously commanded a brigade of the cavalry division at the July 1 Battle of San Juan Hill on the city's approaches.

Wood had charge of the city until December 1899 and proved most effective. As military governor, he was responsible not only for the civilian population of 50,000 people but also for 12,000 Spanish prisoners of war. After Shafter departed for the United States in mid-August, Wood's superior was Major General Henry W. Lawton, who was the military governor of the province of Santiago. Lawton departed in October 1898, and Wood took command of both the city and the province. Wood remained in this post until December 1899, when he became military governor for all of Cuba. He served as the military governor of Cuba for 18 months and then turned the administration of Cuba over to the popularly elected president of Cuba, Tomás Estrada Palma, on May 20, 1901.

Wood's focus and his efforts throughout his three years of service in Cuba followed the model he established in his initial experience as the governor of Santiago de Cuba. When Shafter appointed Wood governor of Santiago de Cuba, the city was in crisis. Local city officials had abandoned their posts, parts of the city had been destroyed by the siege, much of the city's population was sick and starving, and refugees from the countryside, who were even more emaciated than the city's population, were flooding into the city.

Wood immediately took command of the situation using his unlimited powers as military governor, backed up by the occupying American troops. His first task was to reestablish law and order. In so doing, he located former policemen and armed and equipped them under the command of his own American provost marshal. He prohibited the brutal police methods employed under Spanish authority but did not otherwise interfere with local customs of law enforcement. He also reestablished the court system, personally held a weekly Governor's Audience to hear complaints of the population, and headed the Superior Provost Court.

As with the police force, Wood carried out occupation operations employing indigenous officials as much as possible. These were organized and then placed under the supervision of army officers. For example, U.S. Army medical officers organized and supervised all Spanish and Cuban doctors in the city. Wood himself inspected the administration of the city on a daily basis. He rode by horseback throughout the city and often, as a trained physician, intervened to provide aid to sick citizens encountered during his inspections.

Simultaneous with establishing law and order, the military governor attacked the other immediate problems facing the population: famine and disease. When Wood took command, approximately 15,000 of the population were sick, and 200 people were dying in the city each day. To attack the problem of starvation, he immediately arranged for the distribution of Spanish Army rations to the population. During the first weeks of the occupation, his command issued approximately 18,000 rations per day and on one occasion issued some 51,000 rations in a single day. The American occupation authority also instituted strict price controls and ensured that merchants sold available local foodstuffs at reasonable prices. The city governor vigorously prosecuted merchants who attempted to take advantage of the starving population by raising prices or engaging in black market sales.

The American army fought disease in the city using a variety of techniques. The first requirement was through improved sanitation. At the beginning of the occupation, hundreds of dead lay unburied throughout the city, posing a significant health hazard. The Americans organized work parties to move the dead outside the city and then had the bodies burned. Next, work parties tackled the city streets and alleys, which were filled with refuse of all sorts, human and animal excrement, and decaying animal carcasses. This refuse was systematically loaded onto confiscated wagons, moved outside the city, and burned.

The army also published and enforced detailed sanitation regulations. The city was divided up into wards, and each ward was assigned to an army medical officer. The officer systematically inspected all areas in his ward, including house-by-house inspections of homes. The medical officers identified violations of regulations; violators conformed or faced action by the provost.

Lack of potable water also contributed to disease in the city, so army engineers restored and improved the water system. Combat as well as poor maintenance had reduced the system to a shambles. The army repaired broken or nonfunctioning water mains and extended the system into parts of the city that had not previously had functioning water service.

Wood's administration of Santiago was strict, and the population only reluctantly conformed to his authority. However, by the end of August 1898, the city was relatively clean, the people were fed, and law and order had been restored. Also, the disease and death rates within the city had been reduced dramatically. The success that Wood achieved in Santiago de Cuba became a model. Indeed, he replicated it to cover the entire province and later all of Cuba as he subsequently governed at those levels.

Louis A. DiMarco

See also

Cuba, U.S. Occupation of; Estrada Palma, Tomás; V Corps; Lawton, Henry Ware; Medicine, Military; Santiago de Cuba Land Campaign; Shafter, William Rufus; Wood, Leonard

Further Reading

Lane, Jack C. *Armed Progressive: General Leonard Wood*. San Rafael, CA: Presidio, 1978.

McCallum, Jack. *Leonard Wood: Rough Rider, Surgeon, and Architect of American Imperialism*. New York: New York University Press, 2006.

U.S. Army. *Military Government, an Historical Approach*. Training Packet No. 9. Camp Gordon, GA: Provost Marshall General's School, 1951.

Santiago de Cuba Land Campaign
Start Date: May 19, 1898
End Date: June 17, 1898

When Spanish rear admiral Pascual Cervera y Topete's Cádiz Squadron slipped into the harbor of Santiago de Cuba on May 19,

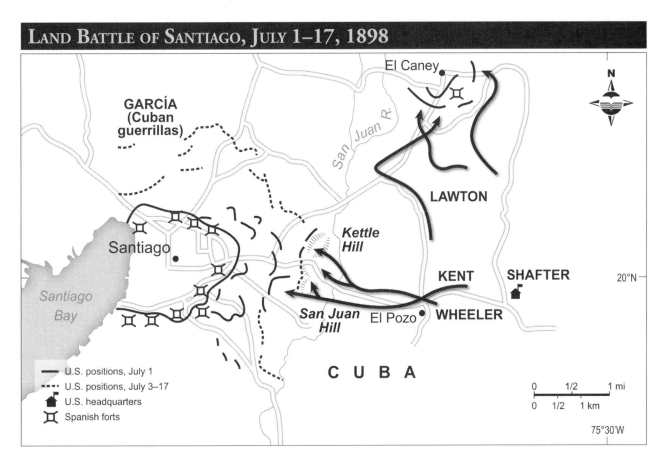

LAND BATTLE OF SANTIAGO, JULY 1–17, 1898

Legend:
— U.S. positions, July 1
---- U.S. positions, July 3–17
U.S. headquarters
U.S. headquarters
Spanish forts

Buildings in Santiago de Cuba damaged by shelling after the capture of the city by U.S. forces. (*Photographic History of the Spanish-American War,* 1898)

1898, U.S. war strategy shifted from capturing Havana to capturing Santiago. Destruction of Cervera's squadron, Washington believed, would help induce Spain to surrender. By June 1, U.S. Navy rear admiral William T. Sampson's North Atlantic Squadron had effectively established a blockade off Santiago Harbor, thereby neutralizing the threat posed by the Spanish fleet, at least temporarily. On June 3, however, Sampson's attempt to blockade the harbor entrance with the collier *Merrimac* failed.

Between June 22 and 26, Major General William Shafter's V Corps landed at Daiquirí and Siboney on the southeastern coast of Cuba. Some 17,000 troops were put ashore, albeit under awkward and confused conditions. Spanish troops were fought at Las Guásimas, but they offered no real obstacle to the American advance. Shafter's assignment was to capture Santiago and in so doing aid the U.S. Navy in destroying Admiral Cervera's squadron. Shafter had two options: he could march from Daiquirí to seize the fort at El Morro, guarding the entrance to Santiago Harbor, or he could drive inland from Siboney directly to Santiago and capture San Juan Heights, which overlooked the port. The advance was to be supported by General Calixto García y Iñiguez's Cuban revolutionary forces. Interservice disagreements and squabbling clouded the

issue from the beginning, both in Cuba between Shafter and Sampson and in Washington, D.C., where Secretary of War Russell Alger and Secretary of the Navy John Long were frequently in dispute.

Sampson believed that Shafter's objective should be El Morro, the capture of which would allow the navy to clear the mines that had been laid in the harbor's entrance. Shafter, by contrast, thought that the navy ought to simply enter the harbor and attack the Spanish fleet. Moreover, reports indicated that the Spanish had established a strong defensive position at El Morro, which gave Shafter pause.

Accordingly, Shafter elected to move inland on Santiago, planning a two-pronged attack on the approaches to Santiago, with Brigadier General Jacob F. Kent's 1st Division and Major General Joseph Wheeler's dismounted cavalry division attacking San Juan Heights on the left and Brigadier General Henry W. Lawton's 2nd Division attacking El Caney on the right. After Wheeler's dismounted cavalry division repulsed the Spaniards at Las Guásimas on June 24, Shafter prepared for a coordinated attack on July 1. Lawton's forces were to strike at El Caney and then move south to support Kent's assault on San Juan Heights. Although stiff Spanish resistance at El Caney resulted in an all-day battle there, Kent suc-

Illustration by William J. Glackens of the scene at El Pozo during the Santiago Campaign in Cuba in 1898. The illustration originally appeared in the October 1898 issue of *McClure's Magazine.* (Library of Congress)

ceeded in taking San Juan Heights in an engagement in which Lieutenant Colonel Theodore Roosevelt's Rough Riders figured prominently. Indeed, Roosevelt's success at Kettle Hill made him a national hero. With the victory at El Caney and the capture of San Juan Heights on July 1, what had been the campaign of Santiago became the siege of Santiago.

The Spanish meanwhile had shifted a limited number of resources to Santiago. On June 22, some 3,700 Spanish troops commanded by Colonel Federico Escario García departed Manzanillo for Santiago, 160 miles distant. Throughout the march, Cuban guerrillas harassed the force constantly. Although the Spanish column finally reached Santiago on the night of July 2, the men did little more than add to the burden on the city's food supply, which by now had reached a critical level, as the city was effectively cut off from supplies or reinforcements. Shafter perceived that Santiago was still much too strong for him to storm and believed that Spanish reinforcements were on their way to the city. In a communiqué to Washington, he requested authorization to withdraw to a more secure position.

Withdrawal was not on the minds of those in Washington, however, and Shafter was promptly directed to hold the heights. The leaders in Washington moved quickly. More troops were ordered to Cuba along with commanding general of the army Major General Nelson Miles with instructions to do whatever he judged necessary to hold San Juan Heights. On the one hand, U.S. authorities, especially Shafter, might have been less concerned had they known of the desperate situation inside Santiago, where the wounded Spanish commander, Lieutenant General Arsenio Linares, had been replaced by Major General José Toral y Vázquez and the city's inhabitants had been reduced to a starvation diet. Although the city's garrison totaled 10,429 men at the end of June, this figure included unreliable militia and volunteers. Morale was also low, with pay for the regulars 11 months in arrears. On the other hand, Shafter's V Corps was suffering an alarming increase in casualties due to fevers brought on by the onset of the tropical disease season.

On July 3, the picture at Santiago was dramatically altered when Cervera's squadron attempted to break out of Santiago Harbor and was destroyed by the U.S. blockading squadron. With the defeat of the Spanish fleet, the military value of Santiago suddenly became questionable. Accordingly, on July 3, Shafter advised General Toral to surrender or the city would be shelled. Toral declined, but negotiations nevertheless continued. Toral then proposed surrendering the city provided that the garrison was allowed to retain its arms and march unopposed to Holguín. Shafter was disposed to accept those terms, but President William McKinley insisted on unconditional surrender.

On July 10 and 11, the two sides engaged in a final battle, with the Spanish sustaining 50 casualties compared to 4 for the Americans. Two days later, on July 13, Shafter and Miles (who had finally arrived) met again with Toral, offering to ship all Spanish troops back to Spain at U.S. expense if Toral agreed to surrender unconditionally. Recognizing that he had little choice, Toral agreed but needed the permission of Lieutenant General Ramón Blanco y Erenas, Spanish captain-general and governor-general of Cuba in Havana. Blanco eventually agreed, and on July 17, Toral surrendered the city of Santiago together with Guantánamo and a number of smaller posts that fell under the authority of the Santiago commander.

The campaign was hardly a military masterpiece. Shafter, who personally suffered from malarial fever and gout during the campaign, was often out of touch with the situation and pessimistic. The Spanish enjoyed superiority in small arms with their Mauser rifles firing smokeless powder cartridges, and American artillery support was negligible at best. In addition, Shafter had made no effort to utilize naval gunfire support or the Spanish guerrilla forces, who he perceived to be little more than laborers.

JERRY KEENAN AND SPENCER C. TUCKER

See also

Alger, Russell Alexander; Blanco y Erenas, Ramón; Cervera y Topete, Pascual; Daiquirí Beachhead, Cuba; El Caney, Battle of; Kettle Hill, Battle of; Las Guásimas, Battle of; Linares y Pombo, Arsenio; Long, John Davis; McKinley, William; Miles, Nelson Appleton; Roosevelt, Theodore; Rough Riders; Sampson, William Thomas; San Juan Heights, Battle of; Santiago de Cuba, Battle of; Shafter, William Rufus; Siboney, Cuba; Toral y Vázquez, José; Wheeler, Joseph

Further Reading

Cosmas, Graham A. *An Army for Empire: The United States Army in the Spanish-American War.* College Station: Texas A&M University Press, 1994.

Leech, Margaret. *In the Days of McKinley.* New York: Harper and Brothers, 1959.

Samuels, Peggy, and Harold Samuels. *Teddy Roosevelt at San Juan: The Making of a President.* College Station: Texas A&M University Press, 1997.

Trask, David F. *The War with Spain in 1898.* Lincoln: University of Nebraska Press, 1996.

Walker, Dale L. *The Boys of '98: Theodore Roosevelt and the Rough Riders.* New York: Forge, 1999.

Savannah, Georgia

See Camp Onward

Schley, Winfield Scott

Birth Date: October 9, 1839
Death Date: October 2, 1911

U.S. admiral. Born on October 9, 1839, in Frederick County, Maryland, and named for U.S. Army brevet major general Winfield Scott, Winfield Scott Schley graduated from the United States Naval Academy, Annapolis, in 1860. His first assignment was aboard the screw frigate *Niagara* when it returned a Japanese delegation to Japan. In May 1861 at the beginning of the American Civil War, the *Niagara* joined the South Atlantic Blockading Squadron operating near Charleston. Schley garnered recognition in bringing a captured prize to Philadelphia. This act brought him promotion to master and assignment to the sailing frigate *Potomac* in the West Gulf Blockading Squadron. In July 1862, he was assigned to the screw gunboat *Winona* and participated in operations along the Mississippi River.

Commodore Winfield Scott Schley, who had actual command of the U.S. blockading warships off Santiago during the Battle of Santiago de Cuba on July 3, 1898. The subsequent controversy between Schley and Rear Admiral William Sampson over who was responsible for the U.S. victory led to much acrimony in the navy. (Library of Congress)

Promoted to lieutenant commander in July 1866, Schley was detailed to the Naval Academy. He then had a variety of assignments during the next 15 years. As commander of the screw sloop *Benica*, he participated in the investigation into the loss of the U.S. merchantman *General Slocum* in Korean waters. He also served under Rear Admiral John Rodgers in the July 1871 action against Korean forts. Promoted to commander in June 1874, Schley was captain of the screw gunboat *Essex* during 1876–1879.

Schley gained public renown for leading the Greeley Relief Expedition to the Artic, which in the summer of 1884 rescued the survivors of an ill-fated army operation. During 1887–1888, he was chief of the Bureau of Equipment and Recruiting, and in March 1888, he was promoted to captain. He then commanded the cruiser *Baltimore*.

On March 26, 1898, Schley took command as commodore of the Flying Squadron, formed to protect the U.S. coast from a possible Spanish attack. The United States declared war on Spain the next month. Leaving Key West, Florida, on May 19, however, Schley failed to locate Spanish rear admiral Pascual Cervera y Topete's Cádiz Squadron, which had departed the Cape Verde Islands on April 29. Convinced that Cervera was at Cienfuegos, Cuba, Schley ignored word from North Atlantic Squadron commander Rear Admiral William T. Sampson that the Spanish squadron was probably at Santiago. Cervera in fact arrived there on May 19. Finally arriving off Santiago on May 26, Schley failed to carry out a reconnaissance and instead departed for Key West, supposedly to coal. During a 17-hour period on May 26–27, Schley disregarded an order from Secretary of the Navy John D. Long to proceed to Santiago and blockade it. Not until May 28 did Schley take up position off Santiago. Cervera thus had ample time to escape from that port but chose not to do so, largely because of the condition of his ships and opposition from his captains.

Following formation of the North Atlantic Fleet on June 21 under Sampson, Schley took command of its 2nd Squadron. Schley is chiefly remembered for his role in the July 3, 1898, Battle of Santiago de Cuba. When the Spanish squadron began exiting the harbor and with Rear Admiral Sampson absent, Schley issued the order for the U.S. ships to open fire. The unorthodox movement of Schley's flagship the *Brooklyn* during the initial stage of the battle, however, almost caused a collision with the battleship *Texas*. The question of which man deserved credit led to one of the worst schisms in U.S. naval history. The resulting media coverage and public scrutiny damaged the reputations of both men and that of the navy.

Although Schley was promoted to rear admiral on March 3, 1899, and took command of the South Atlantic Squadron, his health suffered from the ongoing controversy. He retired from the navy in October 1901. Schley died on October 2, 1911, in New York City.

RICHARD W. PEUSER AND SPENCER C. TUCKER

See also

Cervera y Topete, Pascual; Flying Squadron; Long, John Davis; North Atlantic Squadron; Sampson, William Thomas; Sampson-Schley Controversy; Santiago de Cuba, Battle of

Further Reading

Langley, Harold D. "Winfield Scott Schley: The Confident Commander." In *Admirals of the New Steel Navy*, edited by James C. Bradford, 180–221. Annapolis, MD: Naval Institute Press, 1990.

———."Winfield Scott Schley and Santiago: A New Look at an Old Controversy." In *Crucible of Empire: The Spanish-American War and Its Aftermath*, edited by James C. Bradford, 69–101. Annapolis, MD: Naval Institute Press, 1993.

West, Richard Sedgwick, Jr. *Admirals of American Empire: The Combined Story of George Dewey, Alfred Thayer Mahan, Winfield Scott Schley, and William Thomas Sampson*. Indianapolis: Bobbs-Merrill, 1948.

Schofield, John McAllister

Birth Date: September 29, 1831
Death Date: March 4, 1906

U.S. Army general. John McAllister Schofield was born in Gerry, New York, on September 29, 1831, the son of a Baptist minister. Raised in Illinois, Schofield graduated from the United States Military Academy, West Point, in 1853, ranking seventh out of a class of fifty-four. Commissioned a second lieutenant, he served for

Major General John M. Schofield was commanding general of the U.S. Army during 1888–1895. A capable administrator, he was advanced to lieutenant general upon his retirement. (Chaiba Media)

two years in the 1st U.S. Artillery, then returned to West Point as an instructor of experimental philosophy (physics). He was promoted to first lieutenant in 1855 but, disillusioned by the lack of promotion, secured a leave of absence in 1860 and took a position teaching physics at Washington University in St. Louis.

On the beginning of the American Civil War in April 1861, Schofield was commissioned a major in the 1st Missouri Volunteers. He favorably impressed Major General Nathaniel Lyon, the local Union Army commander, who appointed him his chief of staff. In this capacity, Schofield accompanied Lyon in a series of small Union victories over Southern forces but advised against engaging numerically superior Confederate forces at Wilson's Creek on August 10, 1861. Lyon attacked anyway and was killed. Schofield particularly distinguished himself in the battle, and in 1892 was formally awarded the Medal of Honor for his role.

On November 21, 1861, Schofield was advanced to brigadier general of volunteers. In October 1862, he took command of the Army of the Frontier and the District of Southwest Missouri. Enjoying some success driving Southern guerrillas from Missouri and Kansas, he also sought a more important command. On May 12, 1863, he was named major general of volunteers and given command of the Department of the Ohio and the Army of the Ohio. He then participated in Major General William T. Sherman's Atlanta Campaign during which Schofield did battle with Confederate forces under Lieutenant General John Bell Hood's Confederates. Hood invaded Tennessee and attempted to cut off Schofield's smaller force from Nashville. Schofield eluded Hood and entrenched at Franklin. In the Battle of Franklin on November 30, 1864, Schofield's men destroyed the attacking Confederates. For this victory, Schofield was advanced to brigadier general in the regular army to date from the battle. Moving his forces by sea to Fort Fisher, North Carolina, he occupied Wilmington on February 22, 1865, and then fought at Kinston during March 8–10. He ended the war cooperating closely with Sherman against the remaining Confederate forces under General Joseph E. Johnston.

Following the war, President Andrew Johnson appointed Schofield as a confidential agent of the State Department and sent him to France, charged with negotiating with Emperor Napoleon III the withdrawal of French forces from Mexico. This mission accomplished successfully, Schofield commanded the Department of the Potomac from August 1866 to June 1868. President Johnson then appointed him secretary of war. In March 1869, Schofield advanced to major general of regulars and took charge of the Department of the Missouri until May 1870. He then commanded the Division of the Pacific and in 1873, under secret orders of Secretary of War William Belknap, traveled to Hawaii to evaluate the strategic usefulness of those islands to the United States. Upon his recommendation, the government purchased Pearl Harbor as a naval facility. In September 1876, Schofield returned to West Point as commandant, remaining there until January 1881, when he succeeded to command of the Division of the Gulf. In 1878, he also headed a board that reconsidered the court-martial of Major General Fitz John Porter and absolved him of misconduct at the Second Battle of Bull Run in 1862.

After successive tours with the Division of the Pacific and the Division of the Missouri, in August 1888 Schofield succeeded Lieutenant General Philip H. Sheridan as commanding general of the army. During his seven-year tenure, Schofield pressed for improvements in the life of common soldiers through better rations, higher pay, and improved standards of living. He also sought to foster professionalism among the officer corps by a system of examinations for promotion, the creation of post libraries, and strong support for service schools.

In sharp contrast with his predecessors Sherman and Sheridan, Schofield disagreed with the prevailing national policy toward the Native Americans. Indeed, he urged that they be allowed to join the military as regular soldiers. He believed that in this capacity Native Americans and their dependents could be cared for while at the same time performing useful national service. Owing to the racism prevalent at the time, however, this policy was never adopted.

Schofield proved an able administrator. He clarified the military chain of command by ending a long feud with the secretary of war, subordinating the post of commanding general to the secretary's office, and agreeing to function as his senior military adviser. Schofield's final act was to advocate the adoption of a general staff on the German model to better formulate grand strategic planning. This scheme was not adopted. Schofield, advanced to lieutenant general, retired from the army on February 5, 1895.

On the eve of the Spanish-American War, Schofield argued strongly in favor of U.S. intervention in Cuba in order to end the suffering of the Cuban people. During the war, President William McKinley, who distrusted both Miles and Secretary of War Russell Alger, often sought the counsel of the retired Schofield regarding military issues. Schofield also played a major role in McKinley's decision to call for an increase in the size of the regular army. In 1902, Schofield appeared before a congressional committee to support the creation of a general staff concept, contrary to the opinions of the commanding general of the army, Major General Nelson A. Miles. Schofield died in St. Augustine, Florida, on March 4, 1906. He is generally regarded as one of the finest peacetime commanding generals of the army. Schofield Barracks at Pearl Harbor, Hawaii, is named for him.

JOHN C. FREDRIKSEN AND SPENCER C. TUCKER

See also

Alger, Russell Alexander; McKinley, William; Miles, Nelson Appleton

Further Reading

Connelly, Donald B. *John M. Schofield and the Politics of Generalship.* Chapel Hill: University of North Carolina Press, 2006.

McDonough, James L. *John M. Schofield: Union General in the Civil War and Reconstruction.* Tallahassee: University of Florida Press, 1972.

Schofield, John M. *Forty-Six Years in the Army.* 1897; reprint, Norman: University of Oklahoma Press, 1999.

Schwan, Theodore
Birth Date: July 9, 1841
Death Date: May 27, 1926

U.S. Army brigadier general who served during the American Civil War, the Spanish-American War, and the Philippine-American War. Theodore Schwan was born in Hanover, Germany, on July 9, 1841. Educated in his native country, he immigrated to the United States with his family in 1857.

On June 12, 1857, when he was not yet 16, Schwan enlisted as a private in the 12th U.S. Infantry. He served in the Civil War and rose through the ranks to sergeant until October 31, 1863, when he was commissioned as a second lieutenant. He was advanced to first lieutenant on April 9, 1864, and to captain on March 14, 1866. He was belatedly awarded the Medal of Honor on December 12, 1898, for saving a wounded fellow officer in Virginia during the Civil War in the Battle of Peebles' Farm (October 1, 1864).

Schwan remained in the army after the Civil War and in 1872 participated in Indian campaigns in West Texas. On July 6, 1886, he was promoted to major, serving in the 11th Infantry Regiment. During 1892–1893, he was attached to the U.S. embassy in Berlin, Germany, and on February 19, 1895, he was promoted to lieutenant colonel.

When the Spanish-American War began, Schwan was promoted to colonel on May 18, 1898, and then advanced to brigadier general of volunteers. On June 20, several volunteer regiments from Mobile, Alabama, were transferred to Miami, Florida, where they formed the 1st Division of IV Corps under Schwan's command. On July 1, however, Schwan took command of the Independent Regular Brigade of IV Corps.

On July 31, Schwan sailed with his brigade of some 1,500 men in the transport *Cherokee* for Puerto Rico. He landed with his brigade at Guánica. The brigade remained there until August 6, when Schwan received orders from IV Corps commander Major General Nelson A. Miles to concentrate his brigade at Yauco. Miles hoped to trap Spanish troops by converging on them from three different directions. Schwan's brigade was charged with operations in western Puerto Rico. The brigade occupied Yauco on August 9 and fought in the Battle of Hormigueros on August 10. The next day, Schwan's force entered the town of Mayagüez, which was immediately encircled by Spanish troops. The brigade fought another brief engagement at Las Marías on August 13, the last combat of the Puerto Rico Campaign. Operations by Schwan's brigade had largely cleared Spanish forces from western Puerto Rico. Although Schwan himself was sick during much of the nine-day-long campaign, it was an unqualified success. His men had moved 92 miles, occupied nine towns, and taken 362 prisoners, all at a cost to his own force of 1 dead and 16 wounded.

On August 28, Schwan left for Ponce and then returned to the United States. Transferred to the Philippines, he became chief of staff of VIII Corps there. In October 1899, Schwan's forces helped to crush the Philippine resistance in Cavite and adjacent provinces.

He campaigned for a second time in Cavite during January–February 1900 during which remaining insurgents were dispersed. Schwan retired from the army on February 21, 1901, after more than 40 years in the service. Promoted to major general on the retired list in 1916, he died on May 27, 1926.

KATJA WUESTENBECKER

See also

Cavite, Philippines; Hormigueros, Battle of; Las Marías, Battle of; Mayagüez, Battle of; Miles, Nelson Appleton; Philippine-American War; Philippine Expeditionary Force; Puerto Rico Campaign; Yauco, Battle of

Further Reading

Berbusse, Edward J. *The United States in Puerto Rico, 1898–1900.* Chapel Hill: University of North Carolina Press, 1966.
Carr, Raymond. *Puerto Rico: A Colonial Experiment.* New York: New York University Press, 1984.
Linn, Brian McAllister. *The U.S. Army and Counterinsurgency in the Philippine War, 1899–1902.* Chapel Hill: University of North Carolina Press, 1989.
Millett, Allan R. "The General Staff and the Cuban Intervention of 1906." *Military Affairs* 31(3) (Autumn 1967): 113–119.

Scovel, Henry Sylvester
Birth Date: July 29, 1869
Death Date: February 11, 1905

Born on July 29, 1869, near Pittsburgh, Pennsylvania, Henry Sylvester Scovel (who preferred to be called by his middle name) was one of the best-known newspaper reporters to cover the Spanish-American War. He graduated from Michigan Military Academy in 1887. Sources are confusing concerning Scovel's early life, but he apparently studied at both the College of Wooster in Ohio and the University of Michigan, working part-time as a time-keeper in blast-furnace plants. Some sources claim that he worked on ranches in the West before returning to Ohio to work in the hardware business. He was general manager of the Cleveland Athletic Club and a member of the First Cleveland Troop, an Ohio National Guard unit. Although he was educated in engineering, his passion was writing and journalism.

In 1895, possibly as a result of his penchant for aggressive promoting, the *Pittsburgh Dispatch* and *New York Herald* appointed Scovel to cover the increasing unrest in Spanish-held Cuba. He managed to slip onto the island and locate insurgent leader Máximo Gómez y Iñiguez with whom he spent 10 months in 1896 covering the skirmishes with Spanish troops and the growing Cuban War of Independence. Scovel's mission coincided with the arrival of new captain-general of Cuba Valeriano Weyler y Nicolau, who instituted the infamous *reconcentrado* (reconcentration) policy that proved harsh and deadly to the native population. Scovel's stories detailing Spanish abuses did not endear him to Weyler, who ordered him to leave Cuba. But Scovel ignored this order, leaving for New York only when it suited him.

Scovel's blatant disregard for Weyler led to his hiring by Joseph Pulitzer's paper the *New York World,* which sent Scovel back to Cuba early in 1897. Scovel interviewed Gómez, who publicly rejected the Spanish offer of autonomy for Cuba. Weyler, learning that Scovel was back in Cuba, posted a $5,000 reward for his capture. On February 5, 1897, Scovel was in the port of Tunas trying to send out letters by boat when he was seized by Spanish troops and thrown into prison, accused of communicating with the enemy, crossing Spanish lines, and possessing a false police pass. Once word of his capture reached the United States, the *New York World* began a campaign to secure his release. State legislatures passed resolutions demanding his release, while more than 50 newspapers banded together in a message to Weyler toward the same end. Finally, on March 9, 1897, Weyler, on orders from Madrid, released Scovel.

After briefly covering the Greco-Turkish War, Scovel returned to Cuba late in 1897. This time, the Spanish simply ignored him. He was seated in a waterfront restaurant in Havana on the evening of February 15, 1898, when explosions rocked the U.S. battleship *Maine.* His story appeared two days later in the *New York World.* Scovel, with other American reporters, was expelled from Cuba on April 10, as relations between America and Spain quickly deteriorated.

After war was declared, Scovel befriended Rear Admiral William T. Sampson and placed *New York World* dispatch boats at the navy's disposal, running errands and providing information. The newspaper benefited greatly from this relationship, but on May 18, 1898, Secretary of the Navy John D. Long issued an order banning Scovel from all navy vessels after he was caught stowing away on a navy tug.

Scovel participated in several scouting expeditions along the Cuban coast, helping search for the arrival of the Spanish fleet. Together with reporter Stephen Crane, Scovel landed in Cuba and scouted Santiago Harbor in mid-June, writing a detailed report for both the *New York World* and Sampson who, in spite of Long's edict, continued to make use of Scovel's expertise. Scovel was present at and reported on the American assault on San Juan Heights on July 1, 1898.

American troops entered Santiago de Cuba to accept the formal surrender of the Spanish on July 17. At noon, the Spanish flag was lowered from the governor's palace and the Stars and Stripes raised. In order to be visible in the photos, Scovel had climbed to the palace roof. When some officers saw him, they ordered him down. Once he was on ground level, he began arguing with Major General William R. Shafter and even threw a punch at the general before guards seized him. This incident led to the revocation of Scovel's correspondent's credentials, and he was shipped home.

After the war, Scovel returned to Cuba, serving there until 1902 as a consulting engineer to the Cuban customs service of the U.S. government. Until his death in Havana on February 11, 1905, Scovel was engaged in various commercial enterprises on the island. In many ways, he epitomized the yellow press of the day, but his reporting went beyond that by embedding itself into the local scene and by relying on firsthand (rather than secondhand or thirdhand) reporting.

RICHARD A. SAUERS

See also

Cuban War of Independence; Gómez y Báez, Máximo; Journalism; Newspapers; *Reconcentrado* System; Sampson, William Thomas; San Juan Heights, Battle of; Santiago de Cuba, Battle of; Santiago de Cuba Land Campaign; Shafter, William Rufus; Weyler y Nicolau, Valeriano; Yellow Journalism

Further Reading

Brown, Charles H. *The Correspondents' War: Journalists in the Spanish-American War.* New York: Scribner, 1967.

Milton, Joyce. *The Yellow Kids: Foreign Correspondents in the Heyday of Yellow Journalism.* New York: Harper and Row, 1989.

Seacoast Fortifications
See Coastal Defenses, U.S.

Shafter, William Rufus
Birth Date: October 16, 1836
Death Date: November 12, 1906

U.S. Army general and commander of U.S. forces in Cuba during the Spanish-American War. Born in Galesburg, Kalamazoo County, Michigan, on October 16, 1836, William Rufus Shafter

Major General William Rufus Shafter commanded V Corps in Cuba during the Spanish-American War. (*Photographic History of the Spanish-American War,* 1898)

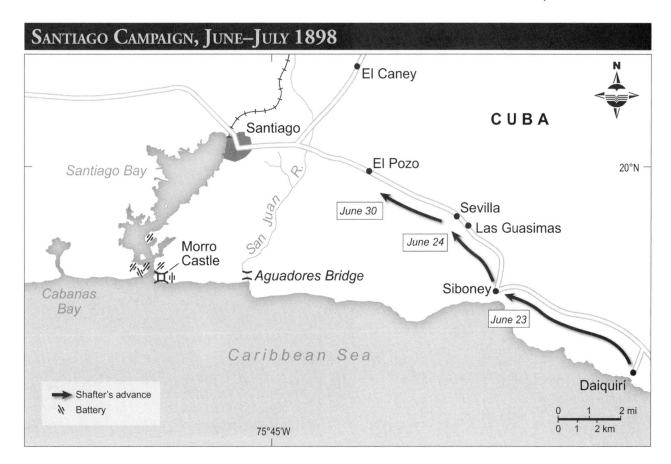

SANTIAGO CAMPAIGN, JUNE–JULY 1898

taught school before the American Civil War. On the outbreak of that war, he secured a commission as a first lieutenant in the 7th Michigan Infantry. He fought in the 1862 Peninsula Campaign and was wounded in the Battle of Seven Pines/Fair Oaks (May 31–June 1). For his role in the battle, he was belatedly awarded the Medal of Honor.

Returning to duty that September, Shafter served as a major in the 19th Michigan Regiment in the western theater. Captured at Thompson's Station, Tennessee, in March 1863, he was exchanged several months later and promoted to lieutenant colonel in June. In April 1864, he assumed command of the 17th United States Colored Infantry as a colonel, leading his unit in the Battle of Nashville in December 1864. In March 1865, he received a brevet promotion to brigadier general in the volunteers.

Offered a regular commission in the army at the end of the war, Shafter reentered the army as a lieutenant colonel of the 41st Infantry, one of the African American regiments, that was merged into the new 24th Infantry in 1869. For the next decade, he served on the West Texas plains. There he supported campaigns led by Colonel Ronald Mackenzie and earned the sobriquet of "Pecos Bill" as commander of the 24th Infantry.

In 1879, Shafter was promoted to colonel of the 1st Infantry Regiment. He held this assignment for almost 18 years. He was stationed with that regiment in the Dakotas, in Texas, and in Arizona. He also headed recruiting in New York, and he commanded the army post at Angel Island, California, during 1891–1897. In May

1897, he received promotion to brigadier general and assumed command of the Department of California.

With the outbreak of the Spanish-American War in 1898, Shafter was advanced to major general of volunteers and received command of V Corps, the U.S. Army force slated to invade Cuba. Age 63 in 1898, Shafter's weight had ballooned to 300 pounds. He was clearly out of shape and in poor health, suffering from persistent gout. In retrospect, he seems to have been a poor choice for the Cuban command, although he was the first pick of the commanding general of the army Major General Nelson A. Miles and Adjutant General Henry Corbin.

In early June 1898, after some indecision by the War Department because of the movement of the Spanish fleet, Shafter received orders to assemble 10,000 men at Tampa, Florida, and prepare to invade Cuba. The original objective was Havana, but upon learning that Spanish rear admiral Pascual Cervera y Topete's Cádiz Squadron had reached Santiago Harbor, the focal point of the campaign became that port city.

From the outset in Tampa, Shafter's ineptness became evident. In his defense, like so many U.S. Army officers of that day, he had no experience managing large numbers of troops. But he also lacked the requisite energy, stamina, health, and organizational skills for such a challenging situation. Fortunately for his command, he had an able staff that made up, at least in part, for his shortcomings.

Departing from Tampa on June 14, 1898, Shafter began landing V Corps at Daiquirí and Siboney on June 22. With orders to capture Santiago, he proposed to move on that city as quickly as possible in the hope of reaching his objective before the beginning of the fever season. Moving inland, Shafter's forces defeated the Spanish in the battles at Las Guásimas, San Juan Heights, and El Caney. Following the U.S. naval victory over Cervera's squadron in the Battle of Santiago de Cuba on July 3, 1898, Shafter began a series of negotiations with Spanish commander General José Toral y Vázquez, who surrendered to Shafter on July 17.

Ill with gout and suffering from the tropical heat, Shafter was barely able to function as commander during the Santiago campaign and was forced to follow the action from the rear, issuing orders through deputies, especially his aide-de-camp Lieutenant John David Miley. Because of Shafter's poor health, a number of his officers believed him unfit for command. Indeed, because of his weight and illness, he occasionally had to be carried about on a door. Finally, he failed to develop a harmonious rapport with his naval counterpart, Commodore William T. Sampson. Fortunately for the United States, the weakness of the Spanish position offset the absence of a strong army-navy relationship. Shafter also drew much criticism in the press for problems associated with the Cuba Campaign, most of which were beyond his control.

Promoted to major general in 1901, Shafter retired from the army several months later. He returned to his farm in California, which was adjacent to his daughter's ranch. Shafter's health continued to deteriorate. He died on November 12, 1906, near Bakersfield, California, of complications from an intestinal obstruction and pneumonia.

JERRY KEENAN

See also

Daiquirí Beachhead, Cuba; El Caney, Battle of; V Corps; Las Guásimas, Battle of; Miley, John David; Sampson, William Thomas; San Juan Heights, Battle of; Santiago de Cuba Land Campaign; Siboney, Cuba; United States Army

Further Reading

Carlson, Paul H. *Pecos Bill: A Military Biography of William R. Shafter.* College Station: Texas A&M University Press, 1989.

Cosmas, Graham A. *An Army for Empire: The United States Army in the Spanish-American War.* College Station: Texas A&M University Press, 1994.

Walker, Dale L. *The Boys of '98: Theodore Roosevelt and the Rough Riders.* New York: Forge, 1999.

Shafter-García Conference

See Aserraderos Conference

Sherman, John

Birth Date: May 10, 1823
Death Date: October 22, 1900

Republican politician, U.S. congressman (1854–1861), U.S. senator (1861–1877, 1881–1897), and U.S. secretary of state (1897–1898).

John Sherman was a congressman and senator. As secretary of state (1897–1898), he was forced to resign by President William McKinley because of his staunch opposition to war with Spain. (Library of Congress)

Born on May 10, 1823, in Lancaster, Ohio, John Sherman, who was the older brother of American Civil War major general William Tecumseh Sherman, began the study of law at age 14. At the same time, John Sherman worked on a number of canal projects in Ohio. He was admitted to the bar in 1844 and established a practice in Mansfield, Ohio, before moving to Cleveland in 1853. Active in politics as a member of the Whig Party and strongly opposed to slavery, Sherman helped to organize the new Republican Party in Ohio after passage of the 1854 Kansas-Nebraska Act. That same year, he was elected to the first of three successive terms in the U.S. House of Representatives. As chairman of the powerful Ways and Means Committee from 1859 to 1861, he quickly rose to political prominence and played an important role in securing passage of the Morrill Tariff of 1861, a protectionist tariff that sharply raised duties on imported goods.

In 1861, Sherman won election to the U.S. Senate, where he served until 1877. As chairman of the Senate Finance Committee, he played a crucial role in formulating government financial policy during the Reconstruction era. Although he had supported the use of paper money (greenbacks) during the Civil War, he deplored the inflationary effects of relying on anything but gold as the foundation of the nation's monetary system. In 1875, he oversaw the enactment of the Specie Resumption Act.

In 1877, Sherman left the Senate to assume the post of secretary of the treasury in the Rutherford B. Hayes administration. While secretary of the treasury, Sherman directed the successful implementation of the Specie Resumption Act in 1879. Once again, the dollar, including the remaining greenbacks in circulation, was redeemable in gold. Sherman served as treasury secretary until March 1881. Later that year, he was once more elected to the U.S. Senate to take up the seat vacated by James A. Garfield, who had been elected president.

Although unsuccessful in securing the Republican presidential nomination for president in 1880, 1884, and 1888, Sherman gave his name to two important pieces of legislation passed in 1890. The first was the Sherman Antitrust Act (1890), which made it a crime for business firms to combine to prevent competition. This legislation was aimed principally at big businesses and trusts, such as John D. Rockefeller's Standard Oil Company. The second piece of legislation was the Sherman Silver Purchase Act (1890), which dramatically increased the amount of silver purchased by the federal government. The silver was to be used to back the printing of paper money, called treasury notes. The goal was to foster debt relief for farmers and debtors through inflation. The consequences of this act proved to be disastrous for the treasury, however, during the economic depression of 1893–1897, because the notes were redeemable in either gold or silver. When the public demanded gold, the treasury's gold reserves fell below the required level of $100 million.

Perhaps as a reward for Sherman's long service to the party and to secure a seat in the U.S. Senate for his political adviser Marcus Alonzo Hanna, President William McKinley appointed Sherman secretary of state in 1897. The move proved to be a poor choice. The combination of Sherman's advanced age (he was then 74), failing memory, and staunch opposition to the acquisition of overseas colonies led McKinley to request that Sherman resign from the Cabinet in April 1898. McKinley replaced him with Assistant Secretary of State William Rufus Day. Sherman thus left the public spotlight after nearly 40 years of public service. He died in Washington, D.C., on October 22, 1900.

PAUL G. PIERPAOLI JR.

See also

Day, William Rufus; Economic Depression; Hanna, Mark; McKinley, William; Rockefeller, John Davison; Silver Standard

Further Reading

Burton, Theodore E. *John Sherman.* Boston and New York: Houghton Mifflin, 1906.

Sherman, John. *Recollections of Forty Years in the House, Senate, and Cabinet: An Autobiography.* 2 vols. Chicago: Werner, 1896.

Thorndike, Rachel Sherman, ed. *The Sherman Letters: Correspondence between General and Senator Sherman, 1837–1891.* New York: Scribner, 1894.

Shimonoseki, Treaty of

Treaty signed between China and Japan on April 17, 1895, that officially ended the First Sino-Japanese War (1894–1895). The peace talks that ended in the treaty had begun in Shimonoseki, Japan, on March 20, 1895, even as hostilities continued between the two nations. At its core, the First Sino-Japanese War was a conflict over the control of Korea. The Treaty of Shimonoseki compelled China to recognize and honor Korean independence and cede large land areas to the Japanese, including the Liaotung (Liaodong) Peninsula in southeastern Manchuria and the islands of Formosa (Taiwan) and the Pescadores (in the Taiwan Straits). The Chinese were also forced to pay Japan an indemnity of 200 million Kuping taels (Chinese currency) over a seven-year period and to sign a new commercial treaty that would open various Chinese rivers and ports to Japanese and Western trade.

The treaty was drafted with the help of former U.S. secretary of state John A. Foster, who had been retained by the Qing dynasty, which was in power in China at the time of the negotiations. On March 24, 1895, just as the negotiations had gotten under way, Chinese representative to the talks Li Hung-Chang was attacked by a Japanese right-wing extremist. The attempted assassination caused a furor in Japan and led the government to temper its demands and agree to a temporary cease-fire. The talks were temporarily suspended until April 10. The treaty was signed a week later, on April 17.

Russia, which had its own aspirations in the Far East over Korea and Manchuria, was very much opposed to the treaty, for if Japan secured Korea, it would control both sides of Tsushima Strait, the southern outlet of the Sea of Japan where the Russian port of Vladivostok was located. Should Japan also secure Port Arthur and the Liaotung Peninsula, it would prevent Russia from having a warm-water port in that region.

Russia secured the assistance of its ally France and also German kaiser Wilhelm II, who sought to divert Russia's attention to Asia. Soon after the conclusion of the treaty of Shimonoseki, Russia, France, and Germany in a joint note advised Japan not to annex any part of the Chinese mainland. Japan had not yet proved its mettle against any of the great European powers and could not easily contemplate war against a coalition of these three great European states. Japan thus gave up her claim to territory on the Asiatic mainland and in return received from China an additional indemnity of some $22.5 million.

In 1896, Russia secured from China a concession to build a railway from China in Siberia across Manchuria to Vladivostok and two years later secured a 25-year lease of about 500 square miles of territory—including part of the land surrendered by Japan in 1895—at the end of the Liaotung Peninsula and the right to construct a branch line to connect this territory with the Chinese Eastern Railway at Harbin. Russian troops maintained security along the line. Soon the Russians were at work building a powerful fortress and naval base at Port Arthur and hoped that it might secure all of Manchuria. The Japanese were furious at these developments, which sparked anti-Russian riots in Japan. In 1902, the Japanese government secured an alliance with Great Britain, and in 1904, Japan went to war against Russia.

Following the Treaty of Shimonoseki, all the major imperialist powers, including the British and Germans secured territorial concessions in China. Thus in 1896, the major powers added an economic addendum to the treaty. Under it, Japanese nationals were allowed to open factories and engage in port trade in China. The same right was extended to the Western powers under the most favored nation clause.

It was clear to American policy makers on the eve of the Spanish-American War that Asia was to be a major cockpit of great power rivalry. American policy makers believed that the Treaty of Shimonoseki and the events that flowed from it demonstrated that the United States must acquire a presence in Asia. This was for geostrategic reasons as well as economic imperatives, such as markets for American goods. But what the Americans did not agree with was the partitioning of China into exclusive spheres of influence. Rather, they saw China as a potential great market that should be open to all foreign trade. Such logic drove Secretary of State John Hay's Open Door Notes of 1899. Be that as it may, the U.S. acquisition of the Philippines in 1898 ensured that the United States would secure an Asian presence.

PAUL G. PIERPAOLI JR. AND ANNA RULSKA

See also

China; China Market; Japan; Open Door Policy; Philippine Islands; Russo-Japanese War; Sino-Japanese War

Further Reading

Ish, Ian, and Aan Ish. *The Origins of the Russo-Japanese War.* London: Longman, 1985.

McCormick, Thomas J. *China Market: America's Quest for Informal Empire, 1893–1901.* Chicago: Quadrangle Books, 1967.

Paine, Sarah C. M. *The Sino-Japanese War of 1894–1895: Perceptions, Power, and Primacy.* New York: Cambridge University Press, 2003.

Siboney, Cuba

Small hamlet located along Cuba's southeastern coast and situated just to the east-southeast of Santiago de Cuba. Siboney was the second beachhead for V Corps after the initial landing at Daiquirí beginning on June 22, 1898. The village is located some seven miles west of Daiquirí, which at the time of the Spanish-American War was accessible via a fairly well-maintained but narrow coastal road. Major General William R. Shafter, commander of V Corps, planned to land at Daiquirí, move up the coast to Siboney, and then turn northwest toward El Caney and Santiago de Cuba.

At midmorning on June 22, V Corps began moving ashore, finding Daiquirí virtually undefended by Spanish troops. By nightfall, some 6,000 U.S. troops had established a beachhead. Although the landing experienced many problems with lost supplies and equipment, just two American soldiers died during the operation, both

Men of the 32nd and 33rd Michigan Volunteer regiments landing near Siboney, Cuba, on June 25, 1898. (*Photographic History of the Spanish-American War,* 1898)

victims of drowning. Shafter immediately assigned Brigadier General Henry Lawton and his brigade the task of marching to Siboney and taking it. At the same time, Shafter decided to make Siboney rather than Daiquirí his headquarters for the eventual assault against Santiago de Cuba.

Lawton's men arrived at Siboney on June 23. They soon realized that the town was undefended and had been abandoned by Spanish troops. Within hours, U.S. troops controlled the hamlet. That same evening, more troops from V Corps began landing at Siboney and were entirely unopposed. By June 26, all of V Corps had disembarked and were well placed to begin the campaign against Santiago de Cuba. American troops were extraordinarily lucky to have landed at two different locations without enemy resistance. As Theodore Roosevelt would later observe, a force of just 500 Spaniards may have foiled the landings.

To care for men wounded in combat and stricken by disease, the U.S. Army established a major hospital operation in Siboney, which was then augmented by several naval ships located off shore. The transport *Olivet,* for example, was converted into a hospital ship in early July. The wounded began pouring into the hospital at Siboney as the campaign for Santiago de Cuba intensified in the last days of June. While Santiago was under siege, on July 6 doctors at Siboney observed the first cases of yellow fever among American troops in Cuba. At the same time, malaria coupled with dysentery was sending more and more soldiers to the now terribly overcrowded hospital. Fearing that V Corps would be decimated by a runaway yellow fever epidemic, the commanding general of the army, Major General Nelson A. Miles, ordered the torching of all buildings in Siboney under the mistaken notion that yellow fever was spread via infected buildings and personal belongings. It was the outbreak of yellow fever at Siboney that served to convince U.S. commanders to seek a rapid end to hostilities.

PAUL G. PIERPAOLI JR.

See also

Daiquirí Beachhead, Cuba; Dysentery; V Corps; Lawton, Henry Ware; Malaria; Miles, Nelson Appleton; Santiago de Cuba Land Campaign; Shafter, William Rufus; Yellow Fever

Further Reading

Cosmas, Graham A. *An Army for Empire: The United States Army in the Spanish-American War.* College Station: Texas A&M University Press, 1994.
Musicant, Ivan. *Empire by Default: The Spanish-American War and the Dawn of the American Century.* New York: Henry Holt, 1998.
Trask, David F. *The War with Spain in 1898.* Lincoln: University of Nebraska Press, 1996.

Sicard, Montgomery

Birth Date: September 20, 1836
Death Date: September 14, 1900

U.S. Navy admiral. Born in New York City on September 20, 1836, Montgomery Sicard became a midshipman after graduating from the United States Naval Academy in 1855. He saw service afloat with both the Home Squadron and the East India Squadron and was promoted to master on November 4, 1858, and to lieutenant on May 31, 1860. With the start of the American Civil War, he was assigned to the West Gulf Coast Blockading Squadron. He participated in flag officer David G. Farragut's run past the Mississippi River forts and capture of New Orleans in April 1862 as well as the runs past Vicksburg that June. Sicard was promoted to lieutenant commander on July 16, 1862. He commanded the screw gunboat *Seneca* during the Union assaults on Fort Fisher in December 1864 and January 1865.

Following the war, Sicard held assignments afloat and ashore, including ordnance duty in Washington, D.C., and New York City. Promoted to commander on March 2, 1870, he served as chief of the Bureau of Ordnance during 1881–1891, being promoted to captain on August 7, 1881. He was named commodore on July 10, 1894, and was advanced to rear admiral and took command of the North Atlantic Squadron on April 6, 1897. However, he was forced to relinquish his command on March 26, 1898, because of poor health. He was replaced by Rear Admiral William T. Sampson.

Upon his partial recovery, Sicard was named the chair of the Naval War Board and served as Secretary of the Navy John D. Long's chief adviser during the Spanish-American War. Sicard played an important role in guiding naval strategy. Fearing loss of capital ships, he opposed V Corps commander Major General William R. Shafter's demand that the navy force the entrance to Santiago Harbor. Rear Admiral Sicard retired from the navy on September 30, 1898. He died at Westernville, New York, on September 14, 1900.

SPENCER C. TUCKER

See also

Long, John Davis; Naval War Board; North Atlantic Squadron; Sampson, William Thomas; Shafter, William Rufus

Further Reading

Coletta, Paolo E. "John Davis Long." In *American Secretaries of the Navy,* edited by Paolo E. Coletto, 1:431–458. Annapolis, MD: Naval Institute Press, 1980.
Trask, David F. *The War with Spain in 1898.* Lincoln: University of Nebraska Press, 1996.

Signal 250

U.S. Navy flag signal used to inform American warships of the departure of Rear Admiral Pascual Cervera y Topete's Spanish squadron from the bay at Santiago de Cuba. Three flags were used, one each for the numbers "2," "5," and "0." The first flag was yellow with a disk in the center, the second one was half yellow and half red, and the third flag was a yellow swallow-tail pennant with a blue cross. The three flags were hoisted as a signal code to mean "The enemy's ships are coming out!" The signal was to be flown by the first U.S. ship to sight the Spanish ships exiting the harbor of Santiago de Cuba, and every other U.S. ship would then fly the same signal to acknowledge receipt and understanding of it. If the

Spanish squadron attempted to elude the U.S. blockade at night, the signal was to have been two red rockets.

The 250 signal was first hoisted by the armored cruiser *Brooklyn*, flagship of Commodore Winfield Scott Schley, to other U.S. ships blockading the port on Sunday morning, July 3, 1898, as two Spanish torpedo boat destroyers and four armored cruisers attempted to break through the American blockade. In the ensuing battle, which lasted for just a few hours, only 1 American was killed. Ten others were wounded, and there were no losses of U.S. warships. Spanish losses were 323 killed and 151 wounded and the sinking or grounding of the entire squadron. A total of 1,720 Spaniards were taken prisoner.

TIMOTHY J. DEMY

See also

Cervera y Topete, Pascual; Santiago de Cuba, Battle of; Schley, Winfield Scott

Further Reading

Azoy, A. C. M. *Signal 250! The Sea Fight Off Santiago.* New York: David McKay, 1964.
Feuer, A. B. *The Spanish-American War at Sea: Naval Action in the Atlantic.* Westport, CT: Praeger, 1995.
Trask, David F. "The Battle of Santiago." In *Great American Naval Battles,* edited by Jack Sweetman, 198–218. Annapolis, MD: Naval Institute Press, 1998.

Sigsbee, Charles Dwight
Birth Date: January 16, 1845
Death Date: July 13, 1923

U.S. Navy officer and captain of the U.S. Navy battleship *Maine,* which exploded in Havana Harbor on February 15, 1898, an event that helped trigger the Spanish-American War. Charles Dwight Sigsbee was born in Albany, New York, on January 16, 1845. Aspiring to a naval career, he graduated from the United States Naval Academy, Annapolis, in the spring of 1863 and soon saw action in the American Civil War.

Sigsbee was first assigned to Rear Admiral David G. Farragut's West Gulf Blockade Squadron and served on the *Brooklyn* and *Monongahela.* While serving on the *Brooklyn,* Sigsbee participated in the Battle of Mobile Bay on August 5, 1864. Transferred to Rear Admiral David D. Porter's North Atlantic Blockading Squadron, Sigsbee participated in the December 1864–January 1865 assaults on Fort Fisher, North Carolina.

Following the war, Sigsbee served on different ships before becoming an instructor at the Naval Academy from 1869 to 1871. In late 1871, he joined the Hydrographic Office. There he invented numerous deep-sea sounding devices and several apparatuses for deep-sea sampling. From 1873 to 1891, he again served afloat as a hydrographer in both the Asiatic Squadron and the European Squadron. While conducting deep-sea explorations in the Gulf of Mexico, ships under his command located the deepest spot in the

U.S. Navy captain Charles D. Sigsbee was commanding the battleship *Maine* when it blew up in Havana Harbor on February 15, 1898. Sigsbee survived the explosion and retired from the navy as a rear admiral. (Library of Congress)

Gulf, which was named the Sigsbee Deep in his honor. He also commanded the screw sloop *Kearsarge* of American Civil War fame. From 1893 to 1897, he was stationed in the navy's Bureau of Navigation as a hydrographer.

Promoted to captain in March 1897, the next month Sigsbee took command of the ill-fated battleship *Maine,* which had been commissioned in 1895. The *Maine* was built as a heavy armored cruiser, but the navy classified it as a second-class battleship. It mounted four 10-inch guns and six 6-inch guns and was capable of a top speed of about 17 knots. On January 24, 1898, with tensions building between the United States and Spain, President William McKinley, upon the recommendations of Secretary of War Russell A. Alger and Secretary of the Navy John D. Long, ordered the *Maine* to Havana, Cuba, as a show of force there and to stand ready to defend U.S. interests if need be.

Sigsbee departed Key West, Florida, that same day. The *Maine* arrived in Havana Harbor the next day, January 25. As instructed, Sigsbee anchored in the harbor. The *Maine* stayed at anchor until 9:40 p.m. on February 15, 1898. Just as Sigsbee was concluding a letter to his wife in his cabin, two massive explosions rocked the ship. With smoke pouring into his cabin, he made his way to an outer deck, where he gave orders to flood the vessel's magazines. The ship sank shortly thereafter. A total of 266 members of the crew perished. Sigsbee promptly cabled Washington about events but urged caution in reaching a conclusion as to the cause of the explosion.

There was immediate suspicion that the ship had fallen victim to a mine planted by the Spanish or a disgruntled Cuban. In his own testimony before the subsequent Navy Court of Inquiry convened at Key West and then before the Senate Foreign Relations Committee, Sigsbee said that he believed the cause of the explosion was indeed a mine, electronically detonated from the shore. The court of inquiry agreed with this conclusion. The court also found that neither Sigsbee nor the crew of the *Maine* had done anything untoward before, during, or after the explosion.

Sigsbee then took command of the armed merchant cruiser *St. Paul*, which had been assigned to blockade duty off the Cuban coast. On June 22, 1898, off San Juan, Puerto Rico, the *St. Paul* engaged and heavily damaged the Spanish destroyer *Terror* and cruiser *Isabella II*. Sigsbee next commanded the battleship *Texas* until 1900.

In February 1900, Sigsbee was named chief intelligence officer for the Office of Naval Intelligence, a position he held until his promotion to rear admiral in August 1903. From late 1903 to mid-1904, he commanded the Philadelphia Navy Yard. He then assumed command of the South Atlantic Squadron in 1904 and the 2nd Division of the North Atlantic Squadron in 1905. He retired from active duty in January 1907. He remained active in retirement, both with speaking and writing engagements. He also wrote several books, including *Deep-Sea Sounding and Dredging* (1880) and *The Maine: An Account of Her Destruction in Havana Harbor* (1899). Sigsbee died in New York City on July 13, 1923.

PAUL G. PIERPAOLI JR.

See also
Maine, USS; *Maine*, USS, Inquiries into the Loss of; "Remember the Maine"; United States Navy

Further Reading
Blow, Michael. *A Ship to Remember: The Maine and the Spanish-American War.* New York: Morrow, 1992.
Rickover, Hyman G. *How the Battleship Maine Was Destroyed.* Annapolis, MD: Naval Institute Press, 1995.
Samuels, Peggy, and Harold Samuels. *Remembering the Maine.* Washington, DC: Smithsonian Institution Press, 1995.
Weems, John Edward. *The Fate of the Maine.* New York: Henry Holt, 1985.

Silver Standard

A monetary system based on the coinage of silver and/or the printing of paper currency that is based upon a specific redeemable silver standard (value). In the years leading up to the Spanish-American War, those advocating so-called free silver (a misnomer because there was nothing free about it), or a currency standard based on gold and silver (bimetalism), believed that a silver standard would cure the nation's economic ills. The Populist Party was most identified with the free silver platform, although segments of the Democratic Party bought into it as well. Indeed, when Democrat William Jennings Bryan ran for president in 1896, the Populists threw their support behind his candidacy.

In 1792, Congress had officially established a gold- and silver-based currency, setting the gold value of the American dollar at a ratio of 15:1 silver to gold, meaning that 15 ounces of silver equaled 1 ounce of gold. The first coins were issued in 1793, but at the time silver was in greater use than gold, which in demand as market bullion had largely disappeared from circulation. This began to change as the result of gold discoveries in North Georgia in 1828. Although the United States officially maintained a bimetal standard, the 1834 Coinage Act Congress changed the ratio of silver to gold to 16:1, a step that overvalued silver at the time. More important, the California Gold Rush of 1849 greatly increased the amount of gold in circulation and virtually eliminated silver from circulation because the cost of silver to the mint was greater than the official value of coins being issued. To meet the escalating costs of the American Civil War, in 1862 the Treasury Department began issuing paper notes, or greenbacks, as legal tender, which caused prices to skyrocket.

In the aftermath of the Civil War, the issue of the monetary standard became one of the most hotly debated issues in American politics. In order to ensure that the United States would have access to foreign financial markets, Republicans championed a slow but steady return to the prewar monetary standard by providing for the gradual redemption of greenbacks in gold. Combined with increased industrial and agricultural production in the 1870s, this resulted in a sharp decline in prices, which had the most adverse impact on American farmers. In addition, new discoveries of silver in the West resulted in a sharp decline in the price of silver, which in turn made gold a far more stable monetary standard. Although the United States would not officially adopt the gold standard until 1900, the country had a de facto gold standard from 1879 onward at an effective ratio of 20:1.

Amid the often heated post–Civil War debate over redemption or resumption of greenbacks, or non–interest-bearing paper that was legal tender in payment of all debts, came the 1873 Coinage Act, which did not provide for further coinage of silver dollars. Passed in the context of falling prices and an economic depression that devastated farmers and debtors, the act was soon labeled the "Crime of '73." More important, in 1876 it led to the formation of the Greenback Party, which sought a return to the paper currency of the Civil War, and the Free Silver Movement, which demanded the unlimited coinage of silver. Both movements essentially advocated an inflationary scheme to put more money into circulation and depreciate the value of the dollar. Farmers, who were often heavily in debt, would benefit from inflation because it would decrease the value of their accumulated debts. Most businessmen and others in the upper and middle classes disdained the free silver movement, however, and the Republican Party ardently opposed it.

After Democrats gained control of the House of Representatives in the congressional elections of 1874, they led an effort to increase the amount of silver in circulation. In 1878, the Bland-Allison Act required the U.S. Treasury to purchase monthly between $2 million and $4 million worth of silver bullion at market prices; this was to be coined into silver dollars with legal tender status. Demands of the so-called free silver forces for unlimited coinage ultimately failed. The Sherman Silver Purchase Act of 1890, passed as a compromise effort with some Republican support, increased the amount of silver purchased by more than 50 percent, authorizing the Treasury to issue notes payable in either gold or silver. The onset of the economic depression of 1893–1897 not only resulted in severe hardships throughout the country but also placed the Treasury's gold reserve in jeopardy when note holders demanded payment in gold instead of silver. President Grover Cleveland, a Bourbon Democrat who firmly supported the gold standard, not only secured the repeal of the Sherman Silver Purchase Act in 1893 but also called upon financier John Pierpont Morgan to help the Treasury purchase enough gold abroad to restore the minimum $100 million gold reserve and maintain the gold standard. Cleveland's stance would ultimately split the Democratic Party in 1896.

Most notable of the groups promoting silver was the Populist Party (also known as the People's Party) of the 1890s. Despite having a wide range of political and economic demands—from direct election of U.S. senators to strict government regulation of railroads—the party made silver its central platform issue in 1892. Its 1892 presidential nominee, former Civil War brevet brigadier general James B. Weaver, who had been the Greenback Party nominee in 1880, received more than 1 million votes. When Democrats nominated William Jennings Bryan of Nebraska in 1896 after his famous "Cross of Gold" speech, Populists decided to nominate him as well. Despite the practical merger of the two parties on a platform of unlimited coinage of silver at a ratio of 16:1 to gold, Bryan lost the 1896 election to Republican William McKinley. The election ushered in an era of Republican dominance that would last until 1932.

As the economy improved in the aftermath of the election of 1896, demands for a silver standard faded. In 1900, Congress passed the Gold Standard Act. Silver continued to circulate as subsidiary coins. Not until the Coinage Act of 1965, however, did Congress vote to reduce or eliminate all silver in American coins (dimes and quarters). By the 1980s, American coins no longer contained silver.

CLAUDINE FERRELL AND JUSTIN D. MURPHY

See also

Bryan, William Jennings; Cleveland, Stephen Grover; Economic Depression; McKinley, William; Morgan, John Pierpont, Sr.; Populist Party; Sherman, John

Further Reading

Cherny, Robert W. *A Righteous Cause: The Life of William Jennings Bryan.* Edited by Oscar Handlin. Boston: Little, Brown, 1985.

Jastram, Roy W. *Silver: The Restless Metal.* New York: Wiley, 1981.

McGrath, Robert C., Jr. *American Populism: A Social History, 1877–1898.* New York: Hill and Wang, 1990.

Nussbaum, Arthur. *A History of the Dollar.* New York: Columbia University Press, 1957.

Timberlake, Richard H. *Monetary Policy in the United States: An Intellectual and Institutional History.* Chicago: University of Chicago Press, 1993.

Wilson, Thomas. *The Power "to Coin" Money: The Exercise of Monetary Powers by the Congress.* Armonk, NY: M. E. Sharpe, 1992.

Sims, William Sowden
Birth Date: October 15, 1858
Death Date: September 25, 1936

U.S. Navy admiral. Born in Port Hope, Ontario, Canada, on October 15, 1858, William Sowden Sims was the son of an American father and a Canadian mother. His family moved to Pennsylvania when he was 10, and he graduated from the United States Naval Academy, Annapolis, in 1880. The transformation of the U.S. Navy in this period to new steel ships and breech-loading guns marked the beginning of his lifelong interest in the development of naval equipment, technology, and doctrine.

From 1880 to 1897, Sims was almost continuously on sea duty, seeing service with the North Atlantic, Pacific, and China squadrons. He had the opportunity to witness firsthand the fine performance of the Japanese Navy in the Sino-Japanese War of 1894–1895, and his intelligence reports sent to the Office of Naval Intelligence analyzed the performance of the various ships involved in the war.

From 1897 to 1900, Sims was the U.S. naval attaché in Paris. From that city, he provided information on European naval innovations and also established an extensive intelligence network that included a number of individuals of widely different backgrounds in a number of nations, including a well-placed doctor in Madrid. Using his network, Sims provided Washington with highly useful intelligence reports about Spanish intentions during the Spanish-American War as well as accurate information on the voyage of Rear Admiral Manuel de la Cámara y Libermoore's squadron. In an effort to secure the recall of that squadron to Spain, Sims carried out a disinformation campaign to the effect that U.S. Navy warships were preparing to assault the Spanish coast.

Sims's activities during the war favorably impressed Assistant Secretary of the Navy Theodore Roosevelt, who became president in 1901. In 1901, Sims served on the staff of the commander of the U.S. Asiatic Fleet and there became friends with British captain Percy Scott and learned from him new techniques of gunnery introduced into the Royal Navy. Sims's efforts to interest the U.S. Navy in these were not successful, leading him to write to President Roosevelt, technically an act of insubordination. Recalled to Washington in 1902 and appointed as inspector of target practice, during 1902–1909 Sims achieved significant success in U.S. naval ordnance reform, reducing the firing time for large-caliber guns from 5 minutes to 30 seconds while at the same time improving accuracy. He was an observer during the 1904–1905 Russo-Japanese War.

Promoted to captain in 1911, Sims was an instructor at the Naval War College during 1911–1912. He then commanded the At-

Admiral William S. Sims commanded U.S. naval forces in European waters during World War I. During the Spanish-American War, he was U.S. naval attaché in Paris, where he established an intelligence network that gathered highly useful information on Spanish naval capabilities and intentions. (Library of Congress)

Benson, to consider him an Anglophile. For his part, Sims ascribed the navy's initially somewhat disappointing wartime performance to his superiors' failure to implement some of his suggestions and what he viewed as their earlier reluctance to prepare the navy for a major conflict, charges he aired to Congress during a 1920 investigation that he largely precipitated and that provoked bitter feuding within the navy.

By November 1917, Sims and his staff were supervising the operations of 350 ships and 75,000 men. Promoted to temporary admiral in December 1918, Sims returned to the United States and reverted to his permanent rank of rear admiral. He then headed the Naval War College from April 1919 until his retirement in October 1922. He continued to speak out on naval and defense issues, publishing his wartime memoirs *The Victory at Sea* (1920), which won the Pulitzer Prize for History, and forcefully urging the development of naval aviation. A dynamic and energetic reformer and proponent of naval expansion, in later life his unfortunate tendency to demonize those who opposed him vitiated his numerous concrete achievements. Sims died in Boston on September 25, 1936.

PRISCILLA ROBERTS

See also

Cámara y Libermoore, Manuel de la; Spain, Navy; United States Navy

Further Reading

Hagan, Kenneth J. "William S. Sims: Naval Insurgent and Coalition Warrior." In *The Human Tradition in the Gilded Age and Progressive Era*, edited by Ballard C. Campbell, 187–203. Wilmington, DE: Scholarly Resources, 2000.

Morison, Elting E. *Admiral Sims and the Modern American Navy*. Boston: Houghton Mifflin, 1942.

Sims, William S. *The Victory at Sea*. 1920; reprint, Annapolis, MD: Naval Institute Press, 1984.

lantic Torpedo Flotilla. Promoted to rear admiral in 1916, the next year he returned to the Naval War College as its president.

With war between the United States and Germany looming, Sims went to Britain in 1917 to discuss naval cooperation with the Allied powers. The United States declared war on Germany on April 6 before his arrival. Promoted temporary vice admiral in May and made commander of U.S. naval forces in European waters, Sims bombarded Washington with recommendations on convoying, antisubmarine warfare, intelligence gathering, and strategic planning. He urged the immediate implementation of convoys, which gained the support of British prime minister David Lloyd George and also urged that American battleships be assigned primarily to escort duties convoying supplies and men for the Allies, ventures that brought drastic reductions in Allied shipping losses but generally involved resigning overall control of American naval operations in Europe to British admirals.

Sims's attitude and his excellent relations with his British counterparts led Washington officials, including Secretary of the Navy Josephus Daniels and Chief of Naval Operations William Shepherd

Sinclair, Upton
Birth Date: September 20, 1878
Death Date: November 25, 1968

American novelist, activist, and socialist whose interest in social and industrial reforms shaped many of his writings. Upton Beall Sinclair Jr. was born in Baltimore, Maryland, on September 20, 1878. He graduated from City College of New York in 1897 and attended Columbia University from 1897 to 1901. He began publishing articles, short stories, and jokes while still a teenager, but he struggled to find a publisher for his first two novels. His third novel, the historically themed *Manassas* (1904), was a minor critical and commercial success.

Sinclair's conversion to socialism inspired *The Jungle*. Published in 1906, the novel's graphic depiction of the Chicago stockyards and America's meatpacking companies provoked public outrage, leading to the passage of the Pure Food and Drug Act (1906) and the Meat Inspection Act (1906). His landmark work was inspired in part by the Embalmed Beef Scandal that had arisen from the Spanish-

596   Sino-Japanese War

Upton Sinclair was a prominent novelist and socialist who pointed out the need for reform in many areas of American life. He is best known for *The Jungle*, a savage exposé of the meatpacking industry. (Library of Congress)

he supported America's intervention in World War I. He believed that the overthrow of Germany's autocratic government was necessary to realize a socialist revolution in Germany. However, he loudly criticized the federal government's suppression of civil liberties during the war and the American military intervention in Russia following the Bolshevik Revolution of November 1917. He was a particularly harsh critic of the so-called Red Scare in the United States that lasted from 1919 to about 1921.

In 1934, during the height of the Great Depression, Sinclair won the Democratic primary for governor in California. Although he lost the general election to the Republican Party candidate, his activism on behalf of the economically disadvantaged may have inspired President Franklin Delano Roosevelt to implement some of the New Deal's most progressive reforms.

In 1940, Sinclair published *World's End,* the first in a series of novels dealing with world affairs from 1914 to 1950 and featuring the fictional protagonist Lanny Budd. The third novel in the cycle, *Dragon's Teeth* (1942), which chronicled German Nazi dictator Adolf Hitler's rise to power, won a Pulitzer Prize. All 11 novels in the Lanny Budd series were best-sellers and were translated into several foreign languages. The Lanny Budd novels reflected Sinclair's shifting politics, which saw him not only embrace orthodox and rightist causes but also renounce his support for the Soviet Union. During the 1960s, he voiced his approval of America's involvement in the Vietnam War as well his support for the nation's Cold War foreign policy.

Sinclair published *My Lifetime in Letters* in 1960 and published his autobiography two years later. During the course of his life, he wrote more than 80 books. Sinclair died on November 25, 1968, in Bound Brook, New Jersey.

TED BUTLER

See also
Eagan, Charles Patrick; Embalmed Beef Scandal; Miles, Nelson Appleton; Progressivism; Roosevelt, Theodore

Further Reading
Arthur, Anthony. *Radical Innocent: Upton Sinclair.* New York: Random House, 2006.
Bloodworth, William A., Jr. *Upton Sinclair.* Boston: Twayne, 1977.
Keuchel, Edward. "Chemicals and Meat: The Embalmed Beef Scandal." *Bulletin of the History of Medicine* 98 (Summer 1974): 65–89.
Mattson, Kevin. *Upton Sinclair and the Other American Century.* Hoboken, NJ: Wiley, 2006.

American War. Several army commanders—most notably the commanding general of the army, Major General Nelson A. Miles—had accused Commissary General Charles P. Eagan of supplying U.S. troops in Cuba and Puerto Rico with 337 tons of refrigerated beef and 198,508 pounds of canned beef that was tainted. The meat allegedly made hundreds of U.S. soldiers sick and may have killed dozens more. The scandal became a national sensation. While the Dodge Commission, the presidential commission tasked with investigating it, could find no hard evidence that the meat had caused the illnesses, President Theodore Roosevelt had believed that the meat was indeed tainted, as he had himself eaten it while on duty in Cuba. Roosevelt's disgust with Sinclair's description in *The Jungle* combined with his suspicion about meat rations during the war led him to prompt Congress to enact the 1906 Meat Inspection Act.

Sinclair used profits from *The Jungle* to found Hellicon Hall, a short-lived socialist commune. He published subsequent novels exposing societal ills, including *King Coal* (1917), *Oil!* (1927), and *Boston* (1928), the latter set during the Sacco and Vanzetti trial.

Sinclair drifted in and out of the American Socialist Party throughout his life. In contrast with most of his socialist brethren,

Sino-Japanese War
Start Date: August 1, 1894
End Date: April 17, 1895

Major Asian confrontation that occurred several years before the Spanish-American War. Unlike China's leaders, the Japanese recognized the need for their nation to Westernize, at least to the point of acquiring advanced Western military technology. Initially, this

Japanese woodcut depicting a Japanese battleship bombarding Chinese shore fortifications during the Sino-Japanese War (1894–1895). (Library of Congress)

process was to prevent the country from falling under the control of a Western power, but by the closing decade of the century, Japan's leaders were ready to embark upon their own program of imperial expansion. They were especially desirous of securing Korea, a tributary kingdom of China across the Tsushima Strait from Japan. As a result of Japanese interference in Korean affairs, war between China and Japan began in 1894.

On July 20, Japan seized control of the Korean government. Then on July 25, Japanese admiral Kozo Tsuboi attacked a Chinese troop convoy bringing reinforcements to Korea, sinking one transport and severely damaging its naval escorts. At the same time, fighting began on land. On August 1, both sides declared war.

The Sino-Japanese War quickly revealed that unarmored wooden ships were no match for the new warships. China's military was antiquated, while that of Japan was modern. Both sides now rushed reinforcements to Korea by sea, although neither attempted to interfere with the other's resupply effort. Chinese admiral Ting Ju-ch'ang (Ding Ruchang) had two newer ironclad battleships, the *Ting Yuen* (Ding Yuen) and *Chen Yuen* (Zhen Yuan). He also had four light cruisers and six torpedo boats. These escorted six transports carrying 4,500 men and 80 guns to the Yalu River. Simultaneously, Admiral Yuko Ito disembarked Japanese troops some 100 miles farther down the Korean coast, after which he sailed north to locate Ting's squadron.

On September 17, 1894, Ito's larger force came upon Ting's ships between the mouth of the Yalu River and Haiyang Island. Ito had four heavy cruisers, four light cruisers, and six torpedo boats. He had the advantage of newer and faster ships, and he enjoyed a considerable advantage in larger (over 5-inch) quick-firing guns. Japanese gunnery and ship handling were superior to those of the Chinese. The Japanese quick-firing guns soon riddled the unprotected Chinese ships, setting their exposed wooden areas ablaze. In the battle, the Chinese lost four or five ships. Although only one of his own ships was seriously damaged, Ito feared the two larger Chinese battleships and did not press his advantage. During the night, the remaining Chinese vessels escaped to Port Arthur.

In March 1895, the Japanese took both Port Arthur (Lüshun) and Wei-hai-wei (Weihaiwei), fortified harbors guarding access to Peking (Beijing). China then sued for peace. In the Japanese-dictated Treaty of Shimonoseki of April 17, 1895, China ceded to Japan the Island of Formosa (Taiwan) and the Liaotung (Liadong) Peninsula in southern Manchuria. China was also forced to pay an indemnity of $150 million and recognize Korea as an independent kingdom, a step toward its absorption by Japan.

Japan's acquisition of a foothold on the Asian mainland was particularly distasteful to Russia's leaders, who secured the support of France and Germany in advising Japan to refrain from annexing any part of the Chinese mainland. Confronted by three powerful European states, Japan gave up claim to territory on the Asian mainland and in return received from China an additional indemnity. Russia then leased from China territory in Manchuria, including Port Arthur (Lüshun), originally assigned to Japan. This action understandably infuriated the Japanese and was a major factor leading to the Russo-Japanese War a decade later.

SPENCER C. TUCKER

See also
Imperialism; Russo-Japanese War; Shimonoseki, Treaty of

Further Reading
Busch, Noel F. *The Emperor's Sword.* New York: Funk and Wagnalls, 1969.
Evans, David C., and Mark R. Peattie. *Kaigun: Strategy, Tactics, and Technology in the Imperial Japanese Navy, 1887–1941.* Annapolis, MD: Naval Institute Press, 1997.

Slums

An area, district, or neighborhood in a town or city in which impoverished and socially disadvantaged people live. Slums can be traced back to antiquity. Indeed, as long as income disparities, growing populations, and racial, ethnic, and religious discrimination have endured, so too have slums. In the 1890s, as now, slums were ubiquitous in both large cities and smaller towns all across the world. They existed in Cuba, the Philippines, Western Europe, and the United States. Slums are generally areas of permanent—albeit substandard—housing as opposed to shanty towns, which have less-permanent housing and are subject to movement or relocation.

"Slum" is also a somewhat generic term to describe an area of impoverishment. Indeed, a ghetto would often be impossible to differentiate from a slum except for the fact that a ghetto is a slum in which one particular racial, ethnic, or religious group predominates. The first true ghetto was located in Venice, Italy, and was reserved for Italian Jews. In addition to being poor and a minority within the larger population, most ghetto dwellers have experienced significant discrimination or persecution, or both, by the larger society. This often precluded them from leaving the ghetto or ameliorating their plight.

Slums are usually blighted areas in which the inhabitants occupy crowded rental housing that is often notorious for its poor sanitation and unsafe living conditions. During the 1890s, many slums, even in relatively wealthy nations such as the United States, had little or no indoor plumbing, which turned streets and alleys into open sewers. Unscrupulous landlords demanded exorbitant rents given the terrible housing they provided, and slum dwellers had little choice but to pay, as rents were still lower than they were anywhere else. In general, unemployment, alcoholism, crime, prostitution, and drug addiction were rampant in slums then as now. Many of those forced to live in the slums had high death rates because of substandard medical care, malnutrition, and diseases of various kinds, many of them communicable in the 1890s.

Most slums were built on shoddy construction with little regard for safety or comfort. Jammed one against the other, apartment slums were notoriously susceptible to fire, which spread quickly because of the close proximity of buildings, almost all of which at the turn of the 20th century were made of wood. Compounding the problem were narrow and clogged streets and alleys that often impeded the arrival of fire-fighting equipment if a slum was lucky enough to be have been served by a fire house. Poor sanitation facilities and overcrowding also made slum housing veritable prone to vermin and rat infestations and communicable diseases of every kind.

In the United States and Western Europe, slums tended to be ghettoized; that is, they were based on racial and ethnic makeup as much as they were on poverty. This was particularly the case in the United States, which witnessed huge influxes of immigrants beginning in the 1840s. Indeed, by the time of the Spanish-American War, immigration to the United States was close to its greatest peak to date. Over time, ghettoes and slums in the United States tended to change based on the most newly arrived ethnic group. At first it was the Irish, then the Germans, then the Italians, then the Eastern Europeans, etc. As each group moved up the socioeconomic ladder, they moved out of the slums, which were then peopled by other groups just arriving. In places such as Cuba and the Philippines, slums tended to be less susceptible to change and more homogenous in makeup, but they were even more ubiquitous because the economies in these areas provided little chance of upward mobility.

The effects of mass immigration and the prevalence of slums in American cities gave rise to the settlement house movement, which had begun in the slums of London in the early 1880s and blossomed in the United States in the 1890s. Settlement houses were established in slum neighborhoods principally to help newly arriving immigrants acculturate to American society. They offered literacy and language programs, educational and vocational training, employment opportunities, health services, socialization programs, and the like. They were essential to mitigating the worst aspects of slum living and helped thousands of individuals better their lives and eventually leave the slum or ghetto.

One of the first and most famous settlement houses in the United States was created by Ellen Starr Gates and Jane Addams in Chicago in 1889. Known as Hull House, this settlement house became the gold standard for the many others that sprang up around the country during the 1890s and into the early 20th century. Almost all of these facilities were created by well-educated, middle-class women who had a genuine desire to mitigate poverty and help newly arriving immigrants. The first settlement house in New York City, known as the Henry Street Settlement, was founded by Lillian Wald in 1893.

The settlement houses and their founders, such as Addams, were the original pioneers in sociology and social work, which would flourish after the turn of the 20th century. At a time in which no government-funded or government-sponsored programs existed for the downtrodden, settlement houses provided invaluable services to those forced to live in slums. The settlement house movement also brought to the public consciousness the problem of poverty, which was quickly spotlighted by the journalists and investigative reporters of the era. In 1890, muckraking journalist Jacob Riis published *How the Other Half Lives: Studies among the Tenements of New York,* shocking genteel American society with his lurid depictions of overcrowded and dangerous tenement houses in

A photograph by Lewis Hine of 233 East 107th Street in New York City, 1912. The rent sign states that these are "Eleganti Apartmenti." (Library of Congress)

which as many as four or five families inhabited a dark, filthy two- or three-room apartment.

Ultimately, the settlement house movement and the exposés of slums in the 1890s gave birth to the Progressive movement in the United States. This was a period of great reform (ca. 1900–1920) during which myriad laws and regulations were passed to ameliorate slum conditions and other dangers associated with low-income housing. Playing a central role in the Progressive movement were journalists, who in the 1880s and 1890s were referred to as yellow journalists. They were redubbed "muckrakers" by President Theodore Roosevelt shortly after the turn of the 20th century. In the end, their innovative reporting did the very same thing: it shone a bright light into the once-dark corners of the human condition.

PAUL G. PIERPAOLI JR.

See also

Addams, Jane; Journalism; Progressivism; Roosevelt, Theodore; Yellow Journalism

Further Reading

Addams, Jane. *Twenty Years at Hull House.* New York: Signet Classics, 1999.

Conant, James B. *Slums and Suburbs.* New York: Signet Books, 1964.

Filler, Louis. *The Muckrakers.* Palo Alto, CA: Stanford University Press, 1993.

Lubove, Roy. *The Progressives and the Slums: Tenement House Reform in New York City, 1890–1917.* Westport, CT: Greenwood, 1974.

Meigs, Cornelia. *Jane Addams: Pioneer for Social Justice.* Boston: Little, Brown, 1970.

Smallpox

A systemic disease caused by the Varicella virus that in its most common form (Varicella major) is fatal in 30 percent of cases. The disease begins with a two-week prodrome of fever, headache, and back pain followed by a widespread raised rash that breaks down into pustules. It is during this time that the disease is most contagious. If the patient survives, the rash subsides although usually leaving scars that are often disfiguring. There is no effective treatment for smallpox, but since Edward Jenner demonstrated in the late 18th century that immunity is conferred by administration of the related but clinically innocuous cowpox virus, vaccination has been so effective that the mild form of the disease had vanished by 1977.

The U.S. Army, under direct orders from General George Washington, had begun prophylactic smallpox inoculations during the Revolutionary War, and at the time of the Spanish-American War, the disease did not exist in American troops. The same could not be said of Cuba, Puerto Rico, or the Philippines. Although Cuban law had mandated vaccination for all citizens under Spanish rule, the statute had been generally ignored. When Brigadier General Leonard Wood assumed command of Santiago in the autumn of 1898, the province was in the throes of an epidemic outbreak of the disease. The town of Holguín, 20 miles inland from Santiago City, had more than 3,000 active cases. Wood sent 100 of his so-called Immunes under Colonel Duncan Hood to disinfect Holguín's buildings and vaccinate the inhabitants. American medical officers supervised local Cuban physicians and established a quarantine hospital that treated 1,185 cases of smallpox between November 1898 and January 1899. By 1901, the American occupation government had mandated and enforced vaccination of all Cuban children by age one and had effectively eliminated the disease on the island. Although the disease was also endemic in Puerto Rico, Major John Van R. Hoff, chief military surgeon on that island, had success similar to that of Wood in Cuba.

The story was less favorable in the Philippines. Lieutenant Colonel Louis Maus, appointed commissioner of health in Manila, attempted an extensive vaccination campaign, but dense jungles, poor roads, and the fact that the Philippines comprised thousands of widely scattered islands made his job much more difficult and prolonged than that in Cuba. The geographic barriers were also complicated by the ongoing insurrection.

JACK McCALLUM

See also

Cuba, U.S. Occupation of; Philippine Islands, U.S. Occupation of; Wood, Leonard

Further Reading

Ashburn, Percy. *A History of the Medical Department of the United States Army.* Boston: Houghton Mifflin, 1929.
Gillett, Mary C. *The Army Medical Department, 1865–1917.* Washington, DC: Center of Military History, United States Army, 1995.
McCallum, Jack. *Leonard Wood: Rough Rider, Surgeon, and Architect of American Imperialism.* New York: New York University Press, 2006.

Smith, Jacob Hurd
Birth Date: 1840
Death Date: March 1, 1918

U.S. Army general notorious for the severity of his campaign in Samar in 1901–1902 during the Philippine-American War. Little is known of Jacob Hurd Smith's childhood. Born in Kentucky in 1840, he enlisted in the U.S. Army in 1861 and was commissioned a second lieutenant a year later. He fought in the American Civil War Battle of Shiloh (April 6–7, 1862) and was badly wounded. Unable to return to field service, he served out the remainder of the war as

a recruiting officer, primarily of African Americans, in Louisville, Kentucky.

Smith secured a regular army commission as captain in 1867. Controversy dogged him, however, for he was soon accused with his father-in-law of being involved in illegal financial dealings that included speculation with funds entrusted to him for enlistment bounties. Revelations of this activity led to his removal from the post of temporary army judge advocate in 1869. Demonstrating a continued propensity both for intemperate remarks and poor judgment, he encountered legal problems for failure to pay debts.

Assigned to the West, he fought in the American Indian Wars. In 1885, however, he was court-martialed in San Antonio, Texas, for failing to pay a sum he had lost playing poker. Found guilty, he was sentenced to be confined to Fort Clark for a year and a half and loss of half his pay. When a number of statements he had made to army authorities regarding the case were determined to be false, he was again court-martialed in 1886 and found guilty. He would have been dismissed from the service had not President Grover Cleveland intervened and changed the sentence to a reprimand.

At the beginning of the Spanish-American War, Smith was a major. He saw service in Cuba and then was assigned to the Philippines as a colonel in command of the 12th Infantry Regiment during the Philippine-American War. Following the Balangiga Massacre on the island of Luzon on September 28, 1901, when villagers and guerrillas attacked 74 American soldiers and killed 48 of them in what was the single worst U.S. military disaster of the war, commander of U.S. forces in the Philippines Major General Adna Chaffee panicked and, in what may have been the worst decision of the war, placed Smith, now a brigadier general, in charge of a punitive campaign on Samar.

Chaffee's decision was no doubt based on Smith's reputation as a commander who was prepared to be tough on guerrillas, but what Chaffee did not seem to realize was Smith's willingness to resort to extralegal means to achieve his ends. Chaffee in 1901 had recommended Smith for promotion to brigadier general, a decision with which civilian governor of the Philippines William Howard Taft had concurred, and given him command of the 6th Separate Brigade precisely because Smith was regarded as being a hard-liner. But Chaffee must have known that Smith had in the past shown a callous disregard for the lives of prisoners and made statements condemning what he believed to be the tendency of officers involved in pacification duties to be too lenient. Typical of this was a letter to the *Manila News* in which Smith blamed the Balangiga Massacre on "U.S. officers who love 'little brown brother.'"

In ordering him to recapture the U.S. weapons taken at Batangas, Chaffee no doubt encouraged Smith to employ harsh methods, but it is by no means clear, as Smith later claimed, that Chaffee ordered him to turn Samar into "a howling wilderness." Clearly, Smith's orders regarding policies to be followed in Samar increased the violence there. Most notoriously, Smith allegedly gave verbal orders to U.S. Marine Corps major Littleton T. Waller, who commanded a marine battalion on loan to Smith, to "kill and burn," to

U.S. Army brigadier general Jacob Hurd Smith, who became notorious for his harsh tactics during fighting on the island of Samar during the Philippine-American War. (Library of Congress)

take no prisoners, to turn the interior of Samar into "a howling wilderness," and to regard every male over the age of 10 as a combatant who could be executed.

Although Waller did not take Smith's orders literally and insisted that the marines not make war on children, the resulting violence of the Samar Campaign attracted considerable unfavorable coverage in the American press. In March 1902, Major Waller was court-martialed for the execution of 10 civilian porters during the Samar Campaign. Waller tried to protect Smith by basing his defense on General Order No. 100 of the American Civil War that dealt with the treatment of guerrillas caught behind the lines. Smith was then called as a witness by the prosecution and, in an act of self-protection, perjured himself by denying that he had issued any special orders to Waller. The defense then rebutted Smith's testimony with three witnesses who had heard the conversation between the two men in which Smith had told Waller not to take prisoners and to execute males above the age of 10. It was by this means that the order became public.

Waller was acquitted, and this forced Secretary of War Elihu Root to order a court-martial for Smith in May 1902. Root sought to reduce the damage by claiming that Smith's orders had never been meant to be taken literally. Always his own worst enemy, Smith contradicted Root and informed reporters that such a course

was the only effective one when dealing with "savages." Root also tried to have Smith declared temporarily insane, but this failed when two of three medical officers appointed by Chaffee to hear the case refused to go along.

Smith's court-martial then proceeded. The charge was not for his orders or for war crimes but rather for "conduct to the prejudice of good order and military discipline." The court found Smith guilty and sentenced him to a verbal reprimand. To mitigate the outcry in the United States over the affair and the lenient sentence, Root recommended that Smith be retired, which President Theodore Roosevelt accepted. Smith retired to Portsmouth, Ohio, and died in San Diego, California on March 1, 1918.

SPENCER C. TUCKER

See also

Atrocities; Balangiga Massacre; Chaffee, Adna Romanza, Sr.; Cleveland, Stephen Grover; Roosevelt, Theodore; Root, Elihu; Samar Campaigns; Waller, Littleton Tazewell

Further Reading

Fritz, David L. "Before the Howling Wilderness: The Military Career of Jacob Hurd Smith, 1862–1902." *Military Affairs* 34 (December 1979): 186–190.

Linn, Brian McAllister. *The Philippine War, 1899–1902*. Lawrence: University Press of Kansas, 2000.

Schott, Joseph L. *The Ordeal of Samar*. Indianapolis: Bobbs-Merrill, 1964.

Smokeless Powder

Smokeless powder, an important development in military technology, made its first appearance in the last two decades of the 19th century. A more efficient propellant than black powder, it helped revolutionize firearms by permitting smaller projectiles with greater muzzle speed than previously possible. The small amount of smoke produced with smokeless powder also impacted battlefield tactics, as it made it easier for riflemen to conceal their positions and prevented the haze associated with black powder that obscured battlefield vision.

For centuries, firearms had used the same basic gunpowder for a propellant. The exact proportions of saltpeter, sulfur, and charcoal might have varied, but the formula remained the same. In the last half of the 19th century, however, scientists began experimenting with new forms of explosive. Individuals such as the Swede Alfred Nobel sought to create a stable and more efficient product. They found that fibrous materials such as cotton or wood pulp could be treated with nitric acid to produce an explosive. Known by such names as guncotton and nitrocellulose, these explosives were stable and could be used safely in engineering projects.

Frenchman Paul Vielle experimented with different ways of treating guncotton to produce a propellant for firing projectiles. He found that a gelatinized nitrocellulose could be mixed with ether and alcohol. The resulting product was rolled into flat sheets, dried, and then cut into small granules or flakes. As with

Spanish troops under the palace colonnade, Havana, Cuba, 1898. The Spanish enjoyed superiority in small arms. Their modern Mauser rifles used smokeless powder cartridges, while U.S. volunteer units still used rifles that fired black powder, which gave away their positions. (Library of Congress)

gunpowder, Vielle's mixture could be loaded into cartridges and ignited by fulminate. Vielle found that when fired his mixture produced a much smaller amount of smoke than regular gunpowder. Powder B, as he called his creation, became better known as smokeless powder. Because the new powder was usually a light color, ordinary gunpowder became known as black powder, a name it still carries.

More important for arms makers, Vielle's smokeless powder was a more efficient propellant than gunpowder. The smokeless powder combined on a molecular level to push a projectile down a gun barrel with greater force. Gun manufacturers soon found that an 8-millimeter (mm) bullet fired with smokeless powder had the same hitting power as an 11-mm bullet fired with ordinary gunpowder. Range was also improved. New bullets appeared as well. Manufacturers quickly introduced weapons to take advantage of the technology. Most European armies, including the Spanish Army, began to rearm with such weapons by 1890.

This transition was incomplete in the U.S. Army at the time of war with Spain. During the conflict, U.S. regulars employed the .30-caliber Krag-Jørgenson (Krag) magazine rifle, but the 150,000 volunteers received old 1873 .45-caliber Springfield Trapdoor rifles that used black powder cartridges. The Americans soon discovered that the Spanish infantrymen, armed with modern 7-mm Mauser rifles firing smokeless powder cartridges, were able to outrange them and remain hidden. U.S. artillery also employed black powder charges. Thus, in the Battle of San Juan Hill on July 1, 1898, the

Spanish were easily able to locate the American guns, and Spanish artillery, firing from behind the heights, soon silenced it. Although the Americans won the battle through bravery and sheer numbers, the experience clearly demonstrated the need in the army for more modern weapons.

TIM J. WATTS

See also
Rifles; San Juan Heights, Battle of

Further Reading
Blair, Claude, ed. *Pollard's History of Firearms.* New York: Macmillan, 1983.
Cocroft, Wayne. *Dangerous Energy: The Archaeology of Gunpowder.* London: English Heritage Publications, 2000.
Kelly, Jack. *Gunpowder: Alchemy, Bombards, and Pyrotechnics: The History of the Explosive That Changed the World.* New York: Basic Books, 2004.
Pauly, Roger. *Firearms: The Life Story of a Technology.* Westport, CT: Greenwood Technographies, 2004.

Socapa Point, Cuba

Promontory located on the western edge of the sea entrance leading to Santiago de Cuba and Santiago Harbor. Socapa Point rises to about 200 feet above sea level and offers a commanding view of the harbor and adjoining waters. Across a 400-yard channel lies Morro Castle (el Castillo de Morro), not to be confused with the castle of the same name located at Havana Harbor. Morro Castle was situated on a similarly high headland and in 1898 contained a small battery of outdated artillery pieces. Socapa Point also contained Socapa Heights and the Socapa Batteries. The upper artillery battery faced Punta Gorda, while the battery faced toward the sea. Both batteries were situated some 150 feet above sea level, but ammunition for them was in short supply.

Socapa Point's lower battery boasted a single 57-millimeter (mm) gun, four 37-mm Hotchkiss guns, and a single machine gun. It was designed chiefly to fire upon vessels attempting a sea invasion and to defend the minefields that lay just in front of the channel between Socapa and Morro.

The upper battery facing land mounted badly outdated guns. These included three 8-inch muzzle-loading howitzers and two 16.3-inch Hontoria guns that had been taken from the Spanish ship *Reina Mercedes.* This battery was supposed to thwart a land-based attack on Santiago.

In spite of the largely antiquated gun batteries, the commander of the North Atlantic Fleet, Rear Admiral William T. Sampson, chose not to force his way into Santiago de Cuba via the harbor, believing that his ships would be imperiled by the Socapa batteries and minefields. Sampson, however, calculated that a land-based assault on Socapa and Morro would be accomplished easily and would leave Santiago open for immediate capture and occupation. The U.S. Army did not see the wisdom in Sampson's plan, however, and thus did not adopt it. Instead, the army preferred a siege to a

U.S. Army Hotchkiss guns at Socapa Point, Cuba, defending Santiago Harbor following its capture by the Americans during the Spanish-American War. (Library of Congress)

frontal assault. After the destruction of the Spanish squadron on July 3, 1898, the Americans besieged Santiago de Cuba, which lasted until the city capitulated on July 17. This marked the end of major hostilities on Cuba during the Spanish-American War.

PAUL G. PIERPAOLI JR.

See also

Artillery; Sampson, William Thomas; Santiago de Cuba, Battle of; Santiago de Cuba Land Campaign

Further Reading

Cosmas, Graham A. *An Army for Empire: The United States Army in the Spanish-American War.* College Station: Texas A&M University Press, 1994.

Trask, David F. *The War with Spain in 1898.* Lincoln: University of Nebraska Press, 1996.

Social Darwinism

A sociological-political construct derived from Charles Darwin's pioneering work on evolution. Social Darwinism is the extension of Darwin's theory of evolution to human societies. It asserts that races, nations, and civilizations evolve in a way that is similar to the evolution of biological species. Social Darwinism holds that because of a process of natural selection, fitter races and societies survive while others are extinguished, the process leading to the progressive improvement of humanity. Social Darwinism was tailor-made for the leaders of industrialized Western states seeking justification for their control of less-developed nations. Thus, when the Spanish-American War raised the question of whether the United States ought to acquire an overseas colonial empire, social Darwinism was used to support the imperialists' position.

In *The Origin of the Species* (1859), Darwin largely avoided extending his theory to human beings, either to their biological evolution or to the understanding of human social relations. His original theory asserts that each species is not permanently fixed; that is, existing species can evolve, new species can develop from existing ones, and species can become extinct. These possibilities arise because all living things are engaged in a struggle for existence and survival. Certain biological variations in an individual member of a species will result in advantages that allow that individual to adapt better to its environment and thereby to survive and procreate. Such individuals

William Graham Sumner was one of the leading exponents of social Darwinism in the United States. Viewing life as a grim struggle in which only the fittest would survive, Sumner glorified the millionaires of his day as products of natural selection and attacked reformers for trying to preserve the unfit. (Hayward Cirker and Blanche Cirker, eds., *Dictionary of American Portraits,* 1967)

transmit these adaptive traits to their offspring, which eventually results in more members of the species who have them. The species as a whole, then, gradually changes, which makes it more likely to survive. Darwin called this process natural selection.

Furthermore, Darwin wrote that "the theory of natural selection is grounded in the belief that each new variety, and ultimately each new species, is produced and maintained by having some advantage over those with which it comes into competition; and the consequent extinction of less favoured forms almost inevitably follows." In *The Descent of Man* (1871), Darwin explicitly applied his theory of evolution to human beings. While Darwin limited himself to discussing the biological development of human beings, he acknowledged that variations in body and mind would prove advantageous to certain individuals and their races.

Working independently of Darwin, the English philosopher and political theorist Hebert Spencer developed a similar theory of evolution, a central feature of which was his concept of the survival of the fittest, a phrase that he (not Darwin) coined. Spencer conceived of human societies as natural organisms to which the theory of evolution would apply. Human societies, too, adapt to their environments. Being engaged in a struggle for existence with one another, societies become ever more complex and advanced. Competition between societies, then, is natural and even essential for progress, with fitter societies becoming dominant and progressive, while those that cannot compete are forced out of existence or are subjugated by the fitter races. When Darwin published his theory of natural selection, which supplied a biological mechanism for evolution, Spencer eagerly incorporated it into his own theory.

Social scientists sought to understand the full implications of Darwin's and Spencer's works for human societies. Incorporating elements of both, their efforts led to the development of social Darwinism. Social Darwinism combines the central concepts of the struggle for existence, natural selection, and the survival of the fittest into a comprehensive account of the evolution of human races and societies. Special attention is given to the dominance of some races and societies and the subjugation or extinction of others. Differences in religions, ethics, and political systems as well as the rise and fall of empires and civilizations are explained by evolutionary forces working at both the biological and social levels. According to social Darwinists, there is nothing exceptional about human beings, then, that excludes them from the evolutionary process, neither having been specially created by God nor having developed unique intellectual capacities that allow them to intervene in the process. Both human biology and human societal development are products of natural and necessary evolutionary processes. To what extent Darwin himself could be deemed to have been a social Darwinist remains a debate among scholars.

The deterministic arguments of social Darwinism, especially the concept of the survival of the fittest, were employed both to justify and to condemn war and its outcome among races and nations. On the one hand, social Darwinism suggests that war is merely part of the universal struggle for existence and that nature tends to hand the victory to the superior race or nation. The winning of wars and the acquiring of empire, then, are evidence of a higher order of evolution of one's race, nation, or civilization, an indication of its biological, social, political, ethical, or intellectual advantages. On the other hand, social Darwinism could suggest that war is dysgenic, ensuring the slaughter of the best individuals (the healthiest, the most courageous, and the most public spirited). From this point of view, war is contrary to natural selection insofar as it destroys the fitter members of society while it is the less fit left at home who survive and procreate. Such arguments both for and against war were common in Europe shortly after the appearance of Darwin's and Spencer's theories and were adopted in American debates about beginning a war with Spain and pursuing a colonial empire abroad.

Social Darwinism became a popular and respected viewpoint in the United States in the last decades of the 19th century, especially as a result of the work of the American sociologist William Graham Sumner. Theories of racial superiority, however, certainly existed before social Darwinism arose. A theory of Anglo-Saxon superiority was already prevalent, and social Darwinism was used to lend support to it and to encourage international expansion. The increasing success of the United States as a result of major struggles (such as the Revolutionary War, the acquisition and settling of the western territories, and the Indian Wars) suggested to social Darwinists that American society was superior to those it was displacing, conquering, or otherwise surpassing. Unlike many other arguments used in support of racial superiority, however, social Darwinism provided a natural, scientific, and universal framework to justify war, conquest, and empire. Like those who adhered to the concept of Manifest Destiny—the belief that the United States was supernaturally ordained to conquer the continent—social Darwinists similarly believed that the United States was naturally ordained to become a colonial power.

American domination and expansion were seen to be natural and inevitable because there were forces of nature at work that were beyond human control. Furthermore, the recognition of the superiority of American society created a moral obligation to bring civilization to people around the world such as in the Philippines, Guam, Puerto Rico, and Hawaii, all of which were acquired as a result of the Spanish-American War. On the other hand, for anti-imperialists opposing expansionist foreign policy, social Darwinism provided arguments against war and empire. For example, some anti-imperialist social Darwinists claimed that war is dysgenic, while others were concerned that the acquisition of colonies would lead to the conferring of American citizenship upon less-advanced or inferior races, resulting in the deterioration of American society. Ultimately, social Darwinism was employed more effectively by imperialists. It lent the authority of science to the justification for war and American empire. While social Darwinism was influential nationally at the end of the 19th century, it was relatively short-lived. After World War I, its popularity declined precipitously as the United States returned to a more isolationist foreign policy.

S. J. LANGE

See also
Imperialism; Manifest Destiny; Racism; Spencer, Herbert

Further Reading
Crook, Paul. *Darwinism, War and History.* New York: Cambridge University Press, 1994.
Hawkins, Mike. *Social Darwinism in European and American Thought, 1860–1945.* New York: Cambridge University Press, 1997.
Hofstadter, Richard. *Social Darwinism in American Thought.* New York: G. Braziller, 1965.

Social Gospel Movement

Broad-based Protestant intellectual and social reform movement that began in the late 19th century and endured well into the 20th century. Among many things, the Social Gospel movement informed Progressivism (ca. 1900–1920), advocated extraterritorial expansion and imperialism on the part of the United States, and launched myriad social reforms aimed at curbing the excesses and dilemmas caused by the Gilded Age. Although the movement lost some of its influence in the late 1930s and early 1940s, it never entirely disappeared and continues in a more modest form in the early 21st century. One of the founders of the Social Gospel movement in America was Josiah Strong, a Congregational minister who wrote several highly popular books in the 1880s and 1890s that systematically laid out much of the movement's philosophical and theological underpinnings.

The Social Gospel movement paralleled a similar—although not identical—movement in Great Britain known as Christian Socialism. In the United States, the concept of socialism as an economic prescription to societal ills was never widely adhered to by those advocating the Social Gospel. Indeed, Strong listed socialism as one of the scourges that had to be eliminated. Other prominent Americans involved with the movement in its early years included Reverend Walter Rauschenbusch, Charles Clayton Morrison, and Charles Sheldon.

The Social Gospel movement was never primarily about theology. Instead, it sought to harness the basic core of Christian theology and apply it to societal ills and problems. In the 1890s, Strong and others viewed mass immigration, urbanization, industrialization, poverty, and radicalism as problems to be solved using Christian principles. In other words, this was an activist movement that sought to move far beyond pulpits and preachers; it was a movement designed to eradicate social problems and establish, ultimately, an ideal society akin to God's kingdom on earth. As such, it invoked the power of the almighty as well as the power of individuals to make choices based upon Christian beliefs that would benefit the whole of society. Most of those involved with the movement also sought Protestant unity and ecumenicalism, although this was not achieved largely because of the large and long-standing chasms dividing many Protestant denominations.

Adherents of the Social Gospel labored on a variety of fronts. They sought better education and housing for the poor, especially for newly arrived immigrants; the imposition of child labor laws; safer factories and workplaces; political reforms aimed at the mitigation of corruption, especially at the municipal level; and public health initiatives, among many others. They worked closely with progressive reformers in both major political parties and counseled a number of leading progressive reformers, including President Theodore Roosevelt. The movement also inspired reformers such as Jane Addams, who established the nation's first settlement house in Chicago to administer to immigrant populations.

There was among some adherents of the Social Gospel movement a healthy strain of American exceptionalism and Anglo-Saxon superiority. This manifested itself most clearly in the many writings and speeches of Strong, who was an unabashed promoter of American imperialist expansionism. Believing the Protestant Anglo-Saxon tradition to be morally and culturally superior to others, he believed that it was a God-given duty for the United States to extend its reach over so-called less-civilized peoples in an effort to introduce them to Christian principles and American ideals. This mind-set became widely accepted within the movement and became a powerful tool for those Americans interested in overseas expansion for strategic, commercial, and political reasons. American imperialism also became a prime motivating factor for Protestant missionaries. Interestingly, although the Catholic Church would also adhere to its own form of the Social Gospel beginning in the 1930s, most Protestants spurned Catholicism in the 1890s and early 1900s, linking it with Mormonism as a scourge to be eliminated.

PAUL G. PIERPAOLI JR.

See also

Addams, Jane; Churches and the War; Expansionism; Gilded Age; Immigration; Imperialism; Missionaries; Progressivism; Slums; Strong, Josiah

Further Reading

Luker, Ralph E. *The Social Gospel in Black and White: American Racial Reform, 1885–1912*. Chapel Hill: University of North Carolina Press, 1998.

Muller, Dorothea R. "Josiah Strong and American Nationalism." *Journal of American History* (December 1966): 487–503.

———. "The Social Philosophy of Josiah Strong: Social Christianity and Progressivism." *Church History* 28(2) (1959): 183–201.

White, Ronald C., and Howard C. Hopkins. *The Social Gospel: Religion and Reform in Changing America*. Philadelphia: Temple University Press, 1975.

Sousa, John Philip
Birth Date: November 6, 1854
Death Date: March 6, 1932

Iconic American musician, composer, band leader, and creator of some of America's most enduring and beloved military marches. John Philip Sousa, who came to be known as the "March King" by the 1890s, was born on November 6, 1854, in Washington, D.C., to a musical family. His father, of Spanish and Portuguese decent, was a trombonist in the U.S. Marine Band and instilled in the young Sousa a fondness for music at a very young age.

When Sousa was just 6 years old, he began violin lessons with several well-respected violinists. In short order, his teachers declared that he had perfect pitch, a gift that many musicians cannot claim. When Sousa was 13 years old, his father secured for him an apprenticeship with the Marine Band. The job allowed him access to many different musical instruments, all of which he learned to master to a substantive degree. In the meantime, he had continued mastering the violin and studied voice, piano, and flute.

At the age of 21, Sousa left the Marine Corps. He almost immediately began touring with various bands and orchestras, playing the violin, conducting, and even arranging musical scores. His conducting jobs included the "HMS *Pinafore*," a Gilbert and Sullivan light opera. At the time, it was one of the most popular and profitable musicals on Broadway.

American composer and bandmaster John Philip Sousa is perhaps best known for his march "The Stars and Stripes Forever." (National Archives)

In 1880, Sousa was honored by being named director of the Marine Band, then perhaps the most famous musical group in the United States. He stayed with the band for 12 years, performing before Presidents Rutherford B. Hayes, James A. Garfield, Chester A. Arthur, Grover Cleveland, and Benjamin Harrison. While Sousa directed the elite band, he kept busy composing and orchestrating many different types of music. Indeed, his talents spanned several musical genres including operettas, waltzes, orchestral suites, short songs, a symphonic poem, and, of course, military marches, for which he is best known today. Sousa and the Marine Band toured all over the world and extensively throughout the United States. Many Americans went to concerts to hear Sousa's music performed live, and as the phonograph gained in popularity, his recordings became very popular.

In a significant sense, Sousa was the right man for the time, musically speaking. His unflinching patriotism, affiliation with the Marine Corps, and rousing marches all fed into the upsurge in American patriotism during the 1890s. His quintessentially American sound also helped the great masses of immigrants become instantly familiar with a key part of American culture. The timing of the Spanish-American War could not have been better, for Sousa's marches were played nearly ad nauseam in civilian parades, military reviews, and the like. His most famous march, "The Stars and Stripes Forever" (1896), was composed less than 18 months before the Spanish-American War began in April 1898. In an age prior to electronic media, with no radio or television, Sousa's music took its place as an auditory form of propaganda of sorts, stirring American patriotism and showcasing Americans' newfound pride as a nation on the edge of greatness.

Among Sousa's prolific scores for marches are "Semper Fidelis" (1888), the official Marine Corps march; "The Washington Post" (1889); "King Cotton" (1895); "El Capitan" (1896); and "The Gallant Seventh" (1922). In all, Sousa composed 136 marches. He also wrote nine full-length operettas. A man of many talents, he wrote his autobiography, five novels, poems, and countless songs and song scraps. He was an unabashed self-promoter, so nearly everything he did ended up being successful.

In 1892, with his popularity akin to a present-day rock star, Sousa left the Marine Corps and began touring extensively with his own band of handpicked musicians. It played to sell-out crowds throughout the rest of the decade and was particularly sought after during and immediately after the Spanish-American War. In 1900, Sousa's band embarked on an extensive tour of Europe after opening at the Paris Exposition of 1900. Interestingly, Sousa was suspicious of radio and refused to conduct any live radio broadcasts for fear that he would lose his connection to the audience. Not until 1929 did he conduct his first radio-broadcast concert. It proved so popular that Sousa found an entire new audience. During World War I, he joined the U.S. Navy Reserve at the age of 62 to show his support for the war effort. He was given the rank of lieutenant and a $1 per month stipend.

Active until the very end of his life, Sousa continued to tour and compose musical scores. By the early 1930s he remained a household name, and while his popularity was not what it was in the 1890s, he nevertheless managed to play to packed houses. Sousa died in Reading, Pennsylvania, on March 6, 1932, while on tour. Fittingly, the last piece he conducted was "The Stars and Stripes Forever."

PAUL G. PIERPAOLI JR.

See also
Music

Further Reading
Gillis, Jennifer Blizen. *John Philip Sousa: The King of March Music.* Portsmouth, NH: Heinemann, 2005.
Newsome, John, ed. *Perspective on John Philip Sousa.* Washington, DC: Library of Congress, 1983.
Zannos, Susan. *The Life and Times of John Philip Sousa.* Hockessin, DE: Mitchell Lane, 2003.

Spain

Nation in southwestern Europe. The Kingdom of Spain, with an area of 194,364 square miles, is the second largest country in Western Europe. Spain, which has extended coastlines on both the Atlantic Ocean and the Mediterranean Sea, occupies the Iberian Peninsula with Portugal, Andorra, and Gibraltar. Spain borders France and the Bay of Biscay to the north, the Gulf of Cádiz and the Alboran Sea to the south, Portugal to the west, and the Mediterranean Sea to the east. Spanish territory includes the Balearic Islands, the Canary Islands, and five small presidios (enclaves), the most important being Ceuta and Melilla in North Africa. At the time of the Spanish-American War, Spain, with a metropolitan population of about 18.6 million, also controlled the Philippines, Cuba, Puerto Rico, and Guam. It was ruled by María Cristina, queen regent of Spain, as a parliamentary monarchy.

The name of the country comes from the Latin word *Hispania,* the term used by the ancient Romans to describe the entire Iberian Peninsula. Although the original inhabitants of the Iberian Peninsula left a slight cultural footprint on the area, six centuries of Roman domination (roughly the second century BCE to the fourth century CE) greatly influenced Spanish culture. It was during this time that Latin-derived languages (such as Castilian, Portuguese, Catalan, and Galician), Roman Catholicism, Roman legal traditions, corporatism, and Mediterranean foodways became prevalent. In 711 CE, the Moors, Muslims of mixed Arab and Berber descent, invaded the peninsula, and ultimately the entire peninsula except for a few small Christian enclaves in the north came under their domination. Trade flourished, religious toleration for Christians and Jews existed, and the rich intellectual tradition from the Middle East was transplanted to Iberia. Notwithstanding seven centuries of fierce Christian resistance, local culture was strongly influenced by the Muslims.

During the 15th century, Christian resistance against the Muslims on the peninsula intensified. The final stage of the seven-centuries-long Reconquista came to fruition with the destruction of the last Moorish kingdom, Grenada, in 1492. This feat was made possible by the dynastic union of the Christian kingdoms of Castile and Aragon, which resulted from the marriage of Isabella of Castile and Ferdinand of Aragon in 1469. The year 1492 also marked the expulsion of the large Jewish community from Spain and the arrival of Christopher Columbus in the New World, which set the stage for an immense Spanish colonial empire in the New World. Precious metals from the New World allowed Spain to become a major world power. Ferdinand and Isabella centralized royal power at the expense of the lesser nobility, and the term *España* (Spain) began to be used to describe the two kingdoms. The Kingdom of Navarre, located in the Basque region of northwestern Spain, was incorporated into the new Spanish kingdom in 1513. Spain, which came to dominate vast territorial possessions in Western Europe, was the most powerful European kingdom during the 16th century and most of the 17th century.

Although still able to assert influence over its vast colonial empire, Spain began a period of seemingly irreversible decline during the 17th century, as the Hapsburg royal family engaged in religious wars that drained the Spanish treasury. Simultaneously, other

European nations, specifically England and France, increased their strength. In 1640, Portugal ended the dynastic union with Spain that had existed since 1580. The reign of King Carlos (Charles) II (1665–1700), the last Hapsburg ruler of Spain, came to symbolize the decline of the country. The childless king's death in 1700 ultimately sparked the War of the Spanish Succession (1701–1714). Although Spain lost its nonpeninsular territorial possessions in Europe, the new Bourbon royal family was able to reestablish order and reinvigorate, albeit temporarily, the Spanish economy.

In 1808, French armies invaded Spain during the Napoleonic Wars and deposed the Spanish monarch. Napoleon then proclaimed his brother, Joseph, the new king of Spain. For eight years, the Spaniards, with the assistance of the British, fought a war of national liberation against the French. At the same time, colonial elites in the New World established autonomous local governments in Latin America that were only nominally loyal to the deposed Spanish monarch. Because Madrid could not assert its authority over its colonies at this time, the colonies began to drift further and further away. Although the Spaniards represented a victorious nation at the Congress of Vienna in 1814–1815, the nation had been economically decimated by the French occupation and was politically divided between liberals and conservatives.

During the reign of King Ferdinand VII (1814–1833), Spain lost all of its New World colonies with the exception of Cuba and Puerto Rico. Latin American colonial elites, realizing that continued colonial dominance by Spain offered neither economic rewards nor military protection, declared independence. Ferdinand, who produced no male heir, died in 1833, sparking a political controversy that plagued Spain for the next five decades. Partisans of Ferdinand's daughter Isabella II, who supported the Pragmatic Sanction of 1830 that abolished the Salic Law and allowed for Isabella's succession, fought the supporters of Ferdinand's brother Carlos, the pretender to the Spanish throne. The result was a series of three Carlist Wars that caused much political and economic confusion.

In 1843, in an attempt to restore political order, the Spanish government declared the 13-year-old Isabella of age and ended the inept regency of her mother. Isabella's reign, however, was plagued by coups, turmoil, and court intrigue. Nevertheless, fiscal reform, especially a revised tax system, established a viable economy that facilitated the revival of the Spanish military. Isabella's incessant political intrigues, however, resulted in the overthrow of the Bourbon monarchy in 1868 by a group of liberal generals, led by General Juan Prim. Isabella went into exile, living in France until she died in 1904.

In the midst of this political turmoil, Spain confronted a major challenge in Cuba, where revolutionaries seeking independence launched the Ten Years' War (1868–1878). Spanish attempts to quell the Cuban revolutionaries placed a considerable drain on the Spanish treasury. In 1870, the liberal generals placed Amadeus, the second son of King Victor Emmanuel II of Italy, on the throne. The 1870 assassination of Prim, the main force behind Amadeus's election as king, however, made Amadeus's hold on power tenuous. The outbreak of the Third Carlist War in 1872 convinced Amadeus that the Spaniards were ungovernable, leading him to abdicate in 1873. On February 11, 1873, the Spanish Cortes (parliament) proclaimed the First Republic. The republic, however, was unable to deal with political and economic chaos at home, the Third Carlist War, and the ongoing revolution in Cuba. In 1874, General Arsenio Martínez de Campos proclaimed the restoration of the Bourbon monarchy under the leadership of Isabella's son, Alfonso XII.

Alfonso XII (1874–1885) was able to defeat the Carlists in 1876 and end the Ten Years' War in Cuba by signing the Pact of Zanjón with the Cuban revolutionaries in 1878. His pragmatic leadership gradually allowed the Spanish government to restore political and economic stability. However, nationalist movements in the Philippines and in Cuba, such as the Guerra Chiquita (Little War) of 1879–1880, continued. Never allowing himself to become the political instrument of either of the two major political parties, Alfonso was able to work with administrations led by Conservative Antonio Cánovas del Castillo as well as Liberal Práxedes Mateo Sagasta. Alfonso's benevolent disposition, which won him the admiration of his people, and his ability to stabilize the economy and implement modernization programs allowed the Bourbon monarchy to withstand the threat of revolution in the aftermath of the Spanish-American War. Following his death by tuberculosis in 1885, his wife, María Cristina, became queen regent for his infant son, Alfonso XIII, who was not crowned until he came of age in 1902.

The outbreak of the Cuban War of Independence in 1895 eventually drew Spain into conflict with the United States. Spanish attempts to quell the Cuban revolutionaries, especially the draconian *reconcentrado* (reconcentration) system unleashed by General Valeriano Weyler y Nicolau, were roundly denounced in American newspapers. The jingoistic rhetoric of American newspapers, commonly referred to as yellow journalism, fueled anti-Spanish sentiment in the United States. Spanish attempts to be conciliatory in finding a peaceful situation to the turmoil in Cuba met with U.S. intransigence. At the same time, Spain was waging a smaller but stubborn struggle with Filipino nationalists, led by Emilio Aguinaldo y Famy.

Notwithstanding Spanish attempts to defuse the situation and great ambivalence in Madrid about a war with the Americans, the United States and Spain went to war in April 1898. Spain and the United States were not evenly matched. The population of Spain was roughly 18.6 million people, while that of the United States was more than 76 million. More problematic still were the American industrial and military capabilities generated by the Industrial Revolution in the United States during the last third of the 19th century. By 1898, the United States led the world in industrial production, including pivotal war materials such as steel. Spanish forces were quickly overwhelmed by superior American forces and manufacturing capacity.

As a result of the 1898 Treaty of Paris, Spain lost its two remaining colonies in the New World—Cuba and Puerto Rico—as well as Guam and the Philippines. Although a political and military disaster for the Spanish, the war actually benefited Spain economically. Large sums of capital held by Spaniards overseas were brought back to Spain and invested in the national economy. Spain's defeat in the Spanish-American War, known as El Desastre (The Disaster) in Spain, also gave rise to a movement in Spain known as the Generation of '98, a group of novelists, scholars, poets, writers, and philosophers who tried to restore the intellectual and literary prominence that Spain had once exerted during the 16th century. Writers such as Miguel de Unamuno, frustrated by Spain's military defeat, initiated a period of critical analysis concerning Spanish identity.

Spain's defeat in the Spanish-American War and the writings of the Generation of '98 weakened the legitimacy of the Bourbon monarchy and contributed to the political instability that eventually resulted in the Spanish Civil War (1936–1939). That in turn led to the establishment of an authoritarian quasi-fascist regime led by General Francisco Franco that endured until the dictator's death in 1975 and the restoration of the Bourbon monarchy under Juan Carlos. Today, Spain is once again a parliamentary monarchy.

MICHAEL R. HALL

See also

Aguinaldo y Famy, Emilio; Alfonso XII, King of Spain; Alfonso XIII, King of Spain; Cánovas del Castillo y Vallejo, Antonio; Carlists; Cuba; Cuba, Spanish Colonial Policies toward; Cuban War of Independence; Guam; María Cristina, Queen Regent of Spain; Martínez de Campos, Arsenio; Philippine Islands; Philippine Islands, Spanish Colonial Policies toward; Puerto Rico; *Reconcentrado* System; Sagasta, Práxedes Mateo; Ten Years' War; Weyler y Nicolau, Valeriano; Yellow Journalism; Zanjón, Pact of

Further Reading

Bowen, Wayne H., and Jose E. Alvarez, eds. *A Military History of Modern Spain: From the Napoleonic Era to the International War on Terror.* Westport, CT: Praeger, 2007.

Carr, Raymond. *Spain: A History.* Oxford: Oxford University Press, 2001.

Crow, John A. *Spain: The Root and the Flower.* Berkeley: University of California Press, 2005.

Pierson, Peter. *The History of Spain.* Westport, CT: Greenwood, 1999.

Spain, Army

The Spanish Army (Ejército de España) was an important and powerful institution in Spain at the end of the 19th century. It consisted of both a regular force and a reserve. Spain had universal military service with young men older than 19 required to serve, although there were a number of exemptions for only sons, for sons supporting their parents or grandparents, and for specialized areas of employment. The so-called blood tax fell predominantly on the poor, as military service could be avoided by payment of as little as 1,200 pesetas, a sum paid by more than 10,000 young men in 1882.

In spite of the fact that the Spanish Army claimed 18 percent of the national budget in 1895, it was chronically short of equipment

Spanish infantry in 1898. (*Photographic History of the Spanish-American War,* 1898)

Distribution of Spain's Overseas Army in 1898

Location	Men	Percent of Total Spanish Army	Military Units
Cuba	278,457	56.60%	101 infantry battalions 4 marine infantry battalions 11 cavalry regiments 2 mountain artillery regiments
Philippines	51,331	10.40%	7 infantry battalions 1 Civil Guard regiment
Puerto Rico	10,005	2.0%	7 infantry regiments 15 independent rifle regiments 1 marine infantry regiment

and supplies in large part because much of the budget was consumed by officer salaries. (Spain had 1 officer for every 6 enlisted men—four times the ratio for the U.S. Army—and 1 general for every 100 enlisted men.) Officers traditionally were drawn from the upper classes and had little contact with their men. Promotion in the Spanish Army was generally slow and was heavily influenced by family connections to the monarchy rather than demonstrated military merit. Under the 1876 constitution, all army captains-general and all navy admirals were given seats in the Cortes (parliament), and all officers were eligible to run for election to the House of Deputies.

In 1898, the Spanish Army numbered 492,077 men, but nearly 70 percent of them were overseas: 278,457 in Cuba, 51,331 in the Philippines, and 10,005 in Puerto Rico. The army had wide recent experience fighting insurgents in both Cuba and the Philippines. While fairly efficient as an antiguerrilla force, the Spanish Army had no recent experience in conventional warfare, and its officers were not skilled in handling large formations. The army was organized into regiments, with the battalion serving as the tactical unit. A regiment consisted of two battalions of six companies each. At full strength, there were 160 men and officers per company, but this strength was not often maintained.

Many of the Spanish officers on the front line were in their late teens and were unable to inspire their men. Although most Spanish units were poorly trained, a number performed well in action against the Americans. Spanish soldiers were armed with the 1893 model Spanish-made Mauser, a bolt-action rifle with a five-cartridge clip that fired a 7-millimeter smokeless powder round. The Mauser was sighted to a maximum range of 2,300 yards and was superior to the American Krag-Jørgensen rifle, but as with much else in the Spanish Army at the time, marksmanship was often poor.

The colonial Spanish army in Cuba consisted of 101 battalions of infantry and four battalions of naval infantry. There were also 11 regiments of cavalry, but they were kept in a garrison role and played no active part in the campaign. There were also two mountain artillery regiments with 70 guns and three fortress artillery battalions. The regular army in Cuba was augmented by 82,000 volunteers.

On the island of Puerto Rico, there were 7 battalions of Spanish regular infantry supported by a regiment of the Civil Guard and about 6,000 additional volunteers. In the Philippines, the Spanish army consisted of 7 regiments of infantry, 15 independent rifle regiments, and a marine infantry regiment. A majority of these troops were stationed on the island of Luzon in and around Manila. There were also another 5,600 native troops.

The war claimed more than 55,000 Spanish troops dead, including those lost fighting against both the Americans and insurgent forces. Although battle losses amounted to some 5,600 killed and more than 10,000 wounded, the majority of fatalities came as a result of disease. When the Spanish Army was repatriated from Cuba, almost all were suffering from various infections and were near starvation.

RALPH BAKER

See also

Cuba; Cuban Revolutionary Army; United States Army

Further Reading

Goldstein, Donald M., and Dillon Katherine V. *The Spanish American War.* Dulles, VA: Brassey's, 2000.
Hendricks, Charles, "The Impact of the 'Disaster' of 1898 on the Spanish Army." Paper presented to the Conference of Army Historians, Bethesda, MD, 1998.
Konstam, Angus. *San Juan Hill, 1898: America's Emergence as a World Power.* Westport, CT: Praeger, 2004.
Nofi, Albert A. *The Spanish-American War: 1898.* Conshohocken, PA: Combined Books, 1996.
O'Toole, G. J. A. *The Spanish War: An American Epic, 1898.* New York: Norton, 1984.

Spain, Navy

When decades of national strife and a failed experiment in republicanism ended with the restoration of 17-year-old Alfonso XII to the Spanish throne in the mid-1870s, the Spanish Navy lay in tatters from neglect. The navy numbered only five armor-plated frigates, a half-dozen wooden ones, a pair of unseaworthy monitors, and a number of lesser auxiliaries. Morale was low, and resources were negligible. Although four new warships emerged from Spanish yards during 1874–1877 and a like number would be built for Spain in France and England over the next four years, all eight were small and outdated in design and capability.

In Spain, a fervent pronaval newspaper campaign began in 1882 that called for the modernization of the Spanish Navy. In accord with these sentiments, conservative Spanish premier Antonio Cánovas del Castillo, himself a former minister of the navy, promoted just such an effort. Two years later, his government secured a major loan to finance the construction of a battleship at the La Seyne shipyards in Toulon, France. The result was the 9,900-ton *Pelayo*, Spain's first modern warship. Its main armament consisted of 2 12.5-inch Spanish González Hontoria guns, each in an armored turret fore or aft, plus 2 11-inch guns. Typical of capital ships of the

The Spanish Navy protected cruiser *Alfonso XIII.* (*Photographic History of the Spanish-American War,* 1898)

time, it mounted a mix of ordnance for long-, medium-, and short-range fire. Its armament also included 1 6.4-inch gun, 12 4.7-inch guns, 12 6-pounder quick-firing guns, 14 machine guns, and 7 torpedo tubes. The ship was rebuilt in 1897 with new boilers and slightly modified armament.

While the *Pelayo* was still being built, Spain's naval allotments had been significantly bolstered because of a diplomatic flap with Germany over the Caroline Islands in the Pacific. This surge in funding permitted Spanish yards to produce during 1885 and 1887 six iron-hulled, 1,150-ton, single-screw, three-masted Velasco-class unprotected cruisers based on the older *Velasco* and *Gravina,* launched in 1881 at the Thames Iron Works at Blackwall in London. These unprotected cruisers mounted a plain armament of four 4.7-inch guns as well as lesser weaponry and two 14-inch torpedo tubes. Their outdated designs and light armament meant that they were really suited only for staking a claim to distant colonial waters, patrolling against native craft or smugglers.

In 1887, the 3,042-ton, single-screw, three-masted unprotected cruisers *Alfonso XII, Reina Mercedes,* and *Reina Cristina* were launched at El Ferrol and Cartagena. They mounted a main armament of six 6.4-inch guns. During 1889–1991, seven 562-ton twin-masted Temerario-class torpedo gunboats were launched from various Spanish yards, and an experimental electric submarine was even tested at Cádiz.

Spain contracted abroad for the more modern 1,030-ton protected cruisers *Isla de Cuba* and *Isla de Luz.* They were launched in

1886 at the Elswick yards in England. A third ship in that class, the *Marqués de la Ensenada,* was launched by La Carraca in Cádiz in 1890. Each boasted a steel hull, 2.5-inch deck armor, and a main armament of six 4.7-inch guns. In January 1887, a swift (more than 20 knots) 348-ton torpedo gunboat emerged from the Thomson yards on the Clyde in Glasgow. It entered the Spanish Navy as the *Destructor.* A half-dozen assorted torpedo boats were also acquired from Britain, Germany, and France.

In 1888, the Thompson yards delivered the 4,725-ton protected cruiser *Reina Regente.* Armed with four 7.9-inch guns, six 4.7-inch guns, multiple lesser pieces, and five torpedo-tubes (two forward, one aft, and one on each broadside), it had a top speed of 18.6 knots. The *Reina Regente* would be copied in the Spanish-built *Alfonso XIII* (Ferrol) and *Lepanto* (Cartagena).

Although this construction program of the mid-1880s had greatly expanded the Spanish Navy, adding more than two dozen new ships, professional officers realized that this number included at least 1 dubious battleship and 10 outmoded cruisers. Even the *Reina Regente* would prove to be dangerously top-heavy, eventually sinking with all hands during a sudden storm on March 10, 1895, while steaming to Cádiz from Tangier. The main batteries of the *Alfonso XIII* and the *Lepanto* were reduced in caliber so as to make them a bit more stable.

Once a long-term budget was approved by the Spanish Cortes (parliament) on January 12, 1887, a more focused approach to naval acquisitions was imposed, allowing for an expenditure of 225 million

The Spanish armored cruiser *Emperador Carlos V.* (*Photographic History of the Spanish-American War,* 1898)

pesetas over the next 10 years. This sum, large by Spanish standards, was small when compared to the amounts being spent in Britain, Germany, France, and the United States. Spanish builders would therefore have to economize so as to maximize their limited funding.

The *Infanta Maria Teresa, Almirante Oquendo,* and *Vizcaya* were all launched at Bilbao in 1890–1891 and were based upon the successful design of HMS *Orlando* with technical assistance from its British shipwright Sir Charles Palmer. Yet despite displacing only 6,890 tons, all three were rated as battleships in the Spanish Navy rather than their true classification of armored cruisers. Heavily armed, they each mounted 2 11-inch and 10 5.5-inch Hontoria pieces, the 11-inch guns mounted fore and aft in barbette mounts with lightly armored hoods and the 5.5-inch guns mounted on the upper deck. The three ships were poorly protected.

The 9,090-ton armored cruiser *Emperador Carlos V* was launched at Cádiz in 1895. It had a main armament of two 11-inch guns along with eight 5.5-inchers and a top speed of about 19 knots. Three other 6,888-ton cruisers, the *Princesa de Asturias, Cardenal Cisneros,* and *Catalu* with a main armament of two 9.4-inch guns along with eight 5.5-inchers, were also laid down in Spanish yards, but they were not completed until 1902, 1903, and 1904, respectively.

As tensions between Spain and the United States escalated in the 1890s, Spanish minister of the navy Vice Admiral José María Beranger secured in 1896 an additional 23 million pesetas to begin construction of an 11,000-ton battleship, two 6,800-ton heavy cruisers, a 5,300-ton light cruiser, two destroyers, and two tugs.

Given the lead time in ship construction and the looming crisis with the United States, Beranger also persuaded the Spanish gov-

ernment to purchase in May 1896 the fine 7,234-ton armored cruiser *Giuseppe Garibaldi* from Italy. Delivered in May 1897 and renamed the *Cristóbal Colón,* it was a swift (20 knots), well-planned warship. The ships of that class mounted 2 10-inch guns and 2 8-inchers along with 14 6-inch guns, 4 17.7-inch torpedo tubes, and assorted smaller armament. Because of a dispute over payment, however, it was delivered without its 10-inch guns, which were never installed.

On the eve of hostilities in April 1898, naval deployments in Spain supposedly consisted of six battleships, although only the ancient *Pelayo* could actually be deemed such, the other five being the armored cruisers *Carlos V, Infanta Maria Teresa, Almirante Oquendo, Vizcaya,* and *Cristóbal Colón.* Spanish ports also held the protected cruisers *Alfonso XIII, Aragón,* and *Navarra;* the auxiliary cruisers *Doña María de Molina, Marqués de la Victoria,* and *Don Alvaro de Bazán;* 8 destroyers; 14 torpedo boats; 15 gunboats; and a dozen assorted transports, coast guard vessels, and lesser craft. These 60 vessels were manned by a total of 6,778 sailors and 5,412 marines.

Overseas, there were on station in Cuba an additional six cruisers, 6 destroyers, 9 gunboats, 29 patrol boats, 3 tugs, and 6 auxiliaries manned by 2,533 sailors and 581 marines. Two additional cruisers and 2 gunboats were assigned to Puerto Rico, with 291 seamen and 23 marines. The destroyer *Temerario* was stationed at Montevideo. Ten cruisers, 15 gunboats, 9 patrol boats, and other auxiliaries were assigned to the Philippines and were manned by 2,479 sailors and 2,515 marines.

This apparent strength on paper was quite deceiving. With the exception of the cruiser *Carlos V* and a handful of destroyers, the vast majority of the Spanish warships were undergunned, too weakly armored and slow, or otherwise technologically outdated. Many inadequate or older vessels had even been refurbished and retained on active duty at considerable expense, while modern warships were either still in the yards or yet to be built. It is little wonder that Spanish rear admiral Pascual Cervera y Topete had no confidence in the outcome when he departed the Cape Verde Islands with his small squadron for the Caribbean. As it worked out, Spain's naval inferiority was glaringly revealed in the two major naval engagements of the war. On May 1, 1898, U.S. Commodore George Dewey's Asiatic Squadron destroyed Spanish rear admiral Patricio Montojo y Pasarón's squadron in the Battle of Manila Bay. Then on July 3, 1898, on the other side of the globe off Santiago de Cuba, U.S. Admiral William T. Sampson's North Atlantic Fleet destroyed Cervera's squadron.

DAVID F. MARLEY AND SPENCER C. TUCKER

See also

Cervera y Topete, Pascual; Dewey, George; Manila Bay, Battle of; Montojo y Pasarón, Patricio; Naval Strategy, Spanish; North Atlantic Squadron; Sampson, William Thomas; Santiago de Cuba, Battle of

Further Reading

Bordejé y Morencos, F. F. de. *Crónica de la Marina española en el siglo XIX, 1868–1898* [Chronicle of the Spanish Navy in the 19th Century, 1868–1898]. Madrid: Marcial Pons, 1995.

Cervera Pery, José. *La guerra naval del 98: a mal planeamiento, peores consecuencias* [The Naval War of 1898: Poor Planning, Worse Consequences]. Madrid: San Martín, 1998.

Chesnau, Roger, and Eugene M. Kolesnik, eds. *Conway's All the World's Fighting Ships, 1860–1905.* New York: Mayflower Books, 1979.

Feuer, A. B. *The Spanish-American War at Sea: Naval Action in the Atlantic.* Westport, CT: Praeger, 1995.

Marolda, Edward J., ed. *Theodore Roosevelt, the U.S. Navy, and the Spanish American War.* New York: Palgrave, 2001.

Smith, Joseph. *The Spanish-American War: Conflict in the Caribbean and the Pacific, 1895–1902.* New York: Longman, 1994.

Spanish-American War, International Reaction to

Reactions in other countries to the war between the United States and Spain ranged from cautious sympathy for the United States on the part of Great Britain to indifference and mild hostility on the part of the governments of the other great powers to dismay among liberal and socialist elements and the general public in Europe and Latin America. These attitudes were largely a product of their perceptions of the war's impact on their own interests.

While most Americans believed that they had gone to war with Spain for humanitarian motives, this was not the perception among European governments. The combination of American belligerence in the First Venezuela Crisis (1895–1897) followed by jingoism in the American press and the U.S. Congress regarding the Cuban crisis and the ensuing American war with Spain triggered considerable anxiety in Europe over U.S. intentions. Except for Britain, where leading members of the government of Prime Minister Robert Gascoyne-Cecil (Lord Salisbury) and other political observers viewed the United States as a potential ally, the other European powers were uneasy about this aggressive American expansionism.

These reactions were, in part, a product of differing political cultures among the European powers. At the end of the 19th century, most of the European states (including Spain) were still headed by monarchies, and these monarchs sympathized with Spanish monarch Queen María Cristina and her ministers. Even Britain's Queen Victoria, the monarch of power otherwise sympathetic with the United States, spoke out against American bellicosity toward Spain. Indeed, Victoria called on other European powers to "unite

Political cartoon titled "The see-saw nations—The Anglo-Saxons balance of power" by Victor Gillam from the April 9, 1898, issue of *Judge.* The cartoon shows Uncle Sam and John Bull sitting at one end of the seesaw, while Turkey, Spain, China, France, Germany, and Russia struggle to stay on the other end, with "History" and a cannon as the fulcrum. (Library of Congress)

against such unheard of conduct" in reference to American war aims. The monarchies of the other great powers (except for Republican France) were also uneasy about the war's possible impact on the Spanish Crown and how a threat to the Spanish monarchy might impact them.

Beyond the reactions of the governments lay the hostility of public opinion and of editorials and essayists across the political spectrum. Conservative political observers took the occasion of the war to revive long-standing images of Americans as greedy, materialistic, selfish, hypocritical, and overbearing. Outside of Britain, few commentators accepted American claims that the war was being waged for humanitarian purposes or to liberate Cuba. Many Europeans saw this as utter hypocrisy carried out by a nation that, as one German press editorial pointed out, conducted "numerous cruel Indian wars and persecutions of 'Negroes.'" There was also virtually no discussion of Cuban aspirations in the European press. Coverage of the war in the continental press was Eurocentric, and throughout the continent, the American war against Spain was perceived as a war against all of Europe.

For liberal and leftist Europeans more in sympathy with U.S. republican values, the war represented a betrayal. They perceived the war and the overseas expansion that accompanied it as an abandonment of America's traditions and core beliefs. Many leftist observers saw the war as evidence of the ascendancy of monopoly capitalism in the United States. There was great concern in liberal internationalist circles that the United States, by intervening in Cuba and seizing the Philippines, had undermined the international legal order.

Public and press outrage over perceived American aggression against Spain did not translate into any kind of united front on the part of the governments of the great powers, however. Of all the European powers, Germany showed the most sympathy toward Spain and, conversely, the most hostility toward the United States. Germany, led by its impetuous Kaiser Wilhelm II, urged a united stand by the European powers against the United States but took no action to bring about collective action by the powers. Germany's actions were governed largely by economic considerations and its overseas ambitions. Indeed, the Germans feared disruption of trade with the United States, then Germany's most important trading partner outside of Europe.

The Germans also had ambitions and concerns regarding the Philippines, where German officials both nursed aspirations about taking over the islands for themselves and feared that Britain might seize the Philippines if the United States did not acquire them. After the outbreak of the war and the American victory in Manila Bay in May 1898, the Germans alternated between hostility toward the United States and moves toward a rapprochement, including feelers about gaining a naval base at Subic Bay and a possible alliance with the United States. When President William McKinley announced the U.S. intention to annex the islands, the Germans acceded without protest.

Similarly, France assumed a stance of ambivalent neutrality, and the French government scarcely commented on the Cuban crisis. After the outbreak of war and the American victory at Manila Bay, press comment in France fearfully acknowledged the new status of the United States as a great power. With its hands tied by domestic political instability, however, the French government could do little more than keep a wary eye on the Americans. As with the Germans, the French sent a naval force to the Philippines and put out feelers concerning a possible sphere of influence in the islands. French foreign minister Théophile Delcassé offered to mediate between Spain and the United States, but when the United States showed no interest, he did not press the offer. When Spain proposed a joint protectorate over the Philippines by all the powers, France refused to support the proposal.

Tsarist Russia, France's ally, followed the same pattern as the other powers. Of all the European powers, Russia should have been the most concerned over the Spanish-American War. The emergence of the United States as a Pacific power clearly affected Russia's ambitions in the Far East. The Russian Foreign Ministry was concerned with the possibility that Britain and the United States might cooperate against a Russian sphere of influence in North China and Manchuria. Nevertheless, apart from expressions of sympathy for the Spanish monarchy from Tsar Nicholas II, the government did not show great concern with the prewar deterioration of Spanish-American relations. Russian diplomats were not enthusiastic about proposals for joint intervention by the powers in support of Spain lest the Americans become even more involved in the Far East.

After the Americans' May 1898 victory at Manila Bay, the Russian government expressed some concern that Britain or Germany, Russia's two chief rivals in both Europe and the Far East, might acquire the Philippines if the United States decided not to take the archipelago. Russian foreign minister Count Mikhail Muraviev approached the French about intervening in the war, forcing Spain to make peace, and taking the Philippines for themselves. The French, however, refused. Muraviev's actions aside, Russia's governing bureaucracy gave little thought during and immediately after the war to policy toward the new world power. If the French had shown more concern and a willingness to mediate between the United States and Spain, it is likely that the Russian government would have vigorously supported a French initiative. As it was, Russia did not seriously rethink relations with the United States until the Americans became more active in China with publication of the Open Door Notes of 1899–1900.

Just as surprising was the ambivalent reaction of another emerging power, Japan. Like the United States, Japan was an emerging Pacific power and had designs on both Hawaii and the Philippines. Expansionist and imperialist ideology was steadily gaining influence in the Japanese press as well as in Japanese government and military circles. In 1893 and 1897, important newspapers representing Japanese political parties had protested American designs on Hawaii. Although Japanese political leaders acquiesced to the U.S. annexation of Hawaii in 1898, many believed that Japan's destiny lay to the south and called for Japan to seize the Philippines if and when the Spanish regime collapsed.

Many European diplomats and other observers also believed that Japan might oppose American acquisition of the Philippines and seek to acquire the islands for itself. On the other hand, many analysts with access to anti-Russian elements in Japan's political establishment believed that the Japanese would seek American assistance, along with that of the British, in contesting Russian and German seizures of Port Arthur and Shantung in North China, respectively.

The Japanese pursued neither course, as domestic political instability brought on by a severe economic depression precluded foreign adventures at this time. In 1898 and 1899, three governments rapidly succeeded one other, each preoccupied with domestic political and economic affairs. None of the three cabinets could afford to take any action that might panic Japanese capitalists or discourage foreign investments. Faced with internal turmoil, the Japanese leadership decided that it could not afford to resist the United States or to court it.

Thus, none of the powers made any serious efforts to unite in support of Spain against the American expansionism. Britain, facing growing isolation in Europe and the approach of war with the Boers in South Africa, elected to strive for American friendship. Germany initially sympathized with Spain but wound up seeking an accommodation with the United States. The other powers displayed neither hostility nor friendship. The powers were all preoccupied with balance of power considerations. Indeed, they feared each other as much as they feared the United States and were faced with internal political and class divisions that limited their ability to act. The result was that decisions regarding America's future in the world were left in the hands of the Americans themselves. As had so often happened in the previous century, the United States benefited from Europe's distress and ambivalence.

WALTER F. BELL

See also

China; China Market; Cuba; Delcassé, Théophile; Diederichs, Ernst Otto von; France; Germany; Great Britain, Policies and Reactions to the Spanish-American War; Imperialism; Japan; Manila Bay, Battle of; McKinley, William; Open Door Policy; Spain; Subic Bay; Venezuela Crisis, First

Further Reading

Hannigan, Robert E. *The New World Power: American Foreign Policy, 1898–1917.* Philadelphia: University of Pennsylvania Press, 2002.

Hilton, Sylvia, and Steve J. S. Ickringill. *European Perceptions of the Spanish-American War.* New York: Peter Lang, 1999.

Kagan, Robert. *Dangerous Nation: America's Place in the World from Its Earliest Days to the Dawn of the Twentieth Century.* New York: Knopf, 2006.

May, Ernest R. *Imperial Democracy: The Emergence of America as a Great Power.* New York: Harcourt, Brace, 1961.

Shippee, Lester Burrell. "Germany and the Spanish-American War." *American Historical Review* 30(4) (July 1925): 754–777.

Spanish-American War, U.S. Financing of

The Spanish-American War cost the U.S. government approximately $250 million, exclusive of the costs associated with the Philippine-American War that began in 1899. This outlay was a significant percentage of the total federal budget and exceeded the total cost of the American Revolution and the War of 1812 combined. While the fighting was brief, the global nature of the conflict proved to be costly in terms of logistics, fuel, supply lines, and troop movements. Fortunately for Americans, the costs associated with the war surfaced at the same time that the U.S. economy was recovering from the disastrous effects of the Panic of 1893 and the economic depression of 1893–1897. The renewed prosperity of the late 1890s allowed the federal government to finance the war with Spain without placing an enormous burden on the entire American economy and without piling up huge debts. The rebounding economy, however, had led many business leaders, including Mark Hanna, President William McKinley's chief political adviser and confidant, to caution against war with Spain because of the potential negative impact on the American economy.

The challenge faced by lawmakers in financing the conflict was trying to increase revenues in the aftermath of the 1895 Supreme Court decision in *Pollock v. Farmers' Loan and Trust Company,* which held that an income tax was a direct tax and thus unconstitutional. This deprived Congress of the option of implementing a wartime income tax that had been quite effective in funding the American Civil War. Moreover, pressure from Wall Street and the business community prompted Congress to reject proposals that would significantly increase tariffs. Given these two major restrictions, the federal government instituted new excise taxes and increased rates on those already in existence.

The need for wartime revenue pressed Congress to pass the War Revenue Act of 1898, an omnibus bill that restored many of the taxes passed during the American Civil War. This legislation generated nearly $344 million in revenue and offset the entire cost of the war.

The most common and profitable source of revenue under this act was excise taxes imposed on a variety of commodities and services. The excise taxes were frequently placed on luxury items or

Comparative Costs of the Spanish-American War (in Millions)

Conflict	Original War Costs	Veterans' Benefits	Repayment of Interest on War Loans	Total
American Revolutionary War	$100	$70	$20	$190
Mexican-American War	$73	$64	$10	$147
Spanish-American War	$400	$6,000	$60	$6,460
World War II	$288,000	$290,000	$86,000	$664,000

took the form of sin taxes on items such as alcohol and tobacco. One famous excise tax was a 3 percent levy on private phone service, which generated approximately $314,000 during the Spanish-American War. This tax was not repealed until 2006, however, and thus continued to raise billions every year. A stamp tax on legal and commercial commodities was another excise tax that was instituted during the war.

The most controversial and widely debated source of wartime revenue was a tax on inheritances. While this type of tax was imposed during the American Civil War, many powerful and wealthy scions of the Gilded Age vociferously opposed this measure, realizing that large amounts of money would transfer from private hands to the federal government. Despite these high-profile opponents, support from prominent economists and industrialist Andrew Carnegie convinced Congress to pass the national inheritance tax in 1898. This graduated tax was placed on all legacies and inherited property. The rate was determined by the size of the inheritance and the relationship of the individual to the deceased. The maximum tax was 15 percent on inheritances that exceeded $1 million. This tax, which was eliminated in 1902, survived legal challenges to its constitutionality.

The federal government was able to finance the short-lived war without imposing taxes that stifled the economy or produced widespread opposition. In most cases, the taxes enacted were specifically for the conduct of the war, and the war revenue reduction bill of 1901 eliminated virtually every tax enacted during the war. The experience of financing the Spanish-American War alerted many astute leaders in the United States that a lengthy and wider war would require more effective and productive sources of revenue. This led to the passage of the 16th Amendment to the U.S. Constitution in 1913, which provided for an income tax just in time for the U.S. entry into World War I.

JAMES T. CARROLL

See also

Carnegie, Andrew; Economic Depression; Gilded Age; Hanna, Mark; McKinley, William

Further Reading

Bradford, James C., ed. *Crucible of Empire: The Spanish-American War and Its Aftermath.* Annapolis, MD: Naval Institute Press, 1993.
Musicant, Ivan. *Empire by Default: The Spanish-American War and the Dawn of the American Century.* New York: Henry Holt, 1998.

Spanish-American War, U.S. Public Reaction to

In the final years of the 19th century, the United States was emerging as a world power and developing a wide array of methods to measure public opinion on specific events. Straw polls, mail solicitations, and random interviews were well established by the 1890s and were quickly embraced by political parties, politicians, newspaper editors, and magazines. The events leading up to the Spanish-

American War, however, prompted a groundswell of public sentiments that frequently moved President William McKinley, members of Congress, and average Americans to take action against Spanish oppression in Cuba, Puerto Rico, and the Philippines. The high degree of support for military action against Spain was a significant reason for the declaration of war in April 1898. Of course, propaganda, instigated chiefly by newspapers and the yellow journalism of the day, also played a significant role in shaping public reaction to events before, during, and after the war.

Reports, both real and imagined, of atrocities committed by the Spanish in Cuba reached a highly sympathetic audience in the United States through newspapers, which had assigned reporters, artists, and photographers to the island nation with the objective of generating graphic accounts of deprivation and mayhem. The arrival in Cuba in the winter of 1896 of General Veleriano Weyler y Nicolau—dubbed "the Beast" and "the Butcher" by American newspapers—provided political cartoonists, writers, and artists with ample accounts to rile American sensibilities and garner support for an American response to the building crisis. The portrayals of mass starvation, murders, and the horrific implementation of the *reconcentrado* (reconcentration) system appealed to a broad spectrum of the American population.

The effective representation of events in Cuba prior to the start of the Spanish-American War shaped American public opinion and motivated a national response to the slaughter. These prewar developments engendered support for Cuban independence, renewed notions of American nationalism, and catapulted yellow journalism to new levels of influence.

The revelation of the Dupuy de Lôme-Canalejas Letter on February 9, 1898, and the explosion of the U.S. Navy battleship *Maine* in Havana Harbor on February 15, 1898, galvanized American public opinion and initiated the process that ultimately led to a formal declaration of war on April 25, 1898, retroactive to April 21, 1898. On February 9, 1898, the San Francisco *Examiner* released details of personal correspondence between Enrique Dupuy de Lôme, Spanish ambassador to the United States, and José Canalejas, a friend and Spanish newspaper reporter, that vilified President William McKinley and indicated that the United States was weak. The letter outraged many Americans. On February 15, 1898, less than a week after the publication of the letter, the destruction of the *Maine* killed 266 U.S. seamen. In short order, it was determined that the tragedy was the result of an external mine explosion, presumably laid by the Spanish.

The shaping of public opinion during the Spanish-American War was heavily influenced by newspapers. In 1898, virtually every town had at least one daily paper, and several major syndicates dominated print media in the major cities of the United States. Some large cities such as New York, Chicago, and Philadelphia had as many as seven daily newspapers. The two most influential editors of the period were William Randolph Hearst, who published the *New York Journal*, and his cross-town rival Joseph Pulitzer, who headed the *New York World*. These newspapers were engaged in a circulation war at the time and employed yellow journalism—often rampant and irresponsible sen-

A Spanish-American War ribbon, "To Hell with Spain." (David J. & Janice L. Frent Collection/Corbis)

sationalism—to win readers and to capture memorable headlines. While many of the assertions in the newspapers were erroneous or exaggerated, they nevertheless shaped public opinion and dictated national policies. The glory of war was good for newspaper circulation and ensured that remarkable headlines were in ready supply during the Spanish-American War.

Both Congress and the White House felt the pressure generated by the press and public opinion, which seemed to be leaning heavily toward war. In the harried weeks prior to the war, pressure mounted on President McKinley to respond to Spanish aggression by taking decisive military action. By the end of March, most Americans believed that war was inevitable, and some factions in Congress threatened to take independent action if the president did not act immediately. Congressmen and senators from both political parties were keenly aware of their constituents' popular support for military intervention and mounted a sustained barrage of pressure on McKinley that led to the war declaration. The Spanish-American War ended up being a highly popular conflict and garnered support from virtually every segment of the American society.

The short duration of the war, its overwhelming military successes, and the large territorial acquisitions to be gained certainly sustained support for the war and swept widespread enthusiasm for the conflict right through to the peace treaty.

JAMES T. CARROLL

See also

Atrocities; Cuban War of Independence; Dupuy de Lôme-Canalejas Letter; Hearst, William Randolph; Journalism; *Maine,* USS; Newspapers; Pulitzer, Joseph; *Reconcentrado* System; Weyler y Nicolau, Valeriano; Yellow Journalism

Further Reading

Gould, Lewis L. *The Presidency of William McKinley.* Lawrence: University Press of Kansas, 1981.

Trask, David F. *The War with Spain in 1898.* Lincoln: University of Nebraska Press, 1996.

Spencer, Herbert
Birth Date: April 27, 1820
Death Date: December 8, 1903

English-born political theorist and philosopher. Herbert Spencer was the 19th century's most ardent proponent of the theory of social evolution (later termed social Darwinism), which relied on scientific findings, particularly those of Charles Darwin and his theory of evolution, to formulate a view of the workings of modern society. Spencer's theories can be said to have driven the Gilded Age and its reliance on industrialization and the search for overseas markets as well as having acted as a validation for the expansionism and imperialism of the late 19th century.

British philosopher Herbert Spencer was the leading proponent of social evolution, later known as social Darwinism. He coined the phrase "survival of the fittest." (Library of Congress)

Born on April 27, 1820, in Derby, England, Spencer came from a family known for its radical politics. His father and uncles had been religious and political dissenters and were fervent believers in the need for widespread reform in British society. Spencer received little formal education, as he was tutored mostly by his father (a former schoolmaster) and uncle. His course of study was unconventional and erratic. He received almost no training in the humanities but instead spent a considerable amount of time exploring the world of science and conducting experiments that gave him great practical knowledge.

At age 17, Spencer became a teacher but quickly became dissatisfied with what he perceived as the stifling limits of formal education. In 1837, he gained a position as a railway engineer through a series of family connections. He excelled in this position, although within a few years he had become restless in this profession as well and in 1841 left the railways.

During the same period that he worked as a railroad engineer, Spencer also became involved in radical politics. He supported electoral reforms and the disestablishment of the Church of England. In concert with such radical politicians as John Bright and Richard Cobden, Spencer fought against the Corn Laws and for expansion of suffrage. In early 1842, he joined the Chartist movement, an organization whose goals included universal male suffrage without the limits of property qualifications, a redefining of electoral districts so that all men in Great Britain were equally represented in the British Parliament, the use of secret ballots in voting, and financial support for members of Parliament so that poor men as well as rich men would be able to hold office. Both the Chartist movement and Spencer's involvement in radical politics were brief, but his activity brought his name into the public eye and earned him a small degree of recognition among Britain's radical circles.

In 1842, Spencer wrote his first political discourse, 12 letters that appeared in a radical newspaper that year and were later published as a pamphlet titled *The Proper Sphere of Government* (1843). In those letters, he argued for the government to adopt a strict attitude of laissez-faire, meaning that it should take no action that in any way regulated the economy, industry, or society. He also declared that governments routinely did more harm than good by interfering in society's workings. This publication brought him praise and the opportunity to publish in other radical publications.

In 1848, Spencer became an assistant editor at the prestigious magazine *The Economist*. He continued to write philosophical tracts during his spare time and in 1851 published *Social Statics: The Conditions Essential to Human Happiness Specified, and the First of Them Developed*. In this work, he advocated not just political but also economic and social laissez-faire. He also reaffirmed that government interference in the economy or the workings of society upset the natural order of the world, where, he believed, the strong survived and the weak perished. This work made his reputation and presented the germ of his social theory that he would refine for the rest of his life.

In 1853, Spencer quit his job at *The Economist* after he received an inheritance from his uncle. His financial independence now allowed him the freedom to develop his social theories and present them to the world by his own fashion. He also dabbled in several inventions during the 1850s, although none amounted to much. However, he wrote prolifically, publishing books in 1885, 1861, 1862, 1864–1867, 1872, 1873–1881, 1882–1896, and 1902.

Throughout those works, Spencer developed his ideas regarding extreme laissez-faire. In 1859, after the publication of Darwin's *On the Origin of Species,* Spencer adopted Darwin's theory of natural selection to bolster his own theories of social science. Although Spencer had already employed this theory and even published a rudimentary version of it in *Social Statics,* Darwin's work on the natural world substantiated Spencer's work on society. Darwin himself never used the phrase "survival of the fittest," but it suited Spencer's needs perfectly. It embodied the idea that policies such as tariffs in the economic world and welfare in the social world were truly unfounded and perverted the order of the natural world. Spencer thus became one of the leading proponents of social Darwinism, an intellectual movement that used Darwin's theories of evolution to explain social and economic phenomena.

Spencer's publications caused a great deal of controversy and debate in Victorian Great Britain and the United States, where his ideas were propagated by William Graham Sumner. In fact, Spencer's theory of social evolution—that society evolved and changed over time just as the natural world did—prompted nearly as much debate as Darwin's theories. Spencer viewed industrialization as progress in society's evolution (itself a highly debatable point in Victorian society) and claimed that the class system existed because some members of society were strong and had therefore succeeded, while others were weak and were therefore being winnowed out. Such an idea that the poor were poor because they lacked the qualities necessary to succeed flew in the face of many of Britain's social reformers at the time, many of whom advocated that the poor were poor because of circumstance and the inequities of capitalism and the factory system. Proponents of Manifest Destiny in the United States used Spencer's findings to advocate their theories, as would Germany in the two world wars in terms of victory of the strong over the weak in society and war.

Indeed, Spencer's worldview was clearly in keeping with social and economic changes taking place in the United States in the late 19th century. The relentless pursuit of technological innovation, industrial conglomeration, and the aggregation of extreme wealth in the hands of a few all fit the patterns of Spencer's social Darwinism. His theories not only helped explain why these trends were developing as they were but also served to validate the trends and the personalities involved. Thus, for Spencer, the robber barons—Andrew Carnegie, John D. Rockefeller, and John Pierpont Morgan, among others—were captains of industry and industrial statesmen rather than shady characters who had accumulated too much wealth and power. As America's industrialization and economic growth began to outpace those of its competitors, the race was on to open overseas markets. Thus, as the Spanish-American War approached, social Darwinists in the United States saw American expansion abroad as a natural extension of its long-standing continental power and search for ever-expanding markets. Social Darwinism certainly fit the mind-set of U.S. imperialists in the 1890s.

Regardless of how Spencer's contemporaries felt about the soundness of his theories, all respected his approach to studying society. Spencer believed that all aspects of intellectual inquiry were ultimately related. Biology, psychology, ethics, economics, and politics made up interlocking parts of society, and therefore none could be studied in isolation. Neither could any branch of study be deemed irrelevant to society. In addition, Spencer advocated that the same rigorous standards that shaped scientific studies must also be applied to studying society. Thus was born the broad field of social science and the more focused field of sociology.

Deeply devoted to his work, Spencer spent his life elaborating on his theories and defending them before the public. He never married and spent much of his life in solitude. Spencer died on December 8, 1903, in Sussex, England.

ELIZABETH DUBRULLE AND PAUL G. PIERPAOLI JR.

See also

Expansionism; Imperialism; Manifest Destiny; Robber Barons; Social Darwinism

Further Reading

Kennedy, James Gettier. *Herbert Spencer.* Boston: Twayne, 1978.
Peel, J. D. Y. *Herbert Spencer: The Evolution of a Sociologist.* New York: Basic Books, 1971.
Wiltshire, David. *The Social and Political Thought of Herbert Spencer.* Oxford Historical Monographs. New York: Oxford University Press USA, 1978.

Spheres of Influence

The phrase "spheres of influence" refers to the attempt by the world's major powers to establish exclusive economic (and sometimes political) domains in areas of the developing world. The new imperialism of the last third of the 19th century and the first part of the 20th century resulted in a remarkable spread of Western domination around the globe. Various methods for securing control of lands in Africa, the Middle East, Asia, and the Pacific were utilized, among them direct colonization, the establishment of protectorates, and the creation of spheres of influence. Spheres of influence may be thought of as economic concessions granted to a stronger power by a weaker one. Spheres of influence allowed the stronger power to exploit the weaker state economically for the profit and benefit of the nation receiving the concession. However, the weaker nation

Queen's Road, the principal thoroughfare of Hong Kong, China, circa 1906. (Library of Congress)

remained nominally in control of its geographical territory, meaning that no direct cession of land was involved.

Although Great Britain established a sphere of influence in Afghanistan in the late 19th century and divided the region that comprised present-day Iraq and Iran into spheres of influence with Russia in 1907, the concept of a sphere of influence is most commonly associated with imperialist competition in China during the late 19th century. The establishment of a number of these would serve as the culmination of the rivalry that was the result of the efforts of the great powers, along with a rising Japan, to take advantage of a declining China.

The combination of Chinese defeats in two Opium Wars (1839–1843 and 1856–1860) with the British and the French and the Sino-French War over Vietnam (1884–1885) was a clear indication of a Chinese state that had become weak and unable to defend itself from increasingly aggressive Western encroachment. In addition, the Taiping Rebellion of 1850–1864 had further sapped the strength of the Chinese Empire. The competition for influence and control in China was further intensified by the emergence of two new players in the game, Germany and Japan, that now joined Britain, France, Russia, and the United States as competitors for the considerable China Market and other economic opportunities. These factors all contributed to increasing encroachment upon China by the Western powers and Japan. The result would be a scramble for concessions between 1895 and 1898. This would formalize the creation of a series of spheres of influence in China that would bring that country to the brink of complete partition by the rival powers.

Two factors in particular contributed to the scramble for concessions. First, increasing Japanese influence in Korea, which China perceived to be under its protection, led to the outbreak in 1894 of the Sino-Japanese War, which concluded in 1895 with a decisive Japanese victory. The ensuing Treaty of Shimonoseki forced China to recognize Korean independence, to cede the island of Taiwan and the Liaodong (Liaotung) Peninsula to Japan, and to allow the Japanese to build factories and industries in Chinese treaty ports. Using the most favored nation status accorded them in their trade agreements with China, the Western powers quickly acquired this privilege as well.

Russia, which had been expanding its interests into Chinese Manchuria with German and French support, forced Japan to restore the Liaodong Peninsula. The Russians then negotiated a treaty with China in 1896 that permitted them to build a railroad to cross Manchuria connecting Vladivostok to the Trans-Siberian Railroad then under construction. This new Chinese Eastern Railway allowed Russia to substantially increase its interests in Manchuria, which threatened Japanese ambitions in the region.

These actions may well have encouraged the other powers to expand their interests in China as they scrambled to take advantage of the "sick old man of Asia" in China. The Germans, who had been interested for some time in acquiring a naval base in the area, initiated the scramble for concessions. The murder of a pair of German missionaries in Shandong Province in November 1897 gave Germany a pretext for action. The Germans seized the port city of Qingdao (Tsingtao) and Jiaozhao Bay, and China was forced to lease the region to Germany for 99 years. The lease also gave the Germans mining rights and permitted the construction of two railroads.

Germany's action set off a new phase of imperialist rivalry as the other powers joined in the scramble. Russia followed up on its earlier actions in Manchuria by occupying the southern Manchurian Peninsula of Liaodong, which Japan had wanted for itself, and leased the region with the harbor cities of Port Arthur (today Lüshunkou) and Dalian for 25 years. Russia also gained permission to link the area to the Chinese Eastern Railway by building a new railroad, the South Manchurian Railway.

In order to block further Russian and German gains, Great Britain acquired a 25-year lease of Weihaiwei, which was located directly across the Bohai Strait from Port Arthur and Dalian, giving the British an excellent location from which to monitor both Russian and German activities in North China. In addition, Britain leased Kowloon, or the New Territories of Hong Kong, for 99 years and effectively held a sphere of influence in the region around the Yangtze River.

The French, meanwhile, were able to coerce a lease of Guangzhou Bay in southern China. The 99-year lease enabled France to create a sphere of influence in Southwest China that included mining rights and permission to construct a railroad linking the area to the French colony in Vietnam. Japan, locked out of North Asia, had to settle for a sphere of influence in Fujian Province across the Taiwan Strait from Taiwan itself. In 1902, Japan also negotiated a naval treaty with Britain that placed Japan in position to challenge Russia for control of Manchuria in the Russo-Japanese War. The Chinese, however, rebuffed an Italian demand to lease a seaport, making Italy the sole European nation to have concession demands rejected by the Qing dynasty.

As for the United States, the war with Spain in 1898 offered the perfect opportunity to expand American influence into East Asia. Having acquired Hawaii and the Philippine Islands during the Spanish-American War, however, the United States made no demands for a sphere of influence in China. Instead, the William McKinley administration responded to the scramble for concessions by enunciating what would become known as the Open Door Policy. In two diplomatic notes circulated to the powers involved in China, Secretary of State John Hay called for equal opportunity for all nations to trade freely in that country and for the powers to respect China's territorial integrity. The Open Door Notes formalized a policy practiced by the United States in regard to international commerce since independence and were designed to ensure American access to ports, investment opportunities, and natural resources located within these new spheres of influence.

While it was feared for a time afterward that the creation of these spheres of influence was a precursor to the ultimate division of China among the great powers, no further significant encroachment occurred during the remaining years of the Qing dynasty. This likely was because the imperial powers and Japan were unable to set aside their competition to come to an agreement regarding dismemberment of the Chinese Empire. When the powers convened to determine China's fate following the Boxer Rebellion (1899–1901), they made no effort to divide Chinese territory among themselves, suggesting simply that they were incapable of agreeing on a formula that would be acceptable to all of them. The competition between the powers in China may well have helped save the empire from a complete collapse.

GREGORY MOORE

See also

Boxer Rebellion; China; China Market; Imperialism; Open Door Policy; Russo-Japanese War; Sino-Japanese War

Further Reading

Darby, Philip. *Three Faces of Imperialism: British and American Approaches to Asia and Africa, 1870–1970*. New Haven, CT: Yale University Press, 1987.

Duus, Peter, Ramon H. Myers, and Mark R. Peattie, eds. *The Japanese Informal Empire in China, 1895–1937*. Princeton, NJ: Princeton University Press, 1989.

Hunt, Michael H. *The Making of a Special Relationship: The United States and China to 1914*. New York: Columbia University Press, 1983.

Spence, Jonathan. *The Search for Modern China*. 2nd ed. New York: Norton, 2001.

Wakeman, Frederic, Jr. *The Fall of Imperial China*. New York: Free Press, 1975.

Splendid Little War

Descriptive phrase used to refer to the Spanish-American War. In a July 27, 1898, personal letter to Colonel Theodore Roosevelt, U.S. ambassador to the United Kingdom John Milton Hay, who subsequently became secretary of state in September 1898, described the Spanish-American War as a "splendid little war." Hay meant that the U.S. victory over Spain was, compared to the long 19th-century wars, relatively short and easy.

The war lasted less than four months, and there were few casualties. It claimed only 379 American combat deaths, although 5,462 American soldiers died of other causes. President William McKinley easily won reelection in November 1900, in large part because of the successful U.S. war with Spain. Most Americans, albeit not all, saw the war as a just and noble cause. Hay's term was duly publicized and became an instantly recognizable term for the Spanish-American War.

As a result of the war, the United States liberated Cuba and annexed Puerto Rico, Guam, and the Philippine Islands. Notwithstanding American victory against Spain, the United States was obliged to fight a protracted and brutal war against Filipino nationalists from 1899 to 1902. Certainly, nobody referred to that conflict as "splendid."

Nevertheless, the Spanish-American War taught the U.S. military important lessons about supplying forces overseas and pro-

jecting military power far from the continental United States. These would prove valuable in World War I. In addition, the splendid little war made the United States a major imperialist power and an Asian power, setting up the ultimate confrontation with Japan in 1941.

MICHAEL R. HALL

See also

Hay, John Milton; Imperialism; McKinley, William; Roosevelt, Theodore

Further Reading

O'Toole, G. J. A. *The Spanish War: An American Epic, 1898*. New York: Norton, 1984.

Trask, David F. *The War with Spain in 1898*. Lincoln: University of Nebraska Press, 1996.

Staging Areas

See Camps, U.S. Army

Steel

Steel production is the lifeblood of a modern industrialized economy. The measure of a nation's steel output, particularly at the turn of the 20th century, was the leading indicator of its economic health and prowess. At the time of the Spanish-American War, the United States was far and away the world's greatest steel producer. America's supremacy in steel production allowed its economy to expand

A steel mill in Homestead, Pennsylvania, circa 1907. (Library of Congress)

exponentially in the years after the American Civil War, permitted the construction of an unparalleled national railroad network, and gave military planners the ability to move toward an ultramodern all-steel navy. All of these developments stood the nation in good stead during the Spanish-American War.

Steel is an alloy that until the mid-19th century was produced by mixing wrought iron with small amounts of carbon. The resulting mixture then had to be laboriously heated for a number of days. This arduous process made large-scale steel production extremely expensive and virtually impossible to attain. Records of steel production—albeit in very small quantities—can be traced to antiquity. However, in 1856, an English inventor, Henry Bessemer, came upon a new process, using a blast furnace, for making steel that allowed the alloy to be fashioned directly from pig iron, a lesser grade of metal than wrought iron. This brought down the labor needed and the amount of coal required to produce steel, which in turn made it significantly less expensive. Even more important, however, the Bessemer process sped up steel production tremendously and allowed producers to make steel in quantities heretofore unthinkable.

In the mid-1850s, the United States produced about 10,000 tons of steel per year. In 1867, only 1,643 tons were being produced by the Bessemer method. However, Andrew Carnegie, who would one day own the world's largest steel-manufacturing facility, witnessed the Bessemer process in action and vowed to put it to use on a large scale in the United States. The results were truly transforming. By 1897, on the eve of the war, the United States was making more than 7.15 million tons of steel per year, an output that was more than double the combined production of both Germany and Great Britain, America's biggest economic rivals. By 1900, the Carnegie Steel Company alone manufactured more steel than all of Great Britain.

Large-scale steel production had a ripple effect on the entire U.S. economy. It greatly increased the need for iron ore mining, rail transportation, coal and coke (a purified coal derivative) production, railcar and ship production, etc. It also fueled the need for hundreds of thousands of new laborers, many of whom were immigrants arriving by the millions to seek a better life in a new world.

Carnegie, an uncannily shrewd businessman, soon cornered the market on steel production. By 1882, he had joined forces with the H. C. Frick Company, which was the nation's largest supplier of coke, a key ingredient in steel production. With the merger of Carnegie Steel and Henry Clay Frick's coke company, the two men were able to vertically integrate their company and force competitors to either match their prices or go out of business. By the mid to late 1880s, Carnegie Steel was the world's largest producer of steel and steel products.

The ready availability of plentiful steel at reasonable prices served to radically transform the United States. In less than a generation, it leaped ahead of its economic competitors and took on the air of a completely modernized nation. Steel, for example, helped the building trades enormously. It gave architects, engi-

neers, and builders infinitely more choices in terms of design and functionality. Until the 1880s, for instance, building heights were limited to usually no more than five or six stories, as anything taller would have required massive masonry walls that were impractical. Steel beams, however, allowed the construction of the world's first skyscrapers, which theoretically had no limit on their size or height. At the same time, steel-framed buildings were stronger and less susceptible to fires. The impact on American cities was spectacular.

By the 1880s, railroads had begun using steel rails rather than wrought iron rails. Steel rails lasted far longer and were much less likely to break, crack, or bend, which increased the railroads' efficiency and allowed them to increase their scope. Indeed, in 1870 the United States had some 53,000 miles of railroad tracks, far more than any other nation. By 1898, this figure had skyrocketed to nearly 190,000 miles of tracks. America's extensive rail network helped keep the economy growing and also served it well during the Spanish-American War, when hundreds of thousands of troops had to be transported to camps and embarkation points and millions of tons of food, clothing, medicine, weapons, and ammunition had to be moved quickly and efficiently to seaports. Telegraph and long-distance phone lines also used the railroads' right-of-way. Before long, these lines had increased at nearly the same pace as the tracks themselves. During the war, railroads proved vitally important to the war effort and, all in all, worked exceedingly well.

It was the U.S. Navy, however, that perhaps benefited most tangibly and directly from the revolution in steel making. By the early 1880s, military and civilian planners decided to begin transforming the navy from a largely preindustrial fleet of wooden ships to an all-steel fleet that would eventually boast steel-hulled ships with steel-plated armor. The advent of relatively inexpensive steel made this an attainable goal, and the first all-steel naval ships had been launched by the mid-1880s. Congress was tight-fisted when it came to military spending, but by the time war broke out in 1898, the U.S. Navy nevertheless boasted an impressive array of thoroughly modern steel warships. The smashing success of U.S. naval forces against the Spanish fleet clearly demonstrated the many advantages of steel ships. Beyond that, steel ships were stronger, far more durable, and required less regular maintenance than wooden-hulled ships. Steel hulls allowed for much larger cargo areas. Steel propellers and other engine parts made them more efficient and reliable as well. In the end, steel transformed the U.S. Navy and in so doing changed the way in which war planners thought about war and war tactics.

It is no exaggeration to say that the American steel industry played a pivotal role in the execution of and quick victory in the Spanish-American War. From improved railroads to artillery guns, ammunition, armor, and ships, steel was the preponderant war material in the conflict with Spain. And as the first U.S. conflict in which steel was cheap and plentiful, the Spanish-American War would prove that industrial prowess, perhaps as much as soldiers in the field and sailors on the seas, wins wars. It is fitting, perhaps, that the world's first billion-dollar company was created in 1901 when the financier John Pierpont Morgan purchased and combined the Carnegie steel conglomeration with several other steel producers to form U.S. Steel, which was valued at $1.4 billion. By comparison, the federal government's revenues in that year amounted to just $586 million.

PAUL G. PIERPAOLI JR.

See also

Carnegie, Andrew; Frick, Henry Clay; Gilded Age; Homestead Steel Strike; Morgan, John Pierpont, Sr.; Railroads; Robber Barons; Telephone and Telegraph; United States Navy

Further Reading

Gordon, John Steele. *An Empire of Wealth: The Epic History of American Economic Power.* New York: Harper Perennial, 2004.

Greenfield, Liah. *The Spirit of Capitalism: Nationalism and Economic Growth.* Cambridge: Harvard University Press, 2001.

Misa, Thomas S. *A Nation of Steel: The Making of Modern America, 1865–1925.* Baltimore: Johns Hopkins University Press, 1995.

Stover, John F. *American Railroads.* 2nd ed. Chicago: University of Chicago Press, 1997.

Wall, Joseph Frazier. *Andrew Carnegie.* New York: Oxford University Press USA, 1970.

George Miller Sternberg, known as the "father of bacteriology," was surgeon general of the U.S. Army during 1893–1902. (Office of Medical History, U.S. Army)

Sternberg, George Miller

Birth Date: June 8, 1838
Death Date: November 3, 1915

U.S. Army physician, pioneering medical researcher, and surgeon general of the U.S. Army from 1893 to 1902. Born on June 8, 1838, at Hartwick Seminary in Orange County, New York, George Miller Sternberg graduated from the Columbia College of Physicians and Surgeons in 1860 and entered the Army Medical Department in 1861. He then held appointments as a battlefield and post surgeon and engaged in considerable pathbreaking medical research. Among many things, he conducted exhaustive research into the pathology of yellow fever, a very serious public health threat at the time. He lectured extensively on his research and by the 1880s was recognized as one of the world's top bacteriologists. In consequence, he was appointed over several more-senior officers to the post of surgeon general on May 30, 1893, and was advanced in rank from lieutenant colonel to brigadier general.

Sternberg strongly advocated the new medicine rooted firmly in science. Over the years, he had witnessed firsthand the scourge of hospital gangrene, erysipelas (a potentially deadly communicable skin disease), and typhoid fever among soldiers at war and peace. Following early work on disinfectants, in 1880 he was the first researcher to identify the *pneumococcus* microbe that causes pneumonia and related diseases, for which he received considerable recognition. Upon taking charge of the Army Medical Department in 1893, he opened the Army Medical School, one of the nation's first postgraduate medical schools, with a dual emphasis on military sanitation and hygiene and microbiology.

From the onset of the Spanish-American War, Sternberg sought to impose some order on the rapid mobilization of volunteers and the political rush for a speedy decision in Cuba. Both Sternberg and commanding general of the army Major General Nelson A. Miles opposed an early invasion of Cuba, preferring to wait for the passing of the rainy season (April to September). Their reservations were overcome by the testimony of Cuban physician Juan M. Guiteras, who opined that careful sanitation preparation by an invading army would keep yellow fever and malaria infections at a minimum. Sternberg next pressed for careful sanitary guidelines with special regard to garbage, latrines, drinking water, and cleanliness in camps.

Despite his efforts to promote higher standards and readiness in the Medical Department, Sternberg remained stubbornly defiant on several issues, particularly on the subject of female nurses and physicians in military service. He outright refused to appoint female physicians as contract surgeons. Before the camp fever crisis exploded in September 1898, he also resisted calls to allow female nurses into the camps. Female nurses, he believed, would present a needless distraction in camp hospitals and were only capable of providing menial support. The typhoid epidemic caused him to reassess this view, and he then took a personal interest in building up a cadre of trained uniformed female nurses to assist in the camps. Ultimately, 1,563 women were selected as contract nurses. Sternberg later gave full support to the permanent establishment of the female Army Nurse Corps on February 2, 1901.

The war revealed that Sternberg's chief failing as a department head came in organization. Reluctant to delegate authority, he spent long hours micromanaging supply shortages, interviewing volunteers for new positions, and making personal recommendations on the conduct of troops in the tropics. As reports of growing chaos reached his office, he issued new circulars to his medical officers. Pleading overwork, he failed to conduct personal inspections of the camps as the crisis unfolded, instead dispatching subordinates who had limited authority to intervene. By September 1898, Sternberg was moved to quick action in authorizing new hospital camps and routing supplies, food, and personnel where needed, but by then the worst was over.

Nevertheless, Sternberg claimed that the overall experience in the war was a triumph for his model of scientific-based medicine, despite the typhoid fever outbreaks. Comparing death rates from disease in the recent conflict with the first year of the American Civil War in 1861, he concluded that the mortality rate from disease during the war (May 1, 1898–April 30, 1899) was half that of the first year of the earlier conflict. However credible Sternberg's efforts were to point out the successes of his department, the fact remained that in the midst of the much-heralded new scientific revolution in medicine, more than five times as many men died of disease than wounds.

In defending his Medical Department, Sternberg garnered criticism for shifting the blame to the volunteer establishment. Civilian physicians in volunteer service frequently owed their appointments to political favors rather than military necessity, he complained, and generally had little if any instruction in hygiene and sanitation. He also noted that the overwhelming preponderance of National Guard and volunteer militia officers had little respect for regimental surgeons. Hence, all essential hygiene recommendations—including those elaborated upon in three different circulars issued by his own office—were generally ignored.

Sternberg's influence on the postwar Medical Department, which he would direct until 1902, was greater than the sum of the criticism against him. His example of scientific medicine and leadership by example also dramatically affected the overall progress of medicine. In the midst of the camp fever crisis, he convened the Typhoid Fever Board, under the leadership of Majors Walter Reed, Edward Shakespeare, and Victor Vaughan. In 1900, Sternberg authorized the formation of the now-famous Yellow Fever Board under Reed's direction. Both boards brought about significant advances in the state of disease etiology and prevention by establishing beyond question the significance of mosquitoes as the vector of yellow fever and the presence of healthy carriers in typhoid fever and disproving once and for all the fomite theory of disease transmission in yellow fever.

Sternberg continued as surgeon general until he retired in June 1902. After his retirement, he lent his name to numerous humani-

tarian causes. Sternberg died in Washington, D.C., on November 3, 1915.

BOB A. WINTERMUTE

See also

Malaria; Medicine, Military; Miles, Nelson Appleton; Reed, Walter; Typhoid Fever; Yellow Fever

Further Reading

Gillett, Mary C. *The Army Medical Department, 1865–1917.* Washington, DC: Center of Military History, United States Army, 1995.

Sternberg, George M. *Sanitary Lessons of the War and Other Papers.* New York: Arno, 1977.

Trask, David F. *The War with Spain in 1898.* Lincoln: University of Nebraska Press, 1996.

Storey, Moorfield
Birth Date: March 19, 1845
Death Date: October 24, 1929

Lawyer, writer, publicist, civil rights advocate, and anti-imperialist. Moorfield Storey was born on March 19, 1845, in Roxbury, Massachusetts, to a well-to-do family that traced its origins to the earliest Puritan settlers of Massachusetts. Several family members were active in the abolitionist movement before the American Civil War, and from an early age Storey learned about and appreciated the work of the abolitionists. He was educated at Harvard University, earning an undergraduate degree there in 1866. From 1867 to 1869, he served as the private secretary to U.S. senator Charles Sumner, a hero of Storey's from Massachusetts who was an ardent abolitionist. This gave Storey the opportunity to view closeup the impeachment proceedings brought against President Andrew Johnson in 1867 and again in 1868. Initially, Storey championed Johnson's impeachment but came to realize that the entire affair was based not on law but rather on politics of the basest kind. Storey went on to study law at Harvard University, receiving his law degree in 1869. That same year, he was admitted to the bar.

Although Storey was not a champion of interventionist government, particularly on matters of business or the economy, over the years he developed a worldview that was quite extraordinary for a man of his time. Indeed, his views were suffused with racial equality, pacifism, and anti-imperialism. The two years working for Sumner also left Storey angry over the amount of greed and corruption in Washington, D.C. Whenever he could, he advocated a return to morally sound government.

In early 1870, Storey established a law practice in Boston that became quite successful over time. He used his stature and wealth to take every opportunity to champion equal rights for African Americans, Native Americans, and immigrants, and he decried congressional attempts to slow the influx of immigrants to the United States.

Long a political maverick, Storey demonstrated his independent streak by defecting from the Republican Party in 1884. This was in

Anti-imperialist and civil rights activist Moorfield Storey investigated war crimes committed by the U.S. military during the Philippine-American War. (Library of Congress)

ted by U.S. troops during the Philippine-American War and in 1902 wrote a briefing book about them that was used by the Senate Committee on the Philippines (Lodge Committee). The Lodge Committee, chaired by Massachusetts Senator Henry Cabot Lodge (an imperialist), had been tasked with investigating allegations of abuses and war crimes committed in the Philippines.

Storey continued to work on issues of social justice well into the latter days of his life. From 1909 to 1915, he served as the head of the National Association for the Advancement of Colored People (NAACP), a civil rights organization conceptualized by W. E. B. Du Bois. On numerous occasions, Storey used his legal acumen to advance the cause of civil rights. In 1917, he was the lead counsel for the NAACP in the Supreme Court case *Buchanan v. Warley,* which dealt with racial discrimination in housing, and ultimately won the case. Storey also chaired the Haiti–Santo Domingo Independence Society in the 1920s. He died in Cranberry Isles, Maine, on October 24, 1929.

PAUL G. PIERPAOLI JR.

See also

Anti-Imperialist League; Atrocities; Bryan, William Jennings; Cleveland, Stephen Grover; Committee on the Philippines; Imperialism; Silver Standard

Further Reading

Hixson, William B., Jr. *Moorfield Storey and the Abolitionist Tradition.* New York: Oxford University Press USA, 1972.
Howe, M. A. DeWolfe. *Portrait of an Independent: Moorfield Storey, 1845–1929.* Freeport, NY: Books for Libraries Press, 1971.

response to the party's nomination of James G. Blaine as its presidential candidate that year. Storey then threw his support behind Democratic nominee Grover Cleveland. Thus, Storey for a time became a mugwump, a Republican who left the party over the 1884 election. Storey ended up being an avid supporter of Cleveland during his two nonconsecutive presidential terms.

In the 1890s, Storey became more and more disgruntled with the Republican Party's support of imperialism and territorial expansionism. However, when William Jennings Bryan ran for president as the candidate of the Democratic and Populist parties, Storey refused to support him because of Bryan's advocacy of the silver standard. In short, Storey believed that the gold standard was the best currency plan for the nation and that a silver standard would wreck the economy. Not wanting to aid and abet the expansionist Republicans, he supported the National Democratic Party, also known as the Gold Democrats, in 1896.

Storey was appalled with the Spanish-American War and feared that it would lead to the acquisition of an American overseas empire. He became involved in the Anti-Imperialist League at the start of the war and spoke at its first large meeting, which took place in Boston in June 1898. He served for a time as vice president of the Anti-Imperialist League of New England and in 1905 became its national president, a position he held until the organization folded in 1921. Most notably, he investigated alleged war crimes commit-

Strong, Josiah
Birth Date: 1847
Death Date: April 28, 1916

Congregational minister, Protestant evangelist, ardent supporter of American imperialism and overseas expansion, and the acknowledged leader of the Social Gospel movement. Josiah Strong was born in 1847 in Illinois and moved with his family at the age of five to Hudson, Ohio. In 1869, he graduated from Western Reserve College in Ohio. He then attended the Lane Theological Seminary and was ordained a minister in the Congregational Church in 1871. He served as a pastor in Wyoming for two years before returning to Western Reserve, where he taught and served as college chaplain. Between 1872 and 1884, he held a number of pastorships, including the Central Congregational Church. There he wrote his seminal work *Our Country* (1885), which began as a manual to be used by the Congregational Missionary Society.

The treatise created a considerable stir and was read widely, far beyond the confines of Congregationalists and missionaries. In the book, Strong developed ideas that would in essence give birth to the Social Gospel movement. He also expounded on U.S. imperialism, of which he was already an ardent proponent. What made Strong's book so influential was that he neatly and eloquently harnessed the power

Congregational minister and Protestant evangelist Josiah Strong led the Social Gospel Movement. He strongly supported U.S. imperialism and overseas expansion. (New York Historical Society)

of religion and religious dogma to the social and economic ills of late 19th-century America. Indeed, he prescribed religiously based solutions for economic and societal problems. He focused on the problems afflicting America's large cities, including slums, crime, and overcrowding, and also proposed that the nation's millions of mostly poor immigrants be attended to via educational opportunities, access to health care, and job training. Indeed, his ideas greatly influenced social reformers such as Jane Addams, who created the nation's first full-service settlement house in Chicago to administer to the city's teeming immigrant population.

Strong did not stop there. A potent part of his message was the concept that the United States, as a nation of white Anglo-Saxon Protestants, was a morally superior nation endowed with a unique God-given mandate to uplift the members of uncivilized and unruly societies. In this regard, his philosophy was squarely in the vanguard of social Darwinism and the idea of the white man's burden, which would later be immortalized by the British poet Rudyard Kipling. What Strong had done was to attach religious overtones to what had been a largely secular call for American overseas imperialism.

Our Country made Strong a celebrity of his era. In 1893, he published *The New Era*, which was also wildly popular. In this book, he elaborated on his earlier work. More specifically, it was to become the blueprint of the Social Gospel movement, which had begun to

gain momentum in the mid-1890s. Strong believed that through social, political, and economic reform, human beings could create a kingdom of God on earth. He subsequently wrote a number of other books, none of which was as successful as his first two.

Nevertheless, Strong was in the vanguard of the Social Gospel movement, which lent an imposing religious and moral force to Progressivism, which blossomed as a national reform movement after 1900. He also sought to unify the various Protestant denominations under the guise of universal social outreach, but his ecumenical vision did not pan out because of the deep and long-standing divisions within the Protestant tradition. All along, he maintained a grueling speaking and writing schedule by which he sought to evangelize nonbelievers and spread the mission of the Social Gospel.

Strong served as the secretary of the American Evangelical Alliance, founded the League for Social Service (after 1902 called the American Institute for Social Service), and was a charter member of the Federal Council of the Churches of Christ. In 1904, he created the British Institute of Social Service, and in the early 1900s, he spearheaded a number of efforts to curb industrial accidents in Central and South America. Throughout his storied career, he remained a staunch supporter of expansionism (he was a close friend of President Theodore Roosevelt) and expounded on what he believed were America's great Gilded Age hazards: socialism, intemperance, Mormonism, Catholicism, poverty, immigration, and urbanization. Strong died in New York City on April 28, 1916.

PAUL G. PIERPAOLI JR.

See also

Addams, Jane; Churches and the War; Expansionism; Gilded Age; Immigration; Imperialism; Missionaries; Slums; Social Darwinism; Social Gospel Movement; White Man's Burden

Further Reading

Luker, Ralph E. *The Social Gospel in Black and White: American Racial Reform, 1885–1912.* Chapel Hill: University of North Carolina Press, 1998.
Muller, Dorothea R. "Josiah Strong and American Nationalism." *Journal of American History* (December 1966): 487–503.
———. "The Social Philosophy of Josiah Strong: Social Christianity and Progressivism." *Church History* 28(2) (1959): 183–201.
Pratt, Julius W. *Expansionists of 1898: The Acquisition of Hawaii and the Spanish Islands.* Baltimore: Johns Hopkins University Press, 1936.

Subic Bay

An inlet with a relatively narrow harbor located on the western coast of Luzon in the Philippines and about 60 miles northwest of Manila. Subic (Subig) Bay is surrounded by Zambales Province. A small islet, known as Grande Island, is located in the bay, while two towns—Subic and Olongapo City—lie along its shores. At one time, Spanish authorities considered Subic Bay a suitable site for a military installation.

With the commencement of hostilities in the Spanish-American War in April 1898, Commodore George Dewey received information leading him to believe that the Spaniards intended to meet his Asiatic Squadron at Subic Bay. Steaming from Chinese waters, Dewey's squadron made landfall at Cape Bolineau, Luzon, at daybreak on April 30. Dewey detached the cruiser *Boston* and the gunboat *Concord,* later reinforced by the cruiser *Baltimore,* to make a quick reconnaissance of Subic Bay. The Americans did not discover any Spanish warships. Indeed, the commander of the Spanish Philippine Squadron, Rear Admiral Patricio Montojo y Pasarón, had abandoned Subic Bay because of limited maneuvering space and insufficient defenses. His plan of berthing ships behind a string of mines proved impractical, and there were no shore batteries to aid his warships. He therefore moved his ships to Manila Bay, where he was nonetheless roundly defeated by U.S. naval forces on May 1, 1898.

The Americans seized weapons at the town of Subic, and in June, Dewey arranged for their transfer to Filipino rebel leader Emilio Aguinaldo y Famy to aid his insurgency against Spain. The next month, when a German warship stopped Aguinaldo's forces from occupying Grande Island in the bay, Dewey dispatched warships to the scene. They secured the island, and the Germans retired.

During the Philippine-American War, Brigadier General Arthur MacArthur ordered U.S. forces to pursue elements of Aguinaldo's Army of Liberation, withdrawing into the southwestern provinces of Pampanga, Bataan, and Zambales. A U.S. column took Iba in western Luzon and advanced southward, reaching the town of Subic on January 12, 1900. Another column marched to Balanga, Bataan's capital, and then approached the bay. Encountering slight opposition and worried about logistics, U.S. commanders split the southern force into three units. Arriving two days earlier than the northern column, the southern force chased Filipino troops out of Olongapo City by the bay, seizing that place and some weapons.

Dewey wanted the United States to retain Luzon after the war. In the meantime, the United States held Manila and Subic, the latter an excellent site for a coal depot or a military base. Following the U.S. decision to retain the Philippines, in 1901 Henry C. Taylor, a member of the General Board of the Navy, requested an anchorage in the Philippines. Dewey endorsed Subic. He liked its deep harbor, situated between hills and behind an island that provided shelter from seaward assault. Possession of Subic, he believed, guaranteed control of Manila, Luzon, and the entire archipelago. On his urging, the General Board and Secretary of the Navy John D. Long were persuaded to build a naval station at Olongapo City. Olongapo, the panel believed, would be vital in a potential contest with Germany over control of the islands. President Theodore Roosevelt likewise favored a base at Subic and issued an executive order that established the Subic Bay Naval Reservation in November 1901. Soon Subic Bay boasted a significant U.S. Navy and U.S. Marine Corps base and was one of the largest such installations in Asia. Well after the Philippines were granted independence in 1946, the United States maintained its base at Subic Bay, which became home to the U.S. Seventh Fleet. In 1992, however, the United States re-

linquished control of Subic to the Philippine government. The end of the Cold War, the devastating June 1991 eruption of Mount Pinatubo that caused major damage to the base, and the Philippines' desire to be rid of the U.S. presence in the region all conspired to close the base permanently.

RODNEY J. ROSS

See also
Aguinaldo y Famy, Emilio; Asiatic Squadron; Dewey, George; Long, John Davis; MacArthur, Arthur; Montojo y Pasarón, Patricio; Philippine-American War; Philippine Islands; Roosevelt, Theodore; Taylor, Henry Clay; Wood, Leonard

Further Reading
Miller, Edward S. *War Plan Orange: The U.S. Strategy to Defeat Japan, 1897–1945.* Annapolis, MD: Naval Institute Press, 1991.
Musicant, Ivan. *Empire by Default: The Spanish-American War and the Dawn of the American Century.* New York: Henry Holt, 1998.
Trask, David F. *The War with Spain in 1898.* Lincoln: University of Nebraska Press, 1996.

Sugar
See Cuban Sugar

Sumner, Samuel Storrow
Birth Date: February 16, 1842
Death Date: July 26, 1937

U.S. Army officer. Samuel Storrow Sumner was born in Carlisle Barracks, Pennsylvania, on February 16, 1842. His father, Edwin Vose Sumner, also a career army officer, was the oldest corps field commander during the American Civil War. When the Civil War began, the younger Sumner eagerly enlisted and saw action in a number of campaigns. For much of the conflict, he served on his father's staff. Sumner remained in the army after the Civil War. He served in the cavalry during the Indian Wars in the American West, eventually rising to the rank of colonel.

When the Spanish-American War began in April 1898, Sumner was advanced to brigadier general of volunteers. He initially led the 1st Brigade of the Dismounted Cavalry Division in V Corps, the U.S. expeditionary forces sent to Cuba. In Cuba, he fought in the June 24, 1898, Battle of Las Guásimas, considered to be the first true land engagement of the war. In the battle, the Americans suffered fairly heavy casualties of nearly 10 percent in what was a minor Spanish victory.

When Major General Joseph Wheeler was stricken by what is believed to have been yellow fever, command of the entire cavalry division fell to Sumner. Sumner distinguished himself during the Santiago Campaign, especially during the Battle of San Juan Hill on July 1, 1898, when his division performed admirably. In the meantime, Wheeler, who reportedly heard the fighting from his sickbed, mustered all of his strength to assume command of the division

Major General Samuel Storrow Sumner distinguished himself in fighting in Cuba, in the international relief expedition to Beijing, and in the Philippine-American War. (Library of Congress)

before the battle was over. For his own leadership under fire in the battle, Sumner was awarded the Silver Star. He then participated in the siege of Santiago (July 3–17, 1898), the end of which marked the conclusion of the hostilities in Cuba.

For his excellent record, Sumner was advanced to major general of volunteers on September 7, 1898. He then was dispatched to London, where he served as military attaché. After the Boxer Rebellion erupted in China in November 1899, Sumner led a brigade as part of the China Relief Expedition, which had been charged with rescuing and protecting foreign nationalists trapped in the legations in Beijing.

In early 1901, Colonel Sumner arrived in the Philippines to help with American pacification efforts and campaigns against Filipino insurgents. While in the Philippines, he commanded the 1st District, Department of Southern Luzon. He achieved impressive results, carrying out highly successful operations in both Cavite and western Batangas in early 1901. In recognition of his accomplishments, he was advanced to brigadier general in the regular army and entrusted with command of the combined 1st and 2nd Districts of Cavite, Batangas, Laguna, and Tayabas. His efforts helped stamp out resistance in southern Luzon and bring an end to the major fighting by 1902. Nonetheless, the new commander of the Department of Southern Luzon, Major General James P. Wade, refused Sumner the resources he requested, and Sumner's efforts to secure creation of a department of military intelligence met with rejection. The military governor of the Philippines, Major General Adna Chaffee, also appeared to have been predisposed to distrust him and did little to provide assistance.

Sumner retired from the army as a major general in 1906. He died in Brookline, Massachusetts, on July 26, 1937.

Paul G. Pierpaoli Jr.

See also

Boxer Rebellion; Chaffee, Adna Romanza, Sr.; V Corps; Las Guásimas, Battle of; Luzon; Luzon Campaigns; San Juan Heights, Battle of; Santiago de Cuba Land Campaign; Wade, James Franklin; Wheeler, Joseph

Further Reading

Feuer, A. B. *The Santiago Campaign of 1898.* Westport, CT: Praeger, 1993.

Peerson, Marie Graham. *Joseph Wheeler: The Fearless Fightin' Joe.* Birmingham, AL: Seacoast Publishing, 2003.

Silbey, David J. *A War of Frontier and Empire: The Philippine-American War, 1899–1902.* New York: Hill and Wang, 2006.

T

Taft, William Howard
Birth Date: September 15, 1857
Death Date: March 8, 1930

Republican politician, jurist, governor-general of the Philippines (1901–1903), secretary of war (1904–1908), president of the United States (1909–1913), and chief justice of the U.S. Supreme Court (1921–1930). The son of future secretary of war Alphonso Taft, William Howard Taft was born in Cincinnati, Ohio, on September 15, 1857. He graduated from Yale University in 1878 and earned his law degree at Cincinnati Law School in 1880 while helping in his father's unsuccessful campaign for governor of Ohio.

President Chester A. Arthur named the younger Taft district collector of internal revenue in 1882. Opposed to the appointment of new people in his department for purely political reasons, he resigned from the office the next year but remained active in local Republican politics. In 1887, at age 30, he was named to fill a vacancy on the Ohio State Superior Court and then won election for a full term the next year.

In 1890, President Benjamin Harrison appointed Taft U.S. solicitor general, the federal government's attorney before the U.S. Supreme Court. The following year, he was appointed a federal superior court judge. As a federal judge, he strengthened the 1890 Sherman Antitrust Act by becoming the first federal judge to state that laborers had a right to strike, which was a radical departure from past court opinions on the matter.

President William McKinley, elected in 1896, knew that Taft coveted a seat on the U.S. Supreme Court and promised to appoint him if he would serve as the first civilian governor of the newly annexed Philippine Islands. The ambitious Taft agreed and arrived in the Philippines in 1901, planning to leave as soon as possible. In-

stead, he ended up enjoying the job and declined two nomination offers to the Supreme Court by President Theodore Roosevelt.

In the Philippines, Taft soon clashed with Major General Arthur MacArthur, commander of the Division of the Philippines and, until Taft's arrival, military governor of the islands. Taft believed strongly in civilian control. He thought, and with considerable justification, that a reforming civilian administration that would win the support of the Filipino people was more likely to bring about law and order than an autocratic military administration. Nonetheless, he supported strong military action when required. Following disagreements between MacArthur and Taft, MacArthur departed the islands.

In 1902, Taft visited Rome to negotiate with Pope Leo XIII the purchase of Catholic Church lands in the Philippines. Taft then worked to secure a congressional appropriation of $7.239 million to purchase the lands, which were then sold to Filipinos on easy terms. Taft remained as governor-general of the Philippines until 1903 and in the process endeared himself to both Americans and Filipinos.

Roosevelt, a close friend since Taft's days as solicitor general, finally managed to get him to return to Washington by appointing him secretary of war in 1904. In Washington, Taft quickly became Roosevelt's most trusted confidant and adviser. Although Roosevelt secured the nomination of Taft as his political successor at the Republican National Convention in 1908, Taft had reluctantly accepted the honor because he could not be appointed chief justice of the Supreme Court. In truth, he did not aspire to the presidency and hated campaigning. Running on a platform that promised to preserve Roosevelt's progressive programs, Taft beat his Democratic rival, William Jennings Bryan, by more than a million votes. Taft was sworn in as president in March 1909.

Having to serve in the shadow of the immensely popular Roosevelt was perhaps Taft's greatest handicap as president. He knew

William Howard Taft was governor-general of the Philippines during 1901–1903 and a strong advocate of civilian control. He went on to become president of the United States during 1909–1913 and chief justice of the Supreme Court during 1921–1930. (Library of Congress)

that the standard to which he was going to be compared was too high for him to match. Indeed, he wrote to Roosevelt shortly after taking office, "I fear that a large part of the public will feel as if I had fallen away from your ideals. . . . I have not the facility for educating the public as you had through talks with correspondents." Taft spoke the truth. He was awkward in public appearances, was supremely uncomfortable with the press, and, to Roosevelt's horror, seemed far too inclined to kowtow to the interests of the big business establishment.

During his four years in office, Taft managed to obtain a slight lowering of tariff rates with the Payne-Aldrich Tariff, although not as low as Progressive Republicans wanted. He vigorously enforced the Sherman Antitrust Act, initiating 80 antitrusts compared to just 25 in Roosevelt's administration. Taft backed the Mann-Elkins Act, which gave the Interstate Commerce Commission jurisdiction over the communications industry and increased railroad rate-setting powers. In the area of government reform, Taft instituted efficiency measures in the federal government; sponsored the Publicity Act, which opened the lists of campaign contributions in races for the U.S. House of Representatives; brought 9,000 assistant postmasters into the civil service; advocated the 16th Amendment, which authorized a federal income tax; and sup-

ported the 17th Amendment, which provided for the direct popular election of U.S. senators.

Taft's problems with the Progressives in his own party began when he developed a close working relationship with their enemy, the conservative and dictatorial Speaker of the House, Joseph G. Cannon. Taft angered conservationists because he believed that the manner in which Roosevelt had conserved huge tracts of land from development in the West—by placing them in the public domain under the guise of water-power or irrigation sites—had been unconstitutional.

In the foreign policy arena, Taft's secretary of state, Philander Chase Knox, is remembered for creating dollar diplomacy as a policy to further American business interests abroad. This policy was designed to replace Theodore Roosevelt's Big Stick with an equally big U.S. dollar. Knox's efforts to secure a reciprocity treaty with Canada were stymied by Canadian fears of annexation, and opposition in the Senate doomed U.S. agreement to settling international disputes through arbitration at The Hague.

Tired of the burdens of the presidency, Taft agreed to run for a second term in 1912 only to prevent the election of his former friend and now rival for the nomination, Roosevelt. Taft was certain that if elected again, Roosevelt would undermine constitutional government. Needless to say, the two men were now avowed enemies. Roosevelt was deeply offended that Taft had not followed in his progressive footsteps. The split in the Republican Party that resulted when Taft won the nomination along with Roosevelt's decision to run on the Progressive Party ticket ensured the victory of Democrat Woodrow Wilson in 1912.

Thoroughly miserable during his last year as president, Taft had added considerable bulk to his already portly figure, and his health suffered accordingly. He happily returned to private life in 1913 at age 53. During World War I, President Wilson named Taft cochairman of the National War Labor Board. In 1921, President Warren G. Harding appointed Taft to the position he had always wanted more than any other, chief justice of the U.S. Supreme Court.

As chief justice, Taft won congressional support for reforms in the federal judiciary that allowed the Supreme Court to have more discretion in selecting which cases it would hear. He wrote the majority opinion in *Myers v. United States* (1926), a decision that asserted the president's right to remove executive appointees without the advice and consent of the Senate. He was part of a majority that denied Congress the right to use taxes as a weapon to restrict practices it disapproved of, and he helped to limit the powers of states in the regulation of commerce and to enlarge federal powers in the same sphere.

The nine years that Taft spent as chief justice were certainly the happiest of his political career. He died in Washington, D.C., on March 8, 1930, just a month after retiring from the Supreme Court.

PAUL G. PIERPAOLI JR.

See also

Bryan, William Jennings; MacArthur, Arthur; McKinley, William; Roosevelt, Theodore

Further Reading
Anderson, Judith Icke. *William Howard Taft: An Intimate History.* New York: Norton, 1981.
Coletta, Paolo E. *The Presidency of William Howard Taft.* Lawrence: University Press of Kansas, 1973.
Mason, Alpheus T. *William Howard Taft: Chief Justice.* New York: Simon and Schuster, 1965.

Tagalogs

Distinct indigenous population within the Philippine Islands primarily inhabiting the island of Luzon. The Tagalogs comprised one of the five major linguistic groups within the Philippine Islands. Many American military commanders during the Philippine-American War (1899–1902) perceived the Tagalogs to be at the center of leadership of the rebellion against American control of the archipelago. The foremost figure of the insurrection, Emilio Aguinaldo y Famy, was a Tagalog, as were many of the inhabitants of the provinces of Luzon, Cavite, Laguna, Batangas, and Tayabas, the sites of much of the fighting in the early years of the war.

In the 19th century, the Tagalogs derived their livelihood almost entirely from sugar and coffee production, but by the 1880s, prices for both commodities had sharply fallen, devastating the local economy. When U.S. forces arrived in the Philippines in 1898, the Tagalogs were already in rebellion against Spain. Then, following the end of the Spanish-American War in 1898, Aguinaldo and his followers refused to accept rule by a new colonial power and began a war against the United States.

During the Second Battle of Manila (February 4–23, 1899), Filipino nationalists skirmished with American occupation forces. Despite their numerical superiority, Aguinaldo's army, composed almost entirely of Tagalogs, proved powerless to stop American advances into the provinces of Laguna and Cavite. After securing the immediate vicinity of Manila, American troops began a campaign north along the major rail line leading into Manila, moving toward Malolos, the capital of Aguinaldo's Philippine Republic. Following six days of heavy fighting particularly at river crossings and at the cost of 500 American casualties, the insurgent capital fell under U.S. control. Another eight months of harsh fighting occurred during which more than 10,000 Tagalogs died in combat.

On November 13, 1899, Aguinaldo announced a shift to guerrilla war in a vain attempt to prevent American occupation of the islands. He was assisted by Mariano Trias, who commanded guerrillas south of Manila, and Miguel Malvar, who established himself as provincial warlord of Batangas. Aguinaldo's personal resistance ended on March 23, 1901, when he was captured by a small party of Macabebe Scouts led by U.S. Army colonel Frederick Funston. Luzon was pacified by troops under the command of Brigadier General J. Franklin Bell, who employed harsh tactics including crop destruction and so-called protected zones, a euphemism for concentration camps, to contain the Filipinos. Over the course of the conventional war and subsequent guerrilla resistance, more

than 20,000 Tagalogs died. The Tagalog economy, already in tatters by 1898, was virtually destroyed by the fighting.

PAUL J. SPRINGER

See also
Aguinaldo y Famy, Emilio; Bell, James Franklin; Funston, Frederick; Pacification Program, Philippine Islands; Philippine-American War

Further Reading
Linn, Brian McAllister. *The Philippine War, 1899–1902.* Lawrence: University Press of Kansas, 2000.
May, Glenn Anthony. *Battle for Batangas: A Philippine Province at War.* New Haven, CT: Yale University Press, 1991.
Miller, Stuart Creighton. *"Benevolent Assimilation": The American Conquest of the Philippines, 1899–1903.* New Haven, CT: Yale University Press, 1982.

Tampa, Florida

City located on the west-central coast of Florida and the principal mobilization and embarkation point for U.S. troops destined for Cuba. Tampa, strategically located in Hillsborough County along the Gulf of Mexico coast, boasts ample deep-water access for large ships and is bordered by Old Tampa Bay and Hillsborough Bay, which converge to form Tampa Bay. The Hillsborough River flows through the city and into Tampa Bay, offering more deep-water access to the city proper and providing the area with much of its drinking water.

Tampa experienced a major population boom beginning in the 1880s, and by 1898 the city's population numbered some 17,000 people, making it the third largest city in Florida at the time. Enhancing its strategic importance was excellent rail service both into and out of the city courtesy of Henry B. Plant's railroad, which had been completed in 1885. The combination of Tampa's abundant deep-water access, excellent rail lines, and relative proximity to Cuba and Puerto Rico made it a natural embarkation point for U.S. soldiers bound for the Caribbean.

As soon as the United States had declared war on Spain on April 24, 1898, the War Department made preparations to transform Tampa into a huge makeshift U.S. Army base. The influx of what would be some 30,000 troops into the city during the late spring and summer of 1898 proved to be a major boon to the local economy and almost overnight transformed the still-sleepy town into a much larger and more cosmopolitan community.

At the time of the war, Tampa's major industry was the manufacture of cigars. Indeed, it boasted one of the largest outputs of fine cigars of any place in the world. The proximity of Cuban tobacco and the large Cuban émigré community in Tampa virtually ensured the success of this lucrative enterprise. A large Italian émigré community in Tampa also provided many workers for the cigar factories. By 1890, an estimated 150 factories produced a staggering 90 million cigars per year for export.

Long before the war broke out, Tampa had been one of the epicenters of support for the Cuban independence movement. Indeed,

Cuban revolutionary José Martí y Pérez visited the area and in 1891 gave a famous speech there concerning the Cuban revolutionary movement. He also drafted the resolutions that would form the basis of the Cuban Revolutionary Party in Tampa.

To accommodate the mass influx of U.S. soldiers, army officials created seven camps in and around Tampa that would serve as temporary housing for the troops. The camps were set up in DeSoto Park, Fort Brooke, Palmetto Beach, Port Tampa, Tampa Heights, Ybor City, and West Tampa. The Tampa Bay Hotel, a fine and modern facility, served as the headquarters for the Cuban expeditionary force commanders. Among those who stayed at the hotel was Lieutenant Colonel Theodore Roosevelt, whose Rough Riders unit passed through Tampa on its way to Cuba. The hotel also served as a makeshift headquarters for journalists covering the war. Most of the soldiers departed Tampa for Cuba on June 7, 1898, but the ships then anchored in Tampa Bay under a hot June sun for several days before the U.S. Navy received word that it was safe for the ships to proceed.

By war's end, a total of 66,000 U.S. troops had moved through Tampa, while 13,000 railcars carrying ammunition, food, and medical supplies had been unloaded in the city. It is estimated that in less than a year, the U.S. government expended $4 million in Florida to support the war effort, the majority of which was spent in Tampa. This massive amount of economic activity transformed Tampa from a relatively small and unimportant town to a large city with considerable importance in Florida and the southeastern United States. The Spanish-American War also marked the beginning of a huge population increase in the area. Tampa's population mushroomed from some 17,000 in 1900 to 37,700 in 1910.

PAUL G. PIERPAOLI JR.

See also

Cuban Revolutionary Party; Martí y Pérez, José Julián; Roosevelt, Theodore; Rough Riders

Further Reading

De Quesada, Alejandro M. *The Spanish-American War in Tampa Bay.* Mount Pleasant, SC: Arcadia, 1998.

Dunn, Hampton. *Tampa: A Pictorial History.* 2nd ed. Virginia Beach, VA: Donning, 1995.

Tampa Tribune. *Tampa and West Central Florida: Portrait of a Community.* Tampa: University of Tampa Press, 1995.

Taussig, Edward David
Birth Date: November 10, 1847
Death Date: January 29, 1921

U.S. Navy officer. Edward David Taussig was born in St. Louis, Missouri, on November 10, 1847. Appointed to the United States Naval Academy as a midshipman on July 24, 1863, he graduated in June 1867 and was commissioned an ensign on December 18, 1868. He saw service at sea in Latin American waters in the gunboat *Wateree.* He was decorated for his actions aboard that ship when it was

Rear Admiral Edward David Taussig. During the Spanish-American War, Commander Taussig claimed Wake Island for the United States. In 1899 he also served as governor of Guam. (Naval Historical Center)

driven some distance on land as a consequence of an earthquake and tidal wave at Arica, then part of Peru, on August 13, 1868.

Taussig was promoted to master on March 21, 1870, and to lieutenant on January 1, 1872. He then saw service aboard the receiving ship *Relief* and then on the screw frigate *Trenton,* flagship of the European Squadron. He was next assigned to survey duty and was promoted to lieutenant commander on June 19, 1892. In 1895, he assumed command of the receiving ship *Richmond.* He then served in the Hydrographic Office and the U.S. Coast Survey.

Promoted to commander on August 10, 1898, Taussig assumed command of the gunboat *Bennington.* In December, he received orders to steam to Wake Island, between Midway Island and Guam, and claim it for the United States. He arrived there on January 17, 1899. The island, which was then uninhabited, had also been claimed by the German government as part of the Marshall Island chain, but Taussig established U.S. control. The island proved useful as a cable station between Hawaii and the Philippines.

On February 1, 1899, Taussig retook the island of Guam for the United States. He set up a local government on the island and served as its governor for some months. On September 1, 1899, he was relieved of command for his criticism of Admiral John C. Watson. Assigned to the Lighthouse Bureau, in 1902 Taussig again received command of a ship, the school ship *Enterprise* at Boston, and subsequently commanded the battleship *Indiana.* He also attended the Naval War College and commanded the Norfolk

Navy Yard and the Fifth Naval District. In May 1908, he was advanced to rear admiral.

Taussig retired in November 1909. He was recalled to active duty during World War I as commandant of the Naval Unit at Columbia University, New York. Taussig died in Newport, Rhode Island, on January 29, 1921. The destroyer *Taussig* (DD 746) was named for him. Taussig's son, Joseph Taussig, was also a U.S. Navy officer who earned distinction in World War I and retired as a vice admiral.

SPENCER C. TUCKER

See also
Guam

Further Reading
Callahan, Edward W., ed. *List of Officers of the Navy of the United States and the Marine Corps from 1775 to 1900.* 1901; reprint, New York: Haskell House, 1969.

Trask, David F. *The War with Spain in 1898.* Lincoln: University of Nebraska Press, 1981.

Taussig, Joseph Knefler
Birth Date: August 30, 1877
Death Date: October 29, 1947

U.S. Navy officer. Joseph Knefler Taussig was born in Dresden, Germany, on August 30, 1877. His father was a U.S. Navy officer serving in the European Squadron who rose to rear admiral and took possession of Wake Island during the Spanish-American War. The younger Taussig graduated from Western High School in Washington, D.C., and from the United States Naval Academy, Annapolis, in 1899. Midshipman Taussig served the required two years at sea during the Spanish-American War and took part in the July 3, 1898, Battle of Santiago de Cuba aboard the flagship, the battleship *New York.*

Taussig served in the Philippines during the Philippine-American War and in China during the Boxer Rebellion (1899–1901), where he was seriously wounded in fighting in June 1900 as the Allied Expeditionary Force ended the siege of the foreign legations in Beijing. He also served in Cuba.

In July 1916, Commander Taussig took command of Division 8, and on April 13, 1917, shortly after the U.S. declaration of war against Germany, he was ordered to prepare his ships for special service. The destroyers departed from Boston for Ireland on April 24 with the mission of assisting naval operations of Entente powers in whatever way possible. They were the first U.S. warships sent to Europe in the war. The destroyers were warmly received at Queenstown following a difficult nine-day Atlantic crossing in gale conditions. The event was immortalized in a painting by Bernard Gribble titled *The Return of the Mayflower.* British commander in chief of the coasts of Ireland Vice Admiral Sir Lewis Bayly asked when the American ships would again be ready for sea. Taussig's

reply entered U.S. Navy lore: "We are ready now, sir, that is as soon as we finish refueling."

Many in the navy marked Taussig as destined for high command. It was not to be, in large part because of a sharp quarrel with Assistant Secretary of the Navy Franklin D. Roosevelt over the latter's desire to improve conditions in naval prisons and for naval trainees. The dispute surfaced in 1920 when Captain Taussig was director of enlisted personnel. Taussig, who disagreed with the planned changes, was relieved of his assignment at his own request and sent to the Naval War College at Newport, Rhode Island. There he read an unsigned article in the *Army and Navy Journal* approving the reforms, and he penned a scathing rebuttal. It turned out that Roosevelt had written the article. Correctly believing his career to be in jeopardy and following unsuccessful efforts to resolve the dispute, Taussig requested but did not receive a court of inquiry.

Taussig remained at the Naval War College after graduation in 1920 except for three years in sea commands. In 1922, his ship, the cruiser *Cleveland,* rendered assistance to victims of an earthquake in Chile. Promoted to rear admiral in 1931, he commanded the battleship *Maryland* and then became chief of staff to the commander of the Battle Fleet and to the commander in chief of the United States Fleet. From 1933 to 1936, Taussig was assistant chief of naval operations. Roosevelt was then president, and after 1936 Taussig did not hold major posts.

From 1938 to 1941, Taussig was commandant of the Fifth Naval District at Norfolk, Virginia. Always outspoken, on April 22, 1940, he testified before a joint House-Senate committee hearing on Pacific fortifications and predicted that events in the Far East would bring war with Japan. His testimony created a considerable stir and led the navy to repudiate his remarks and issue a letter of reprimand, which was rescinded by presidential order on December 8, 1941.

Taussig left the navy at the end of August 1941 at the mandatory retirement age of 64. He was promoted to vice admiral simultaneous with retirement. Recalled to active duty in 1943, he was chairman of the Clemency and Prison Inspection Board during 1943–1946. Although he never made it to the top of the naval hierarchy, he was influential, especially through numerous articles he wrote in *The United States Naval Institute Proceedings.* One of these articles, a 1939 prize essay, recommended the creation of task fleets, a practice adopted by the navy in World War II. Taussig died on October 29, 1947, at the U.S. Naval Hospital in Bethesda, Maryland.

SPENCER C. TUCKER

See also
United States Navy

Further Reading
Freidel, Frank. *Franklin D. Roosevelt: The Ordeal.* Boston: Little, Brown, 1954.

Halpern, Paul G. *A Naval History of World War I.* Annapolis, MD: Naval Institute Press, 1994.

Taylor, Henry Clay
Birth Date: March 4, 1845
Death Date: July 26, 1904

U.S. naval officer. Henry Clay Taylor was born on March 4, 1845, in Washington, D.C. In September 1860, at age 15, he enrolled at the United States Naval Academy, Annapolis. Because of the great demand for naval officers during the American Civil War (1861–1865), Taylor's class was accelerated, and he graduated in 1863. On May 25, he was commissioned an ensign and assigned to the steam sloop *Shenandoah* in the North Atlantic Blockade Squadron. The following year, he transferred to the sloop-of-war *Iroquois.* His tour on the *Iroquois* included duty in the Mediterranean Sea and featured a hunt for Confederate commerce raiders. Taylor continued in the navy after the end of the Civil War in 1865.

During 1866–1867, Taylor served aboard the side-wheel steamer *Rhode Island,* attached to the North Atlantic Squadron. During 1867–1868, he served on the side-wheel frigate *Susquehanna* before he was transferred to the European Squadron aboard the storeship *Guard* until 1869. Over the next decade, he served in a variety of capacities, some at sea and some on shore. From 1869 to 1871, he was an instructor at Annapolis. During 1872, he was the executive officer aboard the side-wheel frigate *Saranac,* which saw duty in the Pacific Squadron. During 1874–1877, Taylor, now a lieutenant commander, commanded the *Hassler,* a steamer attached to the Coast Survey. He then served a short time at the Hydrographic Office in early 1878 before being transferred to Washington Navy Yard, where he was promoted to commander in late 1879. The next year, he commanded the sailing sloop *Saratoga.* He served in several other capacities until 1888, at which time he took a leave of absence.

In 1890, Taylor returned to active duty as commanding officer of the wooden screw sloop *Alliance,* part of the Asiatic Squadron. In September 1891, he took another leave of absence but returned to active duty 15 months later. In 1893, he assumed the presidency of the Navy War College in Newport, Rhode Island. While he was at Newport, the cerebral Taylor developed a war plan in the event of a war with Spain. The plan featured a preemptive move against the Spanish in the Philippines.

In April 1894, Taylor was promoted to captain and was later given command of the *Indianapolis* (also known as Battleship 1), the U.S. Navy's first modern battleship, commissioned in 1895 and first commanded by Taylor's brother-in-law, Captain Robley D. Evans. The battleship was assigned to Rear Admiral William T. Sampson's North American Squadron and took part in the May 1898 bombardment of San Juan, Puerto Rico, at the beginning of the Spanish-American War. The following month, Taylor oversaw the naval convoy that transported V Corps from Tampa, Florida, to Santiago de Cuba. On July 3, 1898, the *Indianapolis* participated in the Battle of Santiago de Cuba and the destruction of Spanish rear admiral Pascual Cervera y Topete's Caribbean Squadron.

Taylor continued in command of the *Indianapolis* through the end of the war and was transferred to shore duty in early 1900. That

Rear Admiral Henry Clay Taylor. As a captain during the Spanish-American War, Taylor commanded the first true modern U.S. battleship, the *Indiana.* (Library of Congress)

March, he was appointed to the navy's General Board, designed to serve as an advisory body to the secretary of the navy. In February 1901, Taylor was advanced to rear admiral, and in April 1902, he became chief of the Bureau of Navigation, a post he held until his death on July 26, 1904, in Ontario, Canada.

PAUL G. PIERPAOLI JR.

See also

Cervera y Topete, Pascual; Evans, Robley Dunglison; V Corps; San Juan, Puerto Rico, Naval Bombardment of; Santiago de Cuba, Battle of; United States Navy

Further Reading

Feuer, A. B. *The Spanish-American War at Sea: Naval Action in the Atlantic.* Westport, CT: Praeger, 1995.
Trask, David F. *The War with Spain in 1898.* Lincoln: University of Nebraska Press, 1996.

Telephone and Telegraph

The telegraph and telephone played prominent roles in the Spanish-American War. The U.S. Army's Signal Corps was responsible for the telegraph and telephone wire lines utilized by the military during the war. Eventually, the Signal Corps set up a nationalized telegraph system, improved field telegraphs, and new telephones to provide rapid communication between the War Department and field telephone stations on the front lines in Cuba.

Beginning with the invention of the telegraph in 1844 by Samuel Morse, messages traveled at near-instantaneous speeds over incredible distances. Presidents and government officials alike were quick to take advantage of this new invention. By the beginning of the American Civil War in 1861, President Abraham Lincoln, utilizing the telegraph, could communicate with his army commanders in St. Louis within an hour. Communications with troops in the field were less swift, however, because they were often away from telegraph lines or because the lines were cut by raiders. However, Lincoln was able to exert far more immediate influence over the conduct of his armies than he otherwise could have.

The telegraph also revolutionized international relations. In 1865, a transatlantic telegraph cable was laid that allowed instant communications between New York and London. Other cables carried messages to the rest of Europe.

After the invention of the telephone in 1876, that instrument supplemented and soon began to replace the telegraph. The telephone's popularity was almost immediate, and by December 1878 a telephone had been installed in the White House. The first telephone in the White House, using the single-digit phone number "1," had been installed on the orders of President Rutherford B. Hayes. As with messages sent by telegraph, telephone communications were limited to those areas connected by communications lines to them.

By 1898 and the Spanish-American War, much of the United States was crisscrossed by telephone lines. While only a few homes had telephones, many businesses and government offices used them daily. Direct conversations at a distance between leaders often impacted how decisions were made and carried out.

As commander in chief, President William McKinley also enjoyed unprecedented communication from the White House with commanders in the field as well as American diplomats abroad. For the first time in U.S. history, the White House rather than the War Department served as the key communications hub in wartime. Indeed, McKinley's effective and extensive use of the telephone and telegraph made him the first modern president in terms of communication.

McKinley greatly expanded the telegraph and telephone system in the White House during his presidency. After taking office in March 1897, he had 15 telephone lines installed in the White House, connecting him to the House of Representatives, the Senate, and eight executive departments. Unlike his successor, Theodore Roosevelt, McKinley preferred to give oral rather than written orders and made maximum use of the telephone to communicate his orders.

When the *Maine* exploded in Havana Harbor on February 15, 1898, McKinley was quickly informed, receiving a call at 3:00 a.m. thanks to an underwater telegraph cable from Cuba. The explosion

Men of the U.S. Army Signal Corps setting up telegraph poles in the Philippines, 1898. (Library of Congress)

escalated tensions between the United States and Spain, and during the next two months McKinley used the telegraph and telephone to search for a peaceful solution to the crisis. Ambassadors in Europe received coded telegrams from Washington and could reply within a few hours. When considering war or further negotiations with Spain, McKinley no longer had to wait for ships to bring the latest information.

When war was declared against Spain on April 25, 1898, McKinley immediately recognized the need for a central clearinghouse for intelligence and operational matters. During the American Civil War, Lincoln often walked next door to the War Department and read the telegrams being sent to the secretary of war and the commanding general. This procedure was inconvenient and left the president out of the decision-making loop. The army and navy had their own intelligence units, but the methods of sharing information with the president remained primitive. When coupled with the fact that the strategy for fighting the Spanish was still developing, McKinley became determined to establish his own center for keeping up on the war.

The first telegraph office in the White House had been installed in 1866 during the presidency of Andrew Johnson. By 1898, there were 20 telegraph wires in the White House connecting the United States to the Caribbean. At the beginning of the Spanish-American War in April 1898, McKinley established a telegraph office on the second floor of the White House to be used solely for war-related communications. The room housing the telegraph office was quickly dubbed the War Room by McKinley's assistants and was the precursor to the current White House Situation Room. The War

Personnel in the White House war room, Washington, D.C., 1898. (Library of Congress)

Room was constantly monitored, and McKinley frequently went there to obtain the most current information on the development of the war against Spain. In constant contact with army and navy officials, McKinley was able to direct the war and chart the war's progress on wall maps in the War Room.

In April 1898, McKinley gave orders to convert a room in the southeast corner of the White House, on the second floor, into a war room or, as McKinley called it, the Operating Room. Formerly known as the Lincoln Sitting Room, the room was part of the family living quarters in the White House. By McKinley's orders, 15 telephone lines were installed, which allowed him to talk to congressmen and department heads in Washington to coordinate policies and invite suggestions. He also ordered 26 telegraph lines installed in the room. The telegraphs permitted McKinley to communicate with virtually any part of the United States. They also brought in information from overseas thanks to transoceanic cables.

To help McKinley function as commander in chief, other equipment was also provided for his war room. Maps were installed on

the walls because for the first time since the Mexican-American War (1846–1848), the United States was fighting a foreign enemy. And because Spanish possessions stretched from the Caribbean to the eastern Pacific, McKinley was directing a two-ocean war. The maps indicated the current situation in each theater, with pins representing ships and troops. Movements were immediately noted on the maps thanks to the information provided by the telephones and telegraphs. McKinley could query commanders about developments or order certain actions with a degree of confidence. The other equipment in the room included desks, typewriters for correspondence, and an early version of a dictating machine. McKinley sometimes used the latter to send orders to nearby departments. A former executive clerk in the White House who was now a lieutenant colonel in the volunteers, Benjamin F. Montgomery, supervised the war room. He recorded all messages in a diary and brought urgent ones to the president's immediate attention. The room was constantly staffed, but its activities remained cloaked in secrecy.

The Operating Room worked well. When American forces landed in Cuba outside Santiago, engineers located the Anglo-French underwater cable between Cuba and Florida. They tied into it and ran a line directly to Major General William Rufus Shafter's headquarters. When all worked as it should, McKinley's messages to his general would be received within 20 minutes. Later when a truce was negotiated in Cuba, the president and Secretary of War Russell Alger could let their military leaders know what was acceptable as they negotiated the particulars with Spanish generals in the field. Other moves, such as ordering occupation troops to the Philippines, were also made possible by the improved communications of the war room.

The war did reveal the danger of wire-based signal systems, however. Commodore George Dewey's decision to cut the Spanish cable between Manila and Hong Kong had the unintended consequence of delaying the arrival of news of the cease-fire protocol that might have rendered unnecessary the First Battle of Manila (August 13, 1898).

Shortly after the war, the Signal Corps implemented the Washington-Alaska Military Cable and Telegraph System, which became the first wireless telegraph in the Western Hemisphere. At a time when telephones were still considered a luxury, the federal government imposed a 1 percent tax, eventually raised to 3 percent, on all long-distance phone calls to help fund the war. Although the war ended in 1898, the federal tax on long distance calls remained in effect until 2006.

MICHAEL R. HALL AND TIM J. WATTS

See also

Alger, Russell Alexander; *Maine,* USS; McKinley, William; War Department, U.S.

Further Reading

Andrew, Christopher M. *For the President's Eyes Only: Secret Intelligence and the American Presidency from Washington to Bush.* New York: HarperCollins, 1995.
Gould, Lewis L. *The Modern American Presidency.* Lawrence: University Press of Kansas, 2003.
———. *The Presidency of William McKinley.* Lawrence: University Press of Kansas, 1981.

Teller, Henry Moore
Birth Date: May 23, 1830
Death Date: February 23, 1914

Influential Colorado politician, U.S. senator (1876–1882, 1885–1909), secretary of the interior (1882–1885), and author of the 1898 Teller Amendment. Henry Moore Teller was born on his family's farm in Allegany County, New York, on May 23, 1830. He attended school only intermittently between farming chores and thus received only a limited education. He later attended academies at Rushford and Alfred, New York. After completing his studies and working for a short period as a teacher, he moved to Angelica, New

U.S. senator Henry Moore Teller was the sponsor of the Teller Amendment of April 19, 1898. The amendment stated that while the United States was willing to use force to end Spanish rule in Cuba, it disclaimed any intent to exercise sovereignty over the island. (Library of Congress)

York, where he read law and was admitted to the New York bar in 1858.

Looking for new opportunities, Teller headed west, first settling in Morrison, Illinois, for three years and finally in Central City, Colorado, in 1861. There he learned the complexities of mining law and served for a time as a major general commanding the Colorado militia, defending Denver from potential Native American attacks. He became one of the leading politicians in Colorado after the American Civil War. He was also a key player in the fight for Colorado statehood following the war and served as president of the Colorado Central Railroad during 1872–1876.

When Colorado was admitted to the Union in 1876, Teller was elected by the state legislature as one of the state's first two U.S. senators. A Republican, he served until 1882, speaking on behalf of western interests and advocating the free coinage of silver. In April 1882, President Chester Arthur named Teller secretary of the interior, replacing the outgoing Samuel Kirkwood. While secretary, Teller established a Court of Indian Offenses to have Native American magistrates judge other Native Americans, urged repeal of the ineffective Timber Culture Act and other related laws, and became embroiled in a scandal involving a railroad land claim that he attempted to grant. His tenure was considered a successful one, however, and he left the post in 1885 with the change in administrations.

The Colorado legislature returned Teller to the U.S. Senate in 1885. He joined with fellow Colorado legislators John C. Bell, John Shafroth, and Edward Wolcott to stymie President Grover Cleveland's attempt to create forestry reserves in 1893. Teller was also a firm supporter of the Pettigrew Act that arose out of the controversy.

Although a conservative Republican, Teller bolted the party in 1896 over the issue of the free coinage of silver and became a founding member of the short-lived Silver Republican Party. Following that group's demise, he switched party affiliation and became a Democrat and remained such for the rest of his political career. During his tenure in the Senate, he served on such committees as Mining and Mines, Public Lands, and Patents.

Teller is most remembered for the landmark Teller Amendment. The amendment was successfully added to the April 19, 1898, Joint Resolution of Congress that authorized President William McKinley to take military action against Spain. Teller's amendment made it clear that the United States supported Cuban independence and would maintain a presence on the island until it was entirely pacified. But the amendment specifically declared that the United States had no long-term claims of sovereignty or jurisdiction over Cuba. The Teller Amendment was subsequently superseded by the 1901 Platt Amendment.

Teller's last years in the Senate were spent on the problems of land distribution, reclamation, and Indian affairs. He retired from the Senate in 1909, served until 1912 as a member of the National Monetary Commission, and then retired to Colorado. Teller died in Denver, Colorado, on February 23, 1914.

PAUL G. PIERPAOLI JR.

See also

Cuba, U.S. Occupation of; Platt Amendment; Silver Standard; Teller Amendment

Further Reading

Ellis, Elmer. *Henry Moore Teller, Defender of the West.* Caldwell, ID: Caxton Printers, 1941.

Smith, Duane A. *Henry M. Teller: Colorado's Grand Old Man.* Boulder: University Press of Colorado, 2002.

Teller Amendment

Sponsored by Democratic senator Henry Moore Teller of Colorado, the Teller Amendment was passed on April 19, 1898, as part of the joint congressional resolution authorizing President William McKinley to take military action against Spanish forces in Cuba and in the other Spanish possessions. McKinley signed the resolution the following day.

The Teller Amendment was a manifestation of both American idealism and ambivalence concerning expansion outside the continental United States on the eve of the Spanish-American War, especially in regard to Cuba. With the authority to take military action in hand, McKinley forwarded an ultimatum to Spain threatening war if Spain did not yield to American demands concerning the unrest in Cuba.

Essentially, the Teller Amendment gave a veneer of altruism to American military endeavors on the island. The amendment stated that the United States was willing to use force to settle the crisis and end Spanish rule on the island but disclaimed any intent to exercise sovereignty, jurisdiction, or control over Cuba "except for the pacification thereof." It also asserted sole U.S. determination as to when that pacification was accomplished so as to "leave the government and control of the island to its people." True to the letter of the amendment, American troops occupied Cuba until 1902, four years after Spain's withdrawal.

Senator Teller's measure grew out of a fierce debate in both the Senate and the House of Representatives over how far the United States should go in supporting Cuban independence following McKinley's April 11 war message to Congress. The amendment represented a compromise between the president, who opposed granting immediate independence, and elements in Congress who wanted immediate recognition of Cuban independence and support of the Cuban insurgents as the governing authority on the island (as voiced in an amendment sponsored by Democratic senator David Turpie of Indiana and Republican senator Joseph Foraker of Ohio). Many congressmen and senators feared that without recognition of some governing authority in Cuba, McKinley was simply priming the island for outright annexation. The president, on the other hand, sought to keep control of Cuban policy in his own hands. He was unsure of the form that an insurgent government might take and strongly believed that the Cuban rebels were incapable of governing the island on their own.

Senator Teller had been a longtime supporter of Cuban independence, but his previous efforts to gain congressional and presidential support for the Cuban insurgents had repeatedly failed. Congressional adoption of his amendment therefore reflected the contradictory currents in American thinking about Cuba. Although public opinion and most leading politicians wished to see Cuba free from Spain's control, no consensus existed on how far the United States should go in asserting its control over the island. Some support for outright annexation of Cuba as a U.S. territory had existed throughout the 19th century, but this had been based mainly on economic considerations. In 1898, opposition to Cuban annexation was widespread for a variety of reasons, racial, cultural, and economic.

By what it did not say, the Teller Amendment also illustrated the limits of American altruism. Its provisions did not apply to other Spanish possessions, such as Puerto Rico, Guam, and the Philippines. And although the amendment precluded direct annexation of Cuba, it did not prevent the establishment of an American protectorate over the island, the acquisition of a naval base at Guantánamo Bay, or the economic domination of the island by American corporations. Indeed, these came to fruition, and until the Communist Revolution in Cuba in 1959, the United States exercised great economic influence in the island nation.

Nor did the amendment prevent further American intervention in Cuban politics. In 1901, the Platt Amendment sponsored by Republican senator Orville Platt of Connecticut superseded the Teller Amendment. Passed in February 1901 as part of the U.S. Army appropriations bill, Platt's measure allowed the United States the right to intervene in Cuba "for the preservation of Cuban independence" and "the maintenance of a government adequate for the protection of life, property, and individual liberty." Taken together, the Teller Amendment and the Platt Amendment cleared the way for continuing American interference in Cuban politics that left a legacy of resentment among the island's people, which had far-reaching consequences when Fidel Castro seized power in 1959.

WALTER F. BELL

See also

Colonial Policies, U.S.; Cuba; Cuba, Spanish Colonial Policies toward; Cuba, U.S. Occupation of; Expansionism; Foraker Amendment; Imperialism; Legacy of the War; McKinley, William; Platt Amendment; Teller, Henry Moore

Further Reading

Gould, Lewis L. *The Spanish-American War and President McKinley.* Lawrence: University Press of Kansas, 1982.

Holbo, Paul S. "Presidential Leadership in Foreign Affairs: William McKinley and the Turpie-Foraker Amendment." *American Historical Review* 72(4) (July 1967): 1321–1335.

McCartney, Paul T. *Power and Progress: American National Identity, the War of 1898, and the Rise of American Imperialism.* Baton Rouge: Louisiana State University Press, 2006.

Morgan, H. Wayne. *William McKinley and His America.* Syracuse, NY: Syracuse University Press, 1963.

Ten Years' War
Start Date: October 10, 1868
End Date: May 28, 1878

The first in a series of three wars of Cuban independence during the 19th century. The Ten Years' War set the stage for the Little War (1879–1880) and the Cuban War of Independence (1895–1898) that directly contributed to U.S. intervention in Cuba's internal affairs and the Spanish-American War in 1898.

Following the overthrow of Spain's Queen Isabella II in September 1868, Carlos Manuel de Céspedes, a wealthy plantation owner in eastern Cuba, became belligerent over Spanish rule and especially increased taxes and the lack of local autonomy. On October 8, the Spanish governor-general of Cuba, learning that Céspedes was plotting rebellion, sent a telegram to the provincial governor ordering Céspedes's arrest. The telegraph clerk was a member of Céspedes's extended family, however, and warned the would-be revolutionary, who then launched a preemptive strike against the Spanish authorities. The Ten Years' War began on October 10, 1868, when Céspedes rang the slave bell on his plantation in eastern Cuba. Once the slaves were assembled, he announced their freedom (and conscription into his revolutionary army) and proclaimed Cuban independence from Spain.

On October 11, Céspedes and a small band of supporters attacked the nearby town of Yara. Although the attack was a failure, the event, commonly known as the Grito de Yara (Shout of Yara), unleashed a war of independence and a slave revolt. The revolutionary spirit quickly spread throughout the eastern half of Cuba. By the end of the year, the rebellion counted more than 10,000 revolutionaries, many of them former slaves. Indeed, for many revolutionaries, emancipation was as important as the liberation of the island. Hoping to win the support of plantation owners in the western half of the island, Céspedes, who preferred gradual emancipation, proclaimed the death penalty for any revolutionary who attacked sugar estates or slave property. In addition, Céspedes favored independence as a prelude to annexation to the United States, a concept that many nationalists found repulsive.

Following the Grito de Yara, Céspedes organized a provisional government. On October 20, 1868, the revolutionaries captured Bayamo, which became the seat of the new government. They held that city until January 11, 1869, when, faced with a superior Spanish force, the revolutionaries burned Bayamo to the ground rather than surrender. Although the revolutionary forces enjoyed moderate success in the countryside, they were unable to capture many cities and towns in the eastern half of the island.

On April 10, 1869, a constitutional assembly convened in Guáimaro. Céspedes was elected president, while Ignacio Agramonte and Antonio Zambrana were elected its secretaries and charged with writing the constitution. Two days later, the assembly transformed itself into the Congress of Representatives. Céspedes was elected president, and his brother-in-law Manuel de Quesada was named the first chief of the armed forces.

In May 1869, Céspedes petitioned the U.S. government for diplomatic recognition. Washington, however, refused to recognize the Céspedes government. The Ulysses S. Grant administration, which was primarily focusing on Reconstruction, feared that recognition of the Cuban rebels would undermine its legal case seeking economic damages from the United Kingdom, which had recognized the belligerency of the Confederate States of America in 1861. In addition, U.S. recognition of the Cuban rebels would absolve Spain from responsibility for damages to American property in Cuba inflicted by Cuban revolutionaries.

Regardless of the official position, many U.S. citizens and officials were openly sympathetic toward the revolutionary cause. In 1870, Quesada, with the collusion of American John Patterson, who was sympathetic to the Cuban rebels, purchased the *Virginius*. This former Confederate blockade runner had been captured by Union forces at the end of the American Civil War.

Flying an American flag and nominally owned by Patterson, the *Virginius* was employed to supply the Cuban revolutionaries with weapons and other matériel. On October 31, 1873, however, the Spanish warship *Tornado* captured the *Virginius* off the coast of

Illustration depicting Spanish volunteers landing in Havana, Cuba, in 1869 during the Ten Years' War of 1868–1878. (Library of Congress)

Jamaica and took the ship to Santiago, Cuba. In early November, following Spanish legal proceedings, 53 men from the *Virginius*, many of them Americans, were executed as pirates. The event, which was well publicized in American newspapers, brought the United States and Spain to the brink of war. Tensions were reduced, however, after the Spanish government promised to pay an indemnity to the families of the executed Americans.

During the revolutionary struggle, Dominican-born Máximo Gómez taught the revolutionary forces, known as Mambi warriors, how to employ the machete against Spanish troops. Although this weapon proved to be quite useful against the Spanish troops, more Spanish soldiers died of disease, primarily yellow fever, than in battle. Nevertheless, by 1873, neither the Spanish nor the revolutionary forces were able to achieve any notable victories. The Spanish had constructed fortifications across the province of Camagüey, which effectively divided the island in half. Céspedes's inability to expand the war into the prosperous western half of the island cost him support. On October 27, 1873, the Congress of Representatives removed Céspedes from power, and Salvador Cisneros became president.

In 1875, Gómez launched an unsuccessful invasion of the western half of the island. The majority of the plantation owners in western Cuba refused to support the revolution. Most of the fighting during the war was therefore confined to the eastern half of the island. Rebels destroyed loyalist plantations, and Spanish troops destroyed insurgent plantations.

Meanwhile, the end of the Third Carlist War (1872–1876) in Spain and the restoration of the Bourbons to the Spanish Crown allowed the Spanish government to dedicate greater resources to fighting the Cuban rebellion. By the end of 1876, King Alfonso XII had sent 100,000 troops to Cuba. On October 19, 1877, Spanish troops captured Cuban president Tomás Estrada Palma. In February 1878 as a result of repeated military misfortunes, the Congress of Representatives opened peace negotiations with Spain. On February 10, 1878, the Cuban revolutionaries signed the Pact of Zanjón, which effectively ended the Ten Years' War.

Spain promised numerous administrative and political reforms in Cuba. All revolutionaries were granted amnesty, and former slaves who served in the revolutionary army were granted their unconditional freedom. Revolutionary general Antonio Maceo Grajales, however, demanded complete emancipation and continued fighting for 10 more weeks, until May 28, 1878. Ultimately, the failure of the Spanish government to fulfill its promise of reform eventually led to the Little War in 1879.

MICHAEL R. HALL

See also

Alfonso XII, King of Spain; Céspedes y del Castillo, Carlos Manuel de; Cuba, Spanish Colonial Policies toward; Estrada Palma, Tomás; Gómez y Báez, Máximo; Spain; *Virginius* Affair

Further Reading

Bradford, Richard H. *The Virginius Affair.* Boulder, CO: Colorado Associated University Press, 1980.

Ferrer, Ada. *Insurgent Cuba: Race, Nation, and Revolution, 1868–1898.* Chapel Hill: University of North Carolina Press, 1999.

Knight, Franklin. *Slave Society in Cuba during the Nineteenth Century.* Madison: University of Wisconsin Press, 1970.

Pérez, Louis A., Jr. *Cuba: Between Reform and Revolution.* New York: Oxford University Press USA, 2006.

Tenerife, Marqués de

See Weyler y Nicolau, Valeriano

Thompson, John Taliaferro
Birth Date: December 31, 1860
Death Date: June 21, 1940

U.S. Army officer and weapons and ordnance designer who is perhaps best known for his development of the Thompson submachine gun. John Taliaferro Thompson was born in Newport, Kentucky, on December 31, 1860, the son of a career army officer. Thompson attended Indiana University during 1876–1877. He then entered the United States Military Academy, West Point, and graduated 11th in his class in 1882 and was commissioned a second lieutenant in the artillery.

Almost immediately, Thompson took a keen interest in weapons, ordnance, and ballistics. He held a number of routine assignments throughout the 1880s. Promoted to first lieutenant in 1889, he graduated from the Artillery School in 1890 and was posted to the U.S. Army Ordnance Department, where he remained for the rest of his military career. Within a year, he had begun research efforts in the area of small arms and ammunition. From 1896 to 1898, he was posted to West Point as senior assistant instructor of ordnance and gunnery. He was promoted to captain in 1898.

During the Spanish-American War, Thompson first earned high praise for his supervision of munitions supplies to U.S. forces in Cuba. When war was declared in April 1898, he was advanced to the rank of lieutenant colonel of volunteers and ordered to Tampa, Florida, the main embarkation point for U.S. troops and supplies bound for the Caribbean. Once there, he was immediately named chief ordnance officer for V Corps, commanded by Major General William R. Shafter and the invasion force destined for Cuba. At a time in which the army was experiencing significant supply problems, Thompson helped ensure the flow of ordnance to Cuba. Indeed, nearly 18,000 tons of weapons and ordnance were dispatched to Cuba with virtually no delays or other problems. During the brief

John Taliaferro Thompson, prominent American arms designer, who invented the Thompson submachine gun. The term "tommy gun" originated with this weapon. (Bettmann/Corbis)

war, Thompson also helped to establish an informal Gatling gun unit. Equipped with 15 Gatling guns, the unit played a key role in the July 1, 1898, Battle of San Juan Hill. For his effective service, Thompson was promoted to colonel of volunteers in the late summer of 1898.

In 1899, Thompson was named chief of small arms in the Ordnance Department, where he was to play a key role in the development of the M1903 Springfield rifle, which replaced the Krag-Jørgenson as the army's small-arms weapon of choice in the early years of the 20th century. The M1903 and its successors would be used well into midcentury and was based on the German-designed Mauser bolt-action rifle employed by many Spanish regulars during the Spanish-American War.

Thompson was promoted to major in 1906. From 1907 to 1914, he was chief assistant to the chief of Army Ordnance. Promoted to lieutenant colonel in January 1909 and to colonel in October 1913, Thompson was then assigned as a lecturer at the Army War College.

Thompson was also instrumental in the adoption of the M1911 Colt pistol, a single-action semiautomatic hand-held weapon that saw service through the Vietnam War. While preparing the army for the adoption of this weapon, Thompson employed animal carcasses and even human cadavers to study the effects of various ammunition and firing patterns and rates on would-be targets. Although they raised eyebrows at the time, Thompson's tests became standard operating procedure whenever new weapons were being developed.

In November 1914, Thompson retired from active duty to take a position with the Remington Arms Company as chief engineer. There he oversaw the construction of the world's newest and most efficient small-arms factory in Chester, Pennsylvania, which produced Enfield rifles for the British and Moisin-Nagant rifles for Russia. By 1916 or so, with the devastating effects of trench warfare fully evident, Thompson began development of various automatic and semiautomatic small arms that would quickly and easily clear an enemy trench. Eventually, he teamed up with John Blish, a navy commander who had designed a prototype automatic weapon that had impressed Thompson.

Thompson and Blish borrowed sufficient capital to begin their own firm, Auto Ordnance Company, in late 1916. Here the two men eventually developed what would become known as the Thompson submachine gun. When the United States entered World War I in April 1917, Thompson was recalled to active duty and in August 1918 was advanced to temporary brigadier general. The army charged him with supervising all its small-arms manufacturing. In December 1918, Thompson was awarded the Distinguished Service Medal and again retired from the army.

Returning to the Auto Ordnance Company, Thompson worked with Blish to secure a patent for what became known as the Thompson submachine gun, or simply the tommy gun, in 1920. A fully automatic shoulder weapon, it fired the same .45-caliber round as in the pistol and was renowned for its rugged construction, ease of use, and absence of malfunctions. At the time, military demand for the new weapon was very low. The U.S. Marine Corps did purchase the weapon for operations in Nicaragua in 1925, while the U.S. Army adopted it for its mechanized cavalry in 1938. The U.S. Navy also purchased it. Much of the sales, however, went to law enforcement, where the Thompson submachine gun became the weapon of choice of the Federal Bureau of Investigation (FBI). It was also much used by gangsters of the period.

In 1928, low sales forced Thompson to leave his post with the Auto Ordnance Company. Subsequently, Thompson Automatic Arms Company, headed by his son, took over manufacture of the Thompson submachine gun. In 1930, Thompson was advanced to brigadier general, retired, by an extraordinary act of the U.S. Congress. He died on June 21, 1940, in Great Neck, New York, just prior to the placing of huge orders for the Thompson submachine gun by the U.S. military as it prepared for World War II. A number of militaries subsequently adopted the Thompson gun, and it was still in use among both military establishments and law enforcement agencies well into the 1980s.

PAUL G. PIERPAOLI JR.

See also
V Corps; Machine Guns; Rifles; San Juan Heights, Battle of; Shafter, William Rufus

Further Reading
Brinkerhoff, Sidney B., and Pierce Chamberlin. "The Army's Search for a Repeating Rifle: 1873–1903." *Military Affairs* 32(1) (Spring 1968): 10–20.
Cosmas, Graham A. *An Army for Empire: The United States Army in the Spanish-American War.* College Station: Texas A&M University Press, 1994.
Hill, Tracie L., et al. *Thompson, the Legend: The First Submachine Gun.* Cobourg, Ontario: Collector Grade Publications, 1996.

Tinio, Manuel
Birth Date: June 17, 1877
Death Date: February 22, 1924

Filipino revolutionary nationalist and general who fought U.S. forces in northern Luzon during the Philippine-American War (1899–1902). Born in Aliaga, Nueva Ecija Province, on June 17, 1877, Manuel Tinio never completed high school, cutting short his studies in April 1896 to join the Katipunan, the secret insurgent organization in support of the revolt against Spain. He entered combat in 1897, engaged the enemy in the provinces of Nueva Ecija and Bulacan, and gained recognition for this leadership. At a revolutionary council in June 1897, he was appointed colonel. Emilio Aguinaldo y Famy, the rebel leader, later commissioned him a brigadier general.

Tinio commanded military operations under Lieutenant General Mamertito Natividad and participated in major engagements at San Rafael in Bulacan, Aliaga in Nueva Ecija, and Tayug in Pangasinan Province. In November 1897, he signed the provisional constitution of the soon-to-be First Philippine Republic and accompanied Aguinaldo to Hong Kong following the December 1897 Pact of Biak-na-Bato, a truce temporarily ending the revolt. With the beginning of the Spanish-American War, Tinio returned with Aguinaldo and other exiles to the Philippines in May 1898 under the orders of Commodore George Dewey.

Once back in the Philippines, Tinio attacked Spanish strong points in his native province. His insurgents captured San Isidro first and then captured Nueva Ecija in July. The next month, he marched northwest and seized San Fernando in La Union Province north of Lingayen Gulf. Aided by the inhabitants of the provinces of Ilocos Sur, Ilocos Norte, Lepanto, Abra, and La Union, Tinio liberated the Ilocan area and placed it under rebel control. He so inspired the residents of one Ilocas Norte community that they took his family name as their place name.

When the Philippine-American War began in February 1899, Tinio commanded Filipino forces in the Ilocano region. He advanced southward to Pangasinan and installed his main base at San Jacinto. He succeeded in ambushing American troops there, but elements of Major Peyton C. March's 33rd Infantry outflanked Tinio's troops, forced their retreat, and seized the village. The Tinio Brigade suffered 134 killed. Incapable of halting the American offensive,

Tinio evacuated San Fernando; withdrew to Tagudin, Ilocos Sur; and then marched north to hold the Tangadan Pass and to protect the Abra Valley in Abra Province.

After setbacks at Vigan, Ilocos Sur, and Tangadan Pass, Tinio retreated into the mountains of Ilocos Norte and resorted to guerrilla operations. Throughout what became known as the American First District, Department of Northern Luzon, unconventional warfare ensued against the American-installed native administrations. Tinio's underground rallied the local home guard and mobilized guerrilla regulars. His troops ambushed small U.S. combat units, seized supplies, severed American communications, and abducted or murdered collaborators. To escape capture, Tinio moved freely, living in various towns.

On October 24, 1900, Tinio's troops won a victory over the Americans at Cosucos in Ilocos Sur. Yet by 1901, Tinio faced failure in the Ilocos region. A strong American military presence and differences among the revolutionaries coupled with supply difficulties and a populace ready to capitulate led to his surrender on April 30, 1901, a little more than a month after Aguinaldo had been captured. Like Aguinaldo, Tinio would in time become loyal to the United States. Later he served as governor of Nueva Ecija. Tinio died in Manila on February 22, 1924.

RODNEY J. ROSS

See also

Aguinaldo y Famy, Emilio; Biak-na-Bato, Pact of; Dewey, George; Katipunan; Philippine-American War; Philippine Islands

Further Reading

Linn, Brian McAllister. *The Philippine War, 1899–1902.* Lawrence: University Press of Kansas, 2000.
———. *The U.S. Army and Counterinsurgency in the Philippine War, 1899–1902.* Chapel Hill: University of North Carolina Press, 1989.
Ochosa, Orlino A. *The Tinio Brigade: Anti-American Resistance in the Ilocos Provinces, 1899–1901.* Quezon City, Philippines: New Day, 1989.

Tirad Pass, Battle of
Event Date: December 2, 1899

An engagement fought on December 2, 1899, during the Philippine-American War (1899–1902) between Filipino rebel forces led by Brigadier General Gregorio del Pilar and the U.S. 33rd Infantry Regiment. The battle occurred at Tirad Pass in northern Luzon, and although the Filipinos incurred heavy casualties, they stalled the U.S. advance long enough for General Emilio Aguinaldo y Famy to evade capture.

After securing Manila in late February 1899, U.S. forces pushed northward in Luzon and seized Malolos, capital of the Philippine Republic, on March 31. U.S. forces continued their northern drive in hopes of capturing Aguinaldo, leader of the rebellion and the republic's president, and his Army of Liberation. Evading U.S. forces, on November 17 Aguinaldo reached Naguillian in La Union Province on the eastern coast of the Lingayen

Gulf. That same day, U.S. brigadier general Samuel B. M. Young, commander of the Cavalry Brigade, mounting an unauthorized dash up the Ilocos coast, set out from Pozorrubio in Pangasinan Province. Down to only about 80 troopers of the 3rd Cavalry Regiment and a few members of Lieutenant Matthew A. Batson's Filipino Macabebe Scouts, Young requested the addition of a battalion of infantry. Reaching the coast on November 19 and making contact with the U.S. gunboat *Samar,* Young took the provincial capital of San Fernando de la Union on November 20. By now, Young's force was at the end of its tether. Difficult terrain, casualties, and the general fatigue of the campaign had all taken their toll. Aguinaldo was then moving up the coast road, his presumed destination the Cagayan Valley.

The additional battalion requested by Young—500 men commanded by Major Peyton C. March of the 33rd Infantry Regiment—arrived at Namacpacan on November 26. March immediately placed his battalion under Young's command. The general then sent March toward Camdon to block Tirad Pass. At Tirad Pass, General Pilar and 60 handpicked men prepared to fight a rearguard action against the advancing Americans so that Aguinaldo would have time to fall back. The Filipinos hastily built a series of fences and dug trenches along the narrow path that ascended toward the Tirad Pass.

On December 2, as March's men proceeded along the zigzag trek over the pass, they encountered a barrier erected by Pilar's men that was blocking the trail. The Filipino riflemen waited to fire until March's troops were within range, then let loose a volley of rifle fire that brought several U.S. casualties. The American vanguard immediately went to the ground. March then assigned a second company to charge ahead, but it too was turned back. March then wisely decided against a full frontal assault and elected to outflank the Filipinos. March deployed sharpshooters to a neighboring hill, where they were positioned behind Pilar's force. He also ordered Company H on a lengthy hike up a gorge to locate a pathway ascending the bluff parallel to the pass, while the rest of his battalion remained on the trail to fix the Filipino defenders in place.

Later in the morning, March's Company H moved up the precipitous cliffs. Close to noon, the unit appeared above Pilar's defenses, attacking down simultaneously as another part of the battalion assaulted the barrier from the front. Pilar's men began to withdraw but were felled in large numbers by the American riflemen on the elevation.

In five hours of fighting, 51 of the Filipino defenders, including young General Pilar, died. U.S. forces suffered 2 dead and 9 wounded in the Battle of Tirad Pass. Nevertheless, this delaying action gave Aguinaldo ample time to escape. The next day, March continued the pursuit, but weariness and illness took a toll. Nevertheless, he drove a great distance into the highlands until his men became too exhausted to continue. He then broke off the chase.

Filipinos consider the Battle of Tirad Pass, or the Filipino Thermopylae as it is also known, as one of the most celebrated engagements of the Philippine-American War. Pilar is celebrated as one of war's great heroes, famed for the courage and sacrifice in this rear-guard action.

RODNEY J. ROSS AND SPENCER C. TUCKER

See also
Aguinaldo y Famy, Emilio; MacArthur, Arthur; Malolos, Philippines, Capture of; Philippine-American War; Pilar, Gregorio del; Young, Samuel Baldwin Marks

Further Reading
Linn, Brian McAllister. *The Philippine War, 1899–1902*. Lawrence: University Press of Kansas, 2000.
Ochosa, Orlino A. *The Tinio Brigade: Anti-American Resistance in the Ilocos Provinces, 1899–1901*. Quezon City, Philippines: New Day, 1989.
Silbey, David J. *A War of Frontier and Empire: The Philippine-American War, 1899–1902*. New York: Hill and Wang, 2006.

Toral y Vázquez, José
Birth Date: 1834
Death Date: July 10, 1904

Spanish general in Cuba during the Spanish-American War who was later court-martialed for his role in the surrender of Santiago. José Toral y Vázquez was born in Spain in 1834. He entered Spanish military service as a young man and rose steadily through the ranks. He was eventually sent to Cuba and held the rank of brigadier general when the Spanish-American War began in April 1898. He served on the commission that oversaw strengthening of the defenses of Santiago. Toral and Brigadier General Joaquín Vara del Rey y Rubio each received command of a division of the two-division Spanish garrison at Santiago on the commencement of hostilities.

On July 1, 1898, when Lieutenant General Arsenio Linares y Pombo was wounded, Toral took command of IV Corps. By then, most of the Spanish troops had fallen back into redoubts located just outside the city of Santiago. Toral ordered Brigadier General Félix Pareja Mesa at Guantánamo, Cuba, to dispatch reinforcements, but Pareja never received the message.

On July 3, 1898, Major General William R. Shafter, commanding V Corps, called on Toral to surrender Santiago. This demand came several hours prior to the defeat of the Spanish Squadron in the Battle of Santiago de Cuba, and Toral ignored the surrender demand. However, the destruction of Rear Admiral Pascual Cervera y Topete's squadron completely changed the strategic situation to the advantage of the Americans. Shafter then again demanded that Toral surrender, this time on the threat of a bombardment of Santiago beginning on July 5. Toral stalled for time, engaging the Americans in further negotiations.

On July 8, Toral offered to quit Santiago but only if Shafter allowed the Spanish IV Corps to retreat to Holguín, some distance from Santiago. After consulting with Washington, Shafter rejected the Spanish offer and threatened to begin shelling Santiago on July 10 if a surrender had not been tendered. Toral rejected the demand, and Shafter called upon U.S. naval vessels to begin shelling the western quadrant of Santiago. The bombardment commended at about 4:00 p.m. on July 10. Shelling was suspended at 1:00 p.m. the next day.

Under incredible pressure, Toral continued to engage the Americans in negotiations when the bombardment stopped. Shafter now offered to return all Spanish prisoners of war to Spain at American expense in return for Toral's unconditional surrender and evacuation of the city. To further pressure the Spanish, Shafter ordered the water supply to Santiago severed. In the meantime, Toral was under increasing pressure from General Ramón Blanco y Erenas, the captain-general of Cuba, to resolve the situation. Blanco believed that Santiago should be surrendered to spare it further bombardment. Even after the Spanish government in Madrid had entered into negotiations with the Americans, Toral stubbornly refused to surrender. Meanwhile, conditions for civilians in the city were rapidly deteriorating. Madrid finally prevailed, and Toral was thus compelled to enter serious negotiations that would bring about the surrender of Santiago.

During the final negotiations with the Americans, Toral appeared more concerned about his personal reputation than the disposition of his troops. Indeed, he insisted that the word "capitulation" be used in lieu of "surrender" and that Spanish troops be permitted to keep their weapons. Finally, with the support of Blanco, Toral signed the surrender papers on July 17, 1898. Effective that day, Santiago was turned over to U.S. forces, and remaining Spanish troops evacuated the city's fortifications.

On September 15, Toral returned to Spain under the terms of the Protocol of Peace of August 12, only to be met there by demonstrations. He was jailed in Madrid and then court-martialed but was acquitted on August 9, 1899. The war and the court-martial proved too much for him, however. Bedeviled by recurring public animosity toward him, Toral soon became mentally unstable, left the army, and spent the last months of his life in a mental hospital in Madrid, where he died on July 10, 1904.

PAUL G. PIERPAOLI JR.

See also
Blanco y Erenas, Ramón; V Corps; Linares y Pombo, Arsenio; Santiago de Cuba, Capitulation Agreement; Santiago de Cuba Land Campaign; Shafter, William Rufus; Vara del Rey y Rubio, Joaquín

Further Reading
Cosmas, Graham A. *An Army for Empire: The United States Army in the Spanish-American War*. College Station: Texas A&M University Press, 1994.
Núñez, Severo Gómez. *The Spanish-American War*. Washington, DC: U.S. Government Printing Office, 1899.

Torpedo Boat Destroyers

During the late 19th century, great improvements were registered in both the range and destructiveness of the automotive torpedo. This and construction of large numbers of high-speed torpedo boats to deliver the torpedoes prompted development of a larger but similar vessel, first called the torpedo boat destroyer and later known simply as the destroyer. The first attempt at a counter to the torpedo boat was the Royal Navy *Polyphemus* of 1881. Known as a torpedo ram, it weighed 2,640 tons, was 240 feet in length, and was capable of 18 knots. It mounted a 2-pounder gun as well as 18 torpedoes for the five torpedo tubes in its largely submerged hull. The chief problem was that the *Polyphemus* had a slow speed.

Initially, the countertorpedo boats were simply larger and faster torpedo boats, mounting guns as well as torpedoes. In 1885, the Royal Navy commissioned the *Swift* (renamed *Torpedo Boat No. 81*) of 125 tons and 157 feet. Although somewhat slower than the torpedo boats, its greater beam allowed it to carry more armament: six quick-firing 3-pounders and three torpedo tubes. The *Swift* soon inspired similar types of torpedo boat catchers or torpedo gunboats.

HMS *Havock*, completed in October 1893, was the first modern torpedo boat destroyer. It displaced 275 tons, was 180 feet long, and was capable of nearly 27 knots. It behaved well in a seaway, had good maneuverability, and in the 1894 fleet maneuvers caught two torpedo boats. It also caught and circled around one of the Swift-class torpedo boat "catchers." The *Havock*'s sister ship, the *Hornet*, was fitted with a new water-tube boiler and could travel at up to 27.3 knots, which made it the fastest ship in the world. At such speeds, the new torpedo boat destroyers were indeed a match for the torpedo boats. Both the *Havock* and *Hornet* were armed with a 12-pounder and three 6-pounder guns as well as three 18-inch torpedo tubes. During 1893–1895, the Royal Navy ordered some 33 destroyers of this type, all capable of 27 knots and later designated Class A and Class B. They were followed by 43 Class C and Class D destroyers built through 1900, all capable of 30 knots. Each was armed with a 12-pounder gun, five 6-pounders, and two 18-inch torpedo tubes.

High speed and the ability to inflict significant damage were the hallmarks of both the torpedo boat and the torpedo boat destroyer. Each new design registered improvements. The French Navy then followed the British lead. The *Forban* of 1895 achieved 31 knots. This was accomplished with a reciprocating engine; speeds with the turbine engine were higher. Generally speaking, the British led this race, laying down vessels that were both larger and faster than those built by the French.

Larger torpedo boats and torpedo boat destroyers could accompany and provide perimeter protection for the battleships. The first of these light ships were subject to hull strain, excessive vibration, wet conditions, and excessive rolling while at sea. They were thus difficult ships for their crews. Some of this was mitigated in later designs that altered the superstructure and weight displacement.

In 1898, the U.S. Navy had yet to commission a torpedo boat destroyer. Spain, however, possessed six: two Furor class (*Furor* and *Terror*) and four improved Audaz class (*Audaz, Osado, Pluton,* and *Prosperpine*). All were built in a British yard during 1896–1897. The first two were 220 feet and displaced 370 tons. The last four were somewhat larger, at 225 feet and 400 tons. Speeds were 28 and 30 knots, respectively. Each was armed with two 14-pounder and two 6-pounder rapid-fire guns, two 1-pounder Maxim guns, and two 14-inch torpedo tubes.

Only three Spanish torpedo boat destroyers saw action in the war. These were the *Furor, Terror,* and *Pluton,* all of which were attached to Rear Admiral Pascual Cervera y Topete's Cape Verde Squadron. Mechanical problems, however, obliged Cervera to leave the *Terror* behind at Martinique when he departed with his squadron for Cuba at the beginning of the war.

Repairs completed, the *Terror* sailed on its own for Puerto Rico. There on June 22, 1898, it sortied from San Juan to engage the blockading U.S. auxiliary cruiser *St. Paul*. Severely damaged by gunfire from the *St. Paul*, the *Terror* was beached. Repaired at San Juan, it returned to Spain in September after the end of the war.

Both the *Furor* and *Pluton* participated in the Battle of Santiago de Cuba on July 3, 1898. The last two ships to exit the harbor, they came under heavy attack. The *Furor* was sunk, and the *Pluton* was run ashore and later blew up. The crews of both Spanish torpedo boat destroyers reportedly fought with great valor.

SPENCER C. TUCKER

See also

Cervera y Topete, Pascual; Mines; Santiago de Cuba, Battle of; Torpedo Boats; Torpedoes, Automotive

Further Reading

George, James L. *History of Warships: From Ancient Times to the Twenty-First Century.* Annapolis, MD: Naval Institute Press, 1998.
Preston, Anthony. *Destroyers.* Englewood Cliffs, NJ: Prentice Hall, 1977.
Tucker, Spencer C. *Handbook of 19th Century Naval Warfare.* Annapolis, MD: Naval Institute Press, 2000.

Torpedo Boats

Small, narrow, lightly built, fast warships designed to operate against an enemy battle fleet. Development of the automotive torpedo beginning in 1865 meant that for the first time in naval history, small vessels could threaten large ships. Successes with the torpedoes led to the development of new warships to deliver them. Such vessels had to be fast and nimble, for they launched their weapons at relatively close range, well within range of an opposing ship's guns. All naval powers built large numbers of torpedo boats. Indeed, the late 19th century was very much the era of the torpedo boat, and some naval strategists believed that it and the torpedo had rendered the battleship obsolete.

The first purpose-built warship to carry the torpedo was the Royal Navy *Lightning* of 1877. Displacing 27 tons, it was 84.5 feet in length. Powered by a 478-horsepower engine, it could make 19 knots and was fitted with a bow-launching tube for a single 14-inch torpedo. At launch, the torpedo boat would be bow-on to its target and present the smallest silhouette to enemy fire. Impressed by the *Lightning*'s early performance, in 1878 the Admiralty ordered 19 similar boats.

The first U.S. Navy torpedo boat, the *Cushing,* commissioned in 1890. (*Photographic History of the Spanish-American War,* 1898)

The French were almost first with a torpedo boat. Their *Torpilleur No. 1* was ordered in 1875 but not completed until 1878. By 1880, the French Navy had 30 torpedo boats built and another 30 under construction. France built the largest number of torpedo boats. By 1890, France had 220 torpedo boats, Britain had 186, Russia had 152, Germany had 143, and Italy had 129.

Although all major naval powers constructed torpedo boats, the early vessels never reached their potential. An essentially offensive weapon was being carried by what amounted to small coastal defensive craft. The early torpedo boats were sharply limited in their capabilities, and their failure as scouting vessels and their poor performance during maneuvers led to the construction of larger vessels of that type. Torpedo boats were made about 50 percent longer while at the same time preserving their slim, narrow lines. These lengthened craft were technically capable of ocean work, although their crews often did not think that to be the case. Nonetheless, torpedo boats came to be regarded as a serious threat to blockading ships.

The initial French torpedo boats were 114.9 feet long and weighed 58 tons, but the failure of such boats led the navy to decide not to build any smaller than 80 tons, even for coastal defense. In 1889, France also decided to build larger boats of about 125 tons each to accompany a squadron at sea. All boats built after 1890 fell into those two categories. In 1892–1893, the French successfully

tried out No. *147,* an 80-ton boat that made 24 knots. In 1895, their 136-ton 144.4-foot *Forban* achieved 31 knots, setting a world record.

The first U.S. Navy torpedo boat was the *Cushing* (TB-1), commissioned in 1890. It was 116 feet in length. By the time of the war with Spain in 1898, the U.S. Navy operated 10 torpedo boats. In addition to the *Cushing,* the others, all launched during 1896–1898, were the *Ericsson, Foote, Rodgers, Winslow, Porter, Du Pont, Talbot, Gwin,* and *McKee.* During the war, all served in the Atlantic, and many of them saw service off Cuba at some point in the conflict, although primarily in dispatch and scouting roles. The *Winslow* sustained some damage in the engagement at Cárdenas, Cuba, on May 11, 1898, and the *Ericsson* participated in the July 3, 1898, Battle of Santiago de Cuba. In 1898, the Spanish Navy operated 19 torpedo craft of all types but did not send any of them to Cuba, Puerto Rico, or the Philippines for fear of leaving Spain itself unprotected.

Navies partially countered the threat posed by torpedo boats by the development of quick-firing Nordenfelt and Gatling machine guns, which now became part of the standard armament of even the largest warships. At night they were used in conjunction with the newly developed searchlight. In a close action with other ships, quick-firing guns might be used to fire at the gunports of an opposing vessel and to repel boarders. Finally, the world's navies developed a new warship type, known first as the torpedo boat destroyer and later as the destroyer.

SPENCER C. TUCKER

See also

Mines; Torpedo Boat Destroyers; Torpedoes, Automotive

Further Reading

George, James L. *History of Warships: From Ancient Times to the Twenty-First Century.* Annapolis, MD: Naval Institute Press, 1998.

Preston, Anthony. *Destroyers.* Englewood Cliffs, NJ: Prentice Hall, 1977.

Tucker, Spencer C. *Handbook of 19th Century Naval Warfare.* Annapolis, MD: Naval Institute Press, 2000.

Torpedoes, Automotive

A self-propelled explosive projectile weapon, launched either above or below the water's surface and designed to explode on or near a target. The word "torpedo" was first used to describe stationary mines and comes from the torpedo, a genus of electric ray that stuns its prey.

The demonstrated success of stationary mines in the Crimean War (1853–1856) and especially in the American Civil War (1861–1865) led to efforts to develop a propelled mine. The first modern automotive mine or torpedo was developed by Captain Giovanni Luppis of the Austrian Navy in 1865. It was perfected two years later by Scottish engineer Robert Whitehead, who managed an engine works in Fiume. The Luppis-Whitehead torpedo was a long cylinder-shaped weapon, streamlined for movement through the water. Armed with an 18-pound dynamite warhead, it was powered by an engine that ran on compressed air and propelled the torpedo just below the surface of the water at a speed of 6–8 knots. It had an effective range of only several hundred yards. The torpedo's secret was a balance chamber that enabled it to remain at a constant depth beneath the surface.

Whitehead traveled to Britain to demonstrate the new weapon. In September–October 1870 trials, the Admiralty was sufficiently impressed with some 1,000 test firings that it purchased rights to his invention for £15,000. In 1872, Whitehead opened a torpedo factory in England. The British concentrated on a 16-inch, 1,000-yard-range version driven by contra-rotating screws at a speed of 7 knots, or 300 yards at 12 knots. The Whitehead torpedo came to be called the "Devil's device." The British first employed the new torpedo in combat in 1877 when the Royal Navy armored frigate *Shah* attacked the Peruvian monitor *Huascar*. The *Shah* launched its torpedo within 600 yards, but the *Huascar* easily avoided it and escaped.

The torpedo meant that for the first time in naval history, small vessels could threaten large ships. This was very much the age of the torpedo boat, and there was even talk in the 1880s that the battleship was obsolete. Such vessels had to be fast and nimble, for they launched their weapons well within range of the opposing ship's guns. All major naval powers built large numbers of small, fast torpedo boats.

Engraving of sailors hoisting a torpedo on board a warship during the Spanish-American War. (James Rankin Young and J. Hampton Moore, *History of Our War with Spain,* 1898)

Whitehead made other improvements in his torpedo, further streamlining it and fitting it with fins to stabilize its movement toward the target. He also increased the explosive charge threefold by replacing gunpowder with guncotton. A three-cylinder gas-powered engine developed by Brotherhood improved torpedo speed to 18 knots, making it more difficult for a targeted vessel to escape. The addition of a gyroscope, adapted for torpedo use by the Austrian Ludwig Obry, was an important advance that made the torpedo more accurate. Range also increased, so that by 1877 torpedoes could reach 800 yards.

The first successful torpedo attack occurred during the Russo-Turkish War of 1877–1878. On January 26, 1878, off Batum on the Black Sea, the Russian torpedo boat *Constantine* fired two torpedoes at a range of some 80 yards to sink the Turkish patrol boat *Intikbah* in Batum Harbor.

Torpedoes had a more spectacular result in 1884 during the Indo-China Black Flag/Tonkin Wars (1882–1885) when France conducted naval operations against China. On August 23, 1884, two small French torpedo craft, motorboats Nos. *45* and *46,* torpedoed and sank the Chinese flagship and damaged a second Chinese warship at the Fuzhou (Foo Chow) naval base on the Minh River.

By the start of the Spanish-American War in April 1898, the Spanish Navy operated as many as 19 torpedo craft of all types, and the U.S. Navy had 10 torpedo boats. During the war, Spain did not send any of its torpedo boats to Cuba, Puerto Rico, or the Philippines, choosing instead to keep them in Spanish waters for home defense. Only 5 of the U.S. torpedo boats saw action. One, the *Ericsson,* participated in the July 3, 1898, Battle of Santiago de Cuba.

Torpedoes became standard armament on all classes of warships. Indeed, all Royal Navy ships launched after 1872 carried them, and in 1876 the Royal Navy established a Torpedo School aboard HMS *Vernon.* Improvements continued to be registered after the war in the range, accuracy, and lethality of torpedoes. With the parallel development of the modern submarine, a unique combination in warfare came into being that would achieve devastating results in both world wars.

SPENCER C. TUCKER

See also
Mines; Torpedo Boat Destroyers; Torpedo Boats; Warships

Further Reading
Gray, Edwyn. *The Devil's Device: Robert Whitehead and the History of the Torpedo.* Rev. and updated ed. Annapolis, MD: Naval Institute Press, 1991.
Middleton, Drew. *Submarine, the Ultimate Naval Weapon: Its Past, Present & Future.* New York: Playboy Press, 1976.
Tucker, Spencer C. *Handbook of 19th Century Naval Warfare.* Annapolis, MD: Naval Institute Press, 2000.

Traprain, Viscount

See Balfour, Arthur James

Treaty of Paris

See Paris, Treaty of

Trocha

A defensive line system employed by the Spanish in their efforts to defeat the insurgents in Cuba. It was used in Cuba during the Ten Years' War (1868–1878) and then again during the Cuban War of Independence (1895–1898). The first trocha was built to contain the anti-Spanish insurrection to the two most eastern provinces of the island. Beginning in 1895, trochas were also utilized to separate Cuban revolutionaries and insurrectionists from the general civilian population. The Spanish word *trocha* means "trench," but the trochas employed in Cuba were far more than mere trenches. The first trocha was about 200 yards wide and featured fortified blockhouses located approximately every half mile along the line. Most trochas had a row of trees lining both sides. Between the blockhouses were stout barbed-wire fencing and smaller fortified redoubts. Where rebels were most likely to attack, the Spanish rigged the trocha with small explosives designed to go off when individuals tried to breach the line.

As originally constructed, the principal Spanish trocha bifurcated Cuba from north to south and ran for about 50 miles. It began at Morón on the northern coast of Cuba and ended at Jucaro on the southern coast. Running roughly parallel to it was an already-existing railroad track. In 1895, when Spanish general Arsenio Martínez de Campos arrived in Cuba to contain the latest rebellion, he once again employed the trocha, ordering it additionally fortified. However, he was unable to quell the insurrection, so Madrid dispatched General Valeriano Weyler y Nicolau to the island in February 1896. Weyler ordered a new line constructed from Mariel to Majana as a means to confine the Cuban insurgents to the western part of the island. Manned by some 14,000 men, it incorporated both electric lights and artillery and proved reasonably effective. He also used the trochas as part of his infamous *reconcentrado* (reconcentration) policy, whereby he rounded up civilians and placed them in concentration centers in an attempt to keep them separated from the rebels. The defensive line was also, at least in theory, supposed to prevent the rebels from moving about the island freely.

During the Ten Years' War, many rebels circumvented the trocha using clever tactics and ploys. During the period of Weyler's command, the trochas were much more effective, and circumvention occurred chiefly by water, as rebels frequently bypassed trochas in small boats at night near the port city of Mariel. Many villages and towns were also surrounded by small trochas, little more than fortified rifle pits to deter rebels from entering the area. Most included a thick stand of barbed-wire fencing.

In the end, the trocha system did little to help the Spanish crush the revolt that began in 1895. Indeed, its presence and its link to Weyler's much-maligned *reconcentrado* policy created more problems for the Spanish as the insurrection endured. Pictures and illustrations in the U.S. press frequently focused on the barbed-wire fencing of the trochas.

PAUL G. PIERPAOLI JR.

See also
Cuba; Cuban War of Independence; Martínez de Campos, Arsenio; *Reconcentrado* System; Ten Years' War; Weyler y Nicolau, Valeriano

Further Reading
Foner, Philip S. *The Spanish-Cuban-American War and the Birth of American Imperialism, 1895–1902.* 2 vols. New York: Monthly Review Press, 1972.
Trask, David F. *The War with Spain in 1898.* Lincoln: University of Nebraska Press, 1996.

Trusts

A term that came into use in the late 19th century to describe business and financial arrangements that sought to create a monopoly in a given industry or service sector. Not all trusts of the 1890s were

WALL STREET BUBBLES;—ALWAYS THE SAME.

Caricature from a 1901 issue of *Puck* of the financier J. P. Morgan as a bull blowing bubbles labeled "inflated values" for which people are reaching. Morgan helped to create some of the largest trusts and monopolies, which exercised great control over prices and competition. (Library of Congress)

monopolies, but the public nevertheless equated the two, and the term "trust" thus took on a pejorative meaning. Most trusts were established when a business leader in a given industry either convinced or pressured the heads of other businesses in the same industry to entrust the shares of their company to a single board of trustees, thus giving the board power over all of the businesses. Sometimes the companies involved would receive periodic dividends from their trust shares, but many times the formation of a trust was a legal maneuver to skirt antimonopoly laws. The board of trustees would manage all of the companies involved simultaneously and in so doing would exercise de facto control over the entire industry.

Many industrialists of the late 19th century turned to trusts as a way to control competition, fix prices, corner a market, or combine their business empires horizontally. Horizontal combination, which was perhaps best practiced by John D. Rockefeller of Standard Oil, enabled many of the so-called robber barons of the era to grow their businesses by either buying or controlling their competition, thereby creating a monopoly. U.S. Steel, created in 1901 by John Pierpont Morgan and Elbert H. Gary by combining Andrew Carnegie's steel works with the Federal Steel Company, was another example of a trust. The 1901 merger also resulted in the first U.S. business to be valued at $1 billion or more. At its zenith, U.S. Steel

controlled almost 68 percent of the nation's steel production. Rockefeller's oil empire had captured 88 percent of the nation's total oil refining capacity by 1890.

Standard Oil was, by most accounts, the best example of a big business trust. Begun in 1870, Rockefeller's Standard Oil set out to quickly destroy, subdue, or buy much of the competition in the oil refining industry. Operating refineries in many midwestern and northeastern states, Rockefeller was ruthless in his pursuit of monopoly, often resorting to price wars and other questionable practices to gain the upper hand. As with most companies that were large enough to form trusts, Standard Oil was a vertically integrated company as well, meaning that it controlled almost all aspects of production, distribution, and sales. Indeed, Rockefeller owned his own rail lines, railcars, steamships, etc. In so doing, he made it virtually impossible for a smaller company that did not have such resources to compete.

Soon, however, a number of states in which Standard Oil was operating began to pass laws that attempted to limit the size and scope of industries to stave off monopoly. In reaction to this pressure, Rockefeller and his managers created what is usually conceded to be the first true trust in 1882 by combining all their companies under the direction of a single board of trustees. Not surprisingly, other companies in other industries began to emulate

Rockefeller's trust. Before long, however, both state governments and the federal government sought ways to break the big business trusts and deter their formation. In 1892, for instance, the State of Ohio brought suit against Standard Oil on the grounds that it had created an illegal monopoly. Undeterred, Standard Oil created a holding company—a legal loophole around antitrust laws—that established a hybrid of a trust, named Standard Oil Company of New Jersey.

Ultimately, the U.S. Justice Department sued Standard Oil of New Jersey using the 1890 Sherman Antitrust Act, alleging that its holding company was a violation of federal law. In 1911, the U.S. Supreme Court ruled on the issue and found that the company had engaged in illegal combination. This forced the mighty corporation to break itself into 34 different companies, each controlled by its own autonomous board of directors.

In 1898, President William McKinley, under pressure from the public and Congress to rein in big business, convened the Industrial Commission. The Industrial Commission was tasked with investigating industry combination, holding companies, trusts, and railroad pricing guidelines, among other things. The commission issued periodic reports to the president and Congress and was operational until 1902. When Theodore Roosevelt became president upon McKinley's assassination in 1901, he used the findings of the Industrial Commission to begin a new push toward business regulation and trust busting, including the dissolution of Morgan's Northern Securities Company.

In 1890s' America, the public—egged on by the sensationalist journalism of the day—seemed at once fascinated and revolted by big business trusts. Many Americans admired, albeit grudgingly, the stratospheric successes of Rockefeller, Carnegie, Morgan, and other business tycoons. At the same time, however, they were alarmed at the unbridled growth and power of their empires and were especially leery of anything that smacked of monopoly. Antimonopoly sentiments have a long history in the United States, and while Americans do not seem to mind large businesses that are vertically integrated, they do view warily those that seek to snuff out competition. Perhaps as an extension of the American pioneering spirit and a long-held belief in healthy economic competition, Americans tend to view any institution that is big and too powerful—be it the government or a private corporation—with great suspicion.

PAUL G. PIERPAOLI JR.

See also

Carnegie, Andrew; McKinley, William; Morgan, John Pierpont, Sr.; Progressivism; Robber Barons; Rockefeller, John Davison; Roosevelt, Theodore

Further Reading

Chandler, Alfred D., Jr. *Strategy and Structure: Chapters in the History of American Industrial Enterprise.* Cambridge, MA: MIT Press, 1990.
———. *The Visible Hand: The Managerial Revolution in American Business.* Cambridge: Belknap Press of Harvard University Press, 1977.
Josephson, Matthew. *The Robber Barons: The Great American Capitalists, 1861–1901.* New York: Harcourt Brace, 1995.
McCraw, Thomas K. *Prophets of Regulation: Charles Francis Adams, Louis D. Brandeis, James M. Landis, Alfred E. Kahn.* Cambridge: Harvard University Press, 1984.

Turbine Propulsion

Turbine propulsion is the most efficient use of steam power to propel ships at sea. American Robert Fulton's *Clermont* of 1807 was the world's first steam-powered ship to prove an economic success. It was followed by other steam-powered vessels, but the new technology was plagued by breakdowns. Steam vessels initially used paddlewheels at the rear or side, but these were inefficient. When these were replaced by screw propellers below the waterline, ocean-going ships powered only by steam and sail became a reality.

The first steam engines were inefficient. At first, the steam drove only one piston. The compound engine introduced in 1854 had the advantage of multiple pistons driving a single crankshaft. Advances in metallurgy permitted boilers that could handle higher steam pressures. Other innovations such as condensers and double-expansion engines extended engine lifetime and conserved fuel. Steam engines grew larger and reached the limit of their capabilities by the 1890s.

In the 1890s, Sir Charles Algernon Parsons achieved a significant breakthrough in steam power propulsion. Parsons had always been fascinated by technology and had invented an epicycloidal engine during the 1870s. He became a junior partner in the firm of Clarke, Chapman and Parsons, heading its electrical department. One of Parsons's projects was the development of a small steam-driven electric lighting unit. He decided to use a steam-driven axial-flow turbine that rotated up to 40,000 revolutions per minute (rpm) to drive a DC generator at 18,000 rpm. He took out patents on both pieces of equipment on April 23, 1884. In 1888, he dissolved his partnership with Clarke, Chapman and Parsons and formed his own engineering firm. He bought back his original patent from his former firm and began his experiments with using a steam turbine as a means of maritime propulsion.

Parsons's turbine used a jet of high-pressure steam directed against blades set at an angle in a drum connected to a propeller shaft. Compared to a reciprocating steam engine, a turbine was simple and had a very favorable power-to-weight ratio. Fewer moving parts made the turbine less likely to break down, but the high speeds at which the turbine turned required a very high degree of precision in all its components.

After experimenting with 2-foot and 6-foot models, Parsons installed steam turbine engines in the *Turbina*, a yacht he built in 1894. The 103-foot *Turbina* was intended to demonstrate the advantage of turbine propulsion to potential customers. Between 1894 and 1897, the yacht was fitted with a number of different steam turbines. The first trials were disappointing, as the *Turbina* could not make more than about 20 knots, comparable to that reached by ships with reciprocating engines. The problem was with cavitation (the creation of voids in the fluid around the propeller), which was little understood at the time. Cavitation prevented the propellers from pushing *Turbina* through the water as rapidly as possible. Parsons studied the problem and ways of making his turbine system more efficient. He redesigned the propellers and shafts, and he installed a three-stage axial steam turbine engine. Three shafts each drove a propeller.

Parsons unveiled the results of his experiments on June 26, 1897, during the British Naval Review at Spithead. The *Turbina* was among the ships passing in review, with Parsons at the wheel. He suddenly rang for full speed and pulled out of line. As thousands watched, the *Turbina* sped down the review line, reaching a speed of 34.5 knots. Guard boats sent to stop the ship were unable to catch it.

Parsons's stunt gained him fame as an engineer and also spurred international interest in turbine propulsion. The Admiralty forgave the embarrassment caused and placed an order for the *Viper* in 1898. Torpedo boats had been built for years, but this ship was a qualitative leap forward. The *Viper* was small and fast and, powered by Parsons's turbines, became the prototype torpedo boat destroyer. Armed with several light guns and torpedoes, the fast turbine-powered destroyer could shield its own battleships from torpedo boats and yet deliver a devastating attack on an opposing enemy battle line. Other countries quickly followed. The first U.S. turbine-propelled destroyer was the *Bainbridge*, laid down in 1899.

Turbines were soon installed in larger ships as well. The first battleship to use turbines was the revolutionary British *Dreadnought*, laid down in 1905. Builders adopted turbines for other ships, including merchant vessels. Turbines were lighter and smaller than the reciprocating steam engines used previously and were also simpler and less prone to breakdowns. The increased speed and efficiency of turbine propulsion outweighed the additional costs.

TIM J. WATTS

See also
Torpedo Boat Destroyers

Further Reading
Canney, Donald L. *The Old Steam Navy: The Ironclads, 1842–1885.* Annapolis, MD: Naval Institute Press, 1993.
Institute of Marine Engineers. *Marine Propulsion: Turbinia and Beyond.* London: Institute of Marine Engineers, 1997.
Leather, John. *World Warships in Review, 1860/1906.* Annapolis, MD: Naval Institute Press, 1976.
Tucker, Spencer C. *Handbook of 19th Century Naval Warfare.* Annapolis, MD: Naval Institute Press, 2000.

Turner, Frederick Jackson
Birth Date: November 14, 1861
Death Date: March 14, 1932

Eminent U.S. historian and writer whose provocative essay "The Significance of the Frontier in American History" (1893) opened

U.S. historian Frederick Jackson Turner's provocative essay "The Significance of the Frontier in American History" of 1893 opened a new period in interpretation of American history and, some say, helped justify U.S. imperialism. (Library of Congress)

up a new period in the interpretation of American history and, some argue, helped justify U.S. overseas expansionism in the 1890s. Frederick Jackson Turner was born on November 14, 1861, in Portage, Wisconsin, and grew up in a family that stressed learning and culture. Educated at local schools, he earned both his bachelor's degree (1884) and master's degree (1888) at the University of Wisconsin in Madison. He received his PhD from Johns Hopkins University, where he studied under Herbert Baxter Adams. Adams was one of a group of American historians who applied social Darwinism to the study of history. Turner retained the evolutionary thrust of Adams's thinking while significantly modifying it.

In 1893, as a young professor at the University of Wisconsin, Turner presented his famous paper "The Significance of the Frontier in American History" at a meeting of the American Historical Association in Chicago. In Turner's view, American democracy had begun in American rather than German forests, as his mentor Adams had postulated. American history, Turner maintained, was to a great extent the history of the conquest of the West, the relentless move westward that had begun when the first English colonists arrived in the New World at the beginning of the 17th century. The availability of free land had drawn settlers farther and farther westward, and as each successive wave of immigrants struggled with the primitive conditions of the frontier, they were transformed by the experience. Thus, if America's national character was to be identified, it was to be found in the individual and shared experiences of the western pioneers. This meant, Turner claimed, that Americans were continually moving away from their European roots and instead moving toward a unique and independent American mind-set. To ignore this powerful movement would be to ignore the very basis of American history.

Turner believed that the frontier had molded the American character. From it stemmed the Americans' toughness, resourcefulness, resiliency, and individualism as well as American democracy itself. He also believed that the frontier had served as a kind of safety valve for Americans, allowing upward mobility and the promise of new opportunities. "So long as free land exists," he wrote, "the opportunity for a competency exists, and economic power secures political power." Turner did not, however, analyze how this westward-looking pioneering spirit affected Native Americans, whose populations were decimated during Anglo America's love affair with Manifest Destiny.

Yet citing a recent bulletin from the superintendent of the census, as of 1893 the western frontier was officially gone, Turner noted. He therefore fretted what the future held in store for Americans without a western frontier, but he hoped that because of their frontier heritage and ingenuity, Americans would avoid many of the social ills that had beset Europeans.

More recent historians have pointed to Turner's so-called Frontier Thesis to argue that while he had announced the end of the frontier, many Americans were looking toward new frontiers to conquer. They included industrialism and economic expansion, inventions and technology, and overseas expansion. While it is not possible to conclude that Turner's thesis prodded America into the Spanish-American War and extraterritorial expansion, it certainly is an instructive way of looking at U.S. expansionism, which Turner might have argued has been part of its character from the very beginning.

Turner's essay catapulted him to instant celebrity. By focusing on an area that until then had been neglected, he brought about a major shift in the interpretation of American history. While previous American historians had concentrated on the nation's European origins, Turner was the first to look for what was unique about the American experience. He was also among the first to apply interdisciplinary techniques and scientific techniques to the study of history in the seminars he taught at the University of Wisconsin.

Turner's dedication to teaching combined with the painstaking process by which he gathered and verified facts meant that his output was relatively slight. In 1906, he published *The Rise of the New West*, covering the period from 1819 to 1829. One other book, a collection of essays titled *The Significance of the Frontier in American History* (1920), appeared during Turner's lifetime. Two additional books were published posthumously: *The Significance of Sections in American History* (1932), which was awarded a Pulitzer Prize, and *The United States, 1830–1850* (1935).

Turner remained at the University of Wisconsin until 1910, when he became a professor at Harvard University. From 1909 to 1910, he served as president of the American Historical Association and from 1910 to 1915 was on the board of the *American Historical Review*. Upon his retirement from Harvard in 1924, he worked as a research associate at the Huntington Library in Pasadena, California. There, he devoted himself to an analysis of such problems as the depletion of natural resources, population explosions, and the prospect of another world war more terrible than the first. Turner died in San Marino, California, on March 14, 1932.

PAUL G. PIERPAOLI JR.

See also
Imperialism; Manifest Destiny

Further Reading
Bogue, Allan G. *Frederick Jackson Turner: Strange Roads Going Down.* Norman: University of Oklahoma Press, 1998.
Jacobs, Wilbur R. *The Historical World of Frederick Jackson Turner.* New Haven, CT: Yale University Press, 1968.
Turner, Jackson, and John Mack Faragher. *Rereading Frederick Jackson Turner: "The Significance of the Frontier in American History" and Other Essays.* New York: Henry Holt, 1995.

Twain, Mark
Birth Date: November 30, 1835
Death Date: April 21, 1910

Iconic American writer, journalist, humorist, social critic, prominent anti-imperialist, and author of *The Adventures of Huckleberry Finn* (1884), a book that many critics consider to be the first truly American novel. Mark Twain was the pseudonym adopted by Samuel Langhorne Clemens at the age of 27. The name derives from a phrase called out on Mississippi riverboats to denote that a channel was two fathoms deep and thus safe for travel. Born on November 30, 1835, in Florida, Missouri, Twain grew up in the small town of Hannibal on the west bank of the Mississippi River. His father, an inveterate dreamer with notions of finding his fortune on the frontier, had wandered west from Virginia. John Marshall Clemens died when his son was just 12, and Twain was apprenticed to a local printer. At age 18 he began selling humorous sketches to newspapers, and at age 21, he began to pursue his childhood dream of becoming a riverboat pilot.

The American Civil War (1861–1865) shut down riverboat service on the Mississippi, and Twain enlisted briefly as a Confederate soldier. He deserted after three weeks, however, and traveled west with his brother Orion Clemens, an abolitionist who had been appointed by President Abraham Lincoln to serve as secretary to the governor of the Nevada Territory. Twain worked briefly for his brother and even tried his hand at mining for gold before taking up

American novelist and humorist Mark Twain (born Samuel Clemens) is best remembered as the author of *The Adventures of Huckleberry Finn.* (Library of Congress)

a succession of reporting jobs, first at the Virginia City, Nevada, *Territorial Enterprise,* where in 1863 he first used the name Mark Twain on a story, and later at the San Francisco *Morning Call.*

Twain's first real success as a writer came with the publication of "The Celebrated Jumping Frog of Calaveras County" in the New York *Saturday Press* in 1865. A folktale current among the miners he knew, the story concerned a bet by Jim Smiley that his frog, Dan'l Webster, could outjump a frog picked by a stranger, a bet that the stranger wins by loading Dan'l Webster with buckshot while Smiley's back is turned. Twain made the tale the title story for his first book, published in 1867.

In 1866, Twain made his debut as a humorous travel writer with a trip to Hawaii for the Sacramento, California, *Union.* The following year, he signed on for a voyage on the steamship *Quaker City* to Europe and the Holy Land. His dispatches for the San Francisco *Alta California* were later rewritten and published as *The Innocents Abroad* (1869), the book that won him an international reputation and made his fortune. Twain's lengthy, energetic parody of the life of the traveler and his irreverence toward the hallowed landmarks of European culture endeared him to American readers, who wished both to be traveling and to feel a sense of their own worth and identity on the international scene. For their part, Europeans

loved Twain's portrayal of Americans and his subtle wit and ribald humor.

In 1870, Twain married Olivia Langdon of Elmira, New York, the daughter of a millionaire who had made his fortune in the coal industry. Twain soon began sharing the drafts of his work with his wife; her role as a censor attuned to the sensibilities of the book-buying classes has been questioned by some critics, although others insist that it has been overstated. The couple settled first in Buffalo, New York, where Twain set himself up as the editor of a local paper, and then in Hartford, Connecticut, where he built an elaborate mansion that drew comparison to a riverboat.

Twain wrote a series of books in quick succession, including *Roughing It* (1872), an account of his adventures in California and Hawaii; *The Gilded Age* (1873), a wonderfully satiric novel of the hectic post–American Civil War big business boom coauthored with Charles Dudley Warner; and *The Prince and the Pauper* (1882), a novel set in Tudor England about two boys who change places in the days before one of them is to be crowned King Edward VI.

During this period, Twain also wrote the three books for which he is most remembered, all of which hearken back to his boyhood in Hannibal, Missouri. *The Adventures of Tom Sawyer* (1876) concerns a mischievous boy and his experiences growing up in St. Petersburg, Missouri, a little town based on Hannibal. The novel recounts Tom's clever pranks on his schoolmates; his wearying effect on his proper Aunt Polly; his infatuation with his first sweetheart, Becky Thatcher; and his misadventures with Huck Finn, with whom Tom both witnesses a murder and eventually finds hidden treasure. *Life on the Mississippi* (1883) is an autobiographical reminiscence of Twain's years training to become a riverboat pilot mingled with an account of his month-long travels along the river as he researched the book.

Twain's acknowledged masterpiece is *The Adventures of Huckleberry Finn.* In this rambling tale, Huck escapes from his father, a violent drunkard who has kidnapped him to gain control of Huck's share of the treasure found at the conclusion of *The Adventures of Tom Sawyer.* Huck teams up with Jim, an escaped slave, and the two head downriver on a raft. The raft becomes a sort of pastoral ideal in which the two find companionship and freedom outside the strictures and racial divisions of Southern society. Their utopian world, however, is invaded by a pair of traveling con men, and the adventure reaches a climax when one of the pair sells Jim into slavery behind Huck's back. Tom Sawyer concocts an elaborate plot to rescue Jim that fails and then reveals that Jim had been freed under the terms of the will of his first owner. At the end of the novel, Huck announces his intention to depart civilization despite his now secure claim to the treasure.

While the novel's apparent moral ambiguity has stirred debate, critics agree that the story remains true to Huck as a character and that Twain's achievement in narrating the tale in Huck's voice was to fully define for the first time an American literary vernacular.

When *The Adventures of Huckleberry Finn* was published, Twain was at the peak of his literary career, but his fortunes reversed soon thereafter. He had invested heavily in the prototype of a new type-setting machine, but its inventor, James Paige, never completed it. Twain wrote furiously in an attempt to stave off bankruptcy, but the project soaked up all the profits from such books as *A Connecticut Yankee in King Arthur's Court* (1889), *Tom Sawyer Abroad* (1894), and *The Tragedy of Pudd'nhead Wilson* (1894). Twain was thus forced into bankruptcy, although fortunately he managed to transfer his copyrights to his wife and thus protected his most valuable assets.

Determined to pay off his debts, Twain began a lecture tour around the world. The death of his daughter Susy of meningitis during his absence depressed him greatly. He continued writing but mostly in fragments. *Following the Equator* (1897) is a record of his tour, and publishing it successfully paid off his debts. This emotional turmoil was compounded by the death of his wife in 1904.

In June 1898, Twain became a prominent member of the Anti-Imperialist League, which served as an outspoken voice against American expansionism both before and after the Spanish-American War. The chief creative works of Twain's twilight years were his short stories and his autobiography, dictated to his secretary, Albert Bigelow Paine, and published posthumously in 1924. Twain died in Redding, Connecticut, on April 21, 1910.

PAUL G. PIERPAOLI JR.

See also
Anti-Imperialist League; Expansionism; Imperialism

Further Reading
Emerson, Everett. *The Authentic Twain: A Literary Biography of Samuel L. Clemens.* Philadelphia: University of Pennsylvania Press, 1984.
———. *Mark Twain: A Literary Life.* Philadelphia: University of Pennsylvania Press, 1999.
Gerber, John C. *Mark Twain.* Boston: Twayne, 1988.

Typewriter

Device used to print letters, forms, orders, etc. in a standardized manner using a standardized font. The typewriter virtually eliminated the need for hand-written documents. The first commercially successful typewriter was invented by Christopher Latham Sholes, Carlos Gliddon, and Samuel W. Soule in 1867 and patented on June 23, 1868. Sholes was encouraged to continue to refine the typewriter over the next five years.

The patent was then sold to George Washington Newton Yost and James Densmore. They introduced the typewriter to Eliphalet Remington, a gunmaker, who had the precision machinery and capacity to mass produce it. The first typewriter, known as the Sholes-Gliddon-Soule Typewriter, was produced on March 1, 1873 in Ilion, New York and had a list price of $125, then a considerable sum. Sholes and Densmore ultimately sold their interest in the typewriter to Remington, who a year later also sold the typewriter business, which became Remington Rand.

The QWERTY keyboard, based on the first row of letters, produced only capital letters, the numbers 2–9, and 10 special characters using two to four fingers and was designed to reduce jamming, having no scientific basis such as the frequency of the letter or ergonomics. The Remington 2, introduced in 1878, included Byron A. Brooks's improvements such as uppercase and lowercase letters on each bar and additional special characters, produced by using the shift key and bringing the total to 78 characters. Although keyboard training was at first provided for free to increase sales, the 10-finger method of keyboarding was not conceived until 1882 and did not become widely adopted until 1888. Other inventors attempted to introduce alternative keyboards designs, but the QWERTY keyboard had already gained widespread acceptance, and typing speed was an important measure in hiring secretaries and clerks.

The intended users of the typewriter were authors, clergy, and telegraph operators; instead, the profession of the typist, or typewriter as they were called in the early days, emerged and was filled largely by women. The position of typist augmented the all-male office staff of secretary, stenographer, copyists, file clerk, and office boys while providing women with an opportunity to work outside the home in a respectable field of commerce. When men did fill the role of typist, however, they made more than their female counterparts. Some women served as public typists, offering their services to traveling businessmen while retaining mobile employment, but the majority of women settled into commercial firms.

Although not originally intended for journalists, the well-worn typewriter did become a status symbol within that profession. Some reporters during the Spanish-American War used a typewriter while on assignment. Mark Twain (Samuel Langhorne Clemens) quickly became enamored with the typewriter in 1876 but lost interest and refused to have his name associated with the machine. He would, however, produce the first typewritten book manuscript. Other communications professionals, such as telegraphers, also abandoned handwritten telegrams by the end of the 19th century in favor of those that had been typed.

Over the course of a quarter of a century, the Remington brand and design all but cornered the typewriter market, thereby setting the standard for design and technique. Its shortcomings, however, would eventually allow the Underwood typewriter, invented in 1898 by Franz X. Wagner, to introduce a front-stroke, full keyboard, visible type design that allowed the typist to see what he or she was writing. These improvements endured, and all competitors followed suit as the Underwood design remained static throughout the 20th century.

The typewriter had immense military applications. In addition to aiding in telegraph and telegram transmission, the typewriter allowed orders to be written in clear, standardized text, thereby eliminating the potential of miscommunication because of handwriting peculiarities. By the 1890s, carbon paper had also become widely used, and in this way military clerks and typists could make copies of official orders and documents simply by inserting carbon paper and extra blank sheets into the typewriter. The military was fairly quick to adopt the new machine because of its efficiency and uniformity. By 1898, the typewriter was used widely in offices and even in the field. Some historians have pointed to the invention and usage of the typewriter as a means by which American society became more impersonalized, a process that began in the 19th century and accelerated rapidly in the 20th and 21st centuries.

MARCEL A. DEROSIER

See also

Journalism; Telephone and Telegraph; Twain, Mark

Further Reading

Beeching, Wilfred A. *Century of the Typewriter.* Bournemouth, UK: British Typewriter Museum, 1990.

Bliven, Bruce, Jr. *The Wonderful Writing Machine.* New York: Random House, 1954.

Gould, Rupert T. *The Story of the Typewriter: From the Eighteenth to the Twentieth Centuries.* London: Office Control and Management, 1949.

Typhoid Board

Commission created by Surgeon General George Sternberg on August 18, 1898, to investigate the typhoid epidemic ravaging military training camps and recommend sanitary measures to alleviate the crisis. The commission comprised Major Walter Reed of the Army Medical Corps and Majors Victor C. Vaughan and Edward O. Shakespeare, both surgeons in the U.S. Volunteers.

The Department of the Army and the American public had been shocked at the morbidity and mortality from fevers in training camps late in the summer of 1898. Losses from febrile disease were greater even than those in the first year of the American Civil War, even though the fact that typhoid was bacterial in origin and that the exact organism responsible for the disease had recently become known.

Reed had been professor of bacteriology and clinical microscopy at the Army Medical School and was a recognized authority on typhoid. Shakespeare had studied the 1885 typhoid epidemic in Plymouth, Pennsylvania, and Vaughan was the founder of formal bacteriologic training in the United States. Between August 20 and September 30, 1898, the three visited every major military training camp in the United States and all of the secondary camps to which men had been moved to escape the disease. They then personally reviewed the sick reports of 107,973 officers and men who had become ill prior to leaving the United States. By the time the work was finished in June of 1900, Shakespeare had died, and Reed had been transferred to Havana, where he was in charge of the Yellow Fever Board.

Although Reed wrote a major essay on the subject, completion of the two-volume *Report on the Origin and Spread of Typhoid Fever in U.S. Military Camps during the Spanish War of 1898* was left to Vaughan. By the time the final report—which remains the most complete study of epidemic typhoid—was published in 1904, Reed had also died, the victim of peritonitis caused by a ruptured appendix.

The Typhoid Board suspected that the disease could be transmitted by asymptomatic carriers, although this would not be definitively demonstrated until 1907. They believed that the disease was transmitted by contaminated water and suspected (incorrectly) that flies played a major role in that spread. They decried the common diagnosis of typho-malarial fever since the serological Widal test could identify typhoid with certainty and since microscopic examination of the blood could do the same for malaria. The board insisted that every camp have a laboratory capable of making the differentiation. They also placed the blame for the epidemic squarely at the feet of line officers who refused to follow the sanitary recommendations of their medical officers.

JACK MCCALLUM

See also

Medicine, Military; Reed, Walter; Sternberg, George Miller; Typhoid Fever

Further Reading

Cirillo, Vincent J. *Bullets and Bacilli: The Spanish-American War and Military Medicine.* New Brunswick, NJ: Rutgers University Press, 2004.

Typhoid Fever

An enteric fever caused by *Salmonella typhi* (formerly *Bacillus typhosus*). The disease is characterized by fever, headache, abdominal pain, diarrhea, and a rose-colored rash sometimes followed by delirium, vascular collapse, and death. There are still 21 million cases of typhoid and 200,000 deaths each year, mostly in developing countries in Africa, Asia, and Latin America. Typhoid was one of the earliest diseases shown to be caused by a specific microorganism, having been cultured by Georg Gaff in 1884 only two years after his mentor Robert Koch elucidated his four postulates for proving infectious causation of an illness. In 1896, Felix Widal demonstrated that serum from a typhoid patient would cause clumping in broth cultures of the causative organism, giving physicians a reliable way to differentiate typhoid from other febrile illnesses. By the beginning of the Spanish-American War, military physicians had access to enough information about the disease that they should have been able to diagnose it accurately and should probably have been able to deploy effective means of prevention. They did neither, and typhoid was by far the major cause of death during the war.

The majority of typhoid cases occurred in training camps among volunteers who never left the United States and was the direct result of abysmal sanitation practices. Sixty thousand men—the number assigned to the I and III Corps at Camp George H. Thomas in Chickamauga Park, Georgia—produce 21,000 gallons of urine and 9.4 tons of feces a day. The dense clay around Camp Thomas could not begin to absorb that volume of waste. The sinks (latrines) quickly overflowed and emanated a nauseating stink. In addition, many of the recruits had come from cities and had no experience with outdoor sanitation. They deposited their waste directly on open ground and

Hospital camp for military victims of typhoid fever in Minnesota, 1898. (Minnesota Historical Society/Corbis)

ignored pleas from medical officers to bury it. A person could not walk anywhere in the surrounding woods without tramping through piles of feces. With the arrival of heavy rains in July and August, the mess spread and was washed into streams that supplied the camp's water.

Camp Alger in Virginia had most of the same problems and, by early September 1898, the entire camp had to be abandoned and the men moved to Camp Meade in Pennsylvania. Camp Cuba Libre in Jacksonville had better soil but no better sanitation and a high water table, and it ultimately had to be abandoned as well.

Because typhoid was endemic in the late 19th-century United States, because the disease can reside in asymptomatic carriers, and because the War Department had opted to congregate its new volunteer regiments in a few camps, an outbreak was virtually inevitable. Typhoid in the camps was not a problem as long as the inhabitants had been members of the regular army, but the story changed when the volunteers came. Within three weeks of their arrival, 82 percent of the volunteer regiments had typhoid, and that number reached 90 percent after eight weeks. Every regiment of the I, II, III, IV, V, and VII Corps eventually had typhoid—a total

of 20,738 cases, of whom 1,590 died (a 7.7 percent mortality rate). In retrospect, 86.8 percent of all deaths from disease during the Spanish-American War were probably from typhoid.

Responsibility for those deaths lies with both line officers and the medical corps. The regimental surgeons had no operational authority outside direct treatment of the sick and wounded. To the extent that they made recommendations on camp sanitation, those suggestions were generally ignored by officers who had little interest in and less understanding of infectious disease. The line officers almost universally viewed sanitary measures as a waste of time. The physicians, however, also contributed to the problem. Because many of them were ancillary to the volunteer regiments, their training and ability were far from uniform. Many had only a sketchy idea of how infectious diseases were transmitted, and a number were still unable to differentiate among various febrile illnesses, with the most obvious result being the widespread use of the diagnosis typho-malarial fever even though William Osler had discredited that diagnosis in 1896 and laboratory tests were readily available to separate the two. Thermometers had been available in the United States since 1866, but many physicians continued to diagnose fever by feeling the patient and had yet to make the connection between febrile illness and body temperature, much less the connection between the amount of temperature elevation and the severity of the disease and the risk of death.

Even the best of physicians in 1898 did not fully understand that typhoid was generally transmitted by contaminating food and water with infected feces. The least educated thought that the disease was transmitted by bad air. The better educated thought that it was primarily waterborne. Even the postwar Typhoid Board persisted in the belief that flies were the main culprit. In fact, most disease came from camp kitchens but not—as line officers and men suspected—from deteriorated food. The disease really came from cooks who failed to wash their hands, and it would be almost a decade before physicians learned that asymptomatic carriers were a primary source of typhoid epidemics.

If diagnosis was bad, treatment was nearly nonexistent. Calomel, strychnine, alcohol, and sedatives were all tried, but none were actually of any use. It was somewhat helpful to treat the fever since the rate of death approached 100 percent in those whose temperature surpassed 107 degrees. Aspirin and cold baths were used to that end but had minimal impact on overall mortality. Fortunately, the disease ran its course as the camps emptied. The incidence peaked in September and was virtually gone by December.

Distress over the unnecessary loss of life was, however, not gone by the end of 1898. Surgeon General George Sternberg had created a special commission—the Typhoid Board chaired by Major Walter Reed—in August 1898. The board personally inspected the camps and reviewed records of those who had suffered from the disease. Its work culminated in a two-volume report released in June 1900. Although the report mistakenly attributed typhoid's spread to flies, it firmly placed responsibility for the debacle on poor sanitation and the blame for that on the line officers who failed to listen to their surgeons' recommendations. At any event, the Spanish-American War was the last American conflict in which the loss of life from disease outweighed that from trauma.

Jack McCallum

See also
Medicine, Military; Reed, Walter; Sternberg, George Miller; Typhoid Board

Further Reading

Ashburn, Percy M. *A History of the Medical Department of the United States Army.* Boston: Houghton Mifflin, 1929.

Cirillo, Vincent J. *Bullets and Bacilli: The Spanish-American War and Military Medicine.* New Brunswick, NJ: Rutgers University Press, 2004.

Gillett, Mary C. *The Army Medical Department, 1865–1917.* Washington, DC: Center of Military History, United States Army, 1995.

U

Uniforms

When the Spanish-American War began in April 1898, the American armed forces were in the midst of a transition from the uniforms worn in the later Indian Wars in the West to the khaki-colored uniforms worn by the American Expeditionary Force during World War I. Perhaps nothing better exemplified the Americans' ill preparation for war than the uniform situation in the spring and summer of 1898. Cloth shortages, procurement difficulties, production bottlenecks, and shoddy workmanship all resulted in thousands of soldiers deploying to a tropical climate in the middle of summer in what were essentially winter uniforms. The Spanish, on the other hand, who had been ruling over lands in tropical climates for several centuries, were well clothed for battle in a hot, humid climate.

The standard U.S. infantry uniform included light-blue pants and a dark-blue shirt, with rank indicated in white markings. Light-brown leggings were sometimes worn along with darker-brown shoes. Tan suspenders were also sometimes worn. A tan, gray, or brown slouch hat creased at the front and rear capped off the infantry uniform. Although attempts were made to do away with the blue pants in favor of khaki, shortages of the material and procurement problems prevented this from becoming widespread until the end of the war in August 1898. Those in the artillery dressed in much the same fashion as those in the infantry, but chevrons were in red rather than white. Some volunteer artillery units wore a khaki-colored jacket with a red collar, cuffs, and epaulets.

The U.S. cavalry, which had already begun to transition to khaki-colored uniforms, generally sported khaki trousers but the same dark-blue shirt worn by the infantry. Rank and chevrons were in yellow. Boots were black leather.

The U.S. Marine Corps wore the standard field uniform, which included a dark-blue jacket with red piping around the collar, at the cuffs, and vertically down the front. Trousers were light blue. Soon after hostilities began, the Marine Corps uniform was changed to more closely resemble that of the infantry. Dark-blue shirts were worn, as were gray-colored slouch hats. Khaki jackets were issued but were rarely used because of the hot battlefield conditions.

American officers had to purchase their own uniforms, which resulted in better uniforms but more variability in appearance. Most officers endeavored to dress in the same manner as the men under their command, but tended to employ more color (branch service color) around the collar and cuffs. The khaki-colored jacket was frequently worn, usually with shoulder straps.

In the spring of 1898, most soldiers in V Corps mustered in with a uniform featuring wool trousers and wool shirts. Commanding general of the army Major General Nelson A. Miles immediately urged the purchase and adoption of khaki uniforms; however, by the time the force deployed to Cuba in June 1898, just 5,000 of the new brown and khaki-colored tropical uniforms had been made available, mainly because of production problems. Indeed, it would not be until August, when the war drew to a close, that most soldiers were outfitted with appropriate tropical-weight uniforms. The uniform shortage resulted in much complaining on the part of American soldiers and most certainly contributed to the high number of heat-related deaths and illnesses in the first weeks of fighting.

By the end of August, the War Department was able to report that more than 80,000 tropical uniforms had been issued. They were not without their problems, however. Most were ill-fitting and poorly made and wore out quickly. Because of a shortage of true khaki material in the United States (khaki is traditionally made of brown cotton), these new uniforms were made of a canvaslike material that was rough, course, and almost as hot as the wool uniforms. U.S. troops serving in the Philippines, however, fared considerably better. There, the U.S. Quartermaster Department was able to contract with excellent garment makers in India, Hong Kong, and Singapore who had for some time been making tropical-weight uniforms for the British.

The procurement of adequate numbers of uniforms in a properly weighted fabric proved to be one of the most vexing supply problems of the short-lived Spanish-American War. Indeed, not until after the August 12 Protocol of Peace had been signed did troops serving in the Caribbean begin wearing tropical uniforms en masse, many of which were as uncomfortable as the wool uniforms they replaced.

Spanish troops all wore a lightweight uniform made of a white cotton cloth known as *rayadillo* that was accented with blue pinstripes. Straw hats with black headbands were worn, some featuring a cockade in red and yellow. Boots and shoes were made of black leather, although many outfits wore rope-soled sandals. Various branches of the service (e.g., cavalry, infantry, and artillery) wore this same basic uniform, the only variance being in accent colors reflecting branch colors. A few Spanish soldiers, recently arrived from Spain, sported the standard continental uniform, featuring billowy red trousers, white gaiters, and a long blue-gray coat. The hat was a low shako, higher in front than the back, and was covered in white cotton and worn with a neck cloth. The Spanish continental uniform was modeled closely after the French uniforms of the same era. Unlike the Americans, the Spanish had no significant issues with uniform procurement, and their standard-issue uniforms were well suited for tropical climates.

PAUL G. PIERPAOLI JR.

See also

Miles, Nelson Appleton; Spain, Army; United States Army; United States Marine Corps

Further Reading

Cosmas, Graham A. *An Army for Empire: The United States Army in the Spanish-American War.* College Station: Texas A&M University Press, 1994.
Field, Ron. *Spanish-American War 1898.* London: Brassey's, 1998.
Trask, David F. *The War with Spain in 1898.* Lincoln: University of Nebraska Press, 1996.

United States

At the time of the Spanish-American War in 1898, the United States was poised to become a significant world power. An exploding population that was principally the result of massive immigration, a rapidly growing industrial economy, an expanding financial system, and a modernized navy had all ensured the United States a place among the world's great powers by the end of the 19th century. The war itself witnessed the United States acquiring a significant overseas empire that included the Philippines, Guam, and Puerto Rico. The Hawaiian Islands had also been annexed in 1898.

Between 1865 and 1898, the United States experienced significant societal and economic transformation. The American Civil War (1861–1865) had resolved the long-standing debate over the relationship between the states and the federal government and had finally abolished slavery. With the end of the Civil War came Reconstruction, the process of rehabilitating the South and reuniting the former Confederacy to the Union, although at the expense of the civil rights of the newly freed slaves. Perhaps the biggest changes in American society came from the effects of heavy industrialization and its consequences. Indeed, by 1898, the United States embarked on a new foreign policy, partly in response to the pressures that industrialization had wrought.

Even though the process of modern industrialization began as early as 1820, it had mainly been limited to the North. After Reconstruction ended in 1877, the United States experienced large-scale industrialization, which impacted all sections of the country. By 1898, the United States had developed much of its economic potential practically unmolested and had woven together a truly national market, an effort that had been aided by its impressive railroad system, second to no other nation in the world. The United States had many advantages from which to draw: rich and vast agricultural land, bountiful raw materials, modern technology (railways, steam engines, mining equipment, telegraph, telephone), geographic isolation, an absence of foreign enemies, a steady labor force fueled by immigration, and am impressive flow of both foreign and domestic investment capital.

Between 1865 and 1898, the United States devoted most of its energies to internal economic development. During the 33 years between the end of the Civil War and the outbreak of the Spanish-American War, productivity in agriculture and industry increased exponentially. Wheat output increased 256 percent, while corn and sugar increased 222 percent and 460 percent, respectively. Coal production grew by 800 percent, while the production of crude petroleum rose from a mere 3 million barrels to 55 million barrels annually. Especially impressive was the increase in steel production, which is the backbone of a modern industrialized economy. In 1850, just 10,000 tons of steel were being produced per year in the United States; by 1898, more than 7.25 million tons were being produced yearly, greater than the output of Great Britain and Germany combined. Greatly aiding American economic growth in these years were the millions of immigrants who joined the labor force. These men and women provided a ready supply of relatively cheap labor, which American industrialists were all too eager to exploit.

American firms such as Singer, Du Pont, Bell, Carnegie Steel, and Standard Oil were leaders in technological innovation and the development of new management techniques and enjoyed a massive domestic market that they dominated without serious competition. American foreign trade proved to be more robust than that of either Britain or Germany, with U.S. exports increasing sevenfold between 1860 and 1914. Indeed, it was the quest for expanded

The Biltmore House in Asheville, North Carolina. Built by George Vanderbilt II, grandson of tycoon Cornelius Vanderbilt, it was modeled on a 16th-century French chateau and was completed in 1895. The largest private residence in America, it boasts 250 rooms, an indoor swimming pool, and a bowling alley. (Library of Congress)

overseas markets that led in part to the demand for extraterritorial possessions.

These admittedly impressive achievements did not tell the whole story, however, for America's enormous economic productivity came at a significant socioeconomic price. The United States experienced increasing social inequality as it moved toward heavy industrialization in the second half of the 19th century. In 1890, just 1 percent of families owned 51 percent of the national wealth, while the bottom 44 percent owned only 1.2 percent of the national wealth. Another 55 percent possessed about 14 percent of the wealth. The poorest one-half of American families received only one-fifth of the nation's wages and salaries, while the wealthiest 2 percent of families received nearly half the national income, often from rents and investments that precluded the need to find work. This growing economic disparity occurred during a time in which there were no federal- or state-sponsored welfare programs. Thus, impoverished individuals were either forced to rely on limited private charitable organizations or, more probably, fend for themselves.

Unfettered economic competition resulted in a wave of corporate mergers and the creation of trusts by which a few companies controlled entire industries. The Gilded Age, as the writer Mark Twain labeled this period in history, witnessed the rise of fantastically wealthy industrialists such as John D. Rockefeller and Andrew Carnegie and financiers such as John Pierpont Morgan. These men made their unprecedented millions by engaging their respective businesses in vertical integration and horizontal combination, enabling them to push out or buy out competitors and gain a virtual monopoly. Lack of government regulation meant low wages and unsafe working conditions

for many factory workers and virtually no oversight of corporate mergers or trusts. The periodic boom and bust cycles made life unpredictable for many working-class families.

With modern industrialization came the rise of the labor movement in the United States. The movement sought to redress the grievances of factory, railway, and mining workers and the like. The Knights of Labor (KoL) originated in 1869 as a fraternal organization of tailors and quickly branched out to embrace workers of all sorts. Uriah S. Stephens was the first leader of the KoL. He believed that it was possible for labor and management to cooperate collectively as producers. The Great Railway Strike of 1877 convinced the KoL to take on an even more prominent profile. Indeed, the KoL's 1878 constitution called for many of the goals that became part and parcel of the modern labor movement, including the establishment of the eight-hour workday, government ownership of railroads, the replacement of private banks with government postal savings banks, and paper currency rather than specie currency. Ultimately, the KoL's agenda was deemed too radical for the American system, and the organization was permanently tarnished for its alleged roll in the 1886 Haymarket Riots in Chicago, which had evolved from an acrimonious labor strike there. In 1886, Samuel Gompers formed the American Federation of Labor (AFL), a confederation of unions representing only skilled workers. Eventually, the AFL broadened its appeal and became the leading labor union in the United States. Vestiges of it still exist today in the form of the American Federation of Labor-Congress of Industrial Organizations (AFL-CIO).

At the same time, major advances in technology, particularly in national transportation, meant that farmers were unable to maintain

A Jacob Riis portrait of an Italian immigrant mother and her child in a New York City tenement in 1890. (Library of Congress)

their livelihoods in the face of decreasing prices for their produce, increasing debts for supplies, and skyrocketing transportation costs for their goods. The Grange and Populist movements ultimately became a means for farmers to organize their interests against the exploitation of the railroads and eastern banking interests that had loaned them money at high interest rates. The Populist Party emerged in the 1890s as a significant third party. The Populists called for government ownership of railroads and telegraphs, government land grants to settlers rather than railroads, a currency based on the silver standard (Free Silver movement), the graduated income tax, postal savings banks instead of private banks, the direct election of U.S. senators, and the eight-hour workday for industrial workers. Though not initially successful in their efforts, the Populists would later see many of their goals gradually realized during the Progressive era (ca. 1900–1920).

By the end of the 19th century, the United States was an industrial giant in search of a new purpose. In 1890, the director of the U.S. Census Bureau had declared the vast western frontier closed. The frontier had served as a traditional safety valve for generations of Americans. This seemed to have had a psychological effect on some

Americans, who now saw their nation as settled from the Atlantic to the Pacific and who eyed the influx of millions of immigrants with considerable trepidation. Some historians have argued that the closing of the American frontier propelled the United States outward in an attempt to create a new frontier (along with new markets) abroad.

Although long a magnet for immigrants (indeed the nation was founded and built by immigrants and descendants of immigrants), the United States now faced the challenge of an entirely new wave of immigrants, most of whom were from Southern and Eastern Europe.

These new immigrants, who began arriving en masse around 1880, differed starkly from earlier immigrants from Northern and Western Europe. Most did not speak English, and they practiced Roman Catholicism, Eastern Orthodoxy, or Judaism, which made it harder for them to acculturate quickly to their adopted nation. These traits also made it easier for native-born Americans to discriminate against them. Nativists, no doubt the descendants of earlier immigrants, often disparaged these new arrivals and doubted their ability to assimilate into American culture. Ultimately, they were proven entirely wrong, and without the immigrants, American industrialization would have taken far longer to achieve.

Because of the general acceptance of Charles Darwin's theory of natural selection by the 1890s, race became a lens through which Americans viewed the world and understood their place in it. English theorist and political philosopher Herbert Spencer appropriated Darwin's theory and applied it in a sociological context, arguing that all humanity was ranked in a hierarchy ranging from superior to inferior races. By the late 19th century, Anglo-Saxonists used history and social Darwinism to justify the superiority of the Anglo-Saxon civilization of Britain and the United States. Anglo-Saxonist historians argued that the ancient Anglo-Saxon race had developed the free institutions of Britain and America by the 19th century and were therefore more fit to rule over so-called inferior peoples.

Theodore Roosevelt was one of the most prominent late 19th-century Anglo-Saxonists. During turn-of-the-century America, his personal charisma and unique rise to power pushed him into national prominence and provided a voice for vigorous American expansion. He belonged to a group of gentlemen historians, men from the East Coast born of privilege who devoted their lives to writing. In the field of Anglo-Saxonism, Roosevelt supported the Teutonist school of thought (i.e., the theory that the Anglo-Saxon race originated in Germany and spread to England and eventually the United States). He thus looked to the Anglo-Saxon and Teutonic traditions for racial affinity. By the turn of the century, Anglo-Saxonism provided a seemingly plausible explanation for America's meteoric success as an industrial nation, setting the stage for a wider international role.

While the United States was indeed a leading economic power in the 1890s, it was not a potent military power. In 1900, the United States had just 96,000 military and naval personnel. In warship tonnage, the United States ranked fifth behind Great Britain, France, Germany, and Russia. American foreign policy still generally held to the tradition of isolationism, thus steering it away from any formal alliances with other nations. Geographic isolation had rendered alliances unnecessary for most of its history. However, the conditions in international politics by the 1890s had forced U.S. policy makers to reappraise President George Washington's 1796 Farewell Address in which he urged the nation to eschew "entangling alliances" with other countries.

During the last third of the 19th century, much of the world was snatched up by the European powers, most notably Britain and France. With the exception of Liberia and Ethiopia, Africa had been partitioned among Britain, France, Germany, and Belgium by 1885. Britain, France, Germany, Russia, and Japan had also begun to carve up China into spheres of influence. The United States had begun to establish an informal empire in Latin America and began its acquisition of islands in the Pacific, such as Midway, Samoa, and Hawaii, for use as coaling stations for its rapidly expanding navy. By the 1890s, the interests of the United States and Great Britain began to coincide, allowing both countries to shed old animosities and embark on a new and different relationship. The First Venezuela Crisis (1895–1897) convinced the leaders of both countries that a third Anglo-American war would have disastrous consequences.

The resulting rapprochement that emerged between America and Britain served as a foundation for the special relationship between both countries that would have powerful ramifications in the years to come.

Without a doubt, the Spanish-American War made the United States a world power with interests that spanned the globe. After the relatively quick and easy victory over the Spanish in Cuba, Puerto Rico, and the Philippines, the United States found itself mired in a bloody war of insurgency against Filipino rebels that lasted until 1902. Even then, sporadic hostilities between U.S. forces and Filipino insurgents continued, not ending until 1913. As a new Pacific power, the United States also dispatched troops to China during 1900 and 1901 to suppress the Boxer Rebellion. For good or ill, the United States now found itself bound to protect its interests far from the continental United States.

DINO E. BUENVIAJE AND PAUL G. PIERPAOLI JR.

See also

American Federation of Labor; Boxer Rebellion; Carnegie, Andrew; Chichester, Edward; Coaling Stations; Dewey, George; Gilded Age; Hawaiian Islands; Hong Kong; Immigration; Knights of Labor; Labor Union Movement; Morgan, John Pierpont, Sr.; Philippine-American War; Philippine Islands, U.S. Occupation of; Populist Party; Progressivism; Railroads; Rockefeller, John Davison; Roosevelt, Theodore; Silver Standard; Social Darwinism; Spencer, Herbert; Steel; Trusts

Further Reading

Anderson, Stuart. *Race and Rapprochement: Anglo-Saxonism and Anglo-American Relations, 1895–1904.* London: Associated University Press, 1981.

Goodwyn, Lawrence. *Democratic Promise: The Populist Movement in America.* New York: Oxford University Press USA, 1976.

Gordon, John Steele. *An Empire of Wealth: The Epic History of American Economic Power.* New York: Harper Perennial, 2004.

Johnson, Paul. *A History of the American People.* New York: HarperCollins, 1998.

Kennedy, Paul. *The Rise and Fall of the Great Powers: Economic Change and Military Conflict from 1500 to 2000.* New York: Random House, 1987.

LaFeber, Walter. *The New Empire: An Interpretation of American Expansion, 1860–1898.* Ithaca, NY: Cornell University Press, 1963.

Painter, Nell Irvin. *Standing at Armageddon: The United States, 1877–1919.* New York: Norton, 1987.

Perkins, Bradford. *The Great Rapprochement: England and the United States, 1895–1914.* New York: Atheneum, 1968.

Summers, Mark Wahlgren. *The Gilded Age, or the Hazard of New Functions.* Upper Saddle River, NJ: Prentice Hall, 1997.

Wiebe, Robert. *The Search for Order, 1877–1920.* New York: Hill and Wang, 1967.

United States Army

The U.S. Army on the eve of the Spanish-American War was minuscule by European standards, numbering just 2,143 officers and 26,040 enlisted men. Its largest unit was the infantry regiment, of which there were 25. Each regiment consisted of 3 battalions of 4 companies each. However, on active service, only 10 companies were fielded, and they generally fought as a single battalion with an average strength of about 530 men per regiment. The army was scattered in garrisons, most often at less than regimental strength, among a large number of posts across the United States.

The army's most recent combat experience was limited to small-scale clashes in the various Indian Wars of the preceding two decades. Generally well trained, it was also for the most part effectively led, its senior commanders having held responsible positions during the American Civil War. The army suffered from lack of larger-unit training and was also handicapped by the lack of either a general staff or agency for carrying out military planning. Authority was divided between the commanding general of the army, Major General Nelson A. Miles, and the civilian secretary of war, Russell Alger. Additional problems included shortfalls in modern equipment, inadequate medical support, the failure to anticipate the immense logistical problems that would come with the war, the lack of joint training with the navy, and the lack of sealift capacity to move substantial forces overseas.

In order to undertake the invasion of Cuba as well as carry out operations in Puerto Rico and the Philippine Islands, the army would have to rely on large numbers of volunteers, most of whom were expected to come from the partially trained National Guard. On April 22, 1898, Congress divided the army into two separate organizations: the regular army and the volunteers. In a three-month span, the army would increase tenfold through the infusion of volunteers, but thanks to the influential National Guard lobby, Congress had limited the regular army to only 65,000 men. By August 1898, the regular army had grown to 59,600 men, selected from some 102,000 applicants. By May 1898, total regular and volunteer strength numbered 168,929 men, with that number rising to 274,717 by August. The volunteer units were organized in a similar way to the regular infantry, and many regular army officers were assigned to command them. Volunteer regiments tended to be larger than those of the regulars, each having an average strength of around 850 men.

On May 7, the War Department formed both the regular and volunteer forces into seven separate corps. On June 21, it created VIII Corps. However, only V Corps and VIII Corps served overseas during the war. V Corps served in Cuba and Puerto Rico, and VIII Corps served in the Philippines. The bulk of the regulars were assigned to V Corps. Each corps was projected to have a strength of about 30,000 men in three divisions of 10,000 men each.

Although the regulars were eventually issued tropical khaki uniforms, most of the volunteers received those of heavy wool, which were totally unsuitable for a tropical climate. The regulars were armed with the .30-caliber Krag-Jørgensen Model 1892 rifle, the army's first magazine rifle. The Krag was a bolt-action weapon with a five-shot magazine employing smokeless cartridges. The volunteers for the most part had to make do with the .45-caliber Springfield Model 1873. Not significantly improved from its American Civil War predecessor, its cartridges still employed black powder that immediately revealed the shooter's firing position.

Comparative Makeup of the U.S. and Spanish Armies on the Eve of the Spanish-American War

	Total Strength	Officers	Enlisted	Ratio of Officers to Enlisted
Spain	492,077	70,297	421,790	1:6
United States	28,183	2,143	26,040	1:12

V Corps took 15 .45-caliber Gatling guns with it to Cuba, and a detachment employing them under Captain John Parker played an important part in the Battle of San Juan Hill. The army had rejected the Colt Model 1895 Automatic Machine Gun, developed by John Browning, but this first automatic machine gun acquired by the U.S. military went to Cuba with the marines and aboard navy ships and provided useful support to marine operations ashore.

The artillery also underwent expansion during the war, from 5 regiments and 10 field batteries to 7 regiments along with 24 volunteer batteries (8 heavy artillery and 16 field artillery). Batteries usually numbered four guns each and 70 men. The basic artillery piece was the quick-firing 3.2-inch gun. These weapons were obsolete and still employed black powder cartridges, which immediately emitted telltale smoke that exposed the batteries to Spanish counterbattery fire.

During the war, African Americans served in segregated units. There were also a number of all-black volunteer regiments (with white officers). These units mostly gave a good account of themselves.

During the period May 1–September 30, 1898, the army suffered 2,910 deaths, a figure representing slightly more than 1 percent of the total force. Actual fighting claimed 23 officers and 257 enlisted men killed in action. Another 4 officers and 612 enlisted men died from their wounds. Most of the dead were from disease (80 officers and 2,485 enlisted men). A total of 113 officers and 1,464 enlisted men were wounded during this period.

The Spanish-American War had a tremendous impact on the U.S. Army and saw it largely transformed from a small frontier force to a far larger organization capable of meeting its new international duties, especially in the Philippines. The war also helped accelerate the acquisition of modern weapons and also brought dramatic changes in the army staff system and organization as well as greater army supervision of the National Guard and its closer identification with the regular army.

RALPH MARTIN BAKER AND SPENCER C. TUCKER

See also
Alger, Russell Alexander; Artillery; Gatling Gun; Machine Guns; Medicine, Military; Miles, Nelson Appleton; Militia Act of 1903; National Guard, U.S.; Rifles

Further Reading
Coffman, Edward M. *Regulars: The American Army from 1898 to 1941.* Cambridge, MA: Belknap, 2004.
Cosmas, Graham A. *An Army for Empire: The United States Army in the Spanish-American War.* College Station: Texas A&M University Press, 1994.

Field, Ron. *Spanish American War, 1898*. London, UK: Brassey's, 1998.

Goldstein, Donald M., and Katherine V. Dillon. *The Spanish American War*. Dulles, VA: Brassey's, 2000.

Nofi, Albert A. *The Spanish-American War: 1898*. Conshohocken, PA: Combined Books, 1996.

Scott, Edward Van Zile. *The Unwept: Black American Soldiers and the Spanish-American War*. Montgomery, AL: Black Belt, 1996.

United States Auxiliary Naval Force

A coast naval defense force initiated by Secretary of the Navy John Davis Long on March 23, 1898, and formalized by a congressional joint resolution on May 26, 1898, following the outbreak of war with Spain. The U.S. Auxiliary Naval Force was sometimes referred to as the Mosquito Flotilla or the Mosquito Squadron, particularly while under Commander Horace Elmer. The force was disbanded shortly after the cessation of hostilities in August 1898.

The U.S. Navy's first serious examination of a possible war with Spain took place at the Naval War College in 1894. Officers at the college developed contingency plans for attacking the Spanish homeland, blockading Cuba, seizing Spain's possessions in the Far East, and protecting America's eastern seaboard. Most U.S. naval officers considered a Spanish attack on American coastal cities unlikely, but as war approached, Secretary of the Navy Long was under pressure not to take any chances in that regard. Accordingly, on March 23, 1898, he ordered Commander Horace Elmer to prepare a scheme for a mosquito flotilla to guard and patrol the East Coast of the United States.

Long directed Elmer to undertake several tasks. First, Elmer was to identify ships that could be outfitted as improvised gun vessels, rams, or torpedo boats. Second, he was to indicate how and where armaments should be obtained and mounted. Third, he was to ascertain how captains and crews for these additional vessels might be secured. Fourth, he was to propose appointments for volunteer officers. And fifth, he was to prepare an organizational structure for the entire flotilla. Elmer immediately detached from duty in Philadelphia and proceeded to the New York Navy Yard, where he established headquarters and commenced his specified assignments.

Elmer, however, died suddenly on April 26, 1898. He left behind well-formulated strategic plans but a force that lacked officers and men. Congress had not yet activated the state naval militias, and the Navy Department hesitated to enlist personnel or appoint officers without proper legal authority. Elmer's successor, Rear Admiral Henry Erben, continued to oversee the acquisition and arming of suitable vessels, but budgetary constraints and the manpower shortage hindered his efforts. Finally, on May 26, 1898, President William McKinley signed into law a joint congressional resolution appropriating $3 million for the purchase, lease, alteration, and repair of vessels. The act also authorized the regular navy to appoint officers and enlist men from the state naval militias and formally established the U.S. Auxiliary Naval Force.

On July 9, 1898, Captain John R. Bartlett relieved Erben as chief of the Auxiliary Naval Force. Bartlett's appointment coincided with two major changes: a transfer of Auxiliary Naval Force headquarters to Washington, D.C., and a reorganization that gave Bartlett command of the navy's coastal defense assets in the Pacific. Bartlett ran the Auxiliary Naval Force with the aid of just 10 junior officers, 9 of whom were in charge of designated coastal districts. Six of these districts were responsible for protecting the Atlantic seaboard, two covered the Gulf of Mexico, and one encompassed the entire Pacific Coast. At its height in August 1898, the Auxiliary Naval Force had 41 ships, including 12 monitors, 10 converted tugs, 9 converted yachts, 4 receiving ships, 4 revenue cutters, and 1 torpedo boat.

The Auxiliary Naval Force saw no combat action during the Spanish-American War. Its principal strategic functions were to deter the Spanish from attacking the North American coast and to give citizens of the states along the Atlantic, Gulf of Mexico, and Pacific coasts a measure of security. Daily operations consisted primarily of guard and patrol duties, the latter of which involved scouting, reconnoitering, and protecting the army's submarine minefields. Captain Bartlett gave high praise to the officers and men performing these patrols even while acknowledging the difficulty of guarding an extended coastline with monitors dating from the American Civil War. In all probability, the Auxiliary Naval Force could not have prevented a concerted Spanish effort to attack one of America's coastal cities.

The Navy Department disbanded the Auxiliary Naval Force after Spain and the United States signed the Protocol of Peace on August 12, 1898. Bartlett sent most of the monitors back to the League Island Navy Yard in Philadelphia, returned all revenue cutters to the Coast Guard, and released the converted yachts and tugs as soon as they were no longer needed to patrol the army's minefields. By September 26, 1898, all vessels of the force had been decommissioned and their crews discharged.

TIMOTHY S. WOLTERS

See also

Coastal Defenses, U.S.; Long, John Davis; Militia, Naval; Naval Strategy, Spanish; Naval Strategy, U.S.; Naval Vessels, U.S. Auxiliary; Spain, Navy; United States Navy; United States Revenue Cutter Service

Further Reading

Bauer, K. Jack, and Stephen S. Roberts. *Register of Ships of the U.S. Navy 1775–1990: Major Combatants*. Westport, CT: Greenwood, 1991.

Canney, Donald L. *The Old Steam Navy: The Ironclads, 1842–1885*. Annapolis, MD: Naval Institute Press, 1993.

Paullin, Charles O. *Paullin's History of Naval Administration, 1775–1911*. Annapolis, MD: Naval Institute Press, 1968.

United States Marine Corps

The U.S. Marine Corps had an active role in the Spanish-American War in Cuba and the Philippines. It was also involved in the subsequent Philippine-American War (1899–1902). In fact, the Spanish-American War and subsequent U.S. interventions in Latin America

U.S. Marines form up in their camp in Cuba in 1898. (Marine Corps Research Center)

helped the Marine Corps define its unique role among the American armed services.

When the United States declared war on Spain in April 1898, only the U.S. Navy was ready for war. Yet the Marine Corps numbered just 78 officers, many of whom were aged veterans of the American Civil War, and barely 2,600 enlisted men. However, with war looming, the corps was allowed to expand to its full authorized strength of 3,073 enlisted men. And when Congress dedicated $50 million for national defense, the corps was able to add 43 second lieutenants and 1,640 enlisted men for the war only.

With an invasion of Cuba imminent, Colonel Charles Heywood, Marine Corps commandant, now raised to brigadier general, reshuffled the East Coast marine posts to create the 1st Marine Battalion at the Brooklyn Naval Yard. Formed on April 26, 1898, the battalion consisted of 23 officers and 623 enlisted men under the command of American Civil War veteran Lieutenant Colonel Robert W. Huntington. Huntington assumed the responsibility for preparing his men for expeditionary duty with the North Atlantic Squadron in Caribbean waters. On April 22, Rear Admiral William T. Sampson's North Atlantic Squadron moved into Cuban waters to establish a blockade. That same evening, Huntington's marines boarded the navy transport *Panther* with their equipment. On April 29, the 1st Battalion established a base camp at Key West, Florida, where Huntington drilled his men.

In the meantime, the first news of U.S. military success arrived from the Spanish colony of the Philippines. On May 1, 1898, Commodore George Dewey's Asiatic Squadron had defeated Rear Admiral Patricio Montojo y Pasarón's squadron in the Battle of Manila Bay. The action was decided at long range, but marines did help man secondary ship batteries and served as ammunition passers

and messengers. On May 3, Dewey sent marines from his ships to occupy the vacated arsenal at Cavite on Manila Bay and to maintain order there. At Cavite, the marines hoisted the first American flag on Spanish soil.

While the entire engagement was a resounding American victory, Dewey lacked the manpower to occupy Manila. Eventually, two additional marine battalions were sent to the Philippines and there organized as a regiment, the first time in U.S. history that the marines fielded a regimental-sized force. By August 1898, adequate American land forces, chiefly the army, were on hand, and they secured Manila.

At the same time that Americans were applauding Dewey's victory in the Philippines, other U.S. warships were carrying out a blockade of Cuba in preparation for an invasion of the island. The ships of Sampson's North Atlantic Squadron blockaded Spanish rear admiral Pascual Cervera y Topete's squadron in the harbor at Santiago de Cuba. Coaling the American ships was a problem, as the nearest coaling station was at Key West, Florida. The navy decided to establish such a facility ashore in Cuba on Guantánamo Bay. On June 7, 1898, the 1st Marine Battalion was ordered to seize Guantánamo and hold the harbor there as a base for the U.S. fleet. On June 10, Huntington and his men went ashore and established a position they named Camp McCalla for Commander Bowman McCalla, captain of the cruiser *Marblehead* and expedition commander. On the evening of June 11, Spanish sniper fire killed 2 marines, and firing continued on and off over the course of the next three days. With the help of Cuban insurgents, Huntington decided to take the offensive. On June 14, Captain George F. Elliot led a force of marines and Cuban insurgents, supported by naval gunfire from the gunboat *Dolphin,* to defeat the Spanish troops and take the fresh water supply at Cuzco Well, two miles distant. In this operation, the attackers sustained casualties of 4 Cubans and 3 marines while inflicting some 160 casualties on the Spaniards, including 18 captured. This operation ended the attacks on Camp McCalla.

Following the U.S. land victory at San Juan Heights and the naval victory at Santiago Bay on July 3, the marines boarded the navy transport *Resolute* on August 5 and headed for Manzanillo, but before the marines could come ashore, the war was over. On August 12, Spain and the United States signed an armistice ending the conflict. The 1st Battalion then returned to the United States and was disbanded on September 19.

In the Philippines, the Marine Corps saw significantly more action, working alongside the army and navy in the Philippine-American War. Duties were wide ranging and included both seeking out insurgent forces and carrying out pacification assignments. This activity was not without controversy because of the reprisal actions taken by Major Littleton Waller following the infamous Balangiga Massacre on Samar of September 28, 1901.

In addition to the aforementioned actions, U.S. marines claimed Apra, Guam, and Ponce, Puerto Rico, as conquests of the United States. Marines also participated in cable-cutting operations in Cuba at the beginning of the Spanish-American War and took part in the naval bombardments of San Juan, Puerto Rico, and Santiago de Cuba.

Certainly the war with Spain and the increased U.S. commitments overseas that accompanied it greatly enhanced the roles of both the U.S. Navy and the U.S. Marine Corps. By 1899, Marine Corps strength was authorized at 211 officers and 6,062 enlisted men.

JEFFERY B. COOK AND SPENCER C. TUCKER

See also

Balangiga Massacre; Camp McCalla; Cuzco Well, Battle of; 1st Marine Battalion; Guantánamo, Battle of; Huntington, Robert Watkinson; McCalla, Bowman Hendry; Philippine-American War; Samar Campaigns; Waller, Littleton Tazewell

Further Reading

Millett, Allan R. *Semper Fidelis: The History of the United States Marine Corps.* New York: Free Press, 1980.
Nalty, Bernard C. *The United States Marines in the War with Spain.* Washington, DC: Historical Branch, G-3 Division, Headquarters, U.S. Marine Corps, 1967.
O'Toole, G. J. A. *The Spanish War: An American Epic, 1898.* New York: Norton, 1984.
Shumlinson, Jack, ed. *Marines in the Spanish American War, 1895–1899: Anthology and Annotated Bibliography.* Washington, DC: History and Museums Division Headquarters, U.S. Marine Corps, 1998.
Trask, David F. *The War with Spain in 1898.* Lincoln: University of Nebraska Press, 1996.

United States Navy

At the close of the American Civil War in 1865, the U.S. Navy was second only to that of Great Britain in terms of size. Between 1866 and 1883, however, the U.S. Navy went from some 700 ships mounting 5,000 guns to the 12th-ranked naval power, with only 52 vessels in commission mounting fewer than 500 obsolete smoothbore guns. This was in part the result of budgetary constraints but may be attributed to a reactionary attitude within the navy itself.

Gradually the reformers won out, and thanks to such proponents of a strong navy as Captain Alfred Thayer Mahan, in 1883 the U.S. Congress authorized construction of three protected cruisers—the *Atlanta, Boston,* and *Chicago*—along with the gunboat *Dolphin.* The so-called ABCDs were the first ships of the new navy. Although unarmored, they had steel decks, were constructed of steel, were powered by compound steam engines or by sails, and were armed with breech-loading rifles firing 8-inch shells. Congress also continued to vote regular appropriations to expand the navy. During 1885–1897, Congress authorized the construction of 74 ships: 11 battleships, 6 monitors, 2 armored cruisers, 13 cruisers, 4 destroyers, 18 torpedo boats, 17 gunboats, and 3 other ships (an armored ram and 2 dynamite cruisers, 1 of which was never built, however). In 1898, the year of the war with Spain, Congress voted to build 36 more ships: 3 battleships, 4 monitors, 16 destroyers, 12 torpedo boats, and 1 gunboat. The Spanish-American War proved to be the first test of this modernization program. The war also signaled the emergence of the United States as a world power, which brought a far more significant role for the navy. This and the splendid record of the navy during the war led to further naval appropriations and additional increases in both the number and capabilities of its ships.

When the war with Spain began in April 1898, Secretary of the Navy John D. Long had charge of the navy. Naval forces were organized into the Northern Patrol Squadron under Commodore John A. Howell, the U.S. Auxiliary Naval Force, the Asiatic Squadron under Commodore George Dewey, the Pacific Squadron, the Flying Squadron under Commodore Winfield S. Schley, and the North Atlantic Squadron under Rear Admiral William T. Sampson. The U.S. Navy was then the world's sixth-largest navy, with 43 principal ships. The most powerful of these were 4 first-class battleships: the *Indiana, Iowa, Massachusetts,* and *Oregon* mounted a mixed battery to enable them to engage opposing ships at long, medium, and short range with their largest guns, 13-inchers. There were in addition 7 small battleships and monitors, 19 cruisers, and 13 torpedo boats. U.S. Navy ship strength continued to rise during the course of the war. By the end of 1898, the U.S. Navy had in commission 196 ships of all types: 73 warships plus 123 auxiliaries, including tugs, tenders, colliers, and even a hospital ship, most of which were acquired by purchase or charter. This sharp increase in the number of ships necessitated additional manpower. At the beginning of the war with Spain, U.S. Navy personnel strength totaled 1,232 officers and 11,750 enlisted men. During the war, personnel doubled to 2,008 officers and 24,123 enlisted men, including marines and the naval militia.

Although relatively small, the U.S. Navy proved entirely sufficient to deal with the Spanish Navy. Even before the start of hostilities, the U.S. Navy had undertaken a blockade of Cuba. Then in

A seaman on the U.S. Navy protected cruiser *Minneapolis* signals to the protected cruiser *Columbia*. (*Photographic History of the Spanish-American War*, 1898)

two major engagements, it destroyed Spain's two overseas squadrons in the Battle of Manila Bay in the Philippine Islands (May 1, 1898) and in the Battle of Santiago de Cuba (July 3, 1898). These battles were far more important than any on land, for they cut off Cuba and the Philippines and induced Spain to make peace. The navy also convoyed the ships carrying the expeditionary forces to Cuba, Puerto Rico, and the Philippines. The navy secured the island of Guam for the United States, and its ships cut underwater cables, disrupting Spanish communications while maintaining those of the United States. The navy also assisted with amphibious operations and provided naval gunfire support to operations ashore.

In contrast to the U.S. Army, the navy suffered few casualties in the war. These numbered only 85 dead, of whom 29 died from injuries and 56 from disease. Just 18 men died in battle or from wounds. Another 68 navy personnel were wounded.

Lessons learned from the war brought changes to the U.S. Navy. The assistance of the Naval War Board and the steady advance of technology proved the need for a permanent advisory board to as-

sist the secretary of navy in war and policy making. The Navy General Board came into being in 1900 and was first chaired by Admiral George Dewey. By 1915, operations of the U.S. Navy had been centralized in the Office of the Chief of Naval Operations. Costly and repeated miscommunications and squabbles between army and navy leaders also led to the creation of the Joint Army and Navy Board in July 1903 to bolster interservice coordination and cooperation. This board was a forerunner to today's Joint Chiefs of Staff. Additionally, an assessment of the forces of the Naval Militia enhanced support for a separate Naval Reserve program.

Although the U.S. Navy had handily won its major battles during the war, much improvement was needed in the area of naval gunnery. Following the war, Lieutenant William Sims studied the accuracy of American gunnery at the Battle of Manila Bay and found it woefully deficient. Dewey's ships had fired nearly 6,000 shells with only 142 hits, a success rate of just 2.4 percent. After attempts to gain the attention of his superiors to initiate reforms failed, Sims wrote directly to President Theodore Roosevelt, who immediately made him inspector of Naval Target Practice. With reforms and the application of new technologies, Sims revolutionized naval artillery capabilities.

MARK C. MOLLAN AND SPENCER C. TUCKER

See also

Asiatic Squadron; Cuba, U.S. Naval Blockade of; Dewey, George; Eastern Squadron; Flying Squadron; Howell, John Adams; Long, John Davis; Mahan, Alfred Thayer; Manila Bay, Battle of; Militia, Naval; Naval Strategy, U.S.; Naval War Board; North Atlantic Squadron; Roosevelt, Theodore; Santiago de Cuba, Battle of; Schley, Winfield Scott; Sims, William Sowden; United States Auxiliary Naval Force; United States Revenue Cutter Service

Further Reading

Chadwick, French Ensor. *The Relations of the United States and Spain V1: The Spanish-American War.* Reprint ed. Kila, MT: Kessinger, 2007.

Chesnau, Roger, and Eugene M. Kolesnik, eds. *Conway's All the World's Fighting Ships, 1860–1905.* New York: Mayflower Books, 1979.

Feuer, A. B. *The Spanish-American War at Sea: Naval Action in the Atlantic.* Westport, CT: Praeger, 1995.

O'Toole, G. J. A. *The Spanish War: An American Epic, 1898.* New York: Norton, 1984.

Trask, David F. *The War with Spain in 1898.* Lincoln: University of Nebraska Press, 1996.

United States Navy Asiatic Squadron

See Asiatic Squadron

United States Revenue Cutter Service

An adjunct service to the U.S. Navy yet not under the purview of the War Department or the navy that was designed chiefly to enforce customs laws, enforce fishing rights, and engage in search and rescue missions close to U.S. shores and on inland lakes and waterways. The U.S. Revenue Cutter Service (also known as the Revenue Marine Service) was created as a division within the Department of Treasury by the Tariff Act of August 4, 1790. Its mission of enforcing collection of import duties and tonnage taxes for customs officials was greatly expanded in the 19th century to include suppressing piracy and the slave trade, conducting lifesaving and rescue operations, enforcing sealing and fishery regulations in Alaska, and many other duties. Since the creation of the U.S. Navy in 1798, the Revenue Cutter Service was mandated to cooperate with naval officials in times of war or as directed by the president, a statute exercised during the Spanish-American War.

On April 9, 1898, President William McKinley signed an executive order directing the cooperation of numerous revenue cutters with the U.S. Navy. The Revenue Cutter Service's involvement in the conflict between Spain and Cuba had actually begun in 1895, when President Grover Cleveland ordered revenue cutters to maintain U.S. neutrality by establishing a patrol of the Florida Strait. The revenue cutters *Forward, McLane, Morrill,* and *Winona* were later joined by the *Boutwell, Colfax,* and *Windom* when the patrol was expanded north to Wilmington, North Carolina. At the time, Cubans and supporters of their cause in the United States were illegally smuggling arms, troops, and supplies to Cuban rebels in support of the revolution. During the patrols, U.S. revenue cutters seized 7 ships for violations of neutrality laws, detained in port 13 other vessels suspected of violating the laws, and thwarted two filibustering expeditions. The destruction of the U.S. battleship *Maine* at Havana on February 15, 1898, however, brought an end to U.S. neutrality and the Revenue Cutter patrol.

Early in the Spanish-American War, the cutter *McCulloch* was on its shakedown cruise from Hampton Roads, Virginia, to San Francisco via the Suez Canal. Upon its arrival in Singapore, Captain D. B. Hodgsdon received orders from the Navy Department via the local U.S. consul to immediately join Commodore George Dewey and the Asiatic Squadron in Hong Kong for their planned attack on the Spanish fleet in the Philippines. At the May 1, 1898, Battle of Manila Bay, Dewey ordered the cutter to protect the *Zafiro* and *Nanshan,* the squadron's supply vessel and collier, respectively. The *McCulloch* also stood ready to assist any vessels damaged in the fighting. After Dewey handily defeated the Spanish in the battle, he sent the *McCulloch* to Hong Kong to send news of the victory and retrieve supplies for the squadron. On a subsequent passage from Hong Kong to Manila, he permitted Emilio Aguinaldo y Famy and 13 of his followers to take passage on the vessel. In addition to these supporting duties, the *McCulloch* captured the gunrunning insurgent vessel *Pasig* before returning to the authority of the Department of Treasury and steaming to San Francisco on October 29, 1898.

In the Caribbean, the Revenue Cutter Service played a broader role. On April 22, 1898, Rear Admiral William T. Sampson, commander of the North Atlantic Squadron, began his blockade of Cuban ports and in the early weeks relied heavily on the eight revenue cutters that served alongside his squadron. While navy ships conducted operations in the Caribbean, searched for Spanish ships, and provided protection for the East Coast of the United States, the revenue cutters provided the needed vessels to initiate and continue the blockade of Cuba.

In addition to supporting the naval cordon, several revenue cutters also engaged in offensive operations. On May 11, 1898, in an exchange of fire between U.S. naval vessels and Spanish shore batteries at Cárdenas Bay, the cutter *Hudson,* commanded by First Lieutenant Frank H. Newcomb, towed the stricken torpedo boat *Winslow* to safety under fire from Spanish shore batteries. In 1900, Congress recognized the valor of its crew by awarding them the Medal of Honor.

The cutter *Manning* provided significant service to U.S. Caribbean operations, including its participation in offensive engagements at Cabañas and Muriel, its convoying of transports, and its support of the blockade off Matanzas and Havana. During the latter duty, the *Manning* chased down the German warship *Geier,* which had attempted to penetrate the naval cordon without communicating with the U.S. Navy. On less dramatic but equally important duty, the cutter *McLane,* stationed near Sanibel Island,

The U.S. revenue cutter *Manning.* (Library of Congress)

Florida, spent the duration of the war protecting the telegraph cable that connected the Key West Naval Station to the mainland, which was Sampson's main conduit for communication with the Navy Department.

Seven cutters also operated with the U.S. Army guarding principal ports and harbors along the East Coast and the Gulf Coast of the United States. One of these vessels, the *Winona,* patrolling the waters off Mobile, Alabama, captured the Spanish steamer *Saturnina* on April 24, 1898, the first such action of the war.

Four cutters, the *Bear, Ruch, Corwin,* and *Grant,* patrolled the West Coast during the war. Additionally, four ships on the Great Lakes, the *Calumet, Algonquin, Gresham,* and *Onondaga,* were transferred to the navy. Because their size was greater than the locks of the Beauharnois Canal of the St. Lawrence River, plans were implemented to split these vessels and reassemble them for use in Atlantic operations. Because of delays, only the *Gresham* made it to the East Coast before the Protocol of Peace was signed on August 12, 1898.

During the Spanish-American War, 131 officers and 725 men of the Revenue Cutter Service served on 20 cutters cooperating with the U.S. Navy and the U.S. Army. They provided valuable support to bolster the power of the U.S. Navy over the statistically equal but comparatively hollow Spanish Navy. The Revenue Cutter Service's

participation and success in the Spanish-American War proved invaluable to solidifying its status as an arm of the U.S. military. In 1902, Congress passed a measure providing the officers of the Revenue Cutter Service with rank, pay, and retirement benefits equal to army and navy officers. This measure helped quell a decades-long legislative dispute over the nature of the Revenue Cutter Service as a civilian or military organ of the government. In 1915, the Revenue Cutter Service merged with the Life-Saving Service to form the U.S. Coast Guard, which was defined by Congress as "a part of the military forces of the United States." The Coast Guard was transferred to the Department of Transportation in 1967 and became part of the Department of Homeland Security in 2003.

MARK C. MOLLAN

See also
Aguinaldo y Famy, Emilio; Cárdenas, Cuba; Cuba, U.S. Naval Blockade of; Cuban War of Independence; Dewey, George; Filibuster; Manila Bay, Battle of; Newcomb, Frank Hamilton; Sampson, William Thomas; United States Navy

Further Reading
Evans, Stephen H. *The United States Coast Guard, 1790–1915: A Definitive History.* Annapolis, MD: Naval Institute Press, 1949.
King, Irving H. *The Coast Guard Expands, 1865–1915.* Annapolis, MD: Naval Institute Press, 1996.

U.S. Coast Guard. *Coast Guard History*. Washington, DC: U.S. Department of Transportation, U.S. Government Printing Office, 1982.

Upton, Emory
Birth Date: August 27, 1839
Death Date: March 15, 1881

U.S. Army officer and military theorist. Emory Upton was born on August 27, 1839, to a farming family in Batavia, New York. After a year at Oberlin College in Ohio, he entered the United States Military Academy, West Point, in 1856, graduating near the top of his class in May 1861. A week later, he was promoted to first lieutenant of artillery.

During the American Civil War, Upton fired the opening gun of the First Bull Run/Manassas (July 21, 1861) and was wounded in the battle. The following year, he fought in the Peninsula Campaign (March–August 1862) and at the Battle of Antietam (September 17, 1862). To avoid an assignment teaching at West Point, he transferred to the infantry as a colonel of the 121st New York Volunteer Regiment. The regiment participated in the Battle of Fredericksburg (December 13, 1862), the Battle of Chancellorsville (May 1–4, 1863), and the Battle of Gettysburg (July 1–3, 1863) but saw little action in those engagements.

Just before the Battle of Gettysburg, Upton received command of a brigade in VI Corps, which he led with great effectiveness at Rappahannock Station (November 7, 1863). He especially distinguished himself during Lieutenant General Ulysses S. Grant's Overland Campaign of 1864 that brought the Union Army to the gates of Richmond.

Upton's experiences on the battlefield led him to advocate an important change in infantry tactics, chiefly advancing the men in columns close to the enemy line, when they would deploy in line and charge. Applying this method, he led 12 regiments in breaking through Confederate defenses during the Battle of Spotsylvania Courthouse (May 7–19, 1864). The attack ultimately failed for lack of support, but Upton had demonstrated its potential for breaking through a strongly defended position.

Still only 24 years old, Upton was rewarded with promotion to brigadier general to date from May 12, 1864. Given command of an infantry division a few months later in Major General Philip H. Sheridan's Shenandoah Valley Campaign, Upton was wounded at Opequon and breveted major general. He was then transferred to Nashville, where he led a cavalry division in a campaign against Selma, Alabama, and Columbus, Georgia.

Following the war, Upton reverted to his permanent rank of captain, but in July 1866 he was appointed lieutenant colonel of the 25th Infantry Regiment. He soon became one of the army's leading intellectuals and reformers. During 1866–1867, he was assigned to West Point as an instructor. There he also produced *A New System of Infantry Tactics* (1867), which was adopted by the army the

Emory Upton, U.S. Army officer, military theorist, and reformer. (Library of Congress)

same year. To solve the dilemma of greatly enhanced infantry defensive firepower, Upton emphasized reliance upon open formations, the basic unit being a squad of four men. Operating under simplified commands, the squads could easily form a battle line in any direction. Attacking infantry would form a skirmish line about 150 yards from the enemy, building it up by squads to a point where an attacking column could advance to about 200 yards away and then rapidly deploy into line and charge. This system essentially served the army in the Spanish-American War and into the two world wars.

From 1870 to 1875, Upton was commandant of cadets and instructor in tactics at West Point. With the United States then involved in fighting Native Americans in the West, commanding general of the army General William T. Sherman sent Upton on a year-long world tour to visit Asia and Europe to study the fighting there, especially the British India campaigns. Upton returned as an admirer of the German model of a strong standing army with a large officer cadre and skeleton formations. In time of need, such an army could be rapidly expanded. This system would do away with volunteer units entirely, for all volunteers would serve in the regular army under its officers. He also applauded the German General Staff system and its frequent rotation of officers between staff and line assignments. He was also an advocate of conscription but dared approach this only indirectly. Upton chiefly wanted the United

States to abandon its dual system of federal and state control in favor of assigning all military duties to the regular army. Upton also argued against civilian control of the military.

Upton presented these views in his report published as *The Armies of Asia and Europe* (1878) and in an influential manuscript work, *The Military Policy of the United States.* The latter, the first professional military history of the United States, was published posthumously in 1904. Congress and the country largely ignored his recommendations.

In 1880, Colonel Upton took command of the 4th Artillery Regiment at the Presidio, San Francisco, where on March 15, 1881, plagued by agonizing headaches perhaps caused by depression heightened by the death of his wife, he took his own life.

NEIL HEYMAN AND SPENCER C. TUCKER

See also

United States Army

Further Reading

Ambrose, Stephen E. *Upton and the Army.* Baton Rouge: Louisiana State University Press, 1964.

Michie, Peter S. *The Life and Letters of Emory Upton, Colonel of the Fourth Regiment of Artillery, and Brevet Major-General, U.S. Army.* New York: D. Appleton, 1885.

Reardon, Carol. *Soldiers and Scholars: The U.S. Army and the Uses of Military History, 1865–1920.* Lawrence: University Press of Kansas, 1990.

Upton, Emory. *The Military Policy of the United States.* Washington, DC: U.S. Government Printing Office, 1904.

Weigley, Russell F. *Towards an American Army: Military Thought from Washington to Marshall.* New York: Columbia University Press, 1962.

Wert, Jeffry. *The Sword of Lincoln: The Army of the Potomac.* New York: Simon and Schuster, 2005.

V

Vara del Rey y Rubio, Joaquín
Birth Date: 1840
Death Date: July 1, 1898

Spanish brigadier general who led the heroic Spanish resistance against U.S. forces at the Battle of El Caney on July 1, 1898. Joaquín Vara del Rey y Rubio was born in 1840 at Ibiza in the Balearic Islands. He entered the army at age 15 and graduated from the Colegio General as a second lieutenant. He was promoted to first lieutenant in 1862. After fighting in Cartagena and Valencia during the Third Carlist War (1872–1876), he was transferred to the Philippines in 1884 and served there until 1890, during which time he was promoted to lieutenant colonel. He was then transferred to the Mariana Islands and held the position of governor from April 20, 1890, to August 14, 1891. He then returned to Spain as commander of the garrison at Avila until 1895.

At the outset of the Cuban War of Independence in 1895, Vara del Rey requested a transfer to Cuba. He commanded forces at Bayamo. His men defeated the insurgents in the Battle of Loma de Gato on July 5, 1896, during which Cuban revolutionary leader José Maceo was killed. Maceo, known as the "Lion of the East," had conducted numerous successful operations against the Spanish forces, and his death was a severe blow to the revolutionary cause and a source of encouragement for the Spanish troops fighting in Cuba.

During the Spanish-American War, Vara del Rey, now a brigadier general, commanded the San Luis Brigade at Santiago. At the end of May 1898, his troops forced Cuban insurgents to withdraw from attacking Palma Soriano. On July 1, his forces then fought the Battle of El Caney against Brigadier General Henry W. Lawton's 2nd Division of the U.S. V Corps. El Caney was a small village located four miles northeast of Santiago. Vara del Rey's defensive line was anchored by the old Spanish fort of El Viso, situated south of the city, and his men also constructed six earthen and wood blockhouses north of the town. The Spanish troops, however, lacked machine guns and artillery and were denied reinforcements from Santiago.

On July 1, 1898, Vara del Rey's 500 infantry withstood attacks by more than 6,600 U.S. troops for more than 10 hours. The Americans had envisioned the fighting at El Caney, which began at 6:35 a.m., as a minor skirmish that would last no more than two hours, after which Lawton would assist in the attack on San Juan Heights. Fierce Spanish resistance, however, resulted in the battle lasting until 5:00 p.m. and prevented the U.S. troops there from arriving at the Battle of San Juan Hill on time. Notwithstanding his heroic efforts, however, Vara del Rey and his two sons fighting under his command were killed in the battle. His brother, a lieutenant colonel, was taken prisoner.

Impressed by Vara del Ray's leadership, U.S. forces accorded him a full military funeral. In November 1898, his remains were exhumed by U.S. authorities and sent to Spain for reburial there with full state and military honors. The Spanish government posthumously conferred on Vara del Rey the Cruz Laureada de San Fernando (Cross of St. Ferdinand), the highest Spanish military decoration.

MICHAEL R. HALL

See also
El Caney, Battle of; V Corps; Mariana Islands; San Juan Heights, Battle of

Further Reading
Alger, Russell A. *The Spanish-American War.* New York: Harper and Brothers, 1901.
Feuer, A. B. *The Santiago Campaign of 1898.* Westport, CT: Praeger, 1993.

Nofi, Albert A. *The Spanish-American War: 1898.* Conshohocken, PA: Combined Books, 1996.

Trask, David F. *The War with Spain in 1898.* Lincoln: University of Nebraska Press, 1996.

Vatican, Role in War

Pope Leo XIII, the first pope elected after the Papal States were lost to Italy in 1870, was also the first pontiff to use diplomacy to augment the Vatican's corresponding increase in moral authority. Concerned about the spiraling war fever sparked by the February 15, 1898, sinking of the U.S. battleship *Maine* in Havana Harbor and lacking diplomatic representation in Washington, Leo XIII, through his secretary of state, Cardinal Mariano Rampolla, telegraphed John Ireland, the influential archbishop of St. Paul and a friend of President William McKinley. The pope urged the archbishop to make every effort to persuade the president to preserve the peace and the United States to arbitrate issues pertaining to the loss of the *Maine*.

Archbishop Ireland, an ardent pro-American patriot, undertook the peace mission reluctantly, concerned that accusations of papal interference might inflame anti-Catholic sentiments in the United States, which in that era still ran long and deep. On April 1, 1898, the one and only direct meeting between Archbishop Ireland and President McKinley occurred. According to the archbishop's telegraph to Rome, McKinley desired both peace and the Vatican's help in securing Spain's acquiescence, either in the sale of Cuba to island nationalists or in committing to an armistice to facilitate negotiations with Cuban insurrectionists.

The Vatican forwarded the request to Madrid. Historians differ as to whether Spain or the Vatican misinterpreted the word "help" in the archbishop's telegram to mean a formal request for Vatican mediation. However, in either case, the jumbled message exposed the president to anti-Catholic attacks. McKinley then distanced himself from Ireland, who nonetheless continued his peace efforts. Ireland used West Virginia senator Stephan Elkins as a presidential intermediary and also met with foreign diplomatic and congressional representatives.

On April 9, 1898, Spain responded to the request and agreed to an armistice, the terms of which were to be decided by the Spanish commander in Cuba but failed to mention Cuban independence. President McKinley, using this Spanish reply in his April 11, 1898, congressional war message, barely kept negotiations alive. Spain's continued failure to address Cuban independence ultimately doomed peace efforts in Congress, leading to the declaration of war on April 25, 1898. At that point, the Vatican declared its neutrality, while American bishops proclaimed Catholic loyalty to the United States.

Pope Leo XIII again tapped Archbishop Ireland to resolve postwar issues in Cuba and the Philippines, such as the composition of the Peace Commission and the new Cuban marriage law. Although Vatican attempts to avert the Spanish-American War failed, Catholic American support in the war helped dispel some anti-Catholic prejudices and established Catholics as loyal U.S. citizens.

DAVID D. JIVIDEN

See also

Churches and the War; *Maine,* USS; McKinley, William

Further Reading

Gould, Lewis L. *The Spanish-American War and President McKinley.* Lawrence: University Press of Kansas, 1982.

Moynihan, James H. *The Life of Archbishop John Ireland.* New York: Harper and Brothers, 1953.

Offner, John. "Washington Mission: Archbishop Ireland on the Eve of the Spanish American War." *Catholic Historical Review* (1987): 562–575.

Wangler, Thomas E. "American Catholics and the Spanish American War." In *Catholics in America,* edited by Robert Trisco, 249–253. Washington, DC: National Conference of Catholic Bishops, 1976.

Venezuela Crisis, First
Start Date: 1895
End Date: 1897

Diplomatic crisis between the United States and Great Britain that began in July 1895 over a disputed boundary line between British Guiana and Venezuela. The crisis ended in 1897, and further arbitration firmly established the boundary in 1899. This boundary had been in dispute as far back as the transfer of the Dutch territory to Great Britain in 1816 and was officially in question since 1841. Gold was discovered in the disputed territory, and the British naturally began to exploit the area. This led the Venezuelan government to break off diplomatic relations with Great Britain and request that the United States arbitrate the controversy.

For almost 20 years, the United States refused to become involved in the boundary dispute. Finally, on February 20, 1895, President Grover Cleveland requested a congressional resolution calling upon Great Britain and Venezuela to solve their border issue through arbitration. Cleveland's newfound resolve was in part the result of growing American economic and military strength, but it was also an acknowledgment that the Democratic Party was losing strength in the West and the South and that a more vigorous foreign policy might help its chances in the 1896 presidential election.

At the time, the president of Venezuela was General Joaquin Crespo, who had seized power from a dictator and then had been elected president to a four-year term beginning in 1894. In April 1895, the Venezuelan government seized two British police inspectors and their party in the disputed zone. Upon their release, they made a report to the British government over the incident. Crespo, concerned that he would be asked by the British to indemnify the inspectors, instructed his ambassador to the United States to call yet again for U.S. arbitration of the boundary dispute.

On July 20, President Cleveland's secretary of state, Richard Olney, issued a strong diplomatic note promulgating what would

Political cartoon depicting Uncle Sam as an armed soldier protecting the Latin American powers of Nicaragua and Venezuela from the European powers of Britain, France, Germany, Spain, and Portugal. The cartoon was published in *Judge*, February 15, 1896. (Library of Congress)

become known as the Olney Doctrine (also known as the Olney Declaration). The note stated unequivocally that Britain was violating the 1823 Monroe Doctrine and that any European (i.e., British) interference in American affairs regarding Venezuela would be viewed by the United States as an unfriendly act. The British were asked to state categorically whether they were opposed to arbitration. Cleveland called Olney's declaration a 20-gun blast and was certain it would bring forth a prompt response. But the British government delayed, and when British prime minister and foreign secretary Robert Gascoyne-Cecil, Lord Salisbury, belatedly replied on December 7, 1895, it was to the effect that the Monroe Doctrine was not applicable in modern conditions and was not recognized by international law. Great Britain could therefore not accept Olney's demand that the issue be submitted to arbitration. Salisbury no doubt erred in not making a counterproposal. This was simply take it or leave it.

The British response prompted Cleveland to deliver a stern message to Congress on December 17, 1895, calling for Great Britain to accept arbitration over this matter or risk the possibility of war. Shortly thereafter, Congress allocated funds for the establishment of an arbitration commission.

In Venezuela, there were many demonstrations of support for Cleveland's position and calls for defiance toward Great Britain.

Appeals were also made to boycott British goods, and the government voted additional funding for the Venezuelan Army. During the crisis, the U.S. military prepared war plans. Theodore Roosevelt, a prominent New York Republican and president of the Board of the New York City Police Commissioners at the time, even spoke of the United States overrunning Canada in the event of war.

In late December 1895, U.S. Navy rear admiral Francis M. Bunce was dispatched with the Flying Squadron to the West Indies. His force consisted of the armored cruiser *New York,* the second-class battleship *Maine,* and the protected cruisers *Columbia, Raleigh, Cincinnati,* and *Montgomery.* This was a regular practice and made the U.S. Navy familiar with West Indian waters on the run-up to the war with Spain.

In Great Britain, most people wanted a peaceful settlement of the issue. Newspapers, however, printed the locations of American warships in both the Atlantic and Pacific. The British Admiralty considered the possibility of sending additional warships to North American waters but did not do so.

The British were worried about the Boers in southern Africa, Canada was open to attack, the British merchant marine was vulnerable, and the British were plainly worried about a German naval buildup. The final straw came in the infamous Kruger Telegram Incident of January 1896 in which Kaiser Wilhelm II congratulated the Boers for defeating a raid into Transvaal. This served to inflame British opinion toward Germany. Salisbury agreed to back down and submit the dispute to arbitration.

The crisis immediately eased. Arbitrators began work on the issue in 1896, and diplomatic relations between Great Britain and Venezuela were finally restored in 1897, thus ending the crisis. The two sides ultimately signed a treaty in February 1899 worked out by the arbitrators. The boundary was set largely in favor of that sought by Great Britain, and Venezuela agreed to pay a moderate indemnity to the British police inspectors. But Venezuela did secure control of the mouth of the Orinoco River, which had been its chief goal.

In the United States, the crisis served to invigorate the Monroe Doctrine. It would be invoked in the future to keep European nations from intervening in the Americas and evolved further with the 1904 Roosevelt Corollary. The First Venezuela Crisis also prompted an increase in U.S. warship construction, some of which would be in service at the time of the Spanish-American War.

JACK GREENE

See also

Cleveland, Stephen Grover; Democratic Party; Gascoyne-Cecil, Robert Arthur Talbot; Monroe Doctrine; Olney, Richard; Roosevelt, Theodore; Roosevelt Corollary

Further Reading

Bailey, Thomas A. *A Diplomatic History of the American People.* 10th ed. New York: Prentice Hall, 1980.
Hagan, J. Kenneth. *The People's Navy.* New York: Free Press, 1991.
Herrick, Walter R., Jr. *The American Naval Revolution.* Baton Rouge: Louisiana State University Press, 1966.
Hood, Miriam. *Gunboat Diplomacy, 1895–1905.* South Brunswick, NJ, and New York: A. S. Barnes, 1977.

Venezuela Crisis, Second
Start Date: 1901
End Date: 1903

Latin American crisis that occurred shortly after the Spanish-American War. The crisis erupted when Great Britain, Germany, and Italy instituted a naval blockade of Venezuela following that nation's refusal to honor its foreign debts. In 1899, General Cipriano Castro seized power in Venezuela. He halted payment on Venezuela's substantial public foreign debt and also ordered the seizure of several British ships for allegedly being involved in supporting opposition forces in the Venezuelan civil war.

Castro assumed that given the Monroe Doctrine, the U.S. government would not allow the European powers to interfere and would not itself intervene on behalf of these states. Yet U.S. president Theodore Roosevelt did not regard mere intervention as a violation of the Monroe Doctrine. Rather, he saw the doctrine as applying to the seizure of territory.

The German government proposed arbitration of its claims by the International Court of Arbitration at The Hague (The Hague

Political cartoon by Clifford Kennedy Barryman addressing the Second Venezuela Crisis (1901–1903). It depicts General Cipriano Castro of Venezuela saying "I won't arbitrate!" to Uncle Sam, who is reading up on the "Venezuelan Case." Uncle Sam replies, "I'm busy now. You'll hear from me later!" (Library of Congress)

Court), but Castro rejected this course out of hand. Encouraged by the attitude of the U.S. government, Germany and Britain, which was owed sums five times that owed Germany, discussed recourse. On December 7, 1902, these two powers instituted a naval pacific blockade of Venezuela, carried out by 12 small warships. Italy joined three days later with 2 additional warships.

The blockading warships captured a number of Venezuelan gunboats, and the Germans sank two. Castro now hastened to accept arbitration, and on December 12, the U.S. government transmitted this word to the governments of Germany, Britain, and Italy, which accepted it but continued the blockade for two additional months until Venezuela had signed a protocol to that effect.

Although British and German warships had bombarded several small Venezuelan forts earlier, the January 1903 German bombardment of Fort San Carlos and destruction of the settlement there caused a considerable negative reaction in the United States against Germany. The ongoing blockade also produced some adverse sentiment toward Britain, which set off alarm bells in London. The blockade was lifted on February 14, 1903.

Ultimately, The Hague Court resolved the dispute in 1904. Although the United States had little role in the crisis, it served to strengthen the Monroe Doctrine because the European states had been careful to make certain that the United States was not opposed to their action before intervening. The crisis also helped secure congressional authorization for the construction of five new U.S. Navy battleships. In addition, the debt crisis contributed to the Roosevelt

Corollary to the Monroe Doctrine in Roosevelt's 1904 message to Congress.

JACK GREENE AND SPENCER C. TUCKER

See also

Monroe Doctrine; Roosevelt, Theodore; Roosevelt Corollary

Further Reading

Challener, Richard D. *Admirals, Generals, and American Foreign Policy, 1898–1914.* Princeton, NJ: Princeton University Press, 1973.

Hood, Miriam. *Gunboat Diplomacy, 1895–1905.* South Brunswick, NJ, and New York: A. S. Barnes, 1977.

McBeth, Brian S. *Gunboats, Corruption, and Claims: Foreign Intervention in Venezuela, 1899–1908.* Westport, CT: Greenwood, 2001.

Morris, Edmund. "A Matter of Extreme Urgency." *Naval War College Review* 55(2) (Spring 2000): 73–86.

Vesuvius, USS

U.S. Navy experimental warship. Conceived as a platform for the so-called dynamite gun, which used compressed air to fire dynamite-filled projectiles, the *Vesuvius* was built by William Cramp and Sons of Philadelphia under a contract from the Pneumatic Gun Company. Designated a dynamite-gun cruiser, the *Vesuvius* was laid down in September 1887, launched in April 1888, and commissioned in June 1890. The ship displaced 750 tons, was some 252 feet in length, and had a crew complement of 70 men and a maximum speed of 21.5 knots. Unarmored, the ship resembled a yacht more than a warship and tended to roll in a seaway. Its armament consisted of three 15-inch pneumatic dynamite guns mounted forward side by side along with three 3-pounder conventional guns. The dynamite guns were immovable at a fixed elevation of 18 degrees and were aimed by turning the ship itself. Fired by compressed air at the rate of about one round per minute, the 966-pound shell had a 500-pound dynamite warhead. Range was only about 1,750 yards but could be tripled with subcaliber ammunition.

Commanded by Lieutenant Commander John E. Pillsbury, the *Vesuvius* was assigned to the North Atlantic Squadron. It arrived off Santiago on June 13, 1898, and the next day shelled Morro Castle on the eastern side of the entrance to the harbor of Santiago. Fire was inaccurate and without significant effect. Following the Battle of Santiago de Cuba, the *Versuvius* participated in the raising of the Spanish warships *Infanta Maria Teresa* and *Reina Mercedes.* Taken out of active service in September 1898, in 1905 the *Vesuvius* became a torpedo target vessel. The ship was sold out of the service in April 1922.

SPENCER C. TUCKER

See also

Dynamite Gun

Further Reading

Bauer, K. Jack. *Ships of the Navy, 1775–1969.* Troy, NY: Rensselaer Polytechnic Institute, 1969.

Hogg, Ian, and John Batchelor. *Naval Gun.* Poole, Dorset, UK: Blandford, 1978.

Veterans of Foreign Wars of the United States

Association dedicated to advancing the agenda of veterans' issues on a national scale and undertaking service missions for active-duty service personnel and retired veterans. The Veterans of Foreign Wars of the United States, or simply the Veterans of Foreign Wars (VFW), was begun in 1899 by veterans of the Spanish-American War and the Philippine-American War. Over the years, the organization has embraced combat veterans from every major overseas conflict, including World War I, World War II, the Korean War, the Vietnam War, the Persian Gulf War, and the Iraq War.

Because the Spanish-American War and the Philippine-American War were the first U.S. conflicts waged overseas, veterans saw the need for a new veterans' group that would bring together former soldiers who had experienced the same combat conditions. Thus, in 1899, the first group for Spanish-American War veterans was organized at the local level in Columbus, Ohio; that same year, the American Veterans of Foreign Service was formed nationally for Spanish-American War veterans. The National Society of the Army of the Philippines, also created in 1899, catered specifically to Americans who had served in the Philippine-American War. In 1914,

Sailors of Rear Admiral George Dewey's Asiatic Squadron pass under the Dewey Arch in a parade in New York City, September 30, 1899. The Veterans of Foreign Wars of the United States (VFW) was begun in 1899 by veterans of the Spanish-American War and the Philippine-American War. (Library of Congress)

these two groups merged to form the VFW, which endures to the present day.

Over the years, the VFW has had a large lobbying presence in Washington, D.C., ensuring that veterans receive top-notch health care and other benefits. In more recent times, the VFW has maintained a number of paid employees whose job is to aid veterans in applying for disability claims. This too is a nationwide program. The VFW is also a service organization and as such donates several million dollars per year to various causes. Its members also perform millions of hours of community service. Currently, its most visible service program is Operation Uplink, which provides free telephone calling cards to American men and women serving abroad.

Members of the VFW must meet certain criteria. First, they must be on current active duty or reserve duty or have been honorably discharged from the armed forces. Members must also have earned either a U.S. government-issued campaign or foreign-expedition medal. Failing that, there are a number of other criteria that would also grant membership, including combat action ribbon, combat medical or action badge, or Korean Defense Service Medal, among others. Today the VFW is a robust organization with a membership of approximately 2.5 million veterans.

PAUL G. PIERPAOLI JR.

See also
Cuba Campaign; Philippine-American War

Further Reading
Bottoms, Bill. *The VFW: An Illustrated History of the Veterans of Foreign Wars of the United States.* Rockville, MD: Woodbine House, 1991.
Silbey, David J. *A War of Frontier and Empire: The Philippine-American War, 1899–1902.* New York: Hill and Wang, 2006.

Victoria, queen of the United Kingdom of Great Britain and Ireland from 1837 and empress of India from 1876 until her death in 1901. She gave her name to the Victorian Age. Although a staunch imperialist, Victoria opposed the U.S. war with Spain. (Library of Congress)

Victoria, Queen of the United Kingdom
Birth Date: May 24, 1819
Death Date: January 22, 1901

Queen of the United Kingdom of Great Britain and Ireland from 1837 and Empress of India from 1876 until her death in 1901. Queen Victoria was the last in the line of the House of Hanover and gave her name to an era known as the Victorian Age, which traditionally refers to the last half of the 19th century. Victoria was born Alexandrina Victoria in London on May 24, 1819, the daughter of Edward, Duke of Kent, and Princess Victore of Saxe-Coburg. Victoria's father died eight months later, and she was reared by her mother, who would have been her regent but for the fact that King William IV of Hanover, Victoria's uncle and ruler since 1830, lived until shortly after her 18th birthday. Although Victoria inherited the crown of Great Britain and ruled over the vast British Empire, the crown of Hanover was barred to her by Salic law (which prevented succession by a woman) and went instead to her uncle

Ernest, Duke of Cumberland. When King William IV died on June 20, 1937, Victoria became queen.

For the first two and a half years of her reign, Victoria remained unmarried, vacillating about becoming betrothed to her cousin, Prince Albert of Saxe-Coburg and Gotha. She married him on February 10, 1840. Commonly known as the Prince Consort, Albert was only formally granted that title in 1857. He became not only Victoria's companion but also an important political adviser and definitely the most important person in her life. The couple had nine children, and Victoria became devoted to Albert.

Plunged into despair by Albert's death from typhoid on December 14, 1861, Victoria actively mourned him for the next 40 years. She also attempted to conduct herself, manage her family, and rule the country as she believed he would have done. These constant references to her late husband became a source of continual strain between herself and her ministers of state, as Albert's previously expressed opinions were not always relevant to current situations. Contemptuous of her son Edward, the future king Edward VII, Victoria refused to turn to him to fill the void left by his father's death; instead, she shut Edward out of all responsibilities associated with governing Great Britain and the empire and refused to consult him about any state affairs.

The Victorian Age was a combination of earnestness and egotism over which Victoria was an unlikely leader. During her reign, she mostly ignored Victorian values, which was more than ironic given that the era was named for her. She loathed pregnancy and disliked motherhood but lived in a period in which motherhood and the nuclear family were seen as societal ideals. The queen was uninterested in social reform, yet 19th-century Britain was an era rife with change and social reforms. She was also ambivalent toward new technologies, even as technological advancements were reordering the world around her.

Victoria's long association with Conservative Party prime minister Benjamin Disraeli and her grating relationship with his rival, Liberal Party prime minister William Gladstone, dominated her political concerns for many years and contributed to the bitter political feud between the two men that consumed British politics for the second half of the 19th century. Disraeli ingratiated himself with Victoria by expressing eternal sympathy for her grief and showing tremendous respect for her thoughts and opinions on affairs of state. Gladstone's attitude toward the queen was just the opposite. Victoria's preference for Disraeli thus made a partisan divide in the political contest between the Conservatives and Liberals. Victoria also found herself disagreeing with Gladstone and the Liberals on many of the issues of the day, particularly Irish home rule, which she viewed as the height of disloyalty to her reign, and social reform.

The British public also grew increasingly intolerant of Victoria's perpetual mourning. Nevertheless, her ambitions for imperialism and her exalted view of Britain's role in the world helped her retain some public support. In a brilliant bit of public relations strategy in 1876, Disraeli secured for her the title "Empress of India," and Victoria became the symbol of the national mood and enthusiasm for expansion and empire building. She actively encouraged this view by importing Indian servants who provided her with tea in an Indian tent set up in the gardens of her various estates. She also supported the many colonial wars that Britain waged during the 19th century, in particular the Crimean War (1854–1856) and the South African Wars (1880–1881, 1889–1902). She loudly endorsed the wartime nursing reforms instituted by Florence Nightingale and frequently visited wounded soldiers in hospitals. During the Crimean War, the queen created the Victoria Cross, which remains the highest honor for a British solider.

Victoria was quite active in the formulation of British foreign policy even into her twilight years in the late 1890s. Although herself a champion of imperial expansionism, Victoria was reportedly horrified by the April 1898 U.S. declaration of war against Spain, which included the Teller Amendment that declared Cuban independence even before the fighting commenced. Indeed, just days after the declaration was made known, Queen Victoria called on other European powers to "unite against such unheard of conduct." Here the queen was most concerned that the United States or other rival nations might take it upon themselves to declare Ireland or other British colonial possessions independent. Regarding the war itself, the queen took a neutral stance, not wishing to provoke a larger conflict by taking sides or commit significant naval assets to the war.

By the very length of her tenure during a time of unprecedented growth, Victoria outlived her detractors and gained the devotion of the nation, although many criticized her dour mood and never-ending mourning. She celebrated both a Golden Jubilee in 1887 and a Diamond Jubilee in 1897. By the time of her death in 1901, she had restored, as Britain's longest-reigning monarch, dignity and respect to as well as affection for the monarchy. In addition, the marriages of her children established links to the ruling families of many European states. Kaiser Wilhelm II, for example, was her grandson. Queen Victoria died on January 22, 1901, at Osborne House on the Isle of Wight. She was succeeded by her eldest son, Edward, who took the title of Edward VII.

GUIDA M. JACKSON

See also
Great Britain; Great Britain, Policies and Reactions to the Spanish-American War; Imperialism

Further Reading
Bolitho, Hector. *The Reign of Queen Victoria.* New York: Macmillan, 1948.
Cecil, Algernon. *Queen Victoria and Her Prime Ministers.* London: Eyre and Spottiswode, 1953.
Farwell, Byron. *Queen Victoria's Little Wars.* New York: Norton, 1985.
Fulford, Roger. *Hanover to Windsor.* New York: Fontana/Collins, 1981.
Hibbert, Christopher. *Queen Victoria: A Personal History.* New York: Viking, 2000.

Virginius Affair
Event Date: 1873

Incident in 1873 that came near to causing war between the United States and Spain. During the Ten Years' War (1868–1878), Cuban patriots living in exile in the United States sought money and weapons from Americans sympathetic to the cause of Cuban independence from Spain. On March 1, 1870, General Rafael Quesada arrived in Washington, D.C., to secure ships that he might then use to transport war matériel to Cuba. Quesada was the brother of Cuban insurgent military commander General Manuel Quesada and the brother-in-law of provisional president Carlos Manuel de Céspedes.

John F. Patterson, a U.S. citizen, agreed to secure a ship on Quesada's behalf. Purchased by Patterson in 1870 and renamed by him the *Virginius,* it was a small, fast iron side-wheel steamer that had been built by Aitken & Mansel in Scotland in 1864, employed as a Confederate blockade runner during the American Civil War, and captured by the U.S. Navy in 1865. Patterson pretended to be the rightful owner and registered the *Virginius* in New York as an American ship.

Illustration from *Frank Leslie's Illustrated Newspaper* depicting the arrival of the Spanish steamer *Tornado* with the captured American steamer *Virginius* at Santiago de Cuba, 1873. (Corbis)

During the next three years, the *Virginius* delivered contraband to Cuban insurrectionists while sailing under the American flag. The supplies were purchased in various South American and Caribbean countries and were chiefly paid for by American supporters. Spanish authorities became suspicious yet were unable to stop the fast ship. In June 1873, the *Virginius* made a narrow escape from its pursuers. It had put in to Aspinwall, Colombia (in present-day Panama), for repairs when the Spanish gunboat *Bazan* intercepted it. The U.S. Navy gunboat *Kansas* intervened and helped the *Virginius* to escape.

In October 1873, the *Virginius* called at Kingston, Jamaica, and then in Haiti to load rifles, cartridges, and gunpowder. The ship was commanded by Joseph Fry, a former Confederate Navy officer. Its 52 crew members and 103 passengers included several American and British nationals. The expedition was under the command of General Barnabé Varona. Members of his staff on board the *Virginius* were Lieutenant Colonels Jesús de Sol and Agustin Santa Rosa. These men, along with other Cubans on board, claimed U.S. citizenship. President Céspedes's younger brother Pedro was also present.

Spanish informers had alerted the authorities about the *Virginius*'s anticipated route, and on October 31, 1873, the Spanish corvette *Tornado* intercepted the ship off the coast of Cuba. The *Vir-*

ginius attempted to escape, and a race ensued between the two ships. The *Tornado* finally overhauled and captured the *Virginius* off Morant Bay, Jamaica, within British territorial waters. Spanish authorities arrested everyone on board on charges of piracy and took the prisoners to Santiago de Cuba. The governments of both the United States and Great Britain protested immediately, but Spanish brigadier general Juan Nepomuceno Burriel, who had charge of the proceedings, refused to let either the American or the British consuls visit the prisoners. After a summary court-martial, all crew members and passengers of the *Virginius* were sentenced to death on charges of piracy and aiding the rebels. Burriel offered to spare the life of Pedro Maria de Céspedes if his brother Carlos Manuel surrendered, but the latter refused. On November 4, Céspedes, Varona, del Sol, and Santa Rosa were shot by a firing squad. Three days later, Captain Fry and other members of the crew met the same fate. The following day, 12 passengers were executed as well. Horses then trampled the bodies of the dead. Thirty-seven crew members and 16 passengers were executed, among them several U.S. and British citizens.

On November 8, the British steam sloop *Niobe* arrived off Santiago de Cuba, and its captain, Sir Lambton Loraine, threatened to bombard the port unless further executions were halted. Meanwhile, public outcry in the United States over these events had brought that nation to the brink of war with Spain. Several former American Civil War generals, Confederate as well as Union, wrote to U.S. president Ulysses S. Grant offering to raise regiments in case of war to avenge the deaths of their fellow officers.

Political events in Spain made it difficult to solve the crisis, however. The monarchy had been overthrown in February 1873, and the new republican government was in a state of flux with the country in near chaos. Royalists had plunged Spain into civil war, and their supporters, such as Burriel in Cuba, simply ignored any orders emanating from Madrid. Former Union general Daniel Sickles, U.S. ambassador to Spain, made the situation worse, as he was an inexperienced diplomat who owed his posting to political patronage. His intemperate attitude strained the already tense relations even more.

Eventually, Secretary of State Hamilton Fish took negotiations out of Sickles's hands and hammered out an agreement with Spanish ambassador to the United States José Polo de Bernabé. The settlement was signed on November 29, 1873. The Spanish government agreed to release the *Virginius* and to return the surviving crew members and passengers to an American warship. Spain also consented to salute the American flag on December 25 and to prosecute its officers if the *Virginius* was proven to have been legitimately flying the American flag at the time of its capture. A hearing at the U.S. Circuit Court for the Southern District of New York revealed, however, that the *Virginius* was the property of Rafael Quesada and had therefore fraudulently flown the American flag.

On December 16, the Spanish Navy towed the *Virginius* to Bahia Honda, west of Havana, and there turned it over to the U.S. Navy screw sloop *Ossipee*. The *Virginius,* which had been wrecked during the fight with the *Torpedo,* sank off Cape Hatteras, North Carolina, during a storm on December 26. On December 18, Spain released the remaining prisoners. On March 5, 1875, the Spanish government signed an indemnity agreement and paid $80,000 to the families of the executed Americans; a smaller indemnity was paid to the British.

The *Virginius* Affair helped fuel American animosity toward Spain and also had a major impact on the U.S. Navy. During the crisis the U.S. Navy had mobilized ships for a possible war with Spain. Merely completing the assembly at Key West, Florida, took three months, however. This fiasco proved an acute embarrassment to the United States and helped spark demands for the creation of a modern navy, something that was realized over the next two and a half decades before the war with Spain.

KATJA WUESTENBECKER

See also

Céspedes y del Castillo, Carlos Manuel de; Ten Years' War

Further Reading

Bradford, Richard. H. *The Virginius Affair.* Boulder: Colorado Associated University Press, 1980.
Crabtree, J. B. *The Passing of Spain and the Ascendency of America.* Springfield, MA: King-Richardson, 1898.
Musicant, Ivan. *Empire by Default: The Spanish-American War and the Dawn of the American Century.* New York: Henry Holt, 1998.

Visayan Campaigns
Start Date: February 11, 1899
End Date: April 9, 1899

Ethnic diversity posed a far greater impediment to U.S. victory in the Philippine-American War than many senior U.S. military officials recognized at the outset. Initially, the primary focus of the war effort was Luzon, largest of the islands in the Philippine archipelago and home of the Tagalogs, the most populous of the archipelago's ethnic groups. The Filipino Nationalist movement was composed mainly of Tagalogs, and the de facto leader of the Republicans, Emilio Aguinaldo y Famy, was himself a Tagalog. Consequently, U.S. military leaders became wedded to the notion that in order to win the war, it was only necessary to defeat Aguinaldo and his Tagalogs. Given this premise, it followed that there would be little or no opposition elsewhere in the archipelago.

As the war evolved, it became increasingly clear to many U.S. military officers that this assessment of the situation was far from realistic. Nowhere in the archipelago was this fact better illustrated than in the Visayas, a cluster of islands in the central Philippines of which the principal islands are Cebu, Samar, Negros, Leyte, Panay, and Bohol. Their inhabitants, although generally in favor of Philippine independence, refused to follow Aguinaldo and his largely Tagalog government, preferring their individual islands' political systems and leaders.

On Panay, leader Martin Delgado formed the Federal State of the Visayas and refused to accept Aguinaldo's authority. With the outbreak of hostilities between Filipino and U.S. forces, Brigadier General Marcus Miller landed his troops from gunboats and seized Iloilo City on February 11, 1899. Resistance was stiff but came mostly in the form of sniper fire. With the city torched, each side blamed the other. Nevertheless, a smoldering Iloilo City was in American hands by dark. The U.S. Army and U.S. Navy argued as to who should get credit for the capture, since the navy believed that it was their gunboat activity that secured the victory. This dispute was indicative of the rivalry that often characterized army-navy relations during the Spanish-American War and the Philippine-American War.

Although Miller occupied and controlled Iloilo City, his position was somewhat tenuous. He lacked sufficient troops to control the entire island and was therefore more or less confined to the city. Patrols were subjected to random attacks by snipers, and banditry flourished. On May 5, 1899, Miller was replaced by Brigadier General Robert P. Hughes, a distinguished soldier who soon discovered that Visayans were no more willing to accept U.S. rule than they were to acquiesce to Aguinaldo's directives. As with his predecessor, Hughes lacked the troops to do more than confine his operations to Iloilo City.

The island of Negros appeared more promising. Enjoying relative wealth because of its many rich sugar plantations, Negros was roughly composed of two parts: Negros Occidental on the west and Negros Oriental on the east. On March 1, Brigadier General James Smith had been named military governor of the new subdistrict of Negros. An able and knowledgeable commander, he worked diligently to develop a strong rapport with the inhabitants, following President William McKinley's policy of benevolent assimilation.

On Negros just as on Panay, a political faction created the Federal Republic of Negros Oriental. General Smith's efforts paid dividends. His work included the creation of a local constabulary to maintain law and order. Yet despite his efforts and the presence of a local police force, he still lacked sufficient manpower to control the outlaw bands that flourished on the island. One such group was composed of former policemen led by a fanatic named Luis Ginete. Yet another group that ravaged and terrorized Negros Occidental was the Babylanes, a militant political sect.

On July 19, 1899, Captain Bernard Byrne, leading two companies of the 6th Infantry Regiment, attacked the Babylane village of Bobong near La Carlota following a difficult march through mud and up steep mountain slopes in drenching rain. When the attack faltered in the face of a sudden charge by Filipino bolomen, Byrne ordered a small detachment of his own exhausted command to charge. The stratagem caught the Filipinos off guard and resulted in a Babylane retreat with heavy casualties. Six weeks later, Byrne destroyed another Babylane camp, continuing a string of army successes that lasted into the fall.

Led by Arcadio Maxilom, the inhabitants of the island of Cebu, like those of other islands, both rejected Aguinaldo's demands and resisted the Americans. On February 21, 1899, the U.S. Navy took control of Cebu City, although again there was some question as to whether the army or navy had taken control. As occurred elsewhere in the Visayas, the U.S. Army simply lacked the strength to control the brigands and revolutionary guerrillas.

In August 1899, a column of the 19th and 23rd Infantry Regiments and the 1st Tennessee moved to seek and destroy the headquarters of revolutionary leader Arcadio Maxilom. Following a torturous march in stifling heat, the column exchanged fire with the rebels but failed to accomplish its main mission.

On the island of Leyte, General Ambrosio Moxica commanded a potent revolutionary force. Opposing him was Colonel Arthur Murray, who had only five companies of the 43rd Infantry Regiment. Detachments sent into the interior were continually harassed by Moxica's troops. Between February and June 1901, there were 125 engagements on Leyte.

In April 1901, Murray received reinforcements and launched a punitive strike against Moxica. During the next several weeks, the revolutionary forces experienced severe losses in battles at Ormoc (April 26) and Hilongas (May 6). Further reinforced in the summer of 1901, Murray finally occupied towns that he had earlier lacked the strength to take. As with Smith on Negros, Murray developed a rapport with the natives and local leaders, attempting to demonstrate why it was to their benefit to work with the Americans.

Although Murray tried hard to implement social reforms, he did get tough when revolutionaries and bandits attacked. During the spring of 1901, punitive columns moved against Moxica and again inflicted heavy losses, destroying stocks of supplies and capturing many prisoners. Moxica himself surrendered after his main camp was attacked on April 9. His surrender officially ended organized resistance on Leyte.

The Visayan Campaigns were conducted as backdoor operations, with the bulk of the army's strength concentrated in Luzon. It was a strange kind of soldiering that ranged from implementing social reforms among the native people to tough, hard-nosed campaigning against brigands and revolutionary groups.

JERRY KEENAN

See also
Aguinaldo y Famy, Emilio; Luzon Campaigns; McKinley, William; Philippine-American War

Further Reading
Gates, John M. *Schoolbooks and Krags: The United States Army in the Philippines, 1898–1902.* Westport, CT: Greenwood, 1973.
Linn, Brian McAllister. *The Philippine War, 1899–1902.* Lawrence: University Press of Kansas, 2000.

W

Wade, James Franklin

Birth Date: April 14, 1843
Death Date: August 23, 1921

U.S. Army officer. James Franklin Wade was born on April 14, 1843, in Jefferson, Ohio. His father, Benjamin F. Wade, was an Ohio state senator and then a U.S. senator. A Radical Republican, during the American Civil War the elder Wade was highly critical of many of President Abraham Lincoln's policies. Upon the 1865 assassination of Lincoln and Vice President Andrew Johnson's ascension to the presidency, Benjamin Wade became acting vice president and president pro tempore of the Senate.

With the outbreak of the Civil War in 1861, James Wade secured a commission as a first lieutenant in the 6th U.S. Cavalry, where he remained throughout most of his military service during the war. He earned a brevet promotion to captain for meritorious service on June 9, 1863, during the Battle of Brandy Station and then earned several more breveted ranks during the war, rising ultimately to the rank of brigadier general of volunteers on February 13, 1865. He remained with the army until April 15, 1866, when he was mustered out. Two weeks later, he was commissioned as a captain in the regular army and a month later was promoted to the rank of major with the 9th Cavalry, an African American unit. He rose slowly through the ranks, attaining the rank of brigadier general in 1887.

With the beginning of the Spanish-American war, Wade was promoted to major general of volunteers on May 26, 1898, and placed in command of III Corps, which was organizing at Camp Thomas. The camp, named for George H. Thomas, had been established on April 14, 1898, on the grounds of Chickamauga National Military Park in North Georgia about nine miles from Chattanooga, Tennessee. Camp Thomas became the assembly point for at least six regiments of regular cavalry transiting to Tampa, Florida, for embarkation to Cuba. By the end of April and President William McKinley's declaration of war, troops began moving into Tampa. With the movement of III Corps from Camp Thomas to Tampa, Wade assumed command of the Tampa mobilization center, which soon took on IV Corps and V Corps. Following the armistice in August 1898, Wade became a member of the Cuban Evacuation Committee, which oversaw the removal of Spanish forces from Cuba and Puerto Rico. He did not see action during the war.

In April 1901, Wade replaced Major General John C. Bates as commander of the Department of Southern Luzon in the Philippine Islands. It encompassed 10,000 square miles and 1.2 million people of Luzon south and east of Manila and an equal area on the islands of Marinduque, Masbate, Mindoro, and Samar. Bates had been criticized by William Howard Taft, the first civilian governor-general of the Philippines and future U.S. president, as a mediocre commander. Wade was more acquainted with irregular warfare and more active than Bates. However, six months into Wade's command, Taft wrote Secretary of War Elihu Root claiming that Wade was incompetent and petitioning for his removal. Wade nonetheless held his command until 1904, when he would take over the Atlantic Division until his retirement on April 14, 1907. He retired to Jefferson, Ohio, where he died on August 23, 1921.

R. RAY ORTENSIE

See also
Bates, John Coalter; Camp Thomas; Luzon; Marinduque; Philippine-American War; Root, Elihu; Samar Campaigns; Taft, William Howard; Tampa, Florida

Further Reading
Linn, Brian McAllister. *The Philippine War, 1899–1902.* Lawrence: University Press of Kansas, 2000.

Titherington, Richard H. *A History of the Spanish-American War of 1898.* 1900; reprint, Freeport, NY: Books for Libraries, 1971.

Trask, David F. *The War with Spain in 1898.* Lincoln: University of Nebraska Press, 1996.

Wagner, Arthur Lockwood
Birth Date: March 16, 1853
Death Date: June 17, 1905

U.S. Army officer. Arthur L. Wagner was born in Ottawa, Illinois, on March 16, 1853. Appointed to the United States Military Academy, West Point, in 1870, he had to repeat his first year and graduated in 1875. Commissioned a second lieutenant, he was assigned to the 6th Infantry Regiment at Fort Buford, Dakota Territory.

Wagner served his first seven years in the army on the western frontier. He participated in numerous campaigns against Native Americans, including the 1876–1877 Great Sioux War, the 1877 Nez Perce War, and the 1880–1881 operations against the Utes in Colorado. In 1882, he was assigned as a military instructor at the East Florida Seminary in Gainesville, Florida.

After three years in Florida, Wagner was detailed to the faculty of the Infantry and Cavalry School at Fort Leavenworth, Kansas. While at Leavenworth, he came to head the Department of Military Art and published two notable books on tactics and drill that became the army's standard texts on the subjects: *The Service of Security and Information* (1892) and *Organization and Tactics* (1894). They remained the foundation of U.S. Army operations and tactics through the first decade of the 20th century, and Wagner did much to transform Leavenworth into an important military educational institution.

Following his assignment at Leavenworth, Wagner was promoted to major and assigned as chief of the military information division at the War Department in 1896. This was the army's first intelligence section. As relations between Spain and the United States became more strained, Wagner dispatched two officers from his department to conduct detailed reconnaissance in Cuba and Puerto Rico. He sent Lieutenant Andrew S. Rowen to Cuba with instructions to link up with Cuban insurgency leader General Calixto García y Iñiguez. Rowen's mission became the inspiration for the well-known essay "A Message to Garcia." Wagner was actually the author of the message in question, a detailed list of questions regarding Cuba and the Spanish forces stationed there.

As war became more likely in early 1898, Wagner was appointed the army representative to the army and navy committee tasked with planning the campaign for the conquest of Cuba. Wagner and his navy counterpart, Captain Albert S. Barker, developed a detailed plan for mobilizing troops, transporting them to Cuba, and taking the capital city of Havana. Although events changed the army's objective from Havana to Santiago de Cuba, Wagner's plan still remained the basis for operations.

As V Corps under U.S. Army major general William Shafter prepared to embark for Cuba, commanding general of the army Major General Nelson Miles authorized Wagner to create a Bureau of Military Intelligence that would accompany Shafter's force to Cuba. Miles's intent, explained in a letter to Shafter, was that Wagner's detachment would be used as the central clearing agency for intelligence and reconnaissance information in support of Shafter's command. However, Shafter had his own ideas regarding the organization of reconnaissance and refused to allow Wagner's detachment to operate.

Now without a mission, Wagner volunteered and was accepted as a member of Brigadier General Henry W. Lawton's 2nd Division staff as the chief of division reconnaissance. In this capacity, Wagner landed with the division in Cuba in June. As the campaign developed, Wagner collected reconnaissance data and commanded the advance guard of the division. However, as U.S. forces approached Santiago de Cuba, Shafter consolidated all division reconnaissance staff at the corps headquarters, once again eliminating Wagner's position. For the remainder of the campaign, Wagner was a frustrated observer who saw American units repeatedly falter in large part because of poorly coordinated or conducted reconnaissance and intelligence gathering.

Following the Cuba Campaign, Wagner wrote a detailed and comprehensive critique of the operation with special emphasis on reconnaissance and intelligence activities. This damning analysis was particularly critical of Shafter and was not released for publication until 1908.

In 1899, Wagner was assigned to the Philippines, where he was promoted to colonel. In 1902, he returned to the United States and was briefly assigned as the deputy commandant of the new General Service and Staff College at Fort Leavenworth. In 1903, he was assigned as the senior director of the new Army War College and concurrently to the Army General Staff as chief of the Third Division. In these roles, he greatly influenced the continued reform of military education until his death from tuberculosis on June 17, 1905, in Asheville, North Carolina. President Theodore Roosevelt was to have signed the orders promoting Wagner to brigadier general on the day of his death.

LOUIS A. DiMARCO

See also

García y Iñiguez, Calixto; Lawton, Henry Ware; "Message to Garcia, A"; Miles, Nelson Appleton; Military Intelligence; Santiago de Cuba Land Campaign; Shafter, William Rufus

Further Reading

Brereton, T. R. *Educating the U.S. Army: Arthur L. Wagner and Reform, 1875–1905.* Lincoln: University of Nebraska Press, 2000.

Trask, David F. *The War with Spain in 1898.* Lincoln: University of Nebraska Press, 1996.

United States Army Center of Military History. *Correspondence relating to the War with Spain, including the Insurrection in the Philippine Islands and the China Relief Expedition, April 15, 1898 to July 30, 1902.* Washington, DC: Center for Military History, 1993.

Wainwright, Richard
Birth Date: December 17, 1849
Death Date: March 6, 1926

U.S. naval officer. Born on December 17, 1849, in Washington, D.C., Richard Wainwright was the son of a naval officer. He received an appointment to the United States Naval Academy, Annapolis, where he showed academic promise but received a low class ranking because of his indifference to the institution's strict disciplinary code. He graduated in 1868.

Although the navy was sharply reduced in numbers of ships in the two decades after the American Civil War, Wainwright built an excellent reputation in a variety of assignments. He was promoted to master in July 1870, to lieutenant in September 1873, and to lieutenant commander in September 1894. Assignments included the battleship *Colorado* and flag lieutenant to the commander in chief of the Asiatic Squadron. Returning to shore duty, he earned a law degree from Columbian University (now George Washington University) in 1884. From 1887 to 1890, he was on the faculty at Annapolis. During 1896–1897, he was intelligence officer of the navy, reporting directly to Assistant Secretary of the Navy Theodore Roosevelt.

In November 1897, Wainwright was assigned as executive officer of the battleship *Maine*. In January 1898, the *Maine* was dispatched to Havana, Cuba, to show the flag during unrest there. Wainwright survived the explosion of the ship on the night of February 15, 1898, and won recognition for his efforts to rescue survivors. In subsequent weeks, he supervised salvage efforts and the return of the *Maine*'s crew members, both living and dead, to the United States. He also testified during the navy's court of inquiry that investigated the explosion.

As war with Spain loomed in the early spring of 1898, Wainwright took command of the gunboat *Gloucester*. The ship, originally a yacht owned by the financier John Pierpont Morgan, was undergoing conversion at a New York shipyard. Wainwright had the task of training an entirely new crew on a lightly armed converted vessel in a very short period of time. The *Gloucester* sailed for Cuba just 25 days after Wainwright had taken command.

Following a month spent patrolling the coast of Cuba, the *Gloucester* took part in the Battle of Santiago de Cuba on July 3, 1898, when Rear Admiral Pascual Cervera y Topete's Spanish squadron attempted to escape the U.S. blockaders. Among the highlights of the subsequent rapid American destruction of the Spanish squadron was the *Gloucester*'s attack on two Spanish destroyers, the *Furor* and *Pluton*, sinking one and forcing the beaching of the other. This was particularly noteworthy in that both vessels were much larger and better armed than the *Gloucester*. Wainwright's crew then assisted in the rescue of Cervera and 200 officers and men from the Spanish flagship. For his actions in the battle, Wainwright was advanced 10 numbers in rank. Wainwright's ship subsequently landed the first U.S. forces in Puerto

Lieutenant Commander Richard Wainwright was the executive officer on the battleship *Maine* when it blew up in Havana Harbor on February 15, 1898. He took part in the Battle of Santiago de Cuba on July 3 and retired from the navy as a rear admiral. (John Clark Ridpath, *Ridpath's History of the World,* 1901)

Rico. In the process, he helped capture Guánica, for which he earned a commendation for gallantry.

Wainwright was promoted to commander in March 1899. During 1900–1902, he was superintendent of the United States Naval Academy. He subsequently commanded the battleship *Louisiana* during 1907–1908 and the Second Division of the Atlantic Fleet during 1908–1909. Promoted to rear admiral in July 1908, he retired from the navy in 1911. Wainwright died on March 6, 1926, in Washington, D.C.

ROBERT M. BROWN

See also
Cervera y Topete, Pascual; Guánica, Puerto Rico; *Maine,* USS; *Maine,* USS, Inquiries into the Loss of; Puerto Rico Campaign; Roosevelt, Theodore; Santiago de Cuba, Battle of

Further Reading
Cummings, Damon E. *Admiral Richard Wainwright and the United States Fleet.* Washington, DC: Office of the Chief of Naval Operations, 1962.
Feuer, A. B. *The Spanish-American War at Sea: Naval Action in the Atlantic.* Westport, CT: Praeger, 1995.
Maclay, Edgar S. *History of the Navy,* Vol. 3. New York: D. Appleton, 1902.

Waller, Littleton Tazewell
Birth Date: September 26, 1856
Death Date: July 13, 1926

U.S. Marine Corps officer. Littleton Tazewell Waller was born on September 26, 1856, in York County, Virginia, to a prominent family. He received an appointment as a second lieutenant in the Marine Corps on June 16, 1880, and was assigned to the U.S. European Naval Squadron in 1881.

In the summer of 1882, Waller participated in a landing at Alexandria, Egypt, as part of a marine contingent sent ashore to protect American interests there following rioting. During the next several years, he served in both sea and shore assignments in Washington, D.C.; in Norfolk, Virginia; and aboard several navy warships. During the Spanish-American War, he was assigned to the battleship *Indiana,* seeing action off Santiago Bay and San Juan, Puerto Rico. During the Battle of Santiago de Cuba on July 3, 1898, in which the entire Spanish squadron was destroyed, Waller helped rescue Spanish crewmen, earning the seldom-awarded Specially Meritorious Service Medal.

Following the war, Waller was transferred to Cavite naval base on Luzon in the Philippines. In 1900, he led a contingent of marines sent to rescue foreign nationals under siege in Tientsin (Tianjin), China, during the Boxer Rebellion of 1899–1901. For his role in this operation, he received commendation and was breveted to lieutenant colonel.

Following the Boxer Rebellion, Waller returned to Cavite. After the September 28, 1901, Balangiga Massacre in which insurgents on Samar killed a number of Americans, Major Waller commanded a battalion of 300 marines temporarily under army command to pacify Samar. His commanding officer, U.S. Army brigadier general Jacob Hurd Smith, allegedly issued verbal orders to Waller to "kill and burn," to take no prisoners, to turn the interior of Samar into "a howling wilderness," and to regard males older than 10 as combatants subject to execution.

Waller did not take Smith's orders literally and indeed insisted that the marines not make war on children. Nonetheless, the ensuing violence of the Samar Campaign attracted considerable negative reportage in the American press. In March 1902, Major Waller was court-martialed for the execution of 10 civilian porters during the Samar Campaign. He sought to protect Smith by basing his defense on General Order No. 100 of the American Civil War concerning guerrillas who were captured behind the lines. Smith was then called as a prosecution witness. In trying to protect himself, Smith committed perjury by denying that he had issued any special orders to Waller. The defense then rebutted Smith's testimony with three witnesses who had heard the conversation between the two men. It was by this means that the order became public. Waller was acquitted, and this forced Secretary of War Elihu Root to order a court-martial for Smith in May 1902. He was found guilty and retired from the army.

Following his own acquittal, Waller returned to the United States and was placed in charge of marine recruiting for Delaware, Pennsylvania, and western New Jersey. In 1904, he took command of a marine regiment in Panama. Two years later, he took part in a U.S. intervention force to restore order in Cuba following fraudulent presidential elections there. By 1911, he commanded a marine brigade on the island, and from 1911 to 1914, he had charge of the marine barracks on Mare Island, California.

In 1914, Waller commanded the 1st Marine Brigade during the occupation of Vera Cruz, Mexico. The following year, he commanded the marines in the occupation of Haiti, remaining there until 1916 and rising to brigadier general. In early January 1917, he became the commander of the Advanced Base Force in Philadelphia. Promoted to major general in August 1918, he retired in June 1920. An obvious candidate for the position of Marine Corps commandant, his connection to Smith and the 1902 court-martial prevented his appointment. Waller died on July 13, 1926, in Philadelphia, Pennsylvania.

GREGORY C. FERENCE

See also

Balangiga Massacre; Boxer Rebellion; Samar Campaigns; Santiago de Cuba, Battle of; Smith, Jacob Hurd

Further Reading

Linn, Brian McAllister. *The Philippine War, 1899–1902.* Lawrence: University Press of Kansas, 2000.

Miller, Stuart Creighton. *"Benevolent Assimilation": The American Conquest of the Philippines, 1899–1903.* New Haven, CT: Yale University Press, 1982.

Schott, Joseph L. *The Ordeal of Samar.* Indianapolis: Bobbs-Merrill, 1964.

War Department, U.S.

The U.S. War Department was the government body responsible for planning, directing, and supporting U.S. Army, National Guard, and Volunteer Army units in the Spain-American War (1898) and the Philippine-American War (1899–1902). Secretary of War Russell A. Alger headed the department, but there were no clear organizational lines of responsibility between Alger and the commanding general of the army, Major General Nelson A. Miles. The War Department was instead a collection of different agencies and bureaus, the chief function of which in peacetime was to keep down costs. These included the powerful Adjutant General's Department, the Engineer Department, the Ordnance Department, the Military Information Division, the Pay Department, the Quartermaster Corps, the Signal Corps, and the Subsistence Department.

The army received $20 million under the Fifty Million Dollar Bill passed by Congress on March 9, 1898, to prepare for war with Spain and spent most of it on coastal defense, largely fortifications and artillery. War Department planners envisioned the navy taking the major role in any war with Spain. They saw only a very limited mobilization, with the National Guard assuming primary responsibility for coastal defense. The department was thus sur-

War Department building, Washington, D.C., 1898. The War Department shared the building with the Navy Department and the State Department. (Library of Congress)

prised when President William McKinley issued a call for 125,000 volunteers at the beginning of the war. This unexpectedly large influx of volunteers produced considerable confusion and created serious logistical problems that were not immediately overcome. During the war, the War Department had to contend with logistical shortfalls to include medical supplies and medical personnel and was compelled to face the issue of African Americans serving as officers and the acquisition of transports to carry large numbers of men overseas.

Following conclusion of the armistice in August 1898, the War Department supervised the demobilization of some 200,000 volunteers, established the Division of Customs and Insular Affairs to administer the newly acquired territories, oversaw garrisons in Cuba and Puerto Rico, and dispatched significant reinforcements to the Philippines.

Complaints during the war of mismanagement by the War Department led Secretary Alger to request an investigation. The resulting War Department Investigating Commission was known as the Dodge Commission for its chairman, former U.S. Army major general and former Republican congressman from Iowa Grenville

Mellen Dodge. The commission held extensive hearings but never brought any formal charges, although McKinley did request Alger's resignation in 1899. Many of the commission's recommendations regarding military hygiene and medical treatment were implemented in fairly short order.

Following the war, new secretary of war Elihu Root endeavored to correct many of the department's shortcomings revealed during the war. These included replacement of the position of commanding general of the army with that of chief of staff and the creation of a General Staff.

SPENCER C. TUCKER

See also

Alger, Russell Alexander; Dodge Commission; McKinley, William; Miles, Nelson Appleton; Root, Elihu; United States Army

Further Reading

Millett, Allan R., and Peter Maslowski. *For the Common Defense: A Military History of the United States of America.* New York: Free Press, 1994.

Trask, David F. *The War with Spain in 1898.* Lincoln: University of Nebraska Press, 1996.

War Department Investigating Committee

See Dodge Commission

Warships

The dominant element driving warship design in the last quarter of the 19th century was ordnance. Reasonably reliable self-propelled torpedoes and moored mines emerged during this period, but their influence on the design of warships was limited to largely ineffective passive defense measures (such as antitorpedo nets) and batteries of light guns for active self-defense. Consequently, the primary weapon for all but dedicated torpedo craft remained the gun.

Three factors drove the emergence of a new panoply of warship types: steel construction, advances in machinery efficiency, and improved artillery design. Steel construction enabled the design of warships that were structurally lighter and stronger than their precursors of similar size. Advances in machinery design, first compounding and then triple expansion, endowed new warships with greater range and reliability and led to the disappearance of sailing rigs from naval fleets. Improved breech-loading guns could fire faster over longer ranges and with greater hitting power. The combination of these advances quickly rendered earlier warships obsolete. In their place emerged battleships for service in the main battle line; an array of cruiser types for reconnaissance, commerce warfare, and distant-force projection; and a variety of small torpedo craft for coastal defense.

The new battleships took advantage of lighter hull structures permitted by steel construction to grow in size to carry heavy armor, powerful heavy main gun batteries, and extensive secondary batteries for close-range action and self-defense against torpedo craft. By the 1890s, a modern battleship, displacing 12–14,000 tons, had a main belt nickel steel armor 10–15 inches thick, gun barbettes and shields of similar thickness, and a main armored deck 3–4 inches thick. Its main armament consisted of four 11–13-inch rifled breech-loading guns, usually mounted in pairs. Secondary armament was a dozen 6-inch or 8-inch quick-firing guns plus a similar number of lighter 3-inch weapons. In addition, it carried 4–6 torpedo tubes. Triple expansion machinery generating 10,000–12,000 horsepower propelled the battleship at 15–18 knots and gave it a normal cruising range of about 8,000 miles.

U.S. cruiser *Marblehead* off Cienfuegos, Cuba. (Library of Congress)

Common Warship Types during the Spanish-American War and the Philippine-American War

Designation	Size (in Tons Displaced)	Guns	Armor (in Inches)	Horsepower	Speed (in Knots)
Battleship	12,000–14,000	four 11–13-inch guns six 6- or 8-inch guns six 3-inch guns four–six torpedo tubes	main belt: 10–15 gun shield: 10–15 deck: 3–4	10,000–12,000	15–18
Armored cruisers	7,000–11,000	six–nine .2-inch guns	side: 3–4; deck: 1–2	15,000–19,000	19–21
Protected cruisers	2,000–11,000	small: eight 4–5-inch guns medium: eight 6-inch guns large: six–nine .2-inch guns	deck: 1–4	5,000–12,000	19–21
Torpedo boats	100–200	two–three 18-inch torpedo tubes four–six 1–3-pounder guns	None	1,500–3,000	24–30

Cruisers, by contrast, displayed a great variety of configurations, although two fundamental types existed: armored cruisers and protected cruisers. Armored cruisers primarily relied on a vertical armor belt for defense against shells, while protected cruisers depended on a turtlelike armor deck over their machinery and magazines. In general, armored cruisers (later heavy cruisers) were large vessels of 7,000–11,000 tons. They were armed with 6, 9.2-inch guns, usually paired heavier guns fore and aft supplemented by lighter guns on the broadside. Armored cruisers often carried a light battery for defense against torpedo craft. Side armor was 3–4 inches thick. There was usually heavier protection for the main guns, and often a 1–2-inch partial or complete armor deck protected machinery and magazines. Armored cruisers also benefited from very powerful machinery, often in the 15,000–19,000 horsepower range, producing top speeds between 19 and 21 knots. Their primary missions were reconnaissance for the battle fleet, serving as a fast wing for the battle line, and independent commerce raiding.

Protected cruisers were far less homogenous in their characteristics, ranging in size from 2,000 tons to as much as 11,000 tons. The smallest ships carried about eight 4–5-inch guns, the medium-size ships carried a similar number of 6-inch weapons, and the largest protected cruisers mounted an armament comparable to that for large armored cruisers. Deck armor was between 1 and 4 inches in thickness; above it, the hull was divided into small compartments, some filled with cellulose or used as coal bunkers to contain damage and resist shells. Protected cruisers usually had powerful machinery, between 5,000 and 12,000 horsepower, producing top speeds of between 19 and 21 knots. Their primary missions were reconnaissance, commerce raiding and protection, and force projection.

Most navies also constructed relatively numerous gunboats, essentially reduced versions of the small cruisers. They rarely carried guns larger than 6 inches in caliber and usually relied on subdivision and side-coal bunkers for protection. Their missions were trade protection and showing the flag to support national interests.

During the 1890s, most navies added quite large numbers of torpedo boats to their fleets. These craft relied on small size, low silhouettes, and speed for survival. Torpedo boats displaced 100–200 tons, and powerful triple-expansion machinery of between 1,500 and 3,000 horsepower drove their very lightly built hulls at between 24 and 30 knots. Their primary armament was two or three 18-inch torpedo tubes, usually on rotating mounts, supplemented by a handful of light 1–3-pounder guns. Their small size, light construction, and voracious appetites for coal largely confined torpedo boat operations to within 300 miles of their bases.

PAUL E. FONTENOY

See also

Spain, Navy; Torpedo Boat Destroyers; Torpedo Boats; United States Navy

Further Reading

Alden, John D. *The American Steel Navy*. Annapolis, MD: Naval Institute Press, 1972.

Chesnau, Roger, and Eugene M. Kolesnik, eds. *Conway's All the World's Fighting Ships, 1860–1905*. New York: Mayflower Books, 1979.

Gardiner, Robert, ed. *Steam, Steel and Shellfire: The Steam Warship, 1815–1905*. London: Conway Maritime Press, 1992.

Washington, Booker T.
Birth Date: April 5, 1856
Death Date: November 14, 1915

U.S. educator, author, and influential civil rights activist. Booker T. Washington was born into slavery in Hale's Ford, Virginia, on April 5, 1856. His mother was a cook and domestic servant for a white family, and his father was a white farmhand about whom little is known but who was not a part of Washington's life while growing up. Because it was illegal for slaves to be educated, the young Washington received no formal education, although his natural intelligence and curiosity as a youngster served as its own form of schooling. When he was just nine years old, the American Civil War ended, and slaves were formally emancipated. In the summer of 1865, Washington relocated to West Virginia, where his mother had already set up house with his stepfather, from whom he took the name Washington.

Anxious to make up for lost time in his education, Washington held a series of menial jobs before he took a job with a fastidious and wealthy white woman as a houseboy. Encouraged by his employer,

Born a slave in 1856, Booker T. Washington became a staunch civil rights activist and one of the most influential educators in American history. (Library of Congress)

he began attending local schools, learned how to read and write flawlessly, and absorbed all the knowledge he could. When he reached age 16, he continued his education by attending the Hampton Normal and Agricultural School in Hampton, Virginia (now Hampton University).

Washington trained as a teacher and from 1878 to 1879 studied at the Weyland Seminary in Washington, D.C. In 1880, he went back to Hampton, where he took a job as a teacher. Here he excelled, and within a year he had been recommended to head a new teaching and vocational school for African Americans in Tuskegee, Alabama. The school, known as the Tuskegee Normal and Industrial Institute (now Tuskegee University), began operations in 1881 and expanded rapidly under Washington's careful supervision. While Tuskegee produced many teachers, its emphasis in those years was on vocational training in occupations such as carpentry, masonry, and mechanics. This fit with Washington's ideas that African Americans should become self-sufficient individuals with good jobs and pride in their work so as to earn the respect of the white community. Only by doing so, he argued, would African Americans be granted the full civil rights enjoyed by white Americans. Washington remained the school's head until his death in 1915 and built the school's investment portfolio from a mere $2,000 in 1881 to more than $1.5 million by 1914.

Washington was a natural politician as well as educator, so he was consulted by many officeholders, most of them Republicans. He was seen as a gradualist in the struggle for black equality, and as such many whites were drawn to his crusade of incrementally introducing black Americans into white-dominated society. In other words, Washington did not immediately threaten the status quo. This also helped him raise millions of dollars and much support for black causes—including the Tuskegee Institute—from the likes of Andrew Carnegie, William Howard Taft, Henry H. Rodgers, and Julius Rosenwald.

In 1895, Washington gave a speech in Atlanta wherein he laid out his so-called Atlanta Compromise. In it, he articulated his belief in the primacy of industrial education for blacks; the importance of blacks becoming self-sufficient, thrifty, productive members of society; and the gradual bestowment of civil rights on African Americans. While this stance played well to liberal-minded whites, some African Americans believed it to be too much of an accommodation with white-dominated society. W. E. B. Du Bois, another renowned black activist, initially supported the Atlanta Compromise. But he soon broke with Washington, believing that formal higher education for a small minority of blacks who would then help lift up the others was the preferred course of action. Du Bois also believed that Washington's platform was too gradualist.

As events in Cuba careened toward war after 1895, a large portion of the African American population found themselves supporting the actions of Cuban rebels. Indeed, they connected their own struggles against a domineering white society in the United States with the Cubans' struggle for independence from colonial Spain. When war did come in 1898, thousands of African Americans served bravely and honorably, albeit in the highly segregated armed forces. When the battleship *Maine* blew up in Havana Harbor on February 15, 1898, among those killed in the tragedy were 22 African American seamen, a point that Washington took great pains to point out as war with Spain loomed.

As the most prominent African American in the country at the time, Washington urged African Americans to support the war effort and to enlist in the armed forces. Indeed, the activist argued that African Americans were uniquely positioned to serve their country in a war with Spain because they were used to the conditions that were to be found in Cuba and were assumed to be immune to mosquito-borne diseases that infested the island. In March 1898, just a month prior to the war declaration, Washington assured Secretary of the Navy John Davis Long that there were "at least 10,000" African Americans in the South alone who were willing to show their gratitude by sacrificing themselves for their country. True to form, African Americans in the thousands fought in Cuba, Puerto Rico, and the Philippines. Washington, however, voiced his opposition to the American pacification and occupation of the Philippines. He asserted that until the United States solved its own social problems, it had little right to solve those of other nations.

In 1901, Washington published his wildly popular autobiography *Up from Slavery.* That same year, President Theodore Roosevelt invited Washington to the White House, much to the consternation of whites in the South. This marked the first time that an African American came to the executive mansion on an official visit.

Washington continued to keep up a daunting pace as head of the Tuskegee Institute, crisscrossing the nation raising money and giving speeches. He also spoke out against the segregationist Jim Crow laws in the South and against lynching, but he maintained his gradualist approach to civil rights until his death. Washington collapsed while giving a speech in New York City and was rushed back to Tuskegee, Alabama, where he died of heart failure on November 14, 1915.

PAUL G. PIERPAOLI JR.

See also

African Americans; Long, John Davis; Roosevelt, Theodore

Further Reading

Harlan, Louis R. *Booker T. Washington: The Making of a Black Leader.* New York: Oxford University Press USA, 1975.

Washington, Booker T. *Booker T. Washington's Own Story of his Life and Work.* Amsterdam: Fredonia Books, 2004.

Watkins, Kathleen Blake
Birth Date: February 20, 1856
Death Date: May 16, 1915

Journalist and war correspondent. Kathleen Watkins, also known as Kit Coleman, was born on February 20, 1856, in Castleblakeney, Ireland, to a middle-class farming family. She received a classical education and completed her studies in her late teens at a finishing school in Belgium. From an early age, she was transfixed by literature and writing. At the age of 20, she married a well-to-do man who was many years older. The marriage was an unhappy one, and when her husband died, his family refused to grant her his estate. Now without funds, she immigrated to Canada in 1884.

In Canada, Blake met and married Thomas Watkins, a Toronto businessman. Kathleen Watkins taught French and music to augment the family's income, but when it became clear that her second husband was an incorrigible philanderer, she left him and took a job as the women's editor for the Toronto *Daily Mail.* To pursue her writing passion and to augment her salary, she also published numerous short stories, the first one appearing in print in 1889.

Watkins's work on the newspaper eventually earned her a daily column, which also began in 1889. Writing under the pen name "Kit," she explored many topics including politics, religion, science, and business. Her superiors at first winced at such topics for a section ostensibly aimed at women, but as readership of her work increased dramatically, they did not dissuade her from such writing.

A naturally restless and curious individual, Watkins began to travel, reporting on what she saw and the people she met. Beginning in 1892, she essentially became a traveling correspondent and regaled her readers about her travels to England, Ireland, the West Indies, and nearly every state in the United States. Indeed, by the mid-1890s, her reporting had made her a household name in Canada and the United States, particularly among women. By 1894, she was without doubt the most influential woman journalist in North America and one of the top reporters for any English-language newspaper. When the Toronto *Daily Mail* and *Empire* merged in 1895, she remained as the women's page editor. This combination increased her visibility and readership.

Watkins gained her greatest fame during the Spanish-American War. Anxious to report on the situation in Cuba and to cover hostilities there, she convinced her newspaper to allow her to go to Cuba and report from that island. She faced an uphill battle, however, in persuading the U.S. War Department to classify her as an official war correspondent. Her persistence paid off, however, for she became the first officially sanctioned female war correspondent. Her superiors at the newspaper had instructed her to write features and interest stories, with the implication that the tough from-the-front reporting should be left to male journalists. Watkins would hear none of that, however. As it turned out, she almost did not make it to Cuba, as male correspondents and military officials, disgruntled by her presence, tried to prevent her passage.

Watkins left Tampa, Florida, in late June 1898, arriving in Cuba in July just prior to the cessation of hostilities there. Characteristically, she made the best of the situation and wrote a long series of reports that detailed the aftereffects of the war in Cuba. Both heart-wrenching and compelling, her reporting from the front made her even more of a celebrity. The human cost of war was a frequent focus of her stories.

Watkins returned to Canada later that year, stopping in Washington, D.C., to speak to a congress of international female journalists. While in Washington, she also met and married Theobold Coleman, a Canadian physician.

Not surprisingly, Watkins was a champion of women's rights and believed that it was foolhardy for women to depend exclusively on men for their economic well-being. In 1911, the *Daily Mail and Empire* revamped its contents and cut back on Watkins's space. She promptly resigned and began writing her own column independently, which was rapidly picked up by newspapers in Canada and the United States on a syndicated basis. Due to fear of retribution from her employers, it was not until 1910 that she publicly voiced her support for women's suffrage. Indeed, the *Daily Mail and Empire* had vociferously opposed women's suffrage. Watkins continued to write until her death in Hamilton, Ontario, Canada, on May 16, 1915.

PAUL G. PIERPAOLI

See also

Journalism; Newspapers

Further Reading

Freeman, Barbara M. *Kit's Kingdom: The Journalism of Kathleen Blake Coleman.* Ottawa: Carleton University Press, 1989.

Smith-Rosenberg, Carroll. *Disorderly Conduct: Visions of Gender in Victorian America.* New York: Oxford University Press USA, 1986.

Watson, John Crittenden
Birth Date: August 24, 1842
Death Date: December 14, 1923

U.S. Navy officer who commanded four different naval squadrons during the Spanish-American War and the Philippine-American War. John Crittenden Watson was born in Frankfort, Kentucky, on August 24, 1842. Appointed an acting midshipman on September 19, 1856, he entered the United States Naval Academy, Annapolis, and graduated on June 15, 1860, as a midshipman.

During the American Civil War, he was promoted to master on September 19, 1861, and lieutenant on July 16, 1862. During the conflict, he served as Rear Admiral David Farragut's flag lieutenant and took part in such engagements as running past Forts Jackson and St. Philip to New Orleans, Vicksburg, Grand Gulf, Port Hudson, and Mobile Bay.

Following the Civil War, Watson held a variety of assignments while continuing to rise in rank. He was promoted to lieutenant commander on July 15, 1866; commander on January 23, 1874; captain on March 6, 1887; and commodore on November 7, 1897. When the Spanish-American War began, he commanded the U.S. Naval Home, Philadelphia, Pennsylvania.

Within days of the declaration of war in April 1898, Watson took command of the Cuban Blockading Squadron. He held this assignment from May 6 to June 21, a critical period during which Spanish rear admiral Pascual Cervera y Topete's squadron was steaming toward Cuba. Following Commodore George Dewey's stunning victory over the Spanish in the Battle of Manila Bay on May 1, Spain ordered a squadron under Rear Admiral Manuel de la Cámara y Libermoore to the Philippines. In response, the Navy Department created the Eastern Squadron, with Watson in command. The new squadron was formed from Rear Admiral William Sampson's North Atlantic Fleet with the assignment of threatening the home waters of Spain and forcing the return of Cámara's squadron or following the squadron to the Philippines should it continue there.

The Eastern Squadron's planned complement of ships varied, but it was to include at least two battleships and a number of cruisers, gunboats, and auxiliary vessels. Sampson was worried about having adequate strength in the Caribbean and sought to delay the deployment of the Eastern Squadron. His strong objections prevented the Eastern Squadron from deploying due to the argument that its ships were needed in Cuba until Cervera's squadron could be destroyed.

On June 21, 1898, Commodore John Howe replaced Watson as commander of the Cuban Blockading Squadron so that Watson could take command of the new Eastern Squadron. Briefly during June 21–27, Watson commanded the 1st North Atlantic Squadron. Awaiting official orders to activate and detach his Eastern Squadron, he utilized the battleship *Oregon* as his flagship and was in that ship during the Battle of Santiago de Cuba on July 3, 1898, during which Cervera's squadron was destroyed.

With Cervera's squadron eliminated, the Eastern Squadron was finally activated on July 7, 1898. However, that same day, Cámara received orders for his squadron, then in the Red Sea, to return to Spain. With Watson's mission to the Philippines ended, the reason for the Eastern Squadron disappeared. Although his squadron was never deployed, he retained his command until September 20, a month after the Protocol of Peace.

Following the conclusion of the Spanish-American War, Watson was promoted to rear admiral on March 3, 1899. In May 1899, he was ordered to Manila, relieving Rear Admiral Dewey on June 20, 1899, as commander of the Asiatic Squadron, then actively involved in the Philippine-American War. Watson's service with the squadron was brief, and in March 1900 he returned to the United States because of ill health.

In 1901, as the Sampson-Schley Controversy was being hotly debated, Watson shocked many by threatening to court-martial anyone who suggested cowardice on Schley's part. In 1902, Watson represented the United States at the coronation of Great Britain's King Edward VII. Watson was later sent to Europe to study naval establishments and personnel policies. He retired from the navy in 1904 and died in Washington, D.C., on December 14, 1923.

PATRICK MCSHERRY

See also

Asiatic Squadron; Cámara y Libermoore, Manuel de la; Cervera y Topete, Pascual; Cuba, U.S. Naval Blockade of; Eastern Squadron; North Atlantic Squadron; Philippine-American War; Sampson, William Thomas; Sampson-Schley Controversy; Santiago de Cuba, Battle of; Schley, Winfield Scott

Further Reading

Clark, Charles E. *My Fifty Years in the Navy*. Reprint ed. Kila, MT: Kessinger, 2007.
Long, John D. *The New American Navy*. 2 vols. New York: Outlook, 1903.
Trask, David F. *The War with Spain in 1898*. Lincoln: University of Nebraska Press, 1996.

Weyler y Nicolau, Valeriano
Birth Date: September 17, 1839
Death Date: October 20, 1930

Spanish Army general and governor-general of Cuba. Valeriano Weyler y Nicolau was born in Palma de Majorca, Spain, on September 17, 1839. Following in the steps of his father, a military doctor, at age 16 he entered the Spanish Army as a cadet at the Infantry College at Toledo. Attending the staff college as a lieutenant, he graduated at the top of his class in 1861. Assigned to Cuba as a captain in 1863, he subsequently took part in the Spanish military expedition to reconquer Dominica.

During 1868–1872, Weyler was again in Cuba, this time taking part in crushing insurgent forces during the Ten Years' War (1868–1878). He returned to Spain in 1872 as a brigadier general, marked as an officer of great promise but known for brutal methods. He

Spanish general Valeriano Weyler, governor-general of Cuba during 1896–1897. His harsh policies did much to bring on the Spanish-American War of 1898. (Library of Congress)

next saw service against the Carlists. Rewarded for his service there, he was advanced to general of division, ennobled as marqués of Tenerife, and appointed to the Spanish Senate. During 1878–1883, he was captain-general of the Canary Islands and in the latter year became captain-general of the Balearic Islands.

In 1888, Weyler secured an appointment as governor-general of the Philippines, a post he held until 1891. He reportedly became wealthy in the Philippines. There he also orchestrated military operations to suppress uprisings in Mindanao and other islands. Returning to Spain in 1892, he took command of the Spanish Army's VI Corps, quelling unrest in Navarre and in the Basque areas of Spain. He was then captain-general of Barcelona, where he took an active role in suppressing socialists and anarchists in this increasing industrial city.

With Cuba again in the midst of an insurgency and liberal pacification policies having failed, conservative Spanish premier Antonio Cánovas del Castillo appointed Weyler as captain-general of Cuba. He served in that post in Cuba during February 1896–October 1897. Arriving on the island with 50,000 Spanish rein-

forcements, he continued his reputation as a stern and uncompromising officer. No friend of the American press, Weyler soon ordered the arrest and expulsion from Cuba of American journalists. In order to isolate the insurgency, he also ordered the construction of trochas (fortified lines) across Cuba. More important, he sought to separate the insurgents from the civilian population in the countryside with his *reconcentrado* (reconcentration) system whereby peasants were removed to fortified towns. The forerunner of the British concentration camps of the South African Boer War and of the U.S. Strategic Hamlet program during the Vietnam War, this program uprooted some 500,000 peasants and concentrated them in hastily constructed and often inadequate communities, where they were prey to unsanitary conditions, disease, and even starvation. Thousands died. Meanwhile, Weyler's troops laid waste to the countryside, destroying crops and livestock and anything else that might be of use to the rebels. These policies, while they had some success against the insurgency, earned Weyler such American press epithets as "the Butcher," "the Beast," "the Mad Dog," and "the Hyena." They also greatly aroused general American opposition to Spanish policies in Cuba.

Sensitive to this criticism and to the sharp deterioration in U.S.-Spanish relations, the government of Premier Práxedes Mateo Sagasta recalled Weyler in October 1897 and replaced him with General Ramón Blanco y Erenas. On Weyler's return to Spain, he was approached about joining a military plot to overthrow the government but rejected it because he believed that it would divide the army.

When the Spanish-American War began, Weyler was optimistic, publicly talking about how an army of 50,000 Spanish troops might invade the United States. Elected to the Spanish Cortes (parliament), he blamed the defeat of Spain on the politicians. He defended both the army and his Cuban policies in his 1906 memoir *Mi mando en Cuba: História militar y política de la última guerra serpartista* (My Command in Cuba: The Military and Political History of the Last Separatist War).

Weyler was military governor of Madrid in 1900 and served as minister of war in several conservative Spanish cabinets (March 1901–December 1902, July–December 1905, and December 1906–January 1907). In 1909, he was again governor-general of Barcelona and helped put down an anarchist rebellion there. During 1921–1923, he was commanding general of the army. Promoted to field marshal, he nonetheless retained his rank after participation in the plot in 1926 to overthrow the regime of Fernando Primo de Rivera y Sobremonte. Weyler died in Madrid on October 20, 1930.

SPENCER C. TUCKER

See also

Blanco y Erenas, Ramón; Cánovas del Castillo y Vallejo, Antonio; Carlists; *Reconcentrado* System; Sagasta, Práxedes Mateo; Spain, Army; Ten Years' War; Trocha

Further Reading

Ferrer, Ada. *Insurgent Cuba: Race, Nation, and Revolution, 1868–1898.* Chapel Hill: University of North Carolina Press, 1999.

Pérez, Louis A., Jr. *Cuba: Between Reform and Revolution*. New York: Oxford University Press USA, 2006.

———. *Cuba between Empires, 1878–1902*. Pittsburgh: University of Pittsburgh Press, 1983.

Tone, John L. *War and Genocide in Cuba, 1895–1898*. Chapel Hill: University of North Carolina Press, 2006.

Wheaton, Lloyd
Birth Date: July 15, 1838
Death Date: September 17, 1918

U.S. Army officer. Born in Penfield, Michigan, on July 15, 1838, Lloyd Wheaton joined the Union Army after the American Civil War began in April 1861. Rising to the rank of captain in the 8th Illinois Infantry Regiment, he was at the Battle of Shiloh in April 1862, where he was wounded. After recuperating, he returned to active duty, rising to the rank of lieutenant colonel by the end of the war. For meritorious actions during an April 9, 1864, assault on Fort Blakely, a Confederate stronghold in Alabama, he received the Medal of Honor in January 1894.

After the Civil War, Wheaton remained in the army, serving in the American West. At the beginning of the Spanish-American War, he received an appointment as brigadier general of volunteers. He commanded the 1st Brigade in Miami, Florida, before sailing with his men to Cuba, where they became part of the occupation forces after the fighting had ended in August 1898.

After the Spanish-American War, Wheaton was placed in charge of two regiments and transferred to the Philippines to help suppress Filipino nationalists led by Emilio Aguinaldo y Famy in the Philippine-American War (1899–1902). Upon landing in Manila in late February 1899, Wheaton took part in an offensive led by Major Generals Elwell S. Otis and Arthur MacArthur to capture the rebel capital at Malolos. The Americans hoped that the campaign would end the war. During the Pasig River Campaign, Wheaton led his troops in clearing the insurgents from an area between Manila and Lake Laguna. During this operation, his force captured several towns, thereby dividing the rebel forces and thus allowing the Americans to move toward the insurgent capital. Under MacArthur's command, Wheaton's men served with distinction during the Malolos Campaign, which ultimately resulted in the rebel capital's capture in March 1899. Although this did not end the war, it did force the rebels to move farther north.

The Americans put another plan into operation to destroy the insurgents in northern Luzon in the autumn of 1899. Two columns would continue to push Aguinaldo's forces farther north, while a third group, led by Wheaton, would sail from Manila, land at San Fabian, and move south to link up at Dagupan with American troops moving north, thereby trapping the Filipinos. Wheaton easily took San Fabian with naval support on November 7, 1899, but did not move with sufficient speed to Dagupan. On November 11, his troops defeated a rebel force at San Jacinto, but Wheaton did not follow up this victory by moving on to Dagupan, instead returning to San Fabian. His column would eventually link up with the other two American groups, but the delay allowed Aguinaldo to escape, turning the conflict into a guerrilla war that lasted into 1902. In 1901, Wheaton became commander of the Department of Northern Luzon, fighting the guerrillas using search and destroy tactics. As his tenure progressed, his tactics became increasingly draconian.

In late March 1901, Wheaton received promotion to major general. On July 15, 1901, he was forced into mandatory retirement because of his age. He moved to Chicago, where he died on September 17, 1918.

GREGORY C. FERENCE

See also

Aguinaldo y Famy, Emilio; Luzon Campaigns; MacArthur, Arthur; Malolos, Philippines, Capture of; Otis, Elwell Stephen; Philippine-American War; Philippine Republic, First

Further Reading

Linn, Brian McAllister. *The Philippine War, 1899–1902*. Lawrence: University Press of Kansas, 2000.

———. *The U.S. Army and Counterinsurgency in the Philippine War, 1899–1902*. Chapel Hill: University of North Carolina Press, 1989.

Welch, Richard E., Jr. *Response to Imperialism: The United States and the Philippine-American War, 1899–1902*. Chapel Hill: University of North Carolina Press, 1979.

Wheeler, Joseph
Birth Date: September 10, 1836
Death Date: January 25, 1906

Major general of U.S. Volunteers in the Spanish-American War. Joseph Wheeler was born on September 10, 1836, near Augusta, Georgia. Graduating from the United States Military Academy, West Point, in the class of 1859, he was commissioned a second lieutenant in the 1st Dragoons Regiment. After training at the Cavalry School in Carlisle, Pennsylvania, he was posted to the American West.

When the American Civil War began, Wheeler resigned his commission in the U.S. Army and accepted a commission as a lieutenant in the Confederate artillery. In September 1861, he was promoted to colonel and took command of the newly formed 19th Alabama Infantry Regiment, fighting with it in the Battle of Shiloh. He then transferred to the cavalry, where he won his greatest renown and came to be nicknamed "Fighting Joe." Initially leading a cavalry brigade in the Army of the Mississippi from September to November 1862, he shifted to the Army of Tennessee. He commanded a brigade during November–December 1862 and saw action in the Battle of Perryville. He was promoted to brigadier general with date of rank of October 30, 1862, and to major general on January 20, 1863. He commanded a division during December 1862–March 1863 and fought at Stone's River (Murfreesboro). He com-

Joseph Wheeler served as a major general in the Confederate Army during the American Civil War. His appointment in 1898 as a major general of volunteers for the Spanish-American War was widely seen as an effort to heal remaining sectional conflict. (Library of Congress)

manded a corps from March 1863 to the autumn of 1864 and March–April 1865 and carried out a masterly raid on Union lines of communication that effectively bottled up at Chattanooga the Union Army of the Cumberland. He also saw service under Lieutenant General James Longstreet in the Siege of Knoxville and opposed Major General William T. Sherman's March to the Sea and then his movement north all the way to Raleigh. Wheeler also briefly commanded a cavalry corps in the Department of South Carolina, Georgia, and Florida from the autumn of 1864 to March 1865.

Following the war, Wheeler became a cotton planter and lawyer near Courtland, Alabama. Entering politics, he ran for Congress from Alabama as a Democrat. His opponent, Greenback Party incumbent William M. Lowe, contested the election. Although Wheeler was seated during 1881–1882, following a legal battle of more than a year Lowe won, taking the seat in June 1882. Lowe, however, died four months later, and Wheeler won a special election to serve out the remainder of the term. Wheeler did not run in 1882 but was reelected in 1884 and served until he resigned in 1900. Throughout his time in Congress, he worked to heal the fissures between the North and the South and supported policies to rebuild the South economically.

With the onset of the Spanish-American War, Wheeler volunteered for service and despite his age (61), President William McKinley appointed him major general of volunteers, an act widely hailed as helping to heal the wounds of the American Civil War. Wheeler commanded the Dismounted Cavalry Division in V Corps, which included the 1st U.S. Volunteers (the Rough Riders), led by Colonel Leonard Wood and Lieutenant Colonel Theodore Roosevelt. Wheeler landed with his division at Daiquirí, Cuba.

In the attack at Las Quásimas on June 24 during the Santiago Campaign, Wheeler was reputed to have shouted, "Come on, we've got the damn Yankees on the run!" He later could not remember saying it, but an aide reported the incident. Although ill at the time of the Battle of San Juan Hill on July 1, Wheeler returned to the front when he heard the sound of the guns. Once the ridge was secured, he assured V Corps commander Major General William R. Shafter that it could be held against possible Spanish counterattacks. Wheeler continued in command of the Cavalry Division for the remainder of the Santiago Campaign and helped negotiate the Capitulation of Santiago Agreement of July 16.

With Cuba secure, Wheeler returned to the United States in mid-August and took command of Camp Wikoff on Montauk Point in Long Island, New York, until the end of September. He then commanded IV Corps at Huntsville, Alabama, until December. He was then assigned to the Philippines to command the 1st Brigade in Major General Arthur MacArthur's 2nd Division. MacArthur refused to send Wheeler forward, however, fearing that the climate and the stress would be too much for him. Arriving back in the United States, Wheeler was commissioned a brigadier general in the regular army with date of rank from September 10, 1900. He retired on his 64th birthday. He wrote several books on military history, including *The Santiago Campaign, 1898* (1899). Wheeler died in Brooklyn, New York, on January 25, 1906, and was buried wearing his U.S. Army uniform at Arlington National Cemetery, one of only a handful of Confederates interred there.

MICHAEL E. LYNCH AND SPENCER C. TUCKER

See also

Camp Wikoff; Daiquirí Beachhead, Cuba; MacArthur, Arthur; Roosevelt, Theodore; San Juan Heights, Battle of; Santiago de Cuba, Capitulation Agreement; Santiago de Cuba Land Campaign; Shafter, William Rufus

Further Reading

Dyer, John P. *From Shiloh to San Juan: The life of "Fightin' Joe" Wheeler.* 1941; reprint, Baton Rouge: Louisiana State University Press, 1992.

Kinney, Anders Michael. "Joseph Wheeler: Uniting the Blue and the Gray, 1880–1900." Unpublished PhD dissertation, Illinois State University, 2000.

Wheeler, Joseph. *The Santiago Campaign, 1898.* 1899; reprint, Port Washington, NY: Kennikat, 1971.

White Man's Burden

Originally the title of a poem by the English writer Rudyard Kipling, the term "white man's burden" refers to a worldview in which the

An illustration by William H. Walker that appeared on the cover of *Life* magazine in 1899 depicting Uncle Sam, John Bull, and Kaiser Wilhelm II being carried on the shoulders of nonwhites. (Library of Congress)

people of civilized (i.e., Western) nations believe that it is their responsibility to bring order, reason, governance, and culture to the native peoples of less-developed regions, such as Africa, Asia, and Latin America. Implicit in this worldview, of course, is the assumption that white Europeans are inherently better and more civilized than other peoples. This concept, which is at once racist and paternalistic, was used to justify colonialism, expansionism, and cultural imperialism.

Kipling's poem was first published in 1899 in *McClure's Magazine* right after the Spanish-American War had ended and during the Philippine-American War. In fact, he subtitled the poem "The United States and the Philippine Islands." Hoping to combat the isolationist views of many Americans, he suggested in the poem that it was the duty of the United States, as a well-meaning world power, to fill the position that Spain had once held in territories such as the Philippines.

As members of a modern and sophisticated world, Americans and Europeans saw themselves as ambassadors who should bring these qualities to the less-enlightened peoples. In their view, only the more civilized peoples had the power to tame the wilderness and raise natives out of savagery. Imperialism was therefore a beneficent rather than an oppressive force, spreading superior Western culture to people who were considered to be so backward and infantile that they were little better than animals. Painting this obligation in altruistic terms helped to obscure the self-serving pur-

pose of an empire. Furthermore, any hardship or resistance encountered while performing these selfless acts was simply the result of an ignorant and ungrateful native population.

This idea relies upon certain aspects of social Darwinism, largely theorized by Herbert Spencer during the 19th century. Social Darwinism, which translates Darwin's theories of natural selection and biological fitness into social terms, allows for social inequality by claiming that particular classes and peoples are disadvantaged through their own innate inferiority. Social Darwinism can thus also be used to justify imperialism. Proponents of the concept of a white man's burden strove to convince themselves and others that their actions were done out of a desire to elevate those who cannot otherwise achieve success.

The ideas expressed by Kipling's poem were not new, of course. In the United States, similar beliefs had driven Christian missionaries to build schools that would teach Native Americans the error of their heathen ways. Southern plantation owners had often viewed slavery in humanitarian terms, claiming that without intervention from whites, Africans would be too lazy and ignorant to survive on their own. Some have suggested that Kipling's poem that coined the term "white man's burden" was more satirical than many people believed at the time of its publication. Others, however, point to the corpus of Kipling's work and his overall worldview, which was strongly imperialistic, to discredit any notions of irony or satire. Kipling, according to these commentators, meant what he wrote.

For a time, at least until World War I tamed the search for glory that was to be found in imperialism and warfare, Kipling's way of thinking was de rigueur, especially among upper-class educated elites in the West. The pervasiveness of this mind-set was famously displayed in an advertisement for hand soap that appeared in mass-consumer magazines in the early years of the 20th century. Pictured at a sink washing his hands was an impeccably groomed man in a starched-white naval officer's uniform. The catch line of the ad read: "The First Step toward Lightening the White Man's Burden Is through Teaching the Virtues of Cleanliness." This ad for Pear's Soap extends the white man's burden to instructing the inferior peoples of the world in the proper ways of personal hygiene.

Today, such ideas are widely denounced as racist and Eurocentric. Many, however, still believe that it is the responsibility of more-developed countries to intervene in the developing world. They argue that without foreign assistance, developing countries could not establish the sort of stable society needed for economic and social prosperity. In the last 50–60 years, this thinking has taken on a different discourse. Instead of trying to civilize people, many Western nations, particularly the United States, argue that it is their mission to spread democracy and protect human rights in the developing world. Yet implicit in this message is a belief in the superiority of Western-style democracy and values. Through trade, economic exchange, and modern communications, the West—and most of all the United States—has regularly practiced cultural imperialism in which Western values are inculcated to vast parts of the globe with more subliminal (but certainly no less powerful) means.

PAUL G. PIERPAOLI JR.

See also

Imperialism; Kipling, Rudyard; Racism; Social Darwinism; Spencer, Herbert

Further Reading

Hobson, J. A. *Imperialism: A Study.* Ann Arbor: University of Michigan Press, 1965.

Jordan, Winthrop D. *White Man's Burden: Historical Origins of Racism in the United States.* Oxford: Oxford University Press, 1974.

Ricketts, Harry. *Rudyard Kipling: A Life.* New York: Carroll and Graf, 2000.

Said, Edward W. *Culture and Imperialism.* New York: Vintage, 1994.

Whitney, Henry Howard

Birth Date: December 25, 1866
Death Date: April 2, 1949

U.S. Army officer who was dispatched to Puerto Rico to conduct reconnaissance there. Born in Glen Hope, Pennsylvania, on December 25, 1866, Henry Howard Whitney graduated from the United States Military Academy, West Point, in 1892 and was commissioned a second lieutenant of artillery and assigned to the 4th Artillery Regiment. A gifted linguist, he was fluent in Spanish and French and had wide knowledge of Latin, ancient and modern Greek, and Italian. Fascinated by technology and its uses for military intelligence, he conducted a number of experiments and wrote numerous reports, some of which attracted the attention of the army hierarchy. In 1896, he was assigned to the Military Information Division.

Because of his facility in languages and interest in military intelligence, Whitney was assigned to West Point in January 1898 to receive advanced training in the use of photography for mapping and reconnaissance purposes. After the Spanish-American War began, he was ordered first to Cuba and then to Puerto Rico to gather intelligence. In Cuba, he acted as a courier to Cuban insurgent leader Major General Máximo Gómez. At Port Charlotte Amalie, St. Thomas, Whitney sailed on a merchant ship that arrived at the port of Ponce, Puerto Rico, on May 15, 1898. With the assistance of the captain, Whitney pretended to be a member of the crew and remained aboard as the ship made stops along the Puerto Rican coast. At each stop, he took photographs and produced detailed maps of the coastline, which stood the U.S. Army in good stead just two months later. He was also able to ascertain detailed information on currents and harbor depths and provide information that residents of Ponce sympathized with the American cause.

Once ashore, Whitney used a number of disguises, including those of a traveling salesman and fisherman, to gather information about inland topography, communications centers, lighthouses, population centers, roads, and bridges. By the end of May

U.S. Army captain Henry H. Whitney, who carried out a reconnaissance assignment in Puerto Rico during the Spanish-American War. (*Photographic History of the Spanish-American War*, 1898)

and after two weeks of intense reconnaissance activity, his work was complete.

Whitney's reports were uncannily accurate and revealed, among other things, that Ponce was defended by just 800 Spanish regulars, of whom half were volunteers; that the city of Guayama was strongly pro-Spanish; and that the town of Vieques would serve well as a site for a U.S. Army camp and hospital. His mission was not without its travails, however. A newspaper mistakenly identified him, nearly blowing his cover, and he had to hide in the boiler room of a British ship when Spanish officials boarded it.

Whitney returned to the United States on June 1, 1898, and personally briefed President William McKinley on his findings. For his good work, Whitney was immediately promoted to captain and was attached to Major General Nelson A. Miles's Puerto Rican Expedition, which landed at Guánica on July 25, 1898, in large part because of Whitney's reconnaissance, which had militated against the originally planned landing at Fajardo. Indeed, his reconnaissance mission had contributed substantially to the relatively easy time that the Americans had assaulting and occupying Puerto Rico with a landing at Guánica. Whitney then served on Miles's staff during the Puerto Rico Campaign.

Whitney remained in the army after the war, serving as chief of staff to Miles and accompanying him during his world tour of 1902–1903. Whitney went on to serve in a variety of administrative positions. He was commander of the Presidio in February 1915 when Brigadier General John J. Pershing's wife and three daughters tragically died in a house fire. During World War I, Whitney was promoted to brigadier general and briefly served as commander of the 38th Division, arriving in France shortly before the armistice. He retired from active duty in 1924 as a brigadier general. Whitney died in Madison, New Jersey, on April 2, 1949.

PAUL G. PIERPAOLI JR.

See also

Gómez y Báez, Máximo; Guánica, Puerto Rico; Miles, Nelson Appleton; Military Intelligence; Ponce, Puerto Rico; Puerto Rico

Further Reading

Cosmas, Graham A. *An Army for Empire: The United States Army in the Spanish-American War.* College Station: Texas A&M University Press, 1994.

Miles, Nelson A. *Personal Recollections and Observations of General Nelson Miles.* 2 vols. Lincoln: University of Nebraska Press, 1992.

Trask, David. "American Intelligence during the Spanish-American War." In *Crucible of Empire: The Spanish-American War and Its Aftermath,* edited by James C. Bradford, 23–46. Annapolis, MD: Naval Institute Press, 1993.

Wikoff, Charles Augustus
Birth Date: 1837
Death Date: July 1, 1898

U.S. Army officer and highest-ranking officer to die during the Spanish-American War. Charles Augustus Wikoff was born in 1837 in Easton, Pennsylvania, and joined the U.S. Army at a young age. During the American Civil War, he was a lieutenant in the Union forces and saw action at a number of battles, among them Shiloh (April 6–7, 1862) during which he was wounded, resulting in permanent blindness in the left eye. For the remainder of his life, he wore a black eye patch.

Now a colonel, Wikoff commanded the 22nd Infantry Regiment at the beginning of the Spanish-American War. He was with the unit from the time it was mobilized at Fort Crook, Nebraska, until it arrived on June 20, 1898, near the mouth of Santiago Bay, Cuba. The 22nd Infantry was the first U.S. Army unit to land in Cuba. Upon arrival, Wikoff was immediately transferred to the 2nd Division of V Corps, under the overall command of Major General William R. Shafter. Wikoff's replacement, Colonel John H. Patterson, took the 22nd Infantry into battle.

As commander of the 13th Infantry Regiment at the beginning of the Battle of San Juan Hill on July 1, Wikoff led his men across the

San Juan River. The regiment came within about 500 yards of the Spanish redoubts at San Juan Hill. Wikoff and his men paused there for a short time to rest and regroup before Wikoff led an advance across an open field, moving toward San Juan Hill. During this movement, he was shot and mortally wounded by Spanish fire. He died on the battlefield before he could be moved to the rear. In less than 10 minutes, two of his succeeding commanders were also shot. Wikoff remained the highest-ranking officer to die in battle during the brief war.

Wikoff's body was returned to the United States and was interred in Easton, Pennsylvania. Camp Wikoff on Long Island, New York, a large army camp dedicated to housing soldiers mustering out at war's end, was named in his honor.

PAUL G. PIERPAOLI JR.

See also

Camp Wikoff; V Corps; San Juan Heights, Battle of; Shafter, William Rufus

Further Reading

Cosmas, Graham A. *An Army for Empire: The United States Army in the Spanish-American War.* College Station: Texas A&M University Press, 1994.

Henry, Will. *San Juan Hill.* Wayne, PA: Dorchester Publishing and Leisure Books, 1996.

Wildman, Rounseville
Birth Date: March 19, 1864
Death Date: February 22, 1901

U.S. diplomat and journalist. Born on March 19, 1864, in Batavia, New York, Rounseville Wildman embarked on a career in journalism after graduating from Syracuse University. He moved to Idaho in the 1880s and became editor of the *Idaho Statesman.* His role in pushing for Idaho's admission to the Union while serving as its territorial delegate to Congress won the notice of Republican president Benjamin Harrison, who in 1889 appointed him consul general to Singapore, where Wildman served for three years before being transferred to Barman, Germany. After Grover Cleveland's election in 1892, Wildman returned to the United States, serving as a commissioner at the Columbian Exposition in 1893 and as editor of the *Overland Monthly* during 1894–1897. Following the election of President William McKinley in 1896, Wildman resumed his diplomatic career, this time serving as consul general in Hong Kong, where he would play an important role in the Spanish-American War.

In 1897, Wildman met in Hong Kong with Felipe Agoncillo, one of the leaders of the Philippine insurgents, who proposed an alliance with the United States against Spain. This was to take effect as soon as Spain and the United States were at war, which Agoncillo believed would occur soon. He suggested that in the meantime, the United States supply arms to the insurgents, which would be paid for as soon as the Philippines secured their independence and gained international diplomatic recognition. Agoncillo assured Wildman that the insurgents were prepared, as the consul put it in a cable to Washington on November 1, 1897, to offer the United States as collateral security "two provinces and the custom-house at Manila."

Wildman's news met with rebuff. Third assistant secretary of state Thomas F. Cridler informed the consul that not only did the United States not enter into such treaties but also that it would be impossible to supply the requested arms and ammunition to the Filipino rebels. Indeed, Cridler was critical of Wildman for meeting with Agoncillo at all and enjoined the consul both to avoid any further talks with him and to "courteously decline to communicate with the Department further regarding his alleged mission."

Wildman had several meetings with Filipino insurgent leader Emilio Aguinaldo y Famy in Hong Kong and in early May 1898 urged that Aguinaldo return to the Philippines. Aguinaldo refused, claiming that he must first have a written agreement with the Americans. Without this, he said, U.S. Navy rear admiral George Dewey might force him to make unfavorable political concessions. But with his colleagues unanimously in favor of his return, Aguinaldo changed his mind, and Wildman arranged passage for him to the Philippines on board the U.S. revenue cutter *McCulloch* when it returned to the Philippines following its delivery of Dewey's dispatches to Hong Kong. Wildman reportedly told Aguinaldo that he should establish a dictatorial government, which would be required in fighting a war with Spain, but that once the war was won, the dictatorial government must be replaced with a democratic government similar to that of the United States. Wildman also reportedly assured Aguinaldo that the U.S. government sympathized with the Filipino aspirations for independence.

Wildman also helped the insurgents secure arms with funds provided by Aguinaldo and reportedly receiving a percentage for his services. On May 27, 1898, a shipment from Amoy of 2,282 Remington rifles and 175,550 rounds of ammunition arrived in the Philippines for the insurgents, secured with the payment by Wildman of 50,000 Mexican pesos that Aguinaldo had provided him from part of the settlement paid by the Spanish government to the insurgent leaders under terms of the Pact of Biak-na-Bato. Wildman also reportedly arranged for a second arms shipment costing 67,000 pesos. It is not clear what became of this shipment or the funds, for the arms were never delivered to the insurgents.

In June, Wildman reported to Washington that most Filipinos favored the Philippines becoming a colony of the United States. In late July, however, he informed Aguinaldo that the United States did not want colonies, and in early August, Wildman insisted to the State Department that he had made no binding political commitments to Aguinaldo on behalf of the United States and that he had treated with him only as a "necessary evil."

Wildman remained at his Hong Kong post during the onset of the Philippine-American War and the Boxer Rebellion. While returning to the United States on leave in February 1901, he and his family perished in the sinking of the *City of Rio de Janeiro* in San Francisco Harbor on February 22, 1901.

SPENCER C. TUCKER

See also

Agoncillo, Felipe; Aguinaldo y Famy, Emilio; Biak-na-Bato, Pact of; Dewey, George; Hong Kong

Further Reading

De Ocampo, Esteban A. *First Filipino Diplomat: Felipe Agoncillo, 1859–1941.* Manila: National Historical Institute, 1977.

Silbey, David J. *A War of Frontier and Empire: The Philippine-American War, 1899–1902.* New York: Hill and Wang, 2006.

Trask, David F. *The War with Spain in 1898.* Lincoln: University of Nebraska Press, 1996.

Wilhelm II, King of Prussia
Birth Date: January 27, 1859
Death Date: June 3, 1941

German emperor and King of Prussia. Born in Berlin on January 27, 1859, Friedrich Wilhelm Viktor Albert of Hohenzollern was the son of Crown Prince Friedrich Wilhelm (briefly Emperor Friedrich III in 1888) and Crown Princess Victoria, eldest daughter of Queen Victoria of Britain. Many historians have focused on Wilhelm II's birth and childhood and particularly his family relations as factors shaping his character. His birth was complicated, leaving attending doctors fearful that he and his mother would die. Some have even speculated that Wilhelm was oxygen deprived at birth, suffering brain damage. He had a withered left arm, the result of damage done to the nerves leading from his neck during the birth. These disabilities posed serious obstacles in a society fixated on physical and mental strength. However, the young Wilhelm overcame them and excelled in sports. Well educated and widely read, he also developed a forceful personality and was determined to have things his own way. Chancellor Otto von Bismarck, who encouraged this tendency in him, said that Wilhelm "wanted every day to be a Sunday."

Wilhelm was fascinated by everything military, including uniforms. As kaiser, he possessed a uniform for every German regiment as well as a warehouse full of German naval uniforms and uniforms from honorary rank in foreign military services. The success of the Prussian Army in wars against Denmark (1864), Austria (1866), and France (1870–1871) not only led to the unification of the German states but also reinforced in Wilhelm the belief that the military was the centerpiece of the state and would be the means whereby Germany would take its rightful place in the world. Yet it should not be said that Wilhelm was inevitably destined for war. He was also affected to a degree by his parents' insistence on a liberal, progressive education from his civilian tutors, out of which grew a genuine sense of social responsibility. In the end, however, the martial tendencies prevailed.

Wilhelm's extended family also had significant bearing on his character. His cousins included Tsar Nicholas II of Russia and King George V of England. Even before he became emperor, Wilhelm was exposed to this family and its diplomacy, heading important

Kaiser Wilhelm II was determined, through his aggressive *Weltpolitik* (world policy), to make Germany the preeminent world power and hoped as a consequence of the Spanish-American War to be able to secure at least part of the Philippines. (Library of Congress)

missions to Russia in 1884 and 1886 at the request of his grandfather, Emperor Wilhelm I, with whom he developed a close relationship. In fact, the connection between the two aggravated Wilhelm's parents to the point that by the mid-1880s, they barely spoke with their son. In effect, Wilhelm and his father became rivals within the German court.

When Wilhelm I died in 1888, Wilhelm's father assumed the throne as Friedrich III but ruled for just 99 days before dying of cancer of the throat on June 15, 1888. Friedrich and his wife Victoria had hoped to take Germany in a liberal direction and make it more in the image of Britain, so his death was a great tragedy for those favoring more liberal institutions.

Wilhelm assumed the throne at age 29 as Wilhelm II, German kaiser and king of Prussia. Initially the new kaiser was dependent on Chancellor Bismarck, who had encouraged his absolutist tendencies in order to annoy Friedrich. Ironically, it was not long before Wilhelm and Bismarck, the "Iron Chancellor," clashed over Wilhelm's initial liberal attitude toward socialism and Bismarck's reactionary opinion on the subject but primarily because of their age difference and forceful personalities. In 1890, Wilhelm forced Bismarck's resignation and in effect began his personal reign. Wil-

helm modeled himself after Bismarck, later admitting that the chancellor was the most important influence on his life.

Wilhelm was, however, no Bismarck. Wilhelm's erratic pursuit of sometimes inconsistent policies alienated would-be allies and ultimately left Germany isolated except for Austria-Hungary. Bismarck had crafted an intricate system of alliances predicated on keeping France in check through secret treaties with Russia and Austria-Hungary. He had also focused on maintaining good ties with Britain, which necessitated that German militarism, especially naval construction, and colonial ambitions be restrained. Wilhelm disregarded both principles and pursued aggressive foreign policies. He was determined, through his *Weltpolitik* (world policy), to make Germany the preeminent world power. In 1890, he allowed the Reinsurance Treaty between Germany and Russia to lapse, casting Russia adrift and into the arms of France.

Wilhelm's attempts to draw Britain into an alliance also failed, largely because of his pursuit of colonies in Africa, the Pacific, and China—where he thought Germany would win its "place in the sun"—but even more significantly because of his decision to expand the German Navy. He aggressively supported the acquisition of a naval base at Jiaozhou (then known as Kiao-Chau, Kiaochow, Kiauchau, or Kiautschou), China, in 1897. During the Spanish-American War, he dispatched Vice Admiral Otto von Diederichs and his powerful Asiatic Squadron to Manila in the hopes of securing a base in the Philippines or even some of the islands. The result of this pressure was a decidedly anti-German stance by the U.S. press and a war of words with U.S. naval commander at Manila Rear Admiral George Dewey that for a time threatened war with the United States. Germany came away with nothing, although it did purchase both the Mariana and Caroline Islands from Spain in 1899.

The kaiser's naval building program was particularly injurious to Germany. Although Wilhelm II and his able minister of marine Admiral Alfred von Tirpitz officially sought a so-called Risk Fleet—a navy powerful enough that no nation would be willing to risk engaging it for fear they might thereby suffer sufficient losses that they could then be defeated by another naval power—the pace of the German naval buildup appeared to the British as nothing less than an attempt to make Germany the world's preeminent naval power. Indeed, the kaiser and Tirpitz sought a powerful battle fleet capable of defeating the Royal Navy and even the Royal Navy and U.S. Navy combined if need be. As the German Army had raised the nation to first place in Europe, so the Imperial Navy would make it a world power. Far from forcing the British into alliance with Germany as Tirpitz claimed it would, this policy drove Britain to side with France. For Britain, an island nation dependent on imports of food and raw materials, maintaining the world's most powerful navy was a necessity. In domestic affairs, Wilhelm's early liberalism gave way to conservatism by 1894.

Because Wilhelm's policies had left Germany with only one faithful ally, Austria-Hungary, they made Germany in effect a prisoner of the Dual Monarchy's policies. This meant that Germany was increasingly dragged into supporting Austria-Hungary in the Balkans, an area that in Bismarck's view was not worth the "bones of a single Pomeranian grenadier." When the Austro-Hungarian leadership decided to embark on a preventive war against Serbia following the June 28, 1914, assassination of Austrian archduke Franz Ferdinand, the kaiser supported it, rashly issuing the so-called blank check without consulting his ministers. When this third war in the Balkans threatened to become a world war, Wilhelm attempted to join Britain in trying to moderate the Dual Monarchy's policies, but his efforts were too little and too late.

During the war, the kaiser receded into the background. By 1916, German Army chief of staff Field Marshal Paul von Hindenburg and first quartermaster general General der Infanterie (equivalent to U.S. lieutenant general) Erich Ludendorff established a virtual military dictatorship in which the two men forced adherence to their own policies by repeatedly threatening to resign. By 1918, Wilhelm was largely a figurehead. With Germany clearly defeated militarily and with civil unrest threatening revolution within Germany itself, chancellor Prince Max of Baden urged him to abdicate. Wilhelm refused, and ultimately this decision was made for him when on November 9, 1918, Chancellor Max in Berlin announced Wilhelm's abdication although in reality the kaiser had done no such thing. When leaders of the Reichstag quickly declared a republic, Wilhelm's hopes to remain as king of Prussia were crushed. He then received permission from the Dutch government to go into permanent exile in the Netherlands and departed Germany on November 10.

Despite subsequent Allied attempts to extradite him as a war criminal, Wilhelm remained in the Netherlands for the next 23 years of his life, long enough to watch Adolf Hitler rebuild the German military and lead the nation into another world war. Controversial to the end, Wilhelm once commented that Hitler represented a "succession of miracles," although on other occasions Wilhelm vehemently denounced Hitler as a dictator and warmonger. Wilhelm never accepted blame for his policies that brought World War I, insisting that he was just one player in a very large and complicated game. Wilhelm died in Doorn, Holland, on June 3, 1941.

ARNE KISLENKO

See also

Bülow, Bernhard Heinrich Martin Karl von; Dewey, George; Diederichs, Ernst Otto von; East Asian Squadron; Germany

Further Reading

Cecil, Lamar. *Wilhelm II.* 2 vols. Chapel Hill: University of North Carolina Press, 1989, 1996.

Clark, Christopher M. *Kaiser Wilhelm II.* Essex: Longman, 2000.

Herwig, Holger H. *Politics of Frustration: The United States in German Naval Planning, 1889–1941.* Boston: Little, Brown, 1976.

Retallack, James. *Germany in the Age of Kaiser Wilhelm II.* Houndsmill, UK: MacMillan, 1996.

Röhl, John C. G. *The Kaiser and His Court: Wilhelm II and the Government of Germany.* Cambridge: Cambridge University Press, 1994.

Van Der Kiste, John. *Kaiser Wilhelm II: Germany's Last Emperor.* Stroud, UK: Sutton, 1999.

Wilson, James Harrison

Birth Date: September 2, 1837
Death Date: February 23, 1925

U.S. Army general. James Harrison Wilson was born near Shawneetown, Illinois, on September 2, 1837. He briefly attended McKendree College before enrolling at the United States Military Academy, from which he graduated seventh in his class in 1860 and was commissioned a 2nd lieutenant of topographical engineers. He spent nearly a year at Fort Vancouver, Washington Territory, before the outbreak of the American Civil War in April 1861 necessitated his transfer east. He participated in the capture of Port Royal, South Carolina, in November 1861 and also distinguished himself during the siege of Fort Pulaski, Georgia, the following April.

Wilson served as an aide-de-camp to Major General George B. McClellan and accompanied him throughout the Peninsula Campaign and at the Battle of Antietam on September 17, 1862. Advanced to lieutenant colonel of volunteers, he joined Major General Ulysses S. Grant's staff as his chief engineer in November 1862. Grant subsequently appointed Wilson inspector general of the Army of the Tennessee.

Wilson played a conspicuous role at the capture of Vicksburg in July 1863 and was promoted to brigadier general of volunteers that October. In November 1863, he distinguished himself in both the Chattanooga Campaign and the relief expedition to Knoxville. Grant then recommended him for the post of chief of the Cavalry Bureau in the War Department, and Wilson assumed that position by January 1864.

Wilson proceeded to overhaul and reequip the army's mounted arm. He believed that the cavalry's days as a shock weapon had passed and that it would be far more effective as mounted infantry. He thus issued rapid-fire Spencer carbines to his troopers and drilled them in tactics emphasizing mobility and firepower. In April 1864, Grant summoned him back as commander of the 3rd Division in Major General Philip H. Sheridan's cavalry corps. Wilson fought well at the battles of the Wilderness and Yellow Tavern that May. In June 1864, Grant entrusted Wilson with the assignment of raiding the outskirts of Petersburg, Virginia, which was then under siege and stoutly defended by Confederate forces. Although Wilson performed effectively in campaigning around Richmond, the Wilson-Kautz Raid that June was a near disaster.

Wilson subsequently fought under Sheridan in the Shenandoah Valley but on September 30 was transferred to command cavalry under Major General William T. Sherman as a major general of volunteers. Wilson accompanied Sherman throughout the Atlanta Campaign until Confederate general John Bell Hood abandoned the city and lunged for the Union supply lines in Tennessee. Wilson then joined Major General John Schofield at the defense of Franklin on November 29, 1864. Hood was repulsed, and both Union generals fell back to join Major General George H. Thomas at Nashville. On December 16, Hood's army was smashed at Nashville, and Wilson destroyed the Confederate remnants in a vigorous pursuit.

Promoted to brevet brigadier general of regulars in March 1865, Wilson was next entrusted with a cavalry corps of three divisions (13,500 men) and ordered to raid the heart of the Confederacy. This was the largest cavalry raid of the war and among the most successful.

Wilson's troopers tangled with renowned cavalry leader Lieutenant General Nathan Bedford Forrest at Ebenezer Church on April 1, 1865, defeating him. The next day, Wilson's troopers again defeated Forrest during the capture of Selma, Alabama. It was the first time that a Union general had outmaneuvered Forrest. Montgomery, Alabama, fell on April 12, as did Columbus, Georgia, on April 20. In all, Wilson's cavalry took more than 7,000 prisoners and 300 cannon before the end of the raid on May 20. Ten days earlier, Wilson had gained distinction when his men captured the fleeing Confederate president Jefferson Davis near Irwinville, Georgia. On June 21, Wilson received his final promotion, to major general of volunteers; he was then only 27 years old.

Following the war, Wilson remained with the army, becoming a lieutenant colonel of the 35th U.S. Infantry in July 1866. He performed engineering duty along the Mississippi River before resigning in December 1870 to pursue railroad construction. He settled in Wilmington, Delaware, in 1883.

When the Spanish-American War commenced in 1898, Wilson immediately volunteered his services and was commissioned as a major general of volunteers and assigned to command VI Corps. That corps was never organized, leaving him frustrated and without a post. In July, he secured command of the 1st Division in I Corps, commanded by Major General Nelson A. Miles.

Wilson's 3,571-man division sailed from Charleston, South Carolina, on July 20 and arrived at Ponce, Puerto Rico, eight days later. Because of a lack of suitable small craft, the debarkation took 10 days. Wilson's command saw little action in the fight for the island before the armistice. A portion under Brigadier General Oswald H. Ernst did fight and win the Battle of Coamo on August 9, and Wilson's command also engaged in a skirmish at Asomante Hills on August 12.

Wilson, who favored the U.S. annexation of both Cuba and Puerto Rico, was then briefly military governor of the Ponce district of Puerto Rico. He returned to the United States to head I Corps at Lexington, Kentucky, and then served in Cuba as military governor of the provinces of Matanzas and Santa Clara. During 1900–1901, he was second-in-command of the Beijing (Peking) relief expedition under Major General Adna R. Chaffee Sr. Wilson led a joint Anglo-American punitive expedition against Patachow, the city of eight temples, but refused to burn the Buddhist pagodas in retribution for the Boxer attacks.

Through a special act of Congress in February 1901, Wilson retired with the rank of brigadier general in the regular army. He represented President Theodore Roosevelt at the coronation of King Edward VII in England in 1902. In 1912, he published his memoirs, titled *Under the Old Flag: Recollections of Military Operations in the War for the Union, the Spanish War, and Boxer Rebellion, Etc.* In March 1915, he was advanced to major general on the retired list. Wilson died in Wilmington, Delaware, on February 23, 1925.

SPENCER C. TUCKER

See also

Asomante Hills, Engagement at; Boxer Rebellion; Coamo, Battle of; Ernst, Oswald Hubert; Miles, Nelson Appleton; Puerto Rico Campaign

Further Reading

Evans, David. *Sherman's Horsemen: Union Cavalry Operations in the Atlanta Campaign.* Bloomington: Indiana University Press, 1996.

Jones, James P. *Yankee Blitzkrieg: Wilson's Raid through Alabama and Georgia.* Athens: University of Georgia Press, 1976.

Keenan, Jerry. *Wilson's Cavalry Corps: Union Campaigns in the Western Theater, October 1864 through Spring 1865.* Jefferson, NC: McFarland, 1998.

Longacre, Edward G. *Grant's Cavalryman: The Life and Wars of General James H. Wilson.* Mechanicsburg, PA: Stackpole, 1996.

Wilson, James Harrison. *Under the Old Flag: Recollections of Military Operations in the War for the Union, the Spanish War, the Boxer Rebellion, Etc.* 2 vols. New York: D. Appleton, 1912.

Wilson, James Moulder
Birth Date: October 8, 1837
Death Date: February 1, 1919

U.S. Army officer and chief of engineers during the Spanish-American War. James Moulder Wilson was born on October 8, 1837, in Washington, D.C. In 1860, he graduated from the United States Military Academy, West Point. He served in the Ordnance Department and in the artillery from 1860 to 1863, seeing action during the American Civil War. He was awarded the Medal of Honor for his conduct in the Battle of Malvern Hill and received brevet promotions three times during the war. In 1864, he transferred to the Corps of Topographical Engineers and remained an engineer for the rest of his career.

Following the Civil War, Wilson undertook numerous projects with the Corps of Engineers, overseeing river and harbor projects throughout the United States. During the Grover Cleveland administrations (1885–1889, 1893–1897), Wilson was in charge of all public buildings in Washington, D.C. From 1889 to 1893, he served as superintendent of West Point.

In February 1897, Wilson was named chief of engineers as a brigadier general. Less than a year later, when the United States was making preliminary preparations for a war with Spain, Wilson and the Corps of Engineers played a key role in the augmentation of coastal defenses in the eastern United States, particularly the Northeast. Indeed, the War Department allotted Wilson $15 million to begin an immediate program to improve and fortify eastern coastal defenses. The program included the procurement and placement of coastal guns, the building of coastal batteries, and the laying of extensive minefields to protect vulnerable ports and cities from attack.

Acting with his customary efficiency, Wilson expedited the program. Ultimately, the Corps of Engineers procured 400 miles of cable wire, 150 tons of explosives, more than 1,600 mine casings, many searchlights, and other accoutrements for coastal defense. To aid friendly ships in navigating the newly laid minefields, Wilson ensured that each port had adequate harbor patrols for this purpose. By July 1898, 185 new mortars and cannon had been mounted at coastal batteries, with an additional 550 more gun emplacements either under construction or near completion. Meanwhile, by the end of June, some 1,500 mines had already been activated in 28 major ports and harbors along the East Coast of the United States.

When the war ended in August, Wilson's Corps of Engineers managed to escape the harsh criticism that had been leveled at other branches. As a result, in September 1898 President William McKinley chose Wilson as one of eight members of the Dodge Commission, which investigated charges of corruption and incompetence during the war effort. Wilson brought a voice of considerable reason to the sometimes-choleric proceedings. After the Dodge Commission had disbanded, he retired from active service on April 30, 1901. Wilson remained in Washington, D.C., where he became a prominent citizen until his death there on February 1, 1919.

PAUL G. PIERPAOLI JR.

See also

Coastal Defenses, U.S.; Dodge Commission; Mines

Further Reading

Ballard, Joe N. *History of the U.S. Army Corps of Engineers.* Alexandria, VA: U.S. Army Corps of Engineers, 1998.

Cosmas, Graham A. *An Army for Empire: The United States Army in the Spanish-American War.* College Station: Texas A&M University Press, 1994.

Major General Leonard Wood. As military governor of Cuba (1899–1902), Wood ended the scourge of yellow fever. He went on to serve as chief of staff of the army and governor-general of the Philippines. (Library of Congress)

Wood, Leonard

Birth Date: October 9, 1860
Death Date: August 7, 1927

Doctor, U.S. Army general, and chief of staff of the U.S. Army. Born on October 9, 1860, in Winchester, New Hampshire, the son of a marginally trained and generally unsuccessful family doctor who died before his children reached adulthood, Leonard Wood was forced by finances to earn a living. Opting for medicine, he earned a degree from Harvard in 1884. He was accepted as an intern at Boston City Hospital but was fired for generally insubordinate behavior before completing his internship.

Wood joined the army as a contract surgeon in 1885 and participated in a protracted pursuit of Apache leader Geronimo through the mountains of southern Arizona and northern Mexico, for which he ultimately received the Medal of Honor. In 1890, Wood married Louise Conditt-Smith, ward of Supreme Court justice Stephen Field. In 1895, after a time at Fort McPherson in Atlanta during which Wood helped organize and served as first coach of the Georgia Tech football team, he was assigned to Washington, D.C. With the assistance of his wife's guardian, he became friends

with President Grover Cleveland. When William McKinley was elected president, Wood became personal physician to McKinley's wife. Wood also became a close friend of the new assistant secretary of the navy, Theodore Roosevelt.

Wood and Roosevelt encouraged McKinley to support war with Spain in 1898, and when he did, they received permission to recruit their friends from both the western territories and the eastern aristocracy into the 1st Volunteer Cavalry Regiment, which, after a number of less attractive alternatives, was nicknamed the Rough Riders. Wood was colonel and commander, and Roosevelt was lieutenant colonel and second-in-command.

Wood commanded the Rough Riders in their first skirmish of the war at Las Guásimas, after which he was promoted to brigadier general. He commanded the 2nd Cavalry Brigade in the Battle of San Juan Hill. Shortly after the Spanish surrendered Santiago, he was made first military governor of the city and then of the province. He used his medical training to bring disease and starvation under control and proved an exceptional and exceptionally stern administrator. His success in Cuba coupled with his Washington ties and a talent for political machinations led to him being named military governor of Cuba in December 1899. As governor, he made notable strides in education, public health, and prison reform and established a fiscally responsible republican government. Perhaps his most notable accomplishment was his sponsorship of and acceptance of responsibility for Walter Reed's yellow fever experiments. Immediately after Reed demonstrated the mosquito's role as a vector for the disease, Wood used his autocratic power to authorize draconian insect control measures carried out by his chief surgeon, Major William Gorgas. The campaign transformed Havana from one of the most dangerous cities in the world to one of the healthiest.

Wood had attained the rank of major general in the volunteer army but was still a captain in the medical corps until 1901 when, in a controversial move, Roosevelt, now the president, secured his promotion to brigadier general in the regular army over 509 more-senior officers.

Wood turned the government of Cuba over to an elected government in 1902 and was named commander of the Department of Mindanao, where he fought to control Islamic insurgents. He was promoted to major general in 1904 and was named commander of the Division of the Philippines in 1906. During his tenure with the army in the Philippines, he was involved in a number of actions against insurgents, several of which were controversial and resulted in the deaths of large numbers of civilians.

Wood was named commander of the Division of the East in 1903 and chief of staff of the army in 1910. In the latter office, which he held until 1914, he rescued the General Staff system from department heads determined to prevent its implementation, introduced techniques of scientific management to the military, and worked to professionalize the officer corps.

From 1914 to 1917, Wood returned to the Department of the East as its commander. Convinced as early as 1910 that the United States would participate in a European war, Wood became a vocal advocate of military preparedness and led the Plattsburg movement, which was designed to train civilians who could be officers in such a war. He advocated universal military training and was a vocal opponent of Woodrow Wilson's pacifism. In 1916, Wood, who repeatedly crossed the traditional line separating military officers from politics, was briefly considered as the Republican candidate for president.

When the United States entered World War I, Wood was passed over for command of the American Expeditionary Force in favor of his former subordinate General John J. Pershing. Wood was relegated to training the 89th Division at Camp Funston, and when that unit was sent to Europe in May 1918, he was (at Pershing's specific request) relieved and reassigned to train the 10th Division. In January 1918, while on an inspection tour of the Western Front, Wood received a minor injury from a mortar shell. In spite of the fact that he never was formally assigned a combat role, he was the most-senior American officer actually wounded by fire.

When Theodore Roosevelt died unexpectedly in 1919, Wood became his political heir and narrowly missed receiving the Republican nomination for president in 1920, even though he was still a general officer on active duty. From 1919 until 1921, he commanded the Central Division and then served on a special mission to the Philippines. He retired from active service in late 1921 and then returned to the Philippines, serving as governor-general until 1927. He died in Boston on August 7, 1927, during surgery to remove a benign brain tumor.

JACK MCCALLUM

See also

Cleveland, Stephen Grover; Gorgas, William Crawford; Las Guásimas, Battle of; Malaria; McKinley, William; Reed, Walter; Roosevelt, Theodore; Rough Riders; Round-Robin Letter; San Juan Heights, Battle of; Yellow Fever; Yellow Fever Board

Further Reading

Hagedorn, Hermann. *Leonard Wood: A Biography.* 2 vols. New York: Harper and Brothers, 1931.
Lane, Jack. *Armed Progressive: General Leonard Wood.* San Rafael, CA: Presidio, 1978.
McCallum, Jack, *Leonard Wood: Rough Rider, Surgeon, and Architect of American Imperialism.* New York: New York University Press, 2006.

Woodford, Stewart Lyndon
Birth Date: September 3, 1835
Death Date: February 14, 1913

Lawyer, American Civil War U.S. Army brevet brigadier general, U.S. representative in Congress (1873–1874), and U.S. minister to Spain (1897–1898). Stewart Lyndon Woodford was born in New York City on September 3, 1835. He studied law at Columbia College (now Columbia University) and graduated in 1854. Admitted to the bar in 1857, he opened a law office in New York City. A member of the Republican Party, he was a delegate to his party's national convention in 1860. He served as assistant U.S. attorney in New York City during 1861–1862. Joining the U.S. Army during the Civil War, he was promoted to lieutenant colonel of the 127th New York Volunteer Regiment on September 8, 1862, and to colonel of the 103rd U.S. Colored Infantry on March 3, 1865. On May 12, 1865, he was advanced to brevet brigadier general of volunteers. He subsequently became the first Union military commander of Charleston, South Carolina, and then of Savannah, Georgia.

Following the Civil War and his stint as a Reconstruction official, Woodford resumed his practice of law. Elected lieutenant governor of New York state in 1867, he served one term (to 1869). He ran unsuccessfully for the governorship of New York in 1870. Elected to Congress in 1872, he served in the House of Representatives from 1873 to 1874, when he resigned. He was appointed U.S. district attorney for the Southern District of New York in 1877 and served in that post until 1883.

Although Woodford lacked diplomatic experience, President William McKinley appointed him U.S. minister to Spain on June 19, 1897. Woodford's instructions of July 16, 1897, from U.S. secretary of state John Sherman called on him to demand an end to

Stewart Lyndon Woodford was U.S. ambassador to Spain during 1897–1898, during which time he worked without success to prevent war between Spain and the United States. (Library of Congress)

the fighting in Cuba on the basis of some sort of autonomy for the island and an end to the "measures of unparalleled security." Woodford was instructed to offer the good offices of the United States in an effort to resolve the Cuban conflict in a manner that would be acceptable to both sides. His release to the press of a portion of his diplomatic instructions brought a reprimand from the McKinley administration.

Woodford took up his duties in Madrid in September 1897. A new Liberal government had just taken over in Spain, headed by Premier Práxedes Mateo Sagasta. He removed the controversial Spanish general Valeriano Weyler y Nicolau as governor of Cuba and promised to grant local autonomy in Cuba. The harsh policies of Weyler were therefore rescinded. Woodford kept McKinley fully informed of developments in Madrid, writing the president 68 personal letters during his eight months in the Spanish capital.

Woodford came to believe as a consequence of his meetings with Spanish government officials that a peaceful solution to the crisis could be achieved if the United States proceeded slowly. In one of his most insightful dispatches, he informed the president that the Liberal ministry could remain in power only so long as its policies were seen as ending the Cuban insurrection. If it appeared that its policies would not work or that the United States was about to intervene, then Queen Regent María Cristina would "have to choose between losing her throne or losing Cuba at the risk of war with us." If Sagasta was forced to choose between war or the overthrow of the dynasty, he would choose war.

At the same time, Woodford became a convert to the idea of U.S. ownership of Cuba. In March 1898, he proposed to the Spanish government that the United States purchase the island from Spain. The queen was opposed to such an arrangement, however.

On the U.S. declaration of war against Spain in April 1898, Woodford turned over U.S. interests to the British ambassador and left the country by train for Paris on April 21, 1898. Woodford formally retained his position as ambassador until September 1898, however. He then returned to his private law practice in New York City. Following the war, he continued to assert that if Congress had not rushed to war, President McKinley could have had a peaceful solution in Cuba. Woodford died in New York City on February 14, 1913.

SPENCER C. TUCKER

See also

Cuban War of Independence; McKinley, William; Sagasta, Práxedes Mateo; Sherman, John; Weyler y Nicolau, Valeriano

Further Reading

Garcia, Juan Ramon Milan. *Sagasta: El Arte de Hacer Politica* [Sagasta: The Art of Making Politics]. Madrid: Biblioteca Nueva, 2001.

Ross, Christopher. *Spain, 1812–1996*. London: Hodder Arnold, 2000.

Trask, David F. *The War with Spain in 1898*. Lincoln: University of Nebraska Press, 1996.

X

Xenophobia

An individual or group attitude characterized by an extreme fear, dislike, or hatred of strangers or foreigners. Not always a phobia in the classic psychological definition, xenophobia can certainly be driven by overt racism, but it can also be driven by a fear or misunderstanding of foreign cultures.

In the closing years of the 19th century, the United States was denying African Americans basic civil rights, limiting the immigration of non-Europeans, and accepting some of the racist notions of social Darwinism. With regard to war and diplomacy, the United States became an imperialist nation with possessions in widely scattered parts of the world. By the beginning of the Spanish-American War in 1898, the social and political culture of the United States was tainted by xenophobia that was buttressed by emerging notions of American power and superiority and by an increasing prevalence of restrictive legislation. The Spanish-American War was a critical juncture in which American racist and xenophobic attitudes became clear as a result of territorial acquisitions and the treatment of subjected peoples.

The Spanish-American War brought the United States into close association with Filipinos, Cubans, Puerto Ricans, and other peoples of color, which prompted debates and discussions on ways of dealing with these so-called inferior and different peoples following the conflict. Journalists, politicians, business leaders, and clergymen contributed to the creation of policies that were at best paternal and at worst overtly racist. Most policy makers accepted the ideas of social Darwinism and agreed that the peoples in the newly acquired territories were backward, inferior, childlike, and generally in need of close supervision and guidance. During this period in the United States, most white Americans accepted racial stereotypes and hierarchies, which strongly influenced social ideas and government poli-

cies. In the aftermath of the war, the United States reflected these prejudices in the way it treated subjected peoples and in the laws enacted to govern and regulate them.

Perhaps the most obvious instance of xenophobia was the U.S. response to the Filipino Insurrection (1900–1902). Throughout the costly guerrilla conflict, prominent political and military officials based their actions on notions of racial superiority rather than sound military or social policy. The U.S. Army pursued a strategic hamlet program to limit the strength of the guerrillas and opened concentration camps that shared much in common with the Spanish concentration camp practices in Cuba, which Americans just a few years before had decried as inhumane. It also endorsed a scorched earth policy and allowed large-scale executions of many Filipinos. Brigadier General Jacob Smith, who was later court-martialed for his actions in the Philippines, ordered his men to make the island of Samar into "a howling wilderness" by executing every male over the age of 10. Another military leader opined that the American objective in the Philippines was to "rawhide these bull-headed Asians until they yell for mercy." These actions and ideas reflected prevalent views that Filipinos were culturally and racially inferior.

While the excesses connected with the Filipino Insurrection were not generally replicated in Cuba or Puerto Rico, U.S. officials still believed that neither country was ready for independence. Regarding Cuban self-government, in 1898 Major General William Shafter opined, "Self-government. Why, these people are no more fit for self-government than gunpowder is for hell." Such basic misapprehensions of the cultures and abilities of subjected peoples resulted in widespread xenophobic prescriptions.

The diplomatic wranglings following the Spanish-American War were also obvious manifestations of American fears regarding

707

the conquered territories and the vexing question of the status of the inhabitants. From the outset, the United States asserted that none of the territories were ready for self-government and would instead require long-term assistance and guidance. In Congress, debate centered on what rights and privileges should be extended to the people of the territories, the bureaucratic structures of colonial administrations, and whether the territories should be considered for statehood. In relation to the rights of colonial peoples, Congress received guidance from the U.S. Supreme Court, which ruled in the Insular Cases (1901–1904) that the inhabitants of U.S. territories had some, but not all, of the rights held by other U.S. citizens under the Constitution and as such were not true members of the U.S. body politic.

In setting up local colonial governments, the United States was careful to ensure the right of liberal intervention in internal affairs of the territory. Finally, Congress clearly indicated that it never intended for any of the new territories to become states of the Union. In limiting rights, advocating intervention, and preventing admission to statehood, Congress reflected the racist and xenophobic fears that gripped American society at the start of the 20th century. The idea of extending complete equality to foreign cultures and a multitude of racial groups was beyond the worldview of most Americans at the time. On a related note, in 1916 Congress promised eventual independence to the Philippines (which occurred in 1946) and in 1917 granted U.S. citizenship to the people of Puerto Rico. American xenophobia would ultimately affect future relations with the territories, which were marked by paternalism and racism.

JAMES F. CARROLL

See also

African Americans; Insular Affairs, Bureau of; Insular Cases; Racism; Samar Campaigns; Shafter, William Rufus; Smith, Jacob Hurd; Social Darwinism

Further Reading

Cosmas, Graham A. *An Army for Empire: The United States Army in the Spanish-American War.* College Station: Texas A&M University Press, 1994.

Love, Eric. *Race over Empire: Racism and U.S. Imperialism, 1865–1900.* Chapel Hill: University of North Carolina Press, 2004.

Smith, Angel, and Emma Davila-Cox, eds. *The Crisis of 1898: Colonial Redistribution and Nationalist Mobilization.* New York: St. Martin's, 1999.

Smith, Joseph. *The Spanish-American War: Conflict in the Caribbean and the Pacific, 1895–1902.* New York: Longman, 1994.

Weston, Rubin Francis. *Racism in U.S. Imperialism: The Influence of Racial Assumptions on American Foreign Policy, 1893–1946.* Columbia: University of South Carolina Press, 1973.

Yauco, Battle of
Event Date: July 26, 1898

Yauco is located in the southwestern part of the island of Puerto Rico some 30 miles west of Ponce and 6 miles northwest of Guánica. Founded in 1756, Yauco was located on the road and railroad to Ponce and was once known as the coffee capital of the world. In 1898, it had about 22,000 inhabitants and was defended by a single company of the Spanish Army's Alfonso XIII Battalion.

U.S. forces landed in Puerto Rico at Guánica on July 25, 1898, and the next day, Brigadier General George A. Garretson proceeded to Yauco with seven companies: six of the 6th Massachusetts Infantry Regiment and one of the 6th Massachusetts Infantry Regiment. Just before their arrival at Yauco, the Americans skirmished briefly with two companies of the Spanish Patria Battalion commanded by Lieutenant Colonel Francisco Puig. The Spanish colonel's orders called on him to merely determine U.S. strength, so he quickly withdrew. This skirmish was, however, the first engagement of the Puerto Rico Campaign.

Yauco was occupied by the Americans on July 27 and 28 without any opposition. Mayor Francisco Mejía issued a proclamation that the American arrival was the intervention of a just god. The town was then garrisoned by Company I, an African American unit of the 6th Massachusetts.

SPENCER C. TUCKER

See also

Garretson, George Armstrong; Guánica, Puerto Rico; Puerto Rico Campaign

Further Reading

Cosmas, Graham A. *An Army for Empire: The United States Army in the Spanish-American War.* College Station: Texas A&M University Press, 1994.

Trask, David F. *The War with Spain in 1898.* Lincoln: University of Nebraska Press, 1996.

Yellow Fever

Lethal systemic disease caused by a *Flavivirus* and transmitted by the bite of the female *Aedes aegyptii* mosquito. Yellow fever begins with a flulike illness and may progress to necrosis of the liver with subsequent diffuse internal and external bleeding, kidney failure, coma, and death. Mortality is still approximately 20 percent, and there is no effective treatment.

The *Aedes* mosquito is not native to the Western Hemisphere and was first introduced to Barbados in 1647 and to Cuba and the Yucatan in 1648 by ships carrying slaves from West Africa, where the disease is endemic. Although the mosquito requires ambient temperatures above the low 70s, yellow fever could be transmitted to northern cities during the summer months, and epidemics were a recurrent event in American seaports. Yellow fever caused more than 100,000 deaths in the United States between 1793 and 1901, and the threat was so serious that Thomas Jefferson was of the opinion that the United States would never be able to support major cities.

Fear of a yellow fever epidemic among American soldiers sent to Cuba and the worry that they would bring the disease home with them played a major role in both the planning and execution of the 1898 invasion of the island. The disease first appeared among American troops at Siboney on July 9, and by August 2 there had been 4,298 cases of fever in Santiago. In retrospect, most of these were probably not yellow fever, but military surgeons in Cuba lacked an accurate diagnostic test for the disease and were quick to call them that. The increasing incidence of fever and the fear of a generalized outbreak led

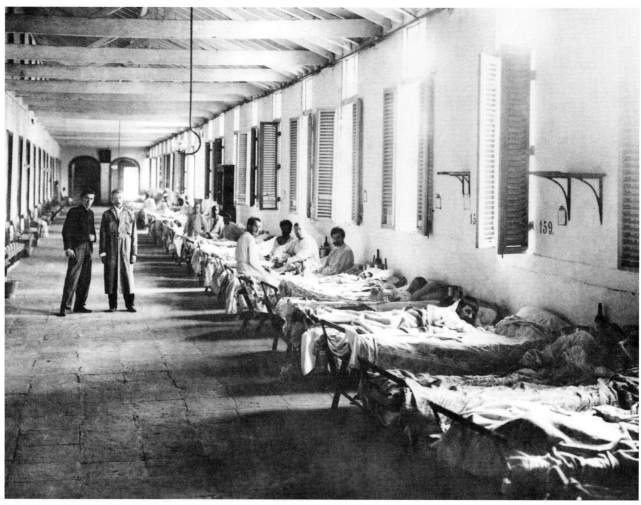

Patients with yellow fever in a hospital in Havana, Cuba, 1899. (Library of Congress)

Major General William Shafter's general officers and Colonel Theodore Roosevelt to write the Round-Robin Letter demanding an immediate withdrawal of American troops from the island.

It was generally assumed that yellow fever was caused by filth, a conviction that led the army to burn Siboney to the ground after the first outbreak. When the Spanish surrendered Santiago, one of the first actions by Brigadier General Leonard Wood as military governor was to institute a draconian public sanitation program. To his great disappointment, 200 new cases appeared in the city in the summer of 1899 with a 22.8 percent mortality rate. Wood was forced to quarantine the city to control the epidemic.

Beginning as early as the June 25 Battle of Las Guásimas, all American wounded were screened for signs of yellow fever before they were allowed to return to the United States. Anyone suspected of having the disease was held in Cuba. By May 22, every returning ship was inspected by the Marine Hospital Service, and anyone with fever was quarantined. Following the Round-Robin Letter, however, public opinion forced the War Department to remove the men from Cuba, and on August 7, ships began moving them to Camp Wikoff, on the eastern end of Long Island, where they could be held in quarantine until free of the risk of yellow fever.

Common Diseases during the Spanish-American War and the Philippine-American War

Disease	Cause	Transmission	Symptoms
Dysentery	Bacteria/amoeba	Contaminated food or water	Bloody diarrhea, abdominal pain, blood poisoning, kidney failure
Malaria	Protozoa	Mosquitoes	Fever, chills, joint pain, anemia, kidney failure, coma
Scurvy	Vitamin C deficiency	Lack of citrus fruit	Liver spots, spongy gums, bleeding from mucus membranes
Smallpox	Virus	Person-to-person	Fever, vomiting, rash, pustules
Typhoid	Bacteria	Contaminated food or water	Fever, chills, weakness, muscle pain, diarrhea, intestinal hemorrhage
Typhus	Bacteria	Fleas, mites, and lice	Fever, chills, muscle pain, rash, delirium, bleeding into the skin, kidney failure
Yellow fever	Virus	Mosquitoes	Fever, muscle ache, vomiting, jaundice, kidney failure

Proof that the *Aedes aegyptii* was the yellow fever vector and that the disease could be controlled by removing mosquito-breeding areas did not come for another three years but did ultimately result in virtual eradication of the disease in Cuba. Yellow fever was not endemic in either Puerto Rico or the Philippines and was not a problem for the American military in either place.

JACK MCCALLUM

See also

Immunes; Reed, Walter; Wood, Leonard; Yellow Fever Board

Further Reading

Cirillo, Vincent J. *Bullets and Bacilli: The Spanish-American War and Military Medicine.* New Brunswick, NJ: Rutgers University Press, 2004.
Gillett, Mary C. *The Army Medical Department, 1865–1917.* Washington, DC: Center of Military History, United States Army, 1995.

Yellow Fever Board

A board of four physicians appointed by Surgeon General George Sternberg on May 23, 1900, to study infectious disease in Cuba. The board, composed of Major Walter Reed and contract surgeons Jesse W. Lazear, Aristides Agramonte, and James Carroll and also known as the Reed Commission, was encouraged by Major Jefferson Keen, a military surgeon who had recently recovered from yellow fever, to concentrate on that disease.

Carroll, who had previously worked with Reed at the Army Medical School, was placed in charge of bacteriology. Lazear, who had trained in entomology with the Italian malaria expert Giovanni Battista Gussi, was eventually given charge of the group's mosquito experiments. Agramonte supervised autopsies and was the group's pathologist.

After a series of false starts, the Yellow Fever Board, as it came to be known, directed its attention to the *Stegomya fasciata* (later renamed *Aedes aegyptii*) mosquito that had been suggested as the disease's vector by Cuban physician Carlos Finlay in 1881. The board designed a remarkable series of controlled experiments that definitively proved not only that the disease was transmitted by the mosquito but also that it was caused by an infectious organism smaller than a bacterium and was therefore the first human infection shown to be viral in origin.

German scientist Robert Koch's postulates requiring passage of an identifiable agent through an experimental animal to prove responsibility for an infectious disease could not be satisfied because no laboratory animal was known to be susceptible to yellow fever. The board was therefore required to design its experiments using human subjects. Since yellow fever at the time had an approximately 30 percent mortality and since there was no treatment for the disease once it was contracted, any human experiment posed significant ethical difficulties. For that reason, the board elected to perform the first experiments on themselves. However, Agramonte was exempted because he had grown up in Cuba and was assumed to have contracted the disease as a child and to be immune. Reed opted out, arguing that at age 47 he was too old to participate safely. Carroll contracted the disease after allowing himself to be bitten by a mosquito that had fed on a yellow fever victim, and although he survived, his health was permanently impaired, and he died seven years later. Lazear also allowed himself to be bitten and did not survive. The board subsequently recruited a series of newly arrived Spanish immigrants and American soldiers as subjects. The ethical questions remained, and the board obtained a written permission—the first formal informed consent—from each potential experimental subject.

Carroll, Agramonte, and Reed—encouraged and funded by military governor Brigadier General Leonard Wood—designed experiments in which they first proved that exposure to clothing, bedding, vomitus, and feces from yellow fever victims did not cause the disease. Next, they divided a small house in half by a screen and placed infected mosquitoes on one side and none on the other with all other conditions being identical. Experimental subjects on the mosquito side contracted yellow fever, while those on the other side of the screen did not. Carroll went on to inject plasma from infected subjects that had been filtered through porcelain known to have small enough pores to capture all bacteria. The filtrate still caused the disease, proving that the responsible agent was smaller than a bacterium.

The results were inconvertible, and Wood promptly used them to justify a draconian antimosquito campaign supervised by Major William C. Gorgas. Within three months, yellow fever, which had plagued Havana for almost 400 years, had disappeared from the city. The Yellow Fever Board's defeat of yellow fever was unquestionably the Army Medical Department's greatest triumph during the Spanish-American War and may well have been the greatest achievement of the war altogether. The methods used in the experiments generated much controversy, however, especially after the death of nurse Clara Maass, who allowed herself to be reinfected after recovering from yellow fever in an effort to determine if prior exposure to the disease produced immunity.

JACK MCCALLUM

See also

Maass, Clara Louise; Reed, Walter; Sternberg, George Miller; Wood, Leonard; Yellow Fever

Further Reading

Altman, Lawrence. *Who Goes First: The Story of Self-Experimentation in Medicine.* New York: Random House, 1987.
Cirillo, Vincent J. *Bullets and Bacilli: The Spanish-American War and Military Medicine.* New Brunswick, NJ: Rutgers University Press, 2004.

Yellow Journalism

A term often used to characterize sensationalist, jingoistic, and sometimes fabricated or embellished news stories by chiefly large-circulation newspapers to stir up support for the Cuban rebels and encourage the United States to go to war with Spain in the 1890s.

Frederic Remington illustration titled "Spaniards Search Women on American Steamers." Yellow journalism sought to cast the Spanish authorities in the worst possible light and used sensationalism to sell newspapers. (*New York Journal,* 1898)

Although many of the tawdry tactics used in yellow journalism well predate the 1890s, the term was struck in the run-up to the Spanish-American War, from about 1895 to 1898, when sensationalist and jingoistic news reporting reached its zenith. Two New York City newspaper publishers—Joseph Pulitzer and William Randolph Hearst—best exemplified yellow journalism in the 1890s.

The circulation war between Pulitzer and Hearst was under way well before the United States declared war on Spain in 1898. After achieving financial success with the *St. Louis-Dispatch,* Pulitzer purchased the *New York World* in 1882. Seeking to tap the immigrant market, the *World* featured illustrations and crime stories often ac-

companied by a sexually titillating angle for only two cents a copy. The politically ambitious and wealthy mining heir Hearst was impressed by how Pulitzer made the *World* the largest-circulation newspaper in New York City. Hearst used similar tactics with the *San Francisco Examiner* and in 1895 decided to compete directly with Pulitzer by purchasing the *New York Journal.* Hearst raided the *World*'s staff and slashed the paper's price to a penny per copy. The term "yellow journalism" is probably derived either from the yellow paper used in the print industry or the Hearst-Pulitzer rivalry over the "Yellow Kid" comic strip, created by cartoonist Richard Outcault.

The fierce struggle for circulation also convinced Hearst that the public clamor for violence might be fed through warmongering. Both Pulitzer and Hearst sought to exploit American sympathies with Cuban revolutionaries seeking independence from Spain. While the newspaper publishers often exaggerated their reports of Spanish atrocities in Cuba, the policies of Spanish governor-general Valeriano Weyler y Nicolau, who herded Cuban peasants into reconcentration camps, provided ample ammunition for the pages of the *World* and the *Journal*.

Reporters and artists such as Richard Harding Davis and Frederic Remington often submitted stories dealing with the Spanish harassment of imprisoned Cuban women as well as the starvation of Cuban children. Although probably apocryphal, a story associated with Remington's January 1897 arrival in Cuba clearly illustrates the nature of yellow journalism. After sizing up the situation, Remington remarked that the military and political situation on the island was quiet and that he was preparing for a return to the United States. Hearst implored Remington to stay in Cuba, allegedly remarking, "You furnish the pictures and I will furnish the war." Anti-Spanish resentment was exacerbated on February 9, 1898, when the *Journal* published a personal letter from the Spanish minister to the United States, Enrique Dupuy de Lôme, to a friend, José Canalejas y Méndez, criticizing President William McKinley.

On February 15, 1898, the U.S. battleship *Maine* was destroyed while anchored in Havana Harbor, resulting in great loss of life. While the exact cause of the explosion was not known, the Pulitzer and Hearst papers immediately labeled the explosion an act of Spanish treachery. On February 17, a *Journal* headline proclaimed, "*Maine* Blown Up by Torpedo." As clamor for war increased around the country, McKinley presented Congress with a declaration of war, which was approved on April 25, 1898. Newspaper coverage also made war heroes of Theodore Roosevelt and Admiral George Dewey.

While the yellow journalism of Hearst and Pulitzer certainly encouraged the jingoism that led to war, it is simplistic to blame the war on these journalists alone, as business interests in the United States certainly supported a policy of territorial and economic expansion in pursuit of overseas markets and more profits. Others sought American expansionism on religious, moral, and chauvinistic grounds.

RON BRILEY

See also

Atrocities; Dupuy de Lôme-Canalejas Letter; Expansionism; Hearst, William Randolph; Jingoism; Journalism; *Maine,* USS; Newspapers; Pulitzer, Joseph; *Reconcentrado* System

Further Reading

Procter, Ben. *William Randolph Hearst.* 2 vols. New York: Oxford University Press USA, 1998, 2007.

Smythe, Ted Curtis. *The Gilded Age Press, 1865–1900.* Westport, CT: Praeger, 2003.

Swanberg, W. A. *Pulitzer.* New York: Scribner, 1967.

Trask, David F. *The War with Spain in 1898.* Lincoln: University of Nebraska Press, 1996.

Young, Samuel Baldwin Marks
Birth Date: January 9, 1840
Death Date: September 1, 1924

U.S. Army officer. Samuel Baldwin Marks Young was born on January 9, 1840, in Pittsburgh, Pennsylvania. He attended Jefferson College in Canonsburg, Pennsylvania, before marrying and enlisting as a private in the U.S. Army in April 1861 upon the outbreak of the American Civil War. Serving with the Army of the Potomac, he rose quickly through the ranks, becoming a captain in 1861, a major in 1862, and a lieutenant colonel and colonel in 1864. In 1865, he was breveted brigadier general of volunteers. He was wounded several times during the conflict.

After returning to civilian life with the end of the Civil War, Young joined the regular army in May 1866 as a second lieutenant in the 12th Infantry Regiment. He received promotion to captain when he transferred to the 8th Cavalry in July 1866. From 1866 to 1879, he fought against various Native American tribes on the western frontier and was breveted colonel.

Young served on the faculty at the Infantry and Cavalry School at Fort Leavenworth, Kansas, in 1882 before being promoted to major and joining the 3rd Cavalry Regiment in California. In 1894, his troops maintained order during labor disputes there. In 1896, he was assigned to Yosemite National Park to protect it from sheepherders and became its acting superintendent. The next year, he took the same position in Yellowstone National Park, where he became friends with Theodore Roosevelt before returning to the 3rd Cavalry as a colonel in June 1897.

At the beginning of the Spanish-American War, Young was appointed brigadier general of volunteers in May 1898 and then major general of volunteers in July 1898. He commanded a cavalry brigade in Major General Joseph Wheeler's division and fought in the first land battle of the war, at Las Guásimas, Cuba, on June 24, 1898. In late July, however, he became quite sick and had to return to the United States the following month. When he had sufficiently recovered, he spent time at Camp Wikoff on Long Island, New York, where he further recuperated.

In 1899, Young, now fully recovered, went to the Philippines as a brigadier general of the volunteers during the Philippine-American War (1899–1902). He took part in the unsuccessful three-pronged attack to destroy the enemy in northern Luzon in the autumn of 1899 during which he led a cavalry brigade. The campaign resulted in the escape of insurgent leader Emilio Aguinaldo y Famy and the beginning of the guerrilla phase of the war. In December 1899, Young became the commander of the District of North Western Luzon (northern Luzon), where he proved an able administrator. He removed incompetent officials, restructured the district, established schools, and improved farming techniques. In January 1900, he was appointed brigadier general of the regular army. However, his harsh, repressive measures against the Filipinos in a failed attempt to end the guerrilla war led to his recall in February 1901.

The same month, Young was promoted to major general and took command of the Department of California, serving there until March 1902. In November 1901, he was named president of the War College Board, and he was appointed the first president of the Army War College in July 1902. The following August, he was promoted to lieutenant general, serving briefly as commanding general of the army. He then became the first chief of staff of the army.

Young retired from the military in January 1904. He served as superintendent of Yellowstone National Park from 1907 to 1908, after which he led the Board of Inquiry of the Brownsville Affair in 1909–1910 that looked into a racial incident between black soldiers and white civilians in Texas. Young died in Helena, Montana, on September 1, 1924.

GREGORY C. FERENCE

See also

Camp Wikoff; Las Guásimas, Battle of; Luzon Campaigns; Philippine-American War; Roosevelt, Theodore; Wheeler, Joseph

Further Reading

Linn, Brian McAllister. *The Philippine War, 1899–1902.* Lawrence: University Press of Kansas, 2000.

Miller, Stuart Creighton. *"Benevolent Assimilation": The American Conquest of the Philippines, 1899–1903.* New Haven, CT: Yale University Press, 1982.

Wheeler, Joseph. *The Santiago Campaign, 1898.* 1899; reprint, Port Washington, NY: Kennikat, 1971.

Z

Zanjón, Pact of

Peace treaty negotiated between Cuban revolutionary nationalists and the Spanish colonial government on February 10, 1878. The Pact of Zanjón officially ended the Ten Years' War (1868–1878), which had begun under the instigation of Carlos Manuel de Céspedes. Also involved in that struggle were other luminaries of the Cuban independence movement, including Máximo Gómez, Antonio Maceo Grajales, and José Martí y Pérez. The uprising began on October 10, 1868, when Céspedes and a small group of revolutionaries launched a failed attack against the city of Yara, which from then on became known as Grito de Yara (Shout of Yara).

That same day, Céspedes, a well-to-do landowner and attorney, brazenly freed his slaves, violating Spanish law. Slavery was still legal in Cuba at the time, but most of the nationalists hoped to rid the island of slavery, which they saw as a Spanish-imposed evil used to benefit absentee Spanish interests. The majority of the rebel nationalists sought economic reforms, increased political autonomy that would lead ultimately to Cuban independence, and an end to slavery.

In its earliest days, the Ten Years' War nearly collapsed, but by 1869, some victories had been won against the Spanish. That same year saw the convening of a revolutionary constitutional assembly, the drafting of a constitution, and the formation of a congress of representatives. On April 10, 1869, the Cuban Republic was established, with Céspedes as its first president. Despite these gains, the rebels were unable to deal a decisive military or political blow to Spanish rule in Cuba. For the next several years, the war ground on with little movement in either direction.

The independence movement was dealt a heavy blow when Spanish soldiers ambushed and killed Céspedes in February 1874. A year earlier, he had been deposed as president because of political infighting within the movement. After 1874, the Ten Years' War went badly for the Cuban rebels, and in 1876, Spain dispatched additional troops to crush the revolt once and for all.

In early February 1878, newly arrived Spanish general Arsenio Martínez de Campos coerced a majority of the rebels to agree to a peace settlement, the Pact of Zanjón, signed on February 10, 1878. Most revolutionaries agreed to its terms, although Maceo, who saw the agreement as a sellout, continued a solitary protest effort until the late spring. Specifically, the treaty was designed to ameliorate Cuba's financial situation so that more of the money generated in Cuba remained in the island. The pact also provided for very modest land reform and land distribution and promised limited Cuban representation in government affairs. Most notably, the pact provided for the emancipation of any slave who had fought during the war. The remainder of the slaves, however, were not to be entirely freed until 1888. Subsequent agreements changed this slightly, and in 1886 slavery was outlawed throughout the island by royal proclamation.

The efficacy of the Pact of Zanjón was a short and fragile one. In less than a year, a new insurgency broke out. Known as the Little War (La Guerra Chiquita), it was led by José Maceo (Antonio's brother) and Calixto García y Iñiguez. That struggle ended in 1879, but the Spanish never made good on their promises of greater reform and autonomy. The result was a period of bitter recriminations and periodic guerrilla warfare by rebel nationalists that would open the way for more general warfare beginning in 1895.

PAUL G. PIERPAOLI JR.

See also
Cuba; García y Iñiguez, Calixto; Gómez y Báez, Máximo; Maceo Grajales, Antonio; Martí y Pérez, José Julián; Martínez de Campos, Arsenio; Ten Years' War

Further Reading

Chapman, Charles E. *A History of the Cuban Republic: A Study in Hispanic American Politics.* New York: Macmillan, 1927.

Pérez, Louis A., Jr. *Cuba between Empires, 1878–1902.* Pittsburgh: University of Pittsburgh Press, 1983.

Thomas, Hugh. *Cuba: The Pursuit of Freedom.* New York: Harper and Row, 1971.

Zapote Line

Spanish-built defensive system surrounding Manila during the Spanish-American War. In 1898, Spain's Manila defenses comprised the walled Intramuros around the old city as well as suburban placements, many of which were part of the Zapote Line. South of the city's Pasig River, the medieval-like Fort Santiago within the walls guarded the river's mouth. Less than two miles to the south of the fort stood the Zapote Line, a complex of trenches and blockhouses, labeled from north to south 1 to 15, anchored by Fort San Antonio de Abad on the extreme south. Past the blockhouses, a mass of brown nipa huts (shelters made from bamboo) spread in all directions.

The avenues of Malate, Manila's southernmost suburb, were barricaded, as were all roads approaching the city. To the south and beside the Calle Real Road, a trench ran from Manila Bay eastward and connected with an unnavigable wetland. Below this position was Fort Malate, built of stone and mounting modern guns. A broad stream ran westward to the beach south of the post. A stone bridge traversed the stream near the fort, with its access blocked by stone barriers, while a trench line joined the bridge with Fort Malate. The trench system extended from the post to the bay westward about 200 feet and then ran eastward in a span of 3,000 feet to Blockhouse No. 14, a stronghold sided by the beach to the west and a marsh to the east.

The Spaniards constructed their blockhouses of uniform design but with various materials: stone, wood and stone, or simply wood. Blockhouse No. 14, a wooden structure, covered a 30-foot-square space, reached two stories in height, and occupied an elevated base, tilting from its foundation out at a 50-degree grade. Ten-inch planks on its corners were covered by nailed boards, continuing from one nook to another and providing a twofold wall of timber. The area between the walls was packed with gravel to make them more impervious to fire and bullets and shells. Each floor had 6-inch-wide peepholes, convenient for the use of small arms. The Spaniards had dug a trench around Blockhouse No. 14 in order to secure the Cingalon Road, another route into Manila.

The Spaniards designed their trenches with a 6-foot-broad and 3-foot-deep gully forward with earth behind and piled to a height of 5 feet. Ranging from 5 to 7 feet deep at the summit, they inclined outward to ground level and were crowned generally with sandbags interspersed with openings for rifle firing. On occasion, a fortification was built with sandbags only. Also, the Spaniards positioned most of their trenches behind swamps and between blockhouses.

In August 1898, General Fermín Jáudenes y Alvarez, the Spanish commander in Manila, still controlled much of the city. But Filipino insurgents, led by General Emilio Aguinaldo y Famy, were deployed in trenches facing the Zapote Line, while American forces to the south prepared for the First Battle of Manila on August 13, 1898. As it turned out, the battle saw most Spanish forces offer only token resistance, while U.S. Navy warships shelled Fort San Antonio de Abad, the southernmost redoubt of the Zapote Line. The token bombardment was part of an agreement worked out in advance between Rear Admiral George Dewey and Jáudenes preceding the Spanish surrender.

RODNEY J. ROSS

See also

Aguinaldo y Famy, Emilio; Dewey, George; Fort San Antonio de Abad; Manila; Manila, First Battle of

Further Reading

Cosmas, Graham A. *An Army for Empire: The United States Army in the Spanish-American War.* College Station: Texas A&M University Press, 1994.

Faust, Karl Irving. *Campaigning in the Philippines.* San Francisco, CA: Hicks-Judd, 1899.

Young, Kenneth Ray. *The General's General: The Life and Times of Arthur MacArthur.* Boulder, CO: Westview, 1994.

Zayas, Juan Alonso
Birth Date: 1869
Death Date: October 8, 1898

Spanish officer who fought in the Philippines for the duration of the Spanish-American War without knowing that a state of war existed between the United States and Spain. Zayas was born in 1869 in San Juan, Puerto Rico. His father was a Spanish Army officer from Barcelona assigned to Puerto Rico. Although Zayas studied photography in his youth, he joined the Spanish Army in 1888. He was sent to Cuba in 1889 and eventually promoted to the rank of sergeant. Prior to the outbreak of the Cuban War of Independence in 1895, he was sent to study at the Spanish Army's School of Sergeants in Madrid.

In 1897, Zayas, who had been promoted to second lieutenant, was sent to the Philippines as part of the effort to quell the Filipino insurrection against Spanish colonial rule. He arrived in Manila in May 1897 and was immediately assigned as second-in-command of the 2nd Expeditionary Rifle Battalion at the remote outpost in Baler on the northeastern shore of the island of Luzon. Although Baler was only 62 miles from Manila, the poor infrastructure and rugged terrain on the island made land travel and communication with that place exceedingly difficult. Indeed, the only feasible method of communication with Manila was by sea.

Filipino resistance to Spanish colonial authority in the Baler area, orchestrated by Calixto Vilacorte, was especially fierce. To protect their battalion of 57 men, Captain Enrique de Las Morenas y Foaai, the battalion commander, and Zayas converted the San Luis de Tolusa church into a fort. Vilacorte demanded the surrender of Spanish troops on June 28, 1898. The demand was rejected, and the insurgents initiated a siege of the garrison, which had occupied the church in the town. The siege lasted for 337 days. Although greatly outnumbered, lacking supplies and reinforcements, and plagued by disease, the Spanish garrison stubbornly refused to capitulate despite several attempts to convince them that the war had ended in August and that a peace treaty had been signed in Paris in December 1898 whereby the Philippines had been transferred to U.S. control. Not until June 2, 1899, did the garrison at Baler surrender. Zayas was not among them. During the siege, he had contracted beriberi, a nervous system disease caused by the lack of thiamine in the diet, that was complicated by injuries sustained in the siege. He died on October 8, 1898. Captain Las Morenas was also among the dead, also felled by beriberi. Zayas and his fallen comrades were buried in the cemetery of San Luis de Tolusa church. The next-ranking officer, Lieutenant Saturnino Martín Cerezo, took command of the battalion upon Zayas's death. The 32 surviving members of Zayas's battalion were returned to Spain, where they received a hero's welcome, military decorations, and pensions. Zayas was among those honored posthumously.

MICHAEL R. HALL

See also

Baler, Philippines, Siege of; Luzon; Paris, Treaty of

Further Reading

Martín Cerezo, Saturnino. *Under the Red and Gold: Notes and Recollections of the Siege of Baler.* Translated by F. L. Dodds. Kila, MT: Kessinger, 2008.

Zogbaum, Rufus Fairchild
Birth Date: August 28, 1849
Death Date: October 22, 1925

Leading artist-correspondent of the American West and the Spanish-American War. Rufus Fairchild Zogbaum was born in Charleston, South Carolina, on August 28, 1849. His father, a manufacturer of musical instruments, moved the family to New York City when Zogbaum was a boy. Zogbaum studied at the Art Students' League, an art school established in 1875, in New York City from 1878 to 1879 and during 1880–1882 at the Académie Julian, an art school established in Paris by Rodolphe Julian in 1868. At the latter, Zogbaum worked from 1880 to 1882 under Léon Bonnat, a leading portraitist whose work showed the influence of Diego Velázquez. Zogbaum was heavily influenced by the works of the French military artist Jean Baptiste Edouard Detaille and the French academic painter Alphonse Marie Adolphe de Neuville.

In 1884, after returning to the United States, Zogbaum traveled to Montana, where he sketched military life on the frontier. From 1883 to 1899, he contributed seven articles to the popular *Harper's Monthly.* In the August 1883 issue of *Harper's Monthly,* his first illus-

trated article, "War Pictures in Times of Peace," was published. The 13-page article about French Army drill tactics was written after the author had spent several months studying the French Army. His second article, "A Home of Tommy Adkins," appeared in the October 1884 issue of *Harper's Monthly.* The 7-page article examined military life in the British Army. His third article, "A Night with the Germans," appeared in the June 1885 issue of *Harper's Monthly.* The 8-page article examined military life in the German Army. The 6-page article "A Days Drive with Montana Cowboys" appeared in the July 1885 issue. "Across Country with a Cavalry Column" was published in the September 1885 issue. The 7-page article glorified the U.S. Cavalry. His sixth article, "With the Bluecoats on the Border," was a 12-page piece that appeared in the May 1886 edition of *Harper's Monthly.* Once again covering the U.S. Cavalry, this time Zogbaum examined the interaction of the settlers on the frontier with the U.S. Cavalry. His seventh and final article for *Harper's Monthly,* "Honor to Whom Honor Is Due," appeared in the April 1899 issue. The 7-page article examined U.S. military life, especially in the navy, during the Spanish-American War.

Zogbaum's seven articles in *Harper's Monthly* were augmented with 24 of his paintings. His painting *Battle of Manila Bay* (1899) vividly depicts Commodore George Dewey directing the battle from his flagship, the cruiser *Olympia.* Zogbaum also published illustrated articles in the *Saturday Evening Post, Harper's Weekly, Scribner's,* and *The North American Review.* He published two illustrated books, *Horse, Foot and Dragoons: Sketches of Army Life at Home and Abroad* (1888) and *All Hands: Pictures of Life in the United States Navy* (1897).

With the coming of the Spanish-American War, Zogbaum's art depicting western scenes disappeared almost entirely. As with fellow artist Frederic Remington, Zogbaum devoted all of his energies to depicting scenes of American heroism for the duration of the war. Unlike Remington, Zogbaum continued to paint military subjects for the rest of his life. Although Remington is better known, Zogbaum's works predate those of Remington and pay greater attention to detail. Zogbaum's paintings, especially his works done in watercolor and gouache of military scenes, set the standard for future military artists. His illustrated articles covering the Spanish-American War were especially popular with the American public. After a prolific career, Zogbaum died on October 22, 1925, in New York City.

MICHAEL R. HALL

See also

Artists and Illustrators; Journalism; Manila Bay, Battle of; Remington, Frederic Sackrider

Further Reading

Goldstein, Donald M., Katherine V. Dillon, J. Michael Wenger, and Robert J. Cressman. *Spanish-American War: The Story and Photographs.* Dulles, VA: Potomac Books, 2000.

Zogbaum, Rufus Fairchild. *All Hands: Pictures of Life in the United States Navy.* New York: Harper and Brothers, 1897.

———. *Horse, Foot and Dragoons: Sketches of Army Life at Home and Abroad.* New York: Harper and Brothers, 1888.

Country Profiles

CUBA

Location: Caribbean
Capital: Havana
Area, Absolute: 42,803 sq. mi.
Area, Relative: Slightly smaller than Pennsylvania

	1896	1898	1900	1902	1904
Population Estimate:	1,800,000	1,570,000	1,600,000	1,758,000	1,879,000
Population Density (People per sq. mi.):	42.05	36.68	37.38	41.07	43.90

Estimated Total Armed Forces (1898): 40,000
Principal Military Bases and Installations: Oriente Province, Santiago de Cuba
Important Agricultural and Industrial Products: Sugar, tobacco, coffee, textiles

PHILIPPINES

Location: Southeastern Asia
Capital: Manila*
Area, Absolute: 500,000
Area, Relative: Slightly smaller than Arizona

	1896	1898	1900	1902	1904
Population Estimate:	6,261,339	7,000,000	7,409,000	7,577,000	7,659,000
Population Density (People per Sq. Mi.):	12.52	14.00	14.82	15.15	15.32

Estimated Total Armed Forces (1898): 50,000
Principal Military Bases and Installations: Malolos, San Isidro
Important Agricultural and Industrial Products: Fruit, fish, textiles, wood products

*Nationalist Army headquartered at Malolos during 1898–1899, moved to San Isidro in 1899.

SPAIN

Location: Southwestern Europe
Capital: Madrid
Area, Absolute: 194,834
Area, Relative: Slightly more than twice the size of Oregon

	1896	1898	1900	1902	1904
Population Estimate:	18,300,000	18,500,000	18,594,000	18,723,000	18,984,000
Population Density (People per Sq. Mi.):	93.93	94.95	95.44	96.10	97.44

Estimated Total Armed Forces (1898): 400,000
Principal Military Bases and Installations:

    Domestic: Madrid, Cádiz

    Abroad: Manila, Philippines; Santiago, Cuba

Important Agricultural and Industrial Products: Wine, olives, livestock, iron, ships

UNITED STATES

Location: North America
Capital: Washington, DC
Area, Absolute: 3,025,600
Area, Relative: Slightly less than half the size of Russia

	1896	1898	1900	1902	1904
Population Estimate:	70,595,000	75,000,000	76,212,000	79,163,000	82,166,000
Population Density (People per Sq. Mi.):	23.33	24.79	25.19	26.16	27.16

Estimated Total Armed Forces (1898): 300,000
Principal Military Bases and Installations:

    Domestic: New Orleans, LA; Tampa, FL; Mobile, AL

    Abroad: Hong Kong; Guantánamo Bay, Cuba; Siboney, Cuba; Manila, Philippines

Important Agricultural and Industrial Products: Grain, vegetables, livestock, ships

Chronology

October 1492
27   Columbus discovers Cuba.

November 1492
19   Puerto Rico is discovered.

1514
       Santiago de Cuba is founded.

1515
       Havana, Cuba, is founded.

1521
       Ferdinand Magellan discovers Guam.

April 1565
27   First Spanish colony is established in the Philippines.

June 1571
24   Spanish Manila (Philippines) is founded.

1668
       Guam is colonized by Spain.

August 1762
13   British forces capture Havana as part of the larger Seven
       Years' War (1756–1763). Havana will be returned to
       Spain in 1763 as part of the peace agreement ending the
       war.

October 1762
5   British forces capture Manila. It will return to Spanish
       control in 1763.

November 1776
5   Spain allows rebel colonists' ships from Britain's North
       American colonies to trade at any Cuban port.

December 1823
2   U.S. president James Monroe enunciates the Monroe
       Doctrine, putting Europe on notice that the United States
       will not permit new colonies in the Americas and will not
       tolerate European interference in the affairs of the newly
       independent nations of Central and South America.

1825
       Secretary of State Henry Clay informs Mexico and
       Venezuela that the United States will block any attempt
       to invade Cuba. The United States takes this position be-
       cause Cuba is viewed as a potential addition to the
       United States. A foreign move on Cuba would also violate
       the Monroe Doctrine.

March 1826
16   First two martyrs for Cuban independence, Francisco
       Agüero y Velazco and Andrés Manuel Sánchez, are
       hanged for inciting rebellion.

June 1848
9   President James Polk offers Spain $100 million for Cuba.

August 1848

15   Spain declines President Polk's offer to sell Cuba to the United States.

1849–1851

Three successive Cuban filibustering expeditions launched from the southern United States end in failure. Many of those captured are hanged or shot before firing squads.

October 1852

22   Spain for a second time refuses to sell Cuba to the United States.

February 1854

28   The U.S.-owned side-wheeler *Black Warrior* is seized in Havana by Spanish authorities. After a fine is paid, the ship is released, but the incident causes a war scare in the United States.

1854

President Franklin Pierce offers Spain $130 million for Cuba.

October 1854

9–11   Ostend Manifesto is written clandestinely in Ostend, Belgium, by American diplomats, who call for the annexation of Cuba.

1855

Spain pays compensation and refunds fine to owners of the *Black Warrior*.

January 1868

6   Comité Revolucionario de Puerto Rico (Revolutionary Committee of Puerto Rico) founded in Puerto Rico by Ramón Emeterio Betances and Segundo Ruiz Belvis.

September 1868

23   Outbreak of the insurrection known as El Grito de Lares (Cry of Lares) in Puerto Rico. It is suppressed the next day by Spanish officials.

October 1868

10   The Ten Years' War breaks out in Cuba, sparked by landowner and slaveholder Carlos Manuel de Céspedes. One of his first of acts of rebellion is to free his slaves.

November 1868

The army of the insurrection in Cuba numbers 12,000 men.

1871

Importation of coolie labor to Cuba from the Far East is halted.

January 1872

20   Cavite Uprising in the Philippines begins and is quickly crushed by Spanish troops.

1873

The U.S. Army adopts the black powder single-shot Springfield M1873 rifle. Many are still in use during the Spanish-American War.

October 1873

31   U.S. side-wheel steamer *Virginius* is captured by Spanish naval forces off Cuba's coast. The vessel was carrying troops and supplies to Cuban rebels fighting the Ten Years' War.

November 1873

8   Forty-three passengers and crew members aboard the *Virginius* are executed in Santiago de Cuba before the executions are stopped by British intervention. Among those executed are British and American citizens. The incident nearly causes a war between Spain and the United States.

February 1878

11   Pact of Zanjón ends the Ten Years' War. Slaves who fought on either side are freed, but slavery is not officially ended in Cuba.

1879–1880

La Guerra Chiquita (Little War) fought by rebels in Cuba and is easily suppressed. Most of Cuba's population, exhausted by the Ten Years' War, refuses to support the new insurgency.

February 1880

13   Gradual abolition of slavery in Cuba begins, to be completed by 1886.

1884

Spain plans on spending 22 million pesetas over several years to build six modern battleships. The battleship *Pelayo,* however, would be the only ship constructed as a result of the plan.

February 1887

5   The Spanish battleship *Pelayo* is launched in France.
     March   *Noli Me Tangere* (Don't Touch Me), authored

by José Rizal, is published in Berlin, Germany, and fans the flames of Filipino nationalism.

October 1888
17   The American battleship *Maine,* which will explode in Havana Harbor on February 15, 1898, is laid down at the Brooklyn Navy Yard in New York.

1890
Captain Alfred T. Mahan's seminal book, *The Influence of Sea Power upon History, 1600–1783,* is published.

August 1890
30   The Spanish armored cruiser *Infanta Maria Teresa* is launched at Bilbao, Spain.

May 1891
7   The American battleship *Indiana,* the first of a class of three, is laid down in Philadelphia, Pennsylvania.

June 1891
17   The American first-class protected cruiser *Olympia* is laid down in San Francisco.

1892
The Norwegian-made Krag-Jørgensen M1892 rifle is adopted by the U.S. Army but is very slowly introduced over the next several years.

January 1892
5   José Martí founds El Partido Revolucionario Cubano (Cuban Revolutionary Party) in New York City and immediately calls for Cuban independence.

July 1892
3   Filipino nationalist José Rizal establishes the short-lived Liga Filipina (Filipino League) in Manila. The organization calls for peaceful reforms in the Philippines. Rizal's vision is for a slow evolution toward independence, to be carried out by Filipinos themselves, and is to be built on the precepts of education and civic and personal responsibility.

July 1892
6   Rizal is arrested and exiled to Mindanao.

July 1892
7   Led by Andrés Bonifacio, the Katipunan (Highest and Most Respected Association of the Sons of the Country) is established in the Philippines and calls for a revolutionary armed struggle to achieve Philippine independence.

January 1893
14   Coup led and inspired by U.S. planters and aided by the U.S. minister to Hawaii and the U.S. Marine Corps successfully overthrows Queen Liliuokalani and the Kingdom of Hawaii. The coup brings pro-American annexation forces to power. Liliuokalani formally abdicates in 1895.

February 1893
1   Americans in Hawaii form a provisional government, name Sanford Dole as its first president, and declare the archipelago a U.S. protectorate.

December 1893
7   Spain adopts the innovative Mauser Model 1893 rifle.

February 1895
5   Commissioning of the American protected cruiser *Olympia.*
24   Cuban War of Independence begins.

April 1895
10   José Martí and Máximo Gómez (general for the revolutionary movement) return to Cuba.

May 1895
19   Martí killed in ambush.

June 1895
12   President Grover Cleveland issues an official proclamation of neutrality in regard to the Cuban War of Independence.

September 1895
17   American battleship *Maine* commissioned. In 1894, while under construction, the *Maine* is redesignated as a second-class battleship.

October 1895
5   Major General Nelson Miles appointed commanding general of the U.S. Army.

November 1895
20   Commissioning of American battleship *Indiana.*

December 1895
8   Dr. José Henna establishes Puerto Rican section of El Partido Revolucionario Cubano.

February 1896
10   General Valeriano Weyler y Nocolau becomes captain-general of Cuba.

February 1896

17   Weyler institutes the highly controversial *reconcentrado* (reconcentration) system in Cuba, which will result in hundreds of thousands of Cuban civilian deaths and alienate U.S. public opinion toward Spain.

February 1896

28   Morgan-Cameron Resolution passes in the U.S. Senate recognizing Cuban belligerency and independence.

March 1896

2   U.S. House of Representatives passes resolution recognizing Cuban belligerency.

August 1896

23   Spanish authorities discover existence of the Katipunan. Hundreds of Filipinos are killed by Spanish vigilantes.

August 1896

26   The Philippine Revolution for independence begins.

September 1896

3   Filipino revolutionary and general Emilio Aguinaldo y Famy wins the Battle of Imus against Spanish forces.

October 1896

17   The Spanish armored cruiser *Princesa de Asturias* is launched at Bilbao, Spain. Construction had begun in 1890 and would be completed in 1902.

December 1896

7   President Cleveland announces that the United States reserves the right to intervene in Cuba if the situation is not soon resolved.

December 1896

30   Spanish authorities execute the internally exiled Filipino nationalist José Rizal.

January 1897

19   Journalist Richard Harding Davis reports in William Randolph Hearst's *New York Journal* on the Spanish firing-squad execution of Cuban rebel Adolfo Rodríguez in Cuba. This and other articles of this ilk inflame American sentiment over the events in Cuba and give rise to yellow journalism.

February 1897

12   Infamous "Does Our Flag Shield Women?" article in Hearst's *New York Journal* is printed. The article includes an imaginative Frederic Remington drawing of the strip search of a woman, which causes outrage throughout the United States.

March 1897

4   William McKinley inaugurated as president of the United States.

April 1897

23   General Fernando Primo de Rivera y Sobremonte replaces General Emilio Garcia de Polavieja as Spanish governor-general of the Philippine Islands.

May 1897

10   Filipino nationalist Andrés Bonifacio is executed by pro-Aguinaldo elements in an internal power struggle.

June 1897

2   Newly installed Assistant Secretary of the Navy Theodore Roosevelt delivers a speech at the Naval War College calling for a much-expanded navy.

August 1897

8   Spanish prime minister Antonio Cánovas del Castillo is assassinated.

October 1897

4   Práxedes Mateo Sagasta becomes prime minister of Spain for the sixth time.
23   Sagasta's government informs the United States that it will grant autonomy to Cuba.
31   General Ramón Blanco y Erenas replaces Weyler as captain-general of Cuba.

November 1897

25   Sagasta formally grants autonomy to Cuba and Puerto Rico.

December 1897

15   The Pact of Biak-na-Bato signed and calls for cessation of hostilities between Filipino rebels and the Spanish.
27   As stipulated by the Pact of Biak-na-Bato, Aguinaldo and a number of his followers and confidants depart the Philippines for Hong Kong, where they are to remain in exile.

January 1898

1   Spain inaugurates limited autonomous government in Cuba.
12   Spanish loyalists in Cuba riot in Havana.

25   U.S. battleship *Maine* arrives at Havana Harbor.

February 1898

9   Enrique Dupuy de Lôme-Canalejas Letter is published in the *New York Journal,* which causes an instant sensation in the United States. Puerto Rico gains limited autonomy.

10   Spanish ambassador to the United States Dupuy de Lôme resigns and is replaced by Luis Polo de Bernabé on February 16.

15   Internal explosion destroys USS *Maine* in Havana Harbor, killing 266 U.S. seamen. Spain is suspected of sabotage, and the disaster fuels the fires of anti-Spanish sentiments in the United States.

17   A U.S. Naval Court of Inquiry is appointed to investigate the loss of the *Maine.*

19   The United States declines a Spanish offer of a joint investigation of the wreckage of the *Maine.*

20   The Spanish armored cruiser *Vizcaya* arrives New York Harbor on a goodwill visit.

25   The *Vizcaya* departs New York Harbor. Commodore George Dewey, commanding the American Asiatic Squadron, is ordered to prepare for possible war with Spain and to destroy the Spanish squadron in the Philippines. Assistant Secretary of the Navy Theodore Roosevelt issues the order while Secretary of the Navy John D. Long is at an afternoon appointment with his physical therapist.

26   The Spanish Cortes (parliament) is dissolved after voting 1 million additional pesetas for the Spanish Navy.

March 1898

3   From information obtained by Spanish intelligence operatives, Spanish governor-general of the Philippines Fernando Primo de Rivera y Sobremonte informs the Spanish minister for the colonies that the American Asiatic Squadron under Dewey has orders to attack Manila in the event of war.

5   Spanish squadron for duty in the Caribbean ordered to assemble at Cádiz, Spain, under the command of Rear Admiral Pascual Cervera y Topete.

7   The gunrunning tug *Dauntless,* on a filibustering mission, is seized by the United States while bound for Cuba.

9   McKinley signs $50 million national defense appropriation bill.

11   The House Committee on Naval Affairs provides for the construction of three new battleships, one to be named the *Maine.*

12   U.S. European Squadron departs Lisbon, Portugal, to escort newly purchased warship and return to the United States.

13   Three Spanish destroyers and three torpedo boats leave Cádiz for the Canary Islands.

17   Small Spanish destroyers and torpedo boats arrive in the Canary Islands.

19   USS *Oregon* leaves San Francisco for the East Coast by steaming around Cape Horn, a voyage of some 14,000 miles. The ship is ordered to rendezvous with the North Atlantic Squadron as part of the naval blockade of Cuba.

22   Spanish destroyers and torpedo boats leave the Canary Islands, but because of breakdowns and coaling problems, they proceed to the Cape Verde Islands and not the West Indies.

24   Captain William Sampson is ordered to take command of the North Atlantic Squadron at Key West, Florida, and is promoted to rear admiral. The Bank of Spain announces a $40 million loan to the Spanish government, presumably to execute a war with the United States if it occurs.

27   Sagasta's government wins parliamentary elections in Spain. Parliamentary elections in Puerto Rico take place.

28   McKinley submits a Naval Court of Inquiry report to Congress that concludes that an external sea mine destroyed the *Maine.* Commodore Winfield Schley takes command of the Flying Squadron.

29   Ultimatum from the United States delivered to the Spanish government demanding that the Spanish leave Cuba.

30   Entire Autonomy Council in Puerto Rico resigns.

April 1898

1   Spain replies to the March 29 U.S. ultimatum, saying it will accept the American demands over leaving Cuba. Spanish armored cruisers *Oquendo* and *Vizcaya* depart Havana with orders to rendezvous with Spanish torpedo craft steaming from the Canary Islands.

3   Rebellion breaks out on the island of Cebu in the Philippines.

4   Steamers dispatched from Key West begin evacuating Americans from Havana. Pope Leo XIII offers to mediate a settlement between the Spanish and the Cuban rebels.

5   U.S. consul general Fitzhugh Lee ordered to leave Havana.

7   Six ambassadors representing the major European powers in Washington, D.C., submit a diplomatic note to McKinley urging peace with Spain.

8   Cervera leaves Cádiz for the Cape Verde Islands with the armored cruisers *Cristóbal Colón* and *Maria Teresa.* Rear Admiral Manuel de la Cámara y Libermoore commands the reserve squadron remaining at Cádiz and made up of largely unready warships.

9   Primo de Rivera replaced by Lieutenant-General Basilio Augustín as governor-general of the Philippines.

Augustín will fail in his attempts to establish autonomy in the Philippines and to reconcile the Filipinos to Spanish rule.

11 McKinley sends war message to Congress.

14 Cervera arrives in the Cape Verde Islands. Italian negotiations with Spain to sell the armored cruiser *Garibaldi* suspended.

15 British government instructs Jamaica that coal will be considered contraband in the event of war between Spain and the United States.

19 Congress passes a joint resolution that is an ultimatum to the Spanish.

20 McKinley signs joint resolution and delivers the ultimatum to the Spanish government. The Spanish ambassador to the United States asks for his passport, and the Spanish legation departs for Canada. Commodore John Howell appointed to command the North Atlantic Patrol squadron.

21 Spain considers the U.S. congressional joint resolution as a declaration of war. Spain mobilizes 80,000 reserve troops and orders 5,000 troops to the Canary Islands. The American ambassador and his staff in Madrid depart for Paris.

22 Rear Admiral William Sampson orders the North Atlantic Squadron to impose a blockade on Cuba. The protected cruiser *Nashville* captures the Spanish merchant ship *Buenaventura* off Havana, which is the first capture of the war.

23 Spain officially declares war. President McKinley calls for 125,000 volunteers.

24 President Bartolomé Masó of the Cuban Republic in Arms issues the Manifiesto de Sebastopol calling for Cuban independence under the motto of "Independence or Death." Cervera ordered to proceed to the Caribbean, and ultimately Cuban waters, with his squadron.

25 Congress declares war on Spain, retroactively to April 21.

27 Commodore Dewey steams with the Asiatic Squadron from Mirs Bay in China for the Philippines. An American squadron bombards coastal defenses at Matanzas, Cuba.

29 The Spanish steamer *Argonauto* is captured off Cienfuegos, and a skirmish is fought between U.S. naval assets and a Spanish warship and shore batteries but with no result. It is nevertheless considered the first naval action of the war. Portugal declares itself neutral in the war. Cervera's Spanish squadron leaves the Cape Verde Islands for the West Indies. Torpedo boats are left behind, however, later to return to Spain.

30 Cuban governor-general Blanco ends truce with Cuban revolutionaries.

May 1898

1 Commodore George Dewey's squadron decimates the Spanish fleet, commanded by Rear Admiral Patricio Montojo y Pasarón, at the Battle of Manila Bay. Lieutenant Andrew S. Rowan delivers his "A Message to Garcia" to General Calixto García y Iñiguez at Bayamo, Cuba.

2 Congress authorizes an additional emergency war loan of more than $35 million. President McKinley formally authorizes sending the U.S. Army to the Philippines. Forces would be sent in several convoys from the West Coast, principally from San Francisco, in the succeeding weeks. Dewey cuts the submarine cable linking Manila and Hong Kong. Cuban revolutionary general Máximo Gómez y Báez communicates with Rear Admiral William Sampson of the U.S. Navy.

3 Opposition forces in the Cortes demand an explanation for the stunning defeat of Spanish naval forces at Manila. Civil unrest in Spain results as news of the defeat spreads.

5 U.S. Senate passes a bill authorizing McKinley to supply munitions to Cuban rebels.

10 Spanish Cortes votes for additional war credits.

11 U.S. torpedo boat *Winslow* heavily damaged in operations off Cárdenas, Cuba. Ensign Worth Bagley, serving on the vessel, is the first American officer killed in the war. An American attempt to sever the undersea cable at Cárdenas is partially successful, and the Medal of Honor will be awarded to 49 troops who took part in the mission. Cervera's squadron arrives at Martinique.

12 Sampson's squadron bombards San Juan. Officials in Washington, D.C., receive report of the arrival of Cervera's squadron at Martinique. U.S. forces land near Port Cabañas, Cuba, with supplies for Cuban rebels, resulting in the first land skirmish with Spanish troops of the Spanish-American War.

14 Partially reconstructed Spanish battleship *Pelayo,* lacking armor plate on its secondary battery, is added to the Reserve Squadron in Spain in preparation for operations in the Far East.

15 In part due to riots in Spain and the defeat at Manila Bay, Spanish prime minister Práxedes Mateo Sagasta reshuffles his cabinet.

16 New army Department of the Pacific is formed, which includes the Philippines and is placed under the command of Major General Wesley Merritt.

18 New government cabinet under Sagasta is formed. McKinley orders Major General Merritt to occupy the Philippines.

19 Cervera's squadron arrives at Santiago de Cuba. Filipino general Emilio Aguinaldo y Famy arrives back on Luzon

after his brief exile in Hong Kong and recommences his revolutionary movement against the Spanish.

20 American War Department begins recruiting six regiments from the South that are made up of men who are allegedly immune to yellow fever. Reports that Spanish rear admiral Cámara's squadron is rumored to have left Spain for the Philippines are given to Dewey.

21 The U.S. monitor *Monterey* along with a collier are ordered from San Diego to reinforce Dewey. A second large monitor would be dispatched shortly thereafter from the West Coast.

23 Beginning on this date and lasting until September 21, 70 secret messages are relayed from a Spanish Montreal-based spy ring to Madrid concerning American military operations and movements.

24 Aguinaldo establishes himself as president and dictator of the Filipino revolutionary government.

25 McKinley calls for an additional 75,000 volunteers.

26 Secretary of the Navy John D. Long orders Dewey not to form alliances with Filipino rebels.

28 Cámara's Reserve Squadron hold maneuvers off Cádiz, Spain.

29 Commodore Winfield S. Schley blockades Santiago de Cuba, bottling up Cervera's vessels in the harbor.

31 Naval skirmish off Santiago de Cuba between Schley's squadron and the *Cristóbal Colón* and Spanish coastal defenses.

June 1898

1 Sampson joins Schley off Santiago de Cuba with overwhelming naval strength.

3 Lieutenant Richmond Hobson, commanding a volunteer crew, fails to block the entrance to Santiago de Cuba by sinking the collier *Merrimac* in the sea channel. The entire crew is captured during the mission.

4 U.S. Secret Service first makes public the existence of a Spanish spy ring based in Canada.

6 Sampson bombards Santiago de Cuba's coastal defenses.

7 American naval squadron cuts submarine cable near Guantánamo Bay and bombards the shore.

9 U.S. marines land at Guantánamo Bay.

9–17 Marines and Cuban rebels skirmish with the Spanish at the Battle of Guantánamo.

12 Aguinaldo declares Filipino independence. German East Asian Squadron begins to concentrate in Manila Bay.

14 Major General William Shafter, V Corps commander, departs Tampa, Florida, for Cuba with an expeditionary force. Battle of Cuzco Well secures Guantánamo for the Americans and a steady supply of fresh water for the marines there.

15 First meeting of Anti-Imperialist League takes place in the United States.

16 Rear Admiral Cámara's naval squadron, bound for the Philippines, departs Cádiz for the Suez Canal.

18 Navy secretary Long orders Sampson to prepare a squadron with battleships to operate off the coast of Spain if Cámara's squadron passes through the Suez Canal. Commodore John Watson is placed in command. Leading merchants in Catalonia, Spain, issue a resolution calling for peace.

20 Shafter's expeditionary force arrives off the coast of Santiago de Cuba. Aserraderos Conference takes place between officials representing the U.S. Army, the U.S. Navy, and Cuban rebels under General García to work out goals and strategies for the unfolding campaign. The protected cruiser *Charleston* with three transports arrives at Spanish-controlled Guam. The island surrenders the next day without a shot being fired.

22 Shafter begins landing on the Cuban coast southeast of Santiago de Cuba near Daiquirí and Siboney, beginning the Cuba Campaign. Direct cable communication between Washington, D.C., and Guantánamo is established. Naval skirmish off San Juan results in minor damage to the Spanish destroyer *Terror.*

24 Battle at Las Guásimas, Cuba, clears the way for an American advance on Santiago de Cuba (Santiago de Cuba Land Campaign). Spanish Cortes is dissolved.

25 First American army troops arrive in the Philippines under Major General Merritt, commander of VIII Corps.

28 McKinley extends the Declaration of Blockade to all of Cuba and San Juan.

29 Brigadier General Simon Snyder's 2nd Division steams for Santiago de Cuba to reinforce Shafter's force.

30 First U.S. troop disembark at Cavite, Philippines.

July 1898

1 Battles of Kettle Hill, San Juan Hill, El Caney, and Aguadores take place. Cuban lieutenant general Arsenio Linares y Pombo, commanding at Santiago de Cuba, is severely wounded and replaced by Major General José Toral y Vázquez.

2 Spanish counterattacks against U.S.-captured positions fail.

3 Battle of Santiago de Cuba destroys Spanish squadron. Shafter gives notice to Toral that U.S. forces will likely bombard Santiago de Cuba and that women and children should leave the city for safety during a temporary truce.

7 Cámara's squadron is recalled to Spain. McKinley signs congressional resolution annexing the Hawaiian Islands.

8 Return of Cámara's squadron to Spain is confirmed by American Intelligence. Among several officers McKinley nominates for promotion is Lieutenant Colonel Theodore Roosevelt to colonel.

8   Toral and Shafter enter into discussions on the surrender of Santiago de Cuba.

11   Major General Nelson Miles arrives at Santiago de Cuba and confers with Shafter and Sampson.

15   Because of continued civil unrest, the Spanish government issues a decree limiting the rights of citizens.

16   Spanish admiral Cervera and other captured Spanish officers are quartered at Annapolis, Maryland.

17   Santiago de Cuba surrenders to American forces, all but ending the fighting in Cuba.

18   Spain requests that France contact the U.S. government to broker a truce. Brigadier General Leonard Wood is appointed military governor of Santiago de Cuba.

20   Major General James Wilson departs Charleston, South Carolina, for Puerto Rico with the 1st Division.

21   American squadron bombards Nipe Bay, Cuba, and sinks two small Spanish warships.

25   Major General Nelson A. Miles commands army that invades Puerto Rico at Guánica. The resulting Puerto Rico Campaign is practically bloodless and will last barely three weeks. Autonomous parliament in Puerto Rico disbands. Spanish forces in Guantánamo region surrender.

26   Peace talks, through French offices, commence in Washington, D.C.

28   Ponce, Puerto Rico, falls to American forces. U.S. government requests that Shafter send back to the United States as many troops as possible, as quickly as possible, from the Santiago de Cuba area to avoid yellow fever epidemic.

29   American troops under Major General Merritt begin their march from Cavite to Manila.

30   McKinley presents truce terms acceptable to the United States to the Spanish.

August 1898

2   Spain, with some reservations concerning the Philippines, accepts American demands.

5   Battle of Guayama fought in Puerto Rico.

9   Battle at Asomante Hills takes place in Cuba. Battle of Coamo occurs in Puerto Rico.

10   Battles of Hormigueros and Mayagüez occur in Puerto Rico.

11   U.S. State Department and French ambassador to the United States Jules-Martin Cambon successfully negotiate the formal Protocol of Peace, which will effectively end hostilities.

12   Armistice takes effect and ends fighting. Manzanillo, Cuba, bombarded.

13   First Battle of Manila occurs, and Manila is captured by U.S. forces. Battle of Las Marías in Puerto Rico is the last battle between the Spanish and Americans.

14   Document for formal surrender of Manila signed.

26   McKinley issues secret decree that Puerto Rico will become a conquered territory of the United States.

September 1898

13   Spanish Cortes ratifies the Protocol of Peace.

15   Revolutionary Malolos (Philippines) Congress meets and later adopts a constitution.

26   Dodge Commission established to investigate mismanagement in the War Department.

October 1898

1   Peace talks in Paris commence.

18   San Juan formally handed over to the American forces, and Major General John Brooke becomes first military governor.

26   McKinley instructs his peace commissioners to demand the annexation of the Philippines at the peace negotiations.

November 1898

11   Rear Admiral Montojo arrives in Madrid for his court-martial. He would be convicted and would serve a short time in prison.

29   Constitution of the First Philippine Republic adopted by the Malolos Congress.

December 1898

10   Treaty of Paris formally ends the war. Cuba officially independent of Spain.

21   McKinley calls for the peaceful annexation of the Philippines.

23   U.S. Navy placed in control of Guam.

January 1899

1   Aguinaldo declared president by Malolos Congress. American officials establish provisional government in Cuba.

17   United States takes formal possession of Wake Island.

February 1899

4   Second Battle of Manila. First shots fired in Philippine-American War between Filipino rebels and U.S. forces. Luzon Campaign begins simultaneously, lasting until December 1899.

6   U.S. Senate ratifies Treaty of Paris in a 52 to 27 vote.

11   Visayan Campaigns commence, lasting until the early summer of 1901.

March 1899

19   Queen Regent María Cristina of Spain breaks stalemate in the Cortes by signing the Treaty of Paris herself.

May 1899

5   Secretary of State John Hay offers autonomy to the Philippines.

July 1899

3   Schools open in Philippines with Spanish, American, and Filipino teachers.

August 1899

10   Bates Treaty finalized between U.S. brigadier general John C. Bates and the sultan of Sulu, Jamalul Kiram II, in the southern Philippines.

September 1899

     Secretary of State John Hay issues a series of diplomatic letters to the world's major colonial powers. The letters, which came to be known as the Open Door Notes, urge that all nations should have free and unfettered access to China's markets. The growing violence of the Boxer Rebellion in China will prompt him to send another letter in July 1900 asking that all nations honor China's territorial and political integrity.

1   General League of Cuban Workers is formed.

December 1899

18   Major General Henry Lawton is killed during the Battle of San Mateo in the Philippines.

20   Brigadier General Leonard Wood is appointed governor of Cuba.

January 1900

17   United States declares Wake Island an unincorporated territory.

26   Samar Campaign begins, lasting until April 27, 1902.

February 1900

22   Hawaii officially becomes a territory of the United States.

May 1900

     To protect their citizens and economic interests in China, now endangered by the ongoing Boxer Rebellion, seven Western nations and Japan dispatch troops to the country to quell the unrest. The United States is one of the nations sending troops.

June 1900

16   First municipal elections in Cuba held since end of the war.

September 1900

13   Battle of Massiquisie is fought in the Philippines.

November 1900

5   Cuban Constitutional Assembly convenes.

March 1901

23   Emilio Aguinaldo y Famy captured by U.S. force led by Brigadier General Frederick Funston.

April 1901

1   Aguinaldo takes oath of allegiance to the United States in Manila.

September 1901

27–28   Balangiga Massacre takes place.

April 1902

16   Surrender of General Miguel Malvar, the last Filipino rebel resisting American occupation, along with his family.

May 1902

     Lake Lanao (Mindanao, Philippines) Campaigns begin, lasting until May 10, 1903.

2   Battle of Bayang (Moro Province) occurs, precipitating the Moro Campaigns that endure sporadically until 1913.

20   Cuba fully independent of American administration.

July 1902

1   U.S. Congress passes the Philippine Organic Act for administering the Philippines.

4   President Theodore Roosevelt declares an end to the Philippine-American War and offers amnesty.

1903

     Resistance by Muslims in the southern Philippines (Jolo) begins. Springfield .30-caliber M1903, based on the Spanish Mauser, adopted by the U.S. Army.

January 1903

21   Militia Act of 1903 (Dick Act) enacted and transforms state militias.

March 1906

5–8   First Battle of Bud Dajo.

December 1911

     Bud Dajo Campaign.

June 1913

11–15   Battle of Bud Bagsak ends Muslim resistance in Jolo.

March 1917

2   Jones-Shafroth Act, making Puerto Ricans citizens of the United States and establishing a native legislature, signed into law.

November 1935

15   Manuel Quezon inaugurated as first president of the Commonwealth of the Philippines. The Philippines will become independent in 1946.

JACK GREENE

Glossary

abaft — Farther aft than; in or toward the stern.

accoutrements — A soldier's gear except for weapons and clothing.

accrocher — French term meaning to board and grapple an enemy vessel.

aft — Near, toward, or at the stern of the ship.

aide-de-camp — The chief military secretary to a superior officer.

aller á l'abordage — A French term meaning to board an enemy vessel.

amidships — The center part of the ship. This is both between the fore and aft sections and between the port and starboard sides.

amphibious warfare — Military activity that involves landing from ships, either directly or by means of landing craft.

army — Military unit, usually consisting of at least 50,000 to 60,000 individuals and commanded by a commissioned officer, usually a general.

assumed position — Position at which the navigator assumes the ship to be when using the intercept method of celestial navigation. This can also be the ship's dead reckoning (DR) position or its estimated position.

astern — Behind a ship.

attack á l'outrance — French term for the doctrine of the offensive to the outer limit. Associated with French philosopher Henri Bergson, it held that offensive spirit and moral supremacy were everything in battle and that defensive operations could not be decisive.

aweigh — Said of an anchor immediately when it is broken out of the ground and when its cable is up and down.

ballast — Additional weight placed low in the hull to improve stability. Ballast can be external (outside the hull) or internal (within the ship) and either permanent (as in concrete) or temporary (as in saltwater tanks).

ballistics — The science of projectiles, divided into interior and exterior ballistics. Its aim is to improve the design of shells or projectiles so that increased accuracy and predictability are the result.

barrage — French term for a barrier formed by artillery fire (land) or an antisubmarine net or mine barrier (sea).

battalion — Military unit, usually consisting of between 300 and 1,000 individuals and commanded by a commissioned officer, usually a lieutenant colonel.

battery — Military unit corresponding to an infantry company, usually composed of about 100 individuals and commanded by a captain.

benevolent assimilation — See entry.

berm	Built-up dirt wall used as a barrier against attack.
bow chase	Cannon mounted on the fore part of the ship that are used in pursuit of an enemy vessel.
brigade	Military unit, usually consisting of between 3,000 and 5,000 individuals and commanded by a commissioned officer, usually a brigadier general (premodern times) or a colonel (modern times).
broadside	The firing of all guns on one side of a vessel as near simultaneously as possible.
cannonade	Application of artillery to naval warfare or a vessel's effort to attack an object.
captain's mast	A hearing at which the captain of the ship dispenses nonjudicial punishments.
cease-fire	A partial or temporary cessation of hostilities. A cease-fire can also involve a general armistice or a total cessation of all hostilities.
"Civilize 'em with a Krag"	See entry.
close hauled	When a vessel has the wind before its beam or is sailing as close to the wind as possible.
coastal defense	The defense of a nation's coast from an enemy sea invasion or blockade, accomplished with heavy artillery, mines, small warships, and nets.
commissioned officer	An officer possessing authority over enlisted men and noncommissioned officers whose rank is conferred by a government document (commission).
company	Military unit, usually consisting of between 70 and 250 individuals and commanded by a commissioned officer, usually a captain.
corps	Military unit, usually consisting of between 30,000 and 50,000 individuals and commanded by a commissioned officer, usually a lieutenant general.
coup d'état	A sudden, decisive use of force in politics, especially in terms of a violent overthrow of an existing government by a small group often assisted by the military.
court-martial	To subject to a military trial with a court consisting of a board of commissioned officers.
dead reckoning	Determining the position of a vessel based on the course steered and distance sailed, not accounting for tides and currents. Dead reckoning (DR) positions are marked on charts.
divided fire	Fire directed by one ship at multiple targets.
division	Military unit, usually consisting of between 10,000 and 20,000 individuals and commanded by a commissioned officer, usually a major general.
economic warfare	Compelling an enemy to submit either by direct action against its economic base or indirectly through blockade or boycott.
enfilade	To fire upon the length rather than the face of an enemy position. Enfilading an enemy allows a varying range of fire to find targets while minimizing the amount of fire the enemy can return.
envelopment	To pour fire along the enemy's line. A double envelopment is an attack on both flanks of an enemy.
estimated position	A vessel's position advanced on the chart from a previous fix of observed position.
executive officer	Second-in-command of a vessel, squadron, etc.
fathom	A unit of measure (often used to describe the depth of water) equal to six feet.
flagship	Ship carrying an admiral who is in command of a fleet or squadron.
flotilla	A grouping of warships, distinctive from a fleet by its smaller size.
forced march	In military usage, a rapid movement of troops over some distance to meet a crisis such as the imperative need to reinforce positions before or during a battle.
gangway	An opening in a ship giving access to a brow or other ladder.
Gilded Age	See entry.
give-way vessel	The vessel that must stay clear of another vessel (the stand-on vessel) in accordance with the rules of navigation.
guerrilla warfare	A form of irregular warfare that is highly flexible and often decentralized. Nontraditional tactics such as raids and ambushes are employed to compensate for a numerical or technological disadvantage.
gunboat	A small armed vessel.
gun deck	The main deck of a frigate that supports the frigate's battery.

gunner	An officer whose duties are to take charge of artillery and ammunition of the ship and to train the crew in the use of its guns.
hegemony	The dominance of one nation over other nations based on the dominant nation's transfer of core values and basic societal institutions rather than through military conquest.
hull	Actual body of a vessel. Excludes superstructure, rigging, masts, and rudder.
hulled	Shot in the hull, normally fired at point-blank range.
in irons	Condition whereby through lack of wind a sailing ship is unable to move while heading into the wind and attempting to tack.
in ordinary	Laid up in reserve (said of a ship).
jetsam	Goods cast out of a ship.
jingoism	See entry.
junta	Rule by a group of military officers who came to national power through a military coup.
league	A unit of measure roughly equivalent to three miles.
lee shore	A shore toward which the wind is blowing (therefore a dangerous shore).
leeward	Downwind, away from the wind.
line of position	A line drawn on a chart to determine a ship's position in relation to an object. The intersection of two or more lines of position (LOPs) provides a fix.
magnetic bearing	Bearing of an object when determined by a compass, the needle of which is aligned with magnetic north.
main battery	A ship's battery made up of its biggest guns or missiles.
Manifest Destiny	See entry.
martial law	Temporary military governance of a civilian population when the civil government has become unable to sustain order.
militarism	The view that military power and efficiency is the supreme ideal of the state.
mobilization	The organization of the armed forces of a nation for active military service in time of war or other national emergency.
Monroe Doctrine	See entry.
Moros	See entry.
nautical mile	Unit of measurement at sea, equal to 6,076 feet.
noncommissioned officer (NCO)	An enlisted soldier who has been promoted to a position of control or authority that is between enlisted men and commissioned officers.
ordnance	Military supplies, particularly weapons and ammunition.
overtaking	Coming up to another vessel from any point abaft the other vessel's beam.
petty officer	Naval rank equivalent to a noncommissioned officer (between officers and enlisted sailors).
platoon	Military unit, usually consisting of between 30 and 50 individuals and commanded by a commissioned officer, usually a lieutenant.
pontoon bridge	A bridge whose deck is supported by flat-bottomed boats.
presidio	Spanish fortress created to protect missions and other important areas.
procurement	The act of purchasing. It often refers to the government's purchasing of military equipment or other supplies.
quarterdeck	Part of the deck that is designated for both official and ceremonial functions. It is also where crew members board the ship by gangways.
quartermaster	A commissioned officer whose duty is to provide clothing and subsistence for a body of troops.
regiment	Military unit, usually consisting of between 2,000 and 3,000 individuals and commanded by a commissioned officer, usually a colonel.
relative bearing	A bearing measure with reference to the ship's longitudinal axis.
relative course	Course steered by another ship when expressed as the angle that course makes with the course of one's own ship.
rudder	Device for steering vessels, usually fitted at the stern.
salvo	The simultaneous firing of a number of guns.
scuttling	The intentional letting of water into a ship's hull in order to sink it.
sea lines of communication	Essential sea routes for military operations.
social Darwinism	See entry.
squad	Military unit, usually consisting of between 8 and 14 individuals and commanded by a noncommissioned officer.

standing army	A permanent military unit of paid soldiers that exists during both peacetime and wartime.
starboard	The right side of a vessel when standing aboard facing forward.
stern chaser	A gun that fires directly astern of the ship.
strike (colors)	To surrender in naval combat by lowering the vessel's flag.
Tagalogs	See entry.
turret ship	Warship carrying main armaments in a turret or turrets.
typhoid fever	See entry.
USS	United States ship; the designation used for vessels of the U.S. Navy.

weather gauge	A windward (upwind) and hence desirable position in relation to an adversary, thus giving the vessel with the weather gauge the advantage of catching the wind first, dictating the speed of approach and the time of engaging.
white man's burden	See entry.
windward	Toward the wind.
yellow fever	See entry.
yellow journalism	See entry.

Selected Bibliography

Abeto, Isidro Escare. *Rizal: The Immortal Filipino (1861–1896)*. Manila: National Book Store, 1984.

Abrahamson, James L. *America Arms for a New Century*. New York: Free Press, 1981.

Adams, Charles Francis, Jr. *Charles Francis Adams, 1835–1915: An Autobiography*. New York: Houghton Mifflin, 1916.

Agoncillo, Teodoro A., and Milagros C. Guerrero. *History of the Filipino People*. 5th ed. Quezon City, Philippines: R. P. Garcia, 1983.

Aguinaldo, Emilio, and Vincente Albano Pacis. *A Second Look at America*. New York: Robert Speller, 1957.

Akin, Edward N. *Flagler: Rockefeller Partner and Florida Baron*. Kent, OH: Kent State University Press, 1988.

Alberts, Don E. *Brandy Station to Manila Bay: A Biography of General Wesley Merritt*. Austin, TX: Presidial, 1980.

Alejandrino, José, trans. *The Price of Freedom (La Senda del Sacrificio): Episodes and Anecdotes of Our Struggles for Freedom*. Manila: Solar Publishing, 1949.

Alger, Russell Alexander. *The Spanish-American War*. New York: Harper and Brothers, 1901.

Alip, Eufronio Melo. *In the Days of General Emilio Aguinaldo: A Study of the Life and Times of a Great Military Leader, Statesman, and Patriot Who Founded the First Republic in Asia*. Manila: Alip, 1969.

Allen, Douglass. *Fredric Remington and the Spanish-American War*. New York: Crown, 1971.

Allen, Frederick Lewis. *The Lords of Creation*. New York: Harper and Brothers, 1935.

Allen, Helena G. *The Betrayal of Liliuokalani, Last Queen of Hawaii, 1838–1917*. Honolulu: Mutual Publishing, 1982.

———. *Sanford Ballard Dole: Hawaii's Only President, 1844–1926*. Glendale, CA: Arthur H. Clark, 1988.

Ambrose, Stephen E. *Upton and the Army*. Baton Rouge: Louisiana State University Press, 1964.

Anderson, David L. *Imperialism and Idealism: American Diplomats in China, 1861–1898*. Bloomington: Indiana University Press, 1985.

Armstrong, David A. *Bullets and Bureaucrats: The Machine Gun and the United States Army, 1861–1916*. Westport, CT: Greenwood, 1982.

Ayala, César J. *American Sugar Kingdom: The Plantation Economy of the Spanish Caribbean, 1898–1934*. Chapel Hill: University of North Carolina Press, 1999.

Azoy, Anastasio C. *Signal 250! The Sea Fight off Santiago*. New York: David McKay, 1964.

Bain, David Haward. *Empire Express: Building the First Transcontinental Railroad*. New York: Viking Penguin, 1999.

———. *Sitting in Darkness: Americans in the Philippines*. New York: Houghton Mifflin, 1984.

Balch, David Arnold. *Elbert Hubbard: Genius of Roycroft*. New York: Frederick A. Stokes, 1940.

Balfour, Sebastian. *The End of the Spanish Empire, 1898–1923*. New York: Oxford University Press USA, 1997.

Bannister, Robert C. *Social Darwinism: Science and Myth in Anglo-American Social Thought*. Philadelphia: Temple University Press, 1979.

Barton, William E. *The Life of Clara Barton, Founder of the American Red Cross*. 2 vols. Boston and New York: Houghton Mifflin, 1922.

Beale, Howard K. *Theodore Roosevelt and the Rise of America to World Power*. Baltimore: Johns Hopkins University Press, 1956.

Beck, Earl R. *A Time of Triumph and Sorrow: Spanish Politics during the Reign of Alfonso XII, 1874–1885.* Carbondale: Southern Illinois University Press, 1979.

Beisner, Robert L. *Twelve against Empire: The Anti-Imperialists, 1898–1900.* New York: McGraw-Hill, 1968.

Benjamin, Jules R. *The United States and Cuba: Hegemony and Dependent Development, 1880–1934.* Pittsburgh: University of Pittsburgh Press, 1977.

———. *The United States and the Origins of the Cuban Revolution: An Empire of Liberty in an Age of National Liberation.* Princeton, NJ: Princeton University Press, 1990.

Bernad, Miguel A. *The Great Island: Studies in the Exploration and Evangelization of Mindanao.* Manila: Ateneo de Manila University Press, 2004.

Berner, Brad K. *The Spanish-American War: A Historical Dictionary.* Lanham, MD: Scarecrow, 1998.

Bigelow, John, Jr. *Reminiscences of the Santiago Campaign.* New York: Harper and Brothers, 1899.

Bigelow, Poultney. *The Children of the Nations: A Study of Colonization and Its Problems.* London: Heinemann, 1901.

Billington, Ray Allen. *Frederick Jackson Turner: Historian, Scholar, Teacher.* New York: Oxford University Press USA, 1973.

Blair, Emma Helen, and James Alexander Robertson, eds. *The Philippine Islands, 1493–1898,* Vol. 52, *1841–1898.* Norman, OK: Arthur H. Clark, 1908.

Blow, Michael. *A Ship to Remember: The Maine and the Spanish-American War.* New York: Morrow, 1992.

Bogue, Allan G. *Frederick Jackson Turner: Strange Roads Going Down.* Norman: University of Oklahoma Press, 1998.

Bolles, Blair. *Tyrant from Illinois: Uncle Joe Cannon's Experiment with Personal Power.* Westport, CT: Greenwood, 1974.

Bonifacio, Andres. *The Trial of Andres Bonifacio: The Original Documents in Tagalog Text and English Translation.* Manila: Ateneo de Manila, 1963.

Boot, Max. *The Savage Wars of Peace: Small Wars and the Rise of American Power.* New York: Perseus, 2002.

Boutwell, George S. *In the Name of Liberty: Imperialism and Anti-Imperialism.* Boston: Anti-Imperialist League, 1899.

Bouvier, Virginia M., ed. *Whose America? The War of 1898 and the Battles to Define the Nation.* Westport, CT: Praeger, 2001.

Bowen, Wayne H., and Jose E. Alvarez, eds. *A Military History of Modern Spain: From the Napoleonic Era to the International War on Terror.* Westport, CT: Praeger, 2007.

Bradford, James C., ed. *Crucible of Empire: The Spanish-American War and Its Aftermath.* Annapolis, MD: Naval Institute Press, 1993.

Bradford, Richard H. *The Virginius Affair.* Boulder: Colorado Associated University Press, 1980.

Braisted, William R. *The United States Navy in the Pacific, 1897–1906.* Austin: University of Texas Press, 1958.

Brands, H. W. *Bound to Empire: The United States and the Philippines.* New York: Oxford University Press USA, 1992.

———. *The Reckless Decade: America in the 1890s.* Chicago: University of Chicago Press, 2002.

Brereton, T. R. *Educating the U.S. Army: Arthur L. Wagner and Reform, 1875–1905.* Lincoln: University of Nebraska Press, 2000.

Brewer, Thomas B. *The Robber Barons: Saints or Sinners?* New York: Holt, Rinehart and Winston, 1970.

Brexel, Bernadette. *The Populist Party: A Voice for Farmers in an Industrialized Society.* New York: Rosen, 2003.

Bridge, James Howard. *The Inside History of the Carnegie Steel Company: A Romance of Millions.* New York: Aldine Book, 1903.

Brody, David. *In Labor's Cause: Main Themes in the History of the American Worker.* New York: Oxford University Press USA, 1993.

Brown, Charles H. *The Correspondents' War: Journalists in the Spanish-American War.* New York: Scribner, 1967.

Brown, E. Richard. *Rockefeller Medicine Men: Medicine and Capitalism in America.* Berkeley: University of California Press, 1979.

Browning, Robert S., III. *Two If by Sea: The Development of American Coastal Defense Policy.* Westport, CT: Greenwood, 1983.

Bülow, Bernhard Fürst von. *Memoirs of Prince von Bülow.* Translated by F. A. Voigt. London: Putnam, 1932.

Burton, David H. *Theodore Roosevelt: Confident Imperialist.* Philadelphia: University of Pennsylvania Press, 1968.

Burton, Theodore E. *John Sherman.* Boston and New York: Houghton Mifflin, 1906.

Callicott, Wilfred H. *The Caribbean Policy of the United States, 1890–1920.* Baltimore: Johns Hopkins University Press, 1942.

Callow, Alexander B., Jr. *The Tweed Ring.* New York: Oxford University Press USA, 1966.

Campbell, Ballard C. *The Human Condition in the Gilded Age and Progressive Era.* Wilmington, DE: SR Books, 1999.

Campbell, Charles S. *Special Business Interests and the Open Door Policy.* New Haven, CT: Yale University Press, 1951.

———. *The Transformation of American Foreign Relations, 1865–1900.* New York: Harper and Row, 1976.

Campbell, W. Joseph. *Yellow Journalism: Puncturing the Myths, Defining the Legacies.* Westport, CT: Praeger, 2003.

Cannon, Joseph Gurney, and L. White Busbey. *Uncle Joe Cannon: The Story of a Pioneer American.* St. Clair Shores, MI: Scholarly Press, 1970.

Canoy, Reuben R. *The History of Mindanao.* Cagayan de Oro, Philippines: International School Publication, 2001.

Carlson, Paul H. *Pecos Bill: A Military Biography of William R. Shafter.* College Station: Texas A&M University Press, 1989.

Carnegie, Andrew. *Autobiography of Andrew Carnegie and the Gospel of Wealth.* New York: Signet Classics, 2006.

Carosso, Vincent P., and Rose C. Carosso. *The Morgans: Private International Bankers, 1854–1913.* Cambridge: Harvard University Press, 1987.

Carpenter, Ronald H. *The Eloquence of Frederick Jackson Turner.* San Marino, CA: Huntington Library, 1983.

Carr, Raymond. *Spain: A History.* Oxford: Oxford University Press, 2001.

Carrion, Arturo Morales. *Puerto Rico: A Political and Cultural History.* New York: Norton, 1984.

Carter, William H. *The Life of Lieutenant General Chaffee.* Chicago: University of Chicago Press, 1917.

Cashman, Sean Dennis. *American in the Gilded Age: From the Death of Lincoln to the Rise of Theodore Roosevelt.* New York: New York University Press, 1984.

Chadwick, French Ensor. *The Relations of the United States and Spain V1: The Spanish-American War.* Reprint ed. Kila, MT: Kessinger, 2007.

Challener, Richard D. *Admirals, Generals, and American Foreign Policy, 1898–1914.* Princeton, NJ: Princeton University Press, 1973.

Champney, Freeman. *Art & Glory: The Story of Elbert Hubbard.* New York: Crown, 1968.

Chandler, Alfred D., Jr. *Strategy and Structure: Chapters in the History of American Industrial Enterprise.* Cambridge, MA: MIT Press, 1990.

———. *The Visible Hand: The Managerial Revolution in American Business.* Cambridge: Belknap Press of Harvard University Press, 1977.

Chapman, Charles E. *A History of the Cuban Republic: A Study in Hispanic American Politics.* New York: Macmillan, 1927.

Chernow, Ron. *Titan: The Life of John D. Rockefeller, Sr.* New York: Random House, 1998.

Cherny, Robert W. *A Righteous Cause: The Life of William Jennings Bryan.* Edited by Oscar Handlin. Boston: Little, Brown, 1985.

Chessman, G. Wallace. *Governor Theodore Roosevelt: The Albany Apprenticeship, 1898–1900.* Cambridge: Harvard University Press, 1965.

Chiang, Hsiang-Tse, et al. *The United States and China.* Chicago: University of Chicago Press, 1988.

Chidsey, Donald Barr. *The Spanish-American War: A Behind-the-Scenes Account of the War in Cuba.* New York: Crown, 1971.

Cirillo, Vincent J. *Bullets and Bacilli: The Spanish-American War and Military Medicine.* New Brunswick, NJ: Rutgers University Press, 2004.

Clements, Kendrick A. *William Jennings Bryan: Missionary Idealist.* Knoxville: University of Tennessee Press, 1983.

Clements, Paul H. *The Boxer Rebellion: A Political and Diplomatic Review.* New York: Longmans, Green, 1914.

Clymer, Kenton J. *John Hay: The Gentleman as Diplomat.* Ann Arbor: University of Michigan Press, 1975.

Coates, Austin. *Rizal: Philippine Nationalist and Martyr.* Oxford: Oxford University Press, 1968.

Coletta, Paolo Enrico. *Admiral Bradley A. Fiske and the American Navy.* Lawrence: Regents Press of Kansas, 1979.

———. *Bowman Hendry McCalla: A Fighting Sailor.* Washington, DC: University Press of America, 1979.

———. *French Ensor Chadwick: Scholarly Warrior.* Lanham, MD: University Press of America, 1980.

———, ed. *Threshold to American Internationalism: Essays on the Foreign Policies of William McKinley.* New York: Exposition Press, 1970.

———. *William Jennings Bryan.* 3 vols. Lincoln: University of Nebraska Press, 1964–1969.

Collin, Richard H. *Theodore Roosevelt's Caribbean: The Panama Canal, the Monroe Doctrine, and the Latin American Context.* Baton Rouge: Louisiana State University Press, 1990.

Connaughton, R. M. *The War of the Rising Sun and the Tumbling Bear: A Military History of the Russo-Japanese War, 1904–5.* New York: Routledge, 1988.

Conroy, Robert. *The Battle of Manila Bay: The Spanish-American War in the Philippines.* New York: MacMillan, 1968.

Corey, Lewis. *The House of Morgan: A Social Biography of the Masters of Money.* New York: G. H. Watt, 1930.

Cosmas, Graham A. *An Army for Empire: The United States Army in the Spanish-American War.* College Station: Texas A&M University Press, 1994.

Couttie, Bob. *Hang the Dogs: The True History of the Balangiga Massacre.* Quezon City: New Day, 2004.

Crosby, Molly Caldwell. *The American Plague: The Untold Story of Yellow Fever, the Epidemic That Shaped Our History.* New York: Berkeley Books, 2006.

Crouch, Thomas W. *A Yankee Guerrillero: Frederick Funston and the Cuban Insurrection, 1896–1897.* Memphis: Memphis State University Press, 1975.

Current, Richard N. *The Typewriter and the Men Who Made It.* Urbana: University of Illinois Press, 1954.

Cushner, Nicholas P. *Spain in the Philippines: From Conquest to Revolution.* Quezon City: Anteneo de Manila University, 1971.

Dagget, A. S. *America in the China Relief Expedition.* New York: Hudson-Kimberly, 1903.

Daniels, Roger. *Coming to America: A History of Immigration and Ethnicity in American Life.* New York: Harper Perennial, 1991.

Davis, Richard Harding. *The Cuban and Porto Rican Campaigns.* New York: Scribner, 1898.

Daws, Gavan. *Shoal of Time: A History of the Hawaiian Islands.* New York: Macmillan, 1968.

Dawson, Joseph G. *The Late 19th Century U.S. Army, 1865–1898: A Research Guide.* New York: Greenwood, 1990.

De La Fuente, Alejandro. *A Nation for All: Race, Inequality and Politics in Twentieth Century Cuba.* Chapel Hill: University of North Carolina Press, 2001.

Delmondo, Sharon. *The Star-Entangled Banner: One Hundred Years of American in the Philippines.* Piscataway, NJ: Rutgers University Press, 2004.

DeMontravel, Peter R. *A Hero to His Fighting Men: Nelson A. Miles, 1839–1925.* Kent, OH: Kent State University Press, 1998.

De Ocampo, Esteban A. *First Filipino Diplomat: Felipe Agoncillo, 1859–1941.* Manila: National Historical Institute, 1977.

Devine, Michael J. *John W. Foster: Politics and Diplomacy in the Imperial Era, 1873–1917.* Athens: Ohio University Press, 1981.

Dewey, George. *The Autobiography of George Dewey.* 1913; reprint, Annapolis, MD: Naval Institute Press, 1987.

Diaz Espino, Ovidio. *How Wall Street Created a Nation: J. P. Morgan, Teddy Roosevelt, and the Panama Canal.* New York: Four Walls Eight Windows, 2001.

Dierks, Jack Cameron. *A Leap to Arms: The Cuban Campaign of 1898.* Philadelphia: Lippincott, 1970.

Dioso, Marconi M. *A Trilogy of Wars: The Philippine Revolutionary Wars of 1896–97, the Spanish-American War in the Philippines in 1898, and the Filipino-American War, 1899–1902.* Pittsburgh: Dorrance, 2004.

Dobson, John M. *Reticent Expansionism: The Foreign Policy of William McKinley.* Pittsburgh: Duquesne University Press, 1988.

Dorwart, Jeffery M. *The Office of Naval Intelligence: The Birth of America's First Agency, 1865–1918.* Annapolis, MD: Naval Institute Press, 1979.

———. *The Pigtail War: American Involvement in the Sino-Japanese War of 1894–1895.* Amherst: University of Massachusetts Press, 1975.

Downey, Fairfax. *Richard Harding Davis: His Day.* New York: Scribner, 1933.

Duncan, Bingham. *Whitelaw Reid: Journalist, Politician, Diplomat.* Athens: University of Georgia Press, 1975.

Dunne, Finley Peter. *Mr. Dooley Remembers: The Informal Memoirs of Finley Peter Dunne.* Boston: Little, Brown, 1963.

Duus, Peter, Ramon H. Myers, and Mark R. Peattie, eds. *The Japanese Informal Empire in China, 1895–1937.* Princeton, NJ: Princeton University Press, 1989.

DuVal, Miles P., Jr. *Cadiz to Cathay: The Story of the Long Struggle for a Waterway across the American Isthmus.* Stanford, CA: Stanford University Press, 1940.

Dyal, Donald H., Brian B. Carpenter, and Mark A. Thomas. *Historical Dictionary of the Spanish-American War.* Westport, CT: Greenwood, 1996.

Dye, Alan. *Cuban Sugar in the Age of Mass Production: Technology and the Economics of the Sugar Central, 1899–1929.* Stanford, CA: Stanford University Press, 1998.

Dyer, John P. *"Fightin' Joe" Wheeler.* Southern Biography Series. Baton Rouge: Louisiana State University Press, 1941.

Dyer, Thomas G. *Theodore Roosevelt and the Idea of Race.* Baton Rouge: Louisiana State University Press, 1980.

Eckley, Grace. *Finley Peter Dunne.* Boston: Twayne, 1981.

Eggert, Gerald G. *Richard Olney: Evolution of a Statesman.* University Park: Pennsylvania State University Press, 1974.

Ellis, Elmer. *Henry Moore Teller: Defender of the West.* Caldwell, ID: Caxton Printers, 1941.

———. *Mr. Dooley's America: A Life of Finley Peter Dunne.* New York: Knopf, 1941.

Ellis, John. *The Social History of the Machine Gun.* 1975; reprint, New York: Arno, 1981.

Endacott, G. B. *Government and People in Hong Kong, 1841–1962.* Hong Kong: Hong Kong University Press, 1964.

Epistola, Silvino V. *Hong Kong Junta.* Quezon City: University of the Philippines Press, 1996.

Esherick, Joseph W. *The Origins of the Boxer Uprising.* Berkeley and Los Angeles: University of California Press, 1989.

Esthus, R. A. *Theodore Roosevelt and Japan.* Seattle: University of Washington Press, 1966.

Farrell, Don A. *The Pictorial History of Guam: The Americanization, 1898–1918.* Tamuning, Guam: Micronesian Productions, 1984.

Faust, Karl Irving. *Campaigning in the Philippines.* San Francisco: Hicks-Judd, 1899.

Ferrer, Ada. *Insurgent Cuba: Race, Nation, and Revolution, 1868–1898.* Chapel Hill: University of North Carolina Press, 1999.

Feuer, A. B. *The Santiago Campaign of 1898.* Westport, CT: Praeger, 1993.

———. *The Spanish-American War at Sea: Naval Action in the Atlantic.* Westport, CT: Praeger, 1995.

Feuer, A. B., and James C. Bradford. *The Spanish-American War at Sea: Naval Action in the Atlantic.* Westport, CT: Praeger, 1995.

Fiske, Bradley A. *From Midshipman to Rear Admiral.* New York: Century, 1919.

———. *War Time in Manila.* Boston: R. G. Badger, 1913.

Fitzgibbon, Russell H. *Cuba and the United States, 1900–1935.* Menasha: George Banta, 1935.

Fletcher, Marvin E. *The Black Soldier and Officer in the United States Army, 1890–1917.* Columbia: University of Missouri Press, 1974.

Flipper, Henry Ossian. *The Colored Cadet at West Point.* New York: Homer and Lee, 1878.

Foner, Jack D. *The United States Soldier between Two Wars: Army Life and Reforms, 1865–1898.* New York: Humanities Press, 1970.

Foner, Philip S. *Antonio Maceo: The "Bronze Titan" of Cuba's Struggle for Independence.* New York: Monthly Review Press, 1978.

———. *The Spanish-Cuban-American War and the Birth of American Imperialism, 1895–1902.* 2 vols. New York: Monthly Review Press, 1972.

Forbes, W. Cameron. *The Philippine Islands.* 1945; reprint, Millwood, NY: Kraus Reprint, 1976.

Franklin, John Hope, Alan M. Kraut, and Abraham S. Eisenstadt, eds. *The Huddled Masses: The Immigrant in American Society, 1880–1921.* Wheeling, IL: Harlan Davidson, 1982.

Freidel, Frank. *The Splendid Little War.* Boston: Little, Brown, 1958.

French, Bryant M. *Mark Twain and the Gilded Age.* Dallas, TX: Southern Methodist University Press, 1965.

Garcia, Mauro, ed. *Aguinaldo in Retrospect: A Volume Issued to Commemorate the Centenary of General Emilio Aguinaldo y Famy with Documents on the Philippine-American War, 1898–1901, and the First Philippine Republic.* Manila: Philippine Historical Association, 1969.

Garraty, John A. *Henry Cabot Lodge: A Biography.* New York: Knopf, 1953.

Gates, John M. *Schoolbooks and Krags: The United States Army in the Philippines, 1898–1902.* Westport, CT: Greenwood, 1973.

Gatewood, William B., Jr. *Black Americans and the White Man's Burden, 1899–1903.* Urbana: University of Illinois Press, 1975.

Gauld, Charles A. *America's First General Overseas: The Story of Thomas M. Anderson.* Vancouver, WA: Fort Vancouver Historical Society, 1973.

Gibert, Stephen P. *East Asia in American Foreign Policy.* Jamaica, NY: St. John's University, 1990.

Gibson, John M. *Physician to the World: The Life of General William C. Gorgas.* Durham, NC: Duke University Press, 1989.

———. *Soldier in White: The Life of General George Miller Sternberg.* Durham, NC: Duke University Press, 1958.

Giddings, Franklin Henry. *Democracy and Empire: With Studies of Their Psychological, Economic, and Moral Foundations.* New York: Macmillan, 1900.

Giffard, Sydney. *Japan among the Powers, 1890–1990.* New Haven, CT: Yale University Press, 1994.

Gillett, Frederick H. *George Frisbie Hoar.* Boston: Houghton Mifflin, 1934.

Gillett, Mary C. *The Army Medical Department, 1865–1917.* Washington, DC: Center of Military History, United States Army, 1995.

Gilmour, David. *The Long Recessional: The Imperial Life of Rudyard Kipling.* New York: Farrar, Straus, and Giroux, 2002.

Goldstein, Donald M., Katherine V. Dillon, J. Michael Wenger, and Robert J. Cressman. *Spanish-American War: The Story and Photographs.* Dulles, VA: Potomac Books, 2000.

Goode, A. M. *With Sampson through the War.* New York: Doubleday and McClure, 1899.

Goodwyn, Lawrence. *Democratic Promise: The Populist Movement in America.* New York: Oxford University Press USA, 1976.

Gordon, John Steele. *An Empire of Wealth: The Epic History of American Economic Power.* New York: Harper Perennial, 2004.

Gordon, Sarah H. *Passage to Union: How the Railroads Transformed American Life, 1829–1929.* Chicago: Ivan R. Dee, 1998.

Gould, Lewis L. *The Presidency of William McKinley.* Lawrence: University Press of Kansas, 1981.

———. *The Spanish-American War and President McKinley.* Lawrence: University Press of Kansas, 1982.

Gowing, Peter Gordon. *Mandate in Moroland: The American Government of Muslim Filipinos, 1899–1920.* Quezon City: University of the Philippines Press, 1977.

Graff, Henry F., ed. *American Imperialism and the Philippine Insurrection: Testimony Taken from Hearings on Affairs in the Philippine Islands before the Senate Committee on the Philippines.* 1902; reprint, Boston: Little, Brown, 1969.

———. *Grover Cleveland.* New York: Time Books, 2002.

Grenville, John A. S., and George Berkeley Young. *Politics, Strategy, and American Diplomacy: Studies in Foreign Policy, 1873–1917.* New Haven, CT: Yale University Press, 1966.

Grodinsky, Julius. *Jay Gould: His Business Career, 1867–1892.* Philadelphia: University of Pennsylvania Press, 1957.

Grosvenor, Edwin W., and Morgan Wesson. *Alexander Graham Bell: The Life and Times of the Man Who Invented the Telephone.* Boston: Harry N. Abrams, 1997.

Guerra, Lillian. *The Myth of José Martí: Conflicting Nationalisms in Early Twentieth-Century Cuba.* Chapel Hill: University of North Carolina Press, 2005.

Hacker, Louis M. *The World of Andrew Carnegie, 1865–1901.* Philadelphia: J. B. Lippincott, 1968.

Hagan, Kenneth J. *American Gunboat Diplomacy and the Old Navy, 1877–1889.* Westport, CT: Greenwood, 1973.

———. *This People's Navy: The Making of American Sea Power.* New York: Free Press, 1991.

Hagedorn, Hermann. *Leonard Wood: A Biography.* 2 vols. New York: Harper and Brothers, 1931.

Hahn, Emily. *The Islands, America's Imperial Venture in the Philippines.* New York: Coward, McCann, Geoghegan, 1981.

Hansen, Jonathan H. *The Lost Promise of Patriotism: Debating American Identity, 1890–1920.* Chicago: University of Chicago Press, 2003.

Hard, Curtis V. *Banners in the Air: The Eighth Ohio Volunteers and the Spanish-American War.* Edited by Robert H. Ferrell. Kent, OH: Kent State University Press, 1988.

Harlan, Louis R. *Booker T. Washington: The Making of a Black Leader.* New York: Oxford University Press USA, 1975.

Harris, Leon. *Upton Sinclair: American Rebel.* New York: Thomas Y. Crowell, 1975.

Harris, Theodore D., ed. *Black Frontiersman: The Memoirs of Henry O. Flipper, First Black Graduate of West Point.* Fort Worth: Texas Christian University Press, 1997.

Harrison, Noel Garraux. *City of Canvas: Camp Russell A. Alger and the Spanish-American War.* Falls Church, VA: Falls Church Historical Commission, Fairfax County History Commission, 1988.

Harrod, Frederick S. *Manning the New Navy: The Development of a Modern Naval Enlisted Force, 1899–1940.* Westport, CT: Greenwood, 1978.

Harvey, Rowland Hill. *Samuel Gompers: Champion of the Toiling Masses.* Stanford, CA: Stanford University Press, 1935.

Haynes, Sam W., and Christopher Morris, eds. *Manifest Destiny and Empire: American Antebellum Expansion.* The Walter Prescott Webb Memorial Lectures 31. College Station: Texas A&M University Press, 1997.

Healy, David. *Drive to Hegemony: The United States in the Caribbean, 1898–1917.* Madison: University of Wisconsin Press, 1988.

———. *The United States in Cuba, 1898–1902: Generals, Politicians and the Search for Policy.* Madison: University of Wisconsin Press, 1963.

———. *U.S. Expansionism: The Imperialist Urge in the 1890s.* Madison: University of Wisconsin Press, 1970.

Hendrick, Burton J. *The Life of Andrew Carnegie.* 2 vols. Garden City, NY: Doubleday, Doran, 1932.

Hendrickson, Kenneth E., Jr. *The Spanish-American War.* Westport, CT: Greenwood, 2003.

Hernández, José M. *Cuba and the United States: Intervention and Militarism, 1868–1933.* Austin: University of Texas Press, 1993.

Herrick, Walter R., Jr. *The American Naval Revolution.* Baton Rouge: Louisiana State University Press, 1966.

Hershkowitz, Leo. *Tweed's New York: Another Look.* Garden City, NY: Anchor, 1977.

Hicks, John Donald. *The Populist Revolt: A History of the Farmers' Alliance and the Peoples' Party.* Lincoln: University of Nebraska Press, 1961.

Higham, John. *Send These to Me: Immigrants in Urban America.* Rev. ed. Baltimore: Johns Hopkins University Press, 1984.

Hilton, Sylvia L., and Steve J. S. Ickringill. *European Perceptions of the Spanish-American War of 1898.* New York: Lang, 1999.

Hirshon, Stanley P. *Grenville M. Dodge: Soldier, Politician, Railroad Pioneer.* Bloomington: University of Indiana Press, 1967.

Hitchman, James H. *Leonard Wood and Cuban Independence, 1898–1902.* The Hague: Martinus Nijhoff, 1971.

Hobson, J. A. *Imperialism: A Study.* Ann Arbor: University of Michigan Press, 1965.

Hofstadter, Richard. *Social Darwinism in American Thought, 1860–1915.* Philadelphia: University of Pennsylvania Press, 1944.

Hoganson, Kristin L. *Fighting for American Manhood: How Gender Politics Provoked the Spanish-American and Philippine-American Wars.* New Haven, CT: Yale University Press, 1998.

Holbrook, Franklin F. *Minnesota in the Spanish-American War and the Philippine Insurrection.* Saint Paul: Minnesota War Records Commission, 1923.

Hood, Miriam. *Gunboat Diplomacy, 1895–1905.* South Brunswick, NJ, and New York: A. S. Barnes, 1977.

Hovey, Carl. *The Life Story of J. Pierpont Morgan: A Biography.* New York: Sturgis and Walton, 1911.

Hovgaard, William. *Modern History of Warships.* Annapolis, MD: Naval Institute Press, 1971.

Howe, M. A. DeWolfe. *Portrait of an Independent: Moorfield Storey, 1845–1929.* Freeport, NY: Books for Libraries Press, 1971.

Hubbard, Elbert. *A Message to Garcia.* Mechanicsburg, PA: Executive Books, 2002.

Huntington, Samuel. *The Soldier and the State: The Theory and Politics of Civil-Military Relations.* Cambridge: Harvard University Press, 1957.

Ignacio, Abe, Enrique De La Cruz, Jorgé Emmanuel, and Helen Toribio. *Forbidden Book: The Philippine-American War in Political Cartoons.* San Francisco: T'Bolli, 2004.

Iriye, Akira. *China and Japan in the Global Setting.* Cambridge: Harvard University Press, 1992.

———. *Japan & the Wider World: From the Mid-Nineteenth Century to the Present.* New York: Longman, 1997.

———. *Pacific Estrangement: Japanese and American Expansion, 1897–1911.* Cambridge: Harvard University Press, 1972.

James, Henry. *Richard Olney and His Public Service.* New York: Houghton Mifflin, 1923.

Jamieson, Perry D. *Crossing the Deadly Ground: United States Army Tactics, 1865–1899.* Tuscaloosa: University of Alabama Press, 1994.

Jeffers, H. Paul. *Colonel Roosevelt: Theodore Roosevelt Goes to War, 1897–1898.* New York: Wiley, 1996.

Jessup, Philip C. *Elihu Root.* 2 vols. New York: Dodd, Mead, 1938.

Johnson, Virginia W. *The Unregimented General: A Biography of Nelson A. Miles.* Boston: Riverside, 1962.

Josephson, Matthew. *Edison: A Biography.* New York: McGraw-Hill, 1959.

———. *The Robber Barons: The Great American Capitalists, 1861–1901.* New York: Harcourt Brace, 1995.

Jrade, Cathy Login, and José Amor y Vazquez. *Imagining a Free Cuba: Carlos Manuel de Céspedes and José Martí.* Occasional Papers of the Watson Institute 24. Providence, RI: Watson Institute for International Studies, Brown University, 1996.

Juergens, George. *Joseph Pulitzer and the New York World.* Princeton, NJ: Princeton University Press, 1966.

Kaplan, Justin. *When the Astors Owned New York: Blue Bloods and Grand Hotels in a Gilded Age.* New York: Viking, 2006.

Karnow, Stanley. *In Our Image: America's Empire in the Philippines.* New York: Random House, 1989.

Karsten, Peter. *The Naval Aristocracy: The Golden Age of Annapolis and the Emergence of Modern American Navalism.* New York: Free Press, 1972.

Keithley, Ralph. *Buckey O'Neill . . . He Stayed with 'em While He Lasted.* Caldwell, ID: Caxton Printers, 1949.

Kennan, George. *Campaigning in Cuba.* New York: Century, 1899.

Kennedy, James G. *Herbert Spencer.* Boston: Twayne, 1978.

Kirk, John M. *José Martí: Mentor of the Cuban Nation.* Gainesville: University Press of Florida, 1983.

Kirkland, Edward C. *Charles Francis Adams, Jr., 1835–1915: The Patrician at Bay.* Cambridge: Harvard University Press, 1965.

Klein, Maury. *The Life and Legend of Jay Gould.* Baltimore: Johns Hopkins University Press, 1986.

Kolko, Gabriel. *Railroads and Regulation, 1877–1916.* Princeton, NJ: Princeton University Press, 1965.

Kramer, Paul. *The Blood of Government: Race, Empire, the United States, and the Philippines.* Chapel Hill: University of North Carolina Press, 2006.

Kraut, Alan M. *The Huddled Masses: The Immigrant in American Society, 1880–1921.* Arlington Heights, IL: Harlan Davidson, 1982.

Krauth, Leland. *Proper Mark Twain.* Athens: University of Georgia Press, 1999.

Kushner, Howard I. *John Milton Hay: The Union of Poetry and Politics.* Farmington Hills, MI: Twayne, 1977.

LaFeber, Walter. *The New Empire: An Interpretation of American Expansion, 1860–1898.* Ithaca, NY: Cornell University Press, 1963.

———. *The Panama Canal: The Crisis in Historical Perspective.* New York: Oxford University Press USA, 1978.

Lambert, John R., Jr. *Arthur Pue Gorman.* Baton Rouge: Louisiana State University Press, 1953.

Lane, Jack C. *Armed Progressive: General Leonard Wood.* San Rafael, CA: Presidio, 1978.

Langley, Lester D. *The Cuban Policy of the United States: A Brief History.* New York: Wiley, 1968.

Leach, Paul Roscoe. *That Man Dawes.* Chicago: Reilly and Lee, 1930.

Leech, Margaret. *In the Days of McKinley.* New York: Harper and Brothers, 1959.

Leopold, Richard W. *Elihu Root and the Conservative Tradition.* Boston: Little, Brown, 1954.

LeRoy, James A. *The Americans in the Philippines: A History of the Conquest and First Years of Occupation, with an Introductory Account of the Spanish Rule.* Introduction by Howard William Taft. 2 vols. Boston and New York: Houghton Mifflin, 1914.

Lewis, Emanuel Raymond. *Seacoast Fortifications of the United States: An Introductory History.* Washington, DC: Smithsonian Institution Press, 1970.

Linderman, Gerald F. *The Mirror of War: American Society and the Spanish-American War.* Ann Arbor: University of Michigan Press, 1971.

Linn, Brian McAllister. *The Philippine War, 1899–1902.* Lawrence: University Press of Kansas, 2000.

———. *The U.S. Army and Counterinsurgency in the Philippine War, 1899–1902.* Chapel Hill: University of North Carolina Press, 1989.

Livesay, Harold C. *American Made: Shapers of the American Economy.* New York: Longman Publishing Group, 2006.

———. *Andrew Carnegie and the Rise of Big Business.* Boston: Little, Brown, 1975.

———. *Samuel Gompers and Organized Labor in America.* Boston: Little, Brown, 1978.

Lodge, Henry Cabot. *The War with Spain.* New York: Harper and Brothers, 1899.

Long, John Davis. *America of Yesterday: As Reflected in the Journal of John Davis Long.* Edited by L. S. Mayo. Boston: Atlantic Monthly Press, 1923.

———. *The Journal of John D. Long.* Edited by Margaret Long. Rindge, NH: Richard R. Smith, 1956.

———. *Papers of John Davis Long, 1897–1904,* Vol. 78. Edited by Gardner Weld Allen. Massachusetts Historical Society Collections. Boston: Massachusetts Historical Society, 1939.

Longacre, Edward G. *Grant's Cavalryman: The Life and Wars of General James H. Wilson.* Mechanicsburg, PA: Stackpole, 1996.

Lorence, James J. *Organized Business and the Myth of the China Market: The American Asiatic Association, 1898–1937.* Transaction of the American Philosophical Society 71, part 4. Philadelphia: American Philosophical Society, 1981.

Lubow, Arthur. *The Reporter Who Would be King.* New York: Scribner, 1992.

Mack, Gerstle. *The Land Divided: A History of the Panama Canal and Other Isthmian Canal Projects.* New York: Knopf, 1944.

Magdalena, Federico V. *The Battle of Bayang and Other Essays on Moroland.* Marawi City, Philippines: Mindanao State University, 2002.

Mahan, Alfred Thayer. *Lessons of the War with Spain: And Other Articles.* Boston: Little, Brown, 1899.

———. *Letters and Papers of Alfred Thayer Mahan.* Edited by Robert Seager II and Doris D. Maguire. 3 vols. Annapolis, MD: Naval Institute Press, 1975.

Malozemoff, Andrew. *Russian Far-Eastern Policy, 1881–1904: With Special Emphasis on the Causes of the Russo-Japanese War.* Berkeley and Los Angeles: University of California Press, 1958.

Mandel, Bernard. *Samuel Gompers: A Biography.* Yellow Springs, OH: Antioch, 1963.

Mannix, Daniel Pratt, III. *The Old Navy.* Edited by Daniel P. Mannix IV. New York: Macmillan, 1983.

Marks, Frederick W., III. *Velvet on Iron: The Diplomacy of Theodore Roosevelt.* Lincoln: University of Nebraska Press, 1979.

Marolda, Edward J., ed. *Theodore Roosevelt, the U.S. Navy, and the Spanish American War.* New York: Palgrave, 2001.

Martin, Albro. *Railroads Triumphant: The Growth, Rejection, and Rebirth of a Vital American Force.* New York: Oxford University Press USA, 1992.

Martín Cerezo, Saturnino. *Under the Red and Gold: Notes and Recollections of the Siege of Baler.* Translated by F. L. Dodds. Kila, MT: Kessinger, 2008.

Masterman, Sylvia. *The Origins of International Rivalry in Samoa, 1845–1884.* London: Allen and Unwin, 1934.

May, Ernest R. *Imperial Democracy: The Emergence of America as a Great Power.* New York: Harcourt, Brace, 1961.

May, Ernest R., and John K. Fairbank, eds. *America's China Trade in Historical Perspective: The Chinese and American Performance.* Cambridge: Harvard University Press, 1986.

May, Glenn Anthony. *Battle for Batangas: A Philippine Province at War.* New Haven, CT: Yale University Press, 1991.

———. *Inventing a Hero: The Posthumous Re-Creation of Andrés Bonifacio.* Madison: University of Wisconsin Press, 1996.

McCalla, Bowman Hendry. *Memoirs of a Naval Career.* 4 vols. Santa Barbara, CA: N.p., 1910.

McCartney, Paul T. *Power and Progress: American National Identity, the War of 1898, and the Rise of American Imperialism.* Baton Rouge: Louisiana State University Press, 2006.

McCormick, Thomas J. *China Market: America's Quest for Informal Empire, 1893–1901.* Chicago: Quadrangle Books, 1967.

McCormick, Thomas J., and Walter LaFeber, eds. *Behind the Throne: Servants of Power to Imperial Presidents, 1898–1968.* Madison: University of Wisconsin Press, 1993.

McCullogh, David. *The Path between the Seas: The Creation of the Panama Canal, 1870–1914.* New York: Simon and Schuster, 1977.

McCullum, Jack. *Leonard Wood: Rough Rider, Surgeon, Architect of American Imperialism.* New York: New York University Press, 2005.

McFerson, Hazel M. *Mixed Blessing: The Impact of the American Colonial Experience on Politics and Society in the Philippines.* Westport, CT: Greenwood, 2002.

McGrath, Robert C., Jr. *American Populism: A Social History, 1877–1898.* New York: Hill and Wang, 1990.

McKee, Delber L. *Chinese Exclusion Versus the Open Door Policy, 1900–1906: Clashes over China Policy in the Roosevelt Era.* Detroit: Wayne State University Press, 1977.

McNeil, William H. *The Pursuit of Power: Technology, Armed Force, and Society Since A.D. 1000.* Chicago: University of Chicago Press, 1982.

Merrill, Horace Samuel. *Bourbon Leader: Grover Cleveland and the Democratic Party.* Boston: Little, Brown, 1957.

Miley, John D. *In Cuba with Shafter.* New York: Scribner, 1899.

Miller, Richard H. *American Imperialism in 1898: The Quest for National Fulfillment.* New York: Wiley, 1970.

Miller, Stuart Creighton. *"Benevolent Assimilation": The American Conquest of the Philippines, 1899–1903.* New Haven, CT: Yale University Press, 1982.

Millett, Allan R. *The General: Robert L. Bullard and Officership in the United States Army, 1881–1925.* Westport, CT: Greenwood, 1975.

Millis, Walter. *The Martial Spirit: A Study of Our War with Spain.* New York: Houghton Mifflin, 1931.

Milton, Joyce. *The Yellow Kids: Foreign Correspondents in the Heyday of Yellow Journalism.* New York: Harper and Row, 1989.

Minger, Ralph Eldin. *William Howard Taft and United States Foreign Policy: The Apprenticeship Years, 1900–1908.* Urbana: University of Illinois Press, 1975.

Mitchell, Donald W. *History of the Modern American Navy: From 1883 through Pearl Harbor.* New York: Knopf, 1946.

Morgan, H. Wayne. *America's Road to Empire: The War with Spain and Overseas Expansion.* New York: Wiley, 1965.

———, ed. *Making Peace with Spain: The Diary of Whitelaw Reid, September–December, 1898.* Austin: University of Texas Press, 1965.

———. *William McKinley and His America.* Syracuse, NY: Syracuse University Press, 1963.

Morison, Elting E. *Admiral Sims and the Modern American Navy.* Boston: Houghton Mifflin, 1942.

Morison, Elting E., et al., eds. *The Letters of Theodore Roosevelt.* 8 vols. Cambridge: Harvard University Press, 1954.

Morris, Charles. *The War with Spain.* Philadelphia: J. B. Lippincott, 1899.

Morris, Charles R. *The Tycoons: How Andrew Carnegie, John D. Rockefeller, Jay Gould, and J. P. Morgan Invented the American Supereconomy.* New York: Times Books, 2005.

Morris, Edmund. *The Rise of Theodore Roosevelt.* New York: Coward, McCann, and Geoghegan, 1979.

———. *Theodore Rex.* New York: Random House, 2001.

Musicant, Ivan. *The Banana Wars: A History of United States Military Intervention in Latin America from the Spanish-American War to the Invasion of Panama.* New York: Macmillan, 1990.

———. *Empire by Default: The Spanish-American War and the Dawn of the American Century.* New York: Henry Holt, 1998.

Muzzey, David Saville. *James G. Blaine: A Political Idol of Other Days.* New York: Dodd, Mead, 1934.

Nalty, Bernard C. *Strength for the Fight: A History of Black Americans in the Military.* New York: Free Press, 1986.

Nasaw, David. *Andrew Carnegie.* New York: Penguin, 2006.

———. *The Chief: The Life of William Randolph Hearst.* Boston: Houghton Mifflin, 2000.

Neale, R. G. *Great Britain and United States Expansion.* East Lansing: Michigan State University Press, 1966.

Neu, Charles E. *An Uncertain Friendship: Theodore Roosevelt and Japan, 1906–1909.* Cambridge: Harvard University Press, 1967.

Nevins, Allan. *Grover Cleveland: A Study in Courage.* American Political Leaders. New York: Dodd, Mead, 1932.

———. *John D. Rockefeller: The Heroic Age of American Enterprise.* 2 vols. New York: Scribner, 1940.

———, ed. *Letters of Grover Cleveland, 1850–1908.* Boston: Houghton Mifflin, 1933.

———. *Study in Power: John D. Rockefeller, Industrialist and Philanthropist.* 2 vols. New York: Scribner, 1953.

Ninkovich, Frank. *The United States and Imperialism.* Oxford, UK: Blackwell, 2000.

Nish, Ian. *The Origins of the Russo-Japanese War.* Edited by Harry Hearder. London: Longman, 1985.

Nofi, Albert A. *The Spanish-American War: 1898.* Conshohocken, PA: Combined Books, 1996.

Ochosa, Orlino A. *The Tinio Brigade: Anti-American Resistance in the Ilocos Provinces, 1899–1901.* Quezon City, Philippines: New Day, 1989.

O'Connor, Harvey. *The Astors.* New York: Knopf, 1941.

Offner, John L. *An Unwanted War: The Diplomacy of the United States and Spain over Cuba, 1895–1898.* Chapel Hill: University of North Carolina Press, 1992.

O'Gara, Gordon Carpenter. *Theodore Roosevelt and the Rise of the Modern Navy.* Princeton, NJ: Princeton University Press, 1943.

Opatrný, Josef. *U.S. Expansionism and Cuban Annexationism in the 1850s.* Prague: Charles University, 1990.

Orejola, Wilmo C. *Ghosts of the Insurrection.* Victoria, Canada: Trafford, 2006.

Osborne, Thomas J. *Empire Can Wait: American Opposition to Hawaiian Annexation, 1893–1898.* Kent, OH: Kent State University Press, 1981.

O'Toole, G. J. A. *The Spanish War: An American Epic, 1898.* New York: Norton, 1984.

Padelford, Norman J. *The Panama Canal in Peace and War.* New York: Macmillan, 1942.

Paine, S. C. M. *The Sino-Japanese War of 1894–1895: Perceptions, Power, and Primacy.* New York: Cambridge University Press, 2003.

Palmer, Frederick. *Bliss, Peacemaker: The Life and Letters of General Tasker Howard Bliss.* 1934; reprint, Freeport, NY: Books for Libraries Press, 1970.

Pando, Magdalen G. *Cuba's Freedom Fighter: Antonio Maceo, 1845–1896.* Gainesville, FL: Felicity, 1980.

Paret, Peter, ed. *Makers of Modern Strategy.* Princeton, NJ: Princeton University Press, 1986.

Paterson, Thomas G., ed. *American Imperialism and Anti-Imperialism.* New York: Thomas Y. Crowell, 1973.

Payne, Stanley G. *Politics and the Military in Early Modern Spain.* Stanford, CA: Stanford University Press, 1967.

Pérez, Louis A., Jr. *Cuba between Empires, 1878–1902.* Pittsburgh: University of Pittsburgh Press, 1983.

———. *Cuba under the Platt Amendment, 1902–1934.* Pittsburgh: University of Pittsburgh Press, 1986.

———. *The War of 1898: The United States & Cuba in History & Historiography.* Chapel Hill: University of North Carolina Press, 1998.

Perkins, Dexter. *The Monroe Doctrine, 1867–1907.* Baltimore: Johns Hopkins University Press, 1937.

Perkins, J. R. *Trails, Rails, and War: The Life of General G. M. Dodge.* Indianapolis: Bobbs-Merrill, 1929.

Petrie, Charles, Sir. *King Alfonso XIII and His Age.* London: Chapman and Hall, 1963.

Pico, Fernando. *Puerto Rico 1898: The War after the War.* Princeton, NJ: Markus Wiener, 2004.

Pierce, John R., and Jim Writer. *Yellow Jack: How Yellow Fever Ravaged America and Walter Reed Discovered Its Deadly Secrets.* Hoboken, NJ: Wiley, 2005.

Pierson, Peter. *The History of Spain.* Westport, CT: Greenwood, 1999.

Pilapil, Vincente. *Alfonso XIII.* New York: Twayne, 1969.

Pomeroy, William J. *American Neo-Colonialism: Its Emergence in the Philippines and Asia.* New York: International Publishers, 1970.

Porter, Glenn. *The Rise of Big Business: 1860–1920.* 2nd ed. Wheeling, IL: Harlan Davidson, 1992.

Post, Charles Johnson. *The Little War of Private Post: The Spanish-American War Seen Up Close.* Lincoln, NE: Bison Books, 1999.

Potter, E. B., and Chester W. Nimitz, eds. *Sea Power: A Naval History.* 2nd ed. Annapolis, MD: Naval Institute Press, 1981.

Powers, Ron. *Mark Twain: A Life.* New York: Free Press, 2005.

Pratt, Julius W. *America's Colonial Experiment: How the United States Gained, Governed, and in Part Gave Away a Colonial Empire.* New York: Prentice Hall, 1950.

———. *Challenge and Rejection: The United States and World Leadership, 1900–1921.* New York: Macmillan, 1967.

———. *Expansionists of 1898: The Acquisition of Hawaii and the Spanish Islands.* Baltimore: Johns Hopkins University Press, 1936.

Pringle, Henry F. *The Life and Times of William Howard Taft.* 2 vols. New York: Farrar and Rinehart, 1939.

Procter, Ben. *William Randolph Hearst.* 2 vols. New York: Oxford University Press USA, 1998, 2007.

Puleston, William D. *Mahan: The Life and Work of Captain Alfred Thayer Mahan.* New Haven, CT: Yale University Press, 1939.

Purcell, Victor. *The Boxer Uprising: A Background Study.* Hamden, CT: Archon Books, 1974.

Rabe, Stephen G., and Thomas G. Patterson, eds. *Imperial Surge: The United States Abroad, the 1890s–Early 1900s.* New York: D. C. Heath, 1992.

Rammelkamp, Julian S. *Pulitzer's Post-Dispatch, 1878–1883.* Princeton, NJ: Princeton University Press, 1967.

Reid, Whitelaw. *Making Peace with Spain: The Diary of Whitelaw Reid, September–December, 1898.* Edited by H. Wayne Morgan. Austin: University of Texas Press, 1965.

Richardson, Leon Burr. *William E. Chandler, Republican.* New York: Dodd, Mead, 1940.

Rickover, Hyman G. *How the Battleship Maine Was Destroyed.* Annapolis, MD: Naval Institute Press, 1995.

Robles, Eliodoro G. *The Philippines in the Nineteenth Century.* Quezon City, Philippines: Malaya Books, 1969.

Röhl, J. C. G. *Germany without Bismarck: The Crisis of Government in the Second Reich, 1890–1900.* London: Batsford, 1967.

Ronning, C. Neale. *José Martí and the Emigré Colony in Key West: Leadership and State Formation.* New York: Praeger, 1990.

Roosevelt, Theodore. *The Rough Riders, an Autobiography.* New York: Library of America, 2004.

Ryden, George Herbert. *The Foreign Policy of the United States in Relation to Samoa.* New Haven, CT: Yale University Press, 1933.

Samuels, Peggy, and Harold Samuels. *Frederic Remington: A Biography.* Garden City, NY: Doubleday, 1982.

———. *Remembering the Maine.* Washington: Smithsonian Institution Press, 1995.

———. *Teddy Roosevelt at San Juan: The Making of a President.* College Station: Texas A&M University Press, 1997.

Saniel, Josefa M. *Japan and the Philippines 1868–1898.* 3rd ed. Manila, Philippines: De La Salle University Press, 1998.

Sargent, Herbert H. *The Campaign of Santiago de Cuba.* 3 vols. Chicago: A. C. McClurg, 1907.

Sargent, Nathan. *Admiral Dewey and the Manila Campaign.* Washington, DC: Naval Historical Foundation, 1947.

Sauers, Richard A. *Pennsylvania in the Spanish-American War: A Commemorative Look Back.* Harrisburg: Pennsylvania Capitol Preservation Committee, 1998.

Saulo, Alfredo B. *Emilio Aguinaldo: Generalissimo and President of the First Philippine Republic, First Republic in Asia.* Quezon City: Phoenix, 1983.

Schirmer, Daniel B. *Republic or Empire: American Resistance to the Philippine War.* Cambridge, MA: Schenkman, 1972.

Schirmer, Daniel B., and Stephen R. Shalom. *The Philippines Reader: A History of Colonialism, Dictatorship, and Resistance.* Cambridge, MA: South End Press, 1987.

Schmidt, Hans. *Maverick Marine: General Smedley D. Butler and the Contradictions of American Military History.* Lexington: University Press of Kentucky, 1987.

Schoonover, Thomas. *Uncle Sam's War of 1898 and the Origins of Globalization.* Lexington: University Press of Kentucky, 2003.

Schott, Joseph L. *The Ordeal of Samar.* Indianapolis: Bobbs-Merrill, 1964.

Schubert, Frank N. *Black Valor: Buffalo Soldiers and the Medal of Honor, 1870–1898.* Wilmington, DE: SR Books, 1997.

Schumacher, John N. *Revolutionary Clergy: The Filipino Clergy and the Nationalist Movement, 1850–1903.* Quezon City: Ateneo de Manila University Press, 1981.

Scott, Rebecca J. *Slave Emancipation in Cuba: The Transition to Free Labor, 1860–1899.* Princeton, NJ: Princeton University Press, 1985.

Seager, Robert. *Alfred Thayer Mahan: The Man and His Letters.* Annapolis, MD: Naval Institute Press, 1977.

Sexton, William Thaddeus. *Soldiers in the Sun: An Adventure in Imperialism.* Harrisburg, PA: Military Service Publishing, 1939.

Shaw, Angel Velasco, and Luis H. Francia. *Vestiges of War: The Philippine-American War and the Aftermath of an American Dream, 1899–1999.* New York: New York University Press, 2002.

Shulimson, Jack. *The Marine Corps' Search for a Mission, 1880–1898.* Lawrence: University Press of Kansas, 1993.

Silbey, David J. *A War of Frontier and Empire: The Philippine-American War, 1899–1902.* New York: Hill and Wang, 2006.

Sinclair, Upton. *The Autobiography of Upton Sinclair.* New York: Harcourt, Brace, and World, 1962.

———. *The Jungle.* 1906; reprint, New York: Longman, 1998.

Smith, Joseph. *The Spanish-American War: Conflict in the Caribbean and the Pacific, 1895–1902.* New York: Longman, 1994.

Smythe, Donald. *Guerrilla Warrior: The Early Life of John J. Pershing.* New York: Scribner, 1973.

Smythe, Ted Curtis. *The Gilded Age Press, 1865–1900.* Westport, CT: Praeger, 2003.

Spears, John R. *Our Navy in the War with Spain.* New York: Scribner, 1899.

Spector, Ronald H. *Admiral of the New Empire: The Life and Career of George Dewey.* Baton Rouge: Louisiana State University Press, 1974.

———. *Professors of War: The Naval War College and the Development of the Naval Profession.* Newport, RI: Naval War College Press, 1977.

Spencer, David R. *The Yellow Journalism: The Press and America's Emergence as a World Power.* Evanston, IL: Northwestern University Press, 2007.

Sprout, Harold, and Margaret Sprout. *The Rise of American Naval Power, 1776–1918.* Princeton, NJ: Princeton University Press, 1946.

Stallman, R. W. *Stephen Crane: A Biography.* New York: G. Braziller, 1968.

Standiford, Les. *Meet You in Hell: Andrew Carnegie, Henry Clay Frick, and the Bitter Partnership That Transformed America.* New York: Crown, 2005.

Staten, Clifford L. *The History of Cuba.* London: Palgrave Macmillan, 2005.

Steinbach, Robert H. *A Long March: The Lives of Frank and Alice Baldwin.* Austin: University of Texas Press, 1989.

Steinberg, David Joel. *The Philippines: A Singular and a Plural Place.* 3rd ed. Boulder, CO: Westview, 1994.

Stephanson, Anders. *Manifest Destiny: American Expansion and the Empire of Right.* New York: Hill and Wang, 1996.

Stephenson, George M. *A History of American Immigration, 1820–1924.* Boston: Ginn, 1926.

Sternlicht, Sanford V. *McKinley's Bulldog: The Battleship Oregon.* Chicago: Nelson-Hall, 1977.

Stevens, John D. *Sensationalism and the New York Press.* New York: Columbia University Press, 1991.

Stevens, Sylvester K. *American Expansion in Hawaii, 1842–1898.* Harrisburg: Archives Publishing, 1945.

Strouse, Jean. *Morgan: American Financier.* New York: Random House, 1999.

Sturtevant, David R. *Popular Uprisings in the Philippines, 1840–1940.* Ithaca, NY: Cornell University Press, 1976.

Styles, T. J., ed. *In Their Own Words: Robber Barons and Radicals.* New York: Perigree Books, 1997.

Summers, Mark Wahlgren. *The Gilded Age, or the Hazard of New Functions.* Upper Saddle River, NJ: Prentice Hall, 1997.

Tan, Samuel K. *The Filipino-American War, 1899–1913.* Quezon City: University of the Philippines Press, 2002.

———. *The Fillipino Muslim Armed Struggle, 1900–1972.* Makati, Philippines: Filipinas Foundation, 1977.

Tate, Merze. *Hawaii: Reciprocity or Annexation.* East Lansing: Michigan State University Press, 1968.

Taylor, John R. M. *The Philippine Insurrection against the United States, 1898–1903: A Compilation of Documents and Introduction.* 5 vols. 1906; reprint, Pasay City, Philippines: Eugenio Lopez Foundation, 1971.

Tebbel, John William. *America's Great Patriotic War with Spain: Mixed Motives, Lies, and Racism in Cuba and the Philippines, 1898–1915.* Manchester Center, VT: Marshall Jones, 1996.

Thomas, Hugh. *Cuba: The Pursuit of Freedom.* New York: Harper and Row, 1971.

Timmons, Bascom Nolly. *Portrait of an American: Charles G. Dawes.* New York: Holt, 1953.

Tomlins, Christopher L. *The State and the Unions: Labor Relations, Law, and the Organized Labor Movement in America, 1880–1960.* New York: Cambridge University Press, 1985.

Tompkins, E. Berkeley. *The Great Debate: Anti-Imperialism in the United States, 1890–1920.* Stanford, CA: Stanford University Press, 1970.

Tone, John Lawrence. *War and Genocide in Cuba, 1895–1898.* Chapel Hill: University of North Carolina Press, 2006.

Trachtenberg, Alan. *The Incorporation of America: Culture and Society in the Gilded Age.* New York: Hill and Wang, 1982.

Trask, David F. *The War with Spain in 1898.* Lincoln: University of Nebraska Press, 1996.

Travis, Ira Dudley. *The History of the Clayton-Bulwer Treaty.* Ann Arbor: Michigan Political Science Association, 1900.

Traxel, David. *1898: Birth of the American Century.* New York: Knopf, 1998.

Trias Monge, José. *Puerto Rico: The Trials of the Oldest Colony in the World.* New Haven, CT: Yale University Press, 1997.

Trimble, Vance H. *The Astonishing Mr. Scripps: The Turbulent Life of America's Penny Press Lord.* Ames: Iowa State University Press, 1992.

Turk, Richard W. *The Ambiguous Relationship: Theodore Roosevelt and Alfred Thayer Mahan.* Westport, CT: Greenwood, 1987.

Turner, Frederick Jackson. *The Frontier in American History.* New York: Holt, Rinehart, and Winston, 1962.

Twain, Mark. *Mark Twain's Weapons of Satire: Anti-Imperialist Writings on the Philippine-American War.* Edited by Jim Zwick. Syracuse, NY: Syracuse University Press, 1992.

Twain, Mark, and Charles Dudley Warner. *The Gilded Age.* 1873; reprint. New York: Modern Library, 2006.

Twitchell, Heath, Jr. *Allen: The Biography of an Army Officer 1859–1930.* New Brunswick, NJ: Rutgers University Press, 1974.

Tyler, Alice Felt. *The Foreign Policy of James G. Blaine.* Minneapolis: University of Minnesota Press, 1927.

Vandiver, Frank E. *Black Jack: The Life and Times of John J. Pershing.* 2 vols. College Station: Texas A&M University Press, 1977.

Van Middeldyk, R. A. *The History of Puerto Rico: From the Spanish Discovery to the American Occupation.* New York: BiblioBazaar, 2006.

Venzon, Anne C. *The Spanish-American War: An Annotated Bibliography.* New York: Garland, 1990.

Wachhorst, Wyn. *Thomas Alva Edison: An American Myth.* Cambridge, MA: MIT Press, 1981.

Wagenheim, Olga Jimenez de. *Puerto Rico: An Interpretative History from Pre-Columbian Times to 1900.* Princeton, NJ: Markus Wiener, 1997.

———. *Puerto Rico's Revolt for Independence: El Grito de Lares.* Boulder, CO: Westview, 1985.

Walker, Dale L. *The Boys of '98: Theodore Roosevelt and the Rough Riders.* New York: Forge, 1999.

Wall, Joseph Frazier. *Andrew Carnegie.* New York: Oxford University Press USA, 1970.

Ward, James A. *Railroads and the Character of America, 1820–1887.* Knoxville: University of Tennessee Press, 1986.

Warfield, Ethelbert Dudley. *Joseph Cabell Breckinridge, Junior, Ensign in the United States Navy: A Brief History of a Short Life.* New York: Knickerbocker, 1898.

Warren, Kenneth. *Triumphant Capitalism: Henry Clay Frick and the Industrial Transformation of America.* Pittsburgh: University of Pittsburgh Press, 1996.

Weems, John Edward. *The Fate of the Maine.* New York: Henry Holt, 1985.

Weigley, Russell F. *History of the United States Army.* New York: Macmillan, 1967.

Weintraub, Stanley. *Victoria: An Intimate Biography.* New York: Dutton, 1987.

Welch, Richard E., Jr. *George Frisbie Hoar and the Half-Breed Republicans.* Cambridge: Harvard University Press, 1971.

———. *The Presidencies of Grover Cleveland.* Lawrence: University Press of Kansas, 1988.

———. *Response to Imperialism: The United States and the Philippine-American War, 1899–1902.* Chapel Hill: University of North Carolina Press, 1979.

Werstein, Irving. *Ninety-Eight: The Story of the Spanish-American War and the Philippine Insurrection.* New York: Cooper Square, 1966.

West, Michael Rudolph. *The Education of Booker T. Washington: American Democracy and the Idea of Race.* New York: Columbia University Press, 2005.

West, Richard Sedgwick, Jr. *Admirals of American Empire: The Combined Story of George Dewey, Alfred Thayer Mahan, Winfield Scott Schley, and William Thomas Sampson.* Indianapolis: Bobbs-Merrill, 1948.

Westermeier, Clifford P. *Who Rush to Glory—The Cowboy Volunteers of 1898: Grisby's Cowboys, Roosevelt's Rough Riders, Torrey's Rocky Mountain Riders.* Caldwell, ID: Caxton Printers, 1958.

Weston, Rubin Francis. *Racism in U.S. Imperialism: The Influence of Racial Assumptions on American Foreign Policy, 1893–1946.* Columbia: University of South Carolina Press, 1973.

Westwood, J. N. *Russia against Japan, 1904–1905: A New Look at the Russo-Japanese War.* Albany: State University of New York Press, 1986.

Wheeler, Joseph. *The Santiago Campaign, 1898.* 1899; reprint, Port Washington, NY: Kennikat, 1971.

White, John R. *Bullets and Bolos: Fifteen Years in the Philippine Islands.* New York: Century, 1928.

Widenor, William C. *Henry Cabot Lodge and the Search for an American Foreign Policy.* Berkeley: University of California Press, 1980.

Wildman, Edwin. *Aguinaldo: A Narrative of Filipino Ambitions.* Boston: Lothrop, 1901.

Wilkerson, Marcus M. *Public Opinion and the Spanish-American War: A Study in War Propaganda.* Baton Rouge: Louisiana State University Press, 1932.

Wilson, Herbert W. *The Downfall of Spain: Naval History of the Spanish-American War.* London: Low, Marston, 1900.

Wilson, James Harrison. *Under the Old Flag: Recollections of Military Operations in the War for the Union, the Spanish War, the Boxer Rebellion, Etc.* 2 vols. New York: D. Appleton, 1912.

Wiltshire, David. *The Social and Political Thought of Herbert Spencer.* Oxford Historical Monographs. New York: Oxford University Press USA, 1978.

Winkler, John K. *Morgan the Magnificent: The Life of J. Pierpont Morgan.* New York: Vanguard, 1930.

Winslow, Erving. *The Anti-Imperialist League: Apologia Pro Vita Sua.* Boston: Anti-Imperialist League, 1908.

Wisan, Joseph E. *The Cuban Crisis as Reflected in the New York Press, 1895–1898.* 1934; reprint, New York: Octagon, 1965.

Wolff, Leon. *Little Brown Brother: How the United States Purchased and Pacified the Philippine Islands at the Century's Turn.* Garden City, NY: Doubleday, 1961.

Wooster, Robert. *Nelson A. Miles and the Twilight of the Frontier Army.* Lincoln: University of Nebraska Press, 1993.

Young, Kenneth Ray. *The General's General: The Life and Times of Arthur MacArthur.* Boulder, CO: Westview, 1994.

Young, Marilyn Blatt. *The Rhetoric of Empire: American China Policy, 1895–1901.* Cambridge: Harvard University Press, 1968.

Yu-Jose, Lydia N. *Japan Views the Philippines 1900–1944.* Manila, Philippines: Ateneo de Manila University Press, 1992.

Zimmermann, Warren. *First Great Triumph: How Five Americans Made Their Country a World Power.* New York: Farrar, Straus, and Giroux, 2002.

Zogbaum, Rufus Fairchild. *All Hands: Pictures of Life in the United States Navy.* New York: Harper and Brothers, 1897.

———. *Horse, Foot and Dragoons: Sketches of Army Life at Home and Abroad.* New York: Harper and Brothers, 1888.

MATTHEW J. WAYMAN

List of Editors and Contributors

Volume Editor
Dr. Spencer C. Tucker
Senior Fellow
Military History, ABC-CLIO, Inc.

Editors, Documents Volume
James Arnold
Independent Scholar

Roberta Wiener
Virginia Military Institute

Associate Editor
Dr. Paul G. Pierpaoli Jr.
Fellow
Military History, ABC-CLIO, Inc.

Assistant Editors
Dr. Jack McCallum
Texas Christian University

Dr. Justin D. Murphy
Howard Payne University

Contributors
Ralph Martin Baker
Independent Scholar

Jeffrey D. Bass
Quinnipiac University

Walter F. Bell
Information Services Librarian
Aurora University

Ron Briley
Assistant Headmaster
Sandia Preparatory School

Robert M. Brown
U.S. Army Historian

Dino E. Buenviaje
University of California, Riverside

Ted Butler
Independent Scholar

Andrew Byers
Duke University

Dr. Stanley D. M. Carpenter
College of Distance Education
United States Naval War College

Dr. James F. Carroll
Iona College

Albert T. Chapman
Government Information and Political
Science Librarian
Purdue University Libraries

Dr. David Coffey
Department of History and Philosophy
University of Tennessee at Martin

Dr. Jeffery B. Cook
North Greenville University

Dr. Timothy J. Demy
Naval War College

Marcel A. Derosier
Independent Scholar

Lieutenant Colonel (Retired) Louis Dimarco
U.S. Army Command and Staff College

Elizabeth Dubrulle
Colonial Society of Massachusetts

Rick Dyson
Information Services Librarian
Missouri Western State University

Dr. Gregory C. Ference
Department of History
Salisbury University

Claudine Ferrell
University of Mary Washington

Paul E. Fontenoy
North Carolina Maritime Museum

Dr. John C. Fredriksen
Independent Scholar

Jack P. Greene
Independent Scholar

Dr. Michael R. Hall
Department of History
Armstrong Atlantic State University

Glenn E. Helm
Navy Department Library

Marco Hewitt
Independent Scholar

Dr. Neil Heyman
Department of History
San Diego State University

Dr. Jesse Hingson
Georgia College and State University

Dr. Charles F. Howlett
Molloy College

Guida M. Jackson
Independent Scholar

David D. Jividen
U.S. Air Force Colonel

Jerry Keenan
Independent Scholar

Dr. Jeff Kinard
Guilford Technical Community College

Dr. Arne Kislenko
Ryerson University
Canada

Matthew Krogman
Independent Scholar

Dr. Stephen J. Lange
Morehead State University

Harold Langley
Curator of Naval History Emeritus
Smithsonian Institution

Michael E. Lynch
Chief of Educational Programs
Army Heritage and Education Center

Rodney Madison
Texas Christian University

Federico Magdalena
University of Hawaii

David F. Marley
Independent Scholar

Dr. Jerome V. Martin
Command Historian
U.S. Strategic Command

Dr. Jack E. McCallum
Department of History and Geography
Texas Christian University

Dr. Stephen McCullough
Mississippi University for Women

James McIntyre
Moraine Valley Community College

Patrick McSherry
Editor
Spanish American War Centennial Website

Mark C. Mollan
Archivist
National Archives and Records Administration

Wesley Moody
Florida Community College at Jacksonville

Dr. Gregory Moore
Department of History
Notre Dame College

Dr. Justin D. Murphy
Department of History, Political Science, and
Geography
Howard Payne University

Dawn Ottevaere Nickeson
Department of History
Michigan State University

Ronald Ray Ortensie
Historian
United States Air Force

Charlene T. Overturf
Armstrong Atlantic State University

Major Jason Palmer
United States Military Academy

Richard W. Peuser
Archivist
National Archives

Dr. Jim Piecuch
Department of History
Kennesaw State University

Dr. Paul G. Pierpaoli Jr.
Associate Editor
Military History, ABC-CLIO, Inc.

Dr. Vincent Kelly Pollard
Asian Studies Program
University of Hawai'i at Manoa

Priscilla Mary Roberts
Department of History
University of Hong Kong
Hong Kong

Charles Rosenberg
Independent Scholar

Rodney J. Ross
Harrisburg Area Community College

Anna Rulska
Old Dominion University

Dr. Richard A. Sauers
Executive Director
Packwood House Museum

Larry Schweikart
Independent Scholar

Robert Shafer
California State University Northridge

James E. Shircliffe Jr.
Analyst
SAIC Inc.

Margaret Sloan
Independent Scholar

Jason M. Sokiera
University of Southern Mississippi

Dr. Paul J. Springer
Department of History
United States Military Academy

Dr. Ian Michael Spurgeon
Independent Scholar

Dr. Stephen K. Stein
Department of History
University of Memphis

Arthur Steinberg
Independent Scholar

Stephen Svonavec
Independent Scholar

David F. Trask
Chief Historian, Ret.
U.S. Army Center of Military History

Dr. Spencer C. Tucker
Senior Fellow
Military History, ABC-CLIO, Inc.

Dallace Unger
Colorado State University

Jose Valente
Independent Scholar

Tim J. Watts
Humanities Librarian
Kansas State University

Matthew J. Wayman
Associate Librarian
Penn State Abington

William Weisberger
Independent Scholar

Jacqueline Whitt
Department of History
University of North Carolina at Chapel Hill

Bob A. Wintermute
Temple University

Timothy S. Wolters
Department of History
Utah State University

Dr. Katja Wuestenbecker
University of Jena
Germany

Categorical Index

Individuals

Places

Ideas and Movements

Index